Fodor's Fourth Edition

The Rockies

The complete guide, thoroughly up-to-date

Packed with details that will make your trip

The must-see sights, off and on the beaten path

What to see, what to skip

Mix-and-match vacation itineraries

City strolls, countryside adventures

Smart lodging and dining options

Essential local do's and taboos

Transportation tips, distances and directions

Key contacts, savvy travel tips

When to go, what to pack

Clear, accurate, easy-to-use maps

Fodor's Travel Publications • New York, Toronto, London, Sydney, Auckland
www.fodors.com

Fodor's The Rockies

EDITOR: Jennifer Levitsky Kasoff

Editorial Contributors: Sasha Abramsky, Candy Moulton, Sharon Niederman, Peter Oliver, Kurt Repanshek, Kristin Rodine
Editorial Production: Linda K. Schmidt
Maps: David Lindroth, *cartographer;* Rebecca Baer, *map editor*
Design: Fabrizio La Rocca, *creative director;* Guido Caroti, *art director;* Jolie Novak, *photo editor*
Cover Design: Pentagram
Production/Manufacturing: Robert Shields
Cover Photograph: Galen Rowell

Copyright

Fourth Edition

ISBN 0-679-00371-1

ISSN 1527-3210

Special Sales

Fodor's Travel Publications are available at special discounts for bulk purchases for sales promotions or premiums. Special editions, including personalized covers, excerpts of existing guides, and corporate imprints, can be created in large quantities for special needs. For more information, contact your local bookseller or write to Special Markets, Fodor's Travel Publications, 201 East 50th Street, New York, NY 10022. Inquiries from Canada should be directed to your local Canadian bookseller or sent to Random House of Canada, Ltd., Marketing Department, 2775 Matheson Boulevard East, Mississauga, Ontario L4W 4P7. Inquiries from the United Kingdom should be sent to Fodor's Travel Publications, 20 Vauxhall Bridge Road, London SW1V 2SA, England.

PRINTED IN THE UNITED STATES OF AMERICA

10 9 8 7 6 5 4 3 2 1

Important Tip

Although all prices, opening times, and other details in this book are based on information supplied to us at press time, changes occur all the time in the travel world, and Fodor's cannot accept responsibility for facts that become outdated or for inadvertent errors or omissions. So **always confirm information when it matters,** especially if you're making a detour to visit a specific place.

CONTENTS

ON THE ROAD WITH FODOR'S

The trips you take this year and next are going to be significant trips, if only because they'll be your first in the new millennium. Acutely aware of that fact, we've pulled out all stops in preparing Fodor's The Rockies. To guide you in putting together your Rockies experience, we've created multiday itineraries and city tours. And to direct you to the places that are truly worth your time and money in these important years, we've rallied the team of endearingly picky know-it-alls we're pleased to call our writers. Having seen all corners of the regions they cover for us, they're real experts. If you knew them, you'd poll them for tips yourself.

Candy Moulton has spent years traveling through Wyoming—her native state—researching her nonfiction books: *Roadside History of Wyoming; Legacy of the Tetons: Homesteading in Jackson Hole; The Grand Encampment: Settling the High Country; Wagon Wheels: A Contemporary Journey on the Oregon Trail; Writer's Guide to Everyday Life in the Wild West From 1840 to 1900;* and *Steamboat: Legendary Bucking Horse.* She has also written *Roadside History of Nebraska* and *Salt Lake City Uncovered.* She is the editor of *Roundup,* the official publication of Western Writers of America, and she is a regular contributor to Fodor's. Presently she is researching and writing *Writer's Guide to Everyday Life: Native Americans in the 1800s.* Moulton makes her home near Encampment, Wyoming.

Sharon Niederman, our Colorado updater, is the author of six books on Southwest travel, cuisine, history, and culture. A full-time writer who travels the backroads and high mountain passes of Colorado and New Mexico, she loves dining in small-town cafés and soaking in the hot springs of Ouray, Durango, and Pagosa. She is a regular contributor to *Sunset* magazine and other regional Western publications. She lived in Colorado for ten years, where she was a professor at Metropolitan State College in Denver. Two of her books, including *A Quilt of Words: Women's Diaries, Letters & Original Accounts of Life in the Southwest, 1860-1960,* received the Border Regional Library Association Southwest Book Award for literary excellence. She lives in Albuquerque, New Mexico.

Peter Oliver, who wrote the two special-interest vacation chapters and the essay in Chapter 1, writes about sports and the outdoors for *Skiing, Bicycling, Backpacker, Outside,* the *Boston Globe,* and the *New York Times,* among other publications. He is also the author of several books on sports and the outdoors. He is currently working on his next book, to be published by *Outside* and W.W. Norton, on skiing around the world. He lives in Warren, Vermont.

Kurt Repanshek, our Utah updater, has roamed the Rockies since 1985 and has lived in Park City, Utah, since 1993 when he embarked on a freelance career after nearly 14 years with The Associated Press. A regular contributor to *Sunset* magazine, he also has written for *National Geographic Traveler, Snow Country,* and *Mountain Living.* When he's not ripping up the powder winter dumps on Utah's ski resorts, you can find Kurt hiking in the Uinta and Wasatch ranges or plying its lakes with his canoe.

Kristin Rodine, a lifelong resident of the Northwest, is city editor of the *Idaho Press-Tribune* in Nampa, Idaho. She worked for daily newspapers in Washington, Idaho, and Arizona before serving eight years as a news editor and feature writer for the University of Montana in Missoula. In 1997 she returned to the *Idaho Press-Tribune* to head its local news division. Although her job is demanding, she rewards herself by revisiting old haunts and exploring new places in Idaho and Montana for Fodor's. She has won state and regional awards for feature writing, investigative reporting, editorial writing, and coordinating special reports.

Don't Forget to Write

Keeping a travel guide fresh and up-to-date is a big job. So we love your feedback—positive and negative—and follow up on all suggestions. Contact the Rockies editor at editors@fodors.com or c/o Fodor's, 201 East 50th Street, New York, New York 10022. And have a wonderful trip!

Karen Cure
Editorial Director

The Rockies

CANADA
MONTANA
IDAHO
WYOMING
NORTH DAKOTA
SOUTH DAKOTA
GLACIER NATIONAL PARK
BLACKFEET INDIAN RES.
FLATHEAD INDIAN RES.
COEUR D'ALENE INDIAN RES.
NEZ PERCE INDIAN RES.
FORT BELKNAP INDIAN RES.
FORT PECK INDIAN RES.
CROW INDIAN RES.
N. CHEYENNE INDIAN RES.
BIGHORN CANYON NAT'L REC. AREA
YELLOWSTONE NAT'L PARK
GRAND TETON NAT'L PARK
SAWTOOTH NAT'L REC AREA
WIND RIVER INDIAN RESERVATION
Milk River
Missouri River
Yellowstone R.
Snake River
Flathead Lake
Fort Peck Lake
Dworshak Res.
Devil's Tower
Sand Point
Libby
Kalispell
Coeur d'Alene
Kellogg
Avery
Moscow
Lewiston
Missoula
Lincoln
Fairfield
Cut Bank
Shelby
Conrad
Havre
Malta
Great Falls
Fort Benton
Helena
Deer Lodge
Anaconda
Butte
Harlowton
Lewistown
Roundup
Ingomar
Jordan
Circle
Glendive
Sidney
Wolf Point
Scobey
Westby
Baker
Miles City
Forsyth
Billings
Livingston
Bozeman
Wisdom
Dillon
Lima
Elk City
Riggins
New Meadows
Salmon
Challis
Stanley
Weiser
Payette
Emmett
Caldwell
Nampa
Boise
Butte City
Hill City
Mountain Home
Gooding
Dubois
Idaho Falls
Shelley
Jackson
Dubois
Cody
Sheridan
Buffalo
Thermopolis
Broadus
Gillette
Newcastle
Midwest
Casper
Rapid City
93
2
95
50
3
90
200
15
89
87
191
12
22
94
26
287
16
25
59
28
21
55
75
84

SMART TRAVEL TIPS A TO Z

Basic Information on Traveling in the Rockies, Savvy Tips to Make Your Trip a Breeze, and Companies and Organizations to Contact

AIR TRAVEL

BOOKING YOUR FLIGHT

When you book **look for nonstop flights** and **remember that "direct" flights stop at least once.** Try to avoid connecting flights, which require a change of plane.

CARRIERS

Chances are, you'll fly into one of the hub cities of Denver or Salt Lake City. Connecting flights all across the Rockies are available most frequently from these two cities. During ski season, some of the major resort towns have increased service and direct flights available.

➤ MAJOR AIRLINES: **American** (☎ 800/433–7300). **Continental** (☎ 800/525–0280). **Delta** (☎ 800/221–1212). **Northwest** (☎ 800/225–2525). **TWA** (☎ 800/221–2000). **United** (☎ 800/241–6522). **US Airways** (☎ 800/428–4322).

➤ SMALLER AIRLINES: **America Trans Air** (☎ 800/225–2995). **America West** (☎ 800/235–9292). **Horizon Air** (☎ 800/547–9308). **Mesa Airlines** (☎ 800/637–2247). **Midwest Express** (☎ 800/452–2022). **SkyWest** (☎ 800/453–9417). **Southwest** (☎ 800/435–9792). **United Express** (☎ 800/241–6522).

CHECK-IN & BOARDING

If you're traveling during snow season, **allow extra time for the drive** to the airport. Weather conditions can slow you down more than you may have predicted. If you'll be checking skis, arrive early for your flight.

Assuming that not everyone with a ticket will show up, airlines routinely overbook planes. When that happens, airlines ask for volunteers to give up their seats. In return these volunteers usually get a certificate for a free flight and are rebooked on the next flight out. If there are not enough volunteers, the airline must choose who will be denied boarding. The first to get bumped are passengers who checked in late and those flying on discounted tickets, so **get to the gate and check in as early as possible,** especially during peak periods.

Always **bring a government-issued photo I.D. to the airport.** You may be asked to show it before you are allowed to check in.

CUTTING COSTS

The least-expensive airfares to the Rockies must usually be purchased in advance and are non-refundable. It's smart to **call a number of airlines, and when you are quoted a good price, book it on the spot**—the same fare may not be available the next day. Always **check different routings** and look into using different airports. Travel agents, especially low-fare specialists (☞ Discounts & Deals, *below*), are helpful.

Consolidators are another good source. They buy tickets for scheduled international flights at reduced rates from the airlines, then sell them at prices that beat the best fare available directly from the airlines, usually without restrictions. Sometimes you can even get your money back if you need to return the ticket. Carefully read the fine print detailing penalties for changes and cancellations, and **confirm your consolidator reservation with the airline.**

When you **fly as a courier** you trade your checked-luggage space for a ticket deeply subsidized by a courier service. There are restrictions on when you can book and how long you can stay.

➤ CONSOLIDATORS: **Cheap Tickets** (☎ 800/377–1000). **Up & Away Travel** (☎ 212/889–2345). **Discount Airline Ticket Service** (☎ 800/576–1600). **Unitravel** (☎ 800/325–2222). **World Travel Network** (☎ 800/409–6753).

ONTARIO
CANADA
QUÉBEC
NEW BRUNSWICK
Fredericton
Québec
MAINE
Augusta
Montréal
Ottawa
Montpelier
VT.
Concord
N.H.
Boston
MASS.
R.I.
Providence
Lake Superior
MINNESOTA
Duluth
WISCONSIN
MICHIGAN
Lake Huron
Lake Michigan
St. Paul
Minneapolis
Green Bay
Toronto
Lake Ontario
Albany
Hudson R.
Buffalo
NEW YORK
Hartford
Milwaukee
Lansing
Lake Erie
CONN.
Madison
Detroit
Cleveland
New York
IOWA
Chicago
PENNSYLVANIA
N.J.
Trenton
Harrisburg
Pittsburgh
Philadelphia
Des Moines
Omaha
OHIO
INDIANA
Columbus
MD
Dover
Baltimore
DEL.
Annapolis
ILLINOIS
Springfield
Indianapolis
WEST VIRGINIA
Washington, D.C.
Mississippi R.
Charleston
Topeka
Cincinnati
Richmond
Kansas City
Jefferson City
St. Louis
Louisville
Frankfort
Norfolk
VIRGINIA
MISSOURI
Ohio R.
KENTUCKY
Raleigh
NORTH CAROLINA
Nashville
TENNESSEE
Tulsa
ARKANSAS
Memphis
Columbia
SOUTH CAROLINA
Savannah R.
Little Rock
Tennessee R.
Atlanta
Birmingham
GEORGIA
ATLANTIC OCEAN
MISSISSIPPI
Savannah
Montgomery
ALABAMA
Jackson
Jacksonville
Baton Rouge
Mobile
Tallahassee
FLORIDA
Orlando
New Orleans
Houston
LOUISIANA
Bahama Islands
Miami
Nassau
Gulf of Mexico
N
0
500 miles
0
800 km
29
94
35
90
80
55
70
65
75
76
87
95
85
40
20
30
16
45
12
10
4
41

The United States

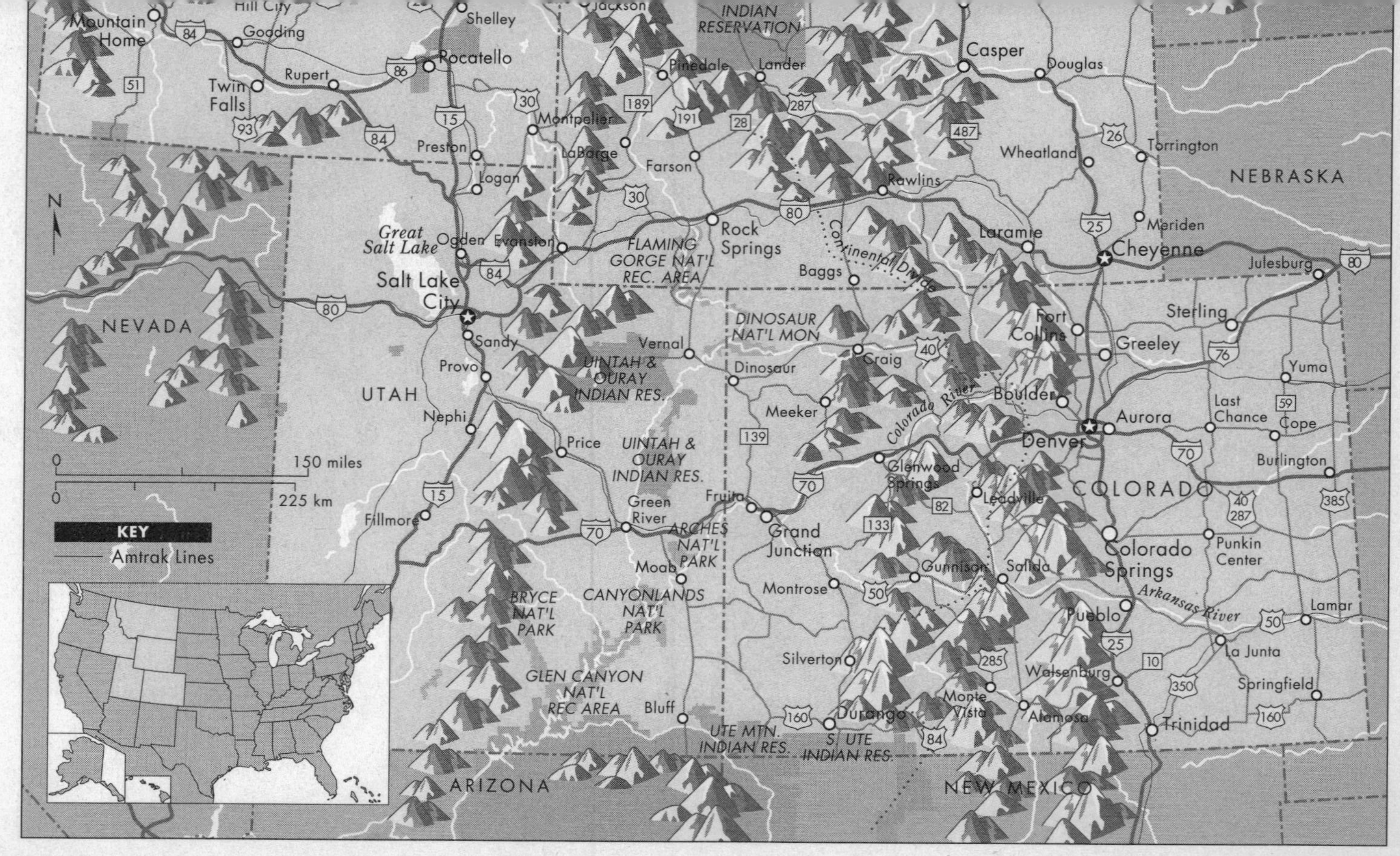
INDIAN RESERVATION
NEBRASKA
NEVADA
UTAH
COLORADO
ARIZONA
NEW MEXICO
Hill City
Mountain Home
Gooding
Twin Falls
Rupert
Shelley
Pocatello
Jackson
Pinedale
Lander
Casper
Douglas
Torrington
Wheatland
Montpelier
LaBarge
Farson
Preston
Logan
Rawlins
Meriden
Great Salt Lake
Ogden
Evanston
Rock Springs
Laramie
Cheyenne
Julesburg
Baggs
Continental Divide
FLAMING GORGE NAT'L REC. AREA
Salt Lake City
Sandy
Provo
Nephi
Vernal
DINOSAUR NAT'L MON
Dinosaur
Craig
Meeker
Fort Collins
Greeley
Sterling
Yuma
Boulder
Aurora
Denver
Last Chance
Cope
Burlington
UINTAH & OURAY INDIAN RES.
Price
Colorado River
Glenwood Springs
Leadville
Fillmore
Green River
Fruita
Grand Junction
ARCHES NAT'L PARK
Moab
Montrose
Gunnison
Salida
Colorado Springs
Punkin Center
Arkansas River
Pueblo
Lamar
La Junta
BRYCE NAT'L PARK
CANYONLANDS NAT'L PARK
Silverton
Walsenburg
Springfield
GLEN CANYON NAT'L REC AREA
Bluff
Durango
Monte Vista
Alamosa
Trinidad
UTE MTN. INDIAN RES.
S. UTE INDIAN RES.
N
0
150 miles
0
225 km
KEY
Amtrak Lines
84
51
86
93
15
30
189
191
28
287
487
26
25
80
40
76
59
139
70
82
133
385
50
285
10
350
160

(4th Thurs. in Nov.); Christmas Eve and Christmas Day (Dec. 24 and 25); and New Year's Eve (Dec. 31).

INSURANCE

The most useful travel insurance plan is a comprehensive policy that includes coverage for trip cancellation and interruption, default, trip delay, and medical expenses (with a waiver for preexisting conditions).

Without insurance you will lose all or most of your money if you cancel your trip, regardless of the reason. Default insurance covers you if your tour operator, airline, or cruise line goes out of business. Trip-delay covers expenses that arise because of bad weather or mechanical delays. Study the fine print when comparing policies.

British and Australian citizens need extra medical coverage when traveling overseas.

Always **buy travel policies directly from the insurance company**; if you buy it from a cruise line, airline, or tour operator that goes out of business you probably will not be covered for the agency or operator's default, a major risk. Before you make any purchase **review your existing health and home-owner's policies** to find what they cover away from home.

➤ TRAVEL INSURERS: In the United States, **Access America** (✉ 6600 W. Broad St., Richmond, VA 23230, ☎ 804/285–3300 or 800/284–8300), **Travel Guard International** (✉ 1145 Clark St., Stevens Point, WI 54481, ☎ 715/345–0505 or 800/826–1300). In Canada, **Voyager Insurance** (✉ 44 Peel Center Dr., Brampton, Ontario L6T 4M8, ☎ 905/791–8700; 800/668–4342 in Canada).

➤ INSURANCE INFORMATION: In the United Kingdom, the **Association of British Insurers** (✉ 51–55 Gresham St., London EC2V 7HQ, ☎ 020/7600–3333, FAX 020/7696–8999). In Australia, the **Insurance Council of Australia** (☎ 03/9614–1077, FAX 03/9614–7924).

LODGING

Accommodations in the Rockies vary from the very posh resorts in ski areas such as Vail, Aspen, Sun Valley, and Jackson Hole, to basic hotels and motels. Dude and guest ranches may be good for families, and bed-and-breakfasts or inns may be more inviting to those on a leisurely schedule.

The lodgings we list are the cream of the crop in each price category. We always list the facilities that are available—but we don't specify whether they cost extra: When pricing accommodations, always ask what's included and what costs extra. Properties indicated by an ✕▣ are lodging establishments whose restaurant warrants a special trip.

Assume that hotels operate on the European Plan (EP, with no meals) unless we specify that they use the Continental Plan (CP, with a Continental breakfast daily), Modified American Plan (MAP, with breakfast and dinner daily), or the Full American Plan (FAP, with all meals).

➤ GENERAL INFORMATION: **Colorado Hotel and Lodging Association** (✉ 999 18th St., Suite 1240, Denver, CO 80202, ☎ 303/297–8335). **Idaho Division of Travel Promotion** (✉ Idaho Department of Commerce, 700 W. State St., Boise, ID 83720, ☎ 800/635–7820). **Travel Montana** (✉ Department of Commerce, 1424 9th Ave., Helena, MT 59620, ☎ 406/444–2654, 800/548–3390 in Montana or 800/847–4868 nationwide). **Utah Hotel & Lodging Association** (✉ 9 Exchange Pl., Suite 115, Salt Lake City, UT 84114, ☎ 801/359–0104). **Wyoming Division of Tourism** (✉ I–25 at College Dr., Cheyenne, WY 82002, ☎ 307/777–7777 or 800/225–5996).

APARTMENT & HOME RENTALS

If you want a home base that's roomy enough for a family and comes with cooking facilities **consider a furnished rental.** These can save you money, especially if you're traveling with a group. Home-exchange directories sometimes list rentals as well as exchanges.

➤ INTERNATIONAL AGENTS: **Hideaways International** (✉ 767 Islington St., Portsmouth, NH 03801, ☎ 603/430–4433 or 800/843–4433, FAX 603/430–4444; membership $99).

TRAVEL AGENCIES

In the United States, although the Americans with Disabilities Act requires that travel firms serve the needs of all travelers, some agencies specialize in working with people with disabilities.

➤ TRAVELERS WITH MOBILITY PROBLEMS: **Access Adventures** (✉ 206 Chestnut Ridge Rd., Rochester, NY 14624, ☎ 716/889–9096) is run by a former physical-rehabilitation counselor. **Accessible Journeys** (✉ 35 W. Sellers Ave., Ridley Park, PA 19078, ☎ 610/521–0339 or 800/846–4537, FAX 610/521–6959). **Accessible Vans of the Rockies, Activity and Travel Agency** (✉ 2040 W. Hamilton Pl., Sheridan, CO 80110, ☎ 303/806–5047 or 888/837–0065, FAX 303/781–2329). **CareVacations** (✉ 5-5110 50th Ave., Leduc, Alberta T9E 6V4, ☎ 780/986–6404 or 877/478–7827, FAX 780/986–8332) has group tours and is especially helpful with cruise vacations. **Flying Wheels Travel** (✉ 143 W. Bridge St., Box 382, Owatonna, MN 55060, ☎ 507/451–5005 or 800/535–6790, FAX 507/451–1685). **Hinsdale Travel Service** (✉ 201 E. Ogden Ave., Suite 100, Hinsdale, IL 60521, ☎ 630/325–1335, FAX 630/325–1342).

➤ TRAVELERS WITH DEVELOPMENTAL DISABILITIES: **Sprout** (✉ 893 Amsterdam Ave., New York, NY 10025, ☎ 212/222–9575 or 888/222–9575, FAX 212/222–9768).

DISCOUNTS & DEALS

Be a smart shopper and **compare all your options** before making decisions. A plane ticket bought with a promotional coupon from travel clubs, coupon books, and direct-mail offers may not be cheaper than the least expensive fare from a discount ticket agency. And always keep in mind that what you get is just as important as what you save.

DISCOUNT RESERVATIONS

To save money **look into discount-reservations services** with toll-free numbers, which use their buying power to get a better price on hotels, airline tickets, even car rentals. When booking a room, always **call the hotel's local toll-free number** (if one is available) rather than the central reservations number—you'll often get a better price. Always ask about special packages or corporate rates.

➤ AIRLINE TICKETS: ☎ **800/FLY-4-LESS.** ☎ **800/FLY-ASAP.**

➤ HOTEL ROOMS: **RMC Travel** (☎ 800/245–5738).

PACKAGE DEALS

Don't confuse packages and guided tours. When you buy a package, you travel on your own, just as though you had planned the trip yourself. Fly/drive packages, which combine airfare and car rental, are often a good deal.

ECOTOURISM

Although the Bureau of Land Management hasn't designated any particular parts of the Rockies to be endangered ecosystems, many areas are open only to hikers, with vehicles and horses banned. For more information contact the **U.S. Bureau of Land Management** (☎ 303/239–3600). Recycling is taken seriously throughout the Rockies and you will find yourself very unpopular if you litter or fail to recycle your cans and bottles.

GAY & LESBIAN TRAVEL

➤ GAY- AND LESBIAN-FRIENDLY TRAVEL AGENCIES: **Different Roads Travel** (✉ 8383 Wilshire Blvd., Suite 902, Beverly Hills, CA 90211, ☎ 323/651–5557 or 800/429–8747, FAX 323/651–3678). **Kennedy Travel** (✉ 314 Jericho Tpk., Floral Park, NY 11001, ☎ 516/352–4888 or 800/237–7433, FAX 516/354–8849). **Now Voyager** (✉ 4406 18th St., San Francisco, CA 94114, ☎ 415/626–1169 or 800/255–6951, FAX 415/626–8626). **Skylink Travel and Tour** (✉ 1006 Mendocino Ave., Santa Rosa, CA 95401, ☎ 707/546–9888 or 800/225–5759, FAX 707/546–9891), serving lesbian travelers.

HOLIDAYS

Major national holidays include New Year's Day (Jan. 1); Martin Luther King, Jr., Day (3rd Mon. in Jan.); President's Day (3rd Mon. in Feb.); Memorial Day (last Mon. in May); Independence Day (July 4); Labor Day (1st Mon. in Sept.); Thanksgiving Day tell someone your destination, if possible. It's also good to carry a cellular phone. Be aware, however, that because of the mountains cell phones don't work everywhere. If you should become stranded **never leave your vehicle.** Instead wait until someone comes looking for you. Most roads are routinely patrolled and plowed.

One of the more unpleasant sights along the highway are roadkills—animals struck by vehicles. Deer, elk, and even bears may try to get to the other side of a road just as you come along, so **watch out for wildlife on the highways.** Exercise caution, not only to save an animal's life, but also to avoid possible extensive damage to your car.

SPEED LIMITS

The speed limit on U.S. interstates is 75 mph in rural areas and 65 mph in urban zones.

WINTER DRIVING

Modern highways make mountain driving safe and generally trouble free even in cold weather. Although winter driving can occasionally present some real challenges, road maintenance is good and plowing is prompt. However, in mountain areas, tire chains, studs, or snow tires are essential. If you're planning to drive into high elevations, be sure to **check the weather forecast** beforehand. Even the mountain passes on main highways can be forced to close because of snow conditions. Each state highway department has a number to call for road conditions. Be prepared for stormy weather: **Carry an emergency kit** containing warm clothes, a flashlight, some food, and perhaps a sleeping bag. If you do get stalled by deep snow, do not leave your car. Wait for help, running the engine only if needed, and remember that assistance is never far away.

➤ ROAD CONDITION INFORMATION: **Colorado Road Condition Information** (☎ 303/639–1111 within a two-hour drive of Denver, 303/639–1234 statewide); **Idaho Road Condition Information** (☎ 208/336–6600); **Montana Road Condition Information** (☎ 406/444–6339 or 800/332–6171); **Utah Road Condition Information** (☎ 801/964–6000 in the Salt Lake City area; 800/492–2400 within Utah); and **Wyoming Road Condition Information** (☎ 307/772–0824).

CHILDREN IN THE ROCKIES

The Rockies are tailor-made for family vacations, offering dude ranches; historic railroads; mining towns; the extreme natural features of national parks such as Yellowstone, Mesa Verde, and Arches; large wildlife; rafting; and many other outdoor activities. Visitor centers and local hotels/motels are often good at recommending places to spend time with children. If you are renting a car don't forget to **arrange for a car seat** when you reserve.

FLYING

If your children are two or older **ask about children's airfares.** As a general rule, infants under two not occupying a seat fly at greatly reduced fares or even for free.

Experts agree that it's a good idea to use safety seats aloft for children weighing less than 40 pounds. Airlines set their own policies: U.S. carriers usually require that the child be ticketed, even if he or she is young enough to ride free, since the seats must be strapped into regular seats. Do **check your airline's policy about using safety seats during takeoff and landing.** And since safety seats are not allowed just everywhere in the plane, get your seat assignments early.

When reserving, **request children's meals or a freestanding bassinet** if you need them. But note that bulkhead seats, where you must sit to use the bassinet, may lack an overhead bin or storage space on the floor.

LODGING

Most hotels in the Rockies allow children under a certain age to stay in their parents' room at no extra charge, but others charge for them as extra adults; be sure to **find out the cutoff age for children's discounts.**

SIGHTS & ATTRACTIONS

Places that are especially good for children are indicated by a rubber duckie icon in the margin.

need a reservation voucher, a passport, a driver's license, and a travel policy that covers each driver, in order to pick up a car.

SURCHARGES

Before you pick up a car in one city and leave it in another **ask about drop-off charges or one-way service fees,** which can be substantial. Note, too, that some rental agencies charge extra if you return the car before the time specified in your contract. To avoid a hefty refueling fee **fill the tank just before you turn in the car,** but be aware that gas stations near the rental outlet may overcharge.

CAR TRAVEL

You'll seldom be bored driving through the Rockies. The most mountainous terrain is in Colorado, but this state is also the region's most populated and accessible. Idaho is home to the rockiest and most rugged stretch of the mountains, with an extraordinarily wild beauty that may be too remote and desolate for some. It is impossible to travel directly through the heart of the state—only two routes go from north to south. Montana's interstate system is more driver-friendly, connecting soaring summits, rivers, glacial valleys, forests, lakes, and vast stretches of prairie, all capped by that endless "Big Sky." It is practically impossible to get around Utah without a car. There are more national parks here than in any other states but Alaska and California, although their interiors are not always accessible by car. Wyoming's interstate links classic, open-range cowboy country and mountain-range vistas with the geothermal wonderland of Yellowstone National Park. In Wyoming, everything is separated by vast distances, so be sure to leave each major city with a full tank of gas and be prepared to see lots of wildlife and few other people.

Before setting out on any driving trip, it's important to **make sure your vehicle is in top condition.** It is best to have a complete tune-up. At the least, you should check the following: lights, including brake lights, backup lights, and emergency lights; tires, including the spare; oil; engine coolant; windshield-washer fluid; windshield-wiper blades; and brakes. For emergencies, take along flares or reflector triangles, jumper cables, an empty gas can, a fire extinguisher, a flashlight, a plastic tarp, blankets, water, and coins for phone calls.

BORDER CROSSING

Driving a car across the U.S.–Canadian border is simple. Personal vehicles are allowed entry into the neighboring country, provided they are not to be left behind. Drivers in rental cars should **bring along a copy of the rental contract when crossing the border,** bearing an endorsement stating that the vehicle is permitted to cross the border.

GASOLINE

Throughout the Rockies, gas prices are roughly similar to the rest of the continental United States. Although gas stations are relatively plentiful in many areas, you can drive more than 100 mi on back roads without finding gas.

ROAD CONDITIONS

The Rockies offer some of the most spectacular vistas and challenging driving in the world. Roads range from multilane blacktop to barely graveled backcountry trails; from twisting switchbacks considerately marked with guardrails to primitive campgrounds with a lane so narrow that you must back up to the edge of a steep cliff to make a turn. Scenic routes and lookout points are clearly marked, enabling you to slow down and pull over to take in the views.

RULES OF THE ROAD

You'll find highways and the national parks crowded in summer, and almost deserted (and occasionally impassable) in winter. Follow the posted speed limit, drive defensively, and **make sure your gas tank is full,** since distances between gas stations could make running on empty (or in the reserve zone) a not-so-pleasant memory of your trip.

In any of these states, **wintertime driving requires that you be prepared.** Take food, water, a can with a candle, extra blankets or a sleeping bag, and

Thursday night. Normal banking hours are weekdays 9–5; some branches are also open on Saturday morning.

CAMERAS & PHOTOGRAPHY

Photographers love the Rockies—and with good reason. The scenery is America's best, and every season offers a multitude of breathtaking images. When you're at Native American sites, be sure to ask if taking pictures is appropriate.

➤ PHOTO HELP: **Kodak Information Center** (☎ 800/242–2424). ***Kodak Guide to Shooting Great Travel Pictures,*** available in bookstores or from Fodor's Travel Publications (☎ 800/533–6478; $16.50 plus $4 shipping).

EQUIPMENT PRECAUTIONS

Always **keep your film and tape out of the sun.** Carry an extra supply of batteries, and **be prepared to turn on your camera or camcorder** to prove to security personnel that the device is real. Always **ask for hand inspection of film,** which becomes clouded after successive exposures to airport X-ray machines, and **keep videotapes away from metal detectors.**

CAR RENTAL

Rates in Denver begin at about $35 a day and $180 a week for an economy car with air-conditioning, an automatic transmission, and unlimited mileage. This does not include tax on car rentals, which is 11.3%. Rates in Boise begin at $28 a day and $173 a week plus a tax of 5%. Rates in Salt Lake City begin at $35 a day and $159 a week plus 15.85% tax. Rates in Jackson Hole begin at $34 a day and $137 a week; the tax is 6%.

➤ MAJOR AGENCIES: **Alamo** (☎ 800/327–9633; 020/8759–6200 in the U.K.). **Avis** (☎ 800/331–1212; 800/879–2847 in Canada; 02/9353–9000 in Australia; 09/525–1982 in New Zealand). **Budget** (☎ 800/527–0700; 0144/227–6266 in the U.K.). **Dollar** (☎ 800/800–4000; 020/8897–0811 in the U.K., where it is known as Eurodollar; 02/9223–1444 in Australia). **Hertz** (☎ 800/654–3131; 800/263–0600 in Canada; 0990/90–60–90 in the U.K.; 02/9669–2444 in Australia; 03/358–6777 in New Zealand). **National InterRent** (☎ 800/227–7368; 0345/222525 in the U.K., where it is known as Europcar InterRent).

CUTTING COSTS

To get the best deal **book through a travel agent who will shop around.** Also **price local car-rental companies,** although the service and maintenance may not be as good as those of a major player. Remember to ask about required deposits, cancellation penalties, and drop-off charges if you're planning to pick up the car in one city and leave it in another. If you're traveling during a holiday period, also make sure that a confirmed reservation guarantees you a car.

Do **look into wholesalers,** companies that do not own fleets but rent in bulk from those that do and often offer better rates than traditional car-rental operations.

INSURANCE

When driving a rented car you are generally responsible for any damage to or loss of the vehicle as well as for any property damage or personal injury that you may cause. Before you rent see what coverage your personal auto-insurance policy and credit cards already provide.

For about $15–$20 per day, rental companies sell protection, known as a collision- or loss-damage waiver (CDW or LDW), that eliminates your liability for damage to the car. In most states you don't need a CDW if you have personal auto insurance or other liability insurance. However, **make sure you have enough coverage to pay for the car.** If you do not have auto insurance or an umbrella policy that covers damage to third parties, purchasing liability insurance and a CDW or LDW is highly recommended.

REQUIREMENTS & RESTRICTIONS

In the Rockies you must be 21 to rent a car, and rates may be higher if you're under 25. You'll pay extra for child seats (about $3 per day), which are compulsory for children under five, and for additional drivers (about $2 per day). Non-U.S. residents will

ENJOYING THE FLIGHT

For more legroom **request an emergency-aisle seat.** Don't sit in the row in front of the emergency aisle or in front of a bulkhead, where seats may not recline. If you have dietary concerns, **ask for special meals when booking.** These can be vegetarian, low-cholesterol, or kosher, for example. On long flights, try to maintain a normal routine, to help fight jet lag. At night **get some sleep.** By day **eat light meals, drink water** (not alcohol), and **move around the cabin** to stretch your legs.

If you love to look out the window during take off and landing, flying in the Rockies provides a special treat. Ask for a window if you want dizzying views of the mountains.

FLYING TIMES

All times are approximate. Flight time from New York to Denver is four hours; New York to Salt Lake City is five hours. Flight time from Chicago to Denver is 2½ hours; Chicago to Salt Lake City is four hours. Flight time from Los Angeles to Denver is 2¼ hours; Los Angeles to Salt Lake City is 3¾ hours.

HOW TO COMPLAIN

If your baggage goes astray or your flight goes awry, complain right away. Most carriers require that you **file a claim immediately.**

➤ AIRLINE COMPLAINTS: U.S. Department of Transportation, **Aviation Consumer Protection Division** (✉ C-75, Room 4107, Washington, DC 20590, ☎ 202/366–2220). **Federal Aviation Administration Consumer Hotline** (☎ 800/322–7873).

AIRPORTS

The major gateways to the Rockies include, in Colorado, Denver International Airport; in Idaho, Boise Air Terminal; in Montana, Missoula Airport and Glacier Park International Airport in Kalispell; in Utah, Salt Lake City International Airport; and in Wyoming, Jackson Hole Airport.

➤ AIRPORT INFORMATION: **Boise Air Terminal** (☎ 208/383–3110). **Denver International Airport** (☎ 303/342–2200 or 800/247–2336, TTY 800/688–1333). **Glacier Park International Airport** (☎ 406/257–5994). **Jackson Hole Airport** (☎ 307/733–3039). **Missoula Airport** (☎ 406/728–4381). **Salt Lake City International Airport** (☎ 801/575–2400).

BIKE TRAVEL

Bike riding, especially mountain biking, is very popular in many parts of the Rockies. Because of the obvious topographical challenges of the terrain, only very fit bicyclists will want to attempt long trips in the region.

BIKES IN FLIGHT

Most airlines accommodate bikes as luggage, provided they are dismantled and boxed. For bike boxes, often free at bike shops, you'll pay about $5 (at least $100 for bike bags) from airlines. International travelers can sometimes substitute a bike for a piece of checked luggage at no charge; otherwise, the cost is about $100. Domestic and Canadian airlines charge $25–$50.

BUS TRAVEL

Greyhound Lines has regular intercity routes throughout the region, with connections from Denver to Cheyenne, Boise, Pocatello, and Missoula. Smaller bus companies provide service within local areas. Regional lines include **Community Rural Transport** (☎ 208/522–2278) in Jackson Hole; **Springs Transit Management** (☎ 719/385–7433) in Colorado Springs; **Boise-Winnemucca Northwestern Bus Lines** (☎ 208/336–3302) in Idaho; **Rimrock/Trailways** (☎ 800/255–7655) in Montana; and **Powder River Transportation** (☎ 800/442–3682) in Wyoming.

➤ BUS INFORMATION: **Greyhound Lines** (☎ 800/231–2222) operates bus service to the Rocky Mountain region from many points in the United States. Smoking is not permitted on any Greyhound bus.

BUSINESS HOURS

Throughout the Rockies, most retail stores are open from 9 AM or 9:30 AM until 6 PM or 7 PM daily in downtown locations and until 9 or 10 in suburban shopping malls. Downtown stores sometimes stay open later

B&BS

➤ Reservation Services: **Montana Bed & Breakfast Association** (✉ 5557 U.S. 93 S, Somers, MT 59932, ☎ 800/453–8870). **Bed & Breakfast Inns of Utah** (✉ Box 2639, Park City, UT 84060, FAX 801/595–0332).

CAMPING

Camping is invigorating and inexpensive. Colorado, Idaho, Montana, Utah, and Wyoming are full of state and national parks and forests with sites that range from rustic (pit toilets and cold running water), to campgrounds with bathhouses with hot showers, paved trailer pads that can accommodate even jumbo RVs, and full hookups. Fees vary, from $6 to $10 a night for tents and up to $21 for RVs, but are usually waived once the water is turned off for the winter.

Sometimes site reservations are accepted, and then only for up to seven days (early birds reserve up to a year in advance); more often, they're not. Campers who prefer a more remote setting may camp in the backcountry; it's free but you'll need a permit, available from park visitor centers and ranger stations. If you're visiting in summer, plan well ahead. *The National Parks: Camping Guide* (Superintendent of Documents, ✉ U.S. Government Printing Office, Washington, DC 20402; $3.50) may be helpful.

The facilities and amenities at privately operated campgrounds are usually more extensive (swimming pools are common), reservations are more widely accepted, and nightly fees are higher: $7 and up for tents, $23 for RVs.

GUEST RANCHES

If the thought of sitting around a campfire after a hard day on the range makes your heart beat faster, **consider playing dude** on a guest ranch. These range from wilderness-rimmed working ranches that accept guests and encourage them to pitch in with chores and other ranch activities to luxurious resorts on the fringes of a small city, with an upscale clientele, swimming pools, tennis courts, and a lively roster of horse-related activities such as breakfast rides, moonlight rides, and all-day trail rides. Rafting, fishing, tubing, and other activities are usually available; at working ranches, you even may be able to participate in a cattle roundup. In winter, cross-country skiing and snowshoeing keep you busy. Lodgings can run the gamut from charmingly rustic cabins to the kind of deluxe quarters you expect at a first-class hotel. Meals may be gourmet or plain but hearty. Many ranches offer packages and children's and off-season rates.

➤ Information: **Colorado Dude/Guest Ranch Association** (✉ Box 2120, Granby, CO 80446, ☎ 970/887–3128). The various state tourism offices also have information on dude ranches.

HOME EXCHANGES

If you would like to exchange your home for someone else's **join a home-exchange organization,** which will send you its updated listings of available exchanges for a year and will include your own listing in at least one of them. It's up to you to make specific arrangements.

➤ Exchange Clubs: **HomeLink International** (✉ Box 650, Key West, FL 33041, ☎ 305/294–7766 or 800/638–3841, FAX 305/294–1448; $93 per year). **Intervac U.S.** (✉ Box 590504, San Francisco, CA 94159, ☎ 800/756–4663, FAX 415/435–7440; $83 for catalogues).

HOSTELS

No matter what your age you can **save on lodging costs by staying at hostels.** In some 5,000 locations in more than 70 countries around the world, Hostelling International (HI), the umbrella group for a number of national youth-hostel associations, offers single-sex, dorm-style beds and, at many hostels, couples rooms and family accommodations. Membership in any HI national hostel association, open to travelers of all ages, allows you to stay in HI-affiliated hostels at member rates (one-year membership is about $25 for adults; hostels run about $10–$25 per night). Members also have priority if the hostel is full; they're eligible for discounts around the world, even on rail and bus travel in some countries.

➤ ORGANIZATIONS: **Australian Youth Hostel Association** (✉ 10 Mallett St., Camperdown, NSW 2050, ☎ 02/9565–1699, FAX 02/9565–1325). **Hostelling International—American Youth Hostels** (✉ 733 15th St. NW, Suite 840, Washington, DC 20005, ☎ 202/783–6161, FAX 202/783–6171). **Hostelling International—Canada** (✉ 400–205 Catherine St., Ottawa, Ontario K2P 1C3, ☎ 613/237–7884, FAX 613/237–7868). **Youth Hostel Association of England and Wales** (✉ Trevelyan House, 8 St. Stephen's Hill, St. Albans, Hertfordshire AL1 2DY, ☎ 01727/855215 or 01727/845047, FAX 01727/844126). **Youth Hostels Association of New Zealand** (✉ Box 436, Christchurch, New Zealand, ☎ 03/379–9970, FAX 03/365–4476). Membership in the United States $25, in Canada C$26.75, in the United Kingdom £9.30, in Australia $44, in New Zealand $24.

HOTELS

Most big-city hotels cater to business travelers, with such facilities as restaurants, cocktail lounges, swimming pools, exercise equipment, and meeting rooms. Room rates usually reflect the range of amenities offered. Most cities also have less expensive hotels that are clean and comfortable but have fewer facilities. A new accommodations trend is the all-suite hotel, which gives you more room for the money; examples include Courtyard by Marriott and Embassy Suites. All five states covered in this book have seen a boom in hotel construction over the past decade.

Many properties offer special weekend rates, sometimes up to 50% off regular prices. However, these deals are usually not extended during peak summer months, when hotels are normally full. All hotels listed have private baths unless otherwise noted.

➤ TOLL-FREE NUMBERS: **Adam's Mark** (☎ 800/444–2326). **Baymont Inns** (☎ 800/428–3438). **Best Western** (☎ 800/528–1234). **Choice** (☎ 800/221–2222). **Clarion** (☎ 800/252–7466). **Colony** (☎ 800/777–1700). **Comfort** (☎ 800/228–5150). **Days Inn** (☎ 800/325–2525). **Doubletree and Red Lion Hotels** (☎ 800/222–8733). **Embassy Suites** (☎ 800/362–2779). **Fairfield Inn** (☎ 800/228–2800). **Forte** (☎ 800/225–5843). **Four Seasons** (☎ 800/332–3442). **Hilton** (☎ 800/445–8667). **Holiday Inn** (☎ 800/465–4329). **Howard Johnson** (☎ 800/654–4656). **Hyatt Hotels & Resorts** (☎ 800/233–1234). **Inter-Continental** (☎ 800/327–0200). **La Quinta** (☎ 800/531–5900). **Marriott** (☎ 800/228–9290). **Le Meridien** (☎ 800/543–4300). **Nikko Hotels International** (☎ 800/645–5687). **Omni** (☎ 800/843–6664). **Quality Inn** (☎ 800/228–5151). **Radisson** (☎ 800/333–3333). **Ramada** (☎ 800/228–2828). **Renaissance Hotels & Resorts** (☎ 800/468–3571). **Ritz-Carlton** (☎ 800/241–3333). **Sheraton** (☎ 800/325–3535). **Sleep Inn** (☎ 800/221–2222). **Stouffer** (☎ 800/468–3751). **Westin Hotels & Resorts** (☎ 800/228–3000). **Wyndham Hotels & Resorts** (☎ 800/822–4200).

INNS

Charm is the long suit of these establishments, which generally occupy a restored older building with some historical or architectural significance. They're generally small, with fewer than 20 rooms, and located outside cities. Breakfast may be included in the rates.

➤ INFORMATION: **Distinctive Inns of Colorado** (✉ Box 10472, Colorado Springs, CO 80932, ☎ 800/866–0621). **Montana Innkeepers Association** (✉ Box 1272, Helena, MT 59624, ☎ 406/449–8408). **Bed and Breakfast Inns of Utah, Inc.** (✉ Box 2639, Park City, UT 84060, FAX 801/595–0332).

MOTELS

The once-familiar roadside motel is fast disappearing from the American landscape. In its place are chain-run motor inns at highway intersections. Some of these establishments offer very basic facilities; others provide restaurants, swimming pools, and other amenities.

➤ MOTEL CHAINS: **Best Western** (☎ 800/528–1234), **Days Inn** (☎ 800/325–2525), **La Quinta Motor Inns** (☎ 800/531–5900), **Motel 6** (☎ 800/466–8356), **Quality Inn** (☎ 800/228–5151), **Rodeway Inns** (☎ 800/228–

2000), **Super 8 Motels** (☏ 800/800–8000), **Travelodge** (☏ 800/578–7878), **Shilo Inn** (☏ 800/222–2244), and **Skyline Motor Inn** (☏ 800/843–8809) are regional chains.

RESORTS

Ski resort towns throughout the Rockies are home to dozens of resorts in all price ranges; the activities lacking in any individual property can usually be found in the town itself—in summer as well as winter. Off the slopes, there are wonderful rustic/luxurious resorts in the national parks: Jackson Lake Lodge and Jenny Lake Lodge in Grand Teton National Park, and Old Faithful Lodge in Yellowstone. The Broadmoor, in Colorado Springs, is a grand old property dating from the late 19th century.

MONEY MATTERS

First-class hotel rooms in Denver, Salt Lake City, Boise, Missoula, and Cheyenne cost from $75 to $175 a night, although some "value" hotel rooms go for $40–$60, and, as elsewhere in the United States, rooms in national budget chain motels go for around $40 nightly. Weekend packages, offered by most city hotels, cut prices up to 50% (but may not be available in peak winter or summer seasons). As a rule, costs outside the major cities are lower, except in the deluxe resorts. A cup of coffee costs between 50¢ and $1, the price for a hamburger runs between $3 and $5, and a beer at a bar generally is between $1.50 and $3. Prices throughout this guide are given for adults. Substantially reduced fees are almost always available for children, students, and senior citizens. For information on taxes, *see* Taxes, *below.*

ATMS

➤ ATM LOCATIONS: **Cirrus** (☏ 800/424–7787). **Plus** (☏ 800/843–7587).

CREDIT CARDS

Throughout this guide, the following abbreviations are used: **AE**, American Express; **D**, Discover; **DC**, Diner's Club; **MC**, Master Card; and **V**, Visa.

NATIONAL PARKS

Look into discount passes to save money on park entrance fees. The Golden Eagle Pass ($50) gets you and your companions free admission to all parks for one year. (Camping and parking are extra.) Both the Golden Age Passport ($10), for those 62 and older, and the Golden Access Passport (free), for travelers with disabilities, entitle holders to free entry to all national parks, plus 50% off fees for the use of many park facilities and services. You must show proof of age and of U.S. citizenship or permanent residency (such as a U.S. passport, driver's license, or birth certificate) and, if requesting Golden Access, proof of disability. All three passes are available at all national park entrances where entrance fees are charged. Golden Eagle Passes are also available by mail.

➤ PASSES BY MAIL: **National Park Service** (✉ National Capitol Area Office, 1100 Ohio Dr. SW, Washington, DC 20242, ☏ 202/208–4747).

OUTDOORS & SPORTS

Opportunities abound in the Rockies. Guest and dude ranches can tailor programs to meet individual needs. Hiking and mountain biking trails are abundant; contact national forests or parks for details about trails. Topographical maps may be available in well-equipped outdoor stores (REI or Eastern Mountain Sports, for example). Maps are also available from the **U.S. Geological Survey** (✉ Distribution Center, Denver, CO 80225). Be specific about the region you're interested in when ordering.

➤ CLIMBING AND MOUNTAINEERING: **American Alpine Institute** (✉ 1515 12th St., Bellingham, WA 98225, ☏ 360/671–1505). **Colorado Mountain School** (✉ Box 1846, Estes Park, CO 80517, ☏ 970/586–5758).

➤ CYCLING: **Adventure Cycling Association** (✉ Box 8308, Missoula, MT 59807, ☏ 406/721–1776) is perhaps the best general source of information on biking in the Rockies—including detailed maps and information on trip organizers.

➤ FISHING: **Colorado Division of Wildlife** (✉ 6060 Broadway, Denver, CO 80216, ☏ 303/297–1192). **Idaho Department of Fish & Game** (✉ Box 25, 600 S. Walnut St., Boise, ID

83707, ☎ 208/334–3700). **Montana Department of Fish, Wildlife & Parks** (✉ 1420 E. 6th St., Helena, MT 59620, ☎ 406/444–2535). **Utah Division of Wildlife Resources** (✉ 1596 W. North Temple St., Salt Lake City, UT 84116, ☎ 801/538–4700). **Wyoming Game & Fish** (✉ 5400 Bishop Blvd., Cheyenne, WY 82006, ☎ 307/777–4600).

➤ HIKING: **The Mountaineers** (✉ 300 3rd Ave. W, Seattle, WA 98119, ☎ 206/284–6310) and **Sierra Club Books** (✉ 85 2nd St., 4th floor, San Francisco, CA 94105, ☎ 415/977–5600) are among the leading publishers of hiking guides for the Rockies.

➤ PACK TRIPS & HORSEBACK RIDING: **All Round Ranch** (✉ Box 153, Jenson, UT 84035, ☎ 800/603–8069, FAX 435/798–5902). **Glacier Wilderness Guides** (✉ Box 535, West Glacier, MT 59936, ☎ 800/521–7238, FAX 406/387–5656). **Rocky Mountain Outdoor Center** (✉ 10281 Hwy. 50, Howard, CO 81233, ☎ 800/255–5784, FAX 719/942–3215).

PACKING

Informality reigns here; jeans, sport shirts, and T-shirts fit in almost everywhere, for both men and women. The few restaurants and performing-arts events where dressier outfits are required, usually in resorts and larger cities, are the exception.

If you plan to spend much time outdoors, and certainly if you go in winter, **choose clothing appropriate for cold and wet weather.** Cotton clothing, including denim—although fine on warm, dry days—can be uncomfortable when it gets wet and when the weather's cold. A better choice is clothing made of wool or any of a number of new synthetics that provide warmth without bulk and maintain their insulating properties even when wet.

In summer, you'll want shorts during the day. But because early morning and night can be cold, and high passes windy, pack a sweater and a light jacket, and perhaps also a wool cap and gloves. Try layering—a T-shirt under another shirt under a jacket—and peel off layers as you go. For walks and hikes, you'll need sturdy footwear. To take you into the wilds, boots should have thick soles and plenty of ankle support; if your shoes are new and you plan to spend much time on the trail, break them in at home. Bring a day pack for short hikes, along with a canteen or water bottle, and don't forget rain gear, a hat, sunscreen, and insect repellent.

In winter, prepare for subzero temperatures with good boots, warm socks and liners, long johns, a well-insulated jacket, and a warm hat and mittens. Dress in layers so you can add or remove clothes as the temperatures fluctuate.

If you attend dances and other events at Native American reservations, dress conservatively—skirts or long pants for women, long pants for men—or you may be asked to leave.

When traveling to mountain areas, **remember that sunglasses and a sun hat are essential at high altitudes**; the thinner atmosphere requires sunscreen with a greater SPF than you might need at lower elevations.

In your carry-on luggage **bring an extra pair of eyeglasses or contact lenses** and **enough of any medication you take** to last the entire trip. You may also want your doctor to write a spare prescription using the drug's generic name, since brand names may vary from country to country. In luggage to be checked, **never pack prescription drugs or valuables.** To avoid customs delays, carry medications in their original packaging. Don't forget to copy down and carry addresses of offices that handle refunds of lost traveler's checks.

CHECKING LUGGAGE

How many carry-on bags you can bring with you is up to the airline. Most allow two, but not always, so make sure that everything you carry aboard will fit under your seat, and get to the gate early. Note that if you have a seat at the back of the plane, you'll probably board first, while the overhead bins are still empty.

If you are flying internationally, note that baggage allowances may be determined not by piece but by weight—generally 88 pounds (40 kilograms) in first class, 66 pounds

(30 kilograms) in business class, and 44 pounds (20 kilograms) in economy.

Airline liability for baggage is limited to $1,250 per person on flights within the United States. On international flights it amounts to $9.07 per pound or $20 per kilogram for checked baggage (roughly $640 per 70-pound bag) and $400 per passenger for unchecked baggage. You can buy additional coverage at check-in for about $10 per $1,000 of coverage, but it excludes a rather extensive list of items, shown on your airline ticket.

Before departure **itemize your bags' contents** and their worth, and label the bags with your name, address, and phone number. (If you use your home address, cover it so that potential thieves can't see it readily.) Inside each bag **pack a copy of your itinerary.** At check-in **make sure that each bag is correctly tagged** with the destination airport's three-letter code. If your bags arrive damaged or fail to arrive at all, file a written report with the airline before leaving the airport.

PASSPORTS & VISAS

➤ U.K. CITIZENS: **U.S. Embassy Visa Information Line** (☎ 01891/200–290; calls cost 49p per minute, 39p per minute cheap rate) for U.S. visa information. **U.S. Embassy Visa Branch** (✉ 5 Upper Grosvenor Sq., London W1A 1AE) for U.S. visa information; send a self-addressed, stamped envelope. Write the **U.S. Consulate General** (✉ Queen's House, Queen St., Belfast BTI 6EO) if you live in Northern Ireland. Write the **Office of Australia Affairs** (✉ 59th floor, MLC Centre, 19-29 Martin Pl., Sydney, NSW 2000) if you live in Australia. Write the **Office of New Zealand Affairs** (✉ 29 Fitzherbert Terr., Thorndon, Wellington) if you live in New Zealand.

PASSPORT OFFICES

The best time to apply for a passport or to renew is during the fall and winter. Before any trip, check your passport's expiration date, and, if necessary, renew it as soon as possible.

➤ AUSTRALIAN CITIZENS: **Australian Passport Office** (☎ 131–232).

➤ NEW ZEALAND CITIZENS: **New Zealand Passport Office** (☎ 04/494–0700 for information on how to apply; 04/474–8000 or 0800/225–050 in New Zealand for information on applications already submitted).

➤ U.K. CITIZENS: **London Passport Office** (☎ 0990/210–410) for fees and documentation requirements and to request an emergency passport.

SAFETY

Regardless of the outdoor activity or your level of skill, safety must come first. Remember: **know your limits!**

Many trails are at high altitudes, where oxygen is scarce. They're also frequently desolate. Hikers and bikers should **carry emergency supplies** in their backpacks. Proper equipment includes a flashlight, a compass, waterproof matches, a first-aid kit, a knife, and a light plastic tarp for shelter. Backcountry skiers should add a repair kit, a blanket, an avalanche beacon, and a lightweight shovel to their lists. Always **bring extra food and a canteen of water** as dehydration is a common occurrence at high altitudes. **Never drink from streams or lakes,** unless you boil the water first or purify it with tablets. Giardia, an intestinal parasite, may be present.

Always **check the condition of roads and trails, and get the latest weather reports** before setting out. In summer, **take precautions against heat stroke or exhaustion** by resting frequently in shaded areas; in winter, **take precautions against hypothermia** by layering clothing. Ultimately, proper planning, common sense, and good physical conditioning are the strongest guards against the elements.

ALTITUDE

You may feel dizzy and weak and find yourself breathing heavily—signs that the thin mountain air isn't giving you your accustomed dose of oxygen. Take it easy and **rest often for a few days until you're acclimatized.** Throughout your stay drink plenty of water and watch your alcohol consumption. If you experience severe headaches and nausea, see a doctor. It is easy—especially in Colorado, where highways climb to 12,000 ft and higher—to go too high too fast. The remedy for altitude-related discomfort is to go down quickly, into heavier air. Other altitude-related problems include dehydration and overexposure to the sun due to the thin air.

SENIOR-CITIZEN TRAVEL

To qualify for age-related discounts **mention your senior-citizen status up front** when booking hotel reservations (not when checking out) and before you're seated in restaurants (not when paying the bill). When renting a car ask about promotional car-rental discounts, which can be cheaper than senior-citizen rates.

➤ EDUCATIONAL PROGRAMS: **Elderhostel** (✉ 75 Federal St., 3rd floor, Boston, MA 02110, ☎ 877/426–8056, FAX 877/426–2166).

SHOPPING

Western memorabilia and clothing can be found all across the Rockies. Choose your souvenir—a cowboy hat, maybe—and take your pick of dozens of choices. You'll also find Native American crafts for sale.

STUDENTS IN THE ROCKIES

➤ STUDENT IDS & SERVICES: **Council on International Educational Exchange** (CIEE, ✉ 205 E. 42nd St., 14th floor, New York, NY 10017, ☎ 212/822–2600 or 888/268–6245, FAX 212/822–2699) for mail orders only, in the United States. **Travel Cuts** (✉ 187 College St., Toronto, Ontario M5T 1P7, ☎ 416/979–2406 or 800/667–2887) in Canada.

TAXES

SALES TAX

Sales taxes are as follows: 3% in Colorado, 4% in Wyoming, 5% in Idaho, and 6.125% in Utah. Montana has no sales tax. Some areas have additional local sales and lodging taxes.

If you are crossing the border into Canada, be aware of Canada's goods and services tax (better known as the GST). This is a value-added tax of 7%, applicable on virtually every purchase except basic groceries and a small number of other items. Visitors to Canada, however, may **claim a full rebate of the GST** on any goods taken out of the country as well as on short-term accommodations. Rebates can be claimed either immediately on departure from Canada at participating duty-free shops or by mail. Rebate forms can be obtained by writing to Revenue Canada (☞ Customs & Duties, *above*). Claims must be for a minimum of $7 worth of tax and can be submitted up to a year from the date of purchase. Purchases made during multiple visits to Canada can be grouped together for rebate purposes.

TELEPHONES

The telephone area codes for the Rocky Mountain region are 303, 970, and 719 for Colorado; 208 for Idaho; 406 for Montana; 801 and 435 for Utah; and 307 for Wyoming.

Pay telephones cost 25¢ for local calls (except in Wyoming, where the cost is 35¢). Charge phones, also common, may be used to charge a call to a telephone-company calling card or a credit card, or for collect calls.

Many hotels place a surcharge on local calls made from your room and include a service charge on long-distance calls. It may be cheaper for you to make your calls from a pay phone in the hotel lobby rather than from your room.

TIME

Idaho, Montana, Utah, and Wyoming are all in the Mountain Time Zone, as is most of Colorado. The southeastern portion of Colorado, east of the Rockies, is in the Central Time Zone. Mountain time is two hours earlier than Eastern time and one hour later than Pacific time. It is one hour earlier than Chicago, seven hours earlier than London and 17 hours earlier than Sydney. Central time is one hour earlier than New York, two hours later than Los Angeles, six hours earlier than London and 16 hours earlier than Sydney.

TOURS & PACKAGES

On a prepackaged tour or independent vacation everything is prearranged so you'll spend less time planning—and often get it all at a good price.

BOOKING WITH AN AGENT

Travel agents are excellent resources. But it's a good idea to collect brochures from several agencies because some agents' suggestions may be influenced by relationships with tour and package firms that reward them for volume sales. If you have a special interest **find an agent with expertise in that area**; ASTA (☞ Travel Agencies, *below*) has a database of specialists worldwide.

Make sure your travel agent knows the accommodations and other services of the place they're recommending. Ask about the hotel's location; room size; beds; and whether it has a pool, room service, or programs for children, if you care about these. Has your agent been there in person or sent others whom you can contact?

Do some homework on your own, too: Local tourism boards can provide information about lesser-known and small-niche operators, some of which may sell only direct.

BUYER BEWARE

Each year consumers are stranded or lose their money when tour operators—even large ones with excellent reputations—go out of business. So **check out the operator.** Ask several travel agents about its reputation, and try to **book with a company that has a consumer-protection program.** (Look for information in the company's brochure.) In the United States, members of the National Tour Association and United States Tour Operators Association are required to set aside funds to cover your payments and travel arrangements in case the company defaults. It's also a good idea to choose a company that participates in the American Society of Travel Agent's Tour Operator Program (TOP); ASTA will act as mediator in any disputes between you and your tour operator.

Remember that the more your package or tour includes the better you can predict the ultimate cost of your vacation. Make sure you know exactly what is covered, and **beware of hidden costs.** Are taxes, tips, and transfers included? Entertainment and excursions? These can add up.

➤ TOUR-OPERATOR RECOMMENDATIONS: **American Society of Travel Agents** (☞ Travel Agencies, *below*). **National Tour Association** (NTA, ✉ 546 E. Main St., Lexington, KY 40508, ☎ 606/226–4444 or 800/682–8886). **United States Tour Operators Association** (USTOA, ✉ 342 Madison Ave., Suite 1522, New York, NY 10173, ☎ 212/599–6599 or 800/468–7862, FAX 212/599–6744).

TRAIN TRAVEL

Amtrak (☎ 800/872–7245) connects the Rockies to both coasts and all major American cities, with trains that run through Boise, Salt Lake City, Cheyenne, and Denver, and other stops in between. Amtrak trains also run through northern Montana, with stops in Essex and Whitefish, along the southern border of Glacier National Park. Connecting bus services to Yellowstone National Park are provided in the summer from Amtrak's stop in Pocatello, Idaho.

Canada's passenger service, **VIA Rail Canada** (☎ 800/561–3949), stops at Jasper, near the Canadian entrance to Waterton/Glacier International Peace Park (☞ Glacier National Park *in* Chapter 6).

SCENIC TRAIN TRIPS

Several Rocky Mountain states have restored unused stretches of track and refurbished turn-of-the-century touring cars. These give you the chance to scout out places beyond the reach of any four-lane freeway.

The American Orient Express Railway Company (✉ 5100 Main St., Downers Grove, WA 60515, ☎ 206/441–2725 or 888/759–3944) operates several trips in the Rockies region—including one that visits a few national parks—aboard its luxury cars.

In Colorado the best-known journeys are to **Pikes Peak** (☎ 719/685–5401) on the highest cog railway in the world and the celebrated **Durango & Silverton** (☎ 970/247–2733) narrow-gauge mining-train trip along the Animas River. For more details on these and other rail excursions, contact the **Colorado Railroad Museum** (✉ 17155 W. 44th Ave., Box 10, Golden, CO 80402, ☎ 303/279–4591, FAX 303/279–4229).

On the **Heber Valley Historic Railroad** (☎ 435/654–5601) in Utah, you can catch the *Heber Creeper,* a turn-of-the-century steam engine train that rides the rails from Heber City across Heber Valley, alongside Deer Creek Reservoir, down Provo Canyon to Vivian Park.

TRAVEL AGENCIES

A good travel agent puts your needs first. Look for an agency that has been in business at least five years, emphasizes customer service, and has someone on staff who specializes in your destination. In addition **make sure the agency belongs to a professional trade organization.** The American Society of Travel Agents (ASTA), with 27,000 agents in some 170 countries, is the largest and most influential in the field. Operating under the motto "Integrity in Travel," it maintains and enforces a strict code of ethics and will step in to help mediate any agent-client disputes if necessary. ASTA also maintains a Web site that includes a directory of agents. Note that if a travel agency is also acting as your tour operator, *see* Buyer Beware *in* Tours & Packages, *above.*

➤ LOCAL AGENT REFERRALS: **American Society of Travel Agents** (ASTA, ☎ 800/965–2782 24-hr hot line, FAX 703/684–8319, www.astanet.com). **Association of British Travel Agents** (✉ 68–271 Newman St., London W1P 4AH, ☎ 020/7637–2444, FAX 020/7637–0713). **Association of Canadian Travel Agents** (✉ 1729 Bank St., Suite 201, Ottawa, Ontario K1V 7Z5, ☎ 613/521–0474, FAX 613/521–0805). **Australian Federation of Travel Agents** (✉ Level 3, 309 Pitt St., Sydney 2000, ☎ 02/9264–3299, FAX 02/9264–1085). **Travel Agents' Association of New Zealand** (✉ Box 1888, Wellington 10033, ☎ 04/499–0104, FAX 04/499–0786).

VISITOR INFORMATION

➤ TOURIST INFORMATION: **Colorado Travel and Tourism Authority** (✉ Box 22005, Denver 80222, ☎ 303/832–6171 or 800/265–6723, FAX 303/832–6174). **Idaho Travel Council** (✉ Department of Commerce, 700 W. State St., Boise 83720, ☎ 208/334–2470 or 800/635–7820, FAX 208/334–2175). **Travel Montana** (✉ Department of Commerce, 1424 9th Ave., Helena 59620, ☎ 406/444–2654 or 800/847–4868, FAX 406/444–1800). **Utah Travel Council** (✉ Council Hall, Capitol Hill, 300 North State St., Salt Lake City 84114, ☎ 801/538–1030 or 800/200–1160 for brochures, FAX 801/538–1399, ☎ 801/521–8102 for ski reports). **Wyoming Tourist Office** (✉ I–25 at College Dr., Cheyenne 82002, ☎ 307/777–7777 or 800/225–5996, FAX 307/777–6904).

WEB SITES

Do **check out the World Wide Web** when you're planning. You'll find everything from up-to-date weather forecasts to virtual tours of famous cities. Fodor's Web site www.fodors.com, is a great place to start your online travels. For more information specifically on the Rockies, visit: colorado.com, visitmt.com, idaho.com, utah.com, and wyoming.com.

WHEN TO GO

Hotels in major tourist destinations book up early, especially in July and August, and hikers crowd the backcountry from June through Labor Day. Temperatures rarely rise above the 80s.

Ski resorts buzz from December to early April, especially during Christmas and President's holiday weeks.

If you don't mind sometimes-capricious weather, spring and fall are opportune seasons to visit. Rates drop and crowds are nonexistent. You may even enjoy a corner of Yellowstone all to yourself. Spring's pleasures are somewhat limited, since snow usually blocks the high country well into June, and mountain-pass roads, such as the famous Going-to-the-Sun Road in Glacier National Park, stay closed into June. But spring is a good time for fishing, rafting on rivers swollen with snowmelt, birding, and wildlife-viewing. In fall, aspens splash the mountainsides with gold, and wildlife come down to lower elevations. The fish are spawning, and the angling is excellent.

CLIMATE

Summer in the Rockies begins in late June or early July. Days are warm, with highs often in the 80s, while nighttime temperatures fall to the 40s and 50s. Afternoon thunderstorms are common over the higher peaks. Fall begins in September, often with a week of unsettled weather around mid-month, followed by four–six gorgeous weeks of Indian summer—frosty nights and warm days. Winter creeps in during November, and deep snows have arrived by December. Temperatures usually hover near freezing by day, thanks to the surprisingly warm mountain sun, dropping considerably overnight, occasionally as low as -60° F. Winter tapers off in March, though snow lingers into April on valley bottoms and into July on mountain passes. The Rockies have a reputation for extreme weather, but that cuts two ways: No condition ever lasts for long.

➤ FORECASTS: **Weather Channel Connection** (☎ 900/932–8437), 95¢ per minute from a Touch-Tone phone.

What follows are the average daily maximum and minimum temperatures for the region.

ASPEN, CO

Jan.	33F	1C	May	64F	18C	Sept.	71F	22C
	6	–14		32	0		35	2
Feb.	37F	3C	June	73F	23C	Oct.	60F	16C
	8	–13		37	3		28	– 2
Mar.	42F	6C	July	80F	27C	Nov.	44F	7C
	15	– 9		44	7		15	– 9
Apr.	53F	12C	Aug.	78F	26C	Dec.	37F	3C
	24	– 4		42	6		8	–13

BOISE, ID

Jan.	37F	3C	May	71F	22C	Sept.	75F	24C
	21	– 6		44	7		46	8
Feb.	42F	6C	June	80F	27C	Oct.	64F	18C
	26	– 3		51	11		39	4
Mar.	53F	12C	July	89F	32C	Nov.	50F	10C
	33	1		57	14		30	– 1
Apr.	62F	17C	Aug.	87F	31C	Dec.	39F	4C
	37	3		55	13		24	– 4

HELENA, MT

Jan.	28F	– 2C	May	62F	17C	Sept.	66F	19C
	12	–11		41	5		44	7
Feb.	32F	0C	June	71F	22C	Oct.	55F	13C
	15	– 9		48	9		35	2
Mar.	42F	6C	July	80F	27C	Nov.	41F	5C
	23	– 5		53	12		24	– 4
Apr.	53F	12C	Aug.	78F	26C	Dec.	32F	0C
	33	1		53	12		17	– 8

SALT LAKE CITY, UT

Jan.	35F	2C	May	73F	23C	Sept.	78F	26C
	17	– 8		44	7		48	9
Feb.	41F	5C	June	82F	28C	Oct.	66F	19C
	24	– 4		51	11		39	4
Mar.	51F	11C	July	91F	33C	Nov.	48F	9C
	30	– 1		60	16		28	– 2
Apr.	62F	17C	Aug.	89F	32C	Dec.	39F	4C
	37	3		60	16		21	– 6

SHERIDAN, WY

Jan.	33F	– 1C	May	66F	19C	Sept.	71F	22C
	6	–14		39	4		41	5
Feb.	35F	2C	June	75F	24C	Oct.	60F	16C
	10	–12		48	9		30	– 1
Mar.	46F	8C	July	86F	30C	Nov.	46F	8C
	21	– 6		53	12		19	– 7
Apr.	55F	13C	Aug.	84F	29C	Dec.	35F	2C
	30	– 1		50	10		10	–12

1 DESTINATION: THE ROCKIES

BETWEEN A ROCK AND A HIGH PLACE

THE ROCKY MOUNTAINS DEFINE America, in both literal and symbolic ways. The sawtooth crest of the Rockies is the backbone of the continent—hence the Continental Divide—and emanating from it are many of America's great rivers, born from trickles of snowmelt that gradually join forces as streams to flow east and west like veins feeding a single, massive organism.

The Rockies also demarcate a line where the East ends and the West begins, a line where old-world principles segue into a still simmering ethos of manifest destiny. From 40,000 ft in transcontinental flight, you can witness in the landscape the earmarks of a cultural transformation. To the east, the orderly mosaic of wheat fields and farmlands represents a rootedness in a stay-at-home, hard-work ethic. To the west, the vast and jumbled open spaces of Colorado, Utah, and Idaho—largely public lands, largely undeveloped—suggest in spirit (if not always in fact) that there is still room in the American Dream for the buffalo to roam and for the antelope to play.

And somewhere within the Rockies themselves resides the essential, unflagging soul of American ruggedness. The country may be hell-bent on urbanizing, modernizing, and multiplying, and in such Rocky Mountain cities as Denver and Salt Lake City, urban sprawl may be spreading like an incurable pox. But that won't stop Americans from hanging on to an intuitive, collective belief in a land of rough-and-tumble vigor at the edge of the frontier. That's where the Rockies come in—rough-and-tumble geology still harboring the American frontier myth.

If there are three geographical features an American ought to see as a rite of citizenship, they are the Atlantic Ocean, the Pacific Ocean, and the Rocky Mountains. But beyond the dull obligations of democratic duty, the Rockies impress in other simple and profound ways: simple, in that they are, simply, big and beautiful; profound, in that they invoke a primordial spirit of wilderness and timelessness. The Rockies can inspire an appreciation that escapes logic, that comes on when alpenglow is the last light of day or when new snow highlights each feathered ledge in a band of rock cliffs. It occurs when the wild bloom of high-alpine meadows exceeds any fair description of color. The sentiment is something close to faith.

It is also something beyond accurate representation. On relief maps, the two-billion-year-old Rockies are often drawn as a single string of mountains—forming blisters on the page—and are defined primarily by the dotted line of the Continental Divide. The plains are over and the mountains begin, and that's that.

But that's *not* that. The Rockies (and here things can get fuzzy, confused by which mountain ranges geologists choose to consider part of the Rockies) cut a swath several hundred miles wide in places and constitute multiple ranges and spurs, each with slightly or markedly differing characteristics. The Colorado Rockies are the highest of the bunch, with the most peaks exceeding 14,000 ft, but ironically they might not seem so because the timberline (the point above which trees won't grow) is unusually high. In short, the Rockies aren't, as the maps might suggest, one big strip of interchangeable rock.

All of these ranges do, however, share a similar history. Uplift (the pressure inflicted by the movements and swelling of ancient oceans through aeons of time) preyed upon weaknesses in the land mass (weaknesses known appropriately if unsympathetically as "faults"); the land squeezed thus could go nowhere but *up*. Couple that phenomenon with volcanic activity and mountains were the result.

Thereafter came the sculpting effects of erosion, with water in various forms (ice, snow, rain, fog, and waterfalls) being the primary chisels. Over the long, long haul, the characteristic formations that we identify as elemental to mountain structure have taken shape: peaks, ridges, bowls, cirques, arêtes, scree slopes, and so on. On lower slopes, depending on the quality and availability of soil as well as the harshness of weather, trees have grown: mainly cottonwoods and aspens (or "quakies," as the cowboys dubbed them because of the shimmering illusion created by their leaves in the sun and wind); higher up, Douglas fir, lodgepole pine, and Engelmann spruce.

Although there are those rare events when the Earth shrugs and mountains heave with cataclysmic suddenness, the Rockies are essentially a stationary spectacle, or, as they appeared to settlers from the East in the 1800s, a stationary obstacle. One can only imagine the thoughts of the pioneers and railroaders on seeing the Rockies for the first time: A mix, presumably of awe and annoyance; inspired by the mountains' beauty yet flustered by the impending (and inevitable) difficulties in finding passage to the other side.

It is somewhat easier to tap the mind-set of prospectors who, after word spread of the discovery of the Comstock lode in western Nevada in the 1850s, came to the Rockies with visions of vast wealth. It's uncertain whether the mountains imposed a ruggedness on the miners and railroad workers, the vanguard of settlement in the Rockies, or whether it was the other way around. Probably a bit of both. These were rowdy men in a rugged country: Civil War deserters, ex-cons, bushwhackers, and miners whose previous claims had come up empty in California, Nevada, or British Columbia. As Glenn Chesney Quiett put it in *They Built the West,* "It was a rough, dangerous, dirty, sweating, hard-working, hard-drinking, free-spending life."

It was not a life made any more comfortable by Native American tribes residing in the mountains—the Cheyenne, the Crow, the Blackfoot, and others—whose homelands had been invaded by these interlopers pick-axing the countryside. Confrontations were numerous; Quiett relates one story in which the natives killed a man by lighting a bonfire on his chest, suggesting—quite obviously—that some natives were going around in very ill humor in regards to the whole idea of the white man's settlement.

Mining, railway construction, lawbreaking, opportunism: The early settlement of the Rockies began taking shape. The route of the railway dictated which Rocky Mountain outposts would become major cities and which wouldn't; that Denver, Colorado, rather than Cheyenne, Wyoming, became the central metropolis of the eastern slope of the Rockies was due largely to politicking by Denver's business elite. It was due also to the paying of a hefty sum to the railroad for the right to have the rail route pass through town. Miners came, established towns, settled in (or some did, anyway), and left their mark and legacy. Indeed, towns that have become popular resorts in the latter half of the 20th century—Aspen, Breckenridge, and Telluride in Colorado and Park City in Utah, for example—have their roots in mining.

UNLIKE GEOLOGY IN ITS incomprehensible slowness, human activity in the Rockies has evolved and changed in a hurry. It has all transpired in little more than 100 years, which isn't even a hiccup's worth of geological time. As precious-metal mining has ebbed (due as much to a swoon in metal prices as a lack of ore) as a mainstay of the Rocky Mountain economy in the last few decades, a boom in tourism has more than filled the gap. Before the 1960s, visitors who spent time in the Rockies were likely to be bohemians, artists, die-hard sportsmen, and national-park visitors in Winnebagos and Airstreams; or passersby broken down in transit—axle busted en route to California and the American Dream. Today the region hosts families and tourists of all means.

As much as any single event in the region, the creation of Vail (the ski resort 100 mi west of Denver) in 1964 issued an evangelical message to the world that tourism in the Rockies was for everyone. In 1963, Vail was an empty valley; today it is a tourism machine generating hundreds of millions of dollars a year in summer and winter business, but not including real-estate turnover, which is hardly small potatoes. No wonder other Rockies resorts, following the Vail model in varying degrees, have sprung up since the mid-1960s to tap the mighty tourism dollar.

Anyone who spends any time in the Rockies is destined to be touched by the exquisite landscape supporting an intricately entwined network of ecosystems—and is subsequently destined to make judgments and establish values accordingly. The high Rockies are full of amazements; for example, on south-facing slopes in April, microscopic buds of wildflowers can be found incubating under shards of warm shale, while the snow on north-facing slopes is likely to be still several feet deep. The lesson here, miraculous as it is, is also quite simple: The land, severe as it is, takes care of itself. It regenerates all on its own. Things work. Unfortunately, once you accept the premise that you are in the presence of nature efficiently and dispassionately going about its own business—a premise that invariably comes in one form or another to anyone who visits or lives in the Rockies—you tend then to proceed to the next obvious question: What to do about it? Here, things turn troublesome.

IN THE LAST DECADE or so the Rocky Mountain states have become the political focus of land grabbers, tree huggers, civilization escapees, resort developers, ranchers, sportspeople, seasonal workers, and the "Hollywood element." Each group has its own sense of righteous propriety and feelings about how the land should be best managed. For whatever reason—and a sheer, alpine beauty comes immediately to mind—almost everyone who comes to the Rockies for any length of time develops an instinctive (if imagined) sense of aboriginal belonging. It's funny: You hear people who have spent barely a year or two of their lives in the Rockies talk wistfully of "the way things used to be," as if their families had lived there for generations. Such reminiscence, of course, implies an attitude about the way things *ought* to be. The upshot is a messy collision of territorial imperatives: Each group is sure it *knows* what is best for the land, and how to defend it against the greed, shortsightedness, or hare-brained thoughtlessness of others. This can lead to such wacky scenarios as ardent wildlife preservationists stalking hunters, who in turn are stalking animals, the idea being that when the hunter gets lined up for a shot, the preservationists make a holy racket, alerting the animal and averting the kill. It is environmental politics right out of *Caddyshack*.

The issues are impossibly, hopelessly complex. In simplest terms the question is: What's the proper formula for balancing the interest of people, the integrity of the land and its resources, and the needs of wildlife? It is a question inevitably muddled in morality, pragmatism, science, self-interest, and the indisputable fact that nobody really knows for sure. As yet, there is no single Grand Unifying Theory. The result, in part, has been a balkanized checkerboard: private land, wilderness areas, national parks, national forests, national monuments, state parks, state forests, wildlife preserves, Native American reservations. Tread carefully. The rules change from one land type to the next, and the borders aren't always obvious (except, mysteriously, to wild animals, who seem to know more accurately than surveyors where national-park borders are, and within which hunting is prohibited). For example, hunting and campfires are legal in national forests but not in national parks; some private landowners are good sports about rights of way, some charge fees, some will have you arrested for just contemplating trespassing. And so on.

When 323,291 acres of forest land burned in Yellowstone in the summer of 1988, fire control was a bitter issue: Would it be better to allow a fire to burn its natural course, even if it might threaten wildlife and human settlements? Fire, the argument goes, is part of a forest's natural way of replenishing itself. Or would it be more correct to fight the fire with every resource at one's disposal, snuffing it out as quickly as possible?

Are mountain resorts scars upon the landscape, as some environmentalists might suggest, or nodes of economic sustenance producing, in most respects, less environmental hazard and impact than mining, ranching, or lumbering? Do visitors to the resorts simply overpopulate an environmentally sensitive region? Or, inspired by the beauty of the land, does their visiting heighten their own environmental sensitivity? And do they then pass that new sensitivity on to others?

The ultimate question is: Who knows?

Fortunately, the Rockies are still big country. There is a lot of room for people to do a lot of shouting, hand-wringing, and placard-waving without upsetting, in any measurable way, the balance of the universe. For all the shouting, for all the resort development that boomed in the '80s and '90s; for all the ranchers fencing in land and upsetting animal migratory patterns; for all the Hollywooders moving to Aspen or to Livingston, Montana, and wrecking the neighborhood, as some residents imply; for all the environmentalists militating against growth—for all of that, and above and beyond all of that, the Rockies remain relatively uncongested, undeveloped country, where the air above 12,000 ft is still clean.

The population density of Colorado, by far the most populous of the Rocky Mountain states, is about 32 people per square mile. Compare that, for example, with 190 people per square mile in California or more than 1,000 per square mile (gasp!) in New Jersey. There are more people living in the borough of Brooklyn, New York, than in the states of Idaho, Montana, and Wyoming combined.

Wandering around in these open spaces, one comes occasionally across the relics of human failure, most likely old mining encampments, now rotting and rusting on their slow way toward vanishing into total decay. They are small reminders that however abusive or misguided people are and have been in their use of this land, the land has the patience to heal itself. Patience that people, with life spans of infinitesimal shortness in geologic terms, can't fathom. If the mountains had a voice in all the land-management yakkety-yak, they would be saying something like: "We can wait. We don't care."

And in the shorter term, the Rockies have one other ace in the hole in withstanding the incursion of man: their own magisterial presence, their ruggedness. The Rockies were the last part of the country to be "settled" and may be the only part of the country that will never be broadly developed. One doesn't build cities on 40-degree slopes raked by rock slides and avalanches. The land is too severe and the growing seasons too short to sustain viable commercial cultivation (except, to some degree, timber crops). In other words, the high-mountain wilderness is a great place to visit but you wouldn't want to live there. And a great place, too, in the summer sun, when the thin air steals breath and the dust settles on old roads, to imagine an America still youthful and inchoate, at the edge of an unexplored frontier.

–Peter Oliver

NEW AND NOTEWORTHY

COLORADO➢ The buzzword in Colorado today is **growth**—and not all of it good, according to locals. Since 1990, more than half a million people have moved to the state's Front Range (the string of such population centers as Denver, Colorado Springs, and Boulder, nudging up against the eastern foothills of the Rockies). Lured by the great outdoors and the opportunities that the state's economic boom offers, they come seeking Utopia and find instead a "brown cloud" of pollution over Denver, and subdivisions that threaten to engulf what used to be ranch land and open space between communities.

Not that this influx should come as a surprise. Denver has aggressively positioned itself as the cultural and entertainment capital of the Rockies—and as the largest city in a 600-mi radius, that hasn't been hard to do. Since 1995, Denver has become a sports lover's mecca, adding the Stanley Cup-winning Colorado Avalanche hockey franchise to the sellout two-time Super Bowl-winning NFL Broncos, the NBA Nuggets, and the wildly popular Rockies baseball team. The $215 million downtown ballpark **Coors Field,** opened in 1995, has revitalized the lower downtown area (LoDo), filling it with brew pubs, cafés, galleries, lofts, and throngs of people on summer nights. **Colorado's Ocean Journey** has brought a gorgeous aquarium to Denver. Other capital improvement highlights have included the construction of the Michael Graves–designed **Denver Public Library,** the relocation of Elitch Gardens Amusement Park into the downtown area, and of course, the controversy-plagued **Denver International Airport.**

And what of the new airport? Coloradans may still be disgruntled at the $4.3 billion money drain and the inconvenience of having to drive a half-hour farther to the airport, but ironically, DIA has proved a boon to out-of-state visitors by spurring lower fares and expanded service elsewhere. The **Colorado Springs Airport** has become a viable alternative to DIA. Vail's **Eagle County Airport** added a new terminal in late '95 and has since almost doubled its number of flights. Indeed, travelers from New York, Chicago, and Los Angeles can now fly nonstop to Vail, often for not much more than flying to Denver.

IDAHO➢ A decade ago, residents of other regions had difficulty distinguishing Idaho from Iowa. That's changed, and longtime residents of the Gem State have decidedly mixed feelings about their discovery. **Real estate** prices are soaring, especially in Idaho's panhandle and in Sun Valley, which have been discovered by city dwellers looking for their own piece of peace. Not only are people moving to Idaho, but they're vacationing there in droves. Tourism ranks third among the state's top industries, and in the past decade lodging revenues have increased well over 50% in many parts of the state. One of the most lucrative spots on the Idaho map is **Sun Valley.** A skiing mecca for decades, the scenic area now holds its own as a summer travel destination, keeping the cash registers ringing year-round.

Boise, too, continues to enjoy growth and rising property values. The late 1990s brought significant improvements to the capital city's entertainment scene: the new Bank of America Center downtown, the Idaho Center in nearby Nampa, and the adjacent Idaho Center Amphitheater pull in major concerts ranging from Lilith Fair to Eric Clapton to Neil Diamond. The acclaimed Idaho Shakespeare Festival finally has a permanent home, a lovely riverside amphitheater shaded by cottonwoods on Boise's eastern edge. In 1999 Boise State University debuted a new spring jazz festival named for local piano legend Gene Harris. Sports fans got a major boost with the introduction of three new professional sports teams based in Boise and Nampa. The Idaho Steelheads slam the hockey puck around the Bank of America Center, while the Idaho Center hosts basketball's Idaho Stampede and the new indoor football league's Idaho Stallions.

MONTANA➢ The big news in Montana is that it's time to slow down. After four years as a haven for gas-pedal stompers and Autobahn wanna-bes, the Big Sky State imposed a daytime speed limit just in time for Memorial Day weekend 1999. When the federal speed limit ended in 1995, Montana chose not to replace it, instead establishing a "basic rule" requiring "reasonable and prudent" behavior behind the wheel. (Not surprisingly, many drivers' definition of "prudent" differed from that of the average state trooper.) Finally, the state Supreme Court ruled that the non-limit limit was too vague, and state lawmakers imposed numerical limits. The new limits are 75 mph for open-area interstates, 70 mph for two-lane highways, and 65 mph for U.S. 93 and interstates in the immediate vicinities of Billings, Great Falls, and Missoula.

Off the highway, life has returned to Big Sky normalcy after several years of unprecedented bad press as a haven for the militantly anti-government and anti-science. The two most prominent such stories came to a close in 1998, when leaders of the anti-government Montana Freemen were convicted of federal charges resulting from an 81-day standoff with the FBI, and Unabomber Ted Kaczynski was sentenced to life in prison. Now Montanans can focus again on the perpetual pressures of their state's beauty and popularity. The influx of upscale out-of-staters to many of Montana's most beautiful and peaceful areas has caused rocketing real estate prices and increased encroachment on wildlife and privacy-loving Montanans. These pressures are particularly acute in the scenic mountain country on either side of the Continental Divide: the Bitterroot Valley and Flathead Lake areas near **Missoula** and **Bigfork,** and the lovely mountain valleys between **Bozeman** and Yellowstone National Park.

UTAH➢ With the 2002 Olympic Winter Games drawing near, Utah is putting the finishing touches on both the sport venues and the state's infrastructure. By mid-2001 a complete rebuild of the Interstate 15 corridor through the Salt Lake Valley, as well as a light-rail system through Salt Lake City, will make it easy to shuttle around the skating venues, while a new road to the Snowbasin Ski Resort will make it quicker to reach the downhill and Super G race courses. Most of the venues are ready to go. At the **Utah Winter Sports Park** just north of Park City, not only can you watch athletes in training and world-class competitions but you can also try ski jumping or riding down the bobsled course with a professional driver and brakeman. The race courses at the Deer Valley, Park City, and Snowbasin resorts also are in place, so you can sample the terrain. Finally, just a week after the close of the 2002 Olympics, Salt Lake will host the **VII Paralympic Winter Games,** the world's top competition for athletes with disabilities. While the **speed-skating oval** in the Salt Lake suburb of Kearns is currently closed until late 2001 as crews enclose it and install seating, you can skate at **The Peaks Ice Arena** in Provo, which will host women's ice hockey. For information on the Games and any of the venues, contact the **Salt Lake Organizing Committee** (☎ 801/212–2002). For lodging information, contact the **Salt Lake Convention and Visitors Bureau** (☎ 877/752–4386).

Designated in September of 1996, the **Grand Staircase–Escalante National Monument** sprawls across 1.7 million acres of Southern Utah. Although few services are offered right now in this pristine area, it is extremely rich in natural and cultural history, as well as geologic values, and it promises intriguing explorations in the future.

WYOMING➢ The most significant change affecting travelers to Wyoming is new **national park entrance fees** for Grand Teton and Yellowstone, as approved in a pilot program intended to generate more money for park maintenance. Park entrance fees are $20 per vehicle, $10 per individual on foot or bicycle, and $15 for motorcycle or snowmobile. The passes are good for seven days in both Grand Teton and Yellowstone parks. Annual passes are $40. Golden Eagle and Golden Age passes are still accepted.

Wyoming's connection to national pioneer **emigrant trails**—the Oregon, California, Mormon, and Pony Express trails all cross the state—continues with new programs at sites along the trail corridor. The 150th anniversary of the Mormon Trail was commemorated in 1997 and led to the addition of trail markers and interpretative exhibits and the development of improved maps and brochures that make it easier find the key trail sites. The Martin's Cove Visitor Center on the historic **Sun Ranch** (60 mi west of Casper on Route 220) opened in May 1997. It offers detailed information about Sun Ranch, the Mormon Trail, and the history of Western migration. Visitors get a chance to push a handcart, as did some 19th-century travelers, along 3½ mi of emigrant trail. The National Historic Trails Center in Casper is now under construction; ground breaking occurred in June 1999 in conjunction with the 150th anniversary of the California Trail. The center is expected to open in the summer of 2001.

WHAT'S WHERE

Colorado

With the Rocky Mountains as its enormous spine, and deep canyons carved by its three main rivers, Colorado is a state of sharp contrasts. The Colorado Rockies offer every possible skiing experience, from the glitter and gossip of Aspen to the skiing purism of Crested Butte. Denver, the Mile High City, has transformed its cow-town aura with a downtown arts district and bustling business centers. To the southwest is the Black Canyon of the Gunnison, whose walls narrow so severely that little sunlight can reach the bottom; as well as the mysterious cliff dwellings of the Anasazi people at Mesa Verde. Near Colorado Springs stands Pikes Peak, the state's most indelible landmark. Katherine Lee Bates wrote "America the Beautiful" while gazing out from its summit.

Idaho

In Idaho, it often seems as if state creed dictates that there is no admittance unless you do something outdoors. Mountain biking, rock climbing, and skiing rank among the most popular pursuits, and the Gem State provides plenty of challenging terrain. That terrain, however, might not seem too hospitable at first. Southern Idaho's flat plains are broken by geysers, hot springs, sand dunes, and lava craters, along with taller-than-Niagara waterfalls and the great gash of the Snake River canyon. In contrast to these stark natural wonders are the plush Sun Valley ski resort and upwardly mobile Boise, with its wine bars, corporate headquarters, and stately mansions warmed by natural hot springs. Northern Idaho has its own extremes in Hells Canyon, a cleft even deeper (though narrower) than the Grand Canyon, and the Salmon River, the longest wild river left in the lower 48 states. These superlatives add up to an outstanding welcome for sports enthusiasts of all stripes. With its impressive terrain, Idaho provides for everything from fly-fishing to white-water river rafting to Alpine skiing.

Montana

The moniker "Big Sky Country" only tells half the story; as the nation's fourth-largest state, Montana has the land to match. More than 30% of this land is publicly owned, making it a gold mine of national forests and parks. (Literal gold mines exist as well—in the late 1800s, gold strikes led to a flood of settlers, which in turn spurred conflict with the Native Americans. The famous Battle of Little Bighorn, otherwise known as Custer's Last Stand, was fought here.) The best trout fishing in the country is found at the Yellowstone, Missouri, Madison, Beaverhead, Gallatin, and Bighorn rivers. Montana's mountainous western half bears the "Crown of the Continent," Glacier National Park, which retains vestiges of the great glaciers that scraped across this majestic landscape, leaving behind impressive lakes, waterfalls, and knife-edge ridges. East of the Continental Divide, rugged mountain country yields to the flowing plains and ranch land that inspired the name "Big Sky Country." The Divide marks a stark separation for more than just topography: Ranching, conservative politics, hunting, and distrust of government regulation continue to dominate the way of life in eastern Montana's far-flung small towns, where locals consider the mountain-bike-and-espresso-set an aberration in their state. Western Montana is generally more liberal and recreation-oriented, with avid environmentalists battling those who strive to preserve the logging and mining economies that built the region's towns.

Utah

Few states can match Utah's topography. In the south, sculpted red-rock desert is showcased in five national parks. In the north, the Wasatch Range stretches from the Idaho border to central Utah and is peppered with ski and summer resorts. Most of Utah's major cities line the base of these mountains, including the capital, Salt Lake City, founded by Mormon pioneers in 1847. Salt Lake City still maintains strong religious ties. Far to the southeast, Moab, along the Colorado River, is headquarters for religion of another kind: mountain biking. With both history and adventure to offer statewide, Utah delivers a surprising blend of recreation and cultural charm.

Wyoming

For most people, Wyoming conjures up images of its northwestern area, dominated by Yellowstone National Park and the Grand Teton mountains. Yellowstone is recovering well from the fires of 1988, and visitors can examine first-hand the ecological renewal process. Not to be entirely outdone by its neighbor, the Teton range harbors one of America's most challenging ski resorts, Jackson Hole. In the southeastern corner of the state, Laramie and Cheyenne still possess a strong frontier flavor—even if they're no longer exactly "hell on wheels."

PLEASURES AND PASTIMES

Climbing and Mountaineering

Climbing in its various forms—mountaineering, rock climbing, ice climbing—is a year-round sport in the Rockies. Many "fourteeners" (peaks over 14,000 ft), such as Long's Peak in Colorado, are a relatively easy (although long) ascent for the well-conditioned and well-prepared, but there are also dozens of highly technical climbs, such as the spires of El Dorado Canyon in Colorado, the City of Rocks in Idaho, and the jagged Grand Teton in Wyoming. In many areas, especially in the national parks, climbing permits are required, primarily for safety reasons. Rangers want to be sure that you have the experience and skill necessary to undertake the challenge at hand. No one should attempt technical rock or mountain climbing without proper skills and equipment.

Cycling

Mountain biking, as a sport and cultural phenomenon, has a huge following in the Rockies and is more popular in the region than touring on paved roads. Moab, Utah, has become the mountain biker's mecca, with its fortuitous spreads of asphalt-smooth sandstone, or slickrock, formations. (The Slickrock Trail has both a practice and a main loop.) For an expedition-length ride, the 100-mi White Rim Trail near Moab offers spectacular views of Canyonlands National Park. In Colorado, Crested Butte vies with Moab as the mountain biking center of the Rockies; the trip over the demanding Pearl Pass is supposedly how the biking craze originated. As for road cycling, the San Juan Mountains loop is as beautiful a ride as there is in the country. Keep in mind that elevations in the Rockies are high, and that they exact their physical toll in an aerobic sport such as cycling. Not only should you be physically fit, but you should be prepared to settle for riding shorter distances than you might be capable of handling at lower elevations. Valley roads tend to be clear of snow by mid- to late-April; roads and trails at higher elevations may not be clear until several months later and may be snow-covered again by early October.

Dining

In 1944, a Denver drive-in owner named Louis Ballast grilled a slice of cheese on top of a hamburger and became famous for patenting his invention, the cheeseburger. It has been suggested that Rocky Mountain cuisine consists of the three *B*s: beef, buffalo, and burritos. Although these items certainly will appear on menus throughout the region, restaurant chefs rise to the challenge and head to market to round out the offerings with seasonal and local specialties.

In addition to mouthwatering steak and tender lamb, this is prime hunting and fishing territory, so antelope, elk, venison, and grouse are no strangers to the Rockies palate. Rainbow trout, salmon, and bass pulled from someone's favorite (and maybe secret) fishing spot find their way onto almost every menu. Colorado's Rocky Mountain oysters (fried bull testicles) are famous—some would say infamous—for their size and taste.

On the flora side of things, Colorado's sugar-sweet Rocky Ford cantaloupe has passionate admirers. Utah's raspberries and cherries make incredible pies, and huckleberries from Montana or Idaho are used in everything from muffins to ice cream. Apples, peaches, and pears from roadside stands are deliciously tree-ripened. And don't forget about potatoes—natives will tell you that if it's not from Idaho, it's just a spud.

Although each state has its share of excellent regional specialties, ethnic foods are finally breaking into the three *B*s circle; the posher ski resorts in particular come equipped with a wide range of international cuisine. With such high-end resort towns as Vail and Aspen, Colorado's dining scene is quite sophisticated. Idaho and Wyoming reputedly have the best steaks; no ties are needed, as almost all establishments are casual—this holds true for Montana as well. Utah's fine restaurants are primarily centered in Salt Lake City and Park City, but there are some surprises to be found scattered in less populated areas as well. The once notoriously strict drinking laws have been significantly altered, so that having a glass of wine with dinner is now common practice.

As for regional beverages, some parts of the Rockies possess excellent vineyards, and local wines are often featured in the best restaurants. Southwest Idaho's Treasure Valley is home to the award-winning Ste. Chapelle and Weston wineries, and the industry is one of the fastest-growing in Colorado. Beer is also popular, and microbreweries are enjoying increasing recognition throughout the area. Often located in or connected with a local pub, some of these breweries produce only enough specialty beers (called microbrews) for their own establishments. Colorado has more microbreweries than any other state, and some of their brews, such as Crested Butte's Fat Tire Ale, are available from regular beer outlets. Other strong entries in the microbrew market are Montana's Black Dog and Idaho's Table Rock.

Dude Ranches

Dude ranches fall roughly into two categories: working ranches and guest ranches. Working ranches, in which guests participate in such activities as round-ups and cattle movements, sometimes require horsemanship experience. Guest ranches, with a wide range of activities in addition to horseback riding, rarely do. The slate of possible activities can vary widely from ranch to ranch. At most establishments, guests will be given some taste of the working-ranch experience with demonstrations of rodeo skills and the like. Fishing tends to be given second priority, and after that, almost anything goes. At a typical dude ranch, guests stay in log cabins and are served meals family-style in a lodge or ranch house. Colorado, Utah, and Wyoming have ranches on both ends of the spectrum.

Fishing

Trout, whether they be cutthroat, brown, rainbow, Mackinaw, brook, or lake, are the prime game fish in the Rockies. This isn't exactly trophy-fish country, but what they lack in size they make up in volume, especially in stocked waters. Western Montana, the setting of Norman Maclean's fishing-permeated book *A River Runs Through It* and the subsequent film, is teeming with fishing holes along the Blackfoot, Madison, Gallatin, and Yellowstone rivers. Just over the state line in eastern Idaho, anglers in drift boats ply the water for trout at Henry's Fork. Silver Creek, a precious little stretch of spring water in the high country of south central Idaho's Picabo Desert, is revered among dry-fly anglers. Provo Canyon in Utah is also an excellent, if over-hyped, fishing spot, and the Snake River in Wyoming has its own unique cutthroat trout strain. Only at Lake Pend Oreille in the far northern reaches of Idaho's Panhandle do anglers catch 30-pound Kamloops trout. Catercorner across the state, in the southeastern corner, is Bear Lake, the only place that Bonneville cisco, also known as Bear Lake sardines, call home. Folks head there with dip nets (it's the only place where net fishing is allowed in the state) for the winter runs.

It is possible to fish year-round in fast-moving streams that don't freeze over; however, summer is by far the most popular fishing season. Fishing licenses, ranging in term from daily to annual, are required in each state and are available in many convenience stores and sporting-goods shops. Local tackle shops are a good place to feel out a region's most effective lures.

Hiking

There are literally thousands of miles of hiking trails in the Rockies. The national parks have particularly well-marked and well-maintained trails, and admittance to all trails is free. In fact, hiking is sometimes the only way to get close to certain highlights on protected land; for example, the famed Mesa Arch rock formation in Canyonlands National Park, Utah, can be reached only on foot. Hiking in the south is usually best in spring, when water is plentiful and before the heat of summer sets in. Primarily for safety reasons, overnight hikers are usually expected to register with park or forest rangers. Also keep in mind that run-ins with bears and mountain lions have become increasingly common, especially in northern regions.

Horse-Pack Trips

Horse-pack trips are a great way to visit the Rockies' backcountry, since horses can travel distances and carry supplies that would be impossible for hikers. Montana's Bob Marshall Wilderness is the perfect example; as the largest stretch of roadless wilderness in an already spacious state, a horse-packing trip is almost the only way to travel the huge expanses. Although horsemanship isn't required for most trips, it is helpful, and even an experienced rider can expect to be a little sore for the first few days. June through August is the peak period for horse-packing trips; before signing up with an outfitter, inquire about the skills and experience they expect.

National Parks

Together, the Rocky Mountain states have a phenomenal amount of national-park land (not to mention the national monuments, national forests, state parks, etc.). Most national parks are open 365 days a year, and they offer a tantalizing range of facilities, including campgrounds, hiking trails, picnic areas, and more. Most parks charge an entrance fee, which varies according to the kind of vehicle. Tight budgets and overcrowding are bringing changes to the national parks. Fees at some parks (such as Yellowstone and Grand Teton) have been increased substantially in an experimental program to raise funds for park upkeep. For more information on any of these parks, *see* Chapters 4–8, or contact the state tourism offices (☞ Visitor Information *in* Smart Travel Tips A to Z).

COLORADO➢ Rocky Mountain National Park is home to 355 mi of hiking trails and sweeping vistas of high-country lakes, meadows, pine forests, alpine tundra, and snow-dusted peaks dotted with small glaciers. The 265,000-acre park attracts more than 3 million visitors annually. Trees grow at right angles, whipped into shape by high winds, and there are minuscule tundra versions of familiar wildflowers. Long's Peak, the highest point in the park, is a surprisingly accessible hike for those in good shape.

IDAHO➢ Unlike every other Rocky Mountain state, Idaho claims no national parks per se. The state does have its share of National Park Service properties and other nationally prominent places, though. Among those is the centerpiece of Hells Canyon National Recreation Area, a chasm even deeper than the Grand Canyon. With a black basalt gash of 8,000 ft, it's the deepest river gorge in the nation. Reportedly the Main Salmon River was nicknamed the "River of No Return" by Lewis and Clark boatmen after they witnessed the waters churn "with great violence from one rock to another on each side foaming and roaring" and decided to backtrack to Montana and pursue an alternative route. Today, the Main Salmon and its Middle Fork are surrounded by the 2-million-acre Frank Church–River of No Return Wilderness Area, the largest such area in the lower 48 states. Selected as a training site for U.S. astronauts owing to its striking, lunarlike appearance, Craters of the Moon National Monument covers 83 square mi near Arco with black-lava spatter cones, caves, and other eerie volcanic-formed features. Other National Park Service properties include: Nez Percé National Historical Park, Hagerman Fossil Beds National Monument, and City of Rocks National Reserve.

MONTANA➢ Glacier National Park is dominated by the Continental Divide, where pure mountain streams form the headwaters of the Columbia and Missouri rivers. Glaciers, pine forests, craggy mountaintops, and lush green meadows can all be seen from the serpentine Going-to-the-Sun Road, which provides dizzying views of the park's 1,600 square mi. The Crown of the Continent is one of the last grizzly bear territories; the park is also home to mountain goats, bighorn sheep, gray wolves, and more than 1,000 species of flowers. Montana also boasts the most awe-inspiring entryway to Yellowstone National Park; the Beartooth Scenic Highway offers breathtaking views en route to the park's northeast corner.

UTAH➢ Arches National Park preserves a 73,378-acre fantasy landscape of red-rock arches. Over the centuries, wind and water eroded the rock into more than 2,000 "windows" and freestanding arches, the largest collection of such formations in the world. A paved road winds through most of the major sites, but some, such as Devil's Garden and Delicate Arch (depicted on the Utah license plate), are accessible only by hiking trails. The arches are especially striking at sunset, when their color deepens to a fiercely burning red. Another beneficiary of sunset's colorful effects is Bryce Canyon National Park. Actually a series of natural amphitheaters, Bryce is famed for the pink-and-cream-color spires that reflect the sun's glow. Queen's Garden is eerily peopled with the "chessmen" formations, so called because the spires resemble human profiles. Ebenezer Bryce, the Mormon settler for whom the park is named, is said to have exclaimed that the area was "a hell of a place to lose a cow!" Canyonlands National Park offers views down to the white-water rapids of the Green and Colorado rivers, as well as red-rock pinnacles, cliffs, and spires. This park is a particular favorite of adventure-sports enthusiasts, since much of the park can be explored only on foot, or by mountain bike or four-wheel drive. In Capitol Reef National Park, a striated reeflike wall juts up 1,000 ft over ground level, with dome-like features reminiscent of the U.S. Capitol building. Visitors can pick fruit at the park's large orchards, drive along the base of the "reef," or hike down the canyons to see the 1,000-year-old Fremont Petroglyphs. Zion National Park, one of the nation's oldest national parks, is famous for its sheer, 2,500-ft-high sandstone walls and its complex desert ecology. The 147,000-acre park includes Zion Canyon and the Gateway to the Narrows, a squeak-through passageway carved by the Virgin River.

WYOMING➢ In the northwestern part of the state, just below Yellowstone National Park, is Grand Teton National Park. (Grand Teton, the highest peak in the Teton Range, was named by French-speaking trappers who thought the mountains resembled breasts.) A handful of glacier-scooped lakes, including Jackson and Jenny lakes, offer ample fishing, canoeing, and even windsurfing possibilities. The majority of visitors, however, are pulled toward Yellowstone National Park, which has two entrances in Wyoming. There are 370 mi of public roads within the park, providing (in theory) access to the park's exceptional sights—the trade-offs are the crawling traffic during tourist season and the fraying road conditions, though with the higher entrance fees, efforts are being made to improve roads, so you might find construction rather than potholes.

Still, the park cannot fail to impress. The Grand Canyon of the Yellowstone has two towering waterfalls; the mercurial Norris Geyser Basin changes every year, as new steam vents erupt and older ones fizzle out. With more than 10,000 geysers, hot springs, fumaroles, and mud pots, the park is the world's largest thermal area. The stunted landscape surrounding a hydrothermal point can seem almost otherworldly, especially in winter, when the skeletons of trees scorched by the heat glitter with icicles. The wealth of animal life is equally awesome—spotting trumpeter swans, grazing bison, or herds of elk is a wonderfully common occurrence.

Shopping

The Rocky Mountain region combines a frontier reverence for nature and the country's past with a fascination for ski-resort glitz and a modern love of megamalls and discount-outlet shopping centers. Boutiques, galleries, and malls are either right in or nearby the many resort towns and cities throughout all five states covered in this book. Colorado sales tax is 3% on average; Idaho, 5%; Utah, 6.25%; and Wyoming, between 5% and 6%. Montana has no sales tax.

ANTIQUES➢ In downtown Denver, Colorado, South Broadway is the main drag as far as antiques are concerned; Western and Native American collectibles are also scattered all over the southwestern part of the state. Idaho is an antiquer's dream, as entire towns can fit the bill; most small towns are rife with old-time street signs, utensils, and other Western goods. In Ogden, Utah, 25th Street (the town's version of a red-light district in the 1870s), is now a chichi shopping district with its fair share of antiques stores.

CRAFTS➢ Remarkable crafts—particularly Native American work—can be bought throughout this part of the country. In Denver, Colorado, the LoDo district is a good place to track down impressive weavings, pottery, jewelry, kachinas, and painting. Southwestern Colorado is generally rumored to be the best place to find both Western and Native American arts and crafts, especially basketry, weaving, and beadwork adapted from Native American methods. In particular, the Toh-Atin Gallery in Durango has a selection mind-boggling in both quantity and quality. As for more esoteric choices, in Coeur d'Alene, Idaho, you can select a custom-made tepee or yurt, while in Missoula, Montana, there is the rare purveyor of indoor trout streams. High-quality Western gear, such as cowboy hats and saddles, can also be found in Montana. Wyoming is admittedly not known for its shopping options, but King's Ropes and Saddlery in Sheridan is where real cowboys come from all over the world for everything a rancher could wish for.

Skiing

Skiing has enormous clout in the Rockies. Downhill skiing is the most popular activity by a large margin, although cross-country skiing and snowboarding have loyal followings. In recent years, resorts have offered an ever-increasing range of special-interest programs, such as classes for women skiers, for skiers with disabilities, or for recreational racing. Rockies resorts may open their lifts as early as October and close as late as July; the ski season, however, usually runs from December until early April. Christmas through New Year's Day and the month of March tend to be the busiest periods for most ski areas. The slower months of January and February often yield good package deals, as do the early and late ends of the season. Cross-country skiing generally has a shorter season owing to lack of snow, but as avalanche risks lessen in April, backcountry skiers may take advantage of the sun-baked snow. Overall, ski resorts are each area's best source of information on everything from lodging to snow conditions.

CHILD CARE➢ Day care can be found at almost all ski areas, often accepting children under a year old. Parents pay a premium for this service, but what they get is peace of mind. Most resorts have a high caretaker-to-children ratio and even offer beepers to parents who want to be notified if their child is unhappy. Normally, parents must supply bottles and diapers for infants, and some young children may want to bring their favorite toys. "Pre-ski" programs (more play than serious instruction) may be offered for children at age three. Reservations are always a good idea.

EQUIPMENT RENTAL➢ Rental equipment is available at all ski areas and at ski shops around resorts or in other cities. It's usually a good idea to rent right at the resort where you'll be skiing; that way you can go back to the shop if something doesn't fit or you want to upgrade. Shop personnel can advise you on the appropriate equipment according to your size and level of ability, and they can make the necessary adjustments. They should also be able to answer questions on how to properly use the gear. Experienced skiers can "demo" (try out) premium equipment to get a feel for new technology before upgrading. Usually the cost of the rental is deducted if you decide to buy.

LESSONS➢ In the United States, the Professional Ski Instructors of America (PSIA) has devised a progressive teaching system that is used with relatively little variation at most ski schools. This allows skiers to take lessons at schools at different ski areas based on the same principles. Classes range in length from 1½ hours to all-day workshops. Many ski areas now offer specialized programs such as powder-skiing courses, mogul clinics, or lessons for women. Of note are the children's ski schools at Vail and Beaver Creek, Colorado; the skiers with disabilities program at Winter Park, Colorado; the "extreme skiing" lessons offered by Doug Coombs (two-time winner of the World Extreme Skiing Championships) at Jackson, Wyoming; and the Mountain Experience Program for challenging, off-trail skiing at Snowbird, Utah.

Most ski schools have adopted the PSIA teaching approach for children, and many also incorporate SKIwee, another standardized teaching technique that includes progress certificates. Classes for children are arranged by ability and age group; often the ski instructor chaperons a meal during the teaching session. Children's ski instruction has come a long way in the last 10 years; instructors specially trained in teaching children, and equipment designed for little bodies now mean that most children can start skiing successfully as young as three or four.

A one-day outing at a nearby ski area is often the best way for first-time skiers to ease their way into the sport. On arrival, go to the base lodge and ask about special beginners' programs. Packages normally include basic equipment (rental skis with bindings, ski boots, ski poles), a lesson lasting at least an hour, and a lift ticket that may be valid only on beginners' slopes.

LIFT TICKETS➢ Lift ticket prices are directly linked to each resort's celebrity profile. In other words, the more popular the resort, the higher the lift ticket's price. Single-day, adult, holiday-weekend passes cost the most, but better bargains can be had through off-site purchase locations, multiple-day passes, stretch weekends (a weekend including a Monday or a Friday), season-long tickets, or other options. You can always call a particular resort's central reservations line to ask where discount lift tickets can be purchased. Occasionally, lift tickets are included in the price of lodging.

LODGING➢ Unless you plan a day trip, lodging is your most important consideration. Although some of the ski areas listed in this book are more suitable for overnight stays than others, most offer several kinds of accommodations—lodges, condominiums, hotels, motels, inns, bed-and-breakfasts—close to or a short distance away from the action. For longer vacations, request the resort area's accommodations brochure, since a package rate may offer the best deal. Combinations can include rooms, meals, lift tickets, ski lessons, rental equipment, parties, or other features.

TRAIL RATING➢ Ski areas have designed fairly accurate standards for rating and marking trails and slopes. Trails are rated Easier (green circle), Intermediate (blue square), Advanced (black diamond), and Expert (double black diamond). Remember that trail difficulty is measured in relation to the other trails *at the same ski area,* not in comparison to trails in other areas; for example, a black-diamond trail in one area may be labeled as a blue square in another area close by. These terrain ratings are most useful in establishing the ratio of trail difficulty at each particular ski area, instead of comparing two or more.

Water Sports

Spring, when rivers are flushed with snowmelt, is the best time of year for white-water enthusiasts. April through June is the best time to run rivers in the south; June through August are the principal months on rivers farther north. In general (except on dammed rivers), the flow of water lessens as the season wears on. River runners seeking the maximum white-water thrills should come early; families and those who want a gentler float should come later.

To prevent overcrowding, almost all major rivers require rafters or kayakers to have permits. For individuals planning their own trips, permits on popular rivers (such as the Middle Fork of the Salmon River or the Selway River in Idaho) can be extremely hard to come by. Permits tend to be awarded first to reputable outfitters, so signing up with an appropriate company is a good way to insure access to the river of your choice.

FODOR'S CHOICE

Flavors

★ **Renaissance, Aspen, Colorado.** The owner-chef of this restaurant calls his cuisine "the alchemy of food," and judging from what comes out of the kitchen, he's probably right. The decor is an abstract imitation of the interior of a sultan's tent. *$$$$*

★ **Syzygy, Aspen, Colorado.** Cuisine, service, and an elegant ambience align perfectly, and the chef somehow manages to harmonize Oriental, Italian, and heartland American influences to create a fabulous alternative to the standard meat-and-potatoes. *$$$$*

★ **Glitretind, Park City, Utah.** This restaurant defines elegant ski-resort dining. Offering seafood, beef, and poultry dishes, Glitretind is worth breaking open the piggy bank for. *$$$–$$$$*

★ **The Tree Room, Sundance, Utah.** For Utah natives, Sundance is as much the home of the Tree Room as it is the home of the film festival. The food changes seasonally, and the presentation, sometimes using fresh flowers, is especially memorable. *$$$–$$$$*

★ **Aerie, Snowbird, Utah.** In what could be Utah's most scenic dining location, Aerie offers a wide range of excellent dishes, an even wider range of wines, and a sushi bar. *$$$*

★ **Antares, Steamboat Springs, Colorado.** An exciting, eclectic cuisine inspired by America's rich ethnic stew is served in this landmark Victorian building. *$$–$$$*

★ **The Bunnery, Jackson, Wyoming.** The breakfasts here are irresistible, and it shows in the brief wait and the elbow-to-elbow seating on busy mornings. *$–$$*

★ **Guy's Lolo Creek Steak House, Lolo, Montana.** For a real taste of Montana, head for this massive log structure 8 mi south of Missoula. The dining room has a hunting-lodge atmosphere, and the crackling open-pit barbecue turns out delectable sirloins and other meats. *$–$$*

★ **John Bozeman's Bistro, Bozeman, Montana.** Tucked into a National Historic Record building, Bozeman's Bistro has everything from Cajun dishes to creative sandwiches. *$–$$*

★ **Buffalo Café, Twin Falls, Idaho.** This tiny café produces an enormous amount of food for breakfast, including the dauntingly sized but delicious Buffalo Chip. *$*

★ **Windbag Saloon & Grill, Helena, Montana.** The cherry-wood interior of this restaurant gives it a comfortable atmosphere that goes over well with the burgers and sandwiches. The Windbag, named for the hot political debate you're likely to hear over lunch, is a popular spot for legislators and families alike. *$*

Comforts

★ **The Broadmoor, Colorado Springs, Colorado.** One of America's truly great hotels, the Broadmoor almost seems like a village unto its own. Besides its luxurious accommodations, it commands a private lake, three world-class championship golf courses, nine restaurants, and a spa. *$$$$*

★ **Cliff Lodge, Snowbird, Utah.** To some, this distinctive hotel might seem to blend in—and that's precisely part of its attraction. Designed to echo the surrounding scenery, the Cliff Lodge has beautiful views from every angle, and it tops it off with the indulgent Cliff Spa. *$$$$*

★ **Wort Hotel, Jackson, Wyoming.** Locals congregate around the Silver Dollar Bar, named for the 1,921, 1921 silver dollars embedded in the S-shape bar counter. The hotel seems to have been around as long as the Tetons, but it feels fresh inside. *$$$$*

★ **Hotel Jerome, Aspen, Colorado.** Built in 1889, the Hotel Jerome is a deep draft of Victorian grandeur. If you tend toward the lavish, the rose damask curtains of the public rooms alone should satisfy. *$$$–$$$$*

★ **B&Bs on North Main Street, Breckenridge, Colorado.** This B&B offers two options: an unabashedly romantic former miner's cottage as well as a new collection of Western primitive rooms in a barnlike structure overlooking the river. The innkeepers are unfailingly generous with their homemade muffins and secret stashes of powder. *$$–$$$$*

★ **SkyRidge Bed and Breakfast, Torrey, Utah.** Near Capitol Reef National Park, this inn is a visual feast both indoors—where the works of Southwestern artists can be purchased right off the walls—and outdoors, with 360 degree views of Capitol Reef, Boulder and the Thousand Lake Mountains, and the verdant Freemont River valley. *$$–$$$$*

★ **Brown Palace, Denver, Colorado.** This is the grande dame of Colorado hotels. Scrupulous attention is paid to the details, and the formal restaurant, the Palace Arms, has won several awards. *$$$*

★ **The Idaho Rocky Mountain Ranch, Stanley, Idaho.** This guest ranch has retained its decades-old character and classic Western-lodge splendor and still offers up awesome views of the spectacular Sawtooth Mountain range across the valley floor. *$$$*

★ **Teton Ridge Ranch, Tetonia, Idaho.** This guest ranch, standing tall and proud in the shadow of the 12,000-ft Grand Tetons, had the courage to call the place a ranch, then to build luxury into every square inch of the dozen guest suites and lodge—and to charge accordingly for a slice of private paradise in the Wild West. *$$$*

★ **Clark House on Hayden Lake, Coeur d'Alene, Idaho.** This hotel was originally a millionaire's eccentric extravagance; after near-demolition, the building was transformed into a giant, sumptuous wedding cake of a place. *$$–$$$*

★ **Lake Yellowstone Hotel, Yellowstone National Park, Wyoming.** This property is one of the oldest and most elegant park resorts. Old-style luxury tourism in the "wilderness" is recalled by the afternoon chamber music in the lobby. *$$–$$$*

★ **Goldsmith's Bed and Breakfast, Missoula, Montana.** Just a footbridge away from the University of Montana campus, this B&B was formerly the university president's home. Right next door is Goldsmith's Premium Ice Cream Café. *$$*

★ **O'Duach'ain Country Inn Bed and Breakfast, Bigfork, Montana.** This lovely log inn sits in a quiet lodgepole-pine forest near Flathead Lake and the Swan River, surrounded by hiking trails. Breakfasts feature such temptations as stuffed Irish toast. *$$*

★ **Grand Hotel, Big Timber, Montana.** The accommodations here are reminiscent of what you might find over the Longbranch Saloon in *Gunsmoke*. *$–$$*

★ **Grist Mill Inn, Monticello, Utah.** Housed in a 1933 flour mill, this B&B has superb suites in the main building and additional guest rooms in the antique caboose out back. *$–$$*

Ski Resorts

★ **Crested Butte, Colorado, for both its rolling intermediate slopes and its Extreme Limits runs.** The main trail network has easy, maneuverable terrain, while Extreme Limits has several hundred acres of steep bowls, tough chutes, and tight tree skiing.

★ **Vail, Colorado, for its back bowls and resort amenities.** On powder days, the back bowls can offer intermediate and expert skiers a small slice of heaven. The resort village is crafted to anticipate every need (or desire).

★ **Sun Valley, Idaho, for bestowing the royal treatment on Baldy Mountain.** A whole host of multimillion-dollar improvements and additions, including new high-speed quad lifts, computerized snowmaking, luxurious new day lodges and mountaintop dining, let the grand dame of U.S. ski resorts reclaim her ranking as queen.

★ **Alta, Utah, for its chance to explore.** Sharing Snowbird's exceptional snowfall, Alta's layout may seem confusing at first. However, Alta is made for exploration, and new discoveries can be made year after year.

★ **Snowbird, Utah, for its expert runs.** The open bowls are already challenging, but even these pale in comparison to chutes such as Upper Cirque. What makes this bearable is the legendary quantity of powder.

★ **Jackson Hole, Wyoming, for its endless variations.** Jackson has literally thousands of skiable routes from top to bottom—all it takes is a little imagination. In addition, its stunning backcountry terrain is some of the most diverse in the U.S.

Views

★ **First glimpse of Vail's sweeping back bowls, Colorado.** The Valhalla of skiers, the back bowls seem like an endless expanse of beckoning snow. In summer, the bowls' enormous cradle works the same magic for mountain bike fanatics.

★ **The cliff dwellings of the Anasazi people at Mesa Verde, Colorado.** These haunting ruins were built into the cliff walls more than 600 years ago, then mysteriously abandoned.

★ **The black basalt columns in Hells Canyon, Idaho.** Deeper than the Grand Canyon, and much narrower, Hells Canyon is flanked with rock formations resembling giant black pencils. By floating or rafting through the chasm, you can also see Native American pictographs along the smooth canyon walls.

★ **The shimmering northern lights in Montana.** Take your pick of open spaces from which to see this exquisite summer phenomenon—sometimes delicately tinting the night sky, other times blazing until dawn.

★ **The views from Going-to-the-Sun Road in Glacier National Park, Montana.** This serpentine, 52-mi-long highway has some of the best views in the world. It crests at Logan Pass, where you can take a short hike to the crystalline Hidden Lake.

★ **Snow clinging to the rock formations in Bryce Canyon National Park, Utah.** The Martianlike landscape of the ruddy pinnacles and spires of Bryce Canyon is incredibly beautiful when dusted with snow. The bristlecone pines along the amphitheaters' rims heighten the colors' effect.

★ **The view over the Island-in-the-Sky district in Canyonlands National Park from Dead Horse Point State Park, Utah.** Where the Green and Colorado rivers come together, towering cliffs stab skyward.

★ **Jackson as seen from the top of Signal Mountain, Wyoming.** A matchless view of the whole of Jackson Hole can be seen from the summit of Signal Mountain.

★ **Erupting geysers and hissing steam vents at the Norris Geyser Basin in Yellowstone National Park, Wyoming.** Norris is the oldest and hottest of Yellowstone's geyser basins; every year its roster of live hydrothermal features changes.

FESTIVALS AND SEASONAL EVENTS

WINTER

DEC.➢ Christmas celebrations blanket most Rockies towns. For the holidays, many ski areas mount **torchlight parades,** with large groups of torch-bearing ski instructors tracing patterns down the mountainside. Contact specific resorts for details.

Colorado: Denver hosts the **World's Largest Christmas Lighting Display** (☎ 303/892–1112), with 40,000 floodlights washing civic buildings in reds, greens, blues, and yellows. Silverton searches for a yule log at its **Yule Log Celebration** (☎ 303/387–5654 or 800/752–4494). Georgetown hosts the **Winter Market** (☎ 800/472–8230), a small-town Christmas fair with sleigh rides through town. The **Vail Festival of Lights** (☎ 970/479–2100) promotes a whole range of attractions including World Cup ski races, Dickensian carolers, brilliant lighting displays, and Christmas ice-skating spectaculars.

Idaho: Sun Valley sparkles as a winter wonderland throughout the month of December with **Christmas in Sun Valley** (☎ 208/726–3423) festivities. The torchlight parade with the ski-school instructors is a decades-old tradition followed by fireworks on Christmas Eve. Sandpoint becomes "Santapoint" for the **Hometown Christmas** (☎ 208/263–0887), a 10-day festival of winter activities.

Montana: Bozeman's **Christmas Stroll** (☎ 406/586–4008) features sleigh rides, carolers, hot-chocolate stands, holiday lights, and late shopping hours.

Utah: Salt Lake City's show is the **Christmas Lights** ceremony ☎ 801/521–2822) at Temple Square.

JAN.➢ Colorado: Denver's two-week **National Western Stock Show and Rodeo** (☎ 303/297–1166), the world's largest livestock show, is one of the month's big events. Ski competitions such as the **Steamboat Springs Annual Cowboy Downhill** (☎ 970/879–6111), the **Aspen Winterskol** (☎ 970/925–1940), and **Breckenridge's Ullr Fest and World Cup Freestyle** (☎ 970/453–6018) keep ski areas lively with races, torchlight skiing, and other events.

Idaho: **Sandpoint Winter Carnival** (☎ 208/263–0887) is a 10-day festival of winter activities. **Winter Olympics Week,** Sun Valley (☎ 800/634–3347), has celebrity ski racing, a food fair, and dances. **McCall** (☎ 208/634–7631) stages a huge winter carnival that stretches into February. You'll find world-class ice sculptures as well as the usual parades, dog-sled races, and fireworks.

Utah: The annual **Sundance Film Festival** (☎ 801/225–4107 or 800/892–1600) based in Park City, lures film aficionados as well as industry executives to seminars, workshops, and previews of films from around the world.

Wyoming: **Wild West Winter Carnival** (☎ 307/856–4801) at Boysen State Park has dog races, a demolition derby, softball, and golf, all on ice, as well as snowmobile races, and a "snowdeo."

FEB.➢ Colorado: Steamboat Springs hosts the oldest continuous **Winter Carnival** (☎ 970/879–0880) west of the Mississippi. The **Ice Fishing Contest** (☎ 970/723–4600) in Walden consists of fishing on four lakes for the eight largest fish.

Idaho: The **Lionel Hampton Jazz Festival** (☎ 208/885–6765) in Moscow attracts some of the world's top jazz musicians.

Montana: **Race to the Sky** (☎ 406/444–2654 or 800/847–4868) near Helena, is a 500-mi dogsled race that crisscrosses the Continental Divide at elevations of up to 7,000 ft. There is also a 300-mi race that the public can watch at check-in sites. The **Western Montana Wine Festival** (☎ 406/543–6623 or 800/526–3465) in Missoula features tastings of regional and west coast wines, accompanied by superb food.

SPRING

MAR.➢ Colorado: More than 70 tribes convene for the **Denver Powwow** (☎ 303/892–1112 or 800/393–8559) with Native American dancers, artisans, and musicians. Charity and celebrity events rope them in at many ski areas, including the **Special Olympics Colorado's** (☏ 303/592–1361) winter events at Copper Mountain, **Jimmie Heuga's Mazda Ski Express** (☏ 970/926–1290 or 800/367–3101) which raises money to fight MS, and the **Beaver Creek American Ski Classic** (☏ 970/949–1999), hosted by former president Gerald Ford.

Idaho: In Pocatello, the **Dodge National Circuit Finals Rodeo** (☏ 208/233–1525) draws the top two cowboys from each of 12 national circuits for four days of bareback-riding, roping, and steer-wrestling competitions.

Montana: Irish folk and other wearers of the green flock to Butte for one of the West's largest and most rollicking **St. Patrick's Day** (☏ 406/723–3177) parades and for other Irish-accented events. Collectors from around the world attend the **C. M. Russell Auction of Original Western Art** (☏ 406/761–6453 or 800/803–3351) held in Great Falls.

APR.➢ Colorado: **A Taste of Vail** (☏ 970/926–1494) showcases that area's superlative restaurants.

Idaho: The citywide **Dogwood Festival** (☏ 208/799–2243) in Lewiston features a rodeo, concerts, and plays.

Montana: The annual **International Wildlife Film Festival** (☏ 406/728–9380) in Missoula is one of two such film festivals in the world.

MAY➢ Colorado: Memorial Day brings the annual **Bolder Boulder** (☏ 303/444–7223) run to Boulder, where top international runners, along with 40,000 ordinary citizens, race through the closed streets of town.

Idaho: Sandpoint marks summer's beginning with a **Waterfest** (☏ 208/263–2161) including a sand-sculpture contest, a regatta, and waterskiing events. The entire town of Wallace, in north central Idaho's silver-mining district, is listed on the National Register of Historic Places, and the town's **Depot Day** (☏ 208/263–2161) celebrates Wallace's heritage with music and a car show in early May.

Montana: Bigfork mounts a laid-back **Cherry Blossom Festival** (☏ 406/837–5888) with a farmers' market, cherry desserts, and various competitions. In Miles City, rodeo stock for the upcoming season is auctioned off at the **Bucking Horse Sale** (☏ 406/232–2890). The horses demonstrate their bucking prowess in rodeo competitions, and the event also features bull riding, a wild-horse race, and street dances. St. Ignatius hosts the **Buffalo Feast and Powwow** (☏ 406/745–2951) with three days of dancing and games capped by a free feast of pit-roasted buffalo. You can sample fine beers from Montana and the northwest at the **Garden City Micro B.R.I.W. Fest** (☏ 406/721–6061) in Missoula.

Wyoming: The huge **Flaming Gorge Fishing Derby** (☏ 307/362–3771) in Rock Springs draws 350 teams of anglers.

SUMMER

JUNE➢ Colorado: The **Silly Home Built River Raft Race** (☏ 719/456–0453) held in Las Animas on the Arkansas River keeps spectators guessing which improbable floating contraptions will reach the finish line. Meanwhile, the season of music festivals and cultural events gets into swing with Telluride's weekend-long **Bluegrass Festival** (☏ 303/449–6007 or 800/624–2422), the **Aspen Music Festival** (☏ 970/925–3254), **Steamboat's Annual Cowboy Roundup Days** (☏ 970/879–0880) with rodeo events, a country-music festival, chili cook-off, Cowboy Poetry gathering, and more, Glenwood Springs' **Strawberry Days** (☏ 970/945–6589) and Grand Junction's **Country Jam** (☏ 970/243–7739 or 800/530–3020). Also popular in summer is Boulder's **Colorado Shakespeare Festival** (☏ 303/492–1527), one of the three most popular in the country.

Idaho: The **Boise River Festival** (☏ 208/338–8887) has a nighttime parade with lit, animated floats; six stages of continuous entertainment; and 300 other events the last week of June. The **International Women's Challenge** (☏ 208/345–7223), statewide, is the nation's premier cycling race for women. Weiser's **National Old-Time Fiddlers Contest** (☏ 208/549–0452) draws the nation's best to compete.

Montana: Helena's **Montana Traditional Dixieland Jazz Festival** (☎ 406/449–7969 or 800/449–0194) is another of the Rockies' summer music festivals. **Custer's Last Stand Reenactment** (☎ 406/665–3577 or 888/450–3577) in Hardin, enlists more than 200 riders.

Wyoming: The **International Barbed Wire Show** ☎ 307/234–5311 or 800/852–1889) in Casper features contemporary and antique wire from all over the world. Note the **Woodchoppers Jamboree & Rodeo** (☎ 307/326–8855) near Saratoga, where competitors make wood chips fly.

JULY➢ Colorado: Arts events galore run throughout July, including **Aspen International Design Conference** (☎ 970/925–2257), Winter Park's **Jazz and American Music Festivals** (☎ 970/726–4118), Vail's **Bravo! Colorado Music Festival** (☎ 970/949–1999), and the Breckenridge **Genuine Jazz** (☎ 970/453–6018). In Crested Butte, the **Fat Tire Festival** (☎ 970/349–6817) runs from late June to early July. There are guided walks and a host of seminars on identification, photography, and cooking at Crested Buttes's **Wildflower Festival** (☎ 970/349–6438 or 800/545–4505).

Idaho: Thirty to forty hot-air balloons are a colorful sight over the mountains at the **Teton Valley Hot-Air Balloon Races** (☎ 208/354–2500) in Driggs, Idaho. The **Snake River Stampede** (☎ 208/466–8497) in Nampa, just west of Boise, is one of the top 20 rodeos in the nation. The **Gooding Basque Association Picnic** (☎ 208/934–4402 or 208/886–2982) celebrates Basque heritage with music, dancing, and food. The **Idaho Shakespeare Festival** (☎ 208/336–9221) in Boise runs all summer, presenting the bard's work under the stars. The **Festival at Sandpoint** (☎ 208/263–0887), the last two weeks of July and the first two weeks of August, is a celebration of music that includes classical, pop, and jazz. The **Sun Valley Ice Shows** (☎ 208/622–4111) feature former Olympians and professional figure skaters carving the ice from June through September.

Montana: The Grant-Kohrs Ranch in Deer Lodge, Montana, celebrates cowboy lore and skills during **Western Heritage Days** (☎ 406/846–2070 or 406/846–3388) with roping, branding, chuck-wagon cooking, and traditional cowboy music and poetry. Classical, jazz, country, and rock music all have their place in Kalispell's ever-growing **Flathead Valley Music Festival** (☎ 406/862–7708). And don't miss the **Montana State Fair** (☎ 406/727–8900) in Great Falls at the end of the month.

Utah: The **Railroaders Festival** (☎ 800/255–8824) in Ogden, is where the spike-driving and buffalo-chip-throwing contests and the Golden Spike Ceremony commemorate the completion of America's first transcontinental railroad.

Wyoming: The old-fashioned **Cody Stampede** (☎ 800/207–0744 or 307/587–5155) in Buffalo Bill Cody's eponymous hometown is one of the Rockies' larger July 4th celebrations. The **Green River Rendezvous** (☎ 307/367–2242), near Pinedale, stages a reenactment of 1830s mountain life. For the king of outdoor rodeos, see the world's largest, **Cheyenne Frontier Days** (☎ 800/227–6336). For something in a more arty line, check out the **Grand Teton Music Festival** (☎ 307/733–1128) in Teton Village.

AUG.➢ Colorado: Rodeos are typical late-summer fare; witness the **Pikes Peak or Bust Rodeo** (☎ 719/635–7506 or 800/368–4748 outside the state) in Colorado Springs, Colorado's largest rodeo. Country fairs are also big business, especially Pueblo's star-studded **state fair** (☎ 800/876–4567). For more high-minded fare, Vail hosts the **International Festival of Dance** (☎ 970/949–1999 or 970/476–2918), set amid the wildflowers in the outdoor Ford Amphitheater. Other top music events include Denver's **Festival of Mountain and Plain: A Taste of Colorado** (☎ 303/534–6161) and Telluride's **Jazz Celebration** (☎ 970/728–7009). The **Wild Mushroom Festival** (☎ 970/728–4431 or 800/525–3455) sponsors seminars on cooking and medicinal uses and forays into the woods around Telluride. Daredevils take to the skies at the **Telluride Hang Gliding Festival** (☎ 970/728–5793).

Idaho: As common as rodeos this month are Native American events that showcase traditional songs, dances, and crafts, such as the **Shoshone-Bannock Indian Festival** (☎ 208/238–3700) in Fort Hall. The **Three Island Crossing** (☎ 208/366–2394), at Glenns Ferry on the first weekend in August, is a re-creation of the pioneers' treacherous Snake River crossing. Boise's **Western Idaho Fair** (☎ 208/376–3247) is the state's biggest and brings in a slate of nationally known entertainers. **Art on the Green** (☎ 208/664–3194), in Coeur d'Alene the first weekend in August, has arts, crafts, and dance and is one of Idaho's largest festivals.

Montana: The **Crow Fair and Rodeo** (☎ 406/638–2601) takes place in Crow Agency—the self-styled tepee capital of the world. At the **Montana Cowboy Poetry Gathering** (☎ 406/538–5436) in Lewistown, U.S. and Canadian performers share verses about a man and a horse following a cow. The **Running of the Sheep** (☎ 406/326–2288) in Reedpoint is a surrealistic version of Pamplona's running of the bulls, with hundreds of sturdy Montana-bred woollies charging down Main Street.

Utah: Who would ever have guessed that the largest outdoor Middle Eastern dance festival in the nation, featuring some 200 dancers from around the country, would be held in Salt Lake City? But there you have it, the **Belly Dancing Festival** (☎ 801/538–1030 or 801/538–1467).

AUTUMN

SEPT.➢ Colorado: Major **film festivals** take place in Aspen (☎ 970/925–6882), Breckenridge (☎ 970/453–6200), and Telluride (☎ 603/643–1255).

Idaho: You'll find lumberjack competitions at the **Clearwater County Fair and Lumberjack Days** (☎ 208/476–4335) in Orofino. **Idaho Spud Day** (☎ 208/357–3390) in Shelley sponsors the World Spud-Picking Championship. The **Nez Percé Cultural Day** (☎ 208/843–2261), in Spalding, celebrates Native American heritage. Bands from around the country come to the **Pocatello Dixieland Jamboree** (☎ 208/233–1525).

Montana: Libby's four-day **Nordicfest** (☎ 406/293–3431 or 800/785–6541) celebrates Scandinavian food, costumes, music, dance, and crafts.

Utah: There's the big **Utah State Fair** (☎ 801/538–8400) in Salt Lake City.

Wyoming: The **Jackson Hole Fall Arts Festival** (☎ 307/733–3316) marks the season with concerts, art, poetry, dance, and crafts workshops and lectures throughout the valley.

OCT.➢ Colorado: Oktoberfests and harvest celebrations dominate October, most notably Carbondale's **Potato Days** (☎ 970/963–1890), Haxtun's **Corn Festival** (☎ 970/774–6104), and the **Cedaredge Applefest** (☎ 800/436–3041). The **Great American Beer Festival** (☎ 303/399–1859) in Denver is the country's largest beer fest, offering samples of more than 1,000 brews.

Idaho: The **Swing 'N' Jazz Jamboree** (☎ 208/726–3423) in Sun Valley presents both big-band and Dixieland music.

Montana: The **Big Mountain Microbrew Festival** (☎ 406/862–2905) at Grouse Mountain Lodge in Whitefish showcases the small-batch beers of local breweries.

NOV.➢ Colorado: Look for **Creede's Chocolate Festival** (☎ 719/648–2374 or 800/327–2102), which puts chocolates of every size, shape, and description imaginable in every corner of the town.

Idaho: Steelhead are the quarry at Idaho's **Great Snake Lake Steelhead Derby** (☎ 208/743–3531 or 800/473–3543) in Lewiston.

Montana: One of the most memorable events is the **eagle watch** (☎ 406/475–3128) near Helena, where majestic bald eagles flock to the Missouri River to dive for kokanee salmon.

2 SPECIAL-INTEREST VACATIONS: WINTER

The special-interest winter activity in the Rockies is downhill skiing, there being (at last count) more than 60 ski areas in the region—each with at least a 1,000-ft vertical drop.

By Peter Oliver

NOT SO LONG AGO IN THE ROCKIES, downhill skiing was the king of winter sports, to the exclusion of almost everything else. To be sure, it is still top dog, but a horde of other activities now share in the spirit of winter fun in the Rockies: dogsledding, snowmobiling, cross-country skiing, ballooning, paragliding, ice climbing, and even fishing. Of course, snowboarding, the nouveau sport of the '80s, continued to boom in the '90s and is still growing in popularity today. A wider array of activities has broadened winter's appeal to a wider population base. Winter vacationers in the Rockies are no longer just hard-core downhill skiing fanatics.

Indeed, in recent years major resorts have bent over backward to accommodate as many people as possible with programs for children, women, snowboarders, skiers with disabilities, recreational racers . . . the list goes on. And it's not all about skiing. Guided snowshoe tours, for example, are gaining in popularity. For the sake of space, only the unique or exemplary programs are described below. If you have a particular interest, call ahead or check at the main ski-school desk. Chances are, you'll find what you're looking for.

The skiing season runs approximately from mid-November to mid-April, depending on the resort and the location. The best package deals usually apply early and late in the season; for packages, check not only with each resort but also with major airlines (American, Continental, Delta, and United) that service the Rockies. Many resorts open late and shut down early, not for lack of snow but for lack of business. In fact, some of the best backcountry skiing can be had in late April and May, when avalanche risks subside and the firmer, sun-baked snow is easier to walk and climb on than midwinter powder. Just because the ski resorts give up on skiing doesn't mean you have to.

Because space is limited, only 23 of the most prominent ski areas are described in this chapter. That omits several terrific but less renowned areas, places such as Purgatory in Colorado, Bogus Basin in Idaho, Bridger Bowl in Montana, and Snowbasin in Utah, where the skiing is usually both crowd-free and budget-priced.

A few notes: terrain ratings (e.g., beginner, intermediate, advanced) are approximate and may vary considerably from one ski area to the next. In other words, an intermediate trail at one area might be rated as expert elsewhere; rating trails is a matter of judgment rather than science. Thus, the terrain ratings might give you a rough idea of the ratio of beginner versus advanced options at a particular area, but they are of much less use in comparing areas with one another. Also, prices were accurate as of spring 1999, but they are subject to change.

COLORADO

Aspen/Snowmass

Aspen is as much a national icon as it is a town—forever in the news as a litmus test of the American public's tolerance of radical-chic politics, conspicuous consumption, and conspicuous love affairs. It's like a scriptless soap opera shot as cinema verité: part resort town, part ski area, part cultural retreat, and part New Age–politics-hedonistic-excess. It is a place where celebrities have affairs and locals have dogs and mountain bikes. It is weird.

In Aspen, high-end clothing boutiques have been known to serve free Campari-and-sodas après-ski, a practice so brazenly elitist that there's a certain charm to it. At the same time, it's a place where people actually live, send their children to school, and work real jobs that may or may not have to do with skiing. It is, arguably, America's original ski-bum destination, a fact that continues to give the town's character an underlying layer of humor and texture. People can come to Aspen, dress much too expensively, and loudly make fools of themselves, as Donald Trump and Barbra Streisand (among others) have done. But a person can also come to Aspen and have a reasonably straightforward, enjoyable ski vacation, because once you've stripped away the veneer, Aspen is not a bad town or a bad place to ski.

Snowmass was built in 1967 as Aspen's answer to Vail—a ski-specific resort—and although it has never quite matched the panache or popularity of Vail, it has gained a certain stature with age. It used to be that if you stayed at Snowmass, dining meant cooking in your condo and entertainment could only be found 15 mi away in Aspen. In recent years, an effort has been made to breathe a little life and pizzazz into Snowmass Village, and the effect has been noticeable. Better restaurants and a livelier après-ski scene have lured people into the village after the lifts close.

In general, Snowmass is the preferred alternative for families with young children, leaving the town of Aspen to a more hard-partying, up-at-the-crack-of-noon kind of crowd. The selling points of Snowmass as an alternative to Aspen are lots of on-slope, ski-in/ski-out lodging, a slow pace, and quiet.

Downhill Skiing and Snowboarding

Aspen and Snowmass are really four ski areas rolled into one resort. Aspen (or Ajax) Mountain, Buttermilk, Snowmass, and Aspen Highlands can all be skied with the same ticket.

Aspen Highlands is essentially a long, long ridge with trails dropping off to either side. A few years ago, two high-speed quad chairs were added to update the antiquated lift system. Highlands has some superb expert terrain. An effort in recent years has been made to extend the ski-area boundary farther into Highlands Bowl, where some of the most dramatic, high-alpine steeps and chutes in Colorado can be found. The steep and often bumpy cluster of trails and small bowls known as Steeplechase is one of the best places to be in the Aspen area on a powder day. One other Highlands bonus: from the summit, the panorama of the Maroon Bells and Pyramid Peak is one of the most dramatic views anywhere in American skiing.

Aspen Mountain is considered a mogul skier's dreamland, and from its Bell Mountain chairlift, that's certainly true. This is a resort where 65% of the trails are rated advanced or expert, and there are no novice runs. However, most Aspen Mountain skiers spend much of their time on intermediate trails off the upper-mountain quad. They also spend their lunchtime on the deck of Bonnie's, the mid-mountain restaurant, which on a sunny day is one of the great people-watching scenes in the world of skiing. After a big snowstorm, there's also Sno-Cat–assisted powder skiing off the back side of the mountain, a treat that can be arranged through the Aspen Skiing Company (*see below*). Aspen Mountain's biggest drawback is that too many trails funnel into Spar Gulch, making the end-of-the-day rush to the bottom chaotic and often dangerous. Aspen is the lone holdout in Colorado that doesn't allow snowboarding—a drawback or a boon, depending on which side of the fence you stand on.

The Rockies Ski Areas

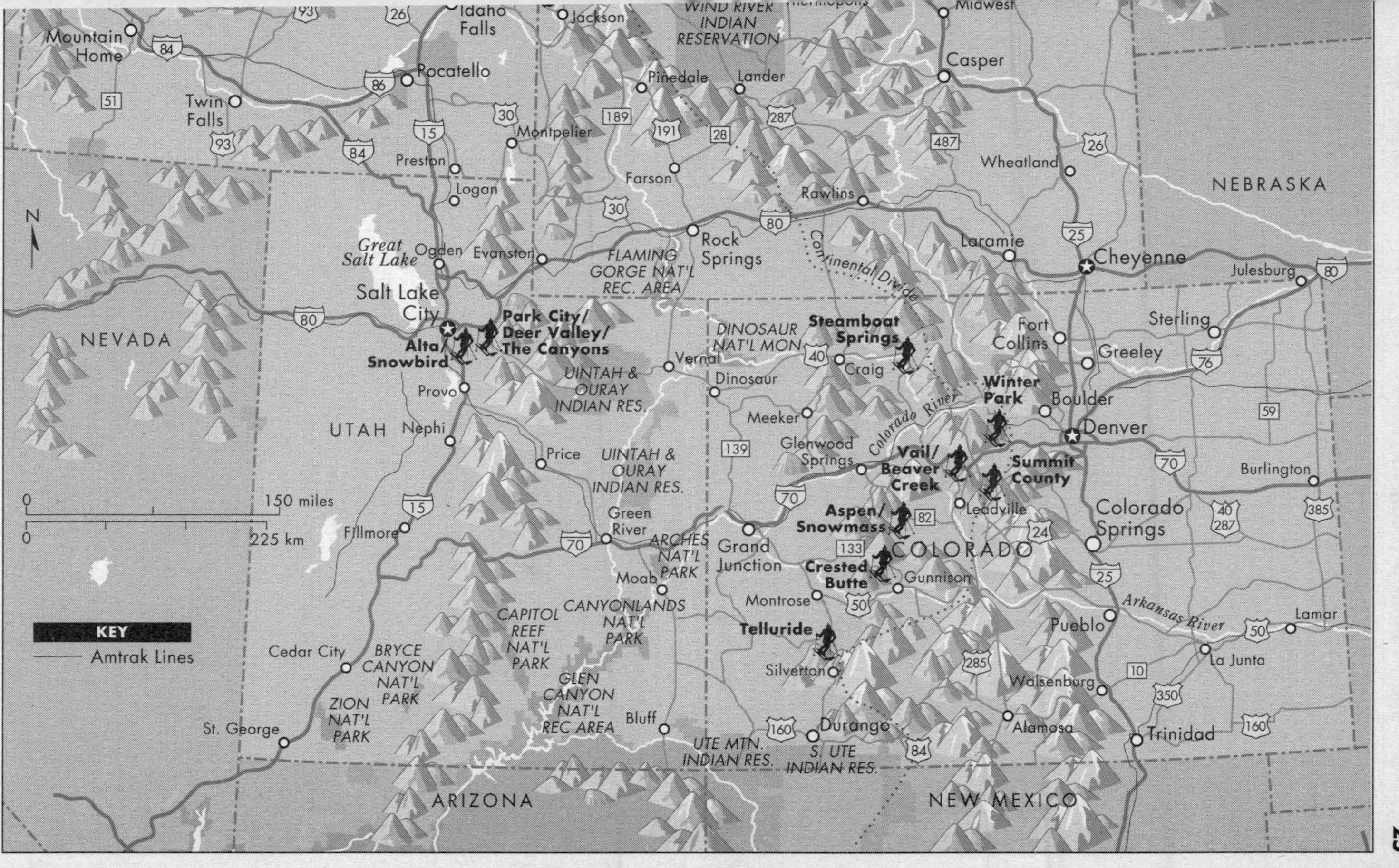
Mountain Home
Idaho Falls
Jackson
WIND RIVER INDIAN RESERVATION
Midwest
Casper
Pocatello
Twin Falls
Pinedale
Lander
Montpelier
Preston
Logan
Farson
Wheatland
Rawlins
NEBRASKA
N
Great Salt Lake
Ogden
Evanston
Rock Springs
FLAMING GORGE NAT'L REC. AREA
Continental Divide
Laramie
Cheyenne
Julesburg
Salt Lake City
Park City/ Deer Valley/ The Canyons
Alta/ Snowbird
NEVADA
DINOSAUR NAT'L MON
Steamboat Springs
Fort Collins
Greeley
Sterling
Vernal
Craig
Dinosaur
UINTAH & OURAY INDIAN RES.
Provo
Winter Park
Boulder
Meeker
Colorado River
Denver
UTAH
Nephi
Glenwood Springs
Vail/ Beaver Creek
Summit County
Burlington
Price
UINTAH & OURAY INDIAN RES.
0
150 miles
225 km
Leadville
Colorado Springs
Fillmore
Green River
Aspen/ Snowmass
ARCHES NAT'L PARK
Grand Junction
COLORADO
Crested Butte
Gunnison
Moab
Montrose
Arkansas River
CAPITOL REEF NAT'L PARK
CANYONLANDS NAT'L PARK
Pueblo
Lamar
KEY
Amtrak Lines
Telluride
Cedar City
BRYCE CANYON NAT'L PARK
La Junta
Silverton
GLEN CANYON NAT'L REC AREA
Walsenburg
ZION NAT'L PARK
Bluff
Durango
Alamosa
Trinidad
St. George
UTE MTN. INDIAN RES.
S. UTE INDIAN RES.
ARIZONA
NEW MEXICO
93
26
84
86
51
30
189
191
28
287
487
15
93
84
30
80
25
26
80
80
40
76
59
139
70
15
70
70
82
40
287
385
133
24
25
50
50
285
10
350
160
160
84

Buttermilk—a place where it is virtually impossible to get into trouble—is terrific for lower intermediates and children. It's a low-key, lighthearted sort of place, an antidote to the kind of skiing machismo you might encounter at Aspen Mountain. Among its featured attractions is a hangout for children named Ft. Frog—a name that ought to tell you something about how seriously the area takes itself. If you're looking for an escape from the Aspen bustle, spend a day at Buttermilk.

Snowmass is a huge sprawl of a ski area, best known for Big Burn, itself a great sprawl of wide-open, intermediate skiing. In general, Snowmass is one of the best ski areas in the Rockies for intermediates. The route variations down Big Burn are essentially inexhaustible, and there are many, many other places on the mountain for intermediates to find entertainment. Although only 38% of the terrain is rated advanced or expert, this is a huge mountain, with enough black runs in the Hanging Valley and Cirque areas to satisfy all but the most demanding skier. The novice and lower-intermediate terrain on the lower part of the mountain makes Snowmass a terrific place for young children.

FACILITIES

Aspen Highlands: 3,635-ft vertical drop; 675 skiable acres; 20% beginner, 33% intermediate, 47% advanced; 2 high-speed quad chairs, 1 triple chair, 3 double chairs. **Aspen Mountain:** 3,267-ft vertical drop; 675 skiable acres; 35% intermediate, 35% advanced, 30% expert; 1 4-passenger gondola, 1 high-speed quad chair, 2 quad chairs, 4 double chairs. **Buttermilk:** 2,030-ft vertical drop; 420 skiable acres; 35% beginner, 39% intermediate, 26% advanced; 1 high-speed quad chair, 5 double chairs, 1 surface lift. **Snowmass:** 4,206-ft vertical drop; 2,655 skiable acres; 10% beginner, 52% intermediate, 18% advanced, 20% expert; 17 lifts.

LESSONS AND PROGRAMS

The **Aspen Skiing Company** (☎ 970/925–1220 or 800/525–6200) gives lessons at all four mountains: Half-day group lessons start at $49, but a noteworthy deal is the three-day guaranteed learn-to-ski or learn-to-snowboard package at Buttermilk, which includes lessons and lift tickets for $199.

LIFT TICKETS

$65, slightly less at Buttermilk. Some savings on multiday tickets.

RENTALS

Numerous ski shops in Aspen and Snowmass rent equipment. **Christy Sports** (☎ 970/920–1170) at the Aspen Mountain gondola base is conveniently located. **Aspen Sports** (☎ 970/923–3566) in Snowmass Village is also convenient. Rentals are also available at the **Buttermilk** base lodge. Rental packages (skis, boots, and poles) start at around $16 per day; snowboard packages (boots and boards) run about $25. Bargain shopping at stores around town may turn up lower-priced deals.

Nordic Skiing

BACKCOUNTRY SKIING

The **Alfred A. Braun Hut System** is one of Aspen's major backcountry networks. The trailhead leads from the Ashcroft Touring Center (☞ Track Skiing, *below*) into the Maroon Bells/Snowmass Wilderness, and it generally covers terrain more prone to avalanche possibilities than the 10th Mountain Division Trail. Huts sleep six–nine people. Reservations are required at least a day in advance, considerably earlier for weekends and peak-season periods. ✉ *Box 7937, Aspen 81612,* ☎ *970/925–6618 or 800/643–8621.* *Hut fee: $17.50 per person per night.*

The **10th Mountain Hut and Trail System,** named in honor of the U.S. Army's skiing 10th Mountain Division, includes 10 huts along the trail connecting Aspen and Vail. The main trail follows a generally avalanche-safe route in altitudes that vary between 8,000 ft and 12,000 ft. This translates to a fair amount of skiing along tree-lined trails and a good bit of high-alpine up and down. You must be in good shape, and some backcountry skiing experience is extremely helpful. The accommodations along the trail are the Hiltons of backcountry huts, supplied with precut wood for wood-burning stoves, mattresses and pillows, and propane stoves and utensils for cooking. Each hut generally sleeps 16 (more if you're willing to cuddle). Reservations are taken beginning in June; weekends in peak ski season fill up very quickly. ✉ *1280 Ute Ave., Aspen 81611,* ☎ *970/925–5775.* 💰 *Hut fee: starts at $22 per person per night.*

If you're either unfamiliar with the hut system or inexperienced in backcountry travel, you should hire a guide. One reliable recommendation is **Aspen Alpine Guides** (✉ Box 5122, Aspen 81612, ☎ 970/925–6618 or 800/643–8621). In Aspen, the best stores for **backcountry-gear rentals** (including ski equipment, climbing skins, packs, sleeping bags, and mountaineering paraphernalia) are the **Hub** (✉ 315 E. Hyman Ave., ☎ 970/925–7970) and **Ute Mountaineer** (✉ 308 S. Mill St., ☎ 970/925–2849).

TRACK SKIING

There is something to be said for a wealthy tax base. Subsidized by local taxes (in most towns, public cross-country ski trails would be considered a fiscal extravagance), the **Aspen/Snowmass Nordic Council** charges no fee for the 80 km (48 mi) of maintained trails (not all interconnected) in the Roaring Fork Valley. Probably the most varied, in terms of scenery and terrain, is the 30-km (18-mi) Snowmass Club trail network. For a longer ski, try the Owl Creek Trail, connecting the Snowmass Club trail system and the Aspen Cross-Country Center trails. More than 16 km (10 mi) long, the trail provides both a good workout and a heavy dosage of woodsy beauty, with many ups and downs across meadows and aspen-gladed hillsides.

Lessons and rentals are available at the **Aspen Cross-Country Center** (✉ 39551 Rte. 82 at the Aspen Golf Course, ☎ 970/925–2145). Diagonal, skating, racing, and light-touring setups are available. Lessons and rentals are also available at the **Snowmass Lodge Cross-Country Touring Center** (✉ Drawer G-2, Snowmass Village, ☎ 970/923–3148) and the **Hub** (☞ Backcountry Skiing, *above*).

Twelve miles from Aspen, the **Ashcroft Touring Center** (✉ Ashcroft Touring Unlimited, Castle Creek Rd., ☎ 970/925–1971) is sequestered in a high alpine basin up Castle Creek, which runs between Aspen Mountain and Aspen Highlands. The 40 km (25 mi) of groomed trails are surrounded by the high peaks of the Maroon Bells/Snowmass Wilderness. It is truly one of the most dramatic cross-country sites in the Rockies.

Other Activities

DOGSLEDDING

Krabloonik (✉ 4250 Divide Rd., Snowmass, ☎ 970/923–4342), with about 200 dogs at its disposal, can put on a good half-day ride (beginning at 8:30 AM or 12:30 PM). The ride is preceded or followed by lunch at the Krabloonik restaurant, among the best in the Aspen/Snowmass area.

SNO-CAT SKIING

Aspen Mountain Powder Tours (☎ 970/925–1220, ext. 3549) provides access to 1,500 acres on the back side of Aspen Mountain via Sno-Cat tours. Most of the terrain is negotiable by confident intermediates, with about 10,000 vertical ft constituting a typical day's skiing. Reservations are required at least a day in advance, but you should book as far in advance as possible during the season. Tours cost $225.

Aspen/Snowmass Essentials

ARRIVING AND DEPARTING

By Car: Generally speaking, driving to Aspen from Denver in the winter is more trouble than it's worth, unless you are on an extended vacation and plan to stop at other resorts such as Vail. With Independence Pass closed in the winter, the drive takes more than three hours at best, depending on road and weather conditions. On the other hand, the drive from the west is relatively easy, with no high-mountain passes to negotiate. Take the Route 82 exit off I–70 at Glenwood Springs.

By Plane: United/United Express has frequent flights between Denver and **Aspen Airport** (☎ 970/920–5385). United Express also has nonstop flights from Chicago, Dallas, and Los Angeles. Most major airlines have numerous flights to and from Denver. Another option is to fly into **Eagle County Airport** (☎ 970/524–9490), 70 mi north of Aspen and served by American, Delta, Northwest, and United.

From the Airports: Colorado Mountain Express (☎ 800/525–6353) and **High Mountain Taxi** (☎ 800/528–8294) provide service to Aspen from Denver, Eagle County, and Glenwood Springs. Avis, Budget, and Hertz, among others, rent cars from the Aspen airport; Hertz and Dollar from Eagle County; and Enterprise from Glenwood Springs (☞ Car Rental *in* Smart Travel Tips A to Z).

GETTING AROUND

A rental car is unnecessary in either Aspen or Snowmass, since both are geared as much for pedestrians as for cars; in many cases it's easier getting around on foot. Furthermore, the Aspen/Snowmass area has perhaps the best free **shuttle-bus** system in skidom. The free shuttles are backed up by **Roaring Fork Transit Agency** (☎ 970/925–8484) buses. The fare is $2–$5, depending on the destination.

VISITOR INFORMATION

Central reservations: ☎ 800/452–2409 for Aspen, 800/214–7669 for Snowmass. **General information: Aspen Skiing Company** (✉ 601 E. Dean St., Aspen 81611, ☎ 970/925–1220 or 800/525–6200); **Aspen Visitors Center** (✉ 425 Rio Grande Pl., Aspen 81611, ☎ 970/925–1940 or 800/262–7736). **Snow reports:** ☎ 970/925–1221 or 888/277–3676.

Crested Butte

Crested Butte has traditionally presented itself as the promised land of ski towns: After you've sold your soul in the Sodom and Gomorrah of Aspen and Vail, you pass through pearly gates and enter Crested Butte. No pretensions. No resort bluster. No fur, except for that worn by living animals. An honest, down-to-earth Rocky Mountain ski town.

The truth is, Crested Butte is more than *one* ski town, and there *are* similarities to the two big shots: There's Crested Butte, a former mining town (not unlike Aspen), and Mount Crested Butte, a recently built resort town (not unlike Vail). But Crested Butte's relaxed, earthy atmosphere is genuine. Its generally youngish and politically left-leaning populace tends toward being "granola," as they say in the West. In other words, things such as natural foods, natural-fiber clothing, and a rugged outdoor spirit are commonplace. For athletic purists, Crested Butte lays claim to sparking the resurgence of telemark skiing about 20 years ago and the emergence, more recently, of mountain biking. You know you're an authentic Crested Butte-ite when you own not one but two mountain bikes: a town bike for hacking around and a performance bike for *serious* hacking around.

Crested Butte has made its mark on the national sporting scene in recent years as winter host in January to ESPN's X Games, a grab bag of sometimes wacky, sometimes avant-garde, often dangerous sports. The event is a tribal gathering of extreme skiers and snowboarders, willing to take on the kind of big air, big speed, and big crashes that make the final edit for national TV. The spirit of the event is quintessentially Crested Butte in exalting youthfulness, talent, and daring. That's not to say you have to be a young hot shot to enjoy Crested Butte's often steep and challenging terrain. There's plenty of relaxed, fun, and easy-going skiing for the whole family. But if you're young and adventurous, you'll fit right in.

Downhill Skiing and Snowboarding

Crested Butte skiing has a split personality, a judgment that is easily made by checking out the skiers who come here. One side of its personality is the primary trail network, characterized by long intermediate and lower-intermediate runs. This is the sort of skiing that attracts vacationers and families, mostly from the Southwest and Texas. They take advantage of, among other things, a wonderful expanse of easy terrain from the Keystone lift—not just a trail network but instead rolling, tree-dotted meadows with plenty of opportunities to poke around off the beaten track.

The other side of Crested Butte's personality is the so-called Extreme Limits, several hundred acres of steep bowls, gnarly chutes, and tight tree skiing. This is an attraction for extreme skiers (and extreme-skiing wanna-bes), so it's not surprising that Crested Butte is the site of the national extreme-skiing championships each year.

The best skiing on the main trail network is on the front side of the mountain. The Silver Queen high-speed quad shoots you up 2,000 vertical ft in just one quick lift ride. On the other side of the mountain, the Paradise high-speed quad accesses some of the mountain's best intermediate terrain.

The Extreme Limits is quirky terrain, capable of being sensational, horrible, or (more often than a lot of experts would like) closed. Until 1987, the only way to get to it was to climb over the ridgeline from the top of the Paradise lift. Although the installation of a Poma lift changed that, it also brought more skiers, some of whom are over their heads on that side of the mountain. This means the fresh snow gets skied up earlier than it used to, especially in those gnarly chutes. Face it: Terrain as steep and rocky as this really requires superb snow conditions to make it truly pleasurable. Otherwise, it can be rough going, and even hazardous.

FACILITIES

2,775-ft vertical drop; 1,160 skiable acres; 13% beginner, 40% intermediate, 47% expert; 3 high-speed quad chairs, 3 triple chairs, 3 double chairs, 4 surface lifts.

LESSONS AND PROGRAMS

A guaranteed learn-to-ski package includes one all-day lesson, plus two two-hour lessons and a three-day lift ticket, for $155. Call the **Crested Butte Ski and Snowboard School** (☎ 970/349–2252) for information on these and other programs. One special program of note is Kim Reichhelm's Women's Ski Adventures. Reichhelm, a former world extreme-skiing champion, leads four-day workshops aimed at "breakthrough" experiences for women of all abilities. Call or write **Women's Ski Ad-**

ventures (✉ 5589 Arapahoe Ave., Suite 208, Boulder 80303, ☎ 303/440–7921 or 888/444–8151) for dates and details.

LIFT TICKETS

$49. Free lift tickets from Thanksgiving week until the week before Christmas and again in mid-April.

RENTALS

Full rental packages (including skis, boots, and poles) are available through **Crested Butte Ski and Snowboard Rental** (☎ 970/349–2241 or 800/544–8448) and start at $14 per day. Substantial discounts are available for multiday rentals.

Nordic Skiing

BACKCOUNTRY SKIING

Considerable avalanche hazards notwithstanding, Crested Butte abounds with backcountry possibilities, from deep-woods touring to above-tree-line telemarking. Keep in mind that this is high-mountain country (the town itself is around 9,000 ft, and things go up from there) and that skiing in certain areas under certain weather conditions can be nothing short of suicidal. To play it safe, your best bet is to arrange a guided tour with the **Crested Butte Nordic Center** (☞ Track Skiing, *below*).

Another possibility is to spend a few days at **Irwin Lodge** (✉ Box 457, Crested Butte 81224, ☎ 970/349–9800), in a high basin about 12 mi from town. In winter, Sno-Cats carry alpine as well as telemark skiers to a ridge offering terrific views of the 14,000-ft peaks of the Maroon Bells/Snowmass Wilderness. From here, it's more than 2,000 vertical ft of bowl and tree skiing back to the lodge. Equally enjoyable is touring on your own (or with a guide) from the lodge.

At the base of the ski area, **Crested Butte Ski and Snowboard** (☎ 970/349–2241) rents downhill ski equipment and snowboards as well as touring and telemark equipment. In town, the **Alpineer** (✉ 419 6th St., ☎ 970/349–5210) is not only a good backcountry equipment source but can also provide information on backcountry routes and snow conditions.

TRACK SKIING

Three track networks totaling approximately 35–40 km (20–24 mi) are maintained by the **Crested Butte Nordic Center.** The largest of the three, the Red Lady Loop, covers mostly flat and rolling terrain across the meadows and through the aspen groves of the valley floor. Views of distant peaks are stunning. The 9 km (5½ mi) of the Bench network include a steep loop through the trees of Gibson Ridge—close to town but seemingly far away in the woods. The 9-km (5½-mi) system set on the Skyland Golf Course, 3 mi out of town, is probably the least interesting of the three, although its worth is enhanced considerably by its on-site restaurant. Lessons and rentals are available. The Nordic Center can also arrange backcountry tours for skiers of all abilities. ✉ *2nd St., Box 1269, Crested Butte 81224,* ☎ *970/349–1707.* *Trail fee: $7.*

Other Activities

HOT-AIR BALLOONING

The conditions must be just right, but on a clear windless morning, this wide-open basin, surrounded on all sides by mountain ranges, must surely be one of the country's best places to be aloft in a balloon. For information, contact **Big Horn Balloon Company** (☎ 970/596–1008). Flights are $125 per person for a ride of 30–60 minutes; $190 per person for a flight of up to two hours.

Crested Butte Essentials

ARRIVING AND DEPARTING

By Car: Crested Butte is 230 mi southwest of Denver. Take U.S. 285 south to U.S. 24 south to U.S. 50 west to Gunnison. From Gunnison, take Rte. 134 north to Crested Butte.

By Plane: American Airlines offers direct flights to **Gunnison County Airport** (☎ 970/641–2304) from Chicago through Dallas/Fort Worth. Delta has direct flights to Gunnison from Atlanta. United Express has regular service from Denver. Western Pacific has flights to Gunnison from about 15 cities nationwide, connecting through Colorado Springs.

From the Airport: Alpine Express (☎ 970/641–5074) offers van service from Gunnison to Crested Butte. Avis, Budget, Hertz, and National (☞ Car Rental *in* Smart Travel Tips A to Z) have car rental counters at the airport.

GETTING AROUND

There is reliable **shuttle-bus** service between the town of Crested Butte and the resort village, which are about 3 mi apart. However, because most lodging is at the resort village and the better restaurants, shopping, and general atmosphere are in town, you can expect to make many resort-to-town trips, and a **car** makes the going much easier.

VISITOR INFORMATION

Central reservations: ☎ 800/544–8448. **General information: Crested Butte Mountain Resort** (✉ 500 Gothic Rd., Box A, Mount Crested Butte 81225, ☎ 970/349–2378 or 888/223–3530); **Crested Butte Chamber of Commerce** (✉ Old Town Hall, Box 1288, Crested Butte 81224, ☎ 970/349–6438 or 800/215–2226). **Snow report:** ☎ 970/349–2323.

Steamboat Springs

Perhaps more than any other ski resort in the United States, Steamboat has linked its identity to a single person: Billy Kidd, the preeminent U.S. ski racer of the '60s. The everlasting image is of Kidd blasting through the powder with a big grin on his face and a cowboy hat that must be glued to his head since it never blows off. That's how Steamboat projects itself: cowboy living and deep-snow skiing—new resort meets the Old West. In large part, Steamboat pulls it off, even if the cowboy business gets a little hokey at times. It is the sort of hokeyness, though, that works for families, which represent the majority of Steamboat's guests.

This is not to suggest that there is no legitimacy to Steamboat's cowboy image, which dates back to the 1800s, when the first ranching communities took root. In fact, these early settlers were also responsible for the advent of skiing in the area, as they strapped wooden boards (vaguely resembling skis) to their feet so they could get around the neighborhood in winter. Later, Steamboat was one of the first ski areas to be developed in the West.

Steamboat carries the banner of "Ski Town, USA," which is simultaneously descriptive and misleading: In reality, this is a modern resort area, sprawling around the base of the ski lifts, and an older town (Steamboat Springs) 2 mi away. The older town indeed has the kind of verve and funkiness you would expect in a real ski town; the resort area, where a good many Steamboat visitors stay, is too spread out—or still too new—to have developed much ski-town character.

Downhill Skiing and Snowboarding

Steamboat is perhaps best known for its tree skiing and "cruising" terrain—the latter term referring to intermediate skiing on wide, groomed runs. The abundance of cruising terrain has made Steamboat immensely popular with intermediates and families who ski only a few times a year and who aren't looking for diabolical challenges to tax their abilities. Set on a predominantly western exposure—most ski areas are situated on north-facing exposures—the resort benefits from intense sun, which contributes to the cruising quality. Moreover, one of the most extensive lift systems in the West allows skiers to take a lot of fast runs without having to spend much time in line. The Storm Peak and Sundown high-speed quads, for example, each deliver about 2,000 vertical ft in less than seven minutes. Do the math, and you can figure that a day of more than 60,000 vertical ft is entirely within the realm of diehards.

All this is not to suggest, however, that Steamboat lacks challenge entirely. Steamboat is renowned as a breeding ground for some of the country's top mogul skiers, and for good reason. The mogul runs might not be steep, but they're numerous. There are also some real steeps, such as Chute One, but they're few and not especially long. The Morningside Park expansion, which added 950 acres to the ski area in 1996–97, encompasses advanced and intermediate terrain. If you're looking for challenging skiing at Steamboat, take on the trees. The ski area has done an admirable job of clearing many gladed areas of such nuisances as saplings, underbrush, and fallen timber, making Steamboat tree skiing a much less hazardous adventure than it can be at some areas. The trees are also where advanced skiers—as well as, in some places, confident intermediates—can find the best of Steamboat's ballyhooed powder. Statistically, Steamboat doesn't report significantly more snowfall than other Colorado resorts, but somehow its numbers seem literally to stack up better than the others. Ask well-traveled Colorado skiers, and they'll confirm that when it comes to consistently good, deep snow, Steamboat is hard to beat.

FACILITIES

3,668-ft vertical drop; 2,939 skiable acres; 14% beginner, 56% intermediate, 30% advanced; 1 8-passenger gondola, 4 high-speed quad chairs, 1 quad chair, 6 triple chairs, 6 double chairs.

LESSONS AND PROGRAMS

Two-hour adult group lessons begin at $38; all-day lessons are $57. Clinics in moguls, powder, snowboarding, and "hyper-carving"—made possible by the relatively new shaped skis—are available. For general **ski school** information, call ☎ 970/879–6111, ext. 531. Intensive two- and three-day "training camps" are offered in racing and advanced skiing through the **Billy Kidd Center for Performance Skiing** (☎ 970/879–6111, ext. 543). Children's programs (lessons and/or day care) are offered for kids 6 months–15 years old through the **Kids' Vacation Center** (☎ 970/879–6111, ext. 218).

LIFT TICKETS

$52. Savings of 5% or less on multiday tickets.

RENTALS

Equipment packages are available at the gondola base as well as at ski shops in town. Packages (skis, boots, and poles) average about $16 a day, less for multiday rentals. Call central reservations (☞ Visitor Information, *below*) for rental information.

Nordic Skiing

BACKCOUNTRY SKIING

The most popular area for backcountry skiing is Rabbit Ears Pass southeast of town, the last pass you must cross if you drive from Denver to Steamboat. Much of its appeal is the easy access to high country; trails emanate from the U.S. 40 roadside. There are plenty of touring routes possible, with limited telemarking opportunity. Arrangements for backcountry tours can be made through the **Steamboat Ski Touring Center** (☞ Track Skiing, *below*).

Another popular backcountry spot is Seedhouse Road, north of the town of Clark and about 25 mi north of Steamboat. A marked trail network covers rolling hills, with good views of distant peaks. For maps, trail suggestions, and information on snow conditions and stability, contact the **Hahn's Peak Ranger Office** (✉ 57 10th St., Box 771212, Steamboat Springs 80477, ☎ 970/879–1870).

Touring and telemarking rentals are available at various ski shops in the Steamboat area. One of the best is the **Ski Haus** (✉ 1450 Lincoln Ave., ☎ 970/879–0385).

TRACK SKIING

The main center for cross-country skiing is the **Steamboat Ski Touring Center,** where most of the 30-km (18½-mi) trail network—laid out on or alongside the Sheraton Steamboat Golf Club—is relatively gentle. The inspiration behind the center is Sven Wiik, a seminal figure in the establishment of cross-country skiing in the United States. A good option for a relaxed afternoon of skiing is to pick up some eats at the Picnic Basket in the touring center building and enjoy lunch at the picnic area along the Fish Creek Trail, a 5-km (3-mi) loop that winds through pine and aspen groves. Rental packages (skis, boots, and poles) are available. ✉ *Box 775401, Steamboat Springs 80477,* ☎ *970/879–8180.* 🎫 *Trail fee: $10.*

Some guest ranches in the area also have groomed track networks. **Home Ranch** (✉ Box 822, Clark 80428, ☎ 970/879–1780), 20 mi north of Steamboat, has 40 km (25 mi) of groomed tracks. **Vista Verde Guest Ranch** (✉ Box 465, Steamboat Springs 80477, ☎ 970/879–3858 or 800/526–7433) also has a groomed trail network, as well as access to adjacent national forest land for touring.

Other Activities

Dogsledding, hot-air ballooning, and snowmobiling can be arranged by calling the activities department at **central reservations** (☎ 800/922–2722, ext. 372).

BOBSLEDDING

The term "bobsledding" might be stretching things, since this isn't quite the 80-mph rush down a twisting gutter of ice that you've seen at the Olympics. However, when riding a soft-shell, four-person sled down the course at **Howelsen Hill** (☎ 970/879–2170), the ski-jumping hill just outside town, it's possible to reach speeds of nearly 50 mph—plenty fast for most people. The cost is $10 per run.

ICE DRIVING

Here's one for anyone who's either been intimidated by snowy roads or gotten teenage thrills from executing doughnuts on icy shopping-mall parking lots. The **Bridgestone Winter Driving School** (☎ 970/879–6104 or 800/949–7543) offers half-day and full-day courses, as well as special, women-only programs.

SLEIGH RIDES

Several ranches in the area offer horse-drawn sleigh rides, dinner rides being the most popular. Call the central reservations number (☞ Visitor Information, *below*) for details. **Windwalker Tours** (☎ 970/879–8065 or 800/748–1642) offers daily afternoon sleigh rides to view elk herds that winter in the area.

SNO-CAT SKIING

Buffalo Pass, northeast of Steamboat, is reputed to be one of the snowiest spots in Colorado, and that's where **Steamboat Powder Cats** (☎ 970/879–5188 or 800/288–0543) operates. The basics are included: open-meadow skiing, deep powder, and a maximum of only 24 skiers. Sno-Cat skiing is the "poor man's" version of helicopter skiing, although at close to $200 a day, it's not exactly skiing for the lunch-pail crowd. One advantage over helicopters: Sno-Cats don't have to worry about landing and can get to places in bad weather that would be inaccessible by helicopter.

Steamboat Springs Essentials

ARRIVING AND DEPARTING

By Car: Steamboat is about a three-hour drive from Denver via I–70 west and U.S. 40 north. The route traverses high-mountain passes, so it's a good idea to check road conditions (☎ 303/639–1234) before you travel.

By Plane: American, Northwest, and United offer service from several U.S. cities to **Yampa Valley Airport** (☎ 970/276–3669), 22 mi from Steamboat. United Express offers connecting flights from Denver.

From the Airport: Central reservations (☞ Visitor Information, *below*) can provide information on rental cars and airport shuttles. **Alpine Taxi** (☎ 970/879–8294) and **Steamboat Taxi** (☎ 970/879–3335) provide transportation from the airport to lodging within the resort community. **Storm Mountain Express** (☎ 877/844–8787) offers daily bus service from Denver International Airport to Steamboat.

GETTING AROUND

Steamboat's public **bus system** is a regular and reliable network that gets you around town and to and from the resort community. Skiers staying in town may find a **rental car** unnecessary; those staying in the more spread-out resort may appreciate the convenience of having one.

VISITOR INFORMATION

Central reservations: ☎ 800/922–2722. **General information: Steamboat Ski & Resort Corporation** (✉ 2305 Mt. Werner Circle, Steamboat Springs 80487, ☎ 970/879–6111). **Snow report:** ☎ 970/879–7300.

Summit County: Arapahoe Basin, Breckenridge, Copper Mountain, Keystone

Summit County is a hard place to get a fix on: four ski areas, three resorts, three towns in between—and Vail just over the pass. Where do you start? This multiplicity is both Summit County's bounty and its curse. It is a curse in that the area seems to have developed without much unified focus or sense of direction. The three major resorts—Breckenridge, Copper Mountain, and Keystone—are caught in that peculiar bind of establishing their own identities while still maintaining an association with the others. Now the mishmash has gotten even more complicated, with the 1997 merger of Breckenridge and Keystone with Vail Associates, and Copper with Intrawest (owner of Blackcomb in Canada). Both corporations are throwing their financial weight behind the respective resorts, trying to outdo one another in on-mountain improvements and base-area construction. The result has been less cohesion among the neighboring resorts than ever; for example, multiday tickets accepted at all Summit county resorts are no longer available.

Frisco, Dillon, and Silverthorne—those three towns in between—have accepted that their mandate calls for function over character. They provide moderately priced lodging and dining at approximately equal distances to the ski areas and are close to the highway. Many Summit County skiers are weekenders from Denver looking for a few days of respite from the city, not a fancy, full-service vacation.

The multimountain, multitown mishmash is not without irony. The one resort with solid historical roots is Breckenridge, built around the Main Street of an old mining town. Yet Breckenridge has become so built up over the years (close to 25,000 beds) that it comes off as the most thoroughly developed resort of the three. The area that *does* have a legitimately unique character, Arapahoe Basin, really hasn't made any effort to buff up its image. Arapahoe is pretty much the ski area it was 20 years ago. It's popular with a generally younger crowd and is especially visited late in the season—April into June. Arapahoe's late-season, on-mountain partying spirit has become legendary.

What does it all add up to? Very briefly: Breckenridge is generally the choice of a young, lively crowd. The skiing focuses mainly on cruising, and so does the nightlife. Copper Mountain is best for skiers committed to skiing. The terrain is the best and most varied in Summit County, and its once antiseptic base village is getting a much-needed makeover from Intrawest. Keystone is a quiet and, by the often slapdash standards of ski-lodging construction, well-built place. It's popular with families and probably wins the Summit County prize for the most genuine mountain resort.

Downhill Skiing and Snowboarding

Let's see—roughly 7,000 skiable acres, 60-some lifts, more than 400 marked trails. What you need in Summit County isn't a lift ticket but a calculator. Despite their proximity, the four ski areas do have distinctly different characters.

What can make **Arapahoe** delightful is also what damns it in bad weather: its elevation. The *base* elevation is 10,800 ft, so that most of Arapahoe's skiing is above tree line. When a storm moves in, you can't tell up from down at Arapahoe, and when the storm passes, skiing can be limited because of avalanche problems.

But if that sounds dreadful, consider the other side of the coin: On sunny spring days, Arapahoe is probably *the* place to be skiing in Colorado. It feels more like skiing in the Alps than Summit County, Colorado, with craggy peaks surrounded by treeless, rolling terrain. Intermediates can have a great time here, although "A-Basin" is best known for its expert challenges: the East Wall, a steep open face with great powder-skiing possibilities; Pallavicini, a wide, steep, tree-lined gutter of a run; and the West Wall cornice, from which young bucks, with varying degrees of bravado and sobriety, like to launch themselves. A typical spring day at Arapahoe: Ski frantically hard in the morning; kick back, catch rays, and swill beers in the afternoon.

For the most part, **Breckenridge** is the sort of area where you can close your eyes and let your skis run; intermediate cruising is the name of the game. It is ideal for people who like a relaxed day on the slopes without having to worry about overworking the challenge meter. Still, there is some more adventurous, above-tree-line bowl skiing, accessible either by hiking or by a hard-to-ride T-bar. When that high-country skiing is good, it's great, but because of Breck's exposure to stormy weather, conditions can often be less than ideal.

Breckenridge's chief drawback is its horizontal layout, spreading across the flanks of four main peaks, named—with great imagination—Peaks

7, 8, 9, and 10. Want to get from the base of Peak 8 to the summit of Peak 10? A couple of lift rides are necessary, and navigational aids would be helpful.

As mentioned, **Copper Mountain** has perhaps the best variety of skiing among the Summit County areas: Good, long cruisers, satisfying mogul runs, above-tree-line bowl skiing, tight tree skiing, and a terrific cluster of lower-intermediate terrain. Furthermore, the layout is such that there's minimal contact (literally) between skiers of differing abilities; you don't have fast skiers sharing the same terrain as beginners, as you do at some areas.

One reason for this is that Copper, like Breckenridge, is a horizontal spread, with novice skiers tending toward the right, intermediates in the middle, and experts toward the left. It's a great choice for a family or group of friends with widely varying skills; there's skiing to keep everyone entertained. In recent years, Copper has been pushing out its boundaries to include open bowls and chutes that add an almost backcountry character to the layout. The runs are relatively short, but that does little to dampen the above-tree-line, high-alpine drama.

Keystone is hard to get a good read on at first, especially since the slopes you see from the base lodge look quite steep—and they are—but they are not indicative of the rest of the trails. About 90% of Keystone Mountain is geared toward novice and lower-intermediate skiing. Yet Keystone Mountain isn't all there is to Keystone. Slip off the back side, and you've got North Peak and the Outback, with skiing for more skilled intermediates and advanced skiers. None of it is real knock-your-socks-off expert terrain, but Keystone has never tried to market itself as an expert's ski area. It's great for families or for people who ski once or twice a year. Better skiers prefer to toss the boards in the car and head for either Copper or Arapahoe, 6 mi up the road.

FACILITIES

Arapahoe Basin: 2,250-ft vertical drop; 490 skiable acres; 10% beginner, 50% intermediate, 40% advanced; 1 triple chair, 4 double chairs. **Breckenridge:** 3,398-ft vertical drop; 2,031 skiable acres; 14% beginner, 26% intermediate, 60% advanced; 6 high-speed quad chairs, 1 quad chair, 1 triple chair, 7 double chairs. **Copper Mountain:** 2,601-ft vertical drop; 2,433 skiable acres; 20% beginner, 24% intermediate, 56% advanced; 1 high-speed six-person chair, 4 high-speed quad chairs, 5 triple chairs, 6 double chairs, 4 surface lifts. **Keystone:** 2,900-ft vertical drop; 1,861 skiable acres; 13% beginner, 36% intermediate, 51% advanced; 2 gondolas, 5 high-speed quad chairs, 1 quad chair, 2 triple chairs, 5 double chairs, 5 surface lifts.

LESSONS AND PROGRAMS

All four areas offer a variety of instructional programs (☞ Visitor Information, *below*), from half-day group lessons to special clinics, notably mogul clinics and women's seminars. Among the better bargains is the $50 all-day class-lesson rate at Breckenridge. One of the better children's programs is at Keystone, with day care and ski groups for children from 2 months to 16 years old. A special program of note is the Mahre Training Center at Keystone, intensive three- or five-day clinics held on various dates during the season and hosted by either Phil or Steve Mahre, both Olympic medalists.

LIFT TICKETS

$50–$52 at Breckenridge, Copper, or Keystone; $26–$40, depending on the time of season, at Arapahoe Basin. Tickets purchased at Keystone and Breckenridge are good at either of the resorts, as well as at

Vail and Beaver Creek (but unfortunately not at Copper, which is under different ownership). Multiday ticket savings can exceed 20%.

RENTALS

Rental shops are at the bases of all four ski areas, with rental packages (skis, boots, and poles) starting at $16 per day. Considerable savings can be found by bargain shopping at ski stores in Breckenridge, Dillon, Frisco, and Silverthorne.

Nordic Skiing

BACKCOUNTRY SKIING

Despite widespread development in Summit County, there are still plenty of opportunities to escape into the backcountry and get away from it all. They don't call it Summit County for nothing; mountain passes above 10,000 ft allow for relatively easy access to high-country terrain and good, high-country snow. This recommendation comes, however, with a word of caution; avalanche-related deaths are all too common in Summit County (more often involving snowmobilers than skiers). Easy access often attracts backcountry travelers whose snow-safety awareness is not what it should be. For information on snow conditions, contact the **Dillon Ranger District Office** (☎ 970/468–5400).

Among the easier, and safer, touring routes is the trip to Boreas Pass, just south of Breckenridge. The trail (about 20 km/12 mi round-trip) follows a former rail route, with good views of distant peaks along the way. Summit County is also developing a system of backcountry huts that will be linked to Aspen's 10th Mountain Hut and Trail System. The first of these huts is Janet's Cabin, about a 10-km (6-mi) ski in from the trailhead off I–70 west of Copper Mountain. For information and reservations, contact the **10th Mountain Hut and Trail System** (☞ Nordic Skiing *in* Aspen/Snowmass, *above*.)

TRACK SKIING

The **Breckenridge Nordic Center** (☎ 970/453–6855), with 30 km (18½ mi) of groomed tracks; the **Copper Mountain Cross-Country Center** (☎ 970/968–2882, ext. 6342), with 25 groomed km (15½ mi); the **Frisco Nordic Center** (☎ 970/668–0866), with 45 groomed km (27 mi); and the **Keystone Cross-Country Center** (☎ 970/468–4275), with 18 groomed km (10 mi), are Summit County's main areas for track skiing. Of these, the Breckenridge terrain is probably the gentlest, the Copper Mountain terrain the most challenging. All offer lessons and rentals.

Other Activities

Dogsledding, sleigh rides, and snowmobiling can be arranged through the central reservation services at Breckenridge, Copper, and Keystone (☞ Visitor Information, *below*).

ICE-SKATING

Keystone has the largest maintained outdoor rink in the country. Actually it is not a true rink but a pond regularly resurfaced by maintenance machinery. At the center of Keystone Village, it is great for a leisurely post-ski skate and is open (and lit in the evening) daily 10–10, with skate rentals available.

Summit County Essentials

ARRIVING AND DEPARTING

By Car: Summit County is approximately 75 mi west of Denver via I–70.

By Plane: Most major carriers fly into **Denver International Airport** (☎ 800/247–2336).

From the Airport: Resort Express (☎ 970/468–7600 or 800/334–7433) provides van service between the airport and the resorts. Rental cars are widely available at the Denver International Airport.

GETTING AROUND

Although there is free shuttle-bus service within Summit County, a **car** is almost essential if you plan to do much traveling between your resort of choice and other points in Summit County. For anyone trying to avoid renting a car, **Summit Stage** ☎ (970/668–0999) provides free bus service around Summit County. Breckenridge, with the widest array of services and a town **shuttle bus,** is a good place for car-less visitors to set up shop.

VISITOR INFORMATION

Central reservations: ☎ 888/830–7669 for Breckenridge or Keystone; 800/458–8386 for Copper Mountain. **General information: Breckenridge Ski Resort** (✉ Box 1058, Breckenridge 80424, ☎ 970/453–6118); **Copper Mountain Resort** (✉ Box 3001, Copper Mountain 80443, ☎ 800/458–8386 or 970/968–2882); **Keystone Resort** (✉ Box 38, Keystone 80435, ☎ 970/468–2316. **Snow reports:** ☎ 800/789–7669 for Breckenridge; 800/789–7609 or 970/968–2100 for Copper Mountain; 970/468–4111 for Keystone.

Telluride

There are at least two Tellurides: Telluride Past and Telluride Future. Squashed in between is a still-evolving concept: Telluride Present. Telluride's distant past—dating to the late 1800s—revolved around mining; more recently, the town had the reputation of being a kind of societal escape hatch. Stuck in a box canyon in Colorado's southwest, Telluride was hard to find and even harder to access. As such, it was a perfect (and perfectly beautiful) hole in the wall of the San Juan Mountains for political and societal recalcitrants (most young and college-educated) who'd had it up to here with the status quo. They weren't bothered too much by the few straggling skiers who made their way to Telluride, and from those roots a ski town developed with a distinctively hip, back-to-nature edge.

Telluride Future has to do with the development of a resort village on the other side of the mountain. The concern is how its existence will mesh with Telluride's already established character. A gondola that runs over the mountain connects the old town and the new village, establishing a physical link if not necessarily a spiritual one. As plans for Telluride Future are beginning to be realized, a number of longtime residents say that the writing is on the wall: Telluride as a ski resort has been "discovered." Real estate values are escalating, encouraging many old-time Telluriders to sell out and move elsewhere. Effectively, some purists believe that Telluride can never again be what it was.

A couple of things are certain. Thanks to very strict zoning ordinances, the old town of Telluride still looks as it always has—a turn-of-the-century mining town against an exquisite backdrop—even if the cost of housing has gone through the roof. The resort village is finally taking shape—a handsome, modern place that could use some of old Telluride's history to lend it the kind of character it has yet to develop on its own.

Downhill Skiing and Snowboarding

Another split image: Telluride is really two ski areas in one. For many years, it had a reputation as being an experts-only ski area. Indeed, the north-facing trails on the town side are impressively steep and long, and by springtime, the moguls are humongous. When the snow is good, this is the site of some of the most outrageous mogul skiing in the world. So reputations are made.

But then there is the other side—literally—of the ski area, the west-facing village, with long, gentle runs. Plans are afoot to upgrade a slow and inefficient lift system, which will make a terrific place for lower-intermediate skiers and young children even better.

What Telluride lacks is much in between the super gentle and the super steep. There is the aptly named See Forever, a great, long cruiser and a few good intermediate runs from Lift 5, but they are, unfortunately, short and have nagging flat spots. The ski area's management hopes that a planned expansion will add more good runs at this level, but the expansion has been languishing on the drawing board for a while.

FACILITIES

3,522-ft vertical drop (3,165 ft lift-serviced); 1,050 skiable acres; 21% beginner, 47% intermediate, 32% advanced/expert; 1 gondola, 2 high-speed quad chairs, 2 triple chairs, 5 double chairs, 1 surface lift.

LESSONS AND PROGRAMS

The **ski school** (☎ 970/728–7533 or 800/801–4832) gives half-day group clinics beginning at $38. First-time beginner lessons are available for alpine and telemark skiers, as well as snowboarders. A five-hour clinic with rentals and restricted beginner lift tickets is available at $85.

LIFT TICKETS

$53. Daily rate as low as $44 on multiday tickets.

RENTALS

Rental packages (skis, boots, and poles) are available from **Telluride Sports** (☎ 970/728–4477) with six locations in town and in the Mountain Village. Rentals are also available from ski shops in town. Packages start at around $20.

Nordic Skiing

BACKCOUNTRY SKIING

About an hour's drive by car from Telluride (though only a few miles as the crow flies) is **St. Paul Lodge** (✉ Box 463, Silverton 81433, ☎ 970/387–5494), a terrific find for anyone enchanted by remote high country. Above 11,000 ft and about a half-hour ski-in from the summit of Red Mountain Pass between Ouray and Silverton, the lodge (a converted mining camp) provides access to a series of above-tree-line bowls and basins. Included in the lodge rates are guide service (essential in this potentially hazardous area), ski equipment, and telemark lessons if necessary, along with meals and lodging.

Among the better backcountry skiing routes in Colorado is the **San Juan Hut System,** leading toward Ridgway along the Sneffels Range. Five huts in the system are about 11 km (7 mi) apart and are well equipped with beds, blankets, wood-burning stoves, and cooking stoves. Previous backcountry experience is not essential (though highly recommended). Rental equipment is available, and reservations are recommended at least two weeks in advance. ✉ *224 E. Colorado Ave. or Box 1663, Telluride 81435,* ☎ *970/728–6935.* 🎫 *$17.*

The San Juan Hut System (☞ *above*) offers a **day-guiding service** as an introduction to backcountry skiing. The best place for backcountry **equipment rentals** in Telluride is Telluride Mountaineer (✉ 219 E. Colorado Ave., ☎ 970/728–6736).

TRACK SKIING

The **Telluride Nordic Association** maintains a hotline (☎ 970/728–7260) on conditions and events at cross-country ski centers in the area.

The 12-km (7½-mi) track along the San Miguel River on the valley floor is relatively flat and good for those who like to develop momentum and rhythm in their skiing. The 5 km (3 mi) of track on the golf course in the Mountain Village are more rolling. For distinctly backcountry flavor, try the groomed trails in the Prospect Basin area (site of the ski area's proposed expansion), reached from the top of the Sunshine Express lift. Many skiers who go into this area wear sturdy touring or telemarking gear and branch off from the groomed tracks. Equipment rentals, for both track skiing and backcountry touring, are available in the Mountain Village at Paragon Ski and Sport (☏ 800/903–4525) or at Telluride Mountaineer (☏ 800/828–7547) and the Telluride Nordic Center (☏ 970/728–7260) in town.

Other Activities

Telluride Outside (☏ 970/728–3895 or 800/831–6230) organizes a variety of winter activities in the Telluride area, among them hot-air ballooning, sleigh rides, snowmobile tours, and even winter fly-fishing excursions.

GLIDER RIDES

For an unusual look at the San Juans, **Telluride Soaring** (☏ 970/728–5424) operates out of the Telluride Airport. Rates are about $80 per half hour, $130 per hour; rides are offered daily, weather permitting.

HELI-SKIING

A day of heli-skiing with **Telluride Helitrax,** operated by **Telluride Outside,** includes five runs (up to 12,000 vertical ft) for $625 per person. Custom and multi-day tours can also be arranged. For reservations, contact Telluride Outside, *see above.*

ICE CLIMBING

Having your body suspended for any extended length of time on a wall of ice would be considered a form of torture by some. For those who think it can be fun, **Fantasy Ridge Alpinism** (✉ 323 N. Oak, Box 1679, Telluride 81435, ☏ 970/728–3546) offers introductory ice-climbing courses. A three-day course, including three nights of lodging and three days of climbing, costs about $900 per person. Guided ice-climbing day trips can also be arranged through **Telluride Outside,** *see above.*

Telluride Essentials

ARRIVING AND DEPARTING

By Car: Telluride is 330 mi southwest of Denver. There is no such thing as a direct route, but the fastest is probably U.S. 285 south to U.S. 24 south to U.S. 50 west to Montrose. Take U.S. 550 south to Ridgway. From Ridgway, take Route 62 west to Placerville and Route 45 south to Telluride.

By Plane: America West and United Express have connecting flights from Denver to **Telluride Regional Airport** (☏ 970/728–5313), just 5 mi from the resort. Telluride is notorious for being one of the hardest ski resorts in the country to fly into, mainly because its airport elevation is well above 9,000 ft. A little turbulence, a few clouds, and the next thing you know, you're landing in Montrose, 67 mi away, and taking a van to Telluride.

From the Airport: Skip's Taxi (☏ 970/728–6667) and **Telluride Transit** (☏ 970/728–6000) offer transportation from the Telluride airport, and Budget, Dollar, and Hertz car-rental agencies have offices there (☞ Car Rental *in* Smart Travel Tips A to Z).

GETTING AROUND

While the separation of the resort village from the town of Telluride has kept the town's historic integrity intact, it created a transportation headache: how to get easily from village to town without causing a huge environmental impact? The opening of a 2½-mi, over-the-mountain free **gondola** in late 1996 solved that problem, and created one of the most beautiful commutes in Colorado.

The gondola makes a car unnecessary for local transportation; both the village and the town are pedestrian-friendly. However, for any out-of-town excursions—and a drive through the spectacular San Juan Mountains is well worthwhile—a **car** is necessary.

VISITOR INFORMATION

Central reservations: ☏ 888/605–2573. **General information: Telluride Visitor Services** (✉ 666 W. Colorado Ave., Box 653, Telluride 81435, ☏ 970/728–3041); **Telluride Ski Resort** (✉ 565 Mountain Village Blvd., Telluride 81435, ☏ 970/728–6900). **Snow report:** ☏ 970/728–7425.

Vail/Beaver Creek

Vail is American skiing's big kahuna, the king of the hills. It is either the most, as they used to say in beatnik talk, or too much, depending on your tastes. Vail logs more "skier days" (the ski industry's measure of ticket sales) than any other resort in the country. You don't do that without being big, both as a ski area and as a resort, and Vail—by ski-resort standards—is enormous. And now, with the merger of Vail with Keystone and Breckenridge, it is the world's largest ski company. It is astounding how much developers have been able to cram into the relatively narrow Vail Valley—and all the more astounding when you consider that a chunk of the valley floor is taken up by a major interstate highway (I–70).

Of course, one valley can only absorb so much, and by the beginning of the '80s, when it became obvious that Vail development had almost maxed out, the satellite resort of Beaver Creek sprang up. "The Beave," as locals call it, has quickly become a substantial resort in its own right—a low-key (relatively speaking) alternative to Vail itself.

Vail and Beaver Creek score high marks on two counts: the total amount of skiing (more than 5,000 skiable acres) and the resort amenities. The two combine as the very definition of full-service resort, a well-oiled service machine that must take care of a bed base of roughly 40,000: restaurants, posh lodging, even ski concierges who will help you put on your skis in the morning. Lacking is a sense of soulful character, but what would you expect with an interstate highway running right through town? The original resort village was developed with a neo-Tyrolean theme, which subsequent development practically ignored. Vail today has more of a neo-suburban atmosphere. You come to Vail and Beaver Creek to ski, eat, and be pampered, but certainly not to have your soul reclaimed by the splendor of the wilderness.

Downhill Skiing and Snowboarding

Neither Vail nor Beaver Creek is renowned for expert terrain. Although **Beaver Creek** has the less of the two, many local experts prefer "the Beave" and the steep runs of Grouse Mountain because far fewer experts ski there than Vail. But the Beave's strong suit remains that it is perhaps one of the best ski areas in America for lower intermediates. The top third of the mountain features a large trail cluster of almost exclusively easygoing stuff, and any skier who doesn't feel up to the slightly steeper lower section of the mountain can ride the lift down to the base. The linking of Beaver Creek's trail system with that of neighboring Arrowhead Resort, and Bachelor Gulch, a new area between the two, has added 30% more novice and intermediate terrain to the area, and has created a European-style "village-to-village" ski experience.

Vail is perhaps best known for its back bowls, a vast expanse (nearly 3,000 acres) of open-bowl skiing that can be sensational on powder days but generally only so-so at other times, after the fresh snow has been tracked up and worked on by sun and wind. For the most part, the back bowls are not extraordinarily steep, and thus are good places for intermediates to learn how to ski powder.

Skiing on the front side of the mountain is a markedly different experience. There's lots of wide-trail skiing, heavily skewed toward groomed intermediate runs. Vail is an ideal mountain for those in the intermediate- and advanced-skier audience who ski a week or two a season and want to be reminded each year that they do know how to turn a ski. Vail skiing has a way of boosting egos. There are a few steep and long mogul runs for experts, but Vail's true expert terrain represents a relatively small chunk of the huge Vail pie.

FACILITIES

Beaver Creek: 4,040-ft vertical drop; 1,625 skiable acres; 27% beginner, 39% intermediate, 34% advanced; 6 high-speed quad chairs, 3 triple chairs, 4 double chairs, 1 surface lift. **Vail:** 3,335-ft vertical drop; 4,644 skiable acres; 21% beginner, 31% intermediate, 48% advanced on the front side; 13% intermediate, 87% advanced in the back bowls; 1 gondola, 10 high-speed quad chairs, 1 regular quad, 3 triple chairs, 5 double chairs, 11 surface lifts.

LESSONS AND PROGRAMS

Half-day group lessons start at $60; full-day lessons start at $70. The ski schools at Vail and Beaver Creek are among the best in the country, with several specialty classes and excellent children's programs. For more information, call the **Vail and Beaver Creek Ski School** (☎ 970/476–3229).

LIFT TICKETS

$59. Multiday tickets (up to seven days) are available, although per-day savings are minimal. Tickets are good at both Vail and Beaver Creek, as well as at Breckenridge and Keystone.

RENTALS

Breeze Ski Rentals, with four locations in the Vail/Beaver Creek area, offers full rental packages for as low as $13 a day for multi-day rentals. Call ☎ 800/525–0314 for advanced reservations. For high-performance rentals, a good choice is **Kenny's Double Diamond** (✉ 520 Lionshead Mall, Vail 81657, ☎ 970/476–5500 or 800/466–2704).

Nordic Skiing

BACKCOUNTRY SKIING

The **10th Mountain Hut and Trail System** reaches far into Vail's backcountry; one route continues to Aspen (☞ Nordic Skiing *in* Aspen/Snowmass, *above*). Maps, equipment, and other information are available and hut reservations should be made at least a month in advance by calling ☎ 970/925–5775. Rates range between $22 and $32 per person per night. If you aren't familiar with the trail system, hiring a guide is highly recommended. In Vail, contact **Paragon Guides** (☎ 970/926–5299).

TRACK SKIING

To reach Beaver Creek's cross-country trail network, **McCoy Park** (☎ 970/845–5313), you must ride the Strawberry Park chairlift. This is a bonus, for it gets you far enough from the resort village that you get a rare sense (around Vail, anyway) that you're in a pristine mountain environment. The 32 km (20 mi) of groomed tracks have a fair amount of ups and downs—or perhaps because the elevation is above 9,500 ft, it just seems that way. The trail fee is $17 for a full day. Lessons, rentals, and snowshoe tours are available through the Vail ski school *see above*. The cross-country skiing at the **Vail Nordic Center** (☎ 970/476–8366) is less inspiring—a network laid out on what in the summer is a golf course—but it's also free.

Other Activities

The **Activities Desk of Vail** (☎ 970/476–9090) or the **Beaver Creek Resort Concierge** (☎ 970/949–9090) can arrange a variety of nonskiing activities, including dogsledding, hot-air ballooning, and Sno-Cat skiing.

BOBSLEDDING

Vail's on-mountain bobsled run, a 2,900-ft course, begins below Mid-Vail (the large restaurant about halfway up the mountain). Neither the course nor the sleds are quite up to an Olympic standard, but speeds of up to 50 mph are still possible. The sleds hold up to four people and cost $14 per person.

SNOWMOBILING

Snowmobile tours are conducted at **Piney River Ranch** (☎ 970/476–9090), just north of Vail. Rates include helmets, snowmobile suits, and boots, and sometimes meals, and range from $72 to $135 per person.

Vail/Beaver Creek Essentials

ARRIVING AND DEPARTING

By Car: Vail and Beaver Creek are about 120 mi west of Denver International Airport, via I–70.

By Plane: Eagle County Airport (☎ 970/524–9490), 35 mi west of Vail, is served by American, Delta, Northwest, and United Express.

From the Airport: Colorado Mountain Express (☎ 800/525–6363) and **Vail Valley Taxi** (☎ 970/476–8294 or 800/882–8872) provide transportation between Vail/Beaver Creek and both the Eagle County Airport and Denver International Airport. Budget, Dollar, Hertz, National, and Thrifty rent cars in the Vail valley (☞ Car Rental *in* Smart Travel Tips A to Z).

GETTING AROUND

A public **shuttle-bus** service is also available within Vail and between Vail and Beaver Creek.

VISITOR INFORMATION

Central reservations: ☎ 800/427–8308. **General information: Vail Resorts, Inc.** (✉ Box 7, Vail 81658, ☎ 970/476–5601); **Vail Valley Tourism and Convention Bureau** (✉ 100 E. Meadow Dr., Vail 81658, ☎ 970/476–1000 or 800/824–5737). **Snow report:** ☎ 970/476–4888.

Winter Park

There is no more aptly named ski area in America than Winter Park. Technically the area—a public park—is owned by the city of Denver and is frequented primarily by skiers who drive 1½ hours from the city for a winter's day or weekend. In an effort to buff up its appeal as a destination resort—to attract multiday vacationers—Winter Park has been undergoing a transformation with the on-going development of the Village at Winter Park. The development is adding lodging, dining, and shopping at the ski-area base—the sort of stuff the day skiers from Denver never really found necessary.

Winter Park isn't Colorado's most scenic resort; the front-range mountains lack the dramatic rocky structure of, say, the San Juans in Colorado's southwest. In large part, that's because proximity to Denver, rather than scenic drama, was most important in choosing the location of the resort. Not that Winter Park is *ugly* by any means; it's all relative.

Finally, Winter Park can attract an unusually eclectic crowd. On any given day, you might have the U.S. Ski Team in training (the 1993 U.S. National Skiing Championships were held here), a large corps of skiers with disabilities (Winter Park has the best program for skiers with disabilities in the country), and busloads of school children from the Denver area, most of them throwing snowballs at one another.

Downhill Skiing and Snowboarding

Winter Park is really three interconnected ski areas: Winter Park flanked by Mary Jane and Vasquez Ridge. That's both good and bad: It's good in that it spreads skiers out on those busy weekend days; it's bad in that it spreads skiers out. It's easy to lose your skiing partners at Winter Park, and once that happens, it's hard to find them.

The skiing at Winter Park and Vasquez Ridge leans heavily toward ultrawide, groomed intermediate trails. It's terrific skiing for families, groups, and schussboomers who enjoy testing the ski patrol's resolve by skiing too fast. On busy weekends, Vasquez Ridge is the best place for escaping crowds, partly because it's difficult to figure out how to get there. For experts *really* trying to escape crowds, the newly opened chutes and headwalls of Vasquez Cirque are the place to run to.

Mary Jane is 1,800 vertical ft of unrelenting moguls, with a couple of groomed runs (if you want groomed, there are more choices at Winter Park). The Timberline lift behind Mary Jane provides access to the above-tree-line skiing of Parsenn Bowl. The pitch is moderate, making the bowl a terrific place for intermediates to try their luck at powder and crud-snow skiing.

FACILITIES

3,060-ft vertical drop; 2,886 skiable acres; 9% beginner, 35% intermediate, 56% advanced; 7 high-speed quad chairs, 5 triple chairs, 8 double chairs.

LESSONS AND PROGRAMS

For adult skiers and snowboarders, the **Winter Park Skier and Rider Improvement Center** (☎ 970/726–1551) offers half-day lessons starting at $20. All-day children's programs, which include lunch, start at $65.

LIFT TICKETS

$50–$52. Savings of up to 30% on multiday tickets.

RENTALS

Rental packages starting at $16 are available at **Winter Park Mountain Sports** (☎ 970/726–1660) at the Winter Park base area. Rental equipment is also available from several shops in downtown Winter Park.

Nordic Skiing

BACKCOUNTRY SKIING

Berthoud Pass, just south of Winter Park, is a hard place to define. As a ski area, it has been opened, closed, and re-opened so often that lifts may or may not be running at any given time. Even when they are, only a portion of the skiing is truly lift-serviced. Much of the best terrain must be hiked to, and skiers and snowboarders get back to the ski-area base via shuttle buses from pick-up points along the highway. Whatever the means of going up and down, Berthoud is well worth a visit for well-conditioned, expert skiers and riders.

TRACK SKIING

The closest groomed tracks to Winter Park are at **Devil's Thumb Ranch,** 7 mi from Winter Park, with a trail system totaling more than 100 km (62 mi). Some skiing is along tree-lined trails, some with more ups and downs and open views. The ranch offers lodging, a restaurant, rentals, lessons, and backcountry tours. ✉ *Box 750, Tabernash 80478,* ☎ *970/726–5632 or 800/933–4339.* *Trail fee: $12.*

Somewhat farther afield is **Snow Mountain Ranch,** 12 mi northwest of Winter Park in Tabernash. The 100-km (62-mi) trail system includes 3 km (almost 2 mi) lit for night skiing. The ranch is a YMCA facility (with discounts for YMCA members) that has such added bonuses as a sauna and an indoor pool. Lessons, rentals, and on-site lodging are available. ✉ *Box 169, Winter Park 80482,* ☎ *970/887–2152.* *Trail fee: $8, $2 evening.*

Other Activities

SNOWMOBILING

Rentals and guided tours are available from **Trailblazer Snowmobile Tours** (✉ Box 3437, Winter Park 80482, ☎ 970/726–8452 or 800/669–0134). Rates range from $40 per hour to $165 for a full-day tour.

SNOW TUBING

A lift-serviced snow-tubing hill? Yes, and it's lit at night, no less. The **Fraser Snow Tubing Hill** (☎ 970/726–5954) has two lifts, groomed trails, and a warming hut to make your experience of riding an inner tube down a snowy hill most enjoyable. The rate is $10 per hour before 6 PM, $11 per hour after 6 PM.

Winter Park Essentials

ARRIVING AND DEPARTING

By Car: Winter Park is about 70 mi west of Denver via I–70 west and U.S. 40 north. However, if you drive, be forewarned that Berthoud Pass on U.S. 40 can be treacherous when winter storms blow in.

By Plane: Most major airlines fly into **Denver International Airport** (☎ 800/247–2336).

From the Airport: Home James Transportation provides van service from the airport to the resort. Reservations can be made through Winter Park Central Reservations *(see below)*. Many car rental companies operate out of the Denver airport.

By Train: Winter Park is the only ski resort in the Rockies with train service right to the slopes. In winter, the *Ski Train* (☎ 303/296–4754) provides round-trip weekend service from Denver's Union Station to the ski area. **Amtrak**'s (☎ 970/726–5587) *California Zephyr* also provides daily service to Winter Park from Chicago and the west coast; some ski packages are available.

GETTING AROUND

A free **shuttle-bus** service runs between most lodges in the Winter Park area and the ski area. Because things are fairly spread out in the Fraser Valley, however, a car is recommended.

VISITOR INFORMATION

Central reservations: ☎ 800/979–0332. **General information: Winter Park Resort** (✉ Box 36, Winter Park 80482, ☎ 970/726–5514); **Winter Park/Fraser Valley Chamber of Commerce** (✉ Box 3236, Winter Park 80482, ☎ 970/726–4118 or 800/903–7275). **Snow report:** ☎ 970/726–7669.

IDAHO

Sun Valley

Before there was Aspen, there was Sun Valley. Long before there were such movies as *Aspen Extreme* (1993) to take Hollywood skiing, there was *Sun Valley Serenade* (1941). Sun Valley's celebrity lineup of yesteryear—Gary Cooper, Claudette Colbert, Erroll Flynn, and Ernest Hemingway, among others—makes Aspen's present-day luster seem dull in comparison. A lot of this can be attributed to the power of astute marketing: When W. Averell Harriman, chairman of the Union Pacific Railroad in the 1930s, decided that the railroad company needed some Western attraction to fill train-car seats with tourists, he had visions of the Saint-Moritz of the Rockies. The location of choice was an old mining town named Ketchum, and imagine how alluring a destination Harriman might have had with a name like that. But his PR team came up with the much sexier name of Sun Valley, flew in a host of Hollywooders for the 1936 opening, and the rest is skiing history.

Sun Valley can still summon up its share of Hollywood glamour; among its regulars are Clint Eastwood and Brooke Shields. But it would be misleading to suggest that this is what Sun Valley is all about. If anything, it is antiglitter, a place where the stardust settled long ago. Today it is a resort of balanced proportions: Well developed but not (yet) overdeveloped, the town of Ketchum and its Harriman-crafted satellite, Sun Valley, effectively mix an air of elegance (and the aura of past glory) with ski-town funkiness.

The ski area is also a well-proportioned mix of trail and open-bowl skiing, easy skiing and tough stuff. The unfortunate rap on Sun Valley has been a lack of snow; not lying in a natural snowbelt and with parts of the mountain exposed to too much of that Sun Valley sun, the ski area has been more likely than most other Western resorts to suffer snow shortages. Recent snowmaking improvements have gone a long way toward solving the problem on 630 of the 2,000 skiable acres. Sun Valley has the largest computer-controlled snowmaking system in the world. Plus, with four high-speed quad lifts and three elegantly furnished log day lodges (one on top and two on the bottom), rounding out the improvements, Sun Valley practically guarantees a good ski. However, seekers of consistently deep powder will have to venture east to Grand Targhee on the Idaho–Wyoming border or south to the Utah resorts.

Downhill Skiing and Snowboarding

Dollar Mountain is Sun Valley's original ski hill (although its amenities are not included in Facilities for the resort, *below*) and when you compare it with the newer Bald Mountain—"Baldy" for short—you get a good idea of how far skiing has come in almost 60 years. Dollar alone was enough to lure celebrities in the '30s and '40s, but it's a short beginner's hill by today's standards, utterly dwarfed by Baldy's 3,400 vertical ft.

Two Baldy attributes are the resort's most noteworthy pluses. One is that its vertical is continuous, and so are its ski runs (uninterrupted by Sno-Cat tracks, long traverses, or extra lift rides). For example, from the Challenger quad alone, you can cover more than 3,000 vertical ft—a rarity in U.S. skiing. The second plus is Baldy's diverse terrain: plenty of good skiing for intermediates and experts; and impeccably groomed trails as well as a good supply of bump runs. A handful of trails, such as the Seattle Ridge and College trails, are suitable for skilled beginners. In all, though, the appeal of Sun Valley's Baldy is challenging terrain that's better suited to intermediate and advanced skiers.

Trails reach down three Baldy exposures (east, north, and west), and the art to skiing Sun Valley (at least on sunny days) is to follow the sun around the mountain. The best skiing for novices and lower intermediates is from the Seattle Ridge quad chair, a nice pod of easy skiing set apart from Sun Valley's more challenging terrain. The best skiing for intermediates are long—*very* long—cruisers, such as River Run. For experts, Sun Valley's mogul skiing is famous: Exhibition has long been regarded as one of the premier mogul runs in America, although the real mogul action tends to be on the Warm Springs side of the mountain, under the afternoon sun. The quality of Sun Valley bowl skiing can vary dramatically according to snow conditions. After a storm, the skiing—about 1,500 vertical ft of wide-open terrain—can be absolutely exhilarating. Otherwise, depending on the time of day, the snow can be soft, crusty, mushy, or slick.

FACILITIES

3,400-ft vertical drop; 2,054 skiable acres; 36% beginner, 42% intermediate, 22% advanced/expert; 7 high-speed quad chairs, 5 triple chairs, 5 double chairs, 1 surface lift.

LESSONS AND PROGRAMS

Two-hour group lessons are $35; four-hour children's group lessons are $69. Daylong child-care programs are available through Sun Valley Company. Race clinics are $60 for three hours of instruction. Throughout the season, special masters racing, snowboarding, and women's clinics are also offered. For more information, call the **ski school** (☏ 208/622–2248).

LIFT TICKETS

$54. Multiday tickets, starting with three-day tickets at $156 (valid three of four consecutive days), offer a slight savings.

RENTALS

Equipment can be rented at a number of shops in Ketchum, Sun Valley, and Warm Springs, and at Sun Valley's base lodges.

Nordic Skiing

TRACK SKIING

The **North Valley Trails** system and nearby trails all along the Wood River Valley are well maintained by the Blaine County Recreation District (☏ 208/788–2117 for trail report), however, KART (the public bus system) does not service these areas, so transportation by car is required. More than 100 mi of trails are groomed for both skating and touring. Dogs are allowed on designated trails. Daily trail fees are reasonable at $7.

The **Sun Valley Nordic Center** (☏ 208/622–2250) grooms 40 km (24½ mi) of trails on the flatlands and rolling meadows of the Sun Valley Golf Course, and adjacent bench and valley areas along Trail Creek. Challenge (ups and downs are minimal compared with trail systems at many other resorts) is not the strong point here, but the groomers do an excellent job of maintaining the tracks for both classical and skating skiers, and instruction is first-rate. Trails for snowshoers have also been recently added. One other noteworthy feature: The Nordic center sets some tracks specifically for children—leaving less space between left- and right-ski tracks to account for smaller legs. Because of the open-valley exposure, late-season (late March and onward) trail conditions can be iffy. The track fee is $15 per day.

BACKCOUNTRY SKIING

The nearby **Sawtooth National Recreation Area** (SNRA; ☎ 208/726–7672) offers plenty of backcountry skiing opportunities. There are several yurts in the Boulder, Smoky, and Sawtooth ranges of the SNRA reached via Route 75 north of Ketchum. There are no roadside signs designating yurt parking areas or trails, so secure maps from the SNRA or cross-country ski shops in town before heading out. Also, check on yurt availability and accessibility (weather and snow conditions can vary considerably between Sun Valley and points north in the SNRA). Guides can be hired for day trips as well as multiday backpack jaunts to the yurts. Once there, skiers can practice their telemark turns or simply tour around frozen alpine lakes and meadows. Tours for skiers of all abilities, from first-time tourers to seasoned telemarkers, can be arranged through guide and outfitter services, such as **Sun Valley Trekking** (☎ 208/726–1002). Among Sun Valley Trekking's highlight trips are hut-to-hut tours and a strenuous "haute route" tour, comparable to similarly named high-mountain journeys in the French Alps.

Other Activities

GLIDING

For a spectacular glimpse of the ski mountain and the valleys below from a different point of view, climb aboard a glider from **Sun Valley Soaring** (☎ 208/788–3054), sit back, and enjoy the ride. Be prepared for breathtaking views while the pilot banks the plane around the top of Baldy, wowing skiers as they catch a few rays on the outdoor terrace of Seattle Ridge Lodge.

ICE-SKATING

Sure, many resorts have a skating rink or two, but the rink at the Sun Valley Lodge is special. The original rink dates back to 1937 and has been a training and performance spot for skaters from Sonja Henie to Kristi Yamaguchi. Katarina Witt has reportedly named this her favorite place to skate. Shows featuring some of the world's great skaters are still staged here regularly (mainly in the summer); when they aren't being staged, the ice is open to the public. For information, call the **Ice Center** (☎ 208/622–2194).

PARAGLIDING

With some help from **Sun Valley Paragliding** (☎ 208/726–3332), you can catch some air under the wing of a paraglider floating over the bowls, and then, hopefully, depending on which way the wind is blowing, make a slow, soft landing on the River Run side of Baldy.

SLEIGH RIDE/DINNER

Bundle up and take a half-hour moonlight ride aboard a horse-drawn 20-passenger sleigh to dinner at a "log cabin" on the northern end of the Sun Valley Golf Course, which doubles as the Nordic ski system in the winter. Leave around 5 PM, to catch the alpenglow on the way out and the stars on the way back. A blast from Sun Valley's past, **Trail Creek Cabin** was built in 1937 and hosted many a party of Harriman and his Hemingway and movie-star entourage. Today, it maintains its original hunting cabin, outdoorsy decor with stuffed pheasants perched overhead and vintage pictures lining the walls. Diners warm themselves by the fire, then settle in for sumptuous prime rib, Idaho trout, pasta, and barbecued-rib dinners. This is one of those schmaltzy must-do activities while playing tourist in Sun Valley. Make reservations well ahead (Sun Valley Reservations, ☎ 208/622–2135); these popular sleigh-ride dinners fill up fast, particularly during the Christmas holidays.

SNOWMOBILING

For those who like the thrill of speed using motorized modes of transportation, numerous snowmobile trails wind through the Sawtooth National Recreation Area. Head up over the Galena Pass to **Smiley Creek Lodge** (☎ 208/774–3547), 37 mi north of Ketchum, and rent a snowmobile. Smiley Creek is on the southern terminus of the jagged Sawtooth range, also known as "America's Alps." When the summit is passable the view of the Sawtooths is well worth the drive. A guide on Idaho snowmobiling trails is available by contacting **Idaho Snowmobiling** (☎ 800/743–7669) or regional travel associations and chambers of commerce.

Sun Valley Essentials

ARRIVING AND DEPARTING

By Car: Sun Valley is about 160 mi (2½ hours) east of Boise via I–84 and U.S. 93/Route 75. It is about 80 mi north of Twin Falls via U.S. 93 and Route 75.

By Plane: Friedman Memorial Airport (☎ 208/788–4956) in Hailey is the closest airport, 12 mi south of Sun Valley. An alternative is to land at **Boise Municipal Airport** (☎ 208/383–3110) and rent a car or go with **Sun Valley Express** (☎ 800/634–6539), which provides van service from the Boise airport to Sun Valley. Sun Valley is served by Horizon and SkyWest. Boise is served by American, Delta, Northwest, and United.

From the Airport: Sun Valley Bell Service (arrangements made through Sun Valley Reservations ☞ Visitor Information, *below*) provides complimentary transportation to the resort from Friedman Memorial Airport. Avis, Budget, and Hertz rent from all three airports. **Sun Valley Stages** (☎ 208/821–9064) is an economical alternative for daily round-trip bus transportation between Twin Falls, Boise, and Sun Valley.

GETTING AROUND

The free **shuttle-bus** system for the Sun Valley–Ketchum area, Ketchum Area Rapid Transit (KART) (☎ 208/726–7140), makes a car unnecessary. However, because the resort community and the North Valley cross-country trail systems are spread throughout the area, a car may be a welcome convenience.

VISITOR INFORMATION

Central reservations: Sun Valley Reservations and Information (☎ 800/786–8259). **General information: Sun Valley Company** (✉ Sun Valley 83353, ☎ 208/622–4111 or 800/786–8259). **Snow report:** ☎ 800/635–4150.

MONTANA

The Big Mountain

The Big Mountain has aspirations of bigness beyond the mountain itself. The owners would like it to be *the* big resort, too, and have been trying aggressively to develop its base area and sell real estate to make this happen. But for the moment, Big Mountain is still a little resort, and that's probably something to be thankful for.

Why hasn't the Big Mountain, with ski-area roots that date back to 1936, grown much? Perhaps for lack of a sexy name, for starters: the Big Mountain, near Whitefish, in Flathead National Forest—how enticing does that sound? Also, Whitefish is still a relatively small, remote town, perhaps best reached by train, that forgotten form of travel. (If you want to check out a curious slice of American life, drop by the Whitefish train station at 6 AM, as a sleepy collection of farmers, cowboys, and skiers awaits the arrival of Amtrak's *Empire Builder,* en route from Seattle to Chicago.) Whitefish isn't a bad town, mind you: Folks are quite friendly, but it hasn't stirred up a swankiness or sizzle in the manner of, say, Colorado resort towns. That, too, might be something to be thankful for.

The ski resort is 8 mi from town up a windy mountain and remains comfortably small, popular among train travelers from the Pacific Northwest and the upper Midwest and others simply seeking more of an escape than an event in their ski vacation.

Downhill Skiing and Snowboarding

At the Big Mountain, snowboarders like running into trees. This says more about the nature of the Big Mountain's terrain than it does about the sanity of snowboarders (which may or may not be suspect). Its most distinctive features are its widely spaced trees, which—when encased in snow—are known as snow ghosts. Snowboarders seem to think sideswiping snow ghosts is quite a lot of fun.

With 3,000 skiable acres, plus out-of-bounds areas for Sno-Cat skiing, the Big Mountain offers a lot of terrain to explore and many different lines to discover among those widely spaced trees. The pleasure of exploration and discovery—such as the finding of a fresh cache of powder many days after a snowstorm—is perhaps the main reason to ski the Big Mountain.

In general, the pitch is in the intermediate to advanced-intermediate range; there's not a whole lot of super-steep or a whole lot of super-easy skiing. A sameness in pitch, however, doesn't mean a sameness in skiing. With trails falling away on all sides of the mountain, there is a tremendous variation in exposure and hence in snow texture; also take into consideration the number of trees to deal with and the views (the best being northeast toward Glacier National Park).

One of the Big Mountain's best features is its long high-speed quad (the "Glacier Chaser"), meaning that runs using most of the mountain's 2,300-ft vertical are interrupted by less than 10 minutes of lift-riding time. A negative is weather; foggy days are not uncommon, and that's when you're thankful that those snow ghosts are around as points of visual reference.

FACILITIES

2,500-ft vertical drop; 3,000 skiable acres; 25% beginner, 50% intermediate, 25% advanced. 2 high-speed quad chairs, 1 quad chair, 4 triple chairs, 1 double chair, 2 surface lifts.

LESSONS AND PROGRAMS

Group instruction in downhill is offered for $23 for a half day ($52, including a lift ticket); cross-country, telemark skiing, and snowboarding lessons are also available. Specialty clinics such as racing, mogul, and telemark techniques are provided, as well as children's programs. For information call the **ski school** (☎ 406/862–2909).

LIFT TICKETS

$40. Night skiing (mid-Dec.–Mar., Wed.–Sun. 4:30–10): $12.

RENTALS

Full rental packages (skis, boots, and poles) start at $15 per day. Snowboard rentals start at $23 per day.

Nordic Skiing

BACKCOUNTRY SKIING

Because of an unusually liberal policy regarding skiing out-of-bounds, backcountry tours are possible from the top of the Big Mountain. For the most part, the Big Mountain ski patrol does not prevent skiers from crossing ski-area boundary ropes, although if you do so and get into trouble, you're responsible for paying rescue costs. Although the avalanche danger (*very* relatively speaking) is usually not high around the Big Mountain, the chances of getting lost are. It is very easy to ski too far down the wrong drainage, creating the prospect of a tiring and excruciating bushwhack back to the base. For an intro to the nearby backcountry, you might want to try the Big Mountain's cat-skiing operation, based near the summit, which takes skiers for as little as $40 per person on a four-hour off-piste adventure.

Guide service for backcountry tours (with some telemarking) in Glacier National Park costs $60–$80 per person per day. Excursions are best made on a clear day, since the mountain views are what make the trip. Contact the **Izaak Walton Inn** (☞ Track Skiing, *below*).

TRACK SKIING

There are two track systems in the Whitefish area: Both systems serve their purpose well enough, but don't expect inspiring views or a sense of wilderness seclusion. One advantage that **Glacier Nordic Touring Center** (☎ 406/862–4369) at Grouse Mountain Lodge in Whitefish has is that 5 km (3 mi) of its 15 km (9 mi) of groomed trail is for night skiing. A $2-per-person donation is suggested. **The Big Mountain Nordic Center** (☎ 406/862–1900) has its own 15 groomed km (9 mi); the daily trail fee is $5. Rentals are available at Grouse Mountain Lodge (☎ 406/862–3000, ext. 436). Arrangements for cross-country lessons can be made through the ski school office (☞ Lessons and Programs, *above*).

Farther afield, the 30 km (18½ mi) of groomed track at **Izaak Walton Inn,** in Essex at the edge of Glacier National Park, *do* combine nicely the pleasures of groomed-trail skiing with the spirit of backcountry skiing. Originally built in 1939 for railroad crews, the inn is now devoted almost exclusively to housing cross-country skiers during the winter. Because it's alongside the railroad tracks, it is also accessible from Whitefish by train. Track, touring, and telemark rentals and multiday packages including skiing, lodging, and meals are available. ✉ *Box 653, Essex 59916,* ☎ *406/888–5700.*

Other Activities

DOGSLEDDING

Dog Sled Adventures (☎ 406/881–2275) leads 12-mi tours in Stillwater State Forest, a few miles northwest of Whitefish.

ICE FISHING

Dangling a line through a sawed hole in the ice isn't the world's most aerobic sport, but because of the many lakes in the Whitefish area, it's a popular pastime. Whitefish Lake is the obvious place to start. The **Tally Lake Ranger District** (☎ 406/862–2508) can recommend other lakes. The best place for ice-fishing gear in Whitefish is **Sportsman & Ski Haus** (✉ 105 Baker Ave., ☎ 406/862–3111).

SNOWMOBILING

There are more than 200 groomed snowmobile trails in the Flathead region. **Glacier Motor Sports** (✉ 30 9th St., Columbia Falls, ☎ 406/892–2195 or 800/221–5098) rents machines and clothing and also leads guided tours.

Big Mountain Essentials

ARRIVING AND DEPARTING

By Car: The Big Mountain is 8 mi from Whitefish and 135 mi north of Missoula via U.S. 93.

By Plane: Delta, Horizon Air, and United Express offer service to **Glacier Park International Airport** (☏ 406/257–5994) in Kalispell, 20 mi from the Big Mountain.

From the Airport: Avis, Budget, Hertz, and National rent cars from the airport.

By Train: Amtrak offers daily service to Whitefish from Chicago and Seattle.

GETTING AROUND

A shuttle bus runs between the resort and Whitefish from 7 AM–10 PM, but having a car—especially if you want to explore Glacier National Park in winter—is more convenient.

VISITOR INFORMATION

Central reservations: ☏ 800/858–3930; for nonresort lodging, **Flathead Convention and Visitors Association** (☏ 406/756–9091 or 800/543–3105). **General information: The Big Mountain Ski and Summer Resort** (✉ Box 1400, Whitefish 59937, ☏ 406/862–1900). **Snow report:** ☏ 406/444–2654 or 800/847–4868.

Big Sky

Lone Peak, the mountain that looms over Big Sky, is an appropriate metaphor for the resort conceived 25 years ago by the renowned TV newscaster Chet Huntley: Big Sky is a solitary node of civilization in otherwise undeveloped country, as much an outpost as a full-service resort. Rugged wilderness areas, huge open ranches, and Yellowstone National Park are the main features of this part of Montana. It is the sort of place where locals are used to driving nearly 50 mi to Bozeman for such simple pleasures as a fresh head of lettuce.

This is not to suggest that Big Sky is uncivilized. Indeed, being just 25 years old and still growing, the resort is quite modern in its design and amenities. It's not as if you can't get a daily newspaper, cable TV, or a substantial, well-prepared meal. Still, Big Sky is one of the most isolated major ski resorts in the country.

This can be both good and bad. It's bad if you're someone who puts a premium on convenient travel arrangements. Getting to Big Sky invariably means at least one plane change en route to Bozeman and about an hour's drive to the resort. It's great, though, if you're someone who appreciates a pervading spirit of the surrounding wilderness and a lack of crowds without having to give up the creature comforts of a warm bed and a good meal.

Recent land transactions around Big Sky have many local people worrying about major real-estate development in the near future that could impinge upon that resort-in-the-wild atmosphere. For the moment, there's a lot more speculation than development activity. It should be some time before hordes of tourists begin descending on Big Sky.

Downhill Skiing and Snowboarding

For many years, the attitude of more advanced skiers toward Big Sky was "big deal." There wasn't nearly enough challenging skiing to keep expert skiers interested for long, and certainly not for an entire ski week. As a remedy, the Big Sky people strung up the Challenger chairlift, one of the steepest in the country, and figured the problem was solved. But it was only a first step in the solution. Shortly thereafter, the resort installed a tram to the summit of Lone Peak, providing access to an array of steep chutes, open bowls, and at least one scary-steep couloir. The tram also gave Big Sky the right to claim the greatest vertical drop—4,180 ft—of any resort in the country. Those big changes now provide big action for experts at Big Sky.

None of that, however, has diminished Big Sky's otherwise easy-skiing reputation. There is, indeed, a good deal of intermediate and lower-intermediate terrain, a combination of wide-open bowl skiing higher up and trail skiing lower down. And as on the Challenger terrain, the skiing on these slopes is pretty unpopulated.

The other plus about skiing Big Sky is its wide variety of exposures. Ski areas tend to be built on north-facing slopes where snow usually stays fresher longer, protected from the sun. In addition to these, Big Sky also has plenty of runs facing south and east, and the differing snow textures as a result make for more interesting skiing.

FACILITIES

4,180-ft vertical drop; 3,500 skiable acres; 10% beginner, 47% intermediate, 43% advanced; 1 aerial tram, 1 4-passenger gondola, 3 high-speed quads, 1 quad chair, 3 triple chairs, 3 double chairs, 3 surface lifts.

LESSONS AND PROGRAMS

Half-day group-lesson rates at the **ski school** (☎ 406/995–5743) are $27; a learn-to-ski package (half-day lesson, equipment rentals, and restricted lift ticket) is $35. Racing, powder, mogul, and snowboarding clinics are also available and start at $22 per person.

LIFT TICKETS

$48. Multiday tickets (up to six of seven days) are available, with savings of up to $5 per day.

RENTALS

The resort's **Performance Rentals** (☎ 406/995–5841) at the base of the mountain offers rental packages (skis, boots, and poles) at $23. Moderate rental packages (starting at $14 per day) are available from **Mad Wolf Ski & Sport** (✉ U.S. 191, 8 mi from ski area, ☎ 406/995–4369).

Nordic Skiing

BACKCOUNTRY SKIING

Lone Mountain Ranch (☞ Track Skiing, *below*) offers guided tours in the nearby backcountry as well as in Yellowstone National Park. Tours near Big Sky tend to cover steeper terrain, with opportunities for telemarking, and are best for experienced skiers. Tours in Yellowstone generally cover flat or gently rolling terrain, for which little or no cross-country skiing experience is necessary. In some cases, snow "coaches" (essentially, snow buses) take skiers from West Yellowstone to scenic parts of the park for skiing.

TRACK SKIING

Lone Mountain Ranch, a full-service cross-country resort about 6 mi from the downhill ski resort, is a rare bird in cross-country circles. Not only are there 65 km (42 mi) of groomed trails, but there are also lodging and dining facilities for 50 guests. The trail network is superb, with everything from a flat, open, golf-course layout to tree-lined trails with as much as 1,600 ft of elevation gain (and loss). Much of the trail network provides a genuine sense of woodsy mountain seclusion. If there is a drawback, it is that moose sometimes wander onto the trails, causing pockmarked tracks and occasional moose-skier confrontations. Rentals (skis, boots, and poles; $12 per day) and weekly lodging/cross-country skiing packages are available. ✉ *Box 160069, Big Sky 59716,* ☎ *406/995–4670 or 800/514–4644.* 🎫 *Trail fee: $12 for a full day, $10 for a half-day.*

Other Activities

FISHING

On almost any day of the winter, no matter how bitter or nasty the weather, there are usually a couple of die-hard anglers laying out lines in the Gallatin River, which runs along U.S. 191. Rivers such as the Madison (one valley west), the Yellowstone (one valley east), and the Gallatin have made southwestern Montana famous among fly fishermen, most of whom visit during the nonwinter months. However, that's not to say the trout stop biting in winter.

Tackle, equipment rentals, and clothing are available at **Gallatin River Guides** (✉ Box 160212, Big Sky 59716, ☎ 406/995–2290), ½ mi south of the Big Sky entrance on U.S. 191. A state fishing license, sold at many local stores, is required. Rental equipment is also offered at **Lone Mountain Ranch** (☞ Nordic Skiing, *above*).

SNOWMOBILING

Far and away the most popular nonskiing activity in the region is snowmobiling into Yellowstone National Park. West Yellowstone (50 mi south of Big Sky) prides itself on being the "Snowmobile Capital of the World," and in winter there are at least as many snowmobiles in town as cars.

The most popular excursion is the 60-mi round-trip between West Yellowstone and Old Faithful. Sightings of buffalo and elk are a certainty along the way, and although you'll have to share the track with plenty of other snowmobilers, the scene is nothing like the crowds that descend upon the park in summer.

Several businesses in West Yellowstone rent snowmobiles on a daily basis. One of the best is **Two Top Snowmobile** (✉ 645 Gibbon Ave., ☎ 406/646–7802 or 800/522–7802). For longer-term rental packages that include lodging, contact **Yellowstone Tour & Travel** (✉ 211 Yellowstone Ave., West Yellowstone 59758, ☎ 800/221–1151). Guide service is available.

Big Sky Essentials

ARRIVING AND DEPARTING

By Car: Big Sky is 45 mi south of Bozeman and 50 mi north of West Yellowstone on U.S. 191.

By Plane: Delta, Horizon, Northwest, and Skywest offer service to **Gallatin Field Airport** (☎ 406/388–8321) in Bozeman, about 45 mi north of Big Sky.

From the Airport: City Taxi (☎ 406/586–2341) provides van service to the resort. Avis, Budget, Hertz, and National rent cars from the airport (☞ Car Rental *in* Smart Travel Tips A to Z).

GETTING AROUND

Although there is free shuttle-bus service, it's best to have a car at Big Sky. The resort comprises two developments, the Meadow Village and the Mountain Village, about 6 mi apart. A car is pretty much essential for exploring beyond the resort area (in Yellowstone National Park, for example).

VISITOR INFORMATION

Central reservations: ☎ 800/548–4486. **General information: Big Sky Ski and Summer Resort** (✉ Box 160001, Big Sky 59716, ☎ 406/995–5000). **Snow report:** ☎ 406/995–5900.

UTAH

Alta/Snowbird

What strange canyon mates Alta and Snowbird make: The two are such close neighbors in Little Cottonwood Canyon that it's possible to ski from one area into the other and back (though not, unfortunately, on the same lift ticket). Yet they are, in almost every way but the quality of their snow, antipodal in character.

Alta is devoutly retro, the sort of place where if the lifts creak (as they often do), the creaks are apt to be revered as part of the Alta legend rather than oiled. Duct tape on ripped nylon pants is Alta chic, and trail signs are exceedingly rare, since only interloping tourists don't know their way around. Alta is so retro that it is one of the few ski areas left in the country that disallows snowboarding, basically because snowboarding seems to Alta skiers just too faddish and MTV-nouveau. Alta also prides itself in being a preternaturally local ski area, a pride shared by Alta skiers. It's a pride worn so openly on fraying wool sleeves that even those skiers who aren't Alta locals have a peculiar habit of dressing the part and pretending they are.

Snowbird, on the other hand, is Euro-modern, its fast tram quietly whisking skiers in stylish powder suits to the summit. Not only does Snowbird have plenty of trail signs, but most come with Japanese translations. Its concrete-and-steel base facilities express an angular, urban efficiency, the most conspicuous structure being the Cliff Lodge, with a ritzy spa in it, no less. A Cliff Lodge–style complex will be built at the base of Alta sometime after the moon falls out of the night sky.

What the two share is snow—lots of it, with a lightness and quantity that is legendary. In the winter of '93, Snowbird got about three or four more seasons' worth than other resorts. (Alta's figure was approximately the same.) Short of heli-skiing, powder skiing in America gets no better on a consistent basis. It had better be good, because skiing is pretty much all there is to do in the winter in Little Cottonwood Canyon. That's why many Alta and Snowbird visitors lodge 30 minutes away in Salt Lake City, where there are—despite rumors to the contrary—things to do at night.

Downhill Skiing and Snowboarding

The common denominator is snow, but the differences in the skiing experience at Alta and Snowbird are otherwise significant. Although Snowbird presents itself unambiguously with 3,240 vertical ft of in-your-face steepness, Alta is an enigma. Within 15 minutes, by riding the tram and simultaneously scoping out more than 2,000 acres of skiable terrain, you can get a pretty good idea of what Snowbird is all about. On the other hand, you can return to Alta year after year and still discover places to ski you never knew existed before.

Alta devotees (of which there are many) believe in this version of Creation: On the first day, God created Heaven and Earth; on the second, He created Alta. (Some, in fact, even question those priorities.) On your first couple of visits to Alta, you might wonder why people feel this way. You must give Alta time to grow on you. It will.

Alta is a ski area made to be explored but hard to get around. There are few trail signs. The lift system seems antiquated and poorly laid out, and a lot of trails seem to flatten out quickly or lead nowhere. This is a complex package of terrain, and the more you explore Alta, the richer your rewards.

Alta sprawls across two large basins, Albion and Wildcat, comprising mostly open bowls and meadows but with some trail skiing, too. There is no clear, easily readable fall line as there is at Snowbird; fall lines drop and roll away in many directions and angles. Furthermore, much of the best skiing (for advanced or expert skiers) requires finding obscure traverses or some hiking.

The only solution is simply to stick with it. One day—one run, even—will be your epiphany, and suddenly Alta will explode upon you with possibilities. On the lower slopes of Albion Basin, Alta has a terrific expanse of novice and lower-intermediate terrain. Rolling meadows combine as perhaps the best place in the country for lesser-skilled skiers to learn to ski powder.

Snowbird is an expert's dream and a novice skier's nightmare. Its open bowls, such as Little Cloud and Regulator Johnson, are challenging, while chutes from the Upper Cirque and the Gad Chutes can be positively hair-raising. They're certainly not for skiers in any way doubtful of their skills. On deep-powder days—not uncommon at the 'Bird—those chutes can also be exhilarating for skiers who like that sense of a cushioned free fall with every turn. If you're looking for intermediate cruising runs, however, there's the long, meandering Chips, a few runs from the Gad chairlifts. For lower-intermediate skiers and down, Snowbird is a waste of time. Head for Alta.

FACILITIES

Alta: 2,100-ft vertical drop; 2,200 skiable acres; 25% novice, 40% intermediate, 35% advanced; 6 double chairs, 2 triple chairs. **Snowbird:** 3,240-ft vertical drop; 2,030 skiable acres; 25% novice, 30% intermediate, 45% advanced; 125-passenger tram, 8 double chairs.

LESSONS AND PROGRAMS

At **Alta** (☎ 801/359–1078), half-day group lessons for adults and children are available (two-hour lessons start at $30). At **Snowbird** (☎ 801/742–2222, ext. 5170), 2½-hour lessons begin at $50. Of note is Snowbird's Mountain Experience Program, a combination of guidance and instruction for expert skiers in challenging, off-slope terrain and variable snow conditions. Full-day workshops start at $85.

LIFT TICKETS

Alta: $34. **Snowbird:** $49 for tram and chairs; $39 for chairlift-only tickets.

RENTALS

Any of several ski shops in the Salt Lake City area offer reasonably priced rental packages, some for less than $10 a day for skis, boots, and poles. Equipment can also be rented at ski shops at Alta and Snowbird; rates range between $13 and $40 per day, depending on equipment and store location. Advance rental reservations are available from **Breeze Ski Rentals** (☎ 800/525–0314), with seven stores in the Salt Lake City area, including one at Snowbird's Upper Tram Plaza.

Nordic Skiing

There are no groomed tracks in Little Cottonwood Canyon, largely because the canyon configuration is too narrow and steep. The bottom line for anyone who puts a high premium on logging lots of track mileage is that Alta and Snowbird are poor destinations. Track junkies can go toward **Park City** (☞ Nordic Skiing *in* Park City/Deer Valley/The Canyons, *below*). The **Solitude Ski Resort** (☎ 801/536–5774 or 800/748–4754), with 20 km (12 mi) of groomed trails is in Big Cottonwood Canyon.

BACKCOUNTRY SKIING

Not surprisingly, retrograde Alta has been a center in the resurgence of telemark skiing. The guided **Ski Utah Interconnect Adventure Tour** (☞ Nordic Skiing *in* Park City/Deer Valley/The Canyons, *below*) is a combination of lift-serviced and backcountry skiing that connects Utah's three major skiing canyons: Parley's, Big Cottonwood, and Little Cottonwood. The trip can be negotiated either on telemark skis or with regular alpine gear. For the most part, however, avalanche risks make backcountry skiing in this area ill-advised for all but those with the proper safety equipment and considerable backcountry experience.

Other Activities

HELI-SKIING

Because the lift-serviced powder skiing at Alta and Snowbird can be so good, heli-skiing here can often be a real extravagance. On the days when you must go farther afield to find powder, or simply for the blessed solitude of the backcountry, **Wasatch Powderbird Guides** has permits for several thousand acres of skiable terrain, mostly in the basins and drainages on the periphery of Alta and Snowbird. The company guarantees seven runs a day (weather permitting), though it doesn't necessarily guarantee the quality of the snow. In general, heli-skiing is an experience most enjoyable for strong intermediate skiers and better. Tours cost $490–$595 per person per day, depending on the season, and reservations are required at least a day in advance, farther ahead during busy periods. ✉ *Box 920057, Snowbird 84092,* ☎ *801/742–2800.*

Alta/Snowbird Essentials

ARRIVING AND DEPARTING

By Car: Alta and Snowbird are about 30 mi from the Salt Lake City airport. Take I–215 to the 6200 South Street exit and follow signs for Alta and Snowbird. Keep in mind that all that wonderful snow can make driving in the canyon treacherous. Parking at the mouth of the canyon and hitchhiking to the ski areas is a standard mode of transport for many locals.

By Plane: Salt Lake City International Airport (☎ 801/575–2400) is a major hub for Delta, with frequent nonstop flights from several U.S. cities. Most other major carriers also fly into Salt Lake.

From the Airport: Canyon Transportation (☎ 801/255–1841 or 800/255–1841) and **Lewis Bros. Stages** (☎ 801/359–8677 or 800/826–5844) provide individual and group transportation service to the resorts. The **Utah Transit Authority** (☎ 801/287–4636) provides bus service between Salt Lake City and the canyon. If you wish to rent a car, most major agencies operate from the Salt Lake airport.

GETTING AROUND

If you're staying at Alta or Snowbird, there's not much need for a **car** unless you're planning frequent visits to Salt Lake City or Park City. The Utah Transit Authority (☞ Arriving and Departing, *above*) public **bus** service between Salt Lake City and the canyon is excellent, the drawback being that buses stop running around 6 PM.

VISITOR INFORMATION

Central reservations: ☎ 888/782–9258 for Alta; 800/232–9542 for Snowbird. **General information:** ☎ 801/742–3333 for **Alta;** ☎ 801/742–2222 for **Snowbird; Ski Utah** (✉ 150 W. 500 South St., Salt Lake City 84101, ☎ 800/754–8824); **Utah Travel Council** (☎ 800/200–1160) for a free *Utah Winter Vacation Planner.* **Snow report:** for **Alta,** ☎ 801/572–3939; for **Snowbird,** ☎ 801/933–2100.

Park City/Deer Valley/The Canyons

Park City, Deer Valley, and the Canyons combine as Utah's one true full-service resort destination, with an old mining town tossed into the package. The skiing might not be as dramatic as elsewhere (e.g., Alta and Snowbird) and the natural snow not quite as plentiful (about 300 inches a winter, compared with about 500 inches in neighboring Big Cottonwood and Little Cottonwood canyons), but there is a lot of skiing for all levels and much to do besides ski. In large part this has been made possible by the Park City area's geography. Although the Cottonwood canyons have a more dramatic beauty, they are too steep and narrow to accommodate much development. Not so in the more rolling and wide-open spaces around Park City, where there are plenty of hotels, restaurants, nightlife, and outdoor activities such as cross-country skiing and snowmobiling.

Park City—sprawling over several square miles—isn't quite a city, as its name implies, but it's not a petite resort, either. Main Street, a protected historic district, adds character to an otherwise rather ordinary-looking collection of hotels, condos, restaurants, and businesses. It's not particularly unattractive, but it's not really inspiring, either.

Deer Valley, 2 mi up the road, was created in the early '80s as the resort that would be skiing's final word in style. The slopes were groomed with a manicurist's attention to detail. Chairlifts had padded seats. "Ski valets" helped you unload your skis. Mountainside lodges actually served something that could be legitimately considered a gourmet lunch. Lots of posh condos and lodges surrounded the resort. The topper was the presence of skiing's master of style and verve, Stein Eriksen. It has all taken time to settle in. After a few early bumps in the developmental road, Deer Valley has at last established itself as Utah's version of stylish (if staid) Vail.

The Canyons is the more-or-less new kid on the block. The ski area once known as Parkwest and later Wolf Mountain has been radically transformed into one of Utah's largest resorts, rivaling neighboring Park City. It is perhaps the most significant development in a resort area that is now booming with development in anticipation of the 2002 Winter Olympic Games.

Downhill Skiing and Snowboarding

Deer Valley's forte is wide, meticulously groomed intermediate runs. It is a ski area for those who want to believe that they can ski with the grace of Stein Eriksen. The moderate pitch of the terrain and the quality of the grooming leads to skiing's version of ballroom dancing. The resort's newest improvement is a new lift in an area called Empire Canyon, with additional expert runs and open bowl skiing. But even with this inviting new terrain, part of the Deer Valley experience for many a skier still includes a two- to three-hour midday interlude of feasting on the Silver Lake Lodge buffet and catching major rays on the snow-covered meadow in front of the lodge—an area known appropriately as McHenry's Beach. The skiing experience, in other words, fits right in with the resort's overall image. After a while, however, a certain sense of sameness can set in. That's why it's nice having Park City Mountain Resort right next door.

The rap on **Park City Mountain Resort** has always been that it lacks legitimate expert skiing. Unfair: The east face of Jupiter Peak features some truly hairy, rock-lined chutes, and Portuguese Gap is an elevator shaft lined by trees. A new "six-pack" chair in McConkey's bowl provides access to additional steeps.

Park City's main drawback isn't lack of steepness but lack of length; despite a vertical drop of 3,100 ft, it's hard putting together a run of more than about 1,400 vertical ft. The ski area is laid out as a series of segments rather than a single unit. That said, however, Park City probably has the best overall terrain mix of any ski area in Utah, enough to keep skiers of all abilities happy for several days.

Skiing at **The Canyons** is comparable to skiing at Park City—a fact that shouldn't be surprising, since the neighboring resorts feature similar mountain terrain. Above-tree-line bowls feed into some fine tree skiing for experts. Intermediates will find cruising runs that, on the whole, are somewhat longer than those found at Park City. As the Canyons grows, however, the base area is a construction-site eyesore, a situation unlikely to be resolved fully for the next few years.

FACILITIES

Deer Valley: 3,000-ft vertical drop; 1,750 skiable acres; 15% beginner, 50% intermediate, 35% advanced; 1 high-speed gondola, 4 high-speed quad chairs, 2 quad chairs, 9 triple chairs, 2 double chairs. **Park City:** 3,100-ft vertical drop; 3,000 skiable acres; 16% beginner, 45% intermediate, 39% advanced; 4 high-speed 6-passenger chairs, 1 high-speed quad chair, 5 triple chairs, 4 double chairs. **The Canyons:** 3,190-ft vertical drop; 3,300 skiable acres; 20% beginner, 40% intermediate, 40% advanced; 1 8-passenger gondola, 5 high-speed quad chairs, 4 quad chairs, 1 triple chair, 1 double chair, 1 surface lift.

LESSONS AND PROGRAMS

At **Deer Valley Resort** (☎ 435/649–1000), five-hour adult group lessons start at $65. Private lessons start at $72 an hour. At **Park City Mountain Resort** (☎ 435/649–8111 or 800/227–7275), a two-hour adult group lesson starts at $45. The resort's popular snowboarding lessons are similarly priced. Children's programs are available. Park City also has an excellent instructional program for skiers with disabilities and group programs for senior citizens or women only. The Perfect Turn program at **The Canyons** (☎ 435/615–3219) bills itself as a "coaching" program rather than an instructional program, for skiers and snowboarders of all ages. One hour private clinics start at $55 per person and $85 for two.

LIFT TICKETS

Park City: $55. **Deer Valley:** $60. **The Canyons:** $39 Monday–Thursday, $52 weekends and holidays.

RENTALS

Several shops in the Park City and Salt Lake City area rent equipment packages, some for as little as $8 a day. Advance rental reservations are available from **Breeze Ski Rentals** (☎ 800/525–0314), with seven stores in the Salt Lake City area, including one in Park City at the resort center. Rates range between $9 and $35 per day, depending on equipment and store. **Jans Mountain Outfitter** (✉ 1600 Park Ave., Park City, ☎ 435/649–4949 or 800/745–1020) offers not only equipment packages ($16 per day; $26 for high-performance) but also clothing-rental packages starting at $25 per day.

Nordic Skiing

BACKCOUNTRY SKIING

The **Ski Utah Interconnect Adventure Tour** is a good trip for alpine skiers who want to get a taste of the backcountry experience. The guided tour covers the three major skiing canyons of the Wasatch Range—Parley's Canyon (in which Park City is located), Big Cottonwood (Brighton and Solitude), and Little Cottonwood (Alta and Snowbird). Ski-area lifts provide uphill transport, and about half of the skiing is within ski-area boundaries. The trip can be negotiated on regular alpine equipment (or on telemark gear) and is recommended only for strong intermediates or better. ✉ *C/o Ski Utah, 150 W. 500 South St., Salt Lake City 84101,* ☎ *801/534–1907.* 🎫 *Fee: $150 per person. Reservations essential.*

Skiers who want to do some unguided skiing on their own can climb the Guardsman's Pass Road, which is between Deer Valley and Park City and is closed to traffic in winter.

TRACK SKIING

The only set tracks in the Park City area are at the **White Pine Ski Touring Center,** between Park City and The Canyons. The 20 groomed km (12 mi) are on a flat golf course that's nothing special as far as either scenery or terrain variation is concerned, but adequate for anyone seeking a quick aerobic workout. Lessons and rentals are available. ✉ *Box 680068, Park City 84068,* ☎ *801/649–8710 or 801/649–8701.* 🎫 *Trail fee: $8.*

Other Activities

HOT-AIR BALLOONING

On a clear day, when the wind is low, it is common to see hot-air balloons rising above Park City. **Park City Balloon Adventures** (✉ Box 1344, Park City, ☎ 801/645–8787 or 800/396–8787) offers half-hour scenic flights and trips up to two hours long. Most flights are just after sunrise, when winds are most predictable.

SKI JUMPING/BOBSLEDDING

Anyone interested in catching some of the 2002 Olympic fever might want to visit the **Utah Winter Sports Park** (☎ 435/647–9650). Bobsled rides (at speeds of up to 50 mph) can be experienced for $27 a ride. Or, for $30, introductory ski-jumping lessons are available.

Park City/Deer Valley/The Canyons Essentials

ARRIVING AND DEPARTING

By Car: Park City is less than 40 mi from Salt Lake City. Take I–80 east to the Park City exit.

By Plane: Salt Lake City International Airport (☎ 801/575–2400) is served by most major carriers.

From the Airport: Lewis Bros. Stages (☎ 801/359–8347 or 800/826–5844), **Park City Transportation** (☎ 435/649–8567 or 800/637–3803), and **Super Express Airport Shuttle** (☎ 801/566–6400 or 800/321–5554) provide individual and group transportation service to these resorts. Most major rental-car companies operate from the Salt Lake City airport.

GETTING AROUND

Because of a free **shuttle-bus** system, a car is not essential when staying at Park City and Deer Valley. But the layout is fairly spread out—it's 5 mi from Deer Valley to The Canyons—so a car can be helpful.

VISITOR INFORMATION

Central reservations: ☎ 800/424–3337 for Deer Valley; ☎ 800/222–7275 or 435/649–0493 for Park City; ☎ 888/226–9667 for the Canyons. **General information: Deer Valley Resort** (✉ Box 1525, Park City 84060, ☎ 435/649–1000); **Park City Mountain Resort** (✉ Box 39, Park City 84060, ☎ 435/649–8111); **The Canyons** 4000 The Canyons Resort Dr., Park City 84060, ☎ 435/649–5400); **Park City Chamber of Commerce** (✉ Box 1630, Park City 84060, ☎ 435/649–6100 or 800/453–1360); **Ski Utah** (✉ 150 W. 500 South St., Salt Lake City 84101, ☎ 801/534–1779); **Utah Travel Council** (☎ 801/538–1030) for a free *Utah Winter Vacation Planner.* **Snow reports:** ☎ 435/649–2000 for Deer Valley; 435/647–5335 for Park City; 435/615–3308 for the Canyons.

WYOMING

Jackson Hole

Jackson Hole is potentially the best ski resort in the United States. The expanse and variety of terrain are awesome. There are literally thousands of ways of getting from top to bottom, and not all of them are hellishly steep, despite Jackson's reputation.

There are two reasons why Jackson might not *absolutely* be the country's best ski resort. The first has to do with the base village, a functional but rather ordinary cluster of buildings with limited lodging. To be sure, there have been improvements and upgrades of the base-area facilities in recent years, but compared with many other major resorts around the country, this is a relatively spartan place. A big reason the base area remains meagerly developed is that it is closely circumscribed by protected land (Grand Teton National Park), limiting expansion possibilities. All things considered, this is probably a plus. The main alternative to staying in Teton Village is staying in the town of Jackson, about 20 minutes away. All in all, it's not a bad town, but it has been somewhat hoked up, primarily for the sake of the many summer tourists on their way to Grand Teton and Yellowstone national parks.

Jackson's second drawback can be snow, or inconsistency thereof. Because of its location on the eastern flanks of the Tetons, it gets on average about 20 ft less snow in a season than does Grand Targhee, a much smaller resort on the western slope. That predominantly eastern exposure often results in snow conditions (at least on the lower half of the mountain) that are less than ideal, either mushy or crusty.

But when the snow is right, this is truly one of the great skiing experiences in America. Jackson is a place to appreciate both as a skier and a voyeur: Every so often you can witness an extreme skier skiing a line that's positively dazzling in its drama and risk. A glimpse of that alone is worth the price of a lift ticket.

Downhill Skiing and Snowboarding

Skiing or snowboarding Jackson is as much a process of imagination as it is the physical process of turning. On the trail map, about 60 squiggly lines have been drawn in and designated as named trails, but this does not even begin to suggest the thousands of different skiable routes from top to bottom. The resort claims 2,500 skiable acres, a figure that seems unduly conservative. And although Jackson is best known for its advanced to extreme skiing, it is also a place where imaginative intermediates can go exploring and have the time of their lives.

The tram to the summit of Rendezvous Peak provides access to 4,139 vertical ft of skiing, resulting in arguably the longest continuous runs in the United States. If there is a drawback to Jackson skiing, it is that the immediate possibilities from the top are somewhat limited: The choice is either Rendezvous Bowl, wide open and moderately steep; or Corbett's Couloir, perhaps the most famous extreme run in America. You must jump into Corbett's or rappel in by rope. If you don't make that first turn, you don't make any; it can be a long and injurious slide to the bottom. Needless to say, the vast majority of skiers choose Rendezvous Bowl. Thereafter, many, many possibilities unfold. There is so much skiing (most of it expert and advanced) that one whole side of the mountain (the Hobacks) is generally opened only on fresh powder days.

Most of Jackson's intermediate skiing is from Après Vous Mountain and in Casper Bowl, between Rendezvous and Après Vous. Casper Bowl tends to attract more skiers, and Après Vous is surprisingly underskied (in part because the chair is long and slow). Après Vous is a great place for intermediates to ski groomed runs and to explore off the beaten track. From the chairlifts on Rendezvous Mountain, Gros Ventre (known by locals simply as GV) is flat-out one of the best intermediate runs in the country—about 2,800 vertical ft of big-turn cruising, with a good, consistent pitch most of the way.

Jackson is not a good place for novice skiers. A small cluster of trails near the base is serviceable, but that's about it. The only way novices get to see the summit is to ride the tram to the top, take in the view (which on a clear day is awesome), and ride the tram down.

FACILITIES

4,139-ft vertical drop; 2,500 skiable acres; 10% beginner, 40% intermediate, 50% expert; 1 aerial tram, 1 gondola, 3 quad chairs, 1 triple chair, 3 double chairs, 1 surface lift.

LESSONS AND PROGRAMS

Half-day group lessons at the **Jackson Hole Ski School** (☎ 307/733–2292 or 800/450–0477) start at $50. For expert skiers, the Tommy Moe All-Mountain Ski Camps, headed by the 1994 Olympic gold medalist, run for five days, teaching everything from big-mountain free-skiing to racing techniques. The cost is $600 per person. The ski school features extensive children's programs, including day care and lessons for kids 6 to 13 years old.

LIFT TICKETS

$51. Savings of about 10% on five- to seven-day tickets.

RENTALS

Equipment can be rented at ski shops in the town of **Jackson**, such as **Jackson Hole Ski Shop** (☎ 307/733–2292, ext. 623), with full-package rates starting at around $13 per day. **Jackson Hole Sports** (☎ 307/733–4005 or 800/443–6931), at the Bridger Center at the ski area, offers ski and snowboard rental packages starting at $12 a day.

Nordic Skiing

BACKCOUNTRY SKIING

Few areas in North America can compete with Jackson Hole when it comes to the breadth, beauty, and variety of backcountry opportunities. For touring skiers, one of the easier areas (because of flatter routes) is along the base of the Tetons toward Jenny and Jackson lakes. In summer, this area can become crowded with national park visitors; solitude is more the order of things in winter. Telemark skiers (or even skiers on alpine gear) can find numerous downhill routes by skiing in from Teton Pass, snow stability permitting. In summer the backcountry excursions along the Teton Crest trail range from easy one-day outings to multiday expeditionary trips (also offered in winter). A guide isn't required for tours to the national park lakes but might be helpful for those unfamiliar with the lay of the land; trails and trail markers set in summer can become obscured by winter snows. When you are touring elsewhere, a guide familiar with the area and avalanche danger is a virtual necessity, for the sake of navigation and safety. The Tetons are big country, and the risks are commensurately large as well.

The **Jackson Hole Nordic Center** (☞ Track Skiing, *below*) leads tours of varying length and difficulty. **Alpine Guides** leads half-day and full-day backcountry tours into the national parks and other areas near the resort, for more downhill-minded skiers. Arrangements can also be made through the Jackson Hole Ski School (☎ 307/733–2292). **Jackson Hole Mountain Guides** (✉ Box 7477T, Jackson 83001, ☎ 307/733–4979) leads more strenuous backcountry tours.

TRACK SKIING

The **Jackson Hole Nordic Center** (☏ 307/739–2629) is at the ski-resort base. The 17 km (10½ mi) of groomed track is relatively flat; scenery rather than heavy aerobic exertion is the main feature. A nice option offered here—because the Nordic Center and the downhill ski area are under the same management—is that downhill skiers with multiday passes can switch over to Nordic skiing in the afternoon for no extra charge. Rentals and lessons are available; alpine lift tickets are also good at the Nordic Center.

Other Activities

DOGSLEDDING

Dogsledding excursions are available through **Iditarod Sled Dog Tours** (☏ 307/733–7388 or 800/554–7388). Frank Teasley, a veteran Iditarod racer, leads half-day introductory trips or full-day trips to Granite Hot Springs.

HELI-SKIING

Daily trips can be arranged through **High Mountain Helicopter Skiing** (☏ 307/733–3274) in Teton Village Sports. In general, a good time to go is when there has been relatively little recent snowfall. For two or three days after a storm, good powder skiing can usually be found within the ski area.

ICE CLIMBING

Among North American climbers, the Tetons are considered a must before hanging up one's ropes and pitons. The mountaineering action continues into winter. Anyone interested in climbing, or learning to climb, can contact **Jackson Hole Mountain Guides** (✉ Box 7477T, Jackson 83001, ☏ 307/733–4979). Offerings range from half-day lessons to multiday trips.

SLEIGH RIDES

The largest herd of elk in North America can be found in winter in the **National Elk Refuge** (☏ 307/733–0277), just north of the town of Jackson. Sleigh rides into the refuge last about 45 minutes and leave from in front of the **National Wildlife Art Museum** daily, 10–4, about every 20 minutes; tickets are available at the museum. Dinner sleigh rides are also offered at **Spring Creek Resort** (☏ 307/733–8833 or 800/443–6139), with dinner at the resort's Granary restaurant.

SNOWMOBILING

Numerous companies in the Jackson area rent snowmobiles. **Rocky Mountain Snowmobile Tours** (1050 S. Highway 89, Box 820, Jackson WY 83001, ☏ 307/733–2237 or 800/647–2561) guides one- to five-day trips. Featured destinations are Granite Hot Springs and Yellowstone National Park.

Jackson Hole Essentials

ARRIVING AND DEPARTING

By Car: Jackson (like the entire Yellowstone/Teton area) is a long way from the interstates and large cities. It's 300 mi from Salt Lake City, via I–15 and U.S. 89. From the east, take U.S. 191 north from I–80 (it's about 175 mi from Rock Springs on I–80 to Jackson).

By Plane: American has daily flights from Chicago, Delta from Salt Lake City, and United from Denver and Los Angeles to **Jackson Hole Airport** (☏ 307/733–7682).

From the Airport: Many lodging facilities offer free airport shuttle-bus service. **All Star Transportation** ☏ (307/733–2888) and **Alltrans** (☏ 307/733–3135 or 800/443–6133) provide van service between the airport and town. Avis, Budget, Hertz, and National rent cars at the airport (☞ Car Rental *in* Smart Travel Tips A to Z).

GETTING AROUND

Given the distances between Teton Village, the town of Jackson, and other points of interest in the area, renting a **car** is a good idea. **Shuttle buses** are available, however. **START Public Shuttle Bus** (☎ 307/733–4521) offers service between Jackson and Teton Village. Nightly shuttle-bus service is provided by **All Star Transportation** (☎ 307/733–2888).

VISITOR INFORMATION

Central reservations: ☎ 800/443–6931. **General information: Jackson Hole Ski Resort** (✉ Box 290, Teton Village 83025, ☎ 307/733–2292 or 800/443–6931); **Jackson Hole Chamber of Commerce** (✉ 990 W. Broadway, Box E, Jackson 83001, ☎ 307/733–3316). **Snow report:** ☎ 307/733–4005.

3 SPECIAL-INTEREST VACATIONS: THE OUTDOORS

It's hard to imagine vacationing or living in the Rockies without becoming hooked on some kind of outdoor recreation. Any excuse *not* to partake in the outdoors is a lousy excuse, seeing as there is a form of recreation to suit everyone's needs and physical condition. Floating gently down a river on a raft, fishing a fast-flowing stream, riding horseback on a pack trip through the high mountains, climbing 14,000-ft peaks or 1,000-ft rock walls—the opportunities are endless.

CHOOSING YOUR VACATION

By Peter Oliver

OUTDOOR ACTIVITIES IN THE ROCKIES are not only plentiful but also easily accessible. Within an hour of leaving their homes and offices, outdoor jocks can be doing their recreational thing, whatever it might be, in the midst of an exquisitely beautiful backcountry environment. These are people who regard the Rockies as America's greatest open-air playground, and their thinking isn't far off the mark.

Under each heading in this chapter, descriptions of suggested trips are included. These activities are among the best the Rockies have to offer, and they have been chosen to give you ideas for planning an off-the-beaten-path vacation. However, these are *not* complete lists. The Rocky Mountain area is immense, and there is simply not enough space to mention all the recreational opportunities the region holds. If one of the listings doesn't quite fit your specifications, contact the outfitter for other itineraries. Local and regional chambers of commerce are also good sources of information about trip organizers or outfitters operating in a particular area. Another consideration is not to feel limited to a single activity. Many organized trips combine activities: Rafting and fishing is an obvious combination, rafting and mountain biking a less conventional one.

Going with a Group

Hiking, pack trips, and river rafting are the recreational activities probably best suited to group travel in the Rockies. Individuals or small groups (four people or fewer), on the other hand, tend to prefer such activities as fishing or mountaineering. Group sizes for organized trips vary considerably, depending on the organizer and the activity. Many trip organizers offer discounts of 10% or more for larger groups, so be sure to inquire. Often, if you are planning a trip with a large group, trip organizers or outfitters are willing to customize. For example, if you're with a group specifically interested in photography or in wildlife, trip organizers have been known to get professional photographers or naturalists to join the group. Recreating as a group gives you leverage with the organizer, and you should use it.

One way to travel with a group is to join an organization before going. Conservation-minded travelers might want to contact the **Sierra Club** (✉ 85 2nd St., San Francisco, CA 94105, ☎ 415/977–5500 or 888/722–6657), a nonprofit organization. An educational alternative is to join a working group; hiking trails tend, for example, to be maintained by volunteers (generally local hiking clubs) that are always recruiting. Park or forest rangers are the best source of information for groups involved in this sort of work. **Hostelling International–American Youth Hostels** (✉ 733 15th St. NW, Suite 840, Washington, DC 20005, ☎ 202/783–6161) provides service for recreational travelers of all ages (despite the name) and is an especially helpful organization for road cyclists.

Two organizations that teach groups and individuals a variety of wilderness skills are **Boulder Outdoor Survival School** (✉ Box 1590, Boulder, CO 80305, ☎ 303/444–9779 or 800/335–7404) and **National Outdoor Leadership School** (✉ 288 Main St., Lander, WY 82520, ☎ 307/332–5300).

Trip Organizers

Many trip organizers specialize in only one type of activity; however, a few companies guide a variety of active trips in the Rockies. (In some cases, these larger companies also act essentially as a clearinghouse or agent for smaller trip outfitters.) At last count, there were something like 5,000 "adventure travel" outfitters operating in North America, a good many of which are here-today, gone-tomorrow operations. Be sure to sign on with a reliable outfitter; getting stuck with a shoddy operator can be disappointing, uncomfortable, and even dangerous. Some sports—white-water rafting and mountaineering, for example—have organizations that license or certify guides, and you should be sure that the guide you're with is properly accredited.

The following are among the most reliable companies that organize active adventures in the Rockies: **American Wilderness Experience** (✉ 2820-A Wilderness Pl., Boulder, CO 80301, ☎ 800/444–0099), **The World Outside** (✉ 2840 Wilderness Pl. F, Boulder, CO 80301, ☎ 303/413–0938 or 800/488–8483), and **Sierra Club Outings** (✉ 85 2nd St., San Francisco, CA 94105, ☎ 415/977–5630).

CANOEING AND KAYAKING

For individual paddlers (as opposed to rafters), the streams and rivers of the Rockies tend to be better suited to kayaking than canoeing. Steep mountains and narrow canyons usually mean fast-flowing water in which the maneuverability of kayaks—especially their ability to roll over and be righted in rough water—is a great asset. A means of transport that has become increasingly popular in recent years for less experienced paddlers is the inflatable kayak.

For true white-water thrill-seekers, June is usually the best month to take on undammed rivers. Before then, high water due to snowmelt runoff can make many rivers dangerous; later in the summer, dwindling flow reduces white-water thrills and exposes rocks. The flow of dammed rivers, of course, can vary at any time of year, according to dam release schedules. Central Idaho and southern Colorado and Utah are where the best rivers for kayaking enthusiasts are found.

It may go without saying that many of the rivers that are good for rafting (☞ Rafting, *below*) are also suitable for kayaking and/or canoeing.

Before You Go

When planning any vacation on a river, it's important to understand that rivers change, presenting different challenges depending on precipitation and the time of year. To help characterize a river's potential, a class system has been established: A Class I river is as calm as pond water; a Class V river churns with rapids that can summon all of the mayhem of a washing machine gone haywire. Like any subjective rating system, this one isn't perfect: Conditions can vary dramatically. For example, a river that earns a Class V rating during the spring runoff may be an impassable trickle by late summer. Nevertheless, the rating system gives you an approximate idea of what sort of thrills or hazards to expect. Anything above a Class II river is probably unsuitable for small children.

Expect to get wet. It's part of the fun. Outfitters often provide waterproof containers for cameras, clothing, and sleeping bags, but passengers remain exposed to the elements. If you don't like getting wet, don't go canoeing or kayaking. Also, bring bug repellent as well as a good hat, sunblock, and warm clothing for overnight trips. The sun on the river can be intense, but once it disappears behind canyon walls, the temperature can drop 30° or more. The best footwear is either a pair of water-resistant sandals or old sneakers. Outfitters provide life jackets and, if necessary, paddles and helmets.

The rivers of the Rockies are fed by snowmelt, meaning that the water can be cold, especially early in the summer. Plan accordingly. Having warm, dry clothing to change into can mean the difference between a pleasurable and a miserable trip. (Dammed rivers, for which chilled, subsurface water from reservoirs is squeezed through dams, can remain cold throughout the summer.)

To minimize environmental impact as well as ensure a sense of wilderness privacy (riverside campgrounds are often limited to one party per night), a reservation policy is used for many rivers of the West. Often, the reserved times—many of the *prime* times—are prebooked by licensed outfitters, limiting your possibilities if you're planning a self-guided trip. For those rivers with restricted-use policies, you're well advised to write for reservations several months or more in advance. Also, try to be flexible about when and where to go; you might find that the time you want to go is unavailable, or you may find yourself closed out altogether from your river of choice. If you insist on running a specific river at a specific time, your best bet is to sign on with a guided trip.

Figure on spending at least $100 a day for a guided trip.

Contacts and Resources

American Outdoors (✉ Box 10847, Knoxville, TN 37939, ☎ 423/558–3597 or 800/524–4814) publishes a list of outfitters. Idaho was one of the first states to license and bond its outfitters and guides. The **Idaho Outfitters and Guides Association** (✉ Box 95, Boise, ID 83701, ☎ 208/342–1919 or 800/494–3246) provides a list and information on guides and outfitters in the state.

For the Family

In general, rafting, which does not necessarily require the paddling skills that kayaking does, is a better way for young children to experience and appreciate river travel (☞ Rafting, *below*).

Instruction

Cascade Kayak School (✉ Rte. 1, Box 117-A, Horseshoe Bend, ID 83629, ☎ 800/292–7238) features Idaho river trips and instruction, including special kid's classes, by former world-class competitors and coaches. **Dvorak Kayak & Rafting Expeditions** (☞ Organizers and Outfitters, *below*) conducts clinics, including certification courses, for kayakers of all abilities.

Organizers and Outfitters

Dvorak Expeditions (✉ 17921 U.S. 285, Nathrop, CO 81236, ☎ 800/824–3795) leads trips on the rivers of southwestern Colorado, Idaho, Wyoming, and eastern Utah. **River Travel Center** (✉ Box 6, Point Arena, CA 95468, ☎ 800/882–7238) arranges trips in Idaho and Utah, among other destinations.

Suggested Trips

Colorado

BLACK CANYON OF THE GUNNISON RIVER

The 12-mi stretch of the Gunnison River through the Black Canyon is so narrow and steep that in some sections the distance from rim to rim at the top is less than the distance from the elevation of the rim to the river. In fact, the Black Canyon—a national monument—earned its name because in places very little sunlight reaches the canyon floor. The stretch of the Gunnison through the canyon is one of the premier kayak challenges in North America, with Class IV and Class V rapids and portages required around bigger drops. It is a section of river that early visitors to the canyon declared unnavigable, and the fact that a few intrepid kayakers are able to make the journey today still stretches belief. This part of the river is only for hardy and experienced paddlers. However, once outside this area designated as a national monument, the canyon opens up, the rapids ease considerably, and the trip becomes more of a quiet float. The canyon itself is administered by the National Park Service; surrounding land is administered by the Forest Service and the Bureau of Land Management. All three agencies can be contacted at the same office (✉ 2465 S. Townsend St., Montrose, CO 81401, ☎ 970/240–5300), but the BLM is the best source of information on kayaking.

Dates: June–October. **River rating:** Class IV–Class V for the upper Gunnison, Class I–Class III for the lower Gunnison. **Trip organizer: Gunnison River Expeditions** (✉ Box 315, Montrose, CO 81402, ☎ 970/249–4441).

Idaho

SALMON RIVER

The Salmon River is not one river but several. As far as kayakers and rafters are concerned, the two Salmons of greatest interest are the Middle Fork (☞ Rafting, *below*) and the Main. The Main is that 80-mi stretch of water with as good a nickname as a river can have: "River of No Return." Although the rapids of the Main are somewhat less fierce and frequent than the rapids on the Middle Fork, the scenery is possibly even more breathtaking. The Main runs through one of the deepest canyons in the country—narrower, certainly, and in places deeper than the Grand Canyon. Running through the heart of the largest wilderness area in the country, the Salmon is a great river for kayakers who appreciate natural beauty and wildlife as much as white-water conquest.

Dates: June–September. **River rating:** Class III. **Trip organizer: Salmon River Outfitters** (✉ Box 519, Donnelly, ID 83615, ☎ 800/346–6204).

SELWAY RIVER

Idaho is famous for its white-water rivers, including the Lochsa, the Payette, the Salmon, and the Snake. But perhaps the river that out-white-waters them all—the one that licensed Idaho boaters generally consider the ultimate test of their skill—is the Selway. All the elements that go into making white water come into play here: a steep drop (up to 125 ft per mile), a shallow riverbed, and a narrow passageway. When the snowmelt feeds the river in earnest in June, the Selway can offer true Class V action. By July, it has usually toned down its act to something more like Class IV. Thereafter, the river can become impassably shallow in places. Running through the Selway-Bitterroot Wilderness Area, this is wild country. The two things you can generally count on from the Selway are that you'll get very wet and that you'll see wildlife. Perhaps the biggest challenge of the Selway, though, is simply getting on it. Permits are issued on a lottery basis, and kayaking groups might have to wait a couple of years before landing a prized permit. (Another possibility is that one of the licensed raft companies that runs the river will agree to allow kayakers to accompany a trip, if space is available.) By all accounts, the wait is well worth it.

Dates: June–July. **River rating:** Class III–Class V in early summer. **Trip organizer:** Kayakers interested in booking a space on a raft trip should contact the **River Travel Center** (☞ Organizers and Outfitters, *above*).

Utah

DESOLATION AND GRAY'S CANYONS

The Green River in southeastern Utah flows through some of the most wildly beautiful desert landscape in the American West. There is a reason why Desolation Canyon gets its name. Within it, there is a sense of complete separation from the civilized world. The only reminders of people having ever been in this area are occasional pictographs and abandoned homesteads. Be prepared in mid-summer to encounter desert heat—although the cool river water is never far away. Because this six-day trip covers fairly easy-flowing water (with no rapids over Class III), this is an excellent option for kayakers just beginning to get the feel for paddling.

Dates: May–September. **River rating:** Class I–Class III. **Trip organizer:** **Dvorak Expeditions** (☞ Organizers and Outfitters, *above*).

CYCLING

The Rockies, not surprisingly, are the land of the mountain bike. In fact, a mountain bike in these parts is as much a cultural statement as it is a recreational vehicle. Not that road bikes are obsolete in the Rockies; many good multiday road tours are possible in the region, although the paved back roads and country inns that make road touring so popular in the Northeast are harder to find in the Rockies.

The mountain bike, on the other hand, has opened up vast stretches of terrain to two-wheelers. A number of ski resorts that run lifts in the summer for sightseers have made arrangements to accommodate mountain bikes, and a popular summer activity for bikers is to ride the lifts up and pedal down. The mountain bike has also provided a new means for exploring the backcountry, a fact that doesn't always sit well with hikers. Mountain bikes are prohibited on many trails, especially in national parks, to limit biker-hiker confrontations, but this still leaves thousands of miles of trails and old logging and mining roads to explore.

Before You Go

High, rugged country puts a premium on fitness. Even if you can ride 40 mi at home without breaking a sweat, you might find yourself struggling terribly on steep climbs and in elevations often exceeding 10,000 ft. If you have an extended tour in mind, you might want to come a couple of days early and try some shorter rides, just to acclimatize yourself to the altitude and terrain. Also, it probably goes without saying that engaging in a little pretrip conditioning is likely to make your trip more enjoyable.

On tours where the elevation may vary 4,000 ft or more, the climate can change dramatically. Although the valleys may be scorching, high-mountain passes may still be lined with snow in summer. Pack clothing accordingly. (Bicycle racers often stuff newspaper inside their jerseys when descending from high passes to shield themselves from the chill.) Although you shouldn't have much problem renting a bike (trip organizers can usually arrange rentals), it's a good idea to bring your own pair of sturdy, stiff-bottom cycling shoes to make riding easier, and your own helmet to make riding safer. Some experienced riders bring not only their own shoes but their pedals if they use an interlocking shoe-and-pedal system. If you do decide to bring your own bike, be prepared to spend as much as $150 in special luggage handling. Airlines are not very bike-friendly. Summer and early fall are the best times to plan a trip; at other times, snow and ice may still obstruct high-terrain roads and trails.

Guided bike trips generally range in price between $80 and $150 a day, depending on lodging and meals.

Contacts and Resources

Adventure Cycling Association (✉ Box 8308, Missoula, MT 59807, ☎ 406/721–1776 or 800/755–2453) is the nation's largest nonprofit recreational cycling organization and is a good source of information on (among other things) bike-tour organizers. **Hostelling International-American Youth Hostels** (✉ 733 15th St. NW, Suite 840, Washington, DC 20005, ☎ 202/783–6161) has a strong focus on lodging and tours for cyclists of all ages.

For the Family

Multiday tours, as well as the trips listed below, are generally not good recreational choices for families with small children. The riding can be strenuous—made all the more so by the altitude—as well as hazardous, on the road and off. Short half-day or full-day trips with plenty of flat riding are, however, possible at many major Rocky Mountain resorts, where bike rentals in summer are easy to come by. Among the better resorts for this sort of riding are Aspen and Steamboat Springs, in Colorado; Sun Valley, Idaho; and Park City, Utah. All are in fairly broad, flat valleys although surrounded—obviously—by mountains. Ask at local bike shops for recommended rides for children. Again, keep in mind that the altitude can be even more taxing on small lungs than on adult lungs, so be conservative in choosing a ride with children.

Instruction

Many ski resorts now have mountain-biking schools in the summer, with the opportunity to ride and learn on ski trails. Among the resorts with good instructional programs is **Winter Park Resort** (✉ Box 36, Winter Park, CO 80482, ☎ 970/726–4118.

For serious road riders, especially would-be racers, the **Carpenter/Phinney Bike Camps** (☎ 303/442–2371) are conducted in Summit County and near Boulder in Colorado by 1984 Olympic road champion Connie Carpenter and her husband, Davis Phinney, also an Olympic medalist and professional racer. One-week sessions focus on riding technique, training methods, and bicycle maintenance.

Organizers and Outfitters

Kaibab Mountain Bike Tours (✉ Box 339, Moab, UT 84532, ☎ 800/451–1133) specializes mainly in mountain-bike touring in Colorado and Utah. **Timberline Adventures** (✉ 7975 E. Harvard, Suite J, Denver, CO 80231, ☎ 303/759–3804 or 800/417–2453) has extensive lists of bike tours in the Rocky Mountain region.

Suggested Trips

Colorado

PEARL PASS

Mountain-bike historians—if there is such a breed—say that this is the route that got the mountain-biking craze started about 20 years ago. A couple of guys, sitting around in Crested Butte without much to do, decided that a great way to entertain themselves would be to ride the rough old road over Pearl Pass to Aspen. Jeeps did it, so why not bikes? They hopped on board their clunky two-wheelers—a far cry from the sophisticated machinery of today—and with that, a sport was born. Today Crested Butte is probably *the* mountain-biking center of the Rockies (vying with Moab, Utah, for the title), a place where there are more bikes than cars, and probably more bikes than residents, too. It is home each summer to **Fat Tire Bike Week** (✉ Box 782, Crested Butte, CO 81224, ☎ 970/349–6817), a week of racing, touring, silly events, and mountain-biker bonding.

The 40-mi trip over Pearl Pass can be done in a day, but you must be in excellent condition to do it. Altitude is the chief enemy of fitness here; the pass itself is close to 13,000 ft. Unless you want to ride back from Aspen—a scenic two-day road ride is the alternative to retracing your route over the pass—you'll need to make return shuttle arrangements by car or by plane.

Montana

GLACIER NATIONAL PARK

Surely one of the great touring routes in the country, whether on a bike or in some less environmentally friendly vehicle, is the renowned Going-to-the-Sun Highway through Glacier National Park. It is by no means easy riding, climbing over 3,000 vertical ft, but the idea is not to blast away in a hyper-aerobic rush. Take your time, breathe in the extraordinary mountain scenery, and appreciate the kind of miraculous natural sculpture that glacial activity can create. Just be prepared in mid-summer to share the road with far too many exhaust-belching RVs—great scenery always seems to come with a price. That's just one day on a seven-day trip that skirts the park's perimeter and ventures into Canada as well, into neighboring Waterton Park. Who says there's no great road riding in the Rockies?

Trip organizer: Timberline Tours (✉ 7975 E. Harvard, Suite J, Denver, CO 80231, ☎ 303/759–3804 or 800/417–2453).

Montana/Wyoming/Colorado/New Mexico

GREAT DIVIDE TRAIL

It had been a grand idea for many years of the Montana-based Adventure Cycling Association to create a mountain-biking trail stretching from Canada to Mexico. The challenge was not in actually creating trails. Rather, it was in finding and mapping existing, interconnecting back roads, logging and forest-service roads, and trails. Opened in sections, the trail was finally completed in 1997. Few people, of course, ride the whole route, which covers close to 2,500 mi. But it's easy to pick a segment to suit any rider's stamina, thirst for challenge, or preferences in mountain scenery. While the route does follow, very approximately, the Continental Divide, the riding is not necessarily all big-mountain climbing and descending. Portions of the trip are negotiable by children as young as 10 (assuming their parents are willing to ride at a leisurely pace). The Adventure Cycling Association guides tours or can provide detailed maps (complete with lodging and/or camping options), information, and advice for self-guided tours.

Trip organizer: Adventure Cycling Association (✉ Box 8308, Missoula, MT 59807, ☎ 406/721–1776 or 800/755–2453).

DUDE RANCHES

Wyoming is obviously not the only Rocky Mountain state in which to find dude ranches, but Wyomingites might want you to think so. No state in the Union exalts cowboy life as Wyoming does, and cowboy life is at the heart of what dude ranching is all about. Wyoming has more dude ranches—more than 80 at last count—than any other state.

It was in Wyoming (around Sheridan) that the first dude ranches were opened for business in the early 1900s, which in all likelihood makes dude ranching the earliest form of organized recreational tourism in the Rockies. The dude ranch was originally conceived as a true East-meets-West phenomenon: Wealthy Easterners curious about the mythic ruggedness of the West accounted for the "dude" part; ranchers eager to cultivate the money of wealthy tourists as well as their own crops and livestock accounted for the ranch part. Railroad companies, in turn, were happy to have their seats filled, going both west and east. It's no wonder the idea took hold.

The original concept was to give those Easterners a taste of real ranch and cowboy life—horseback riding, cattle roping, nights spent in bedrolls by the chuck wagon, and so on. A few dude ranches still promote the working-ranch aspect of the experience, but most have come to realize that there is a larger market in a "softer" ranching experience. In other words, most ranch guests prefer a comfortable bed to sleep in, something more inviting for dinner than jerky and hardtack around the campfire, and recreation other than (or at least in addition to) ranching-related activities. Hence, we get the more modern term "guest ranch." A few old-time dude-ranch owners might insist that there's a difference between a legitimate dude ranch and a guest ranch, but the differences in many cases are more a matter of opinion than definition. In general, though, those ranches that call themselves dude ranches put a heavy emphasis on horseback riding and ranching activities; at guest ranches, such activities share the billing with others, and real ranching is often not part of the mix at all.

The slate of possible activities can vary widely from ranch to ranch. Horseback riding obviously remains Activity Number 1, and at most ranches guests will be given some taste of the working-ranch experience with demonstrations of cowboy (rodeo) skills and the like. Fishing tends to be given second priority, and large ranches usually have access to private waters that otherwise see relatively little fishing activity. After that, almost anything goes: hiking, hunting, mountain biking, tennis, swimming, river rafting (on or off the ranch), and so on. Most ranches try to retain a semblance of ranch life, and at a typical dude ranch, guests stay in log cabins and are served meals family style (everyone eats at the same time, at long tables) in a larger lodge or ranch house. "Family," incidentally, is an important concept here. A dude ranch (or guest ranch) vacation is one of the best ways for a family of widely varying ages and interests to have a shared experience of the Rockies.

Before You Go

Most dude ranches don't require any previous experience with horses, although a few working ranches reserve weeks in spring and fall—when the chore of moving cattle is more intensive than in summer—for experienced riders. No special equipment is necessary, although if you plan to do much fishing, you're best off bringing your own tackle (some ranches have tackle to loan or rent). Be sure to check with the ranch for a list of items you might be expected to bring. If you plan to do much riding, a couple of pairs of sturdy pants, boots, a wide-brimmed hat to shield you from the sun, and outerwear as protection from the possibility of rain or chill should be packed. Casual dress is the norm, for day and evening.

Expect to spend at least $125 per day. Depending on the activities you engage in, as well as accommodations, the price can exceed $250 a day.

Contacts and Resources

Colorado Dude and Guest Ranch Association (✉ Box 300, Tabernash, CO 80478, ☎ 970/887–3128). **Old West Dude Ranch Vacations** (✉ C/o American Wilderness Experiences, Box 1486, Boulder, CO 80306, ☎ 303/444–2622 or 800/444–3833). **Dude Ranchers' Association** (✉ Box F-471, LaPorte, CO 80535, ☎ 970/223–8440). **Idaho Guest and Dude Ranch Association** (✉ HC 72 K, Cascade, ID 83611, ☎ 208/382–4336 or 208/382–3217).

Eugene Kilgore's Ranch Vacations (John Muir Publications, 1994), by Eugene Kilgore, is perhaps the most thorough resource for anyone planning a ranch vacation. State tourism offices (☞ Visitor Information *in* Smart Travel Tips A to Z) can provide lists of dude and guest ranches in the Rocky Mountain region.

For the Family

Although most dude ranches are ideal for children of all ages, not all feature the same types of activities. Some ranches (more likely to be guest ranches), for example, focus more on fishing and river sports, which are usually of less interest to children than ranching activities. Be sure you know not only the activities a ranch offers but also which are emphasized before booking your vacation. Keep in mind, too, that a few ranches may have age restrictions excluding very young children. Fear not if that's the case. There are plenty of toddler-friendly alternatives.

Suggested Ranches

Colorado

FOCUS RANCH

This ranch, in the high-mesa country near the Colorado–Wyoming border, is the real thing: a dude ranch that emphasizes ranching and has been steadfast in maintaining its working-ranch character. If you don't like riding, go elsewhere. The predominant activity is working in small groups with professional cowboys to move cattle from one grazing ground to the next. For guests who need another diversion, there is also good fishing. Although summer activities are skewed toward families, spring and fall are periods reserved for experienced riders and anglers. ✉ *Slater, CO 81653,* ☎ *970/583–2410. 5 cabins; accommodations for 30.* ⏲ *May–mid Oct.*

NORTH FORK GUEST RANCH

The emphasis is on families (newborn infants are even welcome) at this ranch, just 50 mi from Denver in the Mt. Evans Wilderness Area. Programs for children center around riding, hiking, fishing, swimming, and crafts. Guests are assigned a horse for the week for daily rides and an overnight pack trip. Other activities include river rafting, fly-fishing, hiking, and just relaxing in the ranch pool. ✉ *Rte. 285, 1 mi west of Shawnee; Box B, Shawnee, CO 80475,* ☎ *303/838–9873 or 800/843–7895. Accommodations for 40.* ⏲ *May–Sept.*

VISTA VERDE RANCH

Some people are perfectly happy spending a dusty day on horseback, wading for hours waist-deep with fishing tackle in a silty stream, or sweating bricks scrambling up steep, rocky faces. But at night, they want the urbane creature comforts of fine dining and elegant sleeping quarters. For such a clientele, there is Vista Verde, a new-generation guest ranch that offers such activities as kayaking and ballooning—stuff that more traditional working ranches would no doubt shun as being much too nouveau. The food also approaches gourmet, a cultural and gastronomic far cry from more traditional ranch chow. Vista Verde is one of only a handful of Colorado guest ranches open in winter, and the cross-country and telemark skiing opportunities are first-rate. ✉ *Box 465, Steamboat Springs, CO 80477,* ☎ *970/879–3858 or 800/526–7433. Accommodations for 36.* ⏲ *May–Sept., mid-Dec.–mid-Mar.*

Idaho

TETON RIDGE RANCH

Built in 1984 of lodgepole pine, this luxuriously rustic ranch lodge west of the Tetons accommodates just 12 guests, allowing manager Albert Tilt to offer "a wilderness program with lots of personal attention." Ideal for those seeking the utmost in comfort and service at a secluded hideaway, the 10,000-square-ft lodge has cathedral beam ceilings, stone fireplaces, an inviting lounge, and a library with comfy sofas. Situated on 4,000 acres atop a 6,800-ft knoll, the lodge and guest suites offer majestic views of the Tetons. Suites are equipped with woodstoves, hot tubs, and steam showers. Activity programs are tailored to each guest's preferences and can include, among other activities, hiking on 14 mi of marked trails, riding with an experienced wrangler, fishing at two spring-fed stocked ponds, cycling, and shooting at two sporting clay courses. ✉ *200 Valley View Rd., Tetonia, ID 83452,* ☎ *208/456–2650,* FAX *208/456–2218. Accomodations for 12. No credit cards.* ⏲ *Mid-May–Oct., Jan.–Mar.*

TWIN PEAKS RANCH

One of America's first authentic dude guest ranches, Twin Peaks was homesteaded in 1923 and then established as a dude ranch by the E. DuPont family in the mid-1900s. The 2,300-acre ranch 2 mi off U.S. 93 is nestled in a mile-high valley between the Salmon River and the Frank Church–River of No Return Wilderness area, the largest in the lower 48 states. A stately lodge, cabins, the original ranch house, and an apple orchard are set on several acres of lawn. Learn horsemanship from experienced wranglers in the full-size rodeo arena, then venture out for a guided day ride or an overnight pack trip. Stocked trout ponds attract anglers, and guided fishing and white-water rafting trips can be arranged. ✉ *2 mi off Rte. 93, 18 mi south of Salmon; Box 774, Salmon, ID 83467,* ☎ *208/894–2290 or 800/659–4899. Accomodations for 55.* ⏲ *Mid-May–mid-Dec.*

Utah

DALTON GANG ADVENTURES

The fine print for this working cattle ranch reads "Experienced riders, please." That's the first clue that this family operation offering seven-day stints of hands-on participation in ranch chores is not the ranch option for those wanting to be pampered. However, for fulfilling "cowboy" dreams, this is the right place. The Dalton Gang's adventures include sleeping under the stars or in a rustic bunkhouse. Food is simple, but always plentiful. And, there is no denying that running cattle in the stunning alpine and red-rock landscapes of southeastern Utah's LaSal Mountains makes for an unforgettable week. ✉ *U.S. 191, ½ mi north of Monticello; Box 8, Monticello, UT 84535,* ☎ *801/587–2416. Accommodations for 4.* ⏲ *Apr.–Oct.*

HIDDEN SPRINGS RANCH RESORT

This central Utah property is only 100 mi south of Salt Lake City, but it is an entire world apart. Though not a working ranch, Hidden Springs has a full slate of ranch-style recreation, including horseback riding and fishing on mountain lakes and streams. Add guided hiking and mountain biking through the surroundings of the Uinta National Forest, or cross-county skiing in winter, lodging in pleasingly plain lodge suites and cabins with full meal packages, and it's a cinch that this small ranch resort won't stay a locals' secret for long. ✉ *Off Rte. 132 near Fountain Green; 1958 W. Parkway Blvd., Salt Lake City, UT 84119 for reservations,* ☎ *801/977–8776. Accommodations for 30.* ⊙ *Year-round.*

Wyoming

H F BAR RANCH

There is something special about being the original, and this ranch can lay claim to being one of the oldest dude ranches in the West. The emphasis is on horseback riding and fishing, accommodations are in cabins, and meals are served family style in the ranch house. Throw in country dances, hayrides, and barbecues for even more fun. In other words, H F Bar follows the dude-ranch book of rules. Another feature here is a remote camp called Willow Park—a destination for horsepack trips in summer and hunting trips in the fall—15 mi from the ranch in the Big Horn Mountains. ✉ *Saddlestring, WY 82840,* ☎ *307/684–2487. 26 cabins. No credit cards.* ⊙ *June–mid-Sept.*

R LAZY S RANCH

Jackson Hole, with the spectacle of the Tetons in the background, is true dude-ranch country. Although a number of the "ranches" in the state stretch the ranch concept, the R Lazy S does not—it's one of the largest in the Jackson area. Horseback riding and instruction (for adults and children) is the primary activity, with a secondary emphasis on fishing, either in private waters on the ranch or at other rivers and streams in the area. Accommodations are in the dude-ranch tradition—in log-cabin guest cottages, with meals served in the large main lodge. ✉ *Teton Village; Box 308, Teton Village, WY 83025,* ☎ *307/733–2655. Accommodations for 45. No credit cards.* ⊙ *Mid-June–Sept.*

FISHING

Fishing in the Rockies is more than a form of recreation. It is, for many, a secular religion. It breeds the kind of devotion that leads otherwise sane people to stand waist-deep in 35° water in January for hours at a time, or to discuss at length among one another the intricate and intimate details of bug gestation, or to lose their eyesight (as fly–tiers do) fiddling around with pieces of string and lint. It strains marriages. However, when you consider that the thousands of cold streams and lakes of the Rockies are ideal habitats for trout—cutthroats, browns, rainbows, and lake trout—you can understand why people get so enthusiastic. As Brigham Young said about Salt Lake City, so it can be said about the Rockies by trout fishermen: "This is the place."

It is hardly an undiscovered place, though. No longer can you toss a line into almost any Rocky Mountain stream and expect a hit within minutes. Nor is this necessarily trophy-fish country. The fish may be plentiful and lively, especially in stocked waters, but considerable fishing activity assures that most of the older, bigger fish are long gone. A partial remedy is that many popular rivers now have catch-and-release stretches, a measure taken to sustain fish populations and to help smaller fish survive to become bigger fish.

Serious anglers spend a lot of time observing streams to "match the hatch"—that is, to study the insects along a body of water and their state of maturity, then come up with flies from their tackle box that are approximately similar. Less serious anglers can shortcut the process simply by asking tackle-shop proprietors what sort of flies have been working best for a particular area at a particular time and buy flies accordingly. Any angler can make the whole business much, much easier by hiring a knowledgeable guide or signing on with an outfitter.

Before You Go

Fishing licenses, available at tackle shops and a variety of local stores, are required in all Rocky Mountain states. The fishing season may vary from state to state, and from species to species. A few streams are considered "private" streams, in that they are privately stocked by a local club, so be sure you know the rules before making your first cast.

Rocky Mountain water can be cold, especially at higher elevations and especially in spring and fall (and winter, of course). You'd do well to bring waterproof waders or buy them when you arrive in the region. Outfitters and some tackle shops rent equipment, but you're best off bringing your own gear. Lures are another story, though: Whether you plan to fish with flies or other lures, local tackle shops can usually give you a pretty good idea of what works best in a particular region, and you can buy accordingly.

In the mid-1990s, whirling disease—a parasitic infection that afflicts trout—began to reduce fish populations in some Rocky Mountain streams dramatically, particularly in Montana. Efforts to curb the spread of the disease are well underway, but be prepared to face slim pickings in some world-renowned waters. Simply be flexible. There's more than one place to catch a fish.

A guide will cost about $250 per day and can be shared by two anglers if they are fishing from a boat and possibly by three if they are wading. Lunch will probably be included and flies might be, although there may be an extra $15–$20 charge for these.

Contacts and Resources

Colorado Division of Wildlife (⊠ 6060 N. Broadway, Denver, CO 80216, ☎ 303/297–1192). **Idaho Department of Fish and Game** (⊠ 600 S. Walnut St., Box 25, Boise, ID 83707, ☎ 208/334–3700). **Montana Department of Fish, Wildlife and Parks** (⊠ 1420 E. 6th Ave., Helena, MT 59620, ☎ 406/444–2535). **Utah Division of Wildlife Resources** (⊠ 1596 W. North Temple St., Salt Lake City, UT 84116, ☎ 801/538–4700). **Wyoming Game and Fish Department** (⊠ 5400 Bishop Blvd., Cheyenne, WY 82006, ☎ 307/777–4600).

For **lists of guides** to various rivers and lakes of the Rockies, contact the state tourism departments (☞ Visitor Information *in* Smart Travel Trips A to Z). **Montana Board of Outfitters** (⊠ 111 N. Jackson St., Helena, MT 59620, ☎ 406/444–3738). **Idaho Outfitters and Guides Association** (⊠ Box 95, Boise, ID 83701, ☎ 208/342–1919). ***Field and Stream*** magazine is a leading source of information on fishing travel, technique, and equipment.

For the Family

Despite the noble effort of *A River Runs Through It* to project an image of fishing as a family sport, the nuances of fishing, especially the patience required, are often lost on children. Perhaps lakes and reservoirs are better choices than streams and rivers as sites for taking the family fishing, because of the possible alternative activities: swimming, boating, or simply exploring the shoreline.

Instruction

Orvis Fly Fishing Schools (☎ 800/239–2074 ext. 784) runs one of the most respected fishing instructional programs in the country and endorses instructional programs around the country. Rocky Mountain locations are in Evergreen, Colorado, and Coeur d'Alene, Idaho, where 2½-day programs are offered throughout the summer.

Good instruction in the Rocky Mountain region is also offered through: **Bud Lilly's Trout Shop** (✉ 39 Madison Ave., Box 530, West Yellowstone, MT 59758, ☎ 406/646–7801 or 800/854–9559), **Jan's Mountain Outfitters** (✉ 1600 Park Ave., Box 280, Park City, UT 84060, ☎ 801/649–4949 or 800/745–1020), and **Telluride Outside** (✉ 1982 W. Rte. 145, Box 685, Telluride, CO 81435, ☎ 970/728–3895 or 800/831–6230).

Organizers and Outfitters

Local guide services generally provide the best trip leadership when it comes to fishing. In addition, fishing tends not to be a group activity, although it does tend to be a popular peripheral activity on organized river trips (☞ Canoeing and Kayaking, *above,* and Rafting, *below*) and on pack trips (☞ Pack Trips and Horseback Riding, *below*). **Orvis** (☎ 800/548–9548), the eminent purveyor of fishing goods and services, endorses several lodges and outfitters in the Rockies. Consider the Orvis endorsement a stamp of approval and at least some assurance of quality.

Needless to say, in a region with such a wealth of fishing, there are many guide services and outfitters (☞ Contacts and Resources, *above*). For a complete listing of guides or outfitters in a region, probably your best bet is contacting a local or regional chamber of commerce (☞ Chapters 4–8).

Suggested Trips

Colorado

ARKANSAS RIVER

The Arkansas River, as it spills out of the central-Colorado Rockies on its course through the south-central part of the state, reputedly supports a brown-trout population exceeding 3,000 fish per mile. Some of the river's canyon's are deep and some of the best fishing locations difficult to access, making a guide or outfitter a near necessity for anyone wanting to get at all those fish. Browner's is more than a just local fly shop offering good advice. Guided trips on the Arkansas, as well as trips into the backcountry of the Sangre de Cristo mountains, some of Colorado's most ruggedly beautiful, are among services rendered.

Organizer: Browner's Fly Shop and Guide Service (✉ 3745 Hwy. 50, Salida, CO 81201, ☎ 719/539–9350 or 800/826–6505).

Idaho

SILVER CREEK

From the porch of the tiny cabin that houses the Silver Creek Preserve visitor center, the squiggle of a stream that sketches a diminutive course across fields of tall grass looks deceivingly mundane and easy to fish. Longtime dry-fly aficionados and veterans of Silver Creek, though, are quick to compare fishing Silver Creek to golfing at Augusta National the very first time out. It's a humbling experience. Nonetheless, its allure is constant and more than 12,000 fishers find their way to Silver Creek, about 30 mi south of Sun Valley, each year. Fortunately much of Silver Creek and its feeder creeks are protected by the Nature Conservancy, so only catch-and-release fishing is allowed. The creek is an ecologically unique waterway, a high-desert system formed from a series of cold springs that rise from underground aquifers. Smaller feeder streams serve as the ideal spawning ground for trout. Anglers don chest waders or use float tubes in designated areas and try their hands at the legendary rainbows, browns, and brookies, some reaching 20 or more inches in length. The slow-moving, clear water makes skillful fly presentation and masterful execution of casts such as the reach-mend essential. Some say because the fish have been caught so many times, they are very picky and reluctant to eat just any old fly. Add teeny-tiny flies to the formula, and it is easy to see why typically only the experienced dry-fly fishers prevail there. Nevertheless, even beginners enjoy honing their casting techniques, taking in the view, and catching a glimpse—even if from afar—of some of the biggest dorsal fins around.

Information: Fly shops in Sun Valley and Ketchum and the **Sun Valley/Ketchum Chamber of Commerce** (✉ Box 2420, Ketchum, ID 83353, ☎ 800/634–3347 have information on guides and trips. **Trip Organizer: Silver Creek Outfitters** (✉ 500 N. Main St., Ketchum, ID 83340, ☎ 208/726–5282 or 800/732–5687).

Montana

THE SOUTHWEST

This is the land of *A River Runs Through It,* the popular movie based on the acclaimed book by Norman Maclean. Although the book was set in Missoula, to the north, the movie was filmed in this trout-fishing mecca, with the Gallatin River playing the role of Maclean's beloved Big Blackfoot. In fact, several rivers run through the region, notably the Madison, Gallatin, and Yellowstone (which run more or less parallel to one another between Yellowstone National Park and Bozeman), as well as the Big Hole River to the west. All are easily accessible from major roads, which can mean that in summer you might have to drive a ways to find a hole to call your own. However, stream fishing in these parts is a year-round enterprise. Just where the fishing is best along these rivers will vary considerably depending on the source of local knowledge you tap into, but such disagreement no doubt confirms a wealth of opportunity. The Gallatin near Big Sky Ski and Summer Resort; the Madison south of Ennis as well as at its confluence with the Missouri near Three Forks; the Yellowstone south of Livingstone: These are among the spots that get mentioned most often, though it is hard to go wrong in these parts. And even if you never catch a fish, the mountain ranges that separate these rivers (or vice versa) are among the most beautiful in the Rockies. Just being in this part of the world ought to be enough satisfaction; catching a fish is a bonus.

Organizer: Blue Ribbon Flies (✉ Box 1037, West Yellowstone, MT 59758, ☎ 406/646–7642).

Utah

PROVO CANYON

Provo Canyon's reputation for having one of the great trout streams in North America is one that many local fisherman regard dubiously. They claim to know better places in Utah to fish, and they complain that the reputation has resulted in overfishing in Provo Canyon. Maybe they're right, but driving through the canyon at any time of year, and in almost any kind of weather, you're assured of seeing believers in the reputation out there in their waders, laying out lines. They are presumably pulling something out of the river to make that immersion in cold water worthwhile. Wilderness seclusion is not the thing here. A heavily used road parallels the river through the canyon, and its location just a few miles from downtown Provo makes this the sort of river where businesspeople can pull on waders over suit trousers and make a few casts after work. But if there is indeed substance to that reputation, this is one of the great places in the Rockies to catch trout.

Organizer: Spinner Falls Fly Fishing (✉ 2645 E. Parley's Way, Salt Lake City, UT 84109, ☎ 801/466–5801 or 800/959–3474).

Wyoming

WIND RIVER RANGE

For good reason, most visitors to the Jackson Hole area cast their attention westward to the Tetons, as attention-grabbing as any mountain range can be. For that reason, such waters as Jackson and Jenny lakes and the Snake River are heavily fished, especially at the height of the summer tourist season. That's why many local anglers prefer heading eastward into the Wind River Range of Bridger-Teton National Forest. The scenic grandeur of the Bridger Wilderness area here includes 1,300 lakes and more than 800 mi of streams teeming with fish. This is high country—including Gannett Peak, at 13,804 ft the highest point in Wyoming—meaning that some lakes may remain partially frozen even into July. If the Wind River Range has a drawback, it is lack of easy access: Roads lead only to the region, not through it; for the best fishing, you should be prepared to do some hiking. Check at tackle shops in Jackson or Pinedale for recommended fishing spots, but don't necessarily expect to get a straight answer. These are waters Wyomingites would prefer to keep for themselves.

Organizer: Skinner Brothers Guides and Outfitters (✉ Box 859, Pinedale, WY 82941, ☎ 307/367–2270 or 800/237–9138).

HIKING AND BACKPACKING

Hiking is the easiest and least expensive way to experience the Rockies; all you need are a sturdy pair of shoes and a desire to explore. (Even a sturdy pair of shoes isn't essential if you stay on well-maintained trails; hikers have been known to travel comfortably for miles in tennis shoes.) There are literally thousands of miles of marked trails in the Rockies, and they are free of any user's fees, as are most backcountry campgrounds (although permits and/or reservations may be required in some places).

It is surprising, then, how few people take advantage of this wealth of recreational opportunity. Each year, visitor surveys in national parks indicate that less than 5% of all visitors venture more than 1 mi from paved roads. Use of hiking trails outside the national parks is even lighter, and one can only thank the volunteer efforts of local outdoor clubs as well as national organizations for maintaining trails despite such (apparently) little interest among visitors in using them.

There are a couple of things to keep in mind, however. Not all trails are simply hiking trails. On a great many, especially those outside the national parks, don't be surprised to encounter horseback riders, mountain bikers, or even motorized vehicles. Such confrontations can be not only intrusive but also hazardous. Bears, especially in the northern Rockies, present an increasing danger (bear populations have been growing in recent years). Take all bear precautions seriously, and be extra careful traveling in the backcountry in fall, when bears tend to be out foraging in preparation for winter.

Before You Go

In areas (such as national parks) where hiking trails are well marked and well maintained, detailed topographical maps are unnecessary. Rudimentary trail-system maps are usually available at visitor centers or ranger stations for free or for a minimal fee. A good guidebook for the specific region you plan to hike in, however—no matter how well marked the trails—can be extremely helpful. Most guidebooks for hikers provide fairly detailed trail descriptions, including length and elevation gains involved and recommended side trips. Guidebooks to larger areas—a state, for instance—may be helpful in deciding where to go, but they don't serve as well as actual trail guides (☞ Contacts and Resources, *below*).

If you plan to do much scrambling or bushwhacking, or traveling where trails might not be well marked or maintained, you'll need maps and a compass. Topographical maps in several different scales are available from the **U.S. Geological Survey** (✉ Distribution Section, Box 25286, Federal Center, Denver, CO 80225, ☎ 303/202–4700 or 800/435–7627). Before ordering, you will need to request the free index and catalog, from which you can order the specific maps you need. Many local camping, fishing, and hunting stores carry U.S.G.S. and other detailed maps of the surrounding region. The U.S. Forest Service and the BLM also publish useful maps.

One other hiking advantage: It's relatively cheap. Organized-trip costs can be as little as $30 a day. Costs can reach $100 a day for llama trekking.

Contacts and Resources

The **American Hiking Society** (✉ Box 20160, Washington, DC 20041, ☎ 301/565–6704) is a general source of hiking information. **The Mountaineers** (✉ 306 2nd Ave. W, Seattle, WA 98119) and **Sierra Club Books** (✉ 85 2nd St., San Francisco, CA 94105) publish a good selection of Rocky Mountain **hiking guides.** Another great source for hiking guides is the Vermont-based **Adventurous Traveler Bookstore** (☎ 802/860–6667 or 800/282–3963). ***Backpacker*** magazine (Rodale Press) is the leading national magazine that focuses on hiking and backpacking.

For the Family

Several ski resorts in the Rockies run lifts in the summer for sightseers, hikers, and mountain bikers. Riding a lift up and hiking down—or taking short hikes along ridges—can be a relatively easy way for a family to experience both the beauty of the high country and the joys of hiking. Descents are typically between 2 mi and 5 mi. National parks tend to be good places to find short, well-marked trails that lead quickly to spectacular scenery, although such routes usually see plenty of traffic in summer. Some trip organizers arrange backpacking outings specifically geared toward families with small children, especially for family groups of eight or more.

Organizers and Outfitters

Some organizations have extensive listings of guided trips in the Rocky Mountain region, such as **American Wilderness Experiences** (✉ 2820-A Wilderness Pl., Boulder, CO 80301, ☎ 303/444–2622 or 800/444–0099) and **Sierra Club Outings** (✉ 85 2nd St., San Francisco, CA 94105, ☎ 415/977–5630).

One option hikers might consider is llama trekking, where the beasts bear the burden. The **International Llama Association** (✉ Box 1891, Kalispell, MT 59903, ☎ 406/257–0282) publishes a catalog of outfitters throughout the world. **Idaho Outfitters and Guides Association** (✉ Box 95, Boise, ID 83701, ☎ 208/342–1919) has listings of guides and outfitters organizing all types of guided trips, from llama treks to lodge-based hiking packages.

Suggested Trips

The following recommended areas for hiking are rated from easy to strenuous. Easier hiking areas involve little climbing—a rarity in the Rockies. Strenuous hiking may involve as much as 5,000 vertical ft in a day's hike, with steep trail sections included.

Colorado

TELLURIDE

With more 14,000-ft peaks than any other state in the country, Colorado presents an obvious challenge to aggressive hikers: climb to the summit of a so-called fourteener. Many hikers make this challenge a multiple obsession, seeking to bag as many fourteeners as possible. Some summits are easy hike-ups, some require technical climbing skills, and most fall somewhere in between. The peaks of the rugged San Juan Mountains around Telluride require some scrambling, occasionally bordering on real climbing, to get to the top. A local favorite is Mt. Wilson, a roughly 4,000-vertical-ft climb for which only the last 400 vertical ft call for a scramble across steep, shale slopes. Sound a bit too grueling? Try the 13-mi Sneffels Highline Trail through wildflower-covered meadows, or any of numerous other great day hikes in the Telluride area.

Dates: July and August are the most likely snow-free months. **Difficulty:** Strenuous. **Guidebook:** *Telluride Hiking Guide,* by Susan Kees. **Information and permits: San Juan National Forest** (✉ 701 Camino del Rio, Durango, CO 81301, ☎ 970/247–4874). **Uncompahgre National Forest** (✉ 2250 U.S. Hwy. 50, Delta, CO 81416, ☎ 970/874–6600). Nearby **Skyline Ranch** (☎ 970/728–3757 or 888/754–1226) will also provide guide service up Mt. Wilson for intrepid ranch guests. **Trip length:** 8-mi round trip to Mt. Wilson summit.

Idaho

SAWTOOTH MOUNTAINS

At one time, the Sawtooths were in line to become a national park, but it didn't happen: In its zeal to create as much bureaucracy as possible, Congress instead divvied the land up into two parcels—a wilderness area and a national recreation area, each with different regulations. This has not, however, detracted significantly from the beauty of the landscape of rough-edged peaks (hence the name); and perhaps *because* this is not a national park, much of the backcountry here is barely visited, even in the summer. There are 180 lakes, but only the two or three most accessible receive much visitor traffic—mostly locals from the nearby Sun Valley area. Because this is technically national forest, not national park, don't be surprised to encounter mountain bikes and horses on some trails. On many trails, however, don't be surprised if you don't see much of anyone at all.

Dates: Around July–September, when trails are generally clear of snow. **Difficulty:** Moderate. **Guidebook:** *Trails of the Sawtooth and White Cloud Mountains,* by Margaret Fuller. **Information and permits: Sawtooth National Forest** (✉ 2647 Kimberly Rd. E, Twin Falls, ID 83301, ☎ 208/737–3200) or **Sawtooth National Recreation Area** (✉ Star Route, Ketchum, ID 83340, ☎ 208/726–7672). **Trip length:** 5 mi–30 mi.

Montana

ABSAROKA-BEARTOOTH WILDERNESS

While summer visitors swarm into Yellowstone National Park just to the south, relatively few (except for dedicated backcountry travelers) come to the Absaroka-Beartooth Wilderness. One reason is that, unlike Yellowstone, the wilderness area has no paved roads leading into it, although a four-wheel-drive vehicle is not essential for access. Montana's highest mountains, including 12,799-ft Granite Peak, are encompassed by the wilderness boundaries; because of that, the prime hiking season is relatively short. High-mountain lakes may remain partially frozen even into August. Perhaps the most popular hiking is in the East Fork–Rosebud Creek area, featuring numerous lakes in alpine basins above 9,000 ft. One warning: This is bear country.

Dates: August is best. **Difficulty:** Moderate–strenuous. **Guidebook:** *Hiker's Guide to Montana* (Falcon Press). **Information and permits: Custer National Forest** (⊠ 2602 1st Ave. N, Box 2556, Billings, MT 59103, ☏ 406/248–9885) or **Gallatin National Forest** (⊠ Federal Bldg., Box 130, Bozeman, MT 59771, ☏ 406/587–6701). **Trip length:** One-way from East Rosebud Creek to Cooke City is 35 mi.

Utah

CAPITOL REEF NATIONAL PARK

While summer visitors crowd the other national parks of southern Utah—Arches, Bryce Canyon, Canyonlands, and Zion—Capitol Reef is the park few people seem to know about. This is, literally, a reef in Utah's desert country—a giant fold in the earth that stretches for more than 100 mi. White rock domes, multicolor cliffs, deep canyons, and natural bridges are the park's physical features, through which the Fremont River has managed to find its course. In summer, hiking on and through all of this rock can be brutally hot (albeit spectacular); a better time to visit is in spring, when days are warm and nights cool, when side-canyon creeks are still full of water, and when wildflowers and cacti are in bloom. Hikes can range from a couple of miles to a couple of days, although to get to some of the more remote side canyons or trailheads, a four-wheel-drive vehicle may be helpful.

Dates: April–June is best. **Difficulty:** Moderate. **Guidebook:** Trail guide and topographical maps available at the visitor center. **Information and permits: Capitol Reef National Park** (⊠ Superintendent, HC 70, Box 15, Torrey, UT 84775, ☏ 801/425–3791). **Trip length:** 2 mi–15 mi.

Wyoming

TETON RANGE

The plus here is that much of the uphill legwork can be dispensed with by aerial tram, the same one that carries Jackson Hole skiers upward in winter. From the top, you can walk through high-mountain basins filled with wildflowers in summer, or along cliff-line ridges, all the while with the stunning facade of the Tetons as a backdrop. A loop of about 30 mi can be made by picking up the Teton Crest Trail, then branching off on the Death Canyon trail. Longer hikes are also possible. Don't necessarily expect solitude; most of the time, you're in Grand Teton National Park, an exceedingly popular tourist destination. However, this route keeps you well away from the visitor crush at the park's main gate, so you aren't likely to encounter hiker traffic jams, either.

Dates: July–August are best for weather and wildflowers. **Difficulty:** Moderate. **Guidebook:** *Hiking the Teton Backcountry,* by Paul Lawrence (Sierra Club Books). **Information and permits: Grand Teton National Park** (⊠ Drawer 170, Moose, WY 83012, ☏ 307/739–3300). **Trip**

length: 30 mi. **Trip organizer: Jackson Hole Mountain Guides** (✉ Box 7477, Jackson, WY 83001, ☎ 307/733–4979).

PACK TRIPS AND HORSEBACK RIDING

As movies and lore will not let us forget, the horse was the animal that enabled settlement of the West. Despite the use of everything from motorcycles to helicopters, ranches continue to rely on horses as a means of transportation. But horses are also an excellent way to get to the Rocky Mountain backcountry, as they can carry loads and travel distances that would be impossible for hikers. (What backpacker, for example, would carry a heavy iron skillet?) In other words, traveling by horseback is a terrific way to experience the big spaces of Rocky Mountain backcountry—the reason there are hundreds of outfitters that guide pack trips throughout the region.

The length, difficulty, and relative luxury of a pack trip can obviously vary considerably, although anyone who expects true luxury is obviously missing the point. Most pack-trip outfitters try to retain the rough edges that are traditionally a part of the pack-trip experience, and that's as it should be. In other words, tents are the usual overnight accommodations (although backcountry lodges or cabins may be used). Morning coffee is traditionally made from grinds dumped in a big pot of hot water and is powerful enough to keep your eardrums ringing for the rest of the day.

Before You Go

Horsemanship is not a prerequisite for most trips, but it is helpful. If you aren't an experienced rider (and even if you are), you can expect to experience some saddle discomfort for the first day or two. If you're unsure of how much of this sort of thing you can put up with, sign up for a shorter trip (one to three days) before taking on an adventure of a week or longer. Another option is to spend a few days at a dude or guest ranch (☞ Dude Ranches, *above*) to get used to life in the saddle, then try a shorter, overnight pack trip organized by the ranch.

Clothing requirements are minimal. A sturdy pair of pants, a wide-brim sun hat, and outerwear to protect against rain are about the only necessities. Ask your outfitter for a list of items you'll need. You might be limited in the gear (extra clothing) or luxuries (alcoholic beverages) an outfitter will let you bring along. Horses and pack mules are strong but can still carry only so much. Check with your outfitter before showing up at the saddle-up with a trunk full of accessories.

Trip costs typically range between $120 and $180 per day.

Contacts and Resources

Local and regional **chambers of commerce** (☞ Chapters 4–8) are good sources of information on ranches and outfitters. Or, you can get information from: **Colorado Outfitters Association** (✉ Box 1304, Parker, CO 80134, ☎ 303/841–7760), **Idaho Outfitters and Guides Association** (✉ Box 95, Boise, ID 83701, ☎ 208/342–1919), **Montana Board of Outfitters** (✉ 111 N. Jackson St., Helena, MT 59620, ☎ 406/444–3738), **Utah Travel Council** (✉ 300 N. State St., Salt Lake City, UT 84114, ☎ 801/538–1030), and **Wyoming Outfitters and Guides Association** (✉ Box 2284, Cody, WY 82414, ☎ 307/527–7453).

For the Family

Even for adults, an extended pack trip is something best worked up to gradually. That's especially advisable for children. Before launching off on a long trip with younger children (or even teenagers), it's probably a good idea to spend a few days at a dude ranch to find out how well your kids take to horses and riding. The **T Lazy 7 Ranch, Bridger Wilderness Outfitters,** and **Del's Triangle 3 Ranch** (☞ *below*) can arrange **short rides and instruction** for children. The **Alternate Transit Authority** (✉ Box 36, Draper, UT 84020, ☎ 801/567–1188) has an excellent instructional program for children with organized rides in the Wasatch-Cache National Forest.

Instruction

Most ranches and outfitters offer instruction on Western-style riding for those who want it. Near Capitol Reef National Park in Utah, at **Pine Shadows Horse Training Farm** (✉ Box 21, Teasdale, UT 84773, ☎ 801/425–3362), guests polish their riding skills with the competent help of Stan Allen, a fourth generation rancher and "horse whisperer."

Organizers and Outfitters

Pack trips tend to be organized by local outfitters or ranches rather than national organizations. Local chambers of commerce can usually provide lists of outfitters who work in a particular area. The individual state chapters have contact information for local chambers.

Suggested Trips

Colorado

ASPEN

The T Lazy 7 Ranch outside Aspen is a good place to find out if pack tripping is for you, before you commit to a multiday ride. The ranch rents horses by the hour and by the day (with instruction, if you want). The T Lazy 7's convenient location, on Maroon Creek Road, enables short rides into one of the prettiest, and certainly the most photographed, valleys in Colorado's central Rockies, capped by the twin peaks of the Maroon Bells. If that appeals to you, you can sign up for an overnight pack trip, organized by the ranch, into one of Aspen's surrounding wilderness areas. If you want to find out if you can hack some of the cowboy culture that inevitably comes with pack tripping (both the real thing and show-off stuff put on for tourists), combine a ride with a steak dinner at the ranch, enlivened by country musicians.

Dates: Mid-June–mid-October. **Organizer: T Lazy 7 Ranch** (✉ 3129 Maroon Creek Rd., Aspen, CO 81611, ☎ 970/925–7040, 970/925–4625, or 888/875–6343).

STEAMBOAT SPRINGS

The Yampa and Elk River valleys around Steamboat have a long and continuing ranching history. Indeed, Steamboat has successfully used its cowboy heritage as a way of promoting tourism; the area is full of not only real cowboys but also visitors trying to act the part. Horseback riding is a spectator sport as well as a participant sport here. Every weekend in summer, rodeos are held in the evening at the Steamboat Rodeo Grounds. Riding, instruction, and extended pack trips are offered at a number of ranches in the area, although some may require minimum stays of a week. One ranch that offers the full gamut, from hour-long rides to rides of several days into the surrounding mountains, is Del's Triangle 3 Ranch, about 20 mi north of Steamboat.

Dates: Year-round. **Organizer: Del's Triangle 3 Ranch** (✉ Box 333, Clark, CO 80428, ☎ 970/879–3495).

Montana

BOB MARSHALL WILDERNESS

Known by locals simply as "the Bob," this wilderness has remained wild enough to have become popular with bears (including a large grizzly population), mountain goats, bighorn sheep, and elk, as well as pack trippers. It is the largest expanse of roadless land in Montana, and although there are trails to be hiked in the Bob, horse-pack trips are a better way to penetrate this huge wilderness. This tends to be big-country riding, best for (though not restricted to) experienced riders, with stretches of more than 20 mi a day common. Among the highlights of the Bob are wildflowers as well as wildlife; mountain scenery (of course); fishing; and the Chinese Wall, a 120-mi-long, reeflike stretch of cliffs, a kind of natural monument to the powers of tectonic forces.

Dates: July–August. **Organizer: Snowy Springs Outfitters** (✉ 720 Main St., Kalispell, MT 59903, ☎ 406/755–2137). There are dozens of other outfitters who guide horse-pack trips in the Bob. For a list, contact the **Montana Board of Outfitters** (☞ Contacts and Resources, *above*).

Utah

UINTA MOUNTAINS

The Uintas, particularly the High Uintas Wilderness where no vehicles are allowed, are prime country for pack trips and day rides. This range, running east and west in northeastern Utah, claims the state's highest point, King's Peak (13,528 ft). The Uintas are ribboned with streams and have hundreds of small lakes set in rolling meadows. Several ranches clustered on the south slopes of the range offer riding on Uinta trails; the Utah Travel Council (☎ 801/538–1030) publishes a directory. J/L Ranch Outfitters and Guides lead weeklong pack trips into the Uintas and the Ashley National Forest. One thing that sets this operation apart is the extra care taken to assess each rider's ability in a casual way, then offer gentle instruction to participants based on their needs.

Dates: Late June–September. **Organizer: J/L Ranch Outfitters and Guides** (✉ Box 129, Whiterocks, UT 84085, ☎ 801/353–4049).

Wyoming

PINEDALE

Pinedale and Jackson are the twin headquarters of the dude-ranch center of the universe. Not surprisingly, this region is also a center for pack tripping. There are mountains to explore in almost every direction (except due south)—the Tetons being the most obvious (and most populated), the Gros Ventres and the Wind Rivers less famous but no less worthy as pack-trip destinations. And, of course, the wonders of Yellowstone lie to the north. Although Pinedale shares a good bit of Jackson's real and faux Western architecture, it isn't nearly as overcome by the inundation of touristy schlock that is Jackson's summertime curse. In other words, Pinedale's authentic cowboy roots tend to be more apparent, making it a good starting point for pack trips into the Wind River Mountains, in particular. There are several ranches and outfitters in the Pinedale area; half-day trail rides, multiday pack trips—all are possible.

Dates: June–September. **Organizer: Bridger Wilderness Outfitters** (✉ Box 561T, Pinedale, WY 82941, ☎ 307/367–2268 or 888/803–7316).

RAFTING

River rafting is truly one of the great ways to experience the Rockies. It is a relatively easy way to get into the backcountry, whether on a half-day float or a two-week white-water adventure. For most trips, no special skills or physical conditioning are necessary, although you'll probably want to be in good enough shape to make short hikes to explore side canyons along the way. One bonus of river travel is that, by backcountry standards, you can live—or more accurately, you can *eat*—in relatively high style. Heavy food-and-drink items such as beer, soda, refrigerated meats—items that might be cumbersome on a backpacking or horse-pack trip—are easily stashed and carried along on rafts. But don't expect too much luxury: For extended trips, accommodations in virtually all cases are in tents on riverside beaches.

Note that several of the rivers cited in the Canoeing and Kayaking section (*above*) are also suitable for rafting. A good starting point for finding a rafting outfitter is **River Travel Center** (☞ Contacts and Resources, *below*).

Before You Go

Rivers are rated according to the ferocity of their water (☞ Before You Go *in* Canoeing and Kayaking, *above*).

"Raft" can mean any of a number of things: an inflated raft in which passengers do the paddling; an inflated raft or wooden dory in which a licensed professional does the work; a motorized raft on which some oar work might be required. Be sure you know what kind of raft you'll be riding—or paddling—before booking a trip.

Day trips typically run between $30 and $60 per person. Expect to pay between $80 and $120 per day for multiday trips.

Contacts and Resources

ECHO: The Wilderness Company (✉ 6529 Telegraph Ave., Oakland, CA 94609, ☎ 510/652–1600 or 800/652–3246) runs rafting trips in Idaho, among other destinations. **Idaho Outfitters and Guides Association** (✉ Box 95, Boise 83701, ☎ 208/342–1919). **Raft Utah** (✉ 153 E. 7200 South St., Midvale, UT 84047, ☎ 801/566–2662) publishes a comprehensive directory with full descriptions of all of Utah's rivers, and the outfitters who run them. **River Travel Center** (✉ Box 6, Point Arena, CA 95468, ☎ 800/882–7238) arranges trips in Idaho and Utah, among other destinations.

For the Family

Any river can be dangerous, and it is thus not advisable to take children under seven on any extended river trip, except those specifically geared toward young children. Before taking an extended trip with your children, you might want to test the waters with a half-day or one-day excursion. Several outfitters run short trips out of Moab, Utah. For families with younger children, trips aboard larger, motorized rafts are probably safest. Among the trips described here, floating the gentle Snake River is best for young children. The Green is also a fairly gentle river in most places; not so the Dolores or the Middle Fork of the Salmon. Outfitters designate some trips as "adults only," with the cutoff usually being 16 years old.

Organizers and Outfitters

Different companies are licensed to run different rivers, although there may be several companies working the same river. Some organizers combine river rafting with other activities: pack trips, mountain-bike excursions, extended hikes.

The following companies operate Rocky Mountain river trips: **Adrift Adventures** (⊠ Box 192, Jensen, UT 84035, ☎ 800/824–0150), **ARTA River Trips** (⊠ 24000 Casa Loma Rd., Groveland, CA 95321, ☎ 800/323–2782), **Dvorak Expeditions** (⊠ 17921 U.S. Hwy. 285, Nathrop, CO 81236, ☎ 800/824–3795), **Glacier Raft Company** (⊠ Box 210, West Glacier, MT 59936, ☎ 406/888–5454), **Mountain Travel/Sobek** (⊠ 6420 Fairmount Ave., El Cerrito, CA 94530, ☎ 888/687–6235), and **OARS** (⊠ Box 67, Angels Camp, CA 95222, ☎ 800/346–6277).

Suggested Trips

Colorado

DOLORES RIVER

Beginning in the San Juan Mountains of southwestern Colorado, the Dolores runs north for more than 150 mi before joining the Colorado River near Moab, Utah. This is one of those rivers that tend to flow madly in spring and diminish considerably by midsummer, and for that reason trips are usually run between April and June. Sandstone canyons, Anasazi ruins, and the spring bloom of wildflowers and cacti are trip highlights. For the most part, this is a float, interrupted by rapids that—depending on the flow level—can rate a Class IV.

Dates: April–June. **River rating:** Class II–Class IV. **Trip length:** 2–12 days. **Organizer: Dvorak Expeditions** (☞ Organizers and Outfitters, *above*).

Idaho

MIDDLE FORK, SALMON RIVER

The Middle Fork is a true rafting legend. Other than running the Colorado River through the Grand Canyon, the Middle Fork offers perhaps the preeminent rafting experience in North America. It is known less, perhaps, for the seriousness of its rapids (mostly rated Class III and Class IV, although possibly Class V in spring) than for the quantity of rapids. Designated a "wild and scenic river," the 100-plus-mi Middle Fork is not only undammed but also undeveloped; despite the number of river runners who come here each summer, the signs of civilization along the way are exceedingly rare. Steep, tree-studded mountainsides, hot springs, and wildlife are trip highlights—along with all those rapids, of course.

Dates: June–September. **River rating:** Class III–Class IV (higher in June, lower in September). **Trip length:** 6 days. **Organizers: Middle Fork Rapid Transit** (⊠ 160 ISF 2nd St. W, Twin Falls, ID 83301, ☎ 208/734–7890 or 888/433–5628).

Wyoming

SNAKE RIVER

The Snake has earned a strange footnote in history as the river that Evel Knievel tried (and failed miserably) to jump over on a rocket-powered motorcycle. It deserves better. The Snake is a river for river runners who value scenery over white-water thrills. For the most part, floating rather than taking on rapids is the theme of running the Snake (with trips usually incorporating Jackson Lake); as such, it is a good choice for families with younger children. What makes the trip special is the Teton Range, looming as much as 8,000 ft above the river. This float trip can also be combined with two or more days of sea kayaking on Jackson Lake, at the foot of the Tetons.

Dates: June–September. **River rating:** Class I–Class II. **Trip length:** 2 days. **Organizer: OARS** (☞ Organizers and Outfitters, *above*).

ROCK CLIMBING AND MOUNTAINEERING

There are two basic things to know about climbing in the Rockies: (1) The Rockies offer almost unlimited climbing opportunities, as you might expect; and (2) bad things happen to ill-prepared climbers. The first is stated with great appreciation, and the second is not necessarily stated with great foreboding. It is just a fact. There is one good rule in climbing: If you are unsure of your skills or ability to take on a particular climb, don't do it.

That basic precaution given, the question is: What can you expect when climbing in the Rockies? Not all of the climbing requires great technical skills, if any. Many high peaks, such as Long's Peak in Colorado (☞ Rocky Mountain National Park *in* Suggested Trips, *below*) are accessible to anyone in good shape. At the same time, of course, there are numerous highly technical climbs, ranging from rock climbing in the mesa and canyon country of southern Colorado and Utah to alpine-style ascents of the mountains of northern Montana. Rare, however, are the sort of big rock faces a climber might encounter in Yosemite or extensive glaciers similar to those found in the Canadian Rockies or in Alaska. Expeditionary climbers, looking for life-on-the-edge challenges or first ascents, go elsewhere.

Before You Go

Climbing in the Rockies is, for some hardcore alpinists, a year-round sport. Certainly rock climbing in the southern region and ice climbing wherever there are stable icefalls are reasonable wintertime sports. Realistically, though, avalanche risks can persist even into May at higher elevations, and winter can begin in earnest by October. The best months, weather-wise, are June and July; the risk of afternoon thunderstorms (also possible earlier in the summer) throw an additional hazard into August climbing.

Generally speaking, the Rockies do not call for great expeditionary preparation. The range is very accessible and the climbs, by alpine standards, relatively short. In other words, long hikes with heavy packs in order to establish a base are rare, and climbs that typically involve less than 6,000 vertical ft are not like dealing with the 10,000 or more vertical ft involved in climbing, say, Mt. Rainier in Washington. There are few major climbs in the Rockies that can't be accomplished in a day or two.

Guide services usually rent such technical gear as helmets, pitons, ropes, and axes. A good guide service can also provide a gear list of necessary items; be sure to ask for one. Some mountaineering stores also rent climbing equipment. As for clothing, temperatures can fluctuate dramatically, even in summer, at higher elevations. Bringing several thin layers of clothing, including a sturdy, waterproof/breathable outer shell, is the best strategy for dealing with weather variations.

Before you sign on with any trip, be sure to clarify to the trip organizer your climbing skills, experience, and physical condition. Climbing tends to be a team sport, and overestimating your capabilities can endanger not only yourself but other team members. A fair self-assessment of your abilities also helps a guide choose an appropriate climbing route; routes (not unlike ski trails) are rated according to their difficulty. The way to a summit may be relatively easy or brutally challenging, depending on the route selected.

Trip costs when going on an organized climb can vary considerably, depending on group size, length of climb, instruction rendered, and equipment supplied. (Outfitters usually rent equipment on a per-item, per-day basis.) Count on spending at least $80 a day. However, the cost of a small-group multiday instructional climb can push $200 a day.

Contacts and Resources

For technical climbers interested in detailed route descriptions, *The Climber's Guide to North America,* by John Harlin III, is one of the best books on the subject.

Instruction

The **American Alpine Institute** (☞ Organizers and Outfitters, *below*), the **Colorado Mountain School, Fantasy Ridge Alpinism, Jackson Hole Mountain Guides,** and the **Wilderness School** (☞ Suggested Trips, *below*) have **instructional programs** for novices as well as experienced climbers. Another reputable climbing school in the Jackson area is **Exum School of Mountaineering** (✉ Box 56, Moose, WY 83012, ☎ 307/733–2297). Also, climbing walls (both indoor and outdoor) have opened in many places in the United States, and some offer instructional programs, which are helpful preparation for a trip to the Rockies.

Organizers and Outfitters

The **American Alpine Institute** (✉ 1515 12th St., Bellingham, WA 98225, ☎ 360/671–1505) leads trips around the world, ranging from training climbs to expeditionary first ascents. It is one of the most respected climbing organizations in the country.

Suggested Trips

Colorado

ROCKY MOUNTAIN NATIONAL PARK

There are 78 peaks in the park that rise above 12,000 ft, several of which require no technical skills to reach the summit. Via the easiest route, for example, the summit of Long's Peak, the highest point in the park at 14,255 ft, is one of these. This makes the park a good learning and training area for novices.

Climbing in Rocky Mountain National Park has its pros and cons. The pros are variety and ease of access: There are climbs for novices as well as for experienced mountaineers, and most are easily reached from roads leading to and through the park. The cons are (again) ease of access, which can make the park relatively crowded in summer; as many as 800 hikers and climbers have registered to ascend Long's Peak on a single day. Another con is elevation: Not only can the elevation of the park steal one's breath away, but with mountain bases above 9,000 ft, ascents of even the 14,000-footers become relatively short climbs.

Guidebook: *Rocky Mountain National Park: Classic Hikes and Climbs,* by Gerry Roach (Fulcrum). **Information and permits: Rocky Mountain National Park** (✉ Estes Park, CO 80517, ☎ 970/586–1206 or 970/627–3471). **Organizer: Colorado Mountain School** (✉ Box 2062, Estes Park, CO 80517, ☎ 970/586–5758).

SAN JUAN MOUNTAINS

From the mesas of south central Colorado, the San Juans appear to rise up with startling vertical upthrust, and the trip from Montrose to Ouray, less than 50 mi, is like a trip from one planet to another. Whether the San Juans are Colorado's most dramatic mountains is obviously a matter of debate, but a strong case can certainly be made on their behalf. Not surprisingly, this dramatic verticality lends itself to climbing of various sorts: alpine ascents, rock climbing (notably the Ophir Wall near the small town of Ophir), and ice climbing in winter on waterfalls near Ouray and Telluride. The dominant mountain of the range is Mt. Sneffels, 14,150 ft high, although there are several other peaks that rise above 14,000 ft. Because of the San Juans' southerly location, the climbing season (that is, nonwinter climbing) can last somewhat longer than in the northern Rockies.

Information and permits: San Juan National Forest (✉ 701 Camino del Rio, Room 101, Durango, CO 81301, ☎ 970/247–4874). **Organizer: Fantasy Ridge Alpinism** (✉ Nugget Bldg., Suite 204, Box 1679, Telluride, CO 81435, ☎ 970/728–3546).

Utah

WASATCH MOUNTAINS

Accessibility to the canyons of the Wasatch Mountain Range from Salt Lake and other cities along the I–15 corridor is both a blessing and a curse. Because they are easy to get to, these canyons are extremely popular. The curse for climbers is that typically, parking for the most popular routes is along the narrow shoulders of winding canyon roads. However, this problem is not insurmountable in two of the Wasatch Range's best climbing destinations, Little Cottonwood and American Fork Canyons.

Formed by the tireless path of an ancient glacier, **Little Cottonwood** cuts an enormous swath through the Wasatch-Cache National Forest. Canyon walls are composed mostly of striated granite and traditional climbing routes of varied difficulty abound. There are a few bolted routes as well, and Snowbird Ski and Summer Resort (☎ 801/521–6040) has a competition-class outdoor climbing wall open to the public. **American Fork Canyon,** 32 mi south of Salt Lake City in the Uinta National Forest, has northern Utah's best sport climbing with dozens of fixed routes. The canyon's steep walls also offer face, slab, and crack climbs.

Guidebooks: *Wasatch Climbing North* and *Wasatch Climbing South* (Chalkstone Press). **Information and permits: Wasatch–Cache National Forest** (✉ 8236 Federal Bldg., Salt Lake City, UT 84138, ☎ 801/524–5030) and **Uinta National Forest** 88 W. 100 North, Box 1428, Provo, UT 84601, ☎ 801/377–5780. **Organizer: The Wilderness School** (✉ 757 N. State St., Orem, UT 84057, ☎ 801/226–7498).

ZION NATIONAL PARK

In Zion Canyon, huge formations with lofty names, like Angels' Landing and the Great White Throne, rise above the Virgin River. The canyon's towering sandstone cliffs require advanced wall techniques, so novice climbers had better just admire their colleagues' skill, or try out some soft rock bouldering closer to the ground. For proficient climbers, Zion boasts some of the most demanding traditional routes in the state.

Guidebook: *Desert Rock: Rock Climbs in the National Parks,* by Eric Bjornsted (Chalkstone Press). **Information and permits: Zion National Park** (✉ Box 1099, Springdale, UT 84767, ☎ 801/772–3256).

Wyoming

GRAND TETON NATIONAL PARK

In many ways, the 13,770-ft Grand Teton is the most obvious U.S. mountain to climb: 8,000 vertical ft of jagged, exposed rock—more photographed, perhaps, than any other mountain in the nation. It is far from the easiest mountain to climb, however, and there are at least two days of steep rock to deal with on the ascent and rappels of 100 ft (or more) to negotiate on the descent. It is hard to believe that a fellow named Bill Briggs actually skied down the Grand Teton. Fortunately for less experienced climbers, there are other good options in the park, notably 12,325-ft Teewinot Mountain, a more moderate challenge that combines rock, ice, and scrambling. Regardless of the mountain (or route) chosen, the views are as good as they come in the Rockies.

Guidebook: *Climber's Guide to the Tetons* (Grand Teton Natural History Association). **Information and permits Grand Teton National Park:** (✉ Drawer 170, Moose, WY 83012, ☎ 307/739–3300). **Organizer: Jackson Hole Mountain Guides** (✉ Box 7477T, Jackson, WY 83001, ☎ 307/733–4979).

WIND RIVER MOUNTAINS

Much of the appeal of the Wind River Range is the relatively difficult access to major peaks, the most significant of which is Gannett Peak, at 13,804 ft the highest mountain in Wyoming. The trip into the base of the mountain can take two days, with considerable ups and downs and stream crossings that can be dangerous in late spring and early summer. The reward for such effort, however, is seclusion: Climbing Gannett Peak might not be as dramatic as climbing the Grand Teton to the west, but you won't have to face the national park crowds at the beginning or end of the climb. Wind River is a world of granite and glaciers, the latter (though small) being among the last active glaciers in the U.S. Rockies. Other worthy climbs in the Wind River Range are Gannett's neighbors Mt. Sacajawea and Fremont Peak.

Information and permits: Bridger-Teton National Forest (✉ Box 1888, Jackson, WY 83001, ☎ 307/739–5500). **Organizer: Jackson Hole Mountain Guides** (✉ Box 7477T, Jackson, WY 83001, ☎ 307/733–4979).

4 COLORADO

Theodore Roosevelt spoke of Colorado as "scenery to bankrupt the English language." Walt Whitman wrote that its beauty "awakens those grandest and subtlest elements in the human soul." For more than 200 years pioneers, poets, and presidents alike have rhapsodized over what an increasing number of "out-of-towners" are learning: that Colorado is one of America's prime chunks of real estate.

By Jordan Simon

Revised and updated by Sharon Niederman

COLORADO IS A STATE OF STUNNING CONTRASTS. The Rockies create a mountainous spine that's larger than Switzerland, with 52 eternally snowcapped summits towering higher than 14,000 ft. Yet its eastern third is a sea of hypnotically waving grasslands; its southwest, a vibrant multihue desert, carved with pink and mauve canyons, vaulting cinnamon spires, and gnarled red rock monoliths. Its mighty rivers, the Colorado, Arkansas, and Gunnison, etch deep, yawning chasms every bit as impressive as the shimmering blue-tinged glaciers and jagged peaks of the San Juan, Sangre de Cristo, and Front ranges. Add to this glittering sapphire lakes and jade forests, and you have an outdoor paradise second to none.

Much of the state's visual appeal can also be attributed to the legacy of the frontier and mining days, when gold, silver, and railroad barons left an equally rich treasure trove of Victorian architecture in the lavish monuments they built to themselves. The Old West comes alive in Colorado, where you're practically driving through the pages of a history book.

The first Europeans to explore were the Spanish, who left their imprint in the lyrical names and distinctive architecture of the southern part of the state. They were followed by trappers, scouts, and explorers, including some of the legendary names in American history—Zebulon Pike, Kit Carson, Stephen Long, and William Bent—intent on exploiting some of the area's rich natural resources, including vast lodes of gold and silver. In so doing they displaced—and often massacred—the original settlers: Pawnee; Comanche; Ute; and Pueblo, whose ancestors, the Anasazi, fashioned the haunting cliff dwellings of Mesa Verde National Park.

Along with feisty independence, be it right- or left-wing, Coloradans have always displayed an eccentric, even ostentatious streak. State history is animated by stories of fabulous wealth and equally dramatic ruin in the bountiful precious-metal mines. The discovery of gold in 1859 spurred the first major settlement of Colorado, followed by the inevitable railroad lines for transport. When the lodes petered out, many of the thriving communities became virtual ghost towns, until the discovery of black gold in the oil-shale reserves of northwest Colorado and, especially, white gold on the ski slopes.

Today Colorado is a state of unabashed nature lovers and outdoors enthusiasts. Though most people associate the state with skiing, residents have a saying, "We came for the winters, but we stayed for the summers." In addition to skiing and snowmobiling in winter, they climb, hike, bike, fish, and camp in the summer, making Colorado one of America's premier four-season destinations. As a visitor, you'll find plenty to occupy yourself year-round.

Pleasures and Pastimes

Dining

The dining scene in Colorado is quite sophisticated, especially in Denver and the resort towns. Still, restaurants in smaller areas such as Crested Butte rank among the country's most vibrant and creative. Livestock are a main source of livelihood on the eastern plains, where billboards proclaim "Nothing satisfies like beef." However, the calorie- and cholesterol-conscious will appreciate the fresh fish that sometimes appear on menus. Beef, buffalo, and burritos are available in many of the restaurants throughout the state, but a dazzling range of international cuisine from Southwestern to classic French, Italian, and Thai can be found just as easily.

CATEGORY	COST*
$$$$	over $35
$$$	$25–$35
$$	$15–$25
$	under $15

per person, for a three-course meal, excluding drinks, 7.9% tax, and tip

Lodging

Take your pick from the numerous selections across the state: resorts, chain hotels, dude ranches, bed-and-breakfasts, guest houses. Colorado has all sorts of accommodations to match any budget. In many parts of Colorado, particularly the ski areas, condominiums often represent an excellent alternative to the pricier hotels, especially for families and groups. In certain resorts, such as Steamboat, Copper Mountain, and Winter Park, they are often the best lodging, period.

CATEGORY	COST*
$$$$	over $225
$$$	$150–$225
$$	$75–$150
$	under $75

**All prices are for a standard double room in high season, excluding 11.8% tax and service.*

Shopping

You'll find outlets of many top designers in Denver's malls and department stores, as well as in chic resorts such as Aspen and Vail. But the real buys in Colorado are indigenous artifacts, crafts, and specialties. Western and Native American art galleries, ceramics and jewelry shops, and stores specializing in Western memorabilia and cowboy clothing dot the landscape, especially in the southwest. Beware of the numerous "authentic trading posts" that line the roads. Although they're fun and kitschy, they're usually tourist traps with second-rate merchandise.

Ski Areas

Residents and travelers alike claim that the state's snow—champagne powder—is the lightest and fluffiest anywhere. Most ski areas (☞ Skiing *in* Outdoor Activities and Sports sections for each town's facilities; ☞ *also* Chapter 2) permit snowboarding. Many offer special half pipes for performing tricks, in addition to their skiable terrain; Aspen is the lone holdout that does not allow snowboarding. In summer, more and more ski areas are opening their chairlifts to mountain bikers. There are numerous trails winding through the mountain passes, with arduous ascents and exhilarating descents.

Exploring Colorado

Colorado's capital city, Denver, lies smack in the middle of the state. To the west, the High Rockies are home to most of Colorado's many ski resorts. To the east is flat terrain more similar to Kansas than what one typically thinks of as Colorado. The main interest of visitors to eastern Colorado lies in retracing the paths of the pioneers. The southwestern corner of the state has jaggedly beautiful mountains, as well as deserts, canyons, and mesas. The state's second-largest city, Colorado Springs, is found in the South Central area. Farther south is the San Luis Valley, home to the Great Sand Dunes as well as some of the region's oldest towns. The North Central region contains the state's most progressive city—the university town of Boulder—as well as the spectacular alpine scenery of Rocky Mountain National Park. Northwest Colorado is known primarily as dinosaur country.

Numbers in the text correspond to numbers in the margin and on the Denver, North Central Colorado, I–70 and the High Rockies, Southwest Colorado, Colorado Springs Vicinity, South Central Colorado, and Northwest Colorado maps.

Great Itineraries

IF YOU HAVE 3 DAYS

Spend a day and an evening exploring the many attractions of **Denver** ①–⑯. The next day, head up to **Rocky Mountain National Park** ㉑ to take in some alpine scenery and wildlife, and spend the evening in the hip, colorful town of **Boulder** ⑰. The third day, you can head to **Golden,** home of the Coors Brewery; **Central City,** where you can try your hand at gambling or just tour this gold-mining town returned to its glory days (☞ Side Trips West of Denver, *below*); and **Georgetown** ㉕, a charming old silver mining town with a well-preserved downtown. From here, it's just an hour back to Denver.

IF YOU HAVE 7 DAYS

Follow the above itinerary for the first three days, spending the third night in **Georgetown** ㉕. The fourth day, head to **Breckenridge** ㉘—considered by some to be Colorado's prettiest town. No trip to Colorado would be complete without a visit to **Vail** ㉜, so stop there for lunch. Your afternoon destination is **Aspen** ㊲—in summer, you can head south through **Leadville** ㉛ and over Independence Pass; in winter, when the pass is closed, drive west to **Glenwood Springs** ㉟ and south to Aspen. Both are scenic drives with interesting towns along the way; the Glenwood Springs route takes about an hour longer. The next day, when you can tear yourself away from Aspen's chic charms, head north past Carbondale and south to **Redstone** ㊱. In summer, if you have a four-wheel-drive vehicle, you could cut through Kebler Pass for a quick trip to the funky mountain town of **Crested Butte** ㊴ (you can even hike from Aspen to Crested Butte in a day, through the vibrant wildflower meadows of the Maroon Bells Wilderness), but in winter, it's a four-hour drive. Continue on to **Montrose** ㊶ and **Ridgway** ㊷ and into **Telluride** ㊸, a perfectly preserved National Historic District in a stunning box canyon. The sixth day, take your time driving the San Juan Skyway—perhaps the most scenic drive in a state known for breathtaking scenery—through **Dolores** ㊹, **Cortez** ㊺, **Mancos, Durango** ㊼, and **Silverton** ㊿. Each of these towns merits exploring, and if you have time, you'll want to stop at **Mesa Verde National Park** ㊻ for a look at the haunting Native American cliff dwellings. Spend the night in **Ouray** (51), take a soak in the hot springs, and the next day head back to Denver through **Gunnison** ㊵, **Salida** (80), **Buena Vista** (79), and Fairplay.

When to Tour Colorado

Colorado is known for its winter pastimes, but what keeps most locals here are the summers, when meadows are blanketed with wildflowers and snowcapped peaks shimmer in the sunlight. In winter, keep in mind that driving conditions can be treacherous, and you may not be able to cover as much ground as in summer. Of course, if you're a skier, you'll want to spend at least a full day in such resorts as Vail, Aspen, and Telluride to experience some of the best skiing in the country. In summer, you can time your trip to coincide with some of the state's many festivals: June's Shakespeare Festival in Boulder and Bluegrass Festival in Telluride; Crested Butte's Fat Tire Festival in late June and Wildflower Festival in July; the 4th of July celebrations in almost every town; the Aspen Music Festival all summer long; and the Vail International Summer of Dance in August. Temperatures are warmest and wildflowers are at their peak in July and August, and amazingly, resorts are still uncrowded and prices off-peak, since most tourists still don't think of Colorado as a summer destination. Real bargains can be had in spring and fall, but you can count on iffy weather, with at least some snow. Many residents say their favorite month is September, when the changing aspen leaves set the hillsides ablaze with gold.

DENVER

Denver's buildings jut jaggedly into the skyline, creating an incongruous setting in a state that prides itself on its pristine wilderness. And finally, Denver has shed its cow town image, and the new sophistication is more than skin deep. Throughout the 1960s and '70s, when the city mushroomed on a huge surge of oil and energy revenues, Denverites hustled to discard evidence of their Western past to prove their modernity. The last decade, however, has brought an influx of young, well-educated professionals lured by Colorado's outdoor mystique and encouraged by the megalopolis's business prospects. That Denver is a city of cherished and cared-for neighborhoods extends a feeling of community throughout the city and makes it a particularly interesting place to explore. Denver appears to have broken out of its historical boom-and-bust cycle and settled into a period of prosperity and optimism. The two-time Super Bowl champion Denver Broncos have given the city an unparalleled sense of civic pride.

Most Denverites are unabashed nature lovers whose weekends are often spent skiing, camping, hiking, biking, or fishing. (Perhaps as a result of this active lifestyle, Denver is the "thinnest" city in the United States, with less than 20% of the adult population overweight.) For Denverites, preserving the environment and the city's rich mining and ranching heritage are of equally vital importance to the quality of life. Areas such as LoDo—the historic lower downtown—buzz with jazz clubs, restaurants, and art galleries housed in carefully restored century-old buildings. The culturally diverse populace avidly supports the Denver Art Museum, the Museum of Natural History, the Colorado History Museum, and the Museo de las Americas. The expert acting troupe of the Denver Center Theater Company is at home in both traditional mountings of classics and more provocative contemporary works. An excellent public transportation system, including a developing light rail and 400 mi of bike paths, make getting around easy.

Those who don't know Denver may be in for a few big surprises. Although one of its monikers is the "Mile High City," another is "Queen City of the Plains." Denver is flat, with the Rocky Mountains as a backdrop; this combination keeps the climate delightfully mild. Denverites do not spend their winters digging out of fierce snowstorms and skiing out their front doors, though snow may arrive early and leave late. They take advantage of a comfortable climate (over 300 days of sunshine a year), historic city blocks, a cultural center, and sky's-the-limit outdoor adventures just minutes from downtown. All of these factors make this appealing city more than just a layover between home and the Rockies.

Most of Denver's top attractions are concentrated downtown, a remarkably compact area that can be toured on foot. However, a car is recommended for exploring outside of downtown proper. Less than a half-hour's drive from Denver is Golden, which is also a good jumping-off point for the gambling towns of Central City and Black Hawk (☞ Side Trips West of Denver, *below*).

Colorado

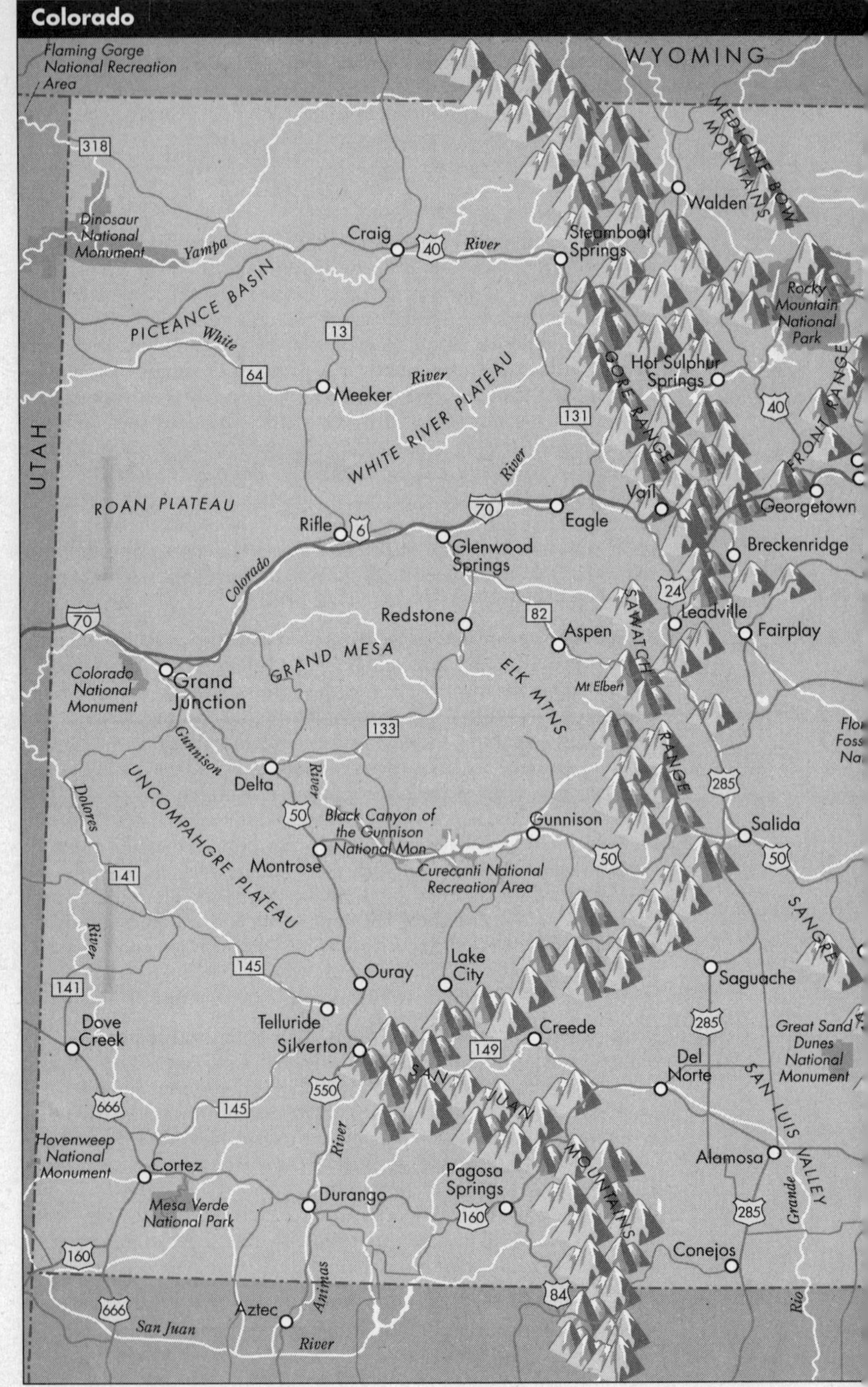
Flaming Gorge National Recreation Area
WYOMING
UTAH
MEDICINE BOW MOUNTAINS
Walden
Dinosaur National Monument
Yampa
Craig
River
Steamboat Springs
PICEANCE BASIN
White
Rocky Mountain National Park
Hot Sulphur Springs
GORE RANGE
Meeker
River
WHITE RIVER PLATEAU
FRONT RANGE
ROAN PLATEAU
River
Vail
Georgetown
Eagle
Rifle
Glenwood Springs
Breckenridge
Colorado
SAWATCH RANGE
Leadville
Fairplay
Redstone
Aspen
Colorado National Monument
Grand Junction
GRAND MESA
ELK MTNS
Mt Elbert
Gunnison
Delta
River
UNCOMPAHGRE PLATEAU
Dolores
Black Canyon of the Gunnison National Mon
Gunnison
Salida
Montrose
Curecanti National Recreation Area
SANGRE
River
Ouray
Lake City
Saguache
Telluride
Dove Creek
Silverton
Creede
Great Sand Dunes National Monument
Del Norte
SAN JUAN MOUNTAINS
SAN LUIS VALLEY
Hovenweep National Monument
Cortez
River
Alamosa
Pagosa Springs
Mesa Verde National Park
Durango
Grande
Conejos
Animas
Aztec
San Juan
River
Rio
318
40
13
64
131
40
70
6
70
82
24
133
285
50
50
50
141
145
141
149
285
550
666
145
160
285
160
666
84

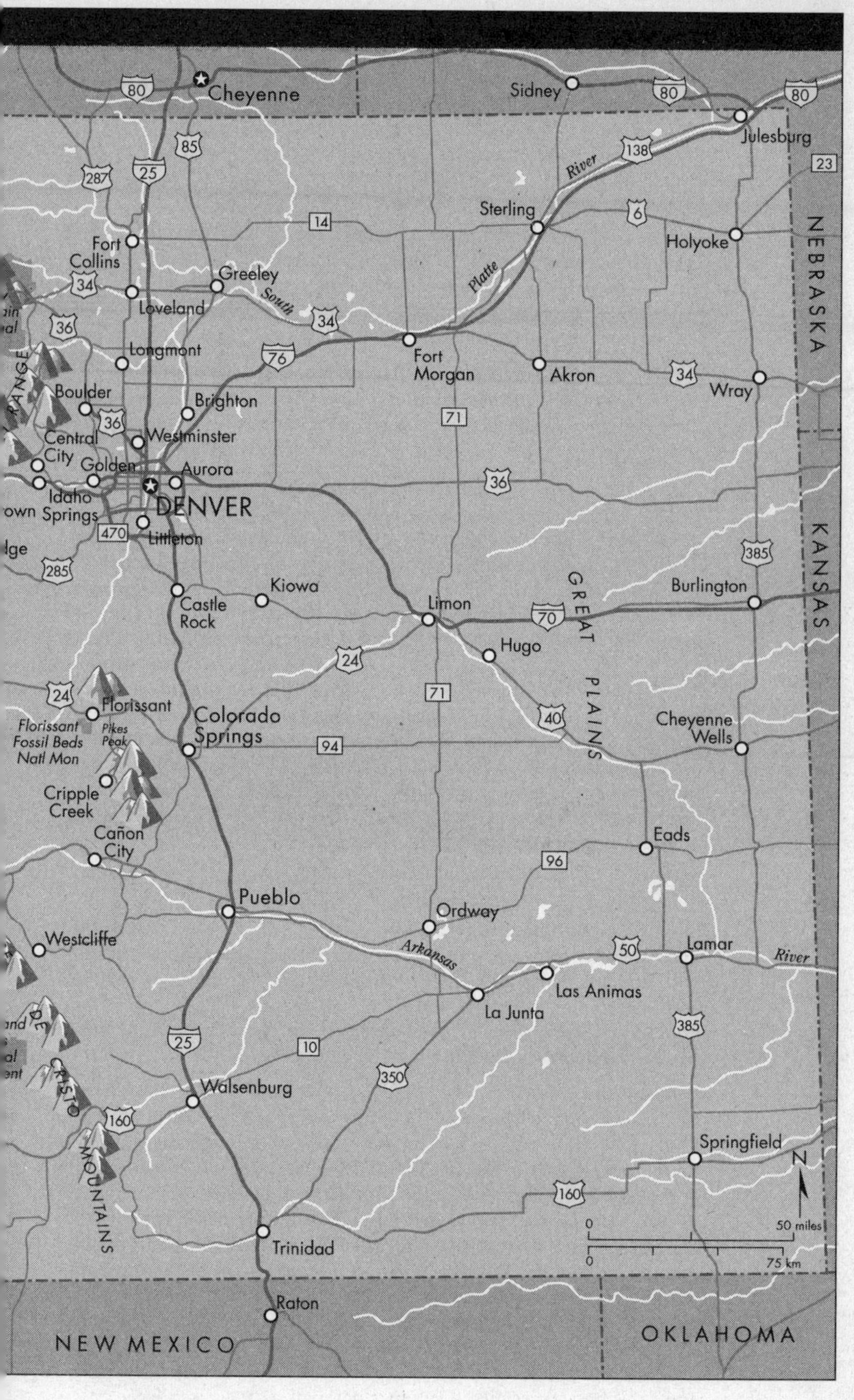
Cheyenne
Sidney
Julesburg
Sterling
Holyoke
Fort Collins
Greeley
Loveland
Longmont
Fort Morgan
Akron
Wray
Boulder
Brighton
Westminster
Central City
Golden
Aurora
Idaho Springs
DENVER
Littleton
Kiowa
Castle Rock
Limon
Burlington
Hugo
Florissant
Florissant Fossil Beds Natl Mon
Pikes Peak
Colorado Springs
Cheyenne Wells
Cripple Creek
Cañon City
Eads
Pueblo
Ordway
Westcliffe
Lamar
Las Animas
La Junta
Walsenburg
Springfield
Trinidad
Raton
NEBRASKA
KANSAS
GREAT PLAINS
South Platte River
Arkansas River
SANGRE DE CRISTO MOUNTAINS
NEW MEXICO
OKLAHOMA
N
0
50 miles
0
75 km

Downtown

Denver's downtown is an intriguing mix of well-preserved monuments from the state's frontier past and modern high-tech marvels. You'll often catch the reflection of an elegant Victorian building in the mirrored glass of a skyscraper. Millions of dollars have been poured into the city since 1995, in such projects as the Coors Field downtown baseball stadium; the relocation of Elitch Gardens—the first amusement park in the country to relocate into a downtown urban area; the new Denver Public Library; and an upgrade of the 16th Street Mall. Lower Downtown, or LoDo, is a Victorian warehouse district revitalized by the new ballpark, loft condominiums, and numerous brew pubs and restaurants. The new downtown Pepsi Center sports arena and the Ocean Journey aquarium are but two more attractions to add to the growing list.

Numbers in the text correspond to numbers in the margin and on the Denver map.

A Good Tour

Denver presents its official face to the world at the **Civic Center,** a three-block-long park that runs from Bannock Street to Broadway south of Colfax Avenue and north of 14th Avenue. Lawns, gardens, and a Greek amphitheater form a serene backdrop for the **State Capitol** ①. Southeast of the Civic Center on Broadway is the vibrant **Colorado History Museum** ②. Head west on 13th Avenue to reach the **Denver Public Library's New Central Library** ③, and cross over Acoma Plaza (or take the underground walkway) to the **Denver Art Museum** ④. The **Byers-Evans House** ⑤, which houses the **Denver History Museum,** is just south of here on Bannock Street. Head back up Bannock to 14th Avenue and turn left (west) to reach the **U.S. Mint** ⑥, the source of all those coins stamped with a *D*. From the mint, continue north on Cherokee Street to Tremont Place and the **Denver Firefighters Museum** ⑦. A block away on 14th Street is the **Trianon Museum and Art Gallery** ⑧.

Continue east on Tremont Place to get to **The Pavillions** ⑨. Nearby is the historic **Brown Palace Hotel** ⑩. Walk or catch a free shuttle up the pedestrian-only **16th Street Mall.** As you head north you'll see the **Daniels and Fisher Tower** ⑪. Just past it is the festive **Tabor Center** ⑫ mall. Across 16th Street from Tabor Center is **Writer Square,** whose shops line the entrance to classy **Larimer Square** ⑬, which runs roughly along the boundary of **LoDo** ⑭. Head southeast on 14th Street to reach the **Denver Performing Arts Complex** ⑮.

TIMING

Although Denver's downtown is easily covered on foot in an hour or less, you'll want to set aside some time to explore its many fine cultural attractions. The Denver Art Museum merits at least two to three hours and the Colorado History Museum can be covered in an hour or two. Monday the Denver Art Museum and Museum of Western Art are closed; the Museum of Western Art is also closed Sunday. Saturday the Denver Art Museum is free. Once you've done the museum rounds, be sure to save some time for browsing and people-watching along the 16th Street Mall and Larimer Square. LoDo is a 30-block-square area that takes several hours to explore on foot. By day, the art galleries and shops are the attraction. At night the many brew pubs and cafés hop, especially in summer baseball season.

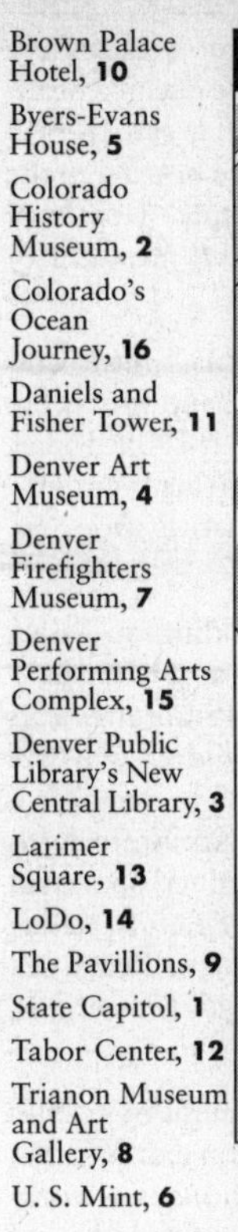
Brown Palace Hotel, **10**
Byers-Evans House, **5**
Colorado History Museum, **2**
Colorado's Ocean Journey, **16**
Daniels and Fisher Tower, **11**
Denver Art Museum, **4**
Denver Firefighters Museum, **7**
Denver Performing Arts Complex, **15**
Denver Public Library's New Central Library, **3**
Larimer Square, **13**
LoDo, **14**
The Pavillions, **9**
State Capitol, **1**
Tabor Center, **12**
Trianon Museum and Art Gallery, **8**
U. S. Mint, **6**

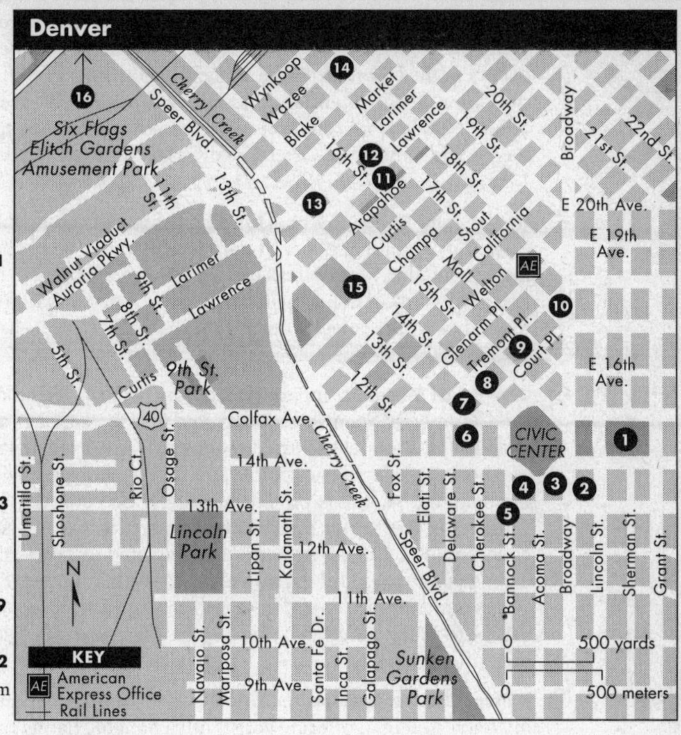

Sights to See

10 **Brown Palace.** Denver's hotel empress was built in 1892 and is still considered the city's most prestigious address. Reputedly this was the first atrium hotel in the United States: Its ornate lobby and nine stories are crowned by a Tiffany stained-glass window (☞ Lodging, *below*). ✉ *321 17th St.*

5 **Byers-Evans House.** This elaborate redbrick Victorian was built in 1883 and restored to its pre–World War I condition in the 1980s. It serves as the **Denver History Museum,** offering exciting interactive video exhibits and history programs about the city. ✉ *1310 Bannock St.,* ☎ *303/620–4933.* 🎫 *$3.* ⏲ *Tues.–Sun. 11–3.*

Civic Center. You'll find a peaceful respite in this three-block park in the cultural heart of downtown, site of the **State Capitol** (☞ below). A Greek amphitheater is set in the middle of one of the city's largest flower gardens. Festivals such as Cinco de Mayo and the People's Fair keep things lively here throughout the summer. ✉ *Bannock St. to Broadway south of Colfax Ave. and north of 14th Ave.*

2 **Colorado History Museum.** The state's frontier past is vibrantly depicted here. Changing exhibits highlight eras such as the Jazz Age and the Gay '90s. Permanent displays include Conestoga wagons, great old touring cars, and an extraordinary time line called "The Colorado Chronicle 1800–1950," which depicts the state's history in amazing detail. The display stretches 112 ft, 6 inches, and dedicates 9 inches to each year. It's crammed with artifacts from rifles to land-grant surveys and old daguerreotypes. ✉ *1300 Broadway,* ☎ *303/866–3682.* 🎫 *$3.* ⏲ *Mon.–Sat. 10–4:30, Sun. noon–4:30.*

16 **Colorado's Ocean Journey.** On the north side of the Platte River across from Elitch Gardens, Ocean Journey is the only million-gallon aquarium between Chicago and the West Coast. It has four sections that show water and aquatic life in all its forms, from the seas to the ocean's headwaters in the Colorado mountains. The journeys of two great rivers—the Colorado River and Indonesia's Kampar River—are housed in the 106,500-square-ft aquarium. Other major displays include "Depths of the Pacific" and "Sea Otter Cove." ⊠ *700 Water St., off Exit 211 of I–25,* ☎ *303/561–4450.* *$14.95.* ⏲ *Daily 10–6.*

11 **Daniels and Fisher Tower.** This 330-ft-high structure was built to emulate the campanile of St. Mark's Cathedral in Venice, and it was the highest building west of the Mississippi when it was built in 1909. Today, it's the city's most convenient clock tower. You can call to arrange entry to the top of the tower to enjoy the view. ⊠ *16th and Arapahoe Sts.,* ☎ *303/892–1505.*

★ 4 **Denver Art Museum.** Superlative, uniquely displayed holdings in Asian, pre-Columbian, Spanish Colonial, and Native American art are the hallmarks of this model of museum design. With dazzling mountain views as a bonus, it's highly accessible and thoughtfully lit. Children will love the imaginative hands-on exhibits and video corners. The new "Adventures in Art" floor offers hands-on art classes and exploration for children and adults. Renovations completed in 1999 added space for extensive special exhibits, as well as a new restaurant, Palettes, which serves contemporary American food. ⊠ *100 W. 14th Ave. Pkwy.,* ☎ *303/640–2793.* *$4.50; free Sat.* ⏲ *Tues.–Sat. 10–5 (Wed. until 8), Sun. noon–5.*

Denver Children's Museum. This is one of the finest museums of its kind in North America, offering constantly changing hands-on exhibits that lure children into discovery. One of the biggest attractions is a working television studio, replete with a weather station, a news desk, and a viewing booth where children can videotape each other and watch the results on "byte"-size monitors. Other interesting aspects of the museum include the Maze-eum, a walk-through maze, the "Indians of the Northwest" display, where children can build their own totem poles, and the outdoor park with climbing equipment, a year-round ski instruction hill, and a trolley ($2) that clatters and clangs the 2 mi down the South Platte River to the Forney Transportation Museum. The trolley also connects to the new Ocean Journey aquarium. ⊠ *2121 Crescent Dr.,* ☎ *303/433–7444.* *$4.* ⏲ *June–Aug., daily 10–5; Sept.–May, Tues.–Sun. 10–5.*

7 **Denver Firefighters Museum.** Occupying the space of Denver's first firehouse, all the original items of the trade are displayed here, including uniforms, nets, fire carts and trucks, bells, and switchboards. ⊠ *1326 Tremont Pl.,* ☎ *303/892–1436.* *$3.* ⏲ *Mon.–Sat. 10–2.*

15 **Denver Performing Arts Complex.** A huge, impressively high-tech group of theaters is connected by a soaring glass archway to a futuristic symphony hall. Guided tours are available, but times vary so call ahead. ⊠ *14th and Curtis Sts.,* ☎ *303/893–4000.*

3 **Denver Public Library's New Central Library.** This Michael Graves-designed building houses a world-renowned collection of books, photographs and newspapers that chronicle the American West, as well as original paintings by Remington, Russell, Audubon, and Bierstadt. The children's library is notable for its captivating design and its unique, child-friendly multimedia computer catálog. The new library is the cornerstone of the Civic Center Cultural Complex, intended to be a center for Western Americana, with shared exhibits and collections with the Denver Art Museum and Colorado History Museum. ⊠ *10 W. 14th Ave.,* ☎ *303/640–6200.* ⏲ *Mon.–Wed. 10–9, Thurs.–Sat. 10–5:30, Sun. 1–5.*

OFF THE BEATEN PATH

FORNEY TRANSPORTATION MUSEUM – Peeling carriages, corroding cabooses, and classic cycles litter the exterior of this odd museum that resembles an abandoned auto yard. It's just outside the downtown loop (west on 15th Street, right past the confluence of the South Platte River and Cherry Creek). Inside not-quite-thought-out exhibit rooms are an 1898 Renault coupe, Teddy Roosevelt's tour car, Aly Khan's Rolls, and a Big Boy steam locomotive, among other collectibles. Strangely enough, there's also a room dedicated to 18th-century military uniforms. Anyone who grew up on model cars or Lionel trains will wander this eccentric museum in a happy daze. ✉ *4303 Brighton Blvd.,* ☎ *303/297–1113.* 🎫 *$4.* ⏲ *Mon.–Sat. 10–5, Sun. 11–5.*

⓭ **Larimer Square.** At **Writer Square** shops line the entrance to the arched redbrick courtyards of Denver's most charming shopping district, where some of the city's oldest retail buildings and toniest specialty shops, such as Overland Sheepskin and Tewksbury & Co., do business. Larimer Square—actually a street—is the oldest street in the city. It was saved from the wrecker's ball by a determined preservationist in the 1960s, when the city went demolition-crazy in its eagerness to present a more youthful image. ✉ *Larimer and 15th Sts.*

⓮ **LoDo.** The historic lower downtown area is now home to art galleries, nightclubs, and restaurants ranging from Denver's most upscale to its most down-home. This part of town was once the city's thriving retail center, then it fell into disuse and slid into slums. Beginning in the late 1980s and early 1990s, LoDo has been undergoing an ongoing, vigorous revival spearheaded not just by avant-garde artists and retailers, but by loft dwellers who have taken over old warehouses here. The handsome **Coors Stadium** (✉ Blake and 20th Sts.), home of baseball's Colorado Rockies, has further galvanized the area. Its old-fashioned brick and grillwork facade, ornamented with 41 blue, green, and white terra-cotta columbines (the state flower), was designed to blend in with the surrounding Victorian warehouses. The brand-new **Pepsi Center** (☎ 303/405–8555) opened nearby in 1999. The new home of the Avalanche and Nuggets has sports fans even more enthused. ✉ *From Larimer St. to the South Platte River, between 14th and 22nd Sts.*

OFF THE BEATEN PATH

MUSEO DE LAS AMERICAS – The region's first museum dedicated to the achievements of Latinos in the Americas has a permanent collection as well as rotating exhibits that cover everything from Hispanics in the state legislature to Latin American women artists in the 20th century. ✉ *861 Santa Fe Dr.,* ☎ *303/571–4401.* 🎫 *$3.* ⏲ *Tues.–Sat. 10–5.*

❾ **The Pavillions.** Denver's newest retail and entertainment center opened in late 1998. This two-city-block complex, with an assortment of restaurants, bookstores, movie theaters, and shops, is located along the 16th Street Mall adjacent to the Adam's Mark Hotel. ✉ *Along the 16th St. Mall near Court Pl.*

Six Flags Elitch Gardens has always been a Denver family tradition, with two hair-raising roller coasters (including one ranked in the nation's top 10); a hand-carved, antique carousel; a 100-ft-high Ferris wheel that provides sensational views of downtown; and flower displays. Now its owner, Premier Parks, is upping the excitement a few notches with a new 10-acre water adventure park, and a suspended inverted looping roller coaster. ✉ *I–25 and Speer Blvd.,* ☎ *303/595–4386.* 🎫 *$28 unlimited ride pass.* ⏲ *June–Labor Day, daily; May, Sept., and Oct, Fri.–Sun.; hrs vary so call ahead.*

★ **16th Street Mall.** Outdoor cafés, historic buildings, and tempting shops line this pedestrian-only 12-block thoroughfare, shaded by red oak and locust trees. You'll find Denver's best people-watching here, with more than 1,000 chairs set out along its length so you can take in the sights. The rose and gray granite mall is scrubbed clean every day. Catch one of the free shuttle buses that run the length of downtown.

❶ **State Capitol.** Built in 1886, the capitol was constructed mostly of materials indigenous to Colorado, including marble, granite, and rose onyx. Especially inspiring is the gold-leaf dome, a reminder of the state's mining heritage. Visitors can climb to the balcony for a panoramic view of the Rockies, or merely to the 18th step, which is exactly 1 mi high (above sea level). ✉ *200 E. Colfax Ave.,* ☎ *303/866–2604.* 🎫 *Free.* ⏲ *Weekdays 9–2:30 (occasionally open Sat. in summer); tours every 45 min.*

⓬ **Tabor Center.** This festive shopping mall has more than 60 stores and attractions, including fast-food eateries, strolling troubadours, jugglers and fire-eaters, and splashing fountains. A concierge desk at the Lawrence Street entrance is staffed with friendly people who offer free walking tours around the city. ✉ *Larimer and Arapahoe Sts. on 16th St.,* ☎ *303/572–6868.*

❽ **Trianon Museum and Art Gallery.** This tranquil museum houses a collection of 18th- and 19th-century European furnishings and objets d'art as well as a rare gun collection, with pieces dating from the 16th century onward. Guided tours are offered on the hour. ✉ *335 14th St.,* ☎ *303/623–0739.* 🎫 *$1.* ⏲ *Mon.–Sat. 10–4.*

❻ **U.S. Mint.** Free tours take guests around this facility, where more than 10 billion coins are minted yearly, and where the nation's second-largest hoard of gold is displayed. ✉ *W. Colfax Ave. and Cherokee St.,* ☎ *303/405–4761.* 🎫 *Free.* ⏲ *Tours weekdays 8–3 every 20 min, except during inventory (usually last 2 wks in June).*

East of Downtown

The area east of downtown is home to two of the city's finest parks, as well as some grand old residential neighborhoods.

A Good Tour

You'll need transportation on this tour, as it covers an area more spread out than downtown. If you don't have a car, Denver has an excellent bus system (☞ Denver A to Z, *below*).

Head east from the **Civic Center** on 14th Avenue to the flamboyant **Molly Brown House.** Continue east on 14th and south on York for a peaceful interlude at the **Denver Botanic Gardens.** Denver's most impressive public space is **City Park,** reached by heading north on York Street. Go east on 23rd Avenue for the main entrance to the **Denver Zoo.** From here it's a short walk across the park (or a drive, on Colorado Boulevard south), to the **Denver Museum of Natural History.** Finish up your day with a stop at the **Black American West Museum and Heritage Center** by getting back on York Street north and going west on 31st Avenue.

TIMING

You'll want to set aside a full day to do these sights justice. If you have children or are an animal lover, you could easily spend half a day in City Park, exploring the Denver Zoo and the Denver Museum of Natural History. Garden enthusiasts could spend half a day in the Denver Botanic Gardens in summer, when the many theme gardens are in full bloom; in the off-season, the conservatory is still a good respite for an hour. There are often evening hours and musical performances in the Denver Botanic Gardens in summer, and the Denver Museum of Natural History stays open late on Friday night. The Molly Brown House and the Black American West Museum and Heritage Center are worthy of at least an hour each. In the off-season (October through April), both are closed Monday and have shortened hours on Sunday. The Black American West Museum and Heritage Center is also closed Tuesday and has shortened hours on Saturday.

Sights to See

Black American West Museum and Heritage Center. The revealing documents here depict the vast contributions that African-Americans made to opening up the West. Nearly a third of the cowboys and many pioneer teachers and doctors were African-Americans. One floor is devoted to black cowboys; another to military troupes such as the Buffalo Soldiers. Changing exhibits focus on topics such as the history of black churches in the West. ✉ *3091 California St.,* ☎ *303/292–2566.* 🎫 *$4.* ⏲ *May–Sept., weekdays 10–5, weekends noon–5; Oct.–Apr., Wed.–Fri. 10–2, weekends noon–5.*

★ **City Park.** Denver's largest public space contains rose gardens, lakes, a golf course, tennis courts, a huge community-built children's playground, and two of the city's most popular attractions: the Denver Zoo and the Denver Museum of Natural History. A shuttle runs between the two.

Denver Botanic Gardens. The horticultural displays in thoughtfully laid-out theme gardens are at their peak during summer, but the tropical conservatory alone is worth a visit in the off-season. Spring brings a brilliant display of wildflowers to the world-renowned alpine rock garden. Tea ceremonies take place some summer weekends in the tranquil Japanese garden. This is a flowering respite from the urban hustle and bustle. ✉ *1005 York St.,* ☎ *303/331–4000.* 🎫 *$4.* ⏲ *Daily 9–5; selected evening hrs in summer.*

★ 🖐 **Denver Museum of Natural History.** This large museum holds a rich combination of traditional collections—dinosaur remains, animal dioramas, a mineralogy display, an Egyptology wing—and intriguing hands-on exhibits such as the "Hall of Life," where you can test your health and fitness on various contraptions. The massive complex includes an IMAX movie theater and the Gates Planetarium. A permanent exhibit, "Prehistoric Journey," covers the seven stages of the earth's development, with each "envirorama" representing the sights and sounds of a specific area of North America or Australia at a particular time. A new interactive children's exhibit is "Cruising the Fossil Freeway." ✉ *2001 Colorado Blvd.,* ☎ *303/322–7009.* 🎫 *$6 museum; $6 IMAX; planetarium included.* ⏲ *Daily 9–5; open 9–7 Fri. in summer.*

🖐 **Denver Zoo.** The 7-acre "Primate Panorama," opened in 1996 for the zoo's centennial, houses 29 species of primates in state-of-the-art environments that simulate the animals' natural habitats. To create a tropical environment in Colorado's climate, heated rocks and hidden steam pipes were incorporated into the design. Other zoo highlights include a nursery for baby animals; seal shows; educational programs on endangered species; and the *Zooliner* train, which snakes through the property as guests are given a safari lecture. ✉ *E. 23rd Ave., between York St. and Colorado Blvd.,* ☎ *303/331–4110.* 🎫 *$6 winter, $8 summer.* ⏲ *Oct.–Mar., daily 10–5; Apr.–Sept., daily 9–6.*

Molly Brown House. This Victorian confection, on Pennsylvania Street between East 13th and 14th avenues, not far from the capitol, celebrates the life and times of the scandalous, "unsinkable" Molly Brown, heroine of the *Titanic* who courageously saved several lives and continued to provide assistance to survivors back on terra firma. Costumed guides and period furnishings in the museum, including flamboyant gilt-edge wallpaper, lace curtains, tile fireplaces, and tapestries, evoke bygone days. A bit of trivia: Margaret Tobin Brown was known as Maggie, not Molly, during her lifetime. Meredith Willson, the composer-lyricist of the musical, *The Unsinkable Molly Brown,* based on Brown's life, thought Molly was easier to sing. ✉ *1340 Pennsylvania St.,* ☎ *303/832–4092.* *$6.* *June–Aug., Mon.–Sat. 10–3:30, Sun. noon–3:30; Sept.–Apr., Tues.–Sat. 10–3:30, Sun. noon–3:30.*

Dining

As befits a multiethnic crossroads, Denver offers a dizzying range of eateries: Head for LoDo, 32nd Avenue in the Highland District, or 17th Street for the more inventive kitchens; try Federal Street for cheap ethnic eats—especially Thai and Vietnamese. Throughout Denver, however, you'll find many trendy restaurants offering New American cuisines with an emphasis on indigenous regional ingredients and light, healthful preparations. Denver's hotels also offer some fine restaurants (☞ Lodging, *below*).

American

$$$$ ✕ **Denver Chophouse & Brewery.** This is the best of the many LoDo brew pubs and restaurants surrounding the ballpark. Housed in the old Union Pacific Railroad warehouse, the restaurant has a clubby atmosphere, with dark wood paneling and exposed brick. The food is basic American food, and plenty of it: steaks, seafood, and chicken served with hot corn bread and honey butter, and "bottomless" salads tossed at the table. ✉ *1735 19th St.,* ☎ *303/296–0800. AE, DC, MC, V.*

$ ✕ **Hotcakes.** This jumping Capitol Hill spot is a breakfast and lunch hangout. Weekend brunch draws crowds of bicyclists and newspaper readers in search of the croissant French toast, "health nut" pancakes, colossal omelettes, and scrumptious skillets. ✉ *1400 E. 18th Ave.,* ☎ *303/830–1090. D, MC, V. No dinner.*

$ ✕ **Rocky Mountain Diner.** Conveniently located in the heart of the downtown business district, you can come in and sample all-American fill-ups of cowboy steak, pan-charred rib eye served with crisp onions, or the very popular buffalo dishes. Don't miss the real mashed potatoes, gravy, and all the fixins'. ✉ *800 18th St.,* ☎ *303/293–8383. AE, D, DC, MC, V.*

$ ✕ **Wazee Supper Club.** Denverites flock to this hip hole for hot jazz and the best pizza in town—crisp yet gooey and bursting with flavor. Some grouse that the Wazee has less ambience since it moved down the street, but the exposed brick walls, jet-black tables, and maroon Naugahyde chairs still convey its ultracool tone. ✉ *1600 15th St.,* ☎ *303/623–9518. AE, MC, V.*

$ ★ ✕ **The Wynkoop Brewing Co.** This trendy yet unpretentious local institution was Denver's first brew pub, and it's still the best. Try the terrific shepherd's pie or charbroiled elk medallions with brandy peppercorns. Wash it down with wilderness wheat ale or sagebrush stout. Then check out the gallery, pool hall, and cabaret for a full night of entertainment. ✉ *1634 18th St.,* ☎ *303/297–2700. AE, DC, MC, V.*

Brazilian

$$ ✕ **Cafe Brazil.** Worth the chase to an outlying neighborhood known as Highlands (just over the viaduct from LoDo) this humble, always-packed, not quite hole-in-the-wall spot is the place for shrimp and scallops sauteed with white wine, garlic, and cream; *feijoda completa,* the Brazilian national dish of black bean stew and smoked meats, accompanied with fried bananas; and grilled chicken breast in a sauce of gin-

ger, raisins, shallots, and coconut milk. This festive, unpretentious spot is favored by locals in the know. ✉ *3611 Navajo St.,* ☎ *303/480–1877. AE, MC. Reservations essential. Closed Sun. and Mon. No lunch.*

Chinese

$$ ✕ **Imperial Chinese.** Papier-mâché lions greet you at the entrance of this sleek Szechuan stunner, probably the best Chinese restaurant in a 500-mi radius. Seafood is the specialty. Try the steamed sea bass in ginger or the spicy, fried Dungeness crab. ✉ *431 S. Broadway,* ☎ *303/698–2800. AE, DC, MC, V. No lunch Sun.*

Contemporary

$$$$ ★ ✕ **Cliff Young's.** Although Young no longer oversees operations here, this refined Art Deco restaurant is still run with meticulous care. Head chef Roberto Ravara serves Asian and Southwestern touches, with such specialties as pinwheels of Chilean sea bass with saffron tomato ragout and pistachio couscous or wild boar loin with potato pancakes. New American standbys, including Colorado rack of lamb and buffalo carpaccio, are also available. ✉ *706 E. 17th Ave.,* ☎ *303/831–8900. Reservations essential. AE, D, DC, MC, V. No lunch.*

$$$$ ✕ **Strings.** This light, airy restaurant with its wide-open kitchen resembles an artist's loft. It's a preferred hangout for Denver's movers and shakers as well as for visiting celebs, whose autographs hang on the walls. The food is billed as casual contemporary; specialties include pan-roasted sea bass in a citrus-cashew crust and penne with chicken, mushrooms, and broccoli in a tomato-cream sauce. ✉ *1700 Humboldt St.,* ☎ *303/831–7310. Reservations essential. AE, D, DC, MC, V. No lunch Sun.*

Continental

$$–$$$ ✕ **European Café.** On the main floor of the Brooks Towers Building, in a space gleaming with polished brass and crystal, the European Café is a mainstay of fine dining in Denver. Many of chef Lupe Gonzalez's dishes pay homage to such French master chefs as Georges Blanc and Paul Bocuse, and all are beautifully presented. Try the lamb chops with roasted garlic sauce. ✉ *1060 15th St.,* ☎ *303/825–6555. AE, D, DC, MC, V. No lunch weekends.*

French

$$$$ ✕ **Tante Louise.** This longtime Denver favorite, just 15 minutes from downtown by car, resembles an intimate French country home. Fireplaces, candlelight, and classical music attract a mostly over-50 crowd. One-third of chef Michael Degenhart's menu is French, one-third is New American, and one-third features low-fat dishes. Try the Maine sea scallops served with carmelized foie gras butter or any of the superlative lamb specials. ✉ *4900 E. Colfax Ave.,* ☎ *303/355–4488. AE, D, DC, MC, V. Closed Sun. No lunch.*

$$ ★ ✕ **Le Central.** This homey bistro calls itself "Denver's affordable French restaurant." The cozy dining room serves excellent mussel dishes; French onion soup; and provincial French specialties, including beef bourguignonne, salmon en croûte, and steak au poivre. Local meat and game are featured. Le Central is a real find. You can depend on fabulous food, great service, and a surprisingly low tab. ✉ *112 E. 8th Ave.,* ☎ *303/863–8094. MC, V.*

Italian

$$$–$$$$ ★ ✕ **Barolo Grill.** This restaurant looks like a chichi farmhouse, as if Martha Stewart went gaga over an Italian count: There are dried flowers in brass urns, hand-painted porcelain, and straw baskets everywhere. The food isn't precious in the least, however. It's more like Santa Monica meets San Stefano—bold yet classic, healthful yet flavorful. Choose from duckling stewed in red wine, mesquite-grilled ostrich, and gnoc-

chi, all well-made and fairly priced. ✉ *3030 E. 6th Ave.,* ☏ *303/393–1040. Reservations essential. AE, D, DC, MC, V. Closed Sun. and Mon. No lunch.*

$ ✕ **Pasquini's Pizzeria.** Come to this informal, popular spot to indulge in fresh, homemade pastas, pizzas, and calzones. Individual pizzas are the house specialty. Don't miss the bakery's fresh Italian breads. ✉ *1310 S. Broadway,* ☏ *303/744–0917. D, DC, MC, V. No dinner Sun.*

Mexican

$ ✕ **Bluebonnet Café and Lounge.** Its location out of the tourist loop, in a fairly seedy neighborhood southeast of downtown, doesn't stop the crowds (mostly tourists) from lining up early for this restaurant. The early Western, Naugahyde decor and fantastic jukebox set an upbeat mood for killer margaritas and some of the best burritos and green chili in town. ✉ *457 S. Broadway,* ☏ *303/778–0147. Reservations not accepted. MC, V.*

$ ✕ **Wahoo's Fish Taco.** California surf decor is the motif at this spot with *taqueria* (taco stand) style. Burritos and soft tacos are made with grilled or blackened fish of the day (or pork, chicken, beef, or grilled vegetables) and served with black beans and fresh salsa with plenty of cilantro. Order at the counter and seat yourself. The margaritas wash it all down nicely. ✉ *1521 Blake St.,* ☏ *303/623–0263. Reservations not accepted. MC, V.*

Steak/Western

$$$$ ✕ **Buckhorn Exchange.** If hunting makes you queasy, don't enter this Denver landmark, a shrine to taxidermy where 500 Bambis stare down at you from the walls. The handsome men's-club decor—with pressed tin ceilings, burgundy walls, red-checker tablecloths, rodeo photos, shotguns, and those trophies—probably looks the same as it did when the Buckhorn first opened in 1893. Rumor has it Buffalo Bill was to the Buckhorn what Norm Peterson was to *Cheers.* The dry-aged, prime-grade Colorado steaks are huge, juicy, and magnificent, as is the game. For an appetizer, try the smoked buffalo sausage or navy bean soup. ✉ *1000 Osage St.,* ☏ *303/534–9505. AE, D, DC, MC, V. No lunch weekends.*

$$$$ ★ ✕ **The Fort.** This adobe structure, complete with flickering luminarias and a piñon bonfire in the courtyard, is a perfect replica of Bent's Fort, a Colorado fur trade center. Buffalo meat and game are the specialties; the elk with huckleberry sauce and tequila-marinated quail are especially good. Intrepid eaters might try the buffalo bone marrow appetizer, jalapeños stuffed with peanut butter, or Rocky Mountain oysters. Costumed characters from the fur trade wander the restaurant, playing the mandolin and telling tall tales. ✉ *U.S. 285 and Rte. 8,* ☏ *303/697–4771. AE, D, DC, MC, V.*

$$$$ ✕ **The Palm Restaurant.** In 1997 the Westin Tabor Center began serving only breakfast and Sunday brunch at its 2nd-floor restaurant, Augusta, and opened the Denver outpost of the longtime New York steak house the Palm, which serves dinner and weekday lunch—meat, seafood, and other American dishes à la carte—on the ground level. The steaks are juicy and the portions grand. ✉ *1672 Lawrence St.,* ☏ *303/825–7256. AE, D, DC, MC, V. No lunch weekdays.*

Vietnamese

$ ✕ **Chez Thuy Hoa.** This simple downtown eatery draws a big lunchtime crowd. The decor isn't much to speak of—a few plants, old-fashioned ceiling fans, and pink table linens—but the savory food keeps it packed during lunchtime (you can usually walk right in at dinner). Try the squid in lemongrass; Dungeness crab salad; or egg rolls bursting with ground pork or shrimp, mint, sprouts, and cucumber. ✉ *1500 California St.,* ☏ *303/623–4809. AE, MC, V. No lunch weekends.*

Lodging

Denver has lodging choices ranging from the stately Brown Palace to the commonplace YMCA, with options such as bed-and-breakfasts and business hotels in between. Unless you're planning a quick escape to the mountains, consider staying in or around downtown, where most of the city's attractions are within walking distance.

$$$ ★ **Brown Palace.** This grande dame of Colorado lodging has housed numerous public figures from President Eisenhower to the Beatles. The details are exquisite: A dramatic nine-story lobby is topped with a glorious stained-glass ceiling, and rooms are decorated with Victorian flair, using sophisticated wainscoting and art-deco fixtures. A much needed refurbishment, completed in early 1997, replaced faded carpets, linens, and upholstery, and added such high-tech touches as in-room Nintendo. The Palace Arms, its formal restaurant, has won numerous awards, including one from *Wine Spectator* magazine. The Churchill cigar bar offers rare cigars and single-malt scotches. ✉ *321 17th St., 80202,* ☎ *303/297–3111 or 800/321–2599,* FAX *303/293–5900. 230 rooms, 25 suites. 4 restaurants, 2 bars, exercise room, concierge. AE, D, DC, MC, V.*

$$$ **Burnsley.** This 16-story, Bauhaus-style tower is a haven for executives seeking peace and quiet close to downtown. The tastefully appointed accommodations are all suites and feature balconies and full kitchens. Floral linens; dusky rose, salmon, and burgundy carpets or upholstery; and old-fashioned riding prints decorate the rooms. Many suites have a sofa bed, making this a good bet for families. The swooningly romantic restaurant is a perfect place to pop the question. ✉ *1000 Grant St., 80203,* ☎ *303/830–1000 or 800/231–3915,* FAX *303/830–7676. 80 suites. Restaurant, bar, pool. AE, D, DC, MC, V.*

$$$ **Warwick Hotel.** This stylish business hotel, ideally located on the edge of downtown, offers oversize rooms and suites and features brass and mahogany Thomasville antique reproductions. Most rooms contain wet bars, full refrigerators, and private balconies. A European breakfast buffet and access to the health club next door are included in the room rate. ✉ *1776 Grant St., 80203,* ☎ *303/861–2000 or 800/525–2888,* FAX *303/839–8504. 194 rooms, 20 suites. Restaurant, bar, pool, concierge. AE, D, DC, MC, V.*

$$$ ★ **Westin Tabor Center.** This sleek, luxurious high-rise opens right onto the 16th Street Mall and all the downtown action. Rooms are oversize and done in grays and taupes, with paisley duvets and prints of the Rockies and the Denver skyline on the walls. The fourth-floor pool has a real-life view of the mountains. Each room has an iron and ironing board, a desk pull-out tray for laptop computers, and cable TV and in-room movies. The hotel even buys blocks of tickets for weekend shows at the Denver Performing Arts Complex for guests' exclusive use. The Palm, a branch of the Manhattan-based steak house, opened in 1997. ✉ *1672 Lawrence St., 80202,* ☎ *303/572–9100,* FAX *303/572–7288. 420 rooms. 2 restaurants, 2 bars, pool, health club, racquetball. AE, D, DC, MC, V.*

$$–$$$ **Adams Mark.** Adams Mark hotels purchased the downtown I. M. Pei–designed Radisson and the old May D&F Department Store across the street in 1994 and spent two years converting them into Denver's first convention-headquarters hotel. The glittering glass hotel—among the 25 largest in the country—includes more than 1,000 rooms and 140,000 square ft of meeting space. The location, at one end of the 16th Street Mall, is ideal. ✉ *1550 Court Pl., 80202,* ☎ *303/893–3333 or 800/444–2326,* FAX *303/626–2543. 1,225 rooms, 100 suites. 3 restaurants, 3 bars, outdoor pool, sauna, steam room, beauty salon, exercise room, dry cleaning, laundry service, concierge, business services, convention center. AE, D, DC, MC, V.*

$$–$$$ ★ **LoDo Inn.** You can't beat the location of this newly refurbished LoDo property that is a cross between an English country B&B packed with tea cozies and doilies and an ultra-sophisticated urban hideaway. Enjoy the business amenities, complimentary beverages and snacks, Continental breakfast, and evening wine and cheese. This posh home away from home is an especially welcome respite for business travelers. ✉ *1612 Wazee St., 80202,* ☎ *303/572–3300,* FAX *303/623–0773. 14 rooms. AE, D, DC, MC, V. Business services.*

$$–$$$ ★ **Loews Giorgio.** The 12-story steel-and-black-glass facade conceals the unexpected and delightful Italian Baroque motif within. Rooms are spacious and elegant, with teal colors and blond wood predominating, and such lovely touches as fresh flowers, fruit baskets, and Renaissance-style portraits. The formal Tuscany restaurant serves sumptuous Italian cuisine. Guests may use a nearby health club, and a Continental breakfast is included. The only drawback of this property is its location: halfway between downtown and the Denver Tech Center, with little in the immediate vicinity. ✉ *4150 E. Mississippi Ave., 80222,* ☎ *303/782–9300 or 800/235–6397,* FAX *303/758–6542. 183 rooms, 20 suites. Restaurant, bar. AE, D, DC, MC, V.*

$$–$$$ ★ **Oxford Hotel.** During the Victorian era this hotel was an elegant fixture on the Denver landscape. Rooms are uniquely furnished with French and English period antiques, while the bar re-creates an art-deco ocean liner. The hotel's location is perfect for those seeking a different, artsy environment. Complimentary shoe shines, afternoon sherry, and morning coffee and fruit are among the civilized touches offered here. Although the Oxford is a notch down from the Brown Palace in most respects, it's also less expensive and is home to McCormick's Fish and Oyster House, Denver's premier seafood restaurant. ✉ *1600 17th St., 80202,* ☎ *303/628–5400 or 800/228–5838,* FAX *303/628–5413. 80 rooms. Restaurant, 2 bars, health club, beauty salon. AE, D, DC, MC, V.*

$$ **Cambridge Club Hotel.** This 1960s-era luxury suites hotel is on a tree-lined street convenient to downtown, one block from the state capitol building. Smart contemporary and traditional furnishings, from Asian to French provincial, decorate the suites; all have wet bars. Local lobbyists, politicos, and CEOs favor the bar. ✉ *1560 Sherman St., 80203,* ☎ *303/831–1252 or 800/877–1252,* FAX *303/831–4724. 33 suites. Restaurant, bar, meeting room. AE, D, DC, MC, V.*

$$ **Castle Marne.** This historic B&B, just east of downtown, sits in a shabbily genteel area. Its balconies, four-story turret, and intricate stone and woodwork present a dramatic facade. Rooms are richly decorated with antiques and artwork. Birdcages, butterfly cases, and old photos of the house are displayed throughout. Most rooms have brass or mahogany beds, throw rugs, tile fireplaces (nonworking), a profusion of dried and fresh flowers, and claw-foot tubs; a few have hot tubs or whirlpool baths. There's a TV in the common room. A full gourmet breakfast—served in the dining room—is included in the room rate, as is afternoon tea. ✉ *1572 Race St., 80206,* ☎ *303/331–0621 or 800/926–2763,* FAX *303/331–0623. 9 rooms. Dining room, business services. MC, V.*

$$ **Comfort Inn/Downtown.** The advantages of this well-used hotel are its reasonable rates and its location in the heart of downtown. Rooms are somewhat cramped, but the corner rooms on the upper floors feature wraparound floor-to-ceiling windows with panoramic views. A complimentary Continental breakfast is offered. ✉ *401 17th St., 80202,* ☎ *303/296–0400 or 800/221–2222,* FAX *303/297–0774. 229 rooms. Restaurant, bar, laundry service. AE, D, DC, MC, V.*

$$ **Holiday Chalet B&B.** Stained-glass windows and homey touches throughout make this Victorian brownstone exceptionally charming. It's also conveniently situated in Capitol Hill, the neighborhood immediately east of downtown. Many of the rooms are furnished with overstuffed Victorian armchairs in light floral fabrics and such cute touches as straw hats. Some units have tile fireplaces, others have small sitting rooms. Each room has a full kitchen. Full breakfast is included. ✉ *1820 E. Colfax Ave., 80218,* ☎ *303/321–9975 or 800/626–4497. 10 rooms. Kitchenettes. AE, D, DC, MC, V.*

$$ **Merritt House.** This beautifully run, antiques-filled 1889 Queen Anne Victorian B&B in Capitol Hill serves a full breakfast with 15 made-to-order items on the menu each day. Large bay windows with window seats frame rooms with canopied beds and vaulted ceilings. Five of the rooms have double whirlpool baths. Locals put their guests up at this find only 10 blocks from downtown. The lovely shaded courtyard is a plus. ✉ *941 E. 17th Ave., 80218,* ☎ *303/861–5230. 10 rooms. AE, D, DC, MC, V.*

$$ ★ **Queen Anne Inn.** Occupying two adjacent Victorians north of downtown in the regentrified Clements historic district (some of the neighboring blocks have yet to be reclaimed), this is a delightful, romantic getaway for B&B mavens. Both houses have handsome oak wainscoting and balustrades, 10-ft vaulted ceilings, numerous bay or stained-glass windows, and such period furnishings as brass and canopy beds, cherry and pine armoires, and oak rocking chairs. The best accommodations are the four "gallery suites" dedicated to Audubon, Rockwell, Calder, and Remington. All rooms have phones. A full breakfast and afternoon tastings of Colorado wines are offered daily. ✉ *2147 Tremont Pl., 80205,* ☎ *303/296–6666 or 800/432–4667,* FAX *303/296–2151. 10 rooms, 4 suites. AE, D, DC, MC, V.*

Nightlife and the Arts

Friday's *Denver Post* and *Rocky Mountain News* publish calendars of the week's events, as does the slightly alternative *Westword*, which is free and published on Tuesday. **Ticketmaster** (☎ 303/830–8497) and **TicketMan** (☎ 303/430–1111 or 800/200–8497) sell tickets by phone to major events, tacking on a slight service charge. The **Ticket Bus** (☎ no phone), on the 16th Street Mall at Curtis Street, sells tickets from 10 until 6 weekdays, and half-price tickets on the day of the performance.

The **Paramount Theater** (✉ 1631 Glenarm Pl., ☎ 303/623–0106) is the site for many large-scale rock concerts. The exquisite **Red Rocks Amphitheater** (☎ 303/640–7300) and **Fiddler's Green** (☎ 303/220–7000) are the primary outdoor concert venues.

Downtown and **LoDo** are where most Denverites make the nightlife scene. Downtown features more mainstream entertainment, whereas LoDo is home to fun, funky rock clubs, and small theaters. Remember that Denver's altitude can intensify your reaction to alcohol.

CABARET

The **Impulse Theater** (✉ 1634 18th St., downstairs in the Wynkoop Brewpub, ☎ 303/297–2111) hosts everything from top-name jazz acts to up-and-coming stand-up comedians, including cabaret numbers.

COMEDY CLUBS

Comedy Works (✉ 1226 15th St., ☎ 303/595–3637) is where Denver comics hone their skills. Well-known performers often drop by. **Chicken Lips Comedy Theater** (✉ 1624 Market St., No. 301, ☎ 303/534–4440) is an improv troupe specializing in topical satire.

COUNTRY MUSIC CLUBS

The **Grizzly Rose** (✉ I–25 at Exit 215, ☎ 303/295–1330) has miles of dance floor, national bands, and offers two-step dancing lessons. **Stam-**

pede Grill & Dance Emporium (✉ 2430 S. Havana St., ☎ 303/337–6909) is the latest boot-scooting spot.

DINNER THEATER

The **Country Dinner Playhouse** (✉ 6875 S. Clinton St., ☎ 303/799–1410) serves a meal before the performance, which is usually a Broadway-style show.

DISCOS

Deadbeat (✉ 404 E. Evans Ave., ☎ 303/758–6853) is where the cool college crowd goes to get carded.

GAY BARS

Charlie's (✉ 900 E. Colfax Ave., ☎ 303/839–8890) offers country-western atmosphere and music at the hottest gay bar in town. **The Elle** (✉ 716 W. Colfax Ave., ☎ 303/572–1710) features go-go dancers, lava lamps, and hot dance parties.

JAZZ CLUBS

El Chapultepec (✉ 20th and Market Sts., ☎ 303/295–9126) is a depressing, fluorescent-lit, bargain-basement Mexican dive. Still, the limos parked outside hint at its enduring popularity: This is where visiting musicians, from former visits of Ol' Blue Eyes to the Marsalis brothers, jam after hours. **Brendan's Pub** (✉ 1624 Market St., ☎ 303/595–0609) attracts local jazz and blues talents. **Vartan's Jazz Club** (✉ 1800 Glenarm Pl., ☎ 303/399–1111) is a comfortable place to listen to a variety of jazz. LoDo's **Vesta Grill** (✉ 1822 Blake St., ☎ 303/296–1970) has live jazz and swing. **Pacific Star** (✉ 1735 Lawrence St., ☎ 303/292–5100) is a gloriously nostalgic recreation of a supper club with smooth crooners on stage.

ROCK CLUBS

There are a number of smoky hangouts in this city, the most popular being the down-home **Herman's Hideaway** (✉ 1578 S. Broadway, ☎ 303/777–5840), which showcases local and national acts, with a smattering of reggae, blues, and alternative music thrown in to keep things lively. Also popular is the **Bluebird Theater** (✉ 3317 E. Colfax Ave., ☎ 303/322–2308). **Cricket on the Hill** (✉ 1209 E. 13th Ave., ☎ 303/830–9020) is yet another club presenting a mix of rock, blues, acoustic, and alternative music. The **Mercury Café** (✉ 2199 California St., ☎ 303/294–9281) triples as a health-food restaurant (sublime tofu fettuccine), fringe theater, and rock club specializing in acoustic sets, progressive, and newer wave music.

SINGLES CLUBS

Rock Island (✉ Wazee and 15th Sts., ☎ 303/572–7625) caters to the young, hip, and restless. Denver's numerous brew pubs are always hopping: **Rock Bottom Brewery** (✉ 1001 16th St., ☎ 303/534–7616) is the flavor-of-the-month, thanks to its rotating special brews and reasonably priced pub grub.

SYMPHONY, OPERA, AND DANCE

The **Colorado Symphony Orchestra** performs at Boettcher Concert Hall (✉ 13th and Curtis Sts., ☎ 303/986–8742). **Opera Colorado** (☎ 303/837–8888) has spring and fall seasons, often with internationally renowned artists, at the Denver Performing Arts Complex. The **Colorado Ballet** (☎ 303/237–8888) specializes in the classics; performances are staged at the Denver Performing Arts Complex (☞ *below*).

THEATER

The **Denver Performing Arts Complex** (✉ 14th and Curtis Sts., ☎ 303/893–3272) houses most of the city's large concert and theater venues. The **Denver Center Theater Company** (✉ 14th and Curtis Sts., ☎ 303/

893–4100) presents high-caliber repertory theater, including new works by promising playwrights, at the Bonfils Theatre Complex (part of the Denver Performing Arts Complex). **Robert Garner Attractions** (☎ 303/893–4100) brings Broadway road companies to Denver. **Eulipions, Inc. Cultural Center** (✉ 1770 Sherman Ave., ☎ 303/863–0019) presents plays by and with African-Americans. Other companies include **Changing Scene Theater** (✉ 1527½ Champa St., ☎ 303/893–5775), **Hunger Artists Ensemble Theater** (✉ Margery Reed Hall, University of Denver, S. University Blvd. and Evans Ave., ☎ 303/893–5438), and **El Centro Su Teatro** (✉ 4725 High St., ☎ 303/296–0219).

Outdoor Activities and Sports

Participant Sports

CYCLING AND JOGGING

Platte River Greenway is a 20-mi-long path for in-line skating, bicycling, and jogging that runs alongside Cherry Creek and the Platte River. Much of it runs through downtown Denver. Paved paths wind through **Matthews-Winters Park,** dotted with plaintive pioneer graves amid the sun-bleached grasses, thistle, and columbine. The **Denver Parks Department** (☎ 303/698–4900) has more suggestions for biking and jogging paths throughout the metropolitan area's 215 parks, including the popular Cherry Creek and Chatfield Lake State Recreation areas. With more than 400 mi of offroad paths in and around the city, cyclists can move easily between urban and rural settings. Popular routes are the **Cherry Creek Bike Path,** which connects Cherry Creek Shopping Center to Larimer Square downtown; the scenic **Highline Canal,** 70 mi of mostly dirt paths through the metro area running an almost completely level grade; the 12 mi of paved paths along the South Platte River heading into downtown; and the **South Platte Canyon,** a graded dirt road closed to traffic.

FITNESS

Denver has more fitness clubs per capita than any other American city. The state-of-the-art **Colorado Athletic Club** (✉ 1630 Welton St., ☎ 303/623–2100) is a 65,000-square-ft, full-service facility featuring more than 60 aerobics classes weekly. The club has cardiovascular and fitness equipment; weight training; racquetball, squash, and basketball courts; and a running track, among other features. Guest passes are available at many major hotels, and free day passes are available.

GOLF

Six courses are operated by the City of Denver and are open to the public: **City Park** (✉ E. 25th Ave. and York St., ☎ 303/295–4420), **Evergreen** (✉ 29614 Upper Bear Creek, Evergreen, ☎ 303/674–4128), **Kennedy** (✉ 10500 E. Hampden Ave., ☎ 303/751–0311), **Overland Park** (✉ S. Santa Fe Dr. and Jewell Ave., ☎ 303/698–4975), **Wellshire** (✉ 3333 S. Colorado Blvd., ☎ 303/692–5636), and **Willis Case** (✉ W. 50th Ave. and Vrain St., ☎ 303/458–4877).

Arrowhead Golf Club (✉ 10850 W. Sundown Trail, Littleton, ☎ 303/973–9614), 45 minutes from downtown in Roxborough State Park, was designed by Robert Trent Jones and is set impressively among red sandstone spires. **Plum Creek Golf and Country Club** (✉ 331 Players Club, Castle Rock, ☎ 303/688–2611) is an 18-hole Pete Dye–designed championship course.

HIKING

Just 15 mi west of Denver, **Red Rocks Park and Amphitheater** is a breathtaking, 70-million-year-old wonderland of vaulting oxblood-and-cinnamon-color sandstone spires. The outdoor music stage is set in a natural

8,000-seat amphitheater (with perfect acoustics, as only nature could have designed) that has awed the likes of Leopold Stokowski and the Beatles. Tickets to concerts are available through Ticketmaster (☞ Nightlife and the Arts, *above*), but hiking in this metro Denver park is free. ✉ *Off U.S. 285 or I–70.*

Lookout Mountain is reached by taking Lariat Look, a winding trail to Buffalo Bill's Grave. Two-thirds of the way up, find the Stapleton Trail that takes you up Lookout Mountain. ✉ *I–70 west to exit 256, and follow signs.*

Roxborough State Park has an easy 2 mi loop trail through rugged rock formations, offering beautiful vistas and a unique look at metro Denver and the plains. This trail is handicap accessible. ✉ *I–25 south to Santa Fe exit, take Santa Fe Blvd., south to Titan Rd. Turn right, and follow signs.*

Mt. Falcon Park looks down on Denver and across at Red Rocks. It's amazingly tranquil, laced with meadows and streams and shaded by conifers. The trails are very well marked. ✉ *Off Rte. 8, Morrison exit, or U.S. 285, Parmalee exit.*

TENNIS

The city has 28 parks with tennis courts. For information call the **Denver Parks Department** (☎ 303/964–2522).

WATER SPORTS

Both **Cherry Creek Marina** (✉ Cherry Creek State Park, Aurora, ☎ 303/779–6144) and **Chatfield Marina** (✉ Chatfield State Park, Littleton, ☎ 303/791–7547) rent sailboats, powerboats, and Windsurfers April–October.

Spectator Sports

The **Colorado Rockies,** Denver's National League baseball team, plays April–October in Coors Stadium (✉ 2001 Blake St., ☎ 303/292–0200 or 800/388–7625). The **Denver Nuggets** of the National Basketball Association and the **Colorado Avalanche** of the National Hockey League play in the new Pepsi Center (1000 Chopper Pl., ☎ 303/405–8555), a 19,000-seat arena The National Football League's **Denver Broncos** play September–December at Mile High Stadium (✉ 1900 Eliot St., exit 210B off I–25, ☎ 303/433–7466).

Arapahoe Park (✉ 26000 E. Quincy Ave., ☎ 303/690–2400) is the venue for betting on horse racing May through August. **Bandimere Speedway** (✉ 3051 S. Rooney Rd., Morrison, ☎ 303/697–6001) features NHRA Championship Drag Racing April–October.

Shopping

Denver may be the best place in the country for shopping for recreational gear and fashions of all stripes. Sporting goods stores hold legendary ski sales around Labor Day.

The **Cherry Creek** shopping district is 2 mi from downtown in a pleasant, predominantly residential neighborhood. On one side of First Avenue at Milwaukee Street is the Cherry Creek Shopping Mall, a granite-and-glass behemoth that houses some of the nation's top retailers, among them: Abercrombie & Fitch, Bally, Banana Republic, Burberry's, Laura Ashley, Lord & Taylor, Louis Vuitton, Neiman Marcus, Polo/Ralph Lauren, and Saks Fifth Avenue. Across from the Cherry Creek Shopping Mall is Cherry Creek North, an open-air development of tree-lined streets and shady plazas, with art galleries, specialty shops, and fashionable restaurants.

Historic **Larimer Square** (✉ 14th and Larimer Sts.), houses distinctive shops and restaurants. **Writer Square** (✉ 1512 Larimer St.) has Tiny Town—a doll-size village inhabited by Michael Garman's inimitable figurines—as well as shops and restaurants. **Tabor Center** (✉ 16th St. Mall) is a light-filled atrium whose 60 specialty shops include retailers such as The Sharper Image and Crabtree & Evelyn, and others that showcase uniquely Coloradan merchandise. It also contains the Bridge Market, which is filled with pushcarts selling everything from Ecuadorean sweaters to endearingly tacky souvenirs. The **Tivoli** (✉ 900 Auraria Pkwy., corner of 9th Ave. and Larimer St.) is a restored historic brewery, with its original pipes and bricks exposed, that houses several moderately priced specialty stores and restaurants.

The **Park Meadows** mall (✉ I–25, 5 mi south of Denver at County Line Rd.) was designed to resemble a ski resort, with a 120-ft-high logbeam ceiling anchored by two massive stone fireplaces. In addition to Colorado's first Nordstrom, the center includes more than 100 specialty shops. On snowy days, "ambassadors" scrape your windshield while free hot chocolate is served inside.

Between Denver and Colorado Springs, **Castle Rock Factory Shops** (✉ Exit 184 off I–25) offers 25%–75% savings on everything from appliances to apparel at its more than 50 outlets.

ANTIQUES

South Broadway between First Avenue and Evans Street, as well as the side streets off this main drag, is chockablock with dusty antiques stores, where patient browsing could net some amazing bargains. The **Antique Mall of Lakewood** (✉ 9635 W. Colfax Ave.) features more than 80 dealer showrooms.

BOOKS

The Tattered Cover (✉ 1st Ave. at Milwaukee St., ☎ 303/322–7727; 1628 16th St., ☎ 303/436–1070) is a must for all bibliophiles. It may be the best bookstore in the United States, not only for the near-endless selection of volumes (more than 400,000 on four stories at the Cherry Creek location and 300,000 in LoDo) and helpful, knowledgeable staff, but also for the incomparably refined atmosphere: overstuffed armchairs, reading nooks, and afternoon readings and lectures.

CRAFT AND ART GALLERIES

LoDo has the trendiest galleries, many in splendidly and stylishly restored Victorian warehouses.

Baobab Tree (✉ 1518 Wazee St., ☎ 303/595–0965) sells South African imports, including astonishing masks. Cherry Creek has its share of chic galleries, including **Pismo** (✉ 235 Filmore St., ☎ 303/333–2879), which showcases exquisite handblown-glass art.

For Native American arts and crafts, head for **Native American Trading Company** (✉ 1301 Bannock St., ☎ 303/534–0771), which has an outstanding collection of weavings, pottery, jewelry, and regional paintings. **David Cook/Fine American Art** (✉ 1637 Wazee St., ☎ 303/623–8181) specializes in historic Native American art and regional paintings, particularly Santa Fe modernists. The **Mudhead Gallery** (✉ 555 17th St., across from the Hyatt, ☎ 303/293–0007; and ✉ 321 17th St., in the Brown Palace, ☎ 303/293–9977) sells museum-quality Southwestern art, with an especially fine selection of Santa Clara and San Ildefonso pottery, and Hopi kachinas. **Old Santa Fe Pottery**'s (✉ 2485 S. Santa Fe Dr., ☎ 303/871–9434) 20 rooms are crammed with Mexican masks, pottery, rustic Mexican furniture—even a salsa room.

DEPARTMENT STORES

The nine **Foley's** department stores throughout metropolitan Denver offer good values; Cherry Creek is their main store (✉ 15 S. Steele St., ☎ 303/333–8555).

SPORTING GOODS

Gart Brothers Sports Castle (✉ 1000 Broadway, ☎ 303/861–1122) is a huge, multistory shrine to Colorado's love of the outdoors. Entire floors are given over to a single sport at this and the many other branches throughout Denver.

WESTERN PARAPHERNALIA

Cry Baby Ranch (✉ 1428 Larimer St., ☎ 303/623–3979) has a rambunctious assortment of '40s and '50s cowboy kitsch. **Denver Buffalo Company Trading Post** (✉ 1109 Lincoln St., ☎ 303/832–0884) has Western duds and high-quality souvenirs, not to mention a restaurant that specializes in buffalo—low in fat and cholesterol. There's also a gourmet deli serving BuffDogs (hot dogs made with buffalo meat), corned buffalo, and other such specialties.

Side Trips West of Denver

Golden

Golden, 15 mi west of Denver via I–70 or U.S. 6 (West 6th Avenue), was once the territorial capital of Colorado. City residents have smarted ever since losing that distinction to Denver by "dubious" vote in 1867, but in 1994, then-Governor Roy Romer restored "ceremonial" territorial-capital status to Golden. Today, the city is one of Colorado's fastest-growing, boosted by the high-tech industry as well as longtime employers Coors Brewery and Colorado School of Mines.

A GOOD TOUR

Start at the **Coors Brewery** and take the free tour and tasting. Then walk west on **12th Street** to the Astor House and the National Historic District. Go south on Arapahoe one block to the Armory, and then continue on Arapahoe into the **Colorado School of Mines.** From here you'll need a car; take 10th Street east out of town about 2 mi to the **Colorado Railroad Museum.** If there are children in the group, get on I–70 West to Colfax Avenue West (U.S. 40) to **Heritage Square.** Otherwise, get off on 6th Avenue West (U.S. 6) to 19th Street to the **Buffalo Bill Grave and Museum.** (From Heritage Square, take Heritage Road [Route 93] north to U.S. 6 west.)

Timing: Golden is a 25-minute drive from Denver. The Coors Brewery tour takes about an hour. The brewery is closed Sunday. You can see downtown and the Colorado School of Mines in another hour or two. To drive to and visit the Colorado Railroad Museum and Buffalo Bill Grave and museum, you'll need another hour or two. The Buffalo Bill Grave is closed Monday in winter. Heritage Square has rides daily in summer, weekends in spring and fall, and most attractions except shops are closed in winter.

SIGHTS TO SEE

Buffalo Bill Grave and Museum. Contrary to popular belief, Bill Cody—Pony Express rider, cavalry scout, and tireless promoter of the West—never expressed a burning desire to be buried here: The *Denver Post* bought the corpse from Bill's sister, and bribed her to concoct a teary story about his dying wish. Apparently, rival towns were so outraged that the National Guard had to be called in to protect the grave from robbers. The drive up Lookout Mountain to the burial site offers a sensational panoramic view of Denver that alone is worth the price of admission. Adjacent to the grave is a small museum with the usual art and artifacts as well as a run-of-the-mill souvenir shop. ✉ *Rte. 5 off I–70 Exit 256, or 19th Ave. out of Golden,* ☎ *303/526–0747.* 🎫 *$3.* ⏲ *May–Oct., daily 9–5; Nov.–Apr., Tues.–Sun. 9–4.*

Colorado Railroad Museum. Just outside Golden is this must-visit for any choo-choo lover. More than 50 vintage locomotives and cars are displayed outside. Inside the replica-1880 masonry depot are historical photos and puffing Billy (nickname for steam trains) memorabilia, along with an astounding model train set that steams through a miniature, scale version of Golden. ✉ *17155 W. 44th Ave.,* ☎ *303/279–4591.* 🎫 *$4.* ⏲ *Daily 9–5.*

Colorado School of Mines. The nation's largest and foremost school of mineral engineering has a lovely campus containing an outstanding geology museum displaying minerals, ore, and gemstones from around the world. Also on campus is the prominent **National Earthquake Center** (✉ 1711 Illinois St., ☎ 303/273–8500; tours by appointment weekdays 9–11 and 1–3), which is responsible for recording continental drift and seismic activity. Free tours are given by appointment and availability Tuesday through Thursday ✉ *16th and Maple Sts.,* ☎ *303/273–3823.* 🎫 *Free.* ⏲ *Mon.–Sat. 9–4, Sun. 1–4; closed Sun. in summer.*

Coors Brewery. Thousands of beer lovers make the pilgrimage to this venerable brewery each year. One of the world's largest, it was founded in 1873 by Adolph Coors, a 21-year-old German stowaway. The free tour lasts a half hour and explains not only the brewing process, but also how "Rocky Mountain mineral water" (or "Colorado Kool-Aid") is packaged and distributed locally. Informal tastings are held at the end of the tour for those 21 and over; souvenirs are available at the gift shop. ✉ *13th and Ford Sts.,* ☎ *303/277–2337.* 🎫 *Free.* ⏲ *Mon.–Sat. 10–4. Children under 18 must be accompanied by an adult.*

Heritage Square. This re-creation of an 1880s frontier town has an opera house, a narrow-gauge railway train ride, a Ferris wheel, a water slide, specialty shops, and a music hall that stages original comedies and musicals as well as traditional melodramas. A vaudeville-style review ends each evening's entertainment. ✉ *U.S. 40 and Rte. 93,* ☎ *303/279–2789.* 🎫 *Admission varies per ride; entrance to the park is free.* ⏲ *Shops open Mon.–Sat. 10–6, Sun. noon–6. Rides open weekends Mar.–May and Sept.–Oct.; daily June–Sept.*

12th Street. This National Historic District has a row of handsome 1860s brick buildings. Among the monuments is the **Astor House** (✉ corner of 12th and Arapahoe Sts., ☎ 303/278–3557), a museum with period furnishings, which is open Tuesday–Saturday 10–3, with a $3 admission fee. Colorado's first **National Guard Armory** (✉ corner of 13th and Arapahoe Sts.) was built in 1913 and is the largest cobblestone building in America.

Central City and Black Hawk

18 mi from Golden via U.S. 6 west and Rte. 119 north.

When limited-stakes gambling was introduced in 1991 to the beautifully preserved old mining towns of Central City and Black Hawk, howls of protest were drowned out by cheers from struggling townspeople. Fortunately, strict zoning laws were legislated to protect the towns' architectural integrity, and by and large the laws have been successful. However, the general atmosphere may be more raucous today than it was in its heyday in the 1860s, thanks to the steady stream of tour buses and loudly jingling coffers. Gaming here is restricted to blackjack, poker, and slots, and the maximum bet is $5.

There are nearly 40 casinos in Black Hawk and Central City. All are in historic buildings—from jails to mansions—and their plush interiors have been lavishly decorated to re-create the Old West era—a period when this town was known as the "Richest Square Mile on Earth." They all serve meals and offer some entertainment. The most popular are Bullwhackers and Harrah's Glory Hole; the Teller House (☞ Sights to See, *below*) is the most historic.

A GOOD TOUR

Both towns can be explored on foot. Starting in Central City, park in one of the pay parking lots in town and begin at the west end of town, at the **Thomas House Museum.** Walk a block down Eureka Street to the **Central City Opera House** and **Teller House.** Take a detour on Main Street to browse the shops and casinos, and then head back down Eureka Street. Just before the Central Palace casino, you'll see a set of steep stairs; take them directly up to the **Gilpin County Historical Society Museum.** Go back down the stairs and walk the downhill mile to Black Hawk, to the **Lace House** at the east end of Main Street. If you're hungry, stop along the way for a bite at the Black Forest Inn (☞ Dining, *below*). If you don't feel like walking back uphill to Central City, catch a free shuttle in front of the Bull Durham or Eureka casinos.

Timing: Both towns are about a 45-minute drive from Denver. Bus transportation is also available from Denver and Golden through most of the casinos and the Opera House. You can cover Central City and Black Hawk's main attractions in a few hours. If you're the gaming type, set aside extra time to try your luck. Although the casinos are open year-round, the museums are open only in the summer.

SIGHTS TO SEE

Central City Opera House. Opera has been staged here almost every year since opening night in 1878. Lillian Gish has acted, Beverly Sills has sung, and many other greats have performed in the Opera House. Because there's no central heating, performances are held in summer only. ✉ *200 Eureka St., Central City,* ☎ *303/292–6700 (Denver box office).*

Gilpin County Historical Society Museum. Photos and reproductions, as well as vintage pieces from different periods of Gilpin County history, paint a richly detailed portrait of life in a typical rowdy mining community. ✉ *228 E. High St., Central City,* ☎ *303/582–5283.* 🎫 *$4.* ⏲ *June–Sept., daily 11–4; Oct.–May, by appt. only.*

Lace House. The most notable attraction in Black Hawk is this superb example of Carpenter Gothic architecture, with signature lacy gingerbread trim, Gothic windows, and hand-sawn scalloped pillars. ✉ *161 Main St., Black Hawk,* ☎ *303/582–5221.* 🎫 *Free.* ⏲ *June–Sept., daily 10–4.*

Teller House Casino, Restaurant, and Museum. This edifice was once one of the West's ritziest hotels. Upstairs is the opulent room that was occupied by President Grant and, later, by Mae West. Downstairs, the floor of the famous Face Bar is adorned with the portrait of a mystery woman named Madeline, painted in 1936 by Herndon Davis. Some say it was created as a lark, others bet it was done for the price of a drink. ✉ *120 Eureka St., Central City,* ☎ *303/440–8446.*

Thomas House Museum. This 1874 house is an example of Victorian mountain elegance. It depicts the life of a middle-class turn-of-the-20th-century family, through family photos and heirlooms such as period quilts and feather hats. ✉ *209 Eureka St., Central City,* ☎ *303/582–5283.* 🎫 *$4.* ⏲ *June–Sept., daily 11–4; Oct.–May, by appt. only.*

DINING

Virtually every casino has a restaurant with the usual mediocre $4.99 daily specials and all-you-can-eat buffets. Nonetheless, there is at least one independent restaurant.

$$ ✕ **Black Forest Inn.** This is an affectionate re-creation of a Bavarian hunting lodge, replete with antlers, tapestries, and cuckoo clocks. Hearty specialties range from fine schnitzel to succulent wild game. Afterward, you can repair to Otto's casino. ✉ *260 Gregory St., Black Hawk,* ☎ *303/279–2333. AE, MC, V; personal checks accepted.*

Denver A to Z

Arriving and Departing

BY BUS

Greyhound Lines (✉ 1055 19th St., ☎ 800/231–2222) serves Denver.

BY CAR

Reaching Denver by car is fairly easy, except during rush hour when the interstates (and downtown) get congested. Interstate Highways 70 and 25 intersect near downtown; an entrance to I–70 is just outside the airport.

BY PLANE

Denver International Airport (☎ 800/247–2336), or DIA, opened its gates in early 1995, replacing Stapleton. It is served by most major domestic carriers and many international ones, including Air Canada, American, America West, Continental, Delta, Frontier, Midway, Mesa, Northwest, Sun Country, TWA, United, and USAir.

Between the Airport and Downtown: Super Shuttle (☎ 303/342–5450), serves downtown and makes door-to-door trips. The region's public bus service, **Regional Transportation District** (RTD, ☎ 303/299–6000 for route and schedule information; 303/299–6700 for other inquiries) runs SkyRide to and from DIA; the trip takes 55 minutes, and the fare is $6. There is a transportation center in the airport just outside baggage claim.

Rental car companies include Advantage, Alamo, Avis, Budget, Dollar, Enterprise, Hertz, and National. All have airport and downtown representatives. Take Peña Boulevard (which later becomes Airport Boulevard) out of the airport to Colfax Avenue west.

A taxi ride costs $45–$50 to downtown from DIA. **Metro Taxi** (☎ 303/333–3333), **Yellow Cab** (☎ 303/777–7777), or **Zone Cab** (☎ 303/444–8888). Rates for **limousine service** average $59 and up, depending on the type of car; try Admiral Limousines (☎ 303/296–2003 or 800/828–8680) or Denver Limousine Services (☎ 303/766–0400 or 800/766–2090).

BY TRAIN

Union Station (✉ 17th Ave. at Wynkoop St., downtown, ☎ 303/534–2812) has Amtrak service.

Getting Around

In downtown Denver, free shuttle-bus service operates about every 10 minutes until 11 PM, running the length of the 16th Street Mall (which bisects downtown) and stopping at two-block intervals. If you plan to spend much time outside downtown, a car is advised, although Denver has one of the best city bus systems in the country (☞ RTD, *above*) and taxis are available. Even downtown, parking spots are usually easy to find; try to avoid driving in the area during rush hour, when traffic gets heavy.

BY BUS OR TRAIN

The region's public bus service, **RTD** (☞ By Plane, *above*) is comprehensive, with routes throughout the metropolitan area. The service also links Denver to outlying towns such as Boulder, Longmont, and Nederland. You can buy bus tokens at grocery stores or pay with exact change on the bus. Fares vary according to time and zone. Within the city limits, buses cost $1.25 during peak hours (6 AM–9 AM, 4 PM–6 PM), 75¢ at other times. You can also buy a **Cultural Connection Trolley** (☎ 303/299–6000) ticket for $3 at several convenient outlets throughout downtown, from the trolley driver, or from most hotel concierges. The trolley operates daily, every half hour 9–6, linking 18 prime attractions from the Denver Performing Arts Complex downtown to the Denver Natural History Museum in City Park. Tickets are good for the entire day. RTD's **Light Rail** service (☎ 303/299–6000) began in October 1994. The original 5⅓ mi track links southwest and northeast Denver to downtown. Routes are continually expanding; the fare is $1.25.

BY CAR

Broadway runs north–south through Denver. Speer Boulevard runs alongside Cherry Creek from northwest to southeast through downtown; numbered streets run parallel to Speer. Colfax Avenue (U.S. 287) runs east–west through downtown; numbered avenues run parallel to Colfax. (It gets confusing—numbered streets intersect numbered avenues at a right angle at Broadway. When you're looking for an address, make sure you know whether it's a street or avenue. To make it more confusing, most numbered streets are one-way.) Other main thoroughfares include Colorado Boulevard (north–south) and Alameda Avenue (east–west). Parking is relatively easy in Denver: metered street parking and many pay lots are available downtown.

BY TAXI

Cabs are available by phone and at the airport and can generally be hailed outside major hotels, for $1.40 minimum, $1.40 per mile. **Metro Taxi** (☎ 303/333–3333). **Yellow Cab** (☎ 303/777–7777).

Contacts and Resources

DOCTORS AND DENTISTS

Clinics and Hospitals: Concentra Medical Centers (✉ 1860 Larimer St., Suite 100, ☎ 303/296–2273) is a full medical clinic. **Exempla Medical Referral** (☎ 303/425–2929) is a free referral service. **Rose Medical Center** (✉ 4567 E. 9th Ave., ☎ 303/320–2121) refers patients to doctors from 8–5:30 and is open 24 hours for emergencies. **St. Joseph Hospital** (✉ 1835 Franklin St., ☎ 303/837–7111) is open 24 hours.

Dentists: Dental Referral Service (☎ 800/428–8773) and **Affordable Dentist USA** (☎ 888/657–6453) offer dental referrals.

GUIDED TOURS

Gray Line Tour (☎ 303/289–2841) of Denver offers a two-hour city tour, a Denver mountain parks tour, and a mountain casino tour. Tours range from $17 to $20 per person.

Lower Downtown District, Inc. (☎ 303/628–5428) offers guided tours of historic Denver. Self-guided walking-tour brochures are available from the Denver Metro Convention and Visitors Bureau (☞ Visitor Information, *below*).

LATE-NIGHT PHARMACIES

Walgreens (✉ 2000 E. Colfax Ave., ☎ 303/331–0917) is open daily, 24 hours. **King Soopers** (✉ 3100 S. Sheridan Blvd., ☎ 303/937–4404) is also open round the clock.

VISITOR INFORMATION

The **Denver Metro Convention and Visitors Bureau** (✉ 225 W. Colfax Ave., Denver 80202, ☎ 303/892–1112 or 800/393–8559), open weekdays 8–5 and Saturday 9–1, is across from the City and County Building, and provides information and free maps, magazines, and brochures.

NORTH CENTRAL COLORADO

North Central Colorado is an appealing blend of Old West and New Age. More a ranching than a mining area, it's strewn with rich evocations of pioneer life, as well as turn-of-the-20th-century resort towns such as Estes Park and Grand Lake. Yet the region is anchored by Boulder, one of the country's most progressive cities and a town virtually synonymous (some might say obsessed) with environmental concern and physical fitness. As the local joke goes, even the dogs jog.

Boulder residents take full advantage of the town's glorious natural setting, nestled against the peaks of the Front Range, indulging in everything from rock climbing to mountain biking. A short drive south brings them to the ski areas along I–70. To the west and north, the Roosevelt and Arapaho national forests and the Great Lakes of Colorado provide a host of recreational opportunities from hiking to fishing to cross-country skiing and snowmobiling. Estes Park is the gateway to America's alpine wonderland—Rocky Mountain National Park, which spans three ecosystems that 900 species of plants, 250 species of birds, and 25 species of mammals—including elk, deer, moose, bobcats, and even black bears—call home.

Boulder

17 *25 mi northwest from Denver via U.S. 36.*

No place in Colorado better epitomizes the state's outdoor mania than Boulder. There are nearly as many bikes as cars in this uncommonly beautiful and beautifully uncommon city embroidered with 25,000 acres of parks and greenbelts laced with jogging tracks and bike trails. You're also more likely to see ponytails than crew cuts: Boulder is a college town with an arty, liberal reputation. Physically fit and environmentally hip, it's a city of cyclists and recyclers who, when they're not out enjoying their natural surroundings, enjoy nothing more than sitting at a sidewalk café, watching the rest of the world jog by.

Boulder's heartbeat is the **Pearl Street Mall,** an eye-catching array of chic shops and trendy restaurants where all of Boulder hangs out. A few blocks away is Mapleton Hill, a historic district of great charm.

Take Broadway north to the **University of Colorado** (☎ 303/492–1411) campus, where spacious lawns separate a handsome collection of stone buildings with red tile roofs. Tours are available weekday afternoons. A favorite nearby student hangout is the bohemian neighborhood called The Hill (around 13th and College streets, west of the campus), home to lots of coffeehouses and hip boutiques, and always happening day or night.

The prettiest views of town can be had by following Baseline Drive (off Broadway) up to **Chatauqua Park,** site of the Colorado Music Festival, and a favorite oasis of locals on weekends. Continue farther up Flagstaff Mountain to Panorama Point and Boulder Mountain Park, where people jog, bike, and climb. The admirable parks system also includes the trademark red sandstone **Flatirons.** These massive structures, so named for their flat rock faces, are popular among rock climbers and hikers. They can be seen from almost every vantage point in town.

North Central Colorado

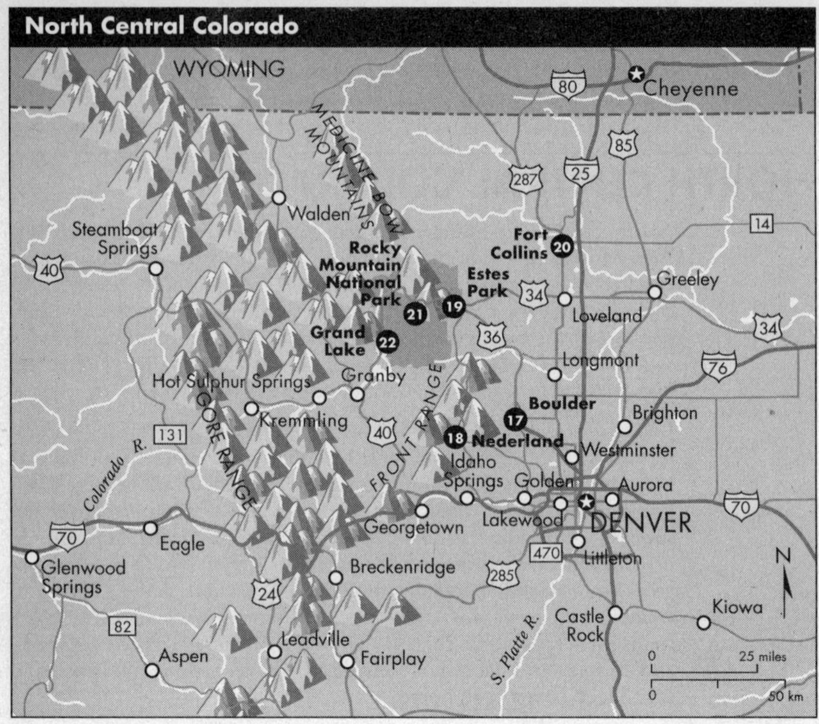

On the outskirts of the city there are three free attractions worth visiting. The first is the **Celestial Seasonings Plant,** offering free tours of this well-known herbal tea company's processing and manufacturing facility. An unmistakable aroma of tea permeates the parking lot. Inside you can see the product ingredients in their raw form (the Mint Room is isolated due to its potent scent) and how they're blended. The tour ends up in the gift shop for a tea-tasting. ✉ *4600 Sleepytime Dr.,* ☎ *303/581–1202.* ⏲ *Tours Mon.–Sat. 10–3.*

Also aromatic are the free tours of the **Rockies Brewing Company** (✉ 2880 Wilderness Pl., ☎ 303/444–8448). These run Monday–Saturday, at 2 PM, and culminate in a tasting.

The last free attraction is the **Leanin' Tree Museum of Western Art**—brought to you by the folks who make wildly popular and humorous western-theme greeting cards—whose superlative collection ranges from traditionalists in the Remington and Bierstadt manner to stylistic innovators of the Western genre. One room is devoted to the paintings of the original greeting-card genius, Lloyd Mitchell. ✉ *6055 Longbow Dr.,* ☎ *303/530–1442.* ⏲ *Weekdays 8–4:30, Sat. 10–4.*

Dining and Lodging

Boulder has almost as impressive a range of ethnic eateries as the much-larger Denver. Prices vary, but most are reasonable, thanks to a large student population that can't afford very expensive meals.

$$$$ ★ ✕ **Flagstaff House.** This refined restaurant atop Flagstaff Mountain is one of Colorado's finest. Sit on the enclosed patio and drink in the sublime views of Boulder while enjoying a selection from the remarkably comprehensive wine list. Chef Mark Monette is noted for his exquisite combinations of ingredients and fanciful, playful presentations. The menu changes daily, but sample inspirations might include lobster

ravioli and shrimp in shiitake broth; potato roll of smoked rabbit and duck with sautéed foie gras; mesquite-smoked alligator and rattlesnake; and elk dumplings with ginger and sweet onion. ✉ *Flagstaff Rd.,* ☎ *303/442–4640. Reservations essential. AE, DC, MC, V.*

$$$ ✕ **Antica Roma.** This trattoria is a virtual stage set for *Marriage of Figaro,* replete with a spotlit balcony, tinkling fountain, exposed brick, painted beams, and ironwork lamps. Breads and appetizers, such as *brescaola* (smoked meats) and *bruschetta* (thick slabs of coarse bread slathered with tomatoes, garlic, olive oil, and cheese), are sensational. Unfortunately, pastas are heavy and undistinguished, just a cut above frozen entrées; stick to such simple dishes as grilled swordfish or salmon, and drink in the ambience. ✉ *1308 Pearl St.,* ☎ *303/442–0378. AE, D, DC, MC, V.*

$$$ ★ ✕ **Redfish New Orleans Brewhouse.** In a warehouse space with exposed brick walls, colorful halogen lamps, an open kitchen, and brew tanks is this very trendy spot—kind of hip-hop meets Cajun. On warm nights, the retractable walls roll back to create a sidewalk café overlooking the Pearl Street Mall. It's real New Orleans–style food: gumbo, crawfish-stuffed grilled quail, and tuna seared with French spices and topped with Creole hollandaise. The Brewhouse's own ales wash it all down. While you wait for your table, you can shoot pool in the bar. ✉ *2027 13th St.,* ☎ *303/440–5858. AE, MC, V. No lunch Mon.–Sat.*

$$$ ✕ **Red Lion Inn.** Up in Boulder Canyon sits this beautiful inn, a local institution for natives and travelers. Ask to be seated in the original dining room—with its fireplace, antlers, Austrian murals, red tablecloths, and white napery—for the feeling of being in the Alps. The stone walls and potbellied stove in the bar make it a cozy place to wait for a table. The Red Lion is revered for its excellent game: Start with rattlesnake cakes or wild game sausage, then try the elk or caribou steak. Or order a satisfying old-fashioned specialty, such as steak Diane or changing specials featuring crab legs, pheasant, and buffalo. ✉ *Boulder Canyon Dr.,* ☎ *303/442–9368. Reservations essential. AE, D, MC, V. No lunch.*

$$$ ★ ✕ **Zolo Grill.** David Query, who once served Malcolm Forbes as his personal chef, now serves happy patrons of Zolo Grill superlative Southwestern cuisine. Its huge picture windows overlook one of Boulder's most active shopping centers and the Flatirons beyond. Blond wood furnishings, striking abstract art, and a high-tech open kitchen complete the urbane decor. The inventive menu offers tortilla-crusted ahi tuna served with chipotle beurre blanc. The margaritas, which may be sipped on the open patio, are sassy, and there's a short but fairly priced wine list (about half the wines are available by the glass). The very cool T-shirts are for sale. ✉ *2525 Arapahoe Blvd.,* ☎ *303/449–0444. AE, DC, MC, V.*

$$–$$$ ★ ✕ **Sushi Zanmai.** The restaurant section is a cool, sleek place to enjoy delectable seafood and very good hibachi items. But the action's really at the zany sushi bar, where the chefs periodically burst into song: "If you knew Sushi" is a popular request. There's always karaoke here, although the official night is Saturday. ✉ *1221 Spruce St.,* ☎ *303/440–0733. AE, MC, V. No lunch weekends.*

$$ ✕ **Bangkok Cuisine.** This very pretty restaurant looks more like a French bistro than a typical Thai place, with cut glass lamps, brass fixtures, and mauve tablecloths. In addition to expertly prepared staples such as satay, lemongrass soup, pad Thai (Thai noodles), and the inimitable curries, try less familiar items such as Gung Pao—juicy shrimp charbroiled with red chili paste. ✉ *2017 13th St.,* ☎ *303/440–4830. AE, D, MC, V.*

$$ ✕ **Dagabi Cucina.** It's well worth the quest to find this jewel of a stylish, contemporary dining spot in the unlikely setting of an out-of-the-way strip mall. Both the hand-tailored food and very personal service are exquisite. Try the homemade black ravioli stuffed with salmon and served in a tomato cream sauce, or the chicken breast in artichoke heart cream sauce. Whether you're looking for candlelight and romance or simply a nice place to meet a friend, you'll find it here. ✉ *3970 N. Broadway,* ☎ *303/786–9004. AE, DC, MC, V.*

$$ ★ ✕ **Gold Hill Inn.** This humble log cabin 10 mi west of Boulder hardly looks like a bastion of haute cuisine, but the six-course, $24 prix-fixe dinner is something to rave about. Sample entrées may be paella or lamb venison marinated for four days in buttermilk, juniper berries, and cloves. The inn also hosts occasional "murder mystery" nights using professional actors. ✉ *Sunshine Canyon, 10 mi from Boulder,* ☎ *303/443–6461. No credit cards.* ⏲ *Open May–Oct. Closed Tues. No lunch.*

$$ ✕ **Mataam Fez.** You eat with your hands at this lavish Moroccan restaurant that looks as if it came straight from *The Arabian Nights.* The prix-fixe dinner ($25) includes five courses, with such fragrant dishes as lamb with honey and almonds and hare paprika couscous. There are branches in Denver, Colorado Springs, and Vail, but this is the original. ✉ *2226 Pearl St.,* ☎ *303/440–4167. AE, D, DC, MC, V. No lunch.*

$$ ✕ **Mediterranean Café.** After work, when all of Boulder shows up to enjoy tapas, "The Med" becomes a real scene (you may feel quite closed in, despite the restaurant's light and airy design). The decor is Portofino meets Santa Fe, with abstract art, terra-cotta floors, and brightly colored tile. The open kitchen turns out daily specials such as barbecued mahi-mahi and horseradish-crusted tuna—dishes complemented by an extensive, well-priced wine list. Come here for a dose of local attitude or stop by just to gaze at all the pretty people. During happy hour from 4 to 6:30, various tapas are just a buck or two. ✉ *1002 Walnut St.,* ☎ *303/444–5335. AE, DC, MC, V. No lunch Sun.*

$$–$$$$ 🏨 **Earl House Historic Inn.** You'll find this 1882 stone Gothic Revival mansion only four blocks from the Pearl Street Mall. Each room has a whirlpool tub or steam shower. Enjoy homemade baked goods at breakfast and afternoon tea, served on marble-top tables near the fireplace. The luxury here is in the details, so much that you may find it difficult to leave your room to sightsee. ✉ *2429 Broadway, 80304,* ☎ *303/938–1400. 6 rooms. AE, D, DC, MC, V.*

$$$ ★ 🏨 **Hotel Boulderado.** This elegant 1909 beauty has been restored to its original splendor. Spend some time in the gracious lobby, with its soaring stained-glass ceiling, or on the mezzanine, with romantic nooks galore—especially suitable for enjoying a quiet drink—or head to the always-hopping Catacombs Blues Bar. When choosing accommodations, opt for the old building, with spacious rooms filled with period antiques and reproductions, over the new wing, which is plush and comfortable but has less character. The gourmet restaurant, Q's, features the stylish New American cuisine of John Platt. Guests have access to the nearby health club, Pulse. ✉ *2115 13th St., 80302,* ☎ *303/442–4344 or 800/433–4344,* FAX *303/442–4378. 160 rooms. 3 restaurants, 2 bars, in-room data ports, business services. AE, D, DC, MC, V.*

$$–$$$ ★ 🏨 **Victoria B&B.** This ideally situated, restored 1870s Victorian offers the most exquisite accommodations in the area. Large rooms, each named after a present or former owner and all with private bath, run toward the English country-home look. Brass beds, down comforters, terrycloth robes, lace curtains, rocking chairs, dried flowers, and period antiques complete the picture. In addition to the complimentary Continental breakfast, baked goods (try the scones or gingersnaps) and tea are served every afternoon in a sunny parlor scented with potpourri. ✉ *1305 Pine St., 80302,* ☎ *303/938–1300. 7 rooms. AE, MC, V.*

$$ 🏨 **Briar Rose B&B.** Innkeeper Margaret Weisenbach makes guests feel completely at home at this appealing bed-and-breakfast. There are five

rooms in the sturdy, 1890s brick main house and four in the adjacent carriage house. The individually decorated rooms abound in froufrou, such as floral carpeting and flowers stenciled above the headboards. All rooms have down comforters and private baths; the most expensive have wood-burning fireplaces. ✉ *2151 Arapahoe Ave., 80302,* ☎ *303/442–3007. 9 rooms. AE, DC, MC, V.*

$$ **Coburn House.** Designer-architect Scott Coburn wanted to create a tasteful lodging offering the services of a hotel and the intimacy of a B&B, and he has succeeded. The grand foyer, with a fieldstone fireplace and a rotating gallery of modern art leads into a coffee bar with saddle stools. Decor, mostly in beige and green, is Scandinavia meets the Old West: hand-carved wood and iron beds, down comforters and pine armoires. A "green" hotel, the Coburn uses low-flush toilets, reduced-flow showerheads, and 100% cotton linens. Enjoy the "Boulder Breakfast" of homemade breads, fruit, and granola. ✉ *2040 16th St., 80302,* ☎ *303/545–5200 or 800/585–5811,* FAX *303/440–6740. 12 rooms. AE, MC, V.*

$$ **Inn on Mapleton Hill.** Cottonwoods shade the sidewalk of this impressive redbrick Victorian with jade trim. The sunny, individually decorated guest rooms are just as elegant, with polished hardwood or brass beds, rocking chairs or armoires, throw rugs, lace curtains, hand-stenciled walls, and a profusion of dried flowers; two also have marble gas-burning fireplaces. The location, on a quiet residential street a few blocks from the Pearl Street Mall, is ideal. A full breakfast is included. ✉ *1001 Spruce St., 80302,* ☎ *303/449–6528. 7 rooms. AE, MC, V.*

$$ **Pearl Street Inn.** The decor is reserved and refined at this B&B, favoring subtle shades of purple, plush carpeting, wildlife prints and antiques, and brass or mahogany four-poster beds. The dining alcove and outdoor patio are fine places to enjoy the complimentary breakfasts. ✉ *1820 Pearl St., 80302,* ☎ *303/444–5584 or 888/810–1302. 7 rooms. AE, MC, V.*

$$ ★ **Regal Harvest House.** This relatively large property has an unusual semicircular design, set amid immaculate gardens dotted with splashing fountains. Spacious rooms are done up in light woods and pastel colors, and some have full baths with a mountain view. In keeping with Boulder's environmental concerns, 32 rooms have been designated as ecologically sound, with all trash recycled and water recirculated and treated. ✉ *1345 28th St., 80302,* ☎ *303/443–3850 or 800/545–6285,* FAX *303/443–1480. 270 rooms. Restaurant, 2 bars, indoor-outdoor pool, hot tub, 15 tennis courts, basketball, exercise room, volleyball, playground, laundry service, meeting rooms, car rental. AE, D, DC, MC, V.*

$ ★ **Foot of the Mountain.** This series of connecting wood cabins is conveniently located across from the city park where the bike path originates. It seems far from Boulder's bustle, yet it's only a few minutes' walk from downtown. Each cozy cabin has either a mountain or stream view and is outfitted with TV, phone, heater, minirefrigerator, and large bath—but no air conditioning. ✉ *200 Arapahoe Ave., 80302,* ☎ *303/442–5688. 18 rooms. AE, D, MC, V.*

Nightlife and the Arts

There are concerts throughout the summer in Boulder's peaceful **Chatauqua Community Hall** (✉ 900 Baseline Rd., ☎ 303/442–3282) including the superb **Colorado Music Festival** (☎ 303/449–1397). **The Boulder Theater** (✉ 2032 14th St., ☎ 303/786–7030) is a venue for top touring bands. **The Boulder Philharmonic** (✉ University of Colorado, Macky Auditorium and Old Main Theatre, ☎ 303/449–1343) presents its own concert season, as well as chamber music concerts, the Boulder Ballet Ensemble, and special performances by visiting divas such as Kathleen Battle.

The **Dept. of Theater and Dance** at the University of Colorado (☎ 303/492–7355) offers excellent student productions throughout the year. The **Colorado Shakespeare Festival** (☎ 303/492–0554) is held in the Mary Rippon outdoor theater on campus each summer. The **Colorado Dance Festival** (☎ 303/442–7666) hits town in June.

BARS AND LOUNGES

The Foundry (✉ 1109 Walnut St., ☎ 303/447–1803) is where the hip hang out—in front is an espresso bar, in back is a cigar room, and in between is the main bar with pool tables and a mezzanine overlooking all the action. The **West End Tavern** (✉ 926 Pearl St., ☎ 303/444–3535), with its rooftop deck, and **Alley Catz** (✉ 1207 Pearl St., ☎ 303/444–3100) are popular after-work hangouts, both with fine pub grub. **Mediterranean Café** (☞ Dining and Lodging, *above*) is the place to see and be seen. The **microbreweries, Rockies Brewing** (✉ 2880 Wilderness Pl., ☎ 303/444–8448), **Walnut Brewery** (✉ 1123 Walnut St., ☎ 303/447–1345), and **Oasis Brewery** (✉ 1095 Canyon Blvd., ☎ 303/449–0363), are also popular. The **Corner Bar** (☎ 303/442–4344) in the Hotel Boulderado (☞ Dining and Lodging, *above*) is a contemporary American pub with outdoor seating and occasional live music. It's a popular place for a business lunch or an after-work cocktail.

DINNER SHOWS

Boulder Dinner Theater (✉ 5501 Arapahoe Ave., ☎ 303/449–6000) presents Broadway-style productions.

MUSIC AND DANCE CLUBS

The **Catacombs Blues Bar** (✉ Hotel Boulderado, ☞ Dining and Lodging, *above*, ☎ 303/443–0486) presents local and national talent. Tulagi (✉ 1129 13th St., ☎ 303/442–1369), Club 156 (✉ University of Colorado campus, ☎ 303/492–8888), and The Sink (✉ 1165 13th St., ☎ 303/444–7465) are where the college set hangs out, listening to rock bands with names such as Small Dog Frenzy, Foreskin 500, the Psychedelic Zombies, and Julius Seizure. The **Fox Theater** (✉ 1135 13th St., ☎ 303/447–0095) is an art deco movie palace that now hosts top touring bands as well as the occasional Disco Inferno. **The Broker** (✉ 555 30th St., ☎ 303/449–1752) has Bentley's Lounge, with salsa, swing, and tango.

Outdoor Activities and Sports

CYCLING

The **Boulder Creek path** winds for more than 20 mi from Eben G. Fine Park, at the base of Boulder Canyon, to Arapahoe and 55th streets, passing gardens and a fish observatory along the way. Just west of town off Baseline Road, head for **Walker Ranch,** a 7 mi loop where some more serious mountain biking is done. The **Foothills Trail,** accessed off North 4th Street offers an 8 mi ride out to Boulder Reservoir. You can rent bikes at **The Bikesmith** (2432 Arapahoe Ave., ☎ 303/443–1132).

GOLF

In Boulder, **Flatirons Golf Course** (✉ 5706 Arapahoe Ave., ☎ 303/442–7851) is an 18-hole public course at the foot of the eponymous mountains. **Lake Valley Golf Club** (✉ Neva Rd., 5 mi north of Boulder, ☎ 303/444–2144) is an 18-hole course with fine views.

HIKING

There is splendid hiking within the **Boulder Mountain Parks** system, including Chatauqua Park and Sunshine Canyon. Locals love the **Mesa Trail,** which follows the Flatirons on a north-south path. With its variations and loops, you can make it a anything from a 15-minute walk to an all-day hike. **Green Mountain** offers an intermediate hike that goes from 6,000 to 8,000 ft. For a two-hour hike, take Flagstaff Rd. to Realization Point. There, you can hike 3½ mi up **Flagstaff Mountain,** where you can connect to the Green Mountain Loop and get a view of the west side of the Continental Divide. For information, call the Boulder Parks and Recreation Department (☎ 303/441–3408).

Shopping

Boulder's **Pearl Street Mall** (✉ Pearl St. between 11th and 15th Sts.) is a shopping extravaganza, with numerous upscale boutiques and galleries. **The Hill** (✉ 13th St. and College Ave.), near the University of Colorado, is a great place for hip duds and CDs. Main Street in the tiny town of **Niwot** (✉ northeast of Boulder on CO 119) is one long strip of antiques stores. Main Street in **Lyons** (✉ north of Boulder on U.S. 36) also has several fine antiques shops.

BOUTIQUES

Alpaca Connection (✉ 1326 Pearl St., ☎ 303/447–2047) offers Indian silks, Bolivian alpaca, and Ecuadorean merino wool garments. **Chico's** (✉ 1200 Pearl St., ☎ 303/449–3381) traffics in funky jewelry and natural fibers and fabrics from around the globe. **Fresh Produce** (✉ 1136 Pearl St., ☎ 303/442–7507) is a Boulder-based company that makes brightly colored and whimsically designed cotton clothing for adults and children. **Pura Vida Imports** (✉ 2012 10th St., Boulder, ☎ 303/440–5601) specializes in women's clothing and accessories with an international accent.

CHILDREN'S ITEMS

Little Mountain (✉ 1136 Spruce St., ☎ 303/443–1757) carries outdoor clothing for children, and rents child-carrier backpacks and all-terrain strollers. **The Printed Page** (✉ 1219 Pearl St., ☎ 970/443–8450) presents unique and exquisite old-fashioned toys.

CRAFT AND ART GALLERIES

Pearl Street Mall, in Boulder, features a number of art galleries and boutiques that carry crafts. **Art Source International** (✉ 1237 Pearl St., ☎ 303/444–4080) is Colorado's largest antique print and map dealer. **Artesanias** (✉ 1420 Pearl St., Boulder, ☎ 303/442–3777) sells Zapotec rugs, Mexican santos, decorative iron, and handcrafted furniture. For the finest selection in cookware, table linen, and kitchen utensils, as well as gourmet items and books, the store to visit is **Peppercorn** (✉ 1235 Pearl St., ☎ 303/449–5847 or 800/447–6905). **Boulder Arts & Crafts Cooperative** (✉ 1421 Pearl St., ☎ 303/443–3683) offers exquisite hand-painted silk scarves, handwoven garments, glass art, and pottery, all by Colorado artists. **Handmade in Colorado** (✉ 1426 Pearl St., ☎ 303/938–8394) sells only the best Colorado-made goods. **Hangouts** (✉ 1328 Pearl St., ☎ 303/442–2533) has splendid handmade hammocks. **McLaren & Markowitz Gallery** (✉ 1011 Pearl St., ☎ 303/449–6807) features fine jewelry, sculpture, paintings, and pottery—primarily with a Southwestern feel.

FOOD

Alfalfa's (✉ Broadway and Arapahoe St., ☎ 303/442–0082) is a New Age organic supermarket, where one-stop shopping will net you everything from "cruelty-free" cosmetics to herbal and homeopathic remedies. The deli offers predictably healthful fare, with a crisp, fresh salad bar, homemade muffins and soups (usually something such as miso), and custom-blended vegetable and fruit juices.

OUTDOOR GEAR

Boulder Mountaineer (✉ 2835 Pearl St., ☎ 303/442–8355) offers the gear to tackle those outdoor pursuits that Boulderites revel in. **McGuckin Hardware** (✉ Village Shopping Center, 2525 Arapahoe St., ☎ 303/443–1822) is a Boulder institution that features a mind-boggling array of merchandise and salespeople who know where everything is.

Nederland

18 *16 mi west from Boulder via Canyon Rd. (Rte. 119).*

A funky mountain hamlet at the top of Boulder Canyon, "Ned" (as locals know it) is the gateway to skiing at Eldora Mountain Resort and summer hiking in the Indian Peaks Wilderness. A small downtown retains the character of gold-mining days and has several good bars and restaurants. **Aspen Kickin'** (✉ Main St., ☎ 303/642–7397) sells handcrafted log furniture.

Dining and Lodging

$ ✕ **Neapolitan's.** "Never eat anything bigger than your head" would not apply here. The meat-filled or vegetarian calzones are monstrous, and included in the price are a salad dripping with Gorgonzola and rolls redolent of garlic. If you're a glutton for punishment, you'll want to order the hot fudge sundae topped with real homemade fudge sauce. The tiny, rustic restaurant is a real local's favorite. ✉ *1 First St.,* ☎ *303/258–7313. MC, V. No lunch weekdays.*

$$ **Best Western Lodge at Nederland.** Although relatively new (1994), and ultramodern within, the lodge is made of rough-hewn timber, giving it a rustic feel. All rooms are spacious and have refrigerators, coffeemakers, hair dryers, and cable TV; rooms upstairs have cathedral ceilings, and those downstairs have gas fireplaces. The enthusiastic staff will help to arrange any outdoor activity you desire—and the possibilities are just about endless. An excellent choice for those who want to be central, the property is within a half-hour's drive of Boulder, Eldora ski area, and Central City. ✉ *55 Lakeview Dr., 80466,* ☎ *303/258–9463 or 800/279–9463,* FAX *303/258–0413. 23 rooms, 1 suite. Hot tub. AE, D, DC, MC, V.*

Outdoor Activities and Sports

There is easily accessible hiking and overnight camping in **Indian Peaks Wilderness.** Contact the Boulder Ranger District Office (☎ 303/444–6600).

SKIING

At **Eldora Mountain Resort** there are 43 trails, 9 lifts, 386 acres, and a 1,400-ft vertical drop; 45 km (72 mi) of groomed track; and ski and snowshoe rentals and lessons. ✉ *Rte. 119,* ☎ *303/440–8700.* ⏲ *Early Nov.–mid-Apr., daily 9–4.*

Estes Park

19 *40 mi from Nederland via Rte. 72 and Rte. 7 (the Peak to Peak Hwy.) north; 36 mi from Boulder via U.S. 36 north.*

The **Peak to Peak Highway,** which winds from Central City to Estes Park (eastern gateway to Rocky Mountain National Park), is not the quickest route but is certainly the most scenic. You'll pass through the old mining towns of Ward and Allenspark and be rewarded with spectacular mountain vistas and, in the fall, golden stands of aspen.

The most direct route to Estes is north along U.S. 36, via the quaint town of Lyons. The scenery gives little hint of the grandeur to come when you reach Estes Park. If ever there was a classic picture-postcard Rockies view, Estes Park has it. Even the McDonald's has glorious views and a facade that complements its surroundings, thanks to strict zoning laws that require all businesses to present a rustic exterior. The town itself is very family-oriented, albeit somewhat kitschy: Many of the small hotels lining the country roads are mom-and-pop outfits that have been passed down through several generations.

As a resort town, Estes attracted the attention of genius entrepreneur F. O. Stanley, inventor of the Stanley Steamer automobile and several photographic processes. In 1905, having been told by his doctors he would soon die of tuberculosis, he constructed the regal **Stanley Hotel** on a promontory overlooking the town. Stanley went on to live another 30-odd years, an extension that he attributed to the fresh air. The hotel soon became one of the most glamorous resorts in the Rockies, a position it holds to this day. Incidentally, the hotel was the inspiration for Stephen King's horror novel, *The Shining,* later made into a movie by Stanley Kubrick starring Jack Nicholson.

From the Stanley, turn left to return to U.S. 36. In two blocks you'll see the **Estes Park Area Historical Museum.** The archeological evidence displayed here makes an eloquent case that Native Americans used the area as a summer resort. The museum also offers the usual assortment of pioneer artifacts and mounts interesting changing exhibits. ⊠ *200 4th St.,* ☎ *970/586–6256.* *$2.50.* ⊙ *May–Oct., Mon.–Sat. 10–5, Sun. 1–5; Jan.–Apr., Fri.–Sat. 10–5, Sun. 1–5.*

Double back on U.S. 36 where it intersects with U.S. 34; follow U.S. 34 to MacGregor Avenue and take it for 1 mi. The **MacGregor Ranch Museum,** in the National Register of Historic Places, offers views of the Twin Owls and Long's Peak (towering more than 14,000 ft). Although the original ranch was homesteaded in 1873, the present house was built in 1896, and it provides a well-preserved record of typical ranch life, thanks to a wealth of material discovered in the attic. ⊠ *MacGregor Ave.,* ☎ *970/586–3749.* *Free.* ⊙ *June–Aug., Tues.–Fri. 10–4.*

Dining and Lodging

$$ ✕ **Nicky's Cattleman Restaurant.** Elegant wood beams, oak paneling, maroon carpeting and upholstery, and a huge picture window fronting the mountain and river make this one of the most sophisticated dining spots in town. They age and cut their own meat here, and specialties include sensational sirloin prepared Greek style with onions, peppers, and feta, and prime rib broiled in rock salt. Nicky's also offers motorlodge rooms, cabins, and condominiums. ⊠ *1350 U.S. 34,* ☎ *970/586–5376. AE, D, DC, MC, V.*

$ ✕ **Ed's Cantina.** Light-hearted antiques adorn the walls here. Huge burritos and tasty burgers are reliable choices at this popular locals' hangout. ⊠ *362 E. Elkhorn Ave.,* ☎ *970/586–2919. AE, D, DC, MC, V.*

$ ✕ **Friar's.** The name refers to the fact that the restaurant occupies a former church. The back room is woodsy and elegant; the front room sunny, with blackboard tables (chalk is supplied). The food ranges from dependable salads and sandwiches to fine daily fish and chicken specials. ⊠ *157 W. Elkhorn Ave.,* ☎ *970/586–2806. AE, D, DC, MC, V.*

$$$$ ★ **Aspen Lodge Ranch Resort and Conference Center.** The main building is the largest log structure in Colorado, with cathedral ceilings, antler chandeliers, and a vaulted stone fireplace. Rustic lodge rooms (variously decorated with Native American weavings and original art) have balconies and thrilling mountain views. There are also 23 nicely appointed cabins with gingerbread trim. Rides are offered to a 2,000-acre working ranch, and you can two-step or square dance in the homey lounge after an excellent dinner. ⊠ *6120 Rte. 7, 80517,* ☎ *970/586–8133 or 800/332–6867. 52 rooms. Restaurant, bar, pool, hot tub, sauna, 2 tennis courts, basketball, exercise room, horseback riding, racquetball, fishing, cross-country skiing, children's programs, laundry service, convention center. AP in summer. 3-night minimum. AE, D, DC, MC, V.*

$$$ ★ **Stanley Hotel.** Perched regally on a hill commanding the town, the Stanley is one of Colorado's great old hotels (☞ *above*). As is often the case, the sunny rooms, decorated with antiques and period reproduc-

tions, are not as sumptuous as they once were. Still, there is an incomparable air of history to this 1909 hotel, along with all the modern conveniences. The McGregor Room is the classiest restaurant in town. ✉ *333 Wonderview Ave., 80517,* ☎ *970/586–3371 or 800/976–1377,* FAX *970/586–3673. 133 rooms. Restaurant, bar, outdoor pool, tennis court, croquet, laundry service, meeting rooms. AE, D, DC, MC, V.*

$$–$$$ **Boulder Brook.** Luxury suites at this secluded spot on the river are tucked in the pines, yet close to town. All feature full kitchen or kitchenette, private deck, gas fireplace, double-headed showers, cable TV, and VCR. Half the units have whirlpool tubs, for which you'll pay a great deal more. ✉ *1900 Fall River Rd., 80517,* ☎ *970/586–0910. 16 suites. Hot tub. AE, D, MC, V.*

$$ **Best Western Lake Estes Resort.** All the well-maintained rooms are good-sized and outfitted with a hodgepodge of furniture; some extremely nice mahogany pieces are mixed with others that would have been better left in someone's attic. All rooms include minirefrigerator and hair dryers, as well as the usual amenities. The newer chalet suites have gas fireplaces. Ask for a unit with a lake view. ✉ *1650 Big Thompson Ave., Hwy. 34, 80517,* ☎ *970/586–3386. 58 rooms. Restaurant, refrigerators, pool, hot tub, sauna, playground, coin laundry. AE, D, DC, MC, V.*

$$ **Estes Park Center/YMCA of the Rockies.** This self-contained property is so huge it's easy to get lost. It even has its own zip code! Both lodge rooms and the 200 cabins are simple, clean, and attractive, and all are constructed of sturdy oak. Cabins also have a full kitchen. ✉ *2515 Tunnel Rd., 80511,* ☎ *970/586–3341. 730 rooms. Restaurant, indoor pool, basketball, exercise room, roller-skating rink, playground, meeting rooms. No credit cards.*

Nightlife and the Arts

Concerts and top-notch semiprofessional theatrical productions are staged periodically at the **Stanley Hotel** (☎ 970/586–3371 or 800/976–1377). Concerts and performances are also staged by **Creative Ensemble Productions** (☎ 970/586–6864); call for current listings.

In Estes Park the venerable **Wheel Bar** (✉ 132 E. Elkhorn Ave., ☎ 970/586–9381) is among the watering holes of choice. The **Gaslight Pub** (✉ Gaslight Sq., ☎ 970/586–0994) has occasional live music. The locals' favorite is **J. R. Chapins Lounge** (✉ Holiday Inn, 101 S. St. Vrain St., ☎ 970/586–2332). **Lonigans** (✉ 110 W. Elkhorn Ave., ☎ 970/586–4346) offers live blues and country bands several nights weekly.

Outdoor Activities and Sports

Camping facilities abound in the 800,000 acres of **Roosevelt National Forest** (✉ 240 W. Prospect Rd., Fort Collins, ☎ 970/498–1100), and there's excellent cycling and hiking here, too. **National Park Village Stables** (☎ 970/586–5269) and **Sombrero Ranch** (☎ 970/586–4577) offer trail rides through the Estes Park region, including Rocky Mountain National Park. Good fishing can be found in the **Big Thompson River** near Estes Park. **Rocky Mountain Adventures** (☎ 970/586–6191) offers guided fly- and float-fishing.

A-1 Wildwater (☎ 970/224–3379 or 800/369–4165), **Rapid Transit Rafting** (☎ 970/586–8852 or 800/367–8523), and **Rocky Mountain Adventures** (☎ 970/586–6191 or 800/858–6808) run trips out of Estes Park up the Poudre River.

Estes Park Golf Club (✉ 1080 S. St. Vrain St., ☎ 970/586–8146) is one of the oldest and prettiest 18-hole courses in the state.

Shopping

In Estes Park, the **Park Theatre Mall** (✉ E. Elkhorn Ave.) and **Old Church Shops Mall** (✉ 157 W. Elkhorn Ave.) feature a wide variety of upscale stores that hawk primarily indigenous crafts.

ART GALLERIES

Michael Ricker Pewter (✉ 2050 Big Thompson, ☎ 970/586–2030) offers free tours of its casting studio and gallery, where you can see the world's largest pewter sculpture. **Glassworks** (✉ 323 Elkhorn Ave., ☎ 970/586–8619) offers glassblowing demonstrations and sells a rainbow of glass creations.

BOUTIQUES

JB Sweaters (✉ 140 E. Elkhorn Ave., ☎ 970/586–6101) features hand-knit sweaters, shirts, and ties for men and women.

GIFTS

The Christmas Shoppe (✉ Park Theatre Mall, Elkhorn Ave., ☎ 970/586–2882) delights children of all ages with every conceivable Noël-related ornament, doll, curio, and knickknack from around the world.

WESTERN PARAPHERNALIA

Rocky Mountain Comfort (✉ 116 E. Elkhorn Ave., ☎ 970/586–0512) has home accessories with the lodge look, including furniture, quilts, baskets, and throws, and even local foodstuffs. **Stage Western Family Clothing** (✉ 104 Moraine Ave., ☎ 970/586–3430), permeated by the pungent aroma of leather, offers imaginative cowboy hats, boots, and belts.

Fort Collins

20 *50 mi from Estes Park via U.S. 34 east and I–25 north.*

Fort Collins was originally established to protect traders from the natives, while the former negotiated the treacherous Overland Trail. Unexpectedly, however, the town grew on two industries: education (Colorado State University was founded here in 1879) and agriculture (rich crops of alfalfa and sugar beets). The Fort Collins Convention & Visitors Bureau (☞ Visitor Information *in* North Central Colorado A to Z, *below*) has designated a historic walking tour of more than 20 buildings, including the original university structures and the stately sandstone **Avery House** (✉ 328 W. Mountain Ave., ☎ 970/221–0533), which is open Wednesday and Sunday, 1–3.

Old Town Square (✉ Mountain and College Aves.) is an urban renewal project that re-creates a pioneer town whose buildings house upscale stores and cafés set around playing fountains.

The **Fort Collins Museum** includes an 1860s stone cabin and an 1884 schoolhouse on the grounds. The collection contains artifacts representing Fort Collins history, from the Native Americans through the fur trappers to the present. ✉ *200 Matthews St.,* ☎ *970/221–6738.* 🎟 *Free.* ⏲ *Tues.–Sat. 10–5, Sun. noon–5.*

The **Swetsville Zoo** is the unique creation of a dairy farmer insomniac who stayed up nights fashioning more than 100 dinosaurs and other creatures from old farm equipment. ✉ *4801 E. Harmony Rd.,* ☎ *970/484–9509.* 🎟 *Free.* ⏲ *Daily, dawn to dusk.*

Dining and Lodging

$ ✕ **Rio Grande Mexican Restaurant.** One of the best Mexican restaurants in the area, the Rio Grande always satisfies with such old favorites as sopaipillas, burritos, and Mexican steak, as well as more fiery Tex-Mex fare. Minimargaritas cost $2.50, and they're strong enough to impart a pleasant buzz. ✉ *143 W. Mountain Ave.,* ☎ *970/224–5428. D, MC, V.*

$–$$ **Fort Collins Plaza Inn.** For a city its size, Fort Collins offers no truly distinctive lodging. This locally owned establishment is unspectacular, but it's a better buy than the nearby competitors, Marriott and Holiday Inn. ✉ *3709 E. Mulberry St., 80524,* ☎ *970/493–7800. 135 rooms. Restaurant, bar, indoor-outdoor pool, hot tub, sauna. AE, D, DC, MC, V.*

Nightlife

BARS AND LOUNGES

A place to hang (usually with the college crowd) is **Coopersmith's Pub & Brewery** (✉ 5 Old Town Sq., ☎ 970/498–0483). You'll also find the college kids at **Lucky Joe's Sidewalk Saloon** (✉ 25 Old Town Sq., ☎ 970/493–2213). The sports bar **Chesterfield, Bottomsley, and Potts** (✉ 1415 W. Elizabeth St., ☎ 970/221–1139) is famous for its burgers and international selection of beers.

ROCK CLUBS

Several clubs in Fort Collins jam with the hottest rock, folk, and blues in the area, including **Lindens** (✉ 214 Linden St., ☎ 970/482–9291) and **The Starlight** (✉ 167 N. College Ave., ☎ 970/484–4974). **Sunset Night Club** (✉ 242 Linden St., ☎ 970/484–4604) is a smoke-free swing club with '80s dance music and stand-up acts on different nights. **Mishawaka Inn** (✉ 13714 Poudre Canyon, 15 mi north of Ft. Collins, ☎ 970/482–4420), an outdoor amphitheater on the banks of the Poudre River, usually corrals some name bands.

Outdoor Activities and Sports

Good **fishing** can be found at the **Horsetooth Reservoir, Red Feather Lakes,** and **Cache la Poudre River** west of Fort Collins. Also west of Fort Collins, in truly unspoiled surroundings, the **Colorado State Forest** (☎ 970/723–8366) offers superb **hiking.** For **cross-country skiers, Never Summer Nordic** (✉ Box 1983, Ft. Collins 80522, ☎ 970/482–9411) is a hut-to-hut system. **Collindale Golf Course** (✉ 1441 E. Horsetooth St., ☎ 970/221–6651) is an 18-hole public **golf** course.

Shopping

Fort Collins's **Old Town Square** (✉ between College and Mountain Aves. and Jefferson St.) is a pleasant collection of cafés and intriguing shops.

Rocky Mountain National Park

❷❶ *5 mi from Estes Park via U.S. 36 or U.S. 34; 55 mi from Fort Collins via I–25 south and U.S. 34 west.*

The real attraction in this neighborhood is the majestic landscape sculpted by violent volcanic uplifts and receding glaciers that savagely clawed the earth. There are three distinct ecosystems in the national park, including verdant subalpine, a cathedral of towering proud ponderosa pines; alpine; and harsh, unforgiving tundra, with wind-whipped trees that grow at right angles and dollhouse-size versions of familiar plants and wildflowers. The park is a splendid place to wander. The world's highest continuous paved highway, **Trail Ridge Road** (U.S. 34, open only in summer), runs 45 mi through the park and accesses several hikes along its meandering way, through terrain filigreed with silvery streams and turquoise lakes. The views around each bend—of moraines and glaciers, and craggy hills framing emerald meadows carpeted with columbine and Indian paintbrush—are truly awesome: nature's workshop on an epic scale. The park also teems with wildlife, from beaver to bighorn sheep, with the largest concentrations of sheep and majestic elk in Horseshoe Meadow. Fine visitor centers at Park Headquarters (✉ U.S. 36, southwest of Estes Park) and on U.S. 34 near Grand Lake at the western entrance offer maps, brochures, newslet-

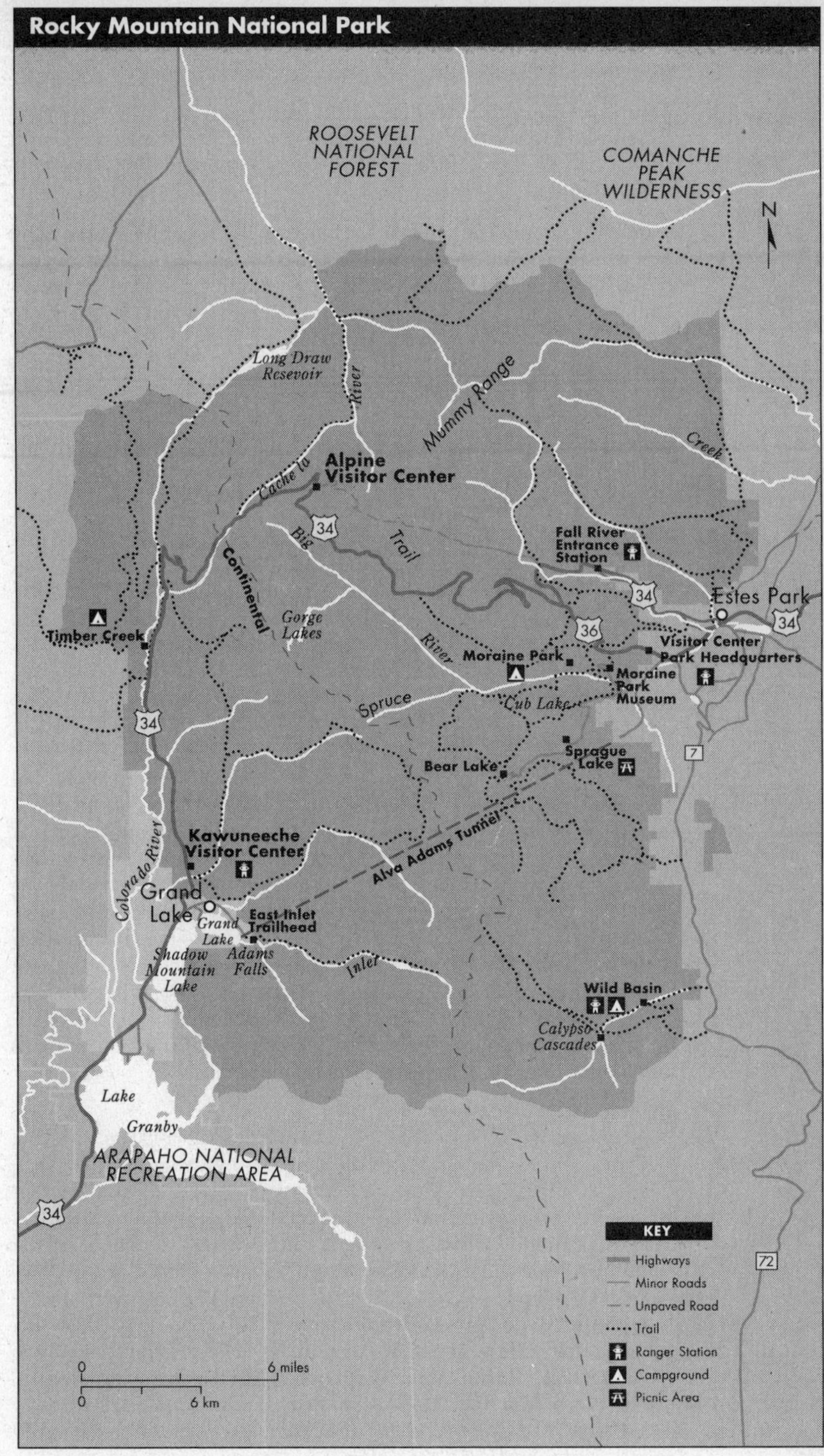
Rocky Mountain National Park
ROOSEVELT NATIONAL FOREST
COMANCHE PEAK WILDERNESS
N
Long Draw Resevoir
River
Mummy Range
Creek
Cache la
Alpine Visitor Center
34
Trail
Big
Continental
Fall River Entrance Station
34
Estes Park
34
36
Gorge Lakes
Timber Creek
River
Moraine Park
Visitor Center
Park Headquarters
Moraine Park Museum
Spruce
Cub Lake
34
Sprague Lake
7
Bear Lake
Alva Adams Tunnel
Colorado River
Kawuneeche Visitor Center
Grand Lake
Grand Lake
East Inlet Trailhead
Shadow Mountain Lake
Adams Falls
Inlet
Wild Basin
Calypso Cascades
Lake Granby
ARAPAHO NATIONAL RECREATION AREA
34
KEY
Highways
Minor Roads
Unpaved Road
Trail
Ranger Station
Campground
Picnic Area
72
0
6 miles
0
6 km

ters, and comprehensive information on the park's statistics and facilities. ✉ *Estes Park, 80517-8397,* ☎ *970/586–1206.* 🎫 *$10 weekly per vehicle.* ⏲ *Year-round, but highway closed in winter.*

Take U.S. 36 south from Park Headquarters for about 4 mi to Bear Lake Road and the **Moraine Park Museum,** which offers lectures, slide shows, and displays on the park's geology and botany. ⏲ *May–Sept., daily 10–6.*

From the museum you can take the twisting, 9-mi-long **Bear Lake Road** as it winds past shimmering waterfalls perpetually shrouded with rainbows. The drive offers superlative views of Long's Peak (Colorado's highest) and the glaciers surrounding Bear Lake. If you choose not to follow Bear Lake Road, head west from the museum on Trail Ridge Road. Many Peaks Curve affords breathtaking views of the crest of the Continental Divide and of the **Alluvial Fan,** a huge gash created in 1982 by a vicious flood after an earthen dam broke. Erosion occurred immediately, rather than over the millions of years that nature usually requires, and today it resembles a lonely lunar landscape.

Outdoor Activities and Sports

There are five top-notch campgrounds in the park, and there's fine hiking as well. The **Colorado Mountain Club** (✉ Estes Park, ☎ 970/586–6623) sponsors day and overnight trips into the park. Rocky Mountain's lower valleys are accessible year-round and have miles of ski trails.

Grand Lake

22 *54 mi from Estes Park via U.S. 34 (Trail Ridge Rd.—closed in winter); 109 mi from Denver via U.S. 40 and 34.*

Grand Lake is the western gateway to Rocky Mountain National Park, and it, too, enjoys an idyllic setting, on the shores of the state's largest natural lake, of the same name. This is the highest-altitude yacht anchorage in America. According to Ute legend, the fine mists that shroud the lake punctually at dawn are the risen spirits of women and children whose raft capsized as they were fleeing a marauding party of Cheyennes and Arapahos. Grand Lake feeds into two much larger man-made reservoirs, Lake Granby and Shadow Mountain Lake, forming the "Great Lakes of Colorado." The entire area is a paradise for hikers and fishermen, and for snowmobilers in winter. Even the town, although it has the usual assortment of souvenir shops and motels, seems less spoiled than many other resort communities.

Dining and Lodging

$$ ✕ **Mountain Inn.** The log cabin interior, decorated with old Singer sewing machines and Rotary Club banners, imparts a pleasant, woodsy feel. The food ranges from fine Rocky Mountain oysters and veggie tempura to flavorful prime rib, beer-batter shrimp, and trout amandine. The Mexican food is also superior, if mild. The real standouts are the bread-bowl stews and chicken pot pies. ✉ *612 Grand Ave.,* ☎ *970/627–3385. MC, V.*

$–$$ 🏨 **Bighorn Lodge.** This downtown motel has a rustic look, which helps it to blend in well with its surroundings. Pride is reflected in the spotless rooms, all with cable TV, phones, ceiling fans, soundproof walls, maroon carpeting, sailing prints, and pastel fabrics and wallpaper. ✉ *613 Grand Ave., 80447,* ☎ *970/627–8101 or 800/341–8000. 20 rooms. Hot tub. AE, D, DC, MC, V.*

$–$$ 🏨 **Grand Lake Lodge.** This rustic retreat, built of lodgepole pine in 1921, calls itself "Colorado's favorite front porch," thanks to its stupendous views of Grand and Shadow Mountain lakes. The restaurant offers the same gorgeous vistas, in addition to fine mesquite-grilled fish. Cabins are comfortably but simply furnished—no TVs or phones—for those who truly want to get away from it all. ✉ *Box 569, 80447, off U.S. 34, north of Grand Lake, ☎ 970/627–3967 or 303/759–5848 off-season. 56 rooms. Restaurant, bar, pool, hot tub, horseback riding. AE, D, MC, V. Closed mid-Sept.–May.*

$–$$ ★ **Rapids Lodge.** This handsome lodgepole-pine structure is one of the oldest hotels in the area. Lodge rooms—each with cable TV and ceiling fan—are frilly, with dust ruffle quilts, floral wallpaper and fabrics, and such mismatched furnishings as old plush chartreuse armchairs, claw-foot tubs, and carved hardwood beds. Cabins, all with kitchenettes, are more rustic. The delightful restaurant is Grand Lake's most romantic, with stained glass, timber beams, and views of the roaring Tonahatu River. The kitchen turns out sumptuous Italian cuisine. ✉ *209 Rapids La., 80447, ☎ 970/627–3707. 6 rooms, 20 suites. Restaurant, bar. AE, MC, V. Closed Nov.–mid-Dec., and Mon. and Tues. mid-Dec.–May.*

$–$$ **Western Riviera.** This friendly motel books up far in advance, thanks to the low prices, affable owners, and comfortable accommodations. Even the cheapest units—although small—are pleasant, done in mauve and earth tones, with lake views and cable TV. Cabins, with a kitchenette (including a microwave), a bedroom, and a living room with a sleeper sofa, are a bargain for families. ✉ *419 Garfield Ave., 80447, ☎ 970/627–3580. 25 rooms. Hot tub. MC, V.*

Nightlife

The hands-down local favorite is the **Stagecoach Inn** (✉ 920 Grand Ave., on the Boardwalk, ☎ 970/627–8079), as much for its cheap booze and good eats as for the live entertainment on weekends.

Outdoor Activities and Sports

BOATING AND FISHING

Grand Lake and Lake Granby are the premier boating centers. Call the **Trail Ridge Marina** (✉ Shadow Mountain Lake, ☎ 970/627–3586) and **Beacon Landing** (✉ 1 mile off Hwy. 34 on CR #64, ☎ 970/627–3671) for information on renting pontoon boats. Great fishing can be found on both lakes. Contact the **Grand Lake Recreation District** (✉ Box 590, 80447, ☎ 970/627–8872) for information.

CROSS-COUNTRY SKIING

For cross-country skiing, the **Grand Lake Metropolitan Recreation Center** (☎ 970/627–8008) offers 18 mi of trails with breathtaking vistas of the Never Summer Range and the Continental Divide.

GOLF

Grand Lake Golf Course (✉ County Rd. 48, ☎ 970/627–8008) is an 18-hole course 8,420 ft above sea level.

HIKING

In Grand County, near Lake Granby, **Indian Peaks Wilderness Area** (☎ 970/887–4100) is a prime location for hiking.

SNOWMOBILING

Grand Lake is considered by many to be Colorado's snowmobiling capital, with more than 130 mi of trails, many winding through virgin forest. Recommended **outfitters** include Alpine Arctic Cat (✉ 902 Grand Ave., ☎ 970/627–8866), Grand Lake Motor Sports (✉ 10438 Hwy. 34, ☎ 970/627–3806), Lone Eagle Rentals (✉ 712 Grand Ave., ☎ 970/627–3310), and Spirit Lake Rentals (✉ 829 Grand Ave., ☎ 970/627–9288).

Shopping

Grand Lake Art Gallery (✉ 1117 Grand Ave., ☎ 970/627–3104) purveys superlative weavings, pottery, stained glass, gourds, and landscapes, primarily by regional artists.

Grand County

20 mi (Granby), 30 mi (Hot Sulphur Springs), and 47 mi (Kremmling) from Grand Lake via U.S. 34 south and U.S. 40 west; 100 mi (Hot Sulphur Springs) and 117 mi (Kremmling) from Denver via I–70 west and U.S. 40 north.

The area west of Grand Lake along U.S. 40 is populated by a number of small towns and some interesting resorts and dude ranches. Hot Sulphur Springs is a faded resort town whose hot springs attracted Hollywood types in the '50s. Now new owners are restoring the springs and spa to their original glory. Kremmling is known as a sportsman's paradise for its year-round recreation, including mountain biking, river rafting, hunting, fishing, and cross-country skiing.

Dining and Lodging

$$ ✕ **Longbranch Restaurant.** *The* restaurant in Granby, this stylish western coffee shop with a warming fireplace, wood paneling, and wagon-wheel chandeliers offers German, Mexican, Continental, and American dishes. Not surprisingly, the quality is uneven. Stick to what the German owners do best—goulash, schnitzel, and sauerbraten, with heavenly homemade spaetzle. ✉ *185 E. Agate Ave. (U.S. 40), Granby,* ☎ *970/887–2209. MC, V.*

$ ✕🏨 **Riverside Hotel.** Colorado is full of fun and funky finds, such as this historic 1903 hotel that you enter through a jungle of plants. The lobby, dominated by a magnificent fieldstone fireplace with cluttered mantel, leads into a grand old mirrored bar and a cozy dining room ($–$$) with a huge potbellied stove, a piano, landscape paintings of the kind charitably called folk art, and views of the Colorado River. Steaks are simple but well prepared and fish is fresh as can be. It's worth having a meal here even if you don't stay at the hotel. The upstairs rooms are filled with iron or oak beds, floral quilts, heavy oak dressers or armoires, and washbasins or sinks. Corner rooms are the sunniest and most spacious. ✉ *509 Grand Ave., Hot Sulphur Springs 80451,* ☎ *970/725–3589. 21 rooms with shared bath. Restaurant, bar, fishing. AE, MC, V.*

$$$$ ★ 🏨 **C Lazy U Guest Ranch.** This is a deluxe dude ranch, attracting an international clientele, including both Hollywood royalty and the real thing. You enjoy your own personal horse, luxurious Western-style accommodations (with hair dryers, coffeemakers, and humidifiers), fine meals, live entertainment, and any outdoor activity you can dream up. The instructors are invariably top-notch, the ratio of guests to staff is nearly one to one, and the children's programs are unbeatable. The C Lazy U seeks to provide the ultimate in hedonism without ostentation, and it succeeds admirably. During the summer, the minimum stay is a week; in winter, it's two nights. All meals are included. ✉ *Box 379, Granby 80446,* ☎ *970/887–3344. 20 cabins, 19 rooms. Restaurant, bar, pool, hot tub, sauna, 2 tennis courts, exercise room, horseback riding, racquetball, fishing, cross-country skiing. No credit cards. Closed Apr.–June, Oct.–Dec. 21. FAP.*

$$$ 🏨 **Latigo Ranch.** Considerably more down-to-earth than many other Colorado guest ranches, Latigo has a caring staff that does everything it can to give you an authentic ranch experience. Accommodations are in comfortable but rather dowdy, one- to three-bedroom cabins fitted out with wood-burning stoves. Although providing fewer amenities than comparable properties, the ranch offers views of the Indian Peaks range, complete seclusion (17 mi—and 30 minutes on heart-stopping roads—to the nearest town), and superb cross-country trails. Owner Jim Yost was an anthropologist and Randy George a chemical engineer; he now engineers the "nouvelle ranch cuisine" (BYOB). ✉ *County Rd. 1911, Box 237, Kremmling 80459,* ☎ *970/724–9008 or 800/227–*

9655. 10 cabins. Dining room, pool, hot tub, horseback riding, fishing, cross-country skiing, tobogganing, recreation room, coin laundry. No credit cards. Closed Apr.–May, mid-Oct.–mid-Dec. FAP.

North Central Colorado A to Z

Arriving and Departing

BY BUS

Greyhound Lines (☎ 800/231–2222) serves most of the major towns in the region.

BY CAR

The region is easily reached via I–25, which runs north–south.

BY PLANE

Boulder and Estes Park are served by **Denver International Airport** (☞ Denver A to Z, *above*); regular shuttles are available from Denver (☞ By Bus, *below*). **Fort Collins-Loveland Municipal Airport** (☎ 970/962–2850) is a private airport.**Airport Express** (✉ Fort Collins, ☎ 970/482–0505) runs shuttles from Denver and to Fort Collins. **Super Shuttle** (☎ 303/444–0808) provides transportation from Denver. **Estes Park Shuttle** (☎ 970/586–5151) offers rides to Estes Park from Denver and Boulder. Costs run from $28 to $50 depending on pick-up location.

Getting Around

BY BUS

In **Fort Collins: Transfort** (☎ 970/221–6620) runs along major thoroughfares.

BY CAR

U.S. 36 North accesses Boulder and Estes Park from Denver. Fort Collins and Longmont can be reached from Denver, via I–25 North. The main thoroughfare through Rocky Mountain National Park, connecting Grand Lake with Estes Park, is U.S. 34, which is partially closed October–May. Grand Lake can also be reached by U.S. 40 into U.S. 34, from Georgetown on I–70.

BY TAXI

Boulder Yellow Cab (☎ 303/442–2277). **Shamrock Taxi** (✉ Fort Collins, ☎ 970/224–2222).

Contacts and Resources

DOCTORS AND DENTISTS

Boulder Community Hospital (✉ 1100 Balsam Ave., Boulder, ☎ 303/440–2037). **Estes Park Medical Center** (✉ 555 Prospect Ave., Estes Park, ☎ 970/586–2317). **Poudre Valley Hospital** (✉ 1024 S. Lemay Ave., Fort Collins, ☎ 970/482–4111).

GUIDED TOURS

Boulder Historical Tours (☎ 303/444–5192) sponsors tours of various Boulder neighborhoods during the summer. **Estes Park Shuttle** (☎ 970/586–5151) runs trips to Rocky Mountain National Park.

VISITOR INFORMATION

Boulder Convention & Visitors Bureau (✉ 2440 Pearl St., Boulder 80302, ☎ 303/442–2911 or 800/444–0447). **Estes Park Area Chamber of Commerce** (✉ Box 3050, Estes Park 80517, ☎ 970/586–4431 or 800/443–7837). **Fort Collins Area Convention & Visitors Bureau** (✉ 420 S. Howes St., Suite 101, Fort Collins 80522, ☎ 970/482–5821 or 800/274–3678). **Grand Lake Area Chamber of Commerce** (✉ Box 57, Grand Lake 80447, ☎ 970/627–3402).

I–70 AND THE HIGH ROCKIES

I–70 is the major artery that fearlessly slices the Continental Divide, passing through or near many of Colorado's most fabled resorts and towns: Aspen, Vail, Breckenridge, Steamboat, Keystone, Snowmass, Copper Mountain, Beaver Creek, Winter Park. True powder hounds intone those names like a mantra to appease the snow gods, speaking in hushed tones of the gnarly mogul runs, the wide-open bowls on top of the world. Here is the image that lingers when most people think of Colorado: a Christmas paperweight come to life, with picture-postcard mining towns and quasi-Tyrolean villages framed by cobalt skies and snowcapped peaks. To those in the know, Colorado is as breathtaking the rest of the year, when meadows are woven with larkspur and columbine, the maroon mountains flecked with the jade of juniper and the white of aspen.

Like most of Colorado, the High Rockies region is a blend of old and new, of tradition and progress. It is historic towns such as Leadville, whose muddy streets still ring with the lusty laughter from saloons, of flamboyant millionaires who built grandiose monuments to themselves before dying penniless. It's also modern resorts such as Vail, whose history began a mere 30 years ago, yet whose founding and expansion involved risk-taking and egos on as monumental a scale. The High Rockies is fur trappers and fur-clad models, rustlers and Rastafarians, heads of cattle and heads of state. One thing links all the players together: a love of the wide-open spaces. Here, those spaces are as vast as the sky.

Most visitors on their way to the magnificent ski resorts along I–70 whiz through the Eisenhower Tunnel and cross the Continental Divide without paying much attention to the extraordinary engineering achievements that facilitate their journey. Interstate 70 and the tunnel are tributes to human ingenuity and endurance: Before their completion in the 1970s, crossing the High Rockies evoked the long, arduous treks of the pioneers.

Idaho Springs

23 *33 mi west of Denver via I–70; 13 mi west of Denver via U.S. 6.*

Idaho Springs was the site of Colorado's first major gold strike, which occurred on January 7, 1859. Today, the quaint old town recalls its mining days, especially along downtown's National Historic Landmark District **Miner Street,** the main drag whose pastel Victorians will transport you back a century without too much imagination.

During the gold rush days, ore was ferried from Central City via a 22,000-ft tunnel to Idaho Springs. The **Argo Gold Mill** explains the milling process and runs public tours. ✉ *2350 Riverside Dr.,* ☎ *303/567–2421.* 🎟 *$10.* ⏲ *Daily.*

Just outside town is the **Phoenix Gold Mine,** still a working site. A seasoned miner leads visitors underground, where they can wield 19th-century excavating tools, and dig or pan for gold. Whatever riches guests find are theirs to keep. ✉ *Off Trail Creek Rd.,* ☎ *303/567–0422.* 🎟 *$9.* ⏲ *Daily 10–6.*

Idaho Springs presently prospers from its **hot springs,** at Indian Springs Resort (✉ 302 Soda Creek Rd., ☎ 303/567–2191). Around the springs, known to the Ute natives as the "healing waters of the Great Spirit," are geothermal caves that were used by several tribes as a neutral meeting site. Hot baths and a mineral-water swimming pool are the primary draws for the resort, but the scenery from here is equally fan-

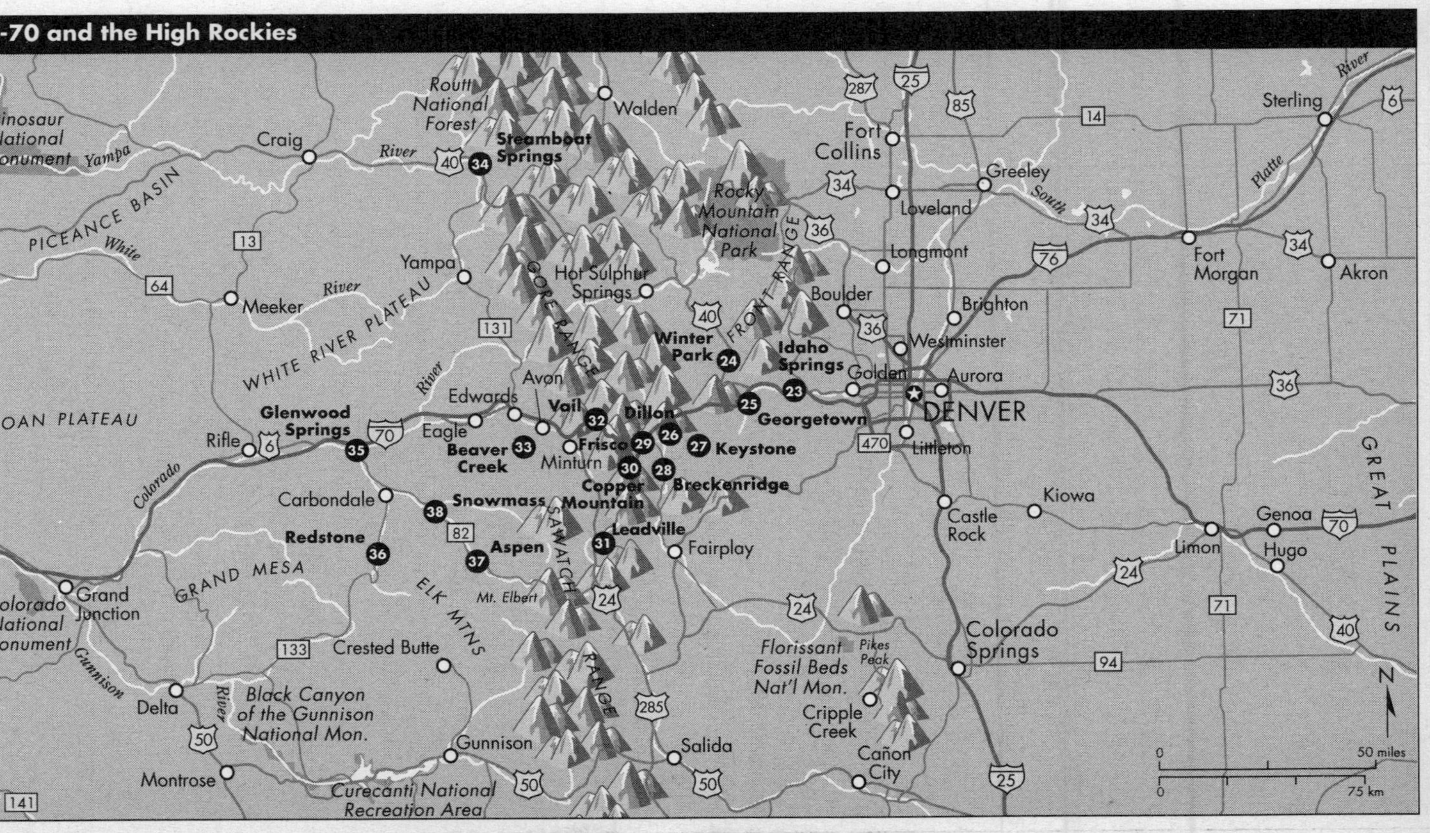
I-70 and the High Rockies
Dinosaur National Monument
Yampa River
Craig
Routt National Forest
Steamboat Springs
Walden
PICEANCE BASIN
White River
Meeker
Yampa
WHITE RIVER PLATEAU
GORE RANGE
Hot Sulphur Springs
Rocky Mountain National Park
FRONT RANGE
Fort Collins
Loveland
Greeley
South Platte River
Longmont
Boulder
Brighton
Westminster
Golden
Aurora
DENVER
Littleton
Sterling
Fort Morgan
Akron
Winter Park
Idaho Springs
Georgetown
Avon
Edwards
Vail
Dillon
Eagle
Frisco
Keystone
Beaver Creek
Minturn
Copper Mountain
Breckenridge
ROAN PLATEAU
Rifle
Glenwood Springs
Colorado
Carbondale
Snowmass
Redstone
Aspen
Leadville
Fairplay
SAWATCH RANGE
Mt. Elbert
ELK MTNS
GRAND MESA
Grand Junction
Colorado National Monument
Gunnison
Delta
Black Canyon of the Gunnison National Mon.
Crested Butte
Gunnison
Montrose
Curecanti National Recreation Area
Salida
Florissant Fossil Beds Nat'l Mon.
Pikes Peak
Cripple Creek
Cañon City
Castle Rock
Kiowa
Colorado Springs
Limon
Genoa
Hugo
GREAT PLAINS
N
0 50 miles
0 75 km

tastic. **Bridal Veil Falls,** within sight of the Indian Springs Resort, are spun out as delicately as lace on the rocks. Also close by is the imposing **Charlie Tayler Water Wheel**—the largest in the state—constructed by a miner in the 1890s who attributed his strong constitution to that fact that he never shaved, took baths, or kissed women.

Drive 2 mi west from Indian Springs Resort up Fall River Road to **St. Mary's Glacier,** a vision of alpine splendor. In summer the sparkling sapphire lake makes a pleasant picnic spot; in winter, intrepid extreme skiers and snowboarders hike up the glacier and bomb down.

For even more glorious surroundings, take the Mt. Evans Scenic and Historic Byway—the highest paved auto road in America—to the summit of the 14,264-ft-high **Mt. Evans.** The pass winds through scenery of incomparable grandeur: past several placid lakes, one after another every few hundred feet; and vegetation galore, from towering Douglas firs to stunted dwarf bristlecone pines.

Dining

$ ✕ **Buffalo Bar and Restaurant.** No surprise as to the specialty here: steaks, burgers, fajitas, chili, Philly steak sandwiches—all made with choice buffalo. It's all part of the western theme, with walls jam-packed with frontier artifacts and memorabilia. The ornate bar dates from 1886. There's often great live music. ✉ *1617 Miner St.,* ☎ *303/567–2729. AE, D, DC, MC, V.*

Winter Park

㉔ *36 mi from Idaho Springs or 67 mi from Denver, via I–70 west and U.S. 40 north.*

Denverites have come to think of Winter Park as their own personal ski area. Although it's owned by the City of Denver and makes a favorite day trip, it is a destination resort on its own. Winter Park is easily accessible, the skiing and setting are superb, and it offers the best value of any major ski area in the state. It's also equally popular in summer for hiking and biking. Since the glory of the area is its natural setting, and most people come here specifically to enjoy the resources, Winter Park otherwise has few tourist attractions.

The three interconnected mountains—Winter Park, Mary Jane, and Vasquez Ridge—offer a phenomenal variety of terrain. Head to Vasquez Ridge for splendid intermediate cruising; Mary Jane for some of the steepest, most thrilling bumps in Colorado; and Winter Park for a pleasing blend of both.

Dining and Lodging

$$$$ ★ ✕ **The Dining Room at Sunspot.** This striking log-and-stone structure at the top of the Winter Park ski area is reached via gondola. Roughhewn log beams and furniture are accented with Southwestern rugs hung on the walls, but the real stunner is the view, so be sure to arrive early enough to catch a glimpse of it. The prix-fixe menu offers game and fish paired with side dishes such as wild rice and potatoes roasted in olive oil and herbs. ✉ *Top of Zephyr Express Lift,* ☎ *970/726–1446. Reservations essential. AE, D, DC, MC, V. Open for dinner Nov.–Apr., Thurs.–Sat. Lunch year-round, but hrs vary.*

$–$$ ✕ **Deno's Mountain Bistro.** In many ways, Deno's is an anomaly: It seems like a casual drinking establishment (there's a sizable selection of beers from around the world), and it is by far the liveliest spot in town, yet it also has an impressive international wine list that's comprehensive and fairly priced. The wine is a labor of love in this unpretentious area, thanks to Deno himself, a charismatic, energetic powerhouse. The menu is as eclectic as the wine list, from angel hair *pomodoro* (tomato) pasta with rock shrimp to grilled Rocky Mountain trout to the best burgers in town, all well prepared and served by a friendly staff, most of whom have been working here for years. ✉ *78911 U.S. 40,* ☎ *970/726–5332. AE, D, DC, MC, V.*

$–$$ ✕ **Last Waltz.** This very homey place is festooned with hanging plants and graced with a crackling fireplace. The huge menu jumps from seafood to burritos, without missing a beat. The south-of-the-border dishes are best: zesty *calientitas* (fried jalapeños filled with cream cheese served with salsa) and black bean tostadas are especially noteworthy. Breakfast and brunch will power you for those mogul runs. ✉ *78336 U.S. 40,* ☎ *970/726–4877. Reservations not accepted. AE, D, DC, MC, V.*

$$–$$$ ★ ✕🏨 **Gasthaus Eichler.** This small hotel encompasses 15 rooms and Winter Park's most romantic dining spot, with quaint Bavarian decor, antler chandeliers, and stained glass, all glowing in the candlelight as Strauss rings softly in the background. Featured are veal and grilled items, in addition to scrumptious versions of German classics such as sauerbraten. The *Rahmschnitzel*—tender veal in a delicate wild mushroom and brandy cream sauce—is extraordinary, as are the feathery-light potato pancakes. The cozy, Old World rooms, with down comforters, lace curtains, armoires, cable TV, and Jacuzzis, are quite economical when you consider that the rate includes breakfast and dinner. Rates without meals included are considerably lower. ✉ *78786 U.S. 40, 80482,* ☎ *970/726–5133 or 800/543–3899. 15 rooms. Restaurant. AE, MC, V.*

$–$$ ✕🏨 **Peck House.** This snug, red-and-white, barnlike inn, Colorado's oldest continually operating hostelry, is actually in the quirky town of Empire, on U.S. 40 a few miles north of I–70. It began in 1860 as a boarding house built for wealthy mine investors, and the dining room ($$–$$$) is crammed with period antiques, including the original etched-glass, gaslight lamp shades from the state capitol, and evocative tinted lithographs. Game is the house specialty: expertly prepared quail and venison (try it with cabernet sauce) are among the standouts. The charming rooms (with Jacuzzis but no TVs) are awash in Victorian splendor. A Sunday brunch is offered. ✉ *U.S. 40, just north of I–70; Box 428, Empire 80438,* ☎ *303/569–9870. AE, D, DC, MC, V.*

$$–$$$ 🏨 **Grand Victorian.** This luxury B&B is a three-story neo-Victorian in downtown Winter Park. Amenities include robes, slippers, and potpourri sachets in the rooms and an afternoon happy hour featuring Colorado wines and beers. The huge breakfast may include potato pancakes, quiches, or delectable macadamia-nut waffles. ✉ *78542 Fraser Valley Pkwy., 80482,* ☎ *970/726–5881 or 800/204–1170. 10 rooms. Meeting room. AE, D, DC, MC, V.*

$$–$$$ 🏨 **Iron Horse Resort Retreat.** This ski-in/ski-out hotel/condominium complex is the deluxe address in Winter Park. There are studios and one- and two-bedroom units; all except the lodge rooms have a full kitchen and balcony and are furnished in an attractive, modern rustic style. ✉ *Box 1286, 80482,* ☎ *970/726–8851 or 800/621–8190;* FAX *970/726–2321. 133 rooms. Restaurant, bar, pool, 4 hot tubs, steam room, health club, ski shop. AE, DC, MC, V.*

$$–$$$ 🏨 **Woodspur Lodge.** This classic log-cabin lodge is on the edge of the Arapahoe National Forest, about 1½ mi from town. The small rooms are more rustic than posh, with furnishings handmade from local lodgepole pines, and the emphasis is on mingling in the common areas. Breakfast, dinner, and afternoon snacks are included in the room rate, and are served in a dining area with a giant fireplace and a soaring roof. Many rooms have adjoining access. ✉ *111 Van Anderson Dr., Box 249, 80482,* ☎ *970/726–8417 or 800/626–6562. 32 rooms. 2 outdoor hot tubs, sauna, recreation room. D, MC, V.*

$$ **Anna Leah.** You'll feel like you're staying at a good friend's house at this B&B, thanks to the congenial owner, Patricia Handel, who will accommodate almost any request. The inn is just past the town of Fraser, about 5 mi from the ski area. With balconies overlooking the national forest and the Continental Divide, it has a wonderfully serene feel. A full breakfast and evening desserts are included in the price. ✉ *1001 County Rd. 8, Fraser 80442,* ☎ *970/726–4414 or 800/237–9913. 5 rooms. Hot tub. No credit cards.*

$$ **Vintage Hotel.** This well-run hotel is Winter Park's other premier resort, offering spacious, comfortable rooms mostly decorated in soothing earth or mountain tones. Configurations range from standard hotel rooms (some with kitchenette and fireplace) to studios (with kitchens) and two-bedroom suites. ✉ *Box 1369, 80482,* ☎ *970/726–8801 or 800/472–7017,* FAX *970/726–9250. 118 rooms. Restaurant, bar, pizzeria, pool, hot tub, sauna, exercise room. AE, D, DC, MC, V.*

$–$$ **Sundowner Motel.** This is probably the nicest motel on the strip, and a great bargain, considering the free shuttle to the ski area. The rooms, decorated in muted earth tones, are slightly threadbare but have the standard amenities. It's right on the main drag, convenient to restaurants and shops. ✉ *78869 U.S. 40; Box 221, 80482,* ☎ *970/726–9451 or 970/726–5452. 22 rooms. Hot tub. AE, DC, MC, V.*

CONDOMINIUMS

The condominiums at Winter Park are an especially good value, particularly those managed by **Condominium Management Co.** (✉ Box 3095, 80482, ☎ 970/726–9421 or 800/228–1025, FAX 970/726–8004). Many feature recreational centers (including pool and hot tub) and laundry facilities. They run the gamut in price.

Nightlife

The Slope (✉ 1161 Winter Park Dr., ☎ 970/726–5727) is Winter Park's most raucous venue, offering everything from rock to jazz to rockabilly.

Outdoor Activities and Sports

Winter Park is one of the leading mountain biking destinations in the Rockies, thanks to the 660-mi trail system created by the **Winter Park Fat Tire Society** (✉ Box 1337, 80482, ☎ no phone). **Mad Adventures** (✉ Box 650, ☎ 970/726–5290 or 800/451–4844) offers 4WD tours. If rafting is your choice, Mad Adventures can help you shoot the rapids of the North Platte, Colorado, and Arkansas rivers. Winter Park's **Pole Creek Golf Club** (✉ County Rd. 51, ☎ 970/726–8847), a 7,000-yard, par-72, 27-hole course designed by Denis Griffiths, is consistently ranked in the top 75 public courses by *Golf Digest.* For horseback riding, contact **Grand Adventure Stables** (☎ 970/726–9247). The **Sulphur Ranger District** (✉ 9 Ten Mile Dr., Granby, ☎ 970/887–4100) can provide information about fishing in Winter Park and the surrounding region.

SKIING

There are 1,414 skiable acres with a vertical of 3,060 ft at **Winter Park/Mary Jane.** The resort's hub is at the base of Winter Park. Twenty chairlifts (including 7 high-speed quads) and 121 trails connect the three mountains and high alpine bowl. ✉ *U.S. 40, 1½ mi east of town; Box 36, 80482,* ☎ *970/726–5514.* 🎫 *$45.* ⏲ *Mid-Nov.–mid-Apr., weekdays 9–4; weekends 8:30–4.*

For cross-country, **Devil's Thumb Ranch** (✉ 10 mi north of Winter Park, ☎ 970/726–5632) is a full-service resort with 65 mi of groomed trails. For additional Winter Park skiing information, *see* the Colorado section *in* Chapter 2.

Shopping

The top **boutiques and galleries** are concentrated in downtown Winter Park at Cooper Creek Square and Crestview Place Mall.

Georgetown

25 *50 mi from Denver via I–70 west; 41 mi from Winter Park, via U.S. 40 south and I–70 west.*

Georgetown rode the crest of the silver boom during the second half of the 19th century. Most of its elegant, impeccably maintained brick buildings, which make up a National Historic District, date from that period. Fortunately, Georgetown hasn't been tarted up at all, so it provides a true sense of what gracious living meant in those rough-and-tumble times.

Just east of the Continental Divide, and just west of the I–70/U.S. 40 junction, Georgetown is close enough to be a day trip from Denver, but its quiet charms warrant more than a hurried visit. You can wander the five-square-block downtown on your own, or explore it on horse-drawn trolley or buggy, courtesy of the **Rutherford Carriage Service** (☎ 303/569–2675), which runs half-hour tours May–December by reservation only.

The **Hamill House,** home of the silver magnate William Arthur Hamill, is a Gothic Revival beauty that displays most of the original wall coverings and furnishings; there's also a unique curved glass conservatory. ✉ *3rd and Argentine Sts.,* ☎ *303/569–2840.* 🎟 *$5.* ⏲ *June–Sept., daily 10–5; Oct.–Dec., weekends noon–4; Jan.–May, by appt.*

The elaborate **Hotel de Paris,** built almost single-handedly by Frenchman Louis Dupuy in 1878, was one of the Old West's preeminent hostelries. Now a museum, the hotel depicts how luxuriously the rich were accommodated: Tiffany fixtures, lace curtains, and hand-carved furniture re-create an era of opulence. ✉ *409 6th St.,* ☎ *303/569–2311.* 🎟 *Donation suggested.* ⏲ *June–Sept., daily 9–5; Oct.–May, weekends noon–4.*

Hop on the **Georgetown Loop Railroad,** a 1920s narrow-gauge steam train that connects the town with the equally historic community of Silver Plume. The 6-mi round-trip excursion takes about 70 minutes and winds through vast stands of pine and fir before crossing the 95-ft-high Devil's Gate Bridge, where the track actually loops back over itself as it gains elevation. In Silver Plume, you can tour the Lebanon Silver Mill and Mine. ✉ *100 Loop Dr.,* ☎ *303/569–2403 or 800/691–4386.* 🎟 *$12.95.* ⏲ *Train operates June–Sept., daily 10–4.*

Dining and Lodging

$$ ✕ **The Red Ram.** This Georgetown landmark has been serving food since the 1950s, in a building dating from almost 100 years before that. Black-and-white photos of Georgetown's heydays bedeck the walls; there's a small cigar bar downstairs and live entertainment on weekends. The fare is basic Western: burgers, ribs, and such Mexican specialties as fajitas, with no entrée costing more than $13. ✉ *606 6th St.,* ☎ *303/569–2300. AE, D, DC, MC, V.*

$$ 🏨 **Hardy House B&B Inn.** This 1877 Victorian has been lovingly restored, and the welcome couldn't be warmer (nor could the potbellied stove that greets you in the parlor). The cozy rooms, all with private bath, are comfortably furnished with antiques and period reproductions, as well as down comforters. ✉ *605 Brownell St., Box 156, 80444,* ☎ *303/569–3388. 4 rooms. MC, V.*

Outdoor Activities and Sports

SKIING

Loveland Ski Area. Loveland is considered small-fry, but only because of its proximity to the megaresorts of Summit County. Actually, Loveland—the nearest ski area to Denver (62 mi, just before the Eisenhower Tunnel)—offers a respectable 965 acres serviced by 10 lifts and spread out over two mountains: Loveland Valley for beginners, and Loveland Basin for everyone else. Basin has some excellent glade and open-bowl skiing, with a 1,680-ft vertical drop. Best of all, it opens early and usually stays open later than any other area except Arapahoe Basin (A-Basin). ✉ *Exit 216 off I–70, 12 mi west of Georgetown,* ☎ *303/569–3203.* ⏲ *Mid-Oct.–May, weekdays 9–4; weekends 8:30–4.*

Shopping

The **Georgetown Antique Emporium** (✉ 501 Rose St., ☎ 303/569–2727) specializes in oak and brass items. The **Trading Post** (✉ 510 6th St., ☎ 303/569–3375) specializes in Western paraphernalia, from pottery to jewelry to moccasins.

OFF THE BEATEN PATH

GUANELLA PASS SCENIC BYWAY – Get in the car and drive the 20-mi loop of Routes 381 and 62 for vistas of the Mt. Evans Wilderness Area. Then park yourself at the wildlife viewing station by Georgetown Lake, from where you can catch a glimpse of the state's largest herd of rare bighorn sheep.

En Route

The western slope of the Rockies past the Continental Divide is where the most—and fluffiest—snow falls. As you travel west along I–70, you'll reach one of the world's engineering marvels, the 8,941-ft-long **Eisenhower Memorial Tunnel.** Most people who drive through take its presence for granted, but until the first lanes were opened in 1973, the only route west was the perilous Loveland Pass, a twisting, roller coaster of a ride. Snow, mud, and a steep grade proved the downfall of many an intrepid motorist. In truly inclement weather, it was impassable, and the east and west slopes were completely cut off from each other. Authorities first proposed the Eisenhower in 1937 (under a different name, of course). At that time, most geologists warned about unstable rock; for more than three decades their direst predictions came true as rock walls crumbled, steel girders buckled, and gas pockets caused mysterious explosions. When the project was finally completed, more than 500,000 cubic yards of solid granite had been removed from Mt. Trelease. The original cost estimate in 1937 was $1 million. By the time the second bore was completed in 1979, the tunnel's cost had skyrocketed to $340 million.

Dillon/Silverthorne

26 *23 mi from Georgetown or 73 mi from Denver via I–70 west.*

Dillon was founded in the 1870s as a stagecoach stop and trading post for miners, but its location has changed twice since the town's conception. In the 1880s Dillon was moved closer to the railroad line. Then, in 1955, plans were drawn up to dam the Blue River, hence forming a reservoir to quench Denver's growing thirst. Dillon would end up submerged under 150 ft of water. Once again the town was moved. Foresighted residents decreed that no building in the new location would be higher than 30 ft, so as not to obstruct the view of the reservoir—now gratefully called Dillon Reservoir, or Lake Dillon. The potential tragedy turned into a boon and a boom for the reborn town, set on pine-blanketed hills mirrored in the sapphire water. There's no pretension to Dillon, just nature lovers and sports enthusiasts who take advantage of all the recreational opportunities their idyllic home affords. The neighboring town of Silverthorne, which straddles I–70, offers recreation of a different sort in its many factory outlet shops.

Dining

$–$$ ✕ **Historic Mint.** Built in 1862, this raucous eatery originally served as a bar and brothel. The old days are still evident in the bar's brass handles and hand-carved wood, as well as in the antiques and vintage photographs covering the walls of the dining area. Red meat and fish are the specialty here; you cook your own on lava rocks sizzling at 1,100 degrees. A well-stocked salad bar complements your entrée. If you prefer to leave the cooking to the chef, there's a prime rib special. ✉ *347 Blue River Pkwy., Silverthorne,* ☏ *970/468–5247. MC, V.*

$ ✕ **Blue Moon Bakery.** In addition to its excellent bagels, this stylish local deli has some tasty soups and pastas and a good selection of cold cuts and cheeses. Breakfast features homemade granola, scones, muffins, and turnovers. You can eat in at one of the five tables or take out, but just get there before closing, at 6 PM. ✉ *253 Summit, Summit Plaza Shopping Center, Silverthorne,* ☏ *970/468–1472. MC, V.*

Outdoor Activities and Sports

Summit Guides (✉ Box 2489, Dillon, ☏ 970/468–8945) offers full- and half-day fishing trips. There's horseback riding at **Eagles Nest Equestrian Center** (✉ Silverthorne, ☏ 970/468–0677).

Shopping

Silverthorne Factory Stores Complex (✉ 145 Stevens Way, Exit 205 off I–70, Silverthorne, ☏ 970/468–5780 or 800/866–5900) includes discount wares from Adolfo, Geoffrey Beene, Liz Claiborne, Evan Picone, Bass Shoe, Royal Doulton, Nike, and many others.

En Route Dillon is the gateway to a string of superb ski areas in **Summit County,** where four mega-areas—Keystone, Arapahoe Basin (A-Basin), Breckenridge, and Copper Mountain—attract skiers from all over the world. There's a saying among Summit County residents: Copper for skiing, Breck for lodging, and Keystone for food. The adage is accurate. So popular is Summit County, thanks to its incomparable setting, incredible variety of ski terrain, multitude of summer activities, and easy accessibility from Denver, that it welcomes more visitors annually than Aspen and Vail combined. Unfortunately, this creates terrible traffic snarls along I–70, especially on weekends and holidays.

Keystone

27 *8 mi from Dillon via U.S. 6 east.*

Keystone was designed to be cruisers' nirvana. With just enough flash to compete with the glamorous resorts, it compares favorably with the stylish if sterile megadevelopments of the Alps—such as France's Les Arcs. For the most part, its planners were sensitive to the environment, favoring mountain colors and materials that blend inconspicuously with the natural surroundings. Keystone has pursued an aggressive policy of expansion, opening the tougher terrain on North Peak (mogul heaven) and the Outback (glade skiing) in an attempt to change its "easy" reputation and provide a balanced ski experience. Keystone has one drawback: its sprawling base area. To improve this situation, an ambitious $700 million redevelopment plan has already begun to, among other things, overhaul the base areas and create more accommodations at the mountain itself. Keystone is becoming a magnet in summer, too, with a small lake for water sports, a top-ranked golf course, and the same premium service visitors can expect in winter.

Dining and Lodging

$$$$ ★ ✕ **Alpenglow Stube.** Without a doubt, this is the finest on-mountain restaurant in Colorado. The decor is warmly elegant, with exposed wood beams, a stone fireplace, and floral upholstery. At night, the gondola ride you take to get here is alone worth the cost of the meal. Dinner is a six-course extravaganza, starting with the signature pine cone paté, followed perhaps by a Stube specialty, such as rack of caribou in Poire William sauce. Lunch is equally delectable, with particularly fine pasta specials. (Removing your ski boots at lunch and putting on the plush slippers reserved for diners is a nice touch.) ✉ *North Peak, the Outpost,* ☎ *970/496–4132. Reservations essential. AE, D, DC, MC, V. No lunch in summer.*

$$$$ ★ ✕ **Keystone Ranch.** This glorious 1930s ranch homestead was once part of an actual working cattle ranch, and cowboy memorabilia is strewn throughout the restaurant, nicely blending with stylish throw rugs and Western craft work. The gorgeous and massive stone fireplace is a cozy backdrop for sipping an aperitif or after-dinner coffee. Chef Christopher Wing's rotating, seasonal six-course menu emphasizes indigenous ingredients, including farm-raised game and fresh fish. You're in luck if the menu includes elk with wild mushrooms in juniper sauce and quince relish or Gorgonzola flan. Finish your meal with a Grand Marnier soufflé drizzled with pistachio cream sauce. ✉ *Keystone Ranch Golf Course,* ☎ *970/496–4161. Reservations essential. AE, D, DC, MC, V. No lunch in winter.*

$$$$ ★ ✕ **Ski Tip Lodge.** In this original ski lodge circa 1800s, almost everything on the menu will melt in your mouth. The four-course, prix-fixe dinner is a favorite in the area for its American cuisine with a Colorado twist. The main course may be a hickory-smoked tenderloin or braised ring-necked pheasant or red trout paupiettes with crab, shrimp, and spinach. The delicious homemade bread and soup in the first course are a meal in themselves. Be sure to adjourn to the cozy lounge for the decadent desserts and special coffees. ✉ *0764 Montezuma Rd., 1 mi off U.S. 6,* ☎ *970/468–4202. AE, D, DC, MC, V.*

$$ ✕ **Gassy Thompson's Food & Spirits.** Imagine a sports bar crossbred with a hunting lodge, and you'll get an idea of the ambience and decor of this popular mountain-base hangout. Gassy Thompson was an 1880s miner said to have made his living by swindling other miners. In his namesake restaurant, hearty American fare is served up in generous portions. Pork barbecue is the specialty, with burgers and extra-large sandwiches vying for second place. Memorabilia from Colorado's mining days—picks, buckets, lamps, and drawings—keeps Gassy's spirit alive despite the honest dealings. ✉ *Mountain House,* ☎ *970/468–4386. Reservations not accepted. AE, D, DC, MC, V. Closed summer.*

$$ ✕ **Kickapoo Tavern.** This rustic bar and grill features Colorado microbrews on tap and big portions of home-style American food such as chili, hearty sandwiches and "a chicken in every pot" pie. The central location, outdoor patio, and TVs tuned to favorite sporting events keep the place hopping both après ski and après night-ski. ✉ *Jackpine Lodge, River Run Plaza,* ☎ *970/468–4601. AE, MC, V.*

$$$$ ★ 🏨 **Keystone Lodge.** The ugly cinder-block structure gives no hint of the gracious, pampered living within this member of Preferred Hotels. Rooms with king-size beds are on the small side, while rooms with two queen-size beds are enormous, with terraces. All units are beautifully appointed in rich mountain colors, with all the amenities. ✉ *Keystone Resort, Box 38, 80435,* ☎ *970/468–4242 or 800/222–0188,* FAX *970/468–4343. 152 rooms. 3 restaurants, bar, outdoor pool, hot tub, 2 tennis courts, health club, children's programs (ages 1–10), convention center. AE, D, DC, MC, V.*

$$–$$$ ★ **Ski Tip Lodge.** The rooms at this charming, elegant log cabin have quaint names such as Edna's Eyrie. They're uniquely decorated with homespun furnishings and accessories such as quilts and hand-knitted throw rugs. Some rooms have four-poster beds. Breakfast is included in the room rate, and, since the kitchen vies for best in Summit County with the Alpenglow Stube and Keystone Ranch, you won't be sorry if you take advantage of the deal. ✉ *Keystone Resort, Box 38, 80435,* ☎ *970/496–4202 or 800/222–0188,* FAX *970/468–4343. 11 rooms, 2 suites. Restaurant. AE, D, DC, MC, V.*

CONDOMINIUMS

Keystone Resort Corporation (☎ 970/468–2316 or 800/222–0188) operates all the lodging facilities at the resort, which range from hotel-style accommodations at Keystone Lodge (☞ *above*) to various condominium properties.

Nightlife

Kickapoo Tavern (☞ Dining and Lodging, *above*) is a popular Keystone hangout. Live music with rockabilly leanings makes the **Snake River Saloon** (✉ 23074 U.S. 6, 1 mi east of Keystone, ☎ 970/468–2788) a good spot to drink beer if you like a loud, music-driven environment. The crowd is generally under 30, but the occasional over-30 senior slips in.

Outdoor Activities and Sports

Mountain bikers in **Arapahoe National Forest** cycle over Loveland Pass and along the Blue River Bikeway and the Tenmile Canyon National Recreation Trail. Keystone boasts the largest maintained outdoor **ice-skating lake** (☎ 800/354–4386) in North America, with skate, sled, and hockey-stick rentals and lessons from late November to early March, daily 10–10. **Keystone Ranch Course** (✉ 22010 Rte. 6, ☎ 970/468–4250) is listed as one of the top 50 resort courses in America by *Golf Digest.* The 7,090-yard, par-72 course, designed by Robert Trent Jones Jr., winds through mountain scenery.

SKIING

Keystone. Three mountains—Keystone (which offers an extensive night-skiing system), North Peak, and the new Outback—make up Keystone Resort. A merger with Vail Associates in 1997 made Keystone part of the world's largest ski company, and means one ticket is good at Keystone, Breckenridge, Vail, and Beaver Creek. In all, Keystone boasts two high-speed gondolas, four high-speed quads, nine other chairs, and five surface lifts to connect this area, which just keeps growing. ☎ *970/468–2316.* ⏲ *Open late Oct.–early May, daily 8:30 AM–10 PM.*

Shopping

Keystone's **Edgewater Mall** and **Argentine Plaza** (✉ both on the shore of the lake at Keystone Village) have **shops** such as Rocky Mountain Chocolates and the upscale ski-clothing store Gorsuch.

Arapahoe Basin

7 mi from Dillon via U.S. 6 east.

Arapahoe was the first ski area to be built in Summit County, in the late '40s. Some say it hasn't changed since; the dig refers, in part, to some of Colorado's slowest lifts. Still, most of A-Basin's dedicated skiers wouldn't have it any other way. It's America's highest ski area, with a *base* elevation of 10,800 ft. Most of the runs are above timberline, giving it an almost otherworldly feel. Aficionados love the short lift lines, the literally breathtaking views (and altitudes), the whopping 90% intermediate and expert terrain, and the wide-open bowls that stay open into June (sometimes July). A-Basin came under new management in the late '70s, but, aside from some upgrading of facilities, it has remained true to its resolutely un-chic, gnarly self.

Outdoor Activities and Sports

SKIING

Arapahoe Basin. A-Basin offers predominantly intermediate and expert terrain (90% of the 490 acres), with a 2,250-ft vertical drop serviced by five lifts. ✉ *Box 8787, 80435,* ☎ *970/468–0718.* ⏲ *Mid-Nov.–mid-June, 8:30–4.*

Breckenridge

28 *22 mi from Keystone via U.S. 6 west, I–70 west, and Rte. 9 south.*

Many people consider Breckenridge the prettiest Colorado town. Gold was discovered here in 1859, and for the next several decades Breckenridge's fortunes rose and fell as its lodes of gold and then silver were mined and exhausted. It's the oldest continuously occupied town on the western slope. Much of its architectural legacy from the mining era remains.

The **downtown** comprises one of Colorado's largest National Historic Districts, with 254 buildings in the National Register of Historic Places. The district is roughly a compact 12 square blocks, bounded by Main, High, and Washington streets and Wellington Road. The Breckenridge Activity Center (✉ 201 S. Main St., ☎ 970/453–5579) and Summit Historical Society (✉ 309 N. Main St., ☎ 970/453–9022) publish guided tours of more than 40 prominent structures, which range from simple log cabins to false-fronts to Victorians with lacy gingerbread trim, all lovingly restored and painted.

The **skiing** at Breckenridge, which opened as a resort in 1961, is varied over Peaks 7, 8, 9, and 10 of the Tenmile Range. The only downside is the strenuous poling required between Breck's four mountains. There are bowls and chutes on Peak 7 and 8, which are above timberline; gentle sweeping runs on Peak 9; and roller-coaster steeps on Peak 10. Consistent with the town's proud heritage, many runs are named for the old mines, including Bonanza, Cashier, Gold King, and Wellington. Nonetheless, Breck has developed a reputation for embracing the new: It was one of the first areas to permit snowboarding, and it has hosted the annual World Cup Freestyle Classic. Also, for one week each January the town declares itself an independent kingdom during the wild revel called Ullr Fest, which honors the Norse God of snow.

Dining and Lodging

$$$–$$$$ ★ ✕ **Café Alpine.** This bright, cheerful place offers terrific soups, salads, and sandwiches at lunch, and more substantial regional American cuisine on a menu that changes daily at dinner. Try the seared salmon with mango pico de gallo or the New York strip steak with scalloped potatoes. At the tapas bar (served after 5) you can sample succulent offerings from around the world, including eggplant crepes, marinated quail breast, blackened tuna sashimi, and lamb chops Szechuan. The recipient of a Wine Spectator Award of Excellence since 1994, Café Alpine serves 20 wines by the glass. ✉ *106 E. Adams Ave.,* ☎ *970/453–8218. AE, D, MC, V.*

$$$ ✕ **Briar Rose.** Named for the old Briar Rose Silver Mine, this restaurant was once a boarding house for miners. Today it still displays a swanky, if somewhat faded, Victorian elegance, with gilt wallpaper and stained glass. Start with the crab-stuffed mushrooms, and choose from such wild game specials as elk tenderloins or sautéed pheasant with pine nut velouté. Prime rib and seafood round out the menu. ✉ *109 E. Lincoln St.,* ☎ *970/453–9948. AE, MC, V.*

$ ✕ **Blue Moose.** Locals flock here for the hearty breakfasts: satisfying eggs, oatmeal, pancakes, and more. Lunch is equally tasty. Choose from one of the sandwiches, burritos, pastas, or salads. Nothing here is fancy—food or decor—but a meal here will hit the spot. ✉ *540 S. Main St.,* ☎ *970/453–4859. MC, V. No dinner.*

$$$–$$$$ 🏨 **Lodge at Breckenridge.** This special property has the disadvantage of being outside town, though shuttle service is provided to the town and ski area. The compensation is the breathtaking panoramas of the Tenmile Range from nearly every angle. Huge, strategically placed picture windows allow full vantage. The look is mountain chalet, with a rustic-modern decor. The well-lit, spacious rooms all have cable TV and full bath. Minisuites also feature fireplace and kitchenette. Continental breakfast is included. The complete spa and health club facility is a bonus. ✉ *112 Overlook Dr., 80424,* ☎ *970/453–9300 or 800/736–1607,* FAX *970/453–0625. 45 rooms. Restaurant, indoor pool, 2 indoor hot tubs, 2 outdoor hot tubs, spa, health club, racquetball, pro shop, meeting rooms. AE, D, DC, MC, V.*

$$$–$$$$ 🏨 **Village at Breckenridge.** The word "village" puts it mildly, at this sprawling, self-contained resort spread over 14 acres, offering several varieties of accommodation from lodge-style rooms to three-bedroom condominiums, all ski-in, ski-out. The decor runs from Southwestern color schemes to gleaming chrome-and-glass units. Studios and efficiencies have fireplaces and kitchenettes. ✉ *Box 8329, 80424,* ☎ *970/453–2000 or 800/800–7829,* FAX *970/453–3116. 347 rooms. 9 restaurants, 3 bars, indoor–outdoor pool, 2 outdoor pools, 9 hot tubs, sauna, 1 health club, ice-skating, ski shop, theater, meeting rooms, car rental. AE, D, DC, MC, V.*

$$–$$$$ ★ 🏨 **B&Bs on North Main Street.** Innkeepers Fred Kinat and Diane Jaynes spent a year restoring an intimate, 1885 miner's cottage, then expanded it with utmost care. In 1994 they opened Willoughby Cottage next door, a romantic retreat complete with a gas-burning fireplace, hot tub, kitchenette, and rustic antique furnishings. A new addition—Barn Above the River—contains five rooms in a timber-frame barn, done in primitive Western decor. Best of all are the affable hosts: Avid skiers ("Cold cereal on powder days," they warn), owners Fred and Diane take guests to their secret ski spots. ✉ *303 N. Main St.,* ☎ *970/453–2975 or 800/795–2975. 12 rooms. AE, DC, MC, V.*

$$–$$$ 🏨 **Great Divide Lodge.** This property is just 50 yards from the base of Peak 9. The only full-service hotel in Breckenridge, it was planned as a condo development, but management ran out of financing. This pays dividends in the enormous bedrooms, which feature pleasing contemporary Southwestern decor in teal, salmon, mauve, and maroon. The one surprising omission: air conditioning (though it's rarely necessary). ✉ *550 Village Rd., 80424,* ☎ *970/453–4500 or 800/321–8444,* FAX *970/453–0212. 208 rooms. Restaurant, bar, indoor pool, 2 hot tubs, health club, ski shop, meeting rooms. AE, D, DC, MC, V.*

$$ 🏨 **Allaire Timbers Inn.** Nestled in a wooded area, this stone-and-timber log cabin inn has a great room anchored by a huge stone fireplace, as well as a reading loft and a sunroom with a green slate floor and handcrafted log furniture. The main deck and hot tub offer spectacular views of the Tenmile Range. A hearty breakfast is included, as is an afternoon happy hour. ✉ *9511 S. Main St., 80424,* ☎ *970/453–7530 or 800/624–4904,* FAX *970/453–8699. 8 rooms, 2 suites. Outdoor hot tub. AE, D, MC, V.*

CONDOMINIUMS

Breckenridge Accommodations (✉ Box 1931, 80424, ☎ 970/453–9140 or 800/872–8789; FAX 970/453–8686). **Breckenridge Central Lodging** (✉ Box 709, 80424, ☎ 970/453–2160 or 800/858–5885; FAX 970/453–

4163). **Breckenridge Resort Chamber Central Reservation System** (☎ 970/453–6018 or 800/221–1091). **East West Resorts/AMR Lodging** (✉ Box 2009, 80424, ☎ 970/453–4222 or 800/525–2258, FAX 970/453–0463). **Summit County Central Reservations** (✉ Box 446, Dillon 80435, ☎ 970/468–6222 or 800/365–6365; FAX 970/468–5660).

Nightlife

BARS AND LOUNGES

Breckenridge Brewery (✉ 600 S. Main St., ☎ 970/453–1550), brews up six premium homemade beers. It's a great après-ski spot. **Hearthstone** (✉ 130 S. Ridge St., ☎ 970/453–1148), set in a former bordello and decorated with maroon velour walls and lace curtains, is a congenial hangout. Skiers and locals scarf down the addictive happy-hour special, jalapeño-wrapped shrimp.

MUSIC CLUBS

Alligator Lounge (✉ 318 S. Main St., ☎ 970/453–7782) is the hot spot for acoustic, blues, Cajun, and reggae sets. **Salt Creek Saloon** (✉ 110 E. Lincoln Ave., ☎ 970/453–4959) offers free dance lessons several nights a week and occasional live C&W bands. **Tiffany's** (✉ 20 Village Rd., ☎ 970/453–6000, ext. 8732) has a DJ and dancing nightly.

Outdoor Activities and Sports

Breckenridge Recreation Center (✉ Kingdom Park, ☎ 970/453–1734) is a state-of-the-art, 62,000-square-ft facility that has a fully equipped health club, two swimming pools, and indoor tennis and racquetball courts. For horseback riding, try **Breckenridge Stables** (☎ 970/453–4438). **Performance Tours Rafting** (✉ Box 7305, Breckenridge 80424, ☎ 970/453–0661 or 800/328–7238) leads rafting trips for families and experienced rafters ready for extremes. **Mountain Anglers** (✉ Breckenridge, ☎ 970/453–4665) organizes fishing trips throughout Summit County. **Good Times** (✉ Breckenridge, ☎ 970/453–7604) will get you snowmobiling.

GOLF

Breckenridge Golf Club (✉ 200 Clubhouse Dr., ☎ 970/453–9104), the only municipally owned Jack Nicklaus–designed course in the world, is a 7,279-yard, par-72 beauty. Dramatically situated, it resembles a nature reserve, with woods and beaver ponds lining the fairways.

SKIING

At **Breckenridge,** 17 lifts (including four speedy "SuperChair" quads) serve 2,023 skiable acres and a 3,398-ft vertical drop. It offers more than half advanced and expert terrain. ☎ *970/453–5000.* ⏲ *Late Oct.–late May, 8:30–3:45.*

For cross-country, **Breckenridge Nordic Ski Center** (☎ 970/453–6855) maintains 18 km (10 mi) of trails in its system.

Shopping

There's high-end shopping in the **Lincoln West Mall** (✉ Main St. and Lincoln Ave.), **Tower Square** (✉ Main St. and Lincoln Ave.), and **La Cima** (✉ Main St. between Jefferson and Ridge Sts.).

CRAFT AND ART GALLERIES

The **Bay Street Company** (✉ 232 S. Main St., ☎ 970/453–6303) carries colorful hand-painted furniture and collectibles in a quaint Victorian house. **Homegrown Creations** (✉ 109 N. Main St., ☎ 970/453–1025) features pottery, jewelry, candles, and sculpture by Colorado artists. **Skilled Hands Gallery** (✉ 110 S. Main St., ☎ 970/453–7818) is the largest arts-and-crafts gallery in Summit County, offering everything from wood carvings to wind chimes.

Frisco

29 *9 mi from Breckenridge via Rte. 9 north.*

Funky, low-key Frisco contains an odd hodgepodge of strip malls near the interstate and a charming downtown district trimmed with restored bed-and-breakfasts and hell-raising bars. The town is a sane, moderate alternative to the glitzier, pricier resorts in Summit County. It's worth exploring even if you're staying elsewhere.

The **Frisco Historic Park** re-creates the boom days with a fully outfitted one-room schoolhouse, jail, and log chapel among the seven authentic 19th-century buildings. ✉ *Main and 2nd Sts.,* ☎ *970/668–3428.* *Free.* *Tues.–Sat. 11–4; Sun. 11–4 in summer only.*

Dining and Lodging

$$ ✕ **El Rio.** On a sunny deck overlooking Tenmile Creek and Gore Range, you can enjoy great margaritas and very fresh south-of-the-border specialties, such as blackened fish tacos, or Taos tacos: a soft flour tortilla with cheese, pinto beans, and roasted vegetables. ✉ *450 W. Main St.,* ☎ *970/668–5043. AE, MC, V.*

$–$$ ✕ **Frisco Bar & Grill.** You'll find no frills here, just juicy burgers (nine varieties), hellacious nachos, buffalo wings, and a lively crowd in this classic pub with neon signs on the walls and sawdust on the floors. ✉ *720 Granite St., Boardwalk Blvd.,* ☎ *970/668–5051. Reservations not accepted. AE, MC, V.*

$–$$$ **Hotel Frisco.** The lobby soars 2½ stories in this mountain-charming, centrally located lodge on historic Main Street. Easy access to Copper Mountain, Breckenridge, Keystone, and Vail/Beaver Creek, in addition to nearby river rafting, hiking, and fly fishing, make this hotel a find in any season. Toast your toes by the river-rock fireplace after a day on the slopes. The owner, a former Colorado ski patroller, happily shares tips. ✉ *308 Main St., 80443,* ☎ *970/668–5009 or 800/262–1002. 14 rooms. Hot tub. AE, D, MC, V.*

Nightlife

The **Moose Jaw** (✉ 208 Main St., ☎ 970/668–3931) is definitely a locals' hangout. Pool tables beckon the unwary, and a plethora of old photographs, trophies, and newspaper articles makes the barn-wood walls all but invisible.

Outdoor Activities and Sports

Breckenridge and Frisco Nordic Center (✉ 18454 N. Summit Blvd., ☎ 970/668–0866) has 45 km (27 mi) of one-way loops for cross-country skiing. Contact **Timber Ridge Tours** (✉ Frisco, ☎ 970/668–8349) for snowmobiling.

Shopping

The **Cactus Patch** (✉ 401 Main St., ☎ 970/668–1240) showcases the work of local artists, from hand-dyed silk scarves to whimsical woodworkings. The **Junk-Tique Antique Barn** (✉ 313 Main St., ☎ 970/668–3040) is filled with odds and ends.

Copper Mountain

30 *7 mi from Frisco via I–70 south.*

Copper Mountain is dedicated to skiing, although it's picking up as a summer resort. Many skiers think the award-winning design, perfectly contoured to the natural terrain, is one of the world's best. The layout is ideal: Beginner runs are concentrated on the right side (facing the mountain) of the area, intermediate runs in the center, and expert terrain to the left. Weaker skiers can't get into trouble unless they look for it. Accommodations here are uniformly excellent, the nightlife lively for singles and younger couples, and the variety of activities and programs perfect for families. That said, the resort lacks a real town, and doesn't have much in the way of personality.

Dining and Lodging

$$$ ✕ **Molly B's Saloon.** This newly opened American bistro serves contemporary dishes with a fresh, flavorful twist. Try the rotisserie chicken, pork loin with ancho chile and peach glaze, Thai beef salad, and pan-roasted mussels. ✉ *102 Wheeler Circle,* ☎ *970/968–2318. AE, D, DC, MC, V.*

$$$ ✕ **Pesce Fresco.** This is *the* spot at Copper, for hearty breakfasts, a surprisingly affordable sit-down lunch, après-ski hors d'oeuvres and evening nightcaps, as well as dinner. The menu is mainly fish, with some solid, if uninspired, pastas. Among the best entrées are seafood fettucine and scaloppini of elk with tomatoes, mushrooms, and Gorgonzola cheese. Other highlights are grilled salmon and Rocky Mountain trout. The understated decor, good service, and weekend piano music make it a popular gathering place. ✉ *Mountain Plaza Bldg.,* ☎ *970/968–2882, ext. 6505. AE, D, DC, MC, V.*

$$–$$$$ 🏨 **Copper Mountain Resort.** The resort runs all 22 lodging facilities, ranging from hotel-style units to condos. All include use of the Copper Mountain Racquet and Athletic Club. The condo-based Central Village complex is the most conveniently located, within easy walking distance of the lifts, and the most favored by families. Units range in size from one to four bedrooms; most have a fireplace and a balcony. Two small subdivisions, the Woods and Legends Town Homes, have some of the largest and most upscale accommodations at the resort, with three or four bedrooms, full kitchens, dining areas, patios, garages, and some private hot tubs. ✉ *Box 3001, Copper Mountain Resort, 209 Tenmile Circle, 80443,* ☎ *970/968–2882 or 800/458–8383,* FAX *970/968–6227. 1,100 rooms. 3 restaurants, 3 cafeterias, coffee shop, pool, sauna, hot tubs, 18-hole golf course, 8 tennis courts, health club, hiking, horseback riding, racquetball, ice-skating, cross-country skiing, downhill skiing, ski shop, playground, business services, convention center. AE, D, DC, MC, V.*

Nightlife

BARS AND LOUNGES

Double Diamond Bar and Grill (✉ base of B-Lift, ☎ 970/968–2880) and **Farley's** (✉ Snowflake Bldg., ☎ 970/968–2577) are hot spots for lunch and **happy hour,** as is the frequently raucous **Sports Bar at O'Shea's** (✉ base of American Eagle, ☎ 970/968–2882, ext. 6504). The best **après-ski** scene is at the always-packed **Kokomo's** (✉ Copper Commons, ☎ 970/968–2318).

MUSIC CLUBS

Club Med (☎ 970/968–2161) offers an international dinner buffet that includes bar games, nightly entertainment and admission to its disco. You can forgo dinner and just hit the show and disco. **Pesce Fresco** (☞ Dining and Lodging, *above*) offers jazz piano weekends in season.

Outdoor Activities and Sports

Vail Fishing Guides (☎ 970/476–3296) provides gear as well as guided tours. **Copper Creek Golf Club** (✉ Wheeler Circle, Copper Mountain, ☎ 970/968–2339), at 9,650 ft, is the highest 18-hole course in North America. Designed by Pete and Perry Dye, the par-70, 6,094-yard course follows the twisting, narrow, natural terrain of Copper's valley. You can get your exercise indoors at **Copper Mountain Racquet and Athletic Club** (☞ Dining and Lodging, *above*).

SKIING

Copper Mountain Resort (☞ Dining and Lodging, above) offers 2,433 acres of skiing on 117 trails and four back bowls, with a 2,601-ft vertical serviced by 20 lifts. The area also provides the "Extreme Experience" on 350 acres of guided adventure skiing. For cross-country, Copper Mountain/Trak Cross-Country Center offers 25 km (15½ mi) of groomed track and skate lanes. ⏲ *Mid-Nov.–late Apr., 8:30–4.*

Leadville

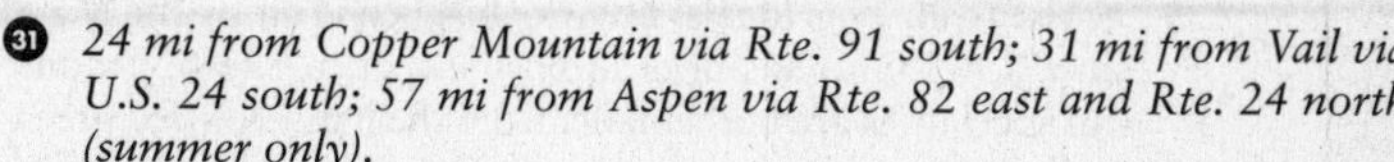

31 *24 mi from Copper Mountain via Rte. 91 south; 31 mi from Vail via U.S. 24 south; 57 mi from Aspen via Rte. 82 east and Rte. 24 north (summer only).*

In the history of Colorado mining, perhaps no town looms larger than Leadville—at 10,152 ft, America's highest incorporated town. (In summer the drive on Route 82 from Aspen over Independence Pass is spectacular.) Two of the state's most fascinating figures are immortalized in Leadville: larger-than-life multimillionaire Horace Tabor and his wife Baby Doe (Elizabeth Doe McCourt), the subject of John La-Touche's Pulitzer Prize–winning opera *The Ballad of Baby Doe.*

Tabor amassed a huge fortune (by 1880s standards) of $12 million, much of which he spent building monuments throughout the state to himself and Baby. His power peaked when he purchased a U.S. Senate seat and replaced Senator Henry Teller, who had been appointed Secretary of the Interior, well into his term. Baby Doe was his ambitious mistress and eventual second wife, after he dumped his first, the faithful Augusta. They made enemies and incurred the scorn of "high society" as only those who throw their money and weight around can. But in 1893 the repeal of the Sherman Act demonetized silver and, like so many other mining magnates, Tabor was ruined. He died a pauper in 1899, admonishing Baby to "hang on to the Matchless," his most famous mine, which he was convinced would once again restore her fortunes. It never did. Baby became a recluse, rarely venturing forth from her tiny unheated cabin beside the Matchless. She froze to death in 1935.

Their legacy can be found in several attractions in town. The **Tabor Home** (✉ 116 E. 5th St., ☎ 719/486–2092) is the modest dwelling where Horace lived with Augusta. Admission is free. Call to arrange a tour, only for groups of 10 or more. The splendiferous **Tabor Opera House** (✉ 308 Harrison St., ☎ 719/486–3900) is $4 and open summers, Sunday–Friday 9–5:30. The **Matchless Mine** (☎ 719/486–1899) and squalid Baby Doe's Cabin are 2 mi east of downtown on 7th Street. Admission is $3.50 and the mine is open in summer from 9 to 5 daily.

The **Mining Hall of Fame and Museum** covers virtually every aspect of mining, including displays of various ores, tools, equipment, and dioramas explaining the extraction processes. ✉ *120 W. 9th St.,* ☎ *719/486–1229.* 🎟 *$3.50.* ⏲ *May–Oct., daily 9–5; Nov.–Apr., weekdays 10–2.*

A museum complex on Harrison Street comprises the **Healy House** and the Dexter Cabin—an 1878 Greek Revival clapboard house and an 1879 log cabin—two of Leadville's earliest houses. The lavishly decorated rooms yield clues as to how the upper crust such as the Tabors lived and played. ✉ *912 Harrison St.,* ☎ *719/486–0487.* 🎟 *$3.50.* ⏲ *Memorial Day–Labor Day, daily 10–4:30.*

The **Heritage Museum** paints a vivid portrait of life in Leadville at its zenith, with dioramas depicting the old mines as well as furniture, clothing, and toys from the Victorian era. ✉ *120 E. 9th St.,* ☎ *719/486–1878.* 🎫 *$2.50.* ⏲ *June–Sept., daily 10–6.*

Eccentricity is still a Leadville trait, as witnessed by the annual **International Pack Burro Race** over Mosquito Pass. The race, held the first weekend of August, ends in Fairplay, another quirky old mining town. The event is immortalized with T-shirts and bumper stickers that read, "Get Your Ass Over the Pass."

Dining and Lodging

$ ✕ **The Grill.** This locals' favorite has been run by the Martinez family since 1965 (and has been in business since 1938). Traditional Mexican specialties are homemade, from the hand-roasted green chili to the stuffed sopaipillas. In summer, you can sip margaritas on the patio while you toss horseshoes. ✉ *715 Elm St.,* ☎ *719/486–9930. MC, V.*

$–$$ 🏨 **Ice Palace Inn Bed & Breakfast.** The original Leadville Ice Palace, built in 1895–96 on 5 acres of 5 tons of ice and housing enormous ice sculptures, was the inspiration for today's Ice Palace, a refurbished Victorian built in 1900 with lumber taken from the original. The rooms are named for the rooms of the original. A full breakfast and afternoon tea are included in the room rate. ✉ *813 Spruce St., 80461,* ☎ *719/486–8272 or 800/754–2840. 6 rooms. AE, D, MC, V.*

$ 🏨 **Hotel Delaware.** This beautifully restored hotel is on the National Register of Historic Places; recent renovations have renewed its original 1888 Victorian condition. The lobby is graced with period antiques, brass fixtures, crystal chandeliers, and oak paneling. The comfortable rooms have lace curtains and antique heirloom quilts, in addition to modern conveniences such as private bath and cable TV. A Continental breakfast is included in the rate. ✉ *700 Harrison Ave., 80461,* ☎ *719/486–1418 or 800/748–2004,* FAX *719/486–2214. 36 rooms. Restaurant, bar, hot tub. AE, DC, MC, V.*

Outdoor Activities and Sports

At **Ski Cooper** 70% of the 385 skiable acres are rated beginner or intermediate, but the area—with a 1,200-ft vertical drop—also runs Sno-Cat tours into 1,800 acres of pristine backcountry powder. ✉ *9 mi west of Leadville on Rte. 24,* ☎ *719/486–3684.* ⏲ *Late-Nov.–early Apr., daily 9–4.*

There's snowmobiling at **2 Mile Hi Ski-Doo** (☎ 719/486–1183).

Vail

32 *20 mi from Copper Mountain or 100 mi from Denver via I–70 west.*

Just a hop, skip, and a jump west of Summit County on I–70 is one of the nation's leading ski destinations, consistently ranked the finest ski resort in North America, if not the world: Vail. The four-letter word means Valhalla for skiers and conjures up images of the rich and famous enjoying their privileges. Actually, Vail is one of the least likely success stories in skiing. Seen from the village, the mountain doesn't look all that imposing. There are no glowering glaciers, no couloirs and chutes slashed from the rock, not even an Olympian summit shrouded in clouds. Even local historians admit that the Gore Creek Valley in which Vail regally sits was an impoverished backwater, too isolated to play a prominent or colorful role in Colorado history, until the resort's opening in 1962.

In truth, the men who lent their names to the valley and resort deserved more notoriety than notice. Sir St. George Gore was a swaggering, filthy rich, drunken lout of a baronet who went on a three-year bacchanal in the 1850s and butchered every herd of elk and buffalo in sight. Charles

Vail, the otherwise obscure chief engineer of the Colorado Highway Department from 1930 to 1945 was—according to townspeople who dealt with him—an ornery cuss who was rumored to accept kickbacks from contractors.

Then, two visionaries appeared on the scene: Pete Seibert, a veteran of the 10th Mountain Division that prepared for alpine warfare in the surrounding Gore and Sawatch ranges during World War II, and Earl Eaton, a uranium prospector who had grown up in and surveyed these very ranges. In 1957 they ascended the mountain now known as Vail, and upon attaining the summit discovered what skiers now salivate over: the Back Bowls, 4,000 acres of open glades formed when the Ute Indians set "spite fires" to the timberland in retaliation for being driven out by ranchers and miners. After five years of bureaucratic red tape and near financial suicide, Seibert's dream became reality, and Vail resort was created.

Former owner George Gillett calls Vail "one of God's special works," and in reality it is an almost perfect example of mountain-and-village design. The development is remarkably compact, divided into the residential East Vail, the upscale Vail Village, and the more modest utilitarian Lionshead. Vail resembles a quaint Bavarian hamlet, with homey inns and lodges nestled against cozy A-frame chalets and clock towers. This, along with a heavy European bias among both the population and clientele, gives Vail perhaps the most international flavor and flair of any Colorado resort. It's crafted to anticipate a guest's every need, so you'll find a wealth of dining, shopping, and entertainment options at your fingertips. Everyone here is thoroughly professional: friendly without being familiar, knowing their business but not yours. Despite its tony reputation, the resort has actively courted the family trade in recent years. Children love the kids-only amusement parks at the ski area, with 15 acres of ski-through tepee villages, gold mines, and other attractions.

Although the mountain has the sheer exhilarating edge in size over nearly every other North American ski area, it's brilliantly and clearly linked by a well-placed network of lifts and trails. There are 1,220 acres of immensely varied runs on the front side alone, but the Back Bowls are truly skiers' heaven: With more than twice the skiable terrain accessed from the front, the back side has eye-popping expanses of fluffy white snow that make both intermediates and experts feel they can ski for days and not run into a single soul. Those same slopes have become a mecca for mountain bike fanatics in summer, and the village now hosts a wide variety of festivals year-round.

At cosmopolitan Vail the emphasis is on luxury, although the pre-fab buildings are beginning to show their age. The best sightseeing is window-shopping, ogling the deluxe merchandise and the consumers—a delightful rather than daunting experience. While you're here, there are two tourist attractions worth visiting. The **Betty Ford Alpine Gardens** (✉ Ford Park, adjacent to the Ford Amphitheater, ☎ 970/476–0103), open daily from snowmelt (around Memorial Day) to snowfall (around Labor Day), are an oasis of forsythia, heather, wild roses, and shrubs, and have the distinction of being the highest public botanic gardens in North America. The **Colorado Ski Museum/Ski Hall of Fame** (✉ 231 S. Frontage Rd., ☎ 970/476–1876), open Tuesday through Sunday, traces the development of the sport throughout the world, with an emphasis on Colorado's contributions. On display are century-old skis and tows, early ski fashions, and an entire room devoted to the 10th Mountain Division.

The rest of Vail Valley is composed of solid working-class towns such as Avon, Eagle, Edwards, and **Minturn,** which is enjoying a renaissance thanks to the influx of savvy artists and entrepreneurs who have opened several superb galleries and the Minturn Cellars winery.

Dining and Lodging

$$$$ ✕ **Alpen Rose Tea Room.** Peter Haller's establishment started as a tearoom and bakery in 1976. The pink, frilly decor is just as sugar-coated. This is rich, luscious, love-handle cuisine with tons of calories and drowned in butter: so good and so bad for you. The schnitzels, steak tartare, and fresh seafood specials are all home cooking at its best. ✉ *100 E. Meadow Dr.,* ☎ *970/476–3194. AE, MC, V. No lunch Tues.*

$$$$ ✕ **Game Creek Club.** Catch a heated gondola and then a Sno-Cat to Vail's exclusive on-mountain lunch club, now open to the public for dinner. In this Bavarian-style lodge, be prepared to linger over a four-course prix-fixe meal. You might start with a salad followed by Chilean sea bass encrusted in *panko* (Japanese bread crumbs), crispy corn-meal-crusted soft shell crabs, veal medallions with foie gras, or the 15-ounce buffalo steak. ✉ *600 Lionshead Circle,* ☎ *970/479–4275. Reservations essential. AE, D, DC, MC, V. No lunch.*

$$$$ ✕ **Michael's American Bistro.** This very sleek, stylish boîte overlooks the atrium of the Gateway Mall, but the space is dramatic: fancifully carved wood columns, lacquered black tables, and striking—almost disturbing—photographs and art on the walls. The hip atmosphere is further accentuated by cool jazz and the slinky, extremely attentive wait staff garbed entirely in black. Try the crab cake with mango chipotle sauce, the seared tuna sashimi with cumin-coriander crust, and the signature dish, tuna pepper steak with ginger and basil pesto. All courses are superbly presented, with festive colors springing from the plate—giving equal weight to the palette and the palate. The fine, extensive wine list has several bargains under $25. ✉ *12 S. Frontage Rd.,* ☎ *970/476–5353. AE, D, DC, MC, V.*

$$$$ ★ ✕ **Sweet Basil.** The understated decor—blond wood chairs and muted teal and buff walls—is enlivened by towering floral arrangements and abstract art. Chef Bruce Yim serves American cuisine with Mediterranean and Asian influences. Try the angel-hair pasta with seafood and double-cut pork chops with Chinese mustard and jasmine rice. ✉ *193 E. Gore Creek Dr.,* ☎ *970/476–0125. AE, MC, V.*

$$$$ ★ ✕ **Terra Bistro.** In the Vail Athletic Club, this sleek, airy space, with a warm fireplace contrasting with black wood chairs and black-and-white photographs, is a sterling addition to the Vail dining scene. Chef Tim Graybill's innovative, seasonal menu caters to both meat-and-potatoes diners and vegetarians. Wild mushroom risotto cake with grilled vegetables and peppered beef tenderloin with shallots in a cabernet reduction with herbed Yukon gold potatoes are headliners. Organic produce and free-range meat and poultry are used whenever possible. ✉ *352 E. Meadow Dr.,* ☎ *970/476–6836. AE, D, MC, V.*

$$$ ✕ **Blu's.** This fun, casual, constantly hopping place is a Vail institution, with an eclectic, affordable menu. The food is always fresh and zippy, from barbecue chicken and asparagus pizza to kick-ass California chicken relleño. Blu's is open for breakfast, lunch, and dinner. Breakfast and lunch are much cheaper than dinner. Blu's is a lively spot, more bistro than restaurant, and enjoys a great location in the heart of Vail Village. ✉ *193 E. Gore Creek Dr.,* ☎ *970/476–3113. Reservations not accepted. D, MC, V.*

$$–$$$ ✕ **Fiesta's!** The Marquez sisters, Debbie and Susan, use family recipes brought to Colorado by their great-grandparents to create Fiesta's authentic Southwestern cuisine. Among the menu favorites are shrimp *carnitas,* marinated shrimp served on a platter with warm hand-made

tortillas; and blue corn enchiladas, served Santa Fe–style with an egg on top. Also try the handmade corn tamales stuffed with pork and smothered in a classic New Mexican chile sauce. Fiesta's is a warm, brightly decorated place with lots of New Mexican folk art and paintings. ✉ *57 Edwards Access Rd., Edwards Plaza, 4 mi west of Beaver Creek,* ☎ *970/926–2121. Reservations essential. AE, D, DC, MC, V.*

$$ ✕ **Minturn Country Club.** This rustic, homey joint is a favorite hangout of racers during World Cup ski competitions, when they literally hang from the rafters. Steaks, prime rib, fish, and chicken preparations vary wildly, but you have only yourself to blame if you wanted it medium rare and it comes out well done: you cook everything yourself. ✉ *Main St., Minturn,* ☎ *970/827–4114. Reservations not accepted. MC, V. No lunch.*

$$ ✕ **The Saloon.** Skiers in the know do the "Minturn Mile" at the end of the day, bushwhacking out the bottom of Game Creek Bowl and ending up a few steps from this venerable gathering place. (Warning: this is not ski area–maintained terrain, and there is no transportation back. Of course, you can always drive here.) The reward is margaritas made with real lime juice, Mexican food in an Old West atmosphere, a children's menu, serve-yourself chips and homemade salsa, such specialties as chili rellenos and the steak and quail plate, and a bar that's always packed with locals. ✉ *146 N. Main St., Minturn,* ☎ *970/827–5954. Reservations not accepted. AE, MC, V. No lunch.*

$ ✕ **Hubcap Brewery and Kitchen.** Vail's first microbrewery offers five regular beers (Vail Pale Ale and Beaver Tail Brown Ale are standouts) and rotating specials. The decor is upscale-diner, with gleaming chrome hubcaps (owner Lance Lucy welcomes additions) adorning the walls. The food is mostly superior pub grub, such as cream cheese and crab-stuffed wontons, chicken wings, and quesadillas. ✉ *Crossroads Shopping Center,* ☎ *970/476–5757. AE, MC, V.*

$$$$ ★ **Sonnenalp.** This property, in the midst of a pseudo-Bavarian village, impresses as the real thing, and for good reason: The owning Fassler family has been in the hotel business in Germany for generations. The Swiss Hotel and Spa is quaint, with Bavarian pine armoires and secretaries and down comforters; and the large, sunny Sonnenalp Resort at Vail suites have an elegant lodge look, with stucco walls, wood beams, and heated marble floors. The superb restaurants include the Western saloon Bully Ranch (great barbecue), the Swiss Chalet (sensational fondue), and the elegant, Continental Ludwig's. ✉ *20 Vail Rd., 81657,* ☎ *970/476–5656 or 800/654–8312,* FAX *970/476–1639. 93 rooms, 93 suites. 3 restaurants, 1 bar, 2 indoor pools, outdoor pool, 2 indoor hot tubs, outdoor hot tub, 2 spas, 3 exercise rooms. AE, DC, MC, V.*

$$$$ **Vail Cascade Hotel and Club.** Down-to-earth yet glamorous is the best way to describe this ski-in/ski-out hotel that manages—despite its fairly large size—to maintain an intimate feel, thanks to the expert staff. Rooms in the older wing are done in mountain colors; those in the newer Terrace Wing have been beautifully redone in burgundy and emerald tones with rich, deep plaid and floral fabrics, wicker beds, and wrought-iron lamps. Alfredo's has long been one of the best Italian restaurants in the valley. Guests have access to the adjoining Cascade Athletic Club. ✉ *1300 Westhaven Dr., 81657,* ☎ *970/476–7111,* FAX *970/479–7020. 290 rooms, 28 suites. Restaurant, bar, pool, beauty salon, 2 hot tubs, spa, 4 indoor tennis courts, health club, ski shop, cinema, meeting rooms. AE, DC, MC, V.*

$$$–$$$$ **Lodge at Vail.** The first hotel to open in Vail remains one of its swankiest. As they say in the hotel business, it has "location, location, location," which translates to ski-in/ski-out status. The medium-size rooms are frilly and floral, a riot of pastels, with mahogany and teak furnishings and marble baths. The 49 suites are individually owned and decorated

condos, but they must meet rigorous standards set by management. Mickey's piano bar is a favored après-ski spot. ✉ *174 E. Gore Creek Dr., 81657,* ☎ *970/476–5011 or 800/331–5634,* FAX *970/476–7425. 76 rooms, 49 suites. 2 restaurants, bar, pool, hot tub, sauna, spa, exercise room, ski shop. AE, D, DC, MC, V.*

$–$$$$ **Minturn Inn.** This 1915 three-story home is older than the town of Vail. The owners have painstakingly restored it into a charming inn with 10 theme rooms (two with shared baths). The Angler, for example, has carved wooden fish and fly-fishing paraphernalia, while the 10th Mountain Division is decorated with skis and snowshoes. The beds are handmade of logs, with quilt coverings. Most rooms have mountain and river views; some have Jacuzzis. The four rooms in the newer lodge across the alley (built in 1998) have private decks or patios overlooking Eagle River. Hearty breakfasts and afternoon wine and cheese are served around a river-rock fireplace. ✉ *442 N. Main St., Box 186, Minturn 81645,* ☎ *970/827–9647 or 800/646–8876,* FAX *970/827–5590. 14 rooms. Sauna. AE, D, MC, V.*

$–$$$$ **Sitzmark Lodge.** This cozy lodge brims with European ambience, thanks to many repeat international guests (it's often booked months in advance). The good-size rooms look out onto either the mountain or Gore Creek. Decor is a hodgepodge, ranging from dark to blond woods and rose, teal, or floral fabrics. Each unit has a balcony, refrigerator, cable TV, hair dryer, and humidifier; some deluxe rooms have gas-burning fireplaces. The staff is ultrafriendly, encouraging guests to congregate in the sunny, split-level living room for complimentary mulled wine. A Continental breakfast is gratis in winter. ✉ *183 Gore Creek Dr., 81657,* ☎ *970/476–5001,* FAX *970/476–8702. 35 rooms. Restaurant, pool, indoor and outdoor hot tubs, sauna. D, MC, V.*

$$–$$$ **Gasthof Gramshammer.** Pepi Gramshammer, a former Austrian Olympic ski racer, is one of Vail's most beloved and respected citizens, whose labor of love—Wedel Weeks—ranks among the country's best intensive ski programs. His charming rooms are done up in pastels, with original oil paintings, and fluffy down comforters. Pepi's and Antlers, the property's two fine restaurants, have a European ambience, with stucco walls, wood-beam ceilings, and waitresses in dirndls. ✉ *231 E. Gore Creek Dr., 81657,* ☎ *970/476–5626 or 800/610–7374,* FAX *970/476–8816. 40 rooms. 2 restaurants, bar, 2 hot tubs, sauna, exercise room, ski shop. AE, MC, V.*

$–$$ ★ **Roost Lodge.** Situated on I–70 and advertising economical rates, comfortable rooms, and a heated pool, this accommodation is true to its promise—and then some, considering the price. The airy rooms are pleasing, many with four-poster beds, all with basic amenities. The staff is helpful, and complimentary Continental breakfast and afternoon wine and cheese are served daily in ski season. ✉ *1783 N. Frontage Rd. W, 81657,* ☎ *970/476–5451 or 800/873–3065,* FAX *970/476–9158. 70 rooms, 2 suites. Pool, hot tub, sauna. AE, D, DC, MC, V.*

CONDOMINIUMS

Vail/Beaver Creek Reservations (☎ 800/525–2257) can handle all calls, requests, and bookings. Among the recommended Vail properties are Cascade Village, Manor Vail, Vail Village Inn, and Simba Resort (all of which have several extras, including restaurants and shops on site). Vail Village Inn is especially notable for the unusual Dieter Menzel-designed woodwork (☞ Shopping, *below*) throughout the property. Top Beaver Creek facilities, also with the above extras, include the Poste Montane, St. James Place, and the Charter. The **Vail Valley Tourism & Convention Bureau** (☎ 800/824–5737) also helps with condominium bookings and information.

Nightlife and the Arts

BARS AND LOUNGES

The coolest, hottest Vail hangout is **Palmo's** (✉ Gateway Plaza, ☎ 970/476–7767), with eye-catching decor that was designed and carved by Dieter Menzel (visible throughout Gateway Plaza; notice the wild stairways) to dazzling effect. The tables alone reputedly cost $3,000 each. There's a selection of hot drinks, brandies, and single malts.

Garfinkel's (✉ 536 W. Lionshead Mall, ☎ 970/476–3789) is a sports bar open until 2 AM. A young crowd can be found scarfing down excellent, cheap pizzas until 2 AM at **Vendetta's** (✉ 291 Bridge St., ☎ 970/476–5070). The **Red Lion** (✉ top of Bridge St., ☎ 970/476–7676), a Vail tradition, attracts a more sedate crowd, with mellow live acts and a wildly popular deck. **Sarah's** (✉ Christiania at Vail, 356 E. Hanson Ranch Rd., ☎ 970/476–5641) showcases Helmut Fricker, a Vail institution who plays accordion while yodeling up a storm. **Mickey's** (✉ Lodge at Vail, 174 E. Gore Creek Dr., ☎ 970/476–5011) is the place for soothing pop standards on the piano.

DANCE

The **Vail International Festival of Dance** (☎ 970/949–1999), in August, hosts ballet and modern dance performers from around the world in the alpine splendor of the Ford Outdoor Amphitheater.

MUSIC AND DANCE CLUBS

Cassidy's Hole in the Wall (✉ 82 E. Beaver Creek Blvd., Avon, ☎ 970/949–9449) is a saloon that offers live country bands nightly, to go with the authentic mouth-watering barbecue. **Club Chelsea** (✉ 304 Bridge St., Vail, ☎ 970/476–5600) has it all: a quiet piano bar that feels like a speakeasy, a raucous disco, and a cigar-smoking room complete with leopard-skin couches around the fire. **Garton's** (✉ 143 East Meadow Dr., Vail, ☎ 970/479–0607) offers everything from rock to reggae, Cajun to country, and attracts a slightly older crowd (pushing 30). In Pepi's (☞ Gasthof Gramshammer *in* Dining and Lodging, *above*), you'll find **Sheika's** (☎ 970/476–1515), where the young are restless on the dance floor.

Outdoor Activities and Sports

Shrine Mountain Adventure (✉ Red Cliff, ☎ 970/827–5363) offers backcountry mountain bike tours, as well as hikes, through the Vail Valley. **A. J. Brink Outfitters** (✉ Sweetwater, north of Vail off exit 133 of I–70, ☎ 970/524–9301) equips horse riders. **Piney River Ranch** (✉ Vail, ☎ 970/476–3941) is another horseback-riding option. **Timberline Tours** (✉ Vail, ☎ 970/476–1414) runs rafting trips throughout the region. **Paragon Guides** (✉ Box 130, 81658, ☎ 970/926–5299) offers llama treks.

Singletree Golf Course (✉ 1265 Berry Creek Rd., Edwards, Vail Valley, ☎ 970/949–4240), a 7,059-yard, par-71 course, is a perennial top-50 resort course, according to *Golf Digest.* The **Cascade Club** (✉ Cascade Village, next to Westin, ☎ 970/476–7400) and the **Vail Athletic Club** (✉ 352 E. Meadow Dr., ☎ 970/476–7960) are full-service fitness facilities and include spas.

SKIING

Vail has an embarrassment of riches: 27 lifts, including a gondola and 10 high-speed quads, with an uphill capacity of 41,855 skiers per hour (and they need it—20,000 is the average skier day!); a vertical of 3,250 ft; and more than 4,000 acres of skiing on 121 runs, divided fairly evenly (32% beginner, 36% intermediate, 32% advanced/expert). ☎ *970/476–5601.* ⏲ *Mid-Nov.–mid-Apr., 8:30–4.*

For cross-country, **Vail/Beaver Creek Cross-Country Ski Centers** (☎ 970/845–5313) provide information on the many trails in the Vail Valley.

SNOWMOBILING

Adventure Ridge at Eagle's Nest (☎ 970/476–9090), at the top of Vail's Lionshead, offers twilight snowmobile excursions, snow inner-tubing, a lighted snowboard terrain garden and half-pipe, and ice skating. For daytime snowmobiling, also try **Nova Guides** (☎ 970/949–4232), **Piney River Ranch** (☎ 970/476–3941), and **Timberline Snowmobile** (☎ 970/476–1414).

Shopping

To some, Vail is one large upscale mall, but for the best of the best, head for **Gateway Plaza** (✉ South Frontage Rd. and Vail Dr., at the roundabout), **Crossroads Shopping Center** (✉ South Frontage Rd., just east of the roundabout), as well as any of the shops along Bridge Street or Gore Creek Drive.

BOUTIQUES

Gorsuch (✉ 263 Gore Creek Dr., Vail, ☎ 970/476–2294; ✉ 70 Promenade, Beaver Creek, ☎ 970/949–7115) is far more than a boutique or a sporting goods store: It offers everything from buffalo coats and pottery to potpourri. **Pepi's Sports** (✉ 231 Bridge St., ☎ 970/476–5202) offers chic ski clothes and accessories, as well as evening wear from Armani to Lauren.

CRAFT AND ART GALLERIES

Aboriginal Arts (✉ 5124 Grouse La., ☎ 970/476–7715) offers ethnic jewelry, resin-cast wood carvings, and feather masks from around the South Pacific and the Americas. **Laughing Monkey** (✉ 223 E. Gore Creek Dr., ☎ 970/476–8809) has Mexican ceramics and women's clothing. **Menzel** (✉ 12 S. Frontage Rd., ☎ 970/476–6617) specializes in fanciful, intricate furniture and interiors crafted from 200-year-old pine. **Two Elk Gallery** (✉ 102 Main St., Minturn, ☎ 970/827–5307) showcases a dizzying array of home furnishings, including items by Colorado artists, from coonskin caps to lodgepole-pine furniture. **Windwood Galleries** (✉ 151 Main St., Minturn, ☎ 970/827–9232) specializes in Colorado artists, as well as ceramics and artifacts.

SPORTING GOODS

Gore Range Mountain Works (✉ Gore Creek Dr., across from the Children's Fountain, ☎ 970/476–7625) carries mountaineering gear for the truly hardcore, as well as mountain fashions for everyone else.

Beaver Creek

33 *12 mi from Vail or 110 mi from Denver via I–70 west.*

Beaver Creek is an exclusive four-season development that gives even Utah's ultra-posh Deer Valley a run for its cash flow. It's been open since 1980 and is finally emerging from big sister Vail's shadow. The rap used to be that Beaver Creek was even more immaculately groomed than its soigné clientele. However, when Beaver Creek developed the 110-acre Grouse Mountain in 1991, the resort's reputation changed. With 38% of its terrain rated advanced, skiers flock here on powder days to seek out Grouse and famed runs such as Birds of Prey. Beginners and intermediates can still find the same pampering on the slopes they receive elsewhere in the resort, which is often blissfully uncrowded even on Vail's most congested days. Linkage with nearby Arrowhead and the Bachelor Gulch area has created one of the state's finest family areas.

Beaver Creek's sublime setting, luxurious accommodations, fine restaurants, and world-class golf course designed by Robert Trent Jones Jr.

make the resort equally popular in summer, especially with families and couples. Elegant without being ostentatious, Vail's quietly glamorous little sister appeals to a select, settled crowd, and everything at Beaver Creek lives up to its billing.

Dining and Lodging

$$$$ ✕ **Beano's Cabin.** Perhaps the ultimate wilderness dining experience is traveling in a snowmobile-drawn sleigh to this tasteful Beaver Creek hunting lodge. During your 2-mi ride, the sled host fills you in on some mountain history. Your destination is a midmountain Montana pine-log cabin, warmed inside by a crackling fire and live dinner music. (In summer, you can reach Beano's by horseback or shuttle van.) Once there, you'll choose from among seven seasonally rotating entrées and six courses. Ever since chef Chad Scothorn left to start his own restaurant (he's since moved to Utah), Beano's has seen a succession of competent chefs, but they've lacked their predecessor's imagination and panache. Scothorn's tradition of witty pizzas has remained a constant, however, and the convivial setting is unmatched. ✉ *Larkspur Bowl,* ☎ *970/949–9090. Reservations essential. AE, MC, V.*

$$$$ ★ ✕ **Mirabelle.** From the crackling fireplace to the burgundy and pink linens, this restaurant has the ultimate in romantic, French-country decor. Belgian Daniel Joly is the superb chef who offers as close to contemporary French haute cuisine as you'll get in Colorado. His preparations are a perfect blend of colors, flavors, and textures. Try the grilled Atlantic salmon with artichokes and roasted peppers, crispy ricotta gnocchi, or the Dover sole meuniere with citrus beurre blanc. Fairly priced wine recommendations are listed beneath each entrée. Desserts are sheer heaven, with caramelized cinnamon pear tart kissed with passion-fruit sorbet and vanilla ice cream the crowning achievement. ✉ *Entrance to Beaver Creek,* ☎ *970/949–7728. AE, D, MC, V. Closed Sun. No lunch.*

$$$$ ★ ✕ **Splendido.** This ultraposh eatery is the height of decadence, probably because of the marble columns and statuary and the custom-made Italian linens that adorn the tables. Chef David Walford, who apprenticed at Northern California's Auberge du Soleil and Masa's, is a master of New American cuisine, borrowing merrily from several different traditions. He is equally adept at turning out rack of lamb with rosemary and carrot-cardamom souffle. Pastry chef Soa Yi excels at such imaginative offerings as caramel-pumpkin *crostata* (puff pastry) with eggnog ice cream. ✉ *17 Chateau La.,* ☎ *970/845–8808. AE, D, DC, MC, V. No lunch.*

$$$ ✕ **TraMonti.** This breezy trattoria in the Charter at Beaver Creek showcases the vibrant progressive cuisine of chef Curtis Cooper. He loves experimenting with bold juxtapositions of flavors and is most successful with creative pizzas such as the roast garlic with basil pesto. Try the lobster ravioli in saffron cream sauce, spaghetti puttanesca, or the osso buco. ✉ *The Charter at Beaver Creek,* ☎ *970/949–5552. AE, MC, V. No lunch.*

$$–$$$ ✕ **The Gashouse.** This classic local hangout, in a 1930s log cabin with trophy-covered walls, draws up-valley crowds who swear by the steaks, delicious ribs, and fresh salmon. Stop in for a brew and some heavenly Buffalo shrimp (a close cousin to wings) and watch how the Vail Valley kicks back. ✉ *Rte. 6, Edwards,* ☎ *970/926–2896. AE, MC, V.*

$$ ✕ **Cassidy's Hole in the Wall.** If you're looking for *the* burger, you're in the right place: The Big-Bob one-pounder should satisfy you. Sandwiches, Mexican dishes, and specialties such as chicken-fried steak and a 2-ft-long rack of ribs head the menu in this western saloon that spans two floors. Looking for the action? Stay at ground zero. If you're partial to watching rather than participating, you'll want to be upstairs. ✉ *82 E. Beaver Creek Blvd., Avon,* ☎ *970/949–9449. AE, D, MC, V.*

$$$$ ★ **Hyatt Regency Beaver Creek.** The lobby at this slope-side hotel, with a magnificent antler chandelier and huge oriel windows opening onto the mountain, manages to be both cozy and grand. Rooms are sizable and decorated in French provincial style, with coffeemakers and heated towel racks. The full spa and health club and nearby golf course (with guest tee times) make it popular with non-skiers, but perhaps the ultimate in pampering is stepping out of the hotel and into your warmed and waiting ski boots and skis. ✉ *136 E. Thomas Pl., 81620,* ☎ *970/949–1234 or 800/233–1234,* FAX *970/949–4164. 275 rooms, 31 suites. 3 restaurants, 2 bars, deli, pool, 8 hot tubs, spa, health club, 5 tennis courts, children's programs, meeting rooms. AE, D, DC, MC, V.*

$$$$ ★ **Lodge & Spa at Cordillera.** Surrounded by a pristine wilderness area, this isolated lodge offers sweeping vistas. The rooms are Old World, in burgundy, buff, and hunter green, with burled pine furnishings. An air of quiet luxury prevails: prints by Picasso and Miró adorn the pine-paneled or exposed-brick walls, and ceilings are of carved recessed wood. You can luxuriate in the spa after a hard day's hiking or cross-country skiing, then sit down to a meal in one of the superlative restaurants serving healthful spa cuisine. The lodge operates a shuttle to the lifts. ✉ *Box 1110, Edwards 81632,* ☎ *970/926–2200 or 800/548–2721,* FAX *970/926–2486. 56 rooms. 4 restaurants, bar, indoor-outdoor pool, 3 hot tubs, spa, health club, 18-hole golf course, cross-country skiing, meeting rooms. AE, D, MC, V.*

$$–$$$$ **The Embassy.** An atrium centerpiece highlights this all-suite property that's charmingly decorated in European alpine style. The units have a sky-blue and forest-green color scheme, and each features a kitchenette and gas-burning fireplace. The casually elegant Fletcher's offers an inventive new American menu, which includes a highly touted scallop bisque, crab cakes, and coconut-wrapped shrimp. ✉ *26 Avondale La., 81620,* ☎ *970/845–9800,* FAX *970/845–8242. 73 suites. Restaurant, bar, indoor-outdoor pool and hot tub, spa, health club, ski shop, meeting rooms. AE, MC, V.*

$$–$$$ **The Pines.** This small, ski-in/ski-out Beaver Creek winner combines posh digs with unpretentious atmosphere—and prices. The rooms are spacious, light, and airy, with blond wood furnishings and pale pink ceilings. Each room has a TV/VCR (tapes are free); several have balconies overlooking the ski area and mountain range. The air of quiet pampering is furthered by such little extras as a ski concierge who arranges complimentary guided mountain tours and a free wax for your skis. The Grouse Mountain Grill serves up superb New American cuisine in an unparalleled setting with huge picture windows. ✉ *Box 18450, Avon 81620,* ☎ *970/845–7900,* FAX *970/845–7809. 60 rooms, 12 suites. Restaurant, bar, refrigerator, pool, hot tub, spa, exercise room, laundry service. AE, D, MC, V.*

Nightlife and the Arts

After attacking the moguls, relax at the Hyatt's **Crooked Hearth Tavern** (☎ 970/949–1234, ext. 2260) and enjoy the lively guitar entertainment. **McCoy's** (☎ 970/949–1234), at the base of the mountain, has live music après-ski.

The **Beaver Creek Center for the Arts** (☎ 970/949–4348) has a 518-seat theater and 2,000 square ft of gallery space in the Market Square pedestrian plaza at the base of the ski area.

Outdoor Activities and Sports

GOLF

Beaver Creek Golf Course (✉ 100 Offerson Rd., ☎ 970/845–5775), befitting the resort's reputation, is a 6,400-yard, par-70 stunner designed by Robert Trent Jones Jr. **Golf Course at Cordillera** (✉ Lodge at

Cordillera, Edwards, ☎ 970/926–2200) is actually three courses. One designed by Hale Irwin is a par-72, 7,444-yard course with open meadows, ponds, and stands of pine and aspen trees. The Dave Pelz short course, par 3, offers irons practice, and the Valley Course, designed by Tom Fazio, is a par-71, 7,500-yard course. Among the challenges of the full courses are wandering elk and brown bears.

SKIING

With 85 trails, 1,529 skiable acres, a 4,040-ft vertical, and 14 lifts (including six high-speed quads), uphill capacity is tremendous at the still-uncrowded, upscale **Beaver Creek Resort.** Now linked to neighboring Arrowhead and Bachelor Gulch ski areas, the resort boasts "village-to-village"-style skiing. ☎ *970/476–5601.* ⏲ *Late Nov.–mid-Apr., daily 8:30–4.*

En Route A few miles west, past the town of Edwards, the narrow, winding Route 131 squirrels north from I–70 through the **Yampa Valley.** The lush, wide-open spaces and vistas are both gorgeous and lonely, relieved only by the occasional odd rock formation thrusting up from the ground. This is cattle country, a land of jade forests, jagged outcroppings, and streams silvered by the sun and skirting the Flat Tops Wilderness Area, a high, flat mountaintop crowned with a lava dome that glaciers have sculpted into a series of steep cliffs and deep gashes.

Steamboat Springs

34 *86 mi from Beaver Creek via I–70 west and U.S. 131 north; 170 mi from Denver via I–70 west, Rte. 9 north, and U.S. 40 north.*

Steamboat is aptly nicknamed Ski Town, U.S.A., since the town has "sent" more athletes—several dozen—to the Winter Olympics than any other ski resort in the nation. The most famous in Steamboat Mountain Village is probably 1972 slalom silver medalist Billy Kidd, whose irrepressible grin and 10-gallon hat are instantly recognizable. When he's around, Kidd conducts daily tours of the mountain.

Speaking of the mountain, keep in mind that the part that's visible from the base area is only the tip of the iceberg, and much more terrain lies concealed in back. Steamboat is famed for its eiderdown-soft snow; in fact, the term "champagne powder" was coined here to describe the area's unique feathery dumps, the result of Steamboat's fortuitous position between the arid desert to the west and the moisture-magnet of the Continental Divide to the east, where storm fronts duke it out.

If you're looking for hellacious steeps and menacing couloirs, you won't find them in Steamboat, but you will find perhaps the finest tree skiing in America. Beginners and intermediates rave about the wide-open spaces of Sunshine Bowl and Storm Peak. Steamboat also earns high marks for its comprehensive children's programs, the Kidd Center for Performance Skiing (where you can learn demanding disciplines such as powder, mogul, and tree skiing), and two of Colorado's best on-mountain restaurants: Hazie's and Ragnar's.

The modern Steamboat Mountain Village is attractive enough, if lacking in personality: a maze of upscale condos, boutiques, and bars. To its credit, though, this increasingly "hot" destination has retained its down-home, Western friendliness, providing the trappings while avoiding the trap of a premium resort. That may have to do with Steamboat Springs itself, a mere 10-minute drive away, where Stetson hats are sold for use and not for souvenirs. Steamboat's origins are not as a mining town but as a ranching and farming community, setting it apart from a Breckenridge or an Aspen. It has its share of Victorian buildings, most of them fronting Lincoln Avenue, the main drag, but they were built to be functional rather than ornamental.

The **Tread of Pioneers Museum,** in a beautifully restored federal building, is an excellent spot to bone up on local history, and includes ski memorabilia dating back to the turn of the 20th century, when Carl Howelsen opened Howelsen Hill, still the country's preeminent ski-jumping facility. ✉ *8th and Oak Sts.,* ☎ *970/879–2214.* *$3.* ⏲ *Apr.–Oct., Tues.–Sat. 11–5; Nov.–Mar., Mon.–Sat. 11–5.*

The entrance to Steamboat from the mountain is roughly marked by the amusingly garish '50s neon sign from the Rabbit Ears Motel, and the unmistakable stench of sulphur. The town got its name from French trappers who, after hearing the bubbling and churning hot springs, mistakenly thought a steamboat was chugging up the Yampa River. There are more than 100 hot springs in the immediate vicinity; the **Steamboat Visitor Center** (✉ 1255 S. Lincoln Ave., ☎ 970/879–0882) publishes a fun and informative walking-tour guide that describes many of the spots. The springs may not be as restorative as legend claims, but the inspiring views of the surrounding pristine forest certainly are. Two springs are the most famous: **Steamboat Springs Health and Recreation Hot Springs** (✉ Lincoln Ave., ☎ 970/879–1828) charges $6 and is open daily 7 AM–9:45 PM. The **Strawberry Park Natural Hot Springs** (✉ Strawberry Park Rd., ☎ 970/879–0342) is 7 mi out of town; it charges $5 and is open daily 10 AM–midnight.

In summer, Steamboat serves as the gateway to magnificent **Medicine Bow/Routt National Forest,** which offers a wealth of activities from hiking to mountain biking to fishing. Among the nearby attractions are the 283-ft **Fish Creek Falls** and the splendidly rugged **Mt. Zirkel Wilderness Area.** To the north, two sparkling man-made lakes, **Steamboat** and **Pearl,** offer a variety of water sports, including fishing and sailing.

Dining and Lodging

$$$–$$$$ ✕ **L'Apogee.** This expert French restaurant is Steamboat's most intimate, with rose-color walls, flickering candlelight, and hanging plants. The classic food, with subtle Asian influences, is well-crafted, especially the half roast duckling glazed with orange-blossom honey; the Alaskan King crab cakes; the foie gras pan seared and topped with warm chèvre; and the fresh Alaskan halibut with a Yampah Valley tomato compote. Still, the menu takes a back seat to the admirable wine list. Oenophile alert: Owner Jamie Jenny is a collector whose magnificent wine cellar—cited by the *Wine Spectator* as one of America's best—contains more than 750 labels (10,000 bottles). ✉ *911 Lincoln Ave.,* ☎ *970/879–1919. AE, MC, V.*

$$$ ★ ✕ **La Montana.** This Mexican/Southwestern establishment is among Steamboat's most popular restaurants. The kitchen incorporates indigenous specialties into the traditional menu. Among the standouts are red chili pasta in a shrimp, garlic, and cilantro sauce; enchiladas layered with Monterey Jack and goat cheese, roasted peppers, and onions; and elk loin crusted with pecan nuts and bourbon cream sauce. The fresh fish is outstanding. ✉ *Après Ski Way and Village Dr.,* ☎ *970/879–5800. AE, D, MC, V. No lunch.*

$$$ ✕ **Mattie Silk's.** Named after a notorious turn-of-the-20th-century madam, this plush split-level charmer, all velour and lace, looks like a prim wife who has loosened her corset and tarted up in an effort to win back her man. The sauces, with fresh pungent herbs and very little butter, are assertive and zippy. Try the tender lemon-pepper veal, pounded thin, breaded, then sautéed in a fragrant lemon-cognac sauce. ✉ *Ski Time Sq., Steamboat Mountain Village,* ☎ *970/879–2441. AE, D, MC, V. No lunch.*

$$–$$$ ★ ✕ **Antares.** Co-owners Paul LeBrun, Ian Donovan, and Doug Enochs, who cut their culinary teeth at Harwig's and L'Apogee, opened this superlative new eatery in the space formerly occupied by Gorky Park. They retained only the fieldstone walls, frosted windows, pressed-tin ceilings, and stained glass, thereby calling attention to the splendid Victorian building itself. LeBrun, the chef, contributes his exciting, eclectic cuisine, which is inspired by America's rich ethnic stew. Hence, you might feast on elk medallions with a Bing cherry-Merlot sauce, or Maine lobster over chili pepper linguine. Doug's encyclopedic knowledge of wines is reflected in the comprehensive, fairly priced list. ✉ *57½ 8th St.,* ☎ *970/879–9939. Reservations essential. AE, MC, V. No lunch.*

$$–$$$ ★ ✕ **Harwig's Grill.** This popular eatery is next door to L'Apogee, and it's run by the same team. The bar offers 40 wines by the glass, including many lesser-known labels, and you can order from L'Apogee's wine list. The menu here reflects owner Jamie Jenny's love of travel, with confidently prepared specialties from around the world: home-cured salmon pastrami to raclette, jambalaya to dim sum. The desserts are predictably sinful. ✉ *911 Lincoln Ave.,* ☎ *970/879–1980. AE, MC, V. No lunch.*

$$ ✕ **Riggio's.** This local favorite is in a dramatic space, whose industrial look (black-and-white tile, exposed pipes) is softened by tapestries, murals, and landscape photos. The menu offers tasty pizzas (one with goat cheese, roasted peppers, and garlic; another with clams, Romano, and herbs) and lighter pastas (the *sciocca,* with rock shrimp, eggplant, tomatoes, and basil sautéed in olive oil, is superb). Standards such as manicotti, chicken cacciatore, and saltimbocca are also well prepared. ✉ *1106 Lincoln Ave.,* ☎ *970/879–9010. AE, D, DC, MC, V. No lunch.*

$$ ✕ **Steamboat Smokehouse.** The loud, raucous scene, brick and wood decor, and occasional live music might fool you into thinking this joint is just a bar. Once you try the phenomenal barbecue or hickory-smoked brisket and turkey, however, you'll realize that this is a place where they really know their beans about home cooking. ✉ *912 Lincoln Ave.,* ☎ *970/879–5570. AE, MC, V.*

$$ ✕ **Yama Chan's.** Most people think you can't get good sushi in Colorado: Wrong. Somehow, the fish tastes fresher in the crisp mountain air at this simple, superlative Japanese restaurant. The rest of the menu is equally well-presented and prepared. ✉ *Old Town Sq., 635 Lincoln Ave.,* ☎ *970/879–8862. AE, MC, V. Closed Mon. year-round; Sun. in winter. No lunch weekends.*

$$$$ ★ 🏨 **Home Ranch.** You won't be roughing it at this all-inclusive retreat (with a seven-night minimum stay), a Relais & Chateaux property nestled among towering stands of aspen outside Clark (just north of Steamboat): The living room, with a magnificent fieldstone fireplace surrounded by plush leather armchairs and sofa, is cozy; the dining room, where Clyde Nelson turns out gourmet Southwestern fare, homey. Accommodations are in the main lodge or in individual cabins with hot tubs and terraces. Decor leans toward Native American rugs and prints, lace curtains, terra-cotta tile or hardwood floors, and stenciled walls. ✉ *Box 822, Clark 80428,* ☎ *970/879–1780 or 800/223–7094. 6 rooms, 8 cabins. Dining room, pool, hot tub, horseback riding, fishing, cross-country skiing, ski shop. AE, D, MC, V. Closed late-Mar.–early June, early Oct.–late-Dec.*

$$$$ ★ 🏨 **Vista Verde Guest Ranch.** Offering similarly deluxe digs and just as many activities as Home Ranch, Vista Verde has lower rates (including activities and three meals) and a more authentic Western ambience. Lodge rooms are huge and beautifully appointed, with lace curtains, Western art, and lodgepole furniture. Cabins are more rustic, with pine paneling and old-fashioned wood-burning stoves, plus refrigerators, coffeemakers, and porches. Chef Jonathon Gillespie serves up sump-

tuous country repasts, which include wild game and fresh produce from his herb and vegetable garden. ✉ *Box 465, 80477,* ☎ *970/879–3858 or 800/526–7433. 3 rooms, 8 cabins. Dining room, 10 hot tubs, sauna, exercise room, horseback riding, fishing, cross-country skiing. No credit cards. Closed mid-Mar.–May and Oct.–Nov.*

$$–$$$$ 🏨 **Ptarmigan Inn.** Convenience and comfort are the keynotes of this appealing property situated on the slopes. The modest rooms, decorated in pleasing pastels and earth tones, have cable TV, balcony, and full bath. If the Ptarmigan is full, consider staying at its inexpensive sister property, **The Alpiner** (✉ 424 Lincoln Ave., ☎ 970/879–1430), a basic but comfortable 32-room lodge downtown, whose guests have full use of the Ptarmigan's facilities. ✉ *2304 Aprés Ski Way, Box 773240, 80477,* ☎ *970/879–1730 or 800/538–7519,* FAX *970/879–6044. 77 rooms. Restaurant, bar, refrigerators, in-room VCRs, pool, hot tub, sauna, ski shop. AE, D, DC, MC, V.*

$–$$$$ ★ 🏨 **Harbor Hotel and Condominiums.** This charming, completely refurbished 1940s hotel is smack in the middle of Steamboat's historic district. The inviting brick and wood-panel lobby sets the tone, further emphasized by the nifty artifacts, such as the old switchboards, that dot the interior of the property. Each room is individually decorated with period furniture, combined with modern amenities for comfort. The property also runs an adjacent motel and condo complex. ✉ *703 Lincoln Ave., 80477,* ☎ *970/879–1522 or 800/543–8888,* FAX *970/879–1737. 113 rooms. 2 hot tubs, sauna, steam room. AE, D, DC, MC, V.*

$–$$$ 🏨 **Sheraton Steamboat Resort & Conference Center.** This bustling deluxe hotel is Steamboat's only true ski-in/ski-out property. Rooms are Sheraton standard, fair-size, with muted decor and most comforts. The hotel handles Sheraton Plaza (not ski-in/ski-out), 26 economy units with kitchens and cable TV, whose guests enjoy full hotel privileges. ✉ *Box 774808, 80477,* ☎ *970/879–2220 or 800/848–8878,* FAX *970/879–7686. 346 rooms. 2 restaurants, 2 bars, pool, 4 hot tubs, sauna, steam room, ski shop, meeting rooms. AE, D, DC, MC, V.*

$$ 🏨 **Sky Valley Lodge.** This homey property is a few miles from downtown, amid glorious scenery that contributes to the get-away-from-it-all feel of the inn. Warm English country–style rooms are decorated in restful mountain colors. Continental breakfast is included. ✉ *31490 E. U.S. 40, 80477,* ☎ *970/879–7749 or 800/538–7519,* FAX *970/879–7752. 24 rooms. Hot tub. AE, D, DC, MC, V.*

$$ 🏨 **Steamboat B&B.** This custard and blue Victorian was originally a church that owner Gordon Hattersley converted into the area's nicest B&B in 1989, cleverly retaining the arched doorways and stained-glass windows. The cozy, comfy rooms have floral wallpaper, lace curtains, landscape photos, potted geraniums, polished hardwood floors, and period antiques and reproductions. A full breakfast is included. ✉ *442 Pine St., 80477,* ☎ *970/879–5724. 7 rooms. Hot tub. AE, D, MC, V.*

$–$$ 🏨 **Rabbit Ears Motel.** The playful, pink-neon bunny sign outside this motel has been a local landmark since 1952, making it an unofficial gateway to Steamboat Springs. The location is ideal for those who want the springs (across the street); the ski area (the town bus stops outside); and the downtown shops, bars, and restaurants. All the rooms are clean and attractive and are equipped with minirefrigerators and coffeemakers. Most have balconies with views of the Yampa River. Continental breakfast is included in the rate. ✉ *201 Lincoln Ave., 80477,* ☎ *970/879–1150 or 800/828–7702,* FAX *970/870–0483. 66 rooms. AE, D, DC, MC, V.*

CONDOMINIUMS

Torian Plum, one of the properties managed by **Steamboat Premier Properties** (✉ 1855 Ski Time Sq., 80487, ☎ 970/879–8811 or 800/228–2458, FAX 970/879–8485), offers elegant one- to three-bedroom units in a ski-in, ski-out location. Each condo has a private balcony, and indoor and outdoor hot tubs are available. **Steamboat Resorts** (✉ Box 2995, 80477, ☎ 800/525–5502, FAX 970/879–8060) and **Mountain Resorts** (✉ 2145 Resort Dr., Suite 100, 80487, ☎ 800/525–2622, FAX 970/879–3228) also manage top properties in the area.

Nightlife

BARS AND LOUNGES

The **Old Town Pub** (✉ 600 Lincoln Ave., ☎ 970/879–2101) has juicy burgers and local flavor, with some great live bands. **Steamboat Brewery** (✉ 5th St. and Lincoln Ave., ☎ 970/879–2233) offers an assortment of homemade ales, lagers, porters, and stouts, as well as superior pub grub. On the mountain, **Mattie Silk's** (☞ Dining and Lodging, *above*) is a favorite après-ski hangout.

MUSIC CLUBS

The Loft section of the **Ore House** restaurant (✉ U.S. 40 and Pine Grove Rd., ☎ 970/879–1190) ropes 'em in for juicy steaks and boot-scooting country music.

In Steamboat (on the mountain), **The Tugboat** (✉ Ski Time Sq., ☎ 970/879–7070) features loud live rock acts. **Heavenly Daze** (✉ Ski Time Sq., ☎ 970/879–8080) has three levels: the ground floor is a brew pub, the second floor a restaurant, and the third floor a combination billiards parlor/rock club/disco.

Outdoor Activities and Sports

Sheraton Steamboat Golf Club (✉ 2000 Clubhouse Dr., ☎ 970/879–1391) is a 6,906-yard, par 72, 18-hole championship course designed by Robert Trent Jones, Jr. For **horseback riding** check out All Seasons Ranch (☎ 970/879–0095) and Sunset Ranch (☎ 970/879–0954). High Adventures (☎ 970/879–8747) runs **rafting** excursions to various rivers. Half-day to two-week trips are offered for all levels.

SKIING

The **Howelsen Ski Area,** a tiny historic area right in Steamboat Springs, is Colorado's oldest. Its three lifts, 15 trails, and 440-ft vertical aren't impressive, but it *is* the largest ski-jumping complex in America, and it's a major Olympic training ground. ✉ *845 Howelsen Pkwy., 80487,* ☎ *970/879–8499.* ⏲ *Dec.–Mar., Mon. 11–6, Tues.–Fri. 11–9, weekends 9–4:30.*

For a taste of that champagne powder, head to **Steamboat Ski Area,** where 20 lifts, including four high-speed quads and a gondola, access 140 trails (2,939 acres), roughly half of them intermediate, with a 3,668-ft vertical drop. ✉ *2305 Mt. Werner Circle, 80487,* ☎ *970/879–6111.* ⏲ *Late-Nov.–mid-Apr., 9–4.*

For cross-country skiing, **Steamboat Ski Touring Center** (☎ 970/879–8180) has 30 km (18 mi) of skiing terrain on the golf course.

SNOWMOBILING

Explore the forests and meadows of the Medicine Bow/Routt National Forest with **High Mountain Snowmobile Tours** (☎ 970/879–9073). **Steamboat Powder Cats** (☎ 970/879–5188) offers tours of the area. **Steamboat Snowmobile Tours** (☎ 970/879–6500) has guided tours.

Shopping

Steamboat's Old Town Square (✉ 7th St. and Lincoln Ave.) is a collection of upscale boutiques and retailers. **On the mountain,** check out Ski Time Square, Torian Plum Plaza, and Gondola Square (✉ all at the base of the ski area, next to one another).

BOOKS

Off the Beaten Path (✉ 56 7th St., ☎ 970/879–6830) is a throwback to the beat generation, with poetry readings, lectures, and concerts. It has an excellent selection of New Age works, in addition to the usual best-sellers and guides.

BOUTIQUES

Amallama (✉ Old Town Sq., ☎ 970/879–9127) offers folk art, jewelry, and clothing from around the world, including Balinese cradle watchers, carved wooden figures believed to keep evil spirits away from sleeping children. You can make your own earrings at the bead counter. **Old Town Leather** (✉ 929 Lincoln Ave., ☎ 970/879–3558) offers every conceivable leather item, most of them handmade.

CRAFT AND ART GALLERIES

Art Quest (✉ 511 Lincoln Ave., ☎ 970/879–1989) offers a variety of works in silver, glass, paper, ceramics, and alabaster, as well as furniture and jewelry. A wide range of Native American art from Alaska to Mexico is featured. **White Hart Gallery** (✉ 843 Lincoln Ave., ☎ 970/879–1015) is a magnificent clutter of Western and Native American paintings and objets d'art.

SPORTING GOODS

Christy Sports (✉ 1724A Mt. Werner Circle, ☎ 970/879–9001) rents and sells ski equipment. **Sport Stalker** (✉ Ski Time Sq., ☎ 970/879–2445) offers the latest fashions and gear.

WESTERN PARAPHERNALIA

F. M. Light and Sons (✉ 830 Lincoln Ave., ☎ 970/879–1822), owned by the same family for four generations, caters to the Marlboro man in us all. If you're lucky you'll find what you're looking for cheaply—how about cowboy hats for $4.98? **Into the West** (✉ 807 Lincoln Ave., ☎ 970/879–8377) is owned by Jace Romick, a former member of the U.S. ski team and a veteran of the rodeo circuit. He crafts splendid, beautifully textured lodgepole furniture, and sells anything tasteful to do with the West: antiques (even ornate potbellied stoves), collectibles, cowhide mirrors, and new handicrafts, such as Native American drum tables and fanciful candleholders made from branding irons. **Two Rivers Gallery** (✉ 56 9th St., ☎ 970/879–0044) sells such cowboy collectibles as antler chandeliers and cow-skull lamps, as well as vintage photographs, prints, sculpture, and paintings.

En Route Return the way you came and head west on I–70 to reach the natural and man-made 15-mi-long **Glenwood Canyon.** Nature began the work as the Colorado River carved deep buff-tint granite, limestone, and quartzite gullies—brilliantly streaked with lavender, rose, and ivory. This process took a half-billion years. Then man stepped in, seeking a more direct route west. In 1992, the work on I–70 through the canyon was completed at a cost of almost $500 million. Much of the expense was attributable to the effort to preserve the natural landscape as much as possible. When contractors blasted cliff faces, for example, they stained the exposed rock to simulate nature's weathering. Biking trails were also created, providing easy access to the hauntingly beautiful **Hanging Lake Recreation Area.** Here Dead Horse Creek sprays ethereal flumes from curling limestone tendrils into a startlingly turquoise pool, as jet-black swifts dart to and fro. It's perhaps the most transcendent of several idyllic spots now reachable on bike or foot. The intrepid can scale the delicate limestone cliffs, pocked with numerous caverns and embroidered with pastel-hue gardens.

Glenwood Springs

35 *110 mi from Steamboat Springs via U.S. 131 south and I–70 west; 160 mi from Denver via I–70 west.*

I–70 snakes through the canyon on its way to a famed spa that forms the western apex of a triangle with Vail and Aspen. Once upon a time, Glenwood Springs was every bit as tony as those chic resorts are today, attracting a faithful legion of the pampered and privileged who came to enjoy the waters (the world's largest natural hot springs), said to cure everything from acne to rheumatism.

Today the entrance to town and its once-splendid prospects of a fertile valley fringed by massive peaks is marred by the proliferation of malls, motels, and fast-food outlets. Remnants of her glory days can still be seen in the grand old **Hotel Colorado** (✉ 526 Pine St., ☎ 970/945–6511), regally commanding the vaporous pools from a patrician distance. Modeled after the Villa de Medici in Italy, the property opened its doors in 1893 to become the fashionable retreat of its day. Teddy Roosevelt even made it his unofficial "Little White House" in 1905.

The **Yampah Hot Springs,** near the hotel, were discovered by the Ute Indians (Yampah is Ute for "Big Medicine"), and are still popular today. Even before the heyday of the Hotel Colorado, western notables from Annie Oakley to Doc Holliday came to take the curative waters. In Doc's case, however, the cure didn't work, and six months after his arrival in 1887 he died broke, broken-down, and tubercular. (He lies in Linwood Cemetery, ½ mi east of town.) The smaller pool is 100 ft long and maintained at 104 degrees. The larger is more than two city blocks long (405 ft), and contains in excess of a million gallons of constantly filtered water that is completely refilled every six hours and maintained at a soothing 90 degrees. ✉ *Pine St.,* ☎ *970/945–7131.* 🎫 *$8.* ⏲ *Memorial Day–Labor Day, daily 7:30 AM–10 PM; Labor Day–Memorial Day, daily 9 AM–10 PM.*

Two blocks down the street, the **Yampa Spa and Vapor Caves** is a series of three natural underground steam baths. The same 124-degree springs that supply the pool flow under the cave floors. Each chamber is successively hotter than the last; you can scoop mud from the walls for a cleansing facial, as you purify your body (and soul, according to Ute legend). A variety of spa treatments from massages to body wraps is also available. ✉ *709 E. 6th St.,* ☎ *970/945–0667.* 🎫 *$8.75 for caves alone, more for various treatments.* ⏲ *Daily 9–9.*

Dining and Lodging

$$$$ ✕ **Florinda's.** The peach walls of this handsome space are graced by changing exhibits of local artists. The chef has a deft hand with Northern and Southern Italian dishes. Try the veal chops sautéed with shiitake mushrooms in marsala, garlic, and sun-dried tomatoes, and topped with Romano cheese. ✉ *721 Grand St.,* ☎ *970/945–1245. MC, V. Closed Sun. No lunch Sat.*

$$–$$$ ★ ✕ **The Bayou.** "Food so good you'll slap yo' mama," trumpets the menu at this casual eatery, whose most distinctive attribute is its frog awning (two bulbous eyes beckon you in). Choose from "pre-stuff, wabbit stuff, udder stuff," such as lip-smacking gumbo that looks like mud (and is supposed to), étouffée and blackened fish, or lethal Cajun martinis. On summer weekends live music is played on the patio. ✉ *52103 Rte. 6, at Rte. 24,* ☎ *970/945–1047. AE, MC, V.*

$ ✕ **Daily Bread.** For years, locals have been packing this little café, where you can get some of the best food at the best prices in town. Hearty breakfasts such as the veggie skillet or breakfast burrito are favorites, while lunch features creative sandwiches, soups, and burgers. Many items are low-fat or vegetarian. The bakery also offers their homemade breads to go. ✉ *729 Grand Ave.,* ☎ *970/945–6253. D, MC, V. No dinner. No lunch Sun.*

$$ **Hotel Colorado.** The exterior of this building, listed in the National Historic Register, is simply exquisite, with graceful sandstone colonnades and Italianate campaniles. The impression of luxury continues in the imposing, yet gracious, marble lobby and public rooms. Unfortunately, the sunny, individually decorated rooms and suites—most with high ceilings, fireplaces, gorgeous period wainscoting, and balconies affording superlative vistas—are a little threadbare and oddly configured. But everyone, whether notable or notorious, from Teddy Roosevelt to Doc Holliday to Al Capone, stayed here in its halcyon days. ✉ *526 Pine St., 81601,* ☎ *970/945–6511 or 800/544–3998,* FAX *970/945–7030. 128 rooms, 32 suites. Restaurant, coffee and juice bar, bar, beauty salon, health club, meeting rooms. AE, D, DC, MC, V.*

$$ **Hot Springs Lodge.** This lodge is perfectly located right by the Springs, which are used to heat the property. The attractive rooms, decorated in jade, teal, buff, and rose, stress a Southwestern motif. Deluxe rooms offer a minirefrigerator and tiny balcony, in addition to standard conveniences such as cable TV and full bath. ✉ *415 E. 6th St., 81601,* ☎ *970/945–6571 or 800/537–7946 (in CO only),* FAX *970/947–2950. 107 rooms. Restaurant, bar, hot tub. AE, D, DC, MC, V.*

$–$$ **Hotel Denver.** Although this hotel was originally built in 1806, its most striking features are the numerous art-deco touches throughout. Most rooms open onto a view of the springs or a three-story New Orleans–style atrium bedecked with colorful canopies. The accommodations are ultraneat, trim, and comfortable and are decorated predominantly in maroon and teal. Glenwood's only microbrewery—the Glenwood Canyon Brewing Company—is the hotel restaurant. ✉ *402 7th St., 81601,* ☎ *970/945–6565 or 800/826–8820,* FAX *970/945–2204. 60 rooms. Restaurant, bar, beauty salon, exercise room, meeting rooms. AE, D, DC, MC, V.*

$ **Sunlight Mountain Inn.** This charming traditional ski lodge a few hundred feet from the Sunlight Mountain Resort lifts brims with European country ambience, from the delightful lounge (with a carved fireplace and wrought-iron chandeliers) and Western-flair restaurant to the cozily rustic rooms, all with pine-board walls and rough-hewn armoires. The restaurant specializes in apple dishes, made from local apples whenever possible. Sunlight is a true get-away-from-it-all place, with no TVs in the rooms. A full breakfast is included. ✉ *10252 County Rd. 117, 81601,* ☎ *970/945–5225. 24 rooms. Restaurant, bar, hot tub. AE, D, DC, MC, V.*

Outdoor Activities and Sports

Roaring Fork Anglers (☎ 970/945–0180) leads wade and float trips throughout the area. **Blue Sky Adventures** (☎ 970/945–6605) and **Rock Garden Rafting** (☎ 970/945–6737) run trips down the Colorado and Roaring Fork rivers. Also try **Whitewater Rafting** (☎ 970/945–8477). Indoors, **Hot Springs Athletic Club** (✉ 401 N. River Rd., Glenwood Springs, ☎ 970/945–7428) offers Nautilus, saunas, tanning beds, and racquetball.

SKIING

Sunlight Mountain Resort, 20 minutes south of Glenwood Springs, has 63 trails, including the super-steep glades of the East Ridge, serviced by four lifts with a drop of 2,010 vertical ft. The varied terrain, sensational views, and lack of pretension make this a local favorite. The ratio of shredders to downhillers here is quite high, as Sunlight has a reputation for "radical air." ✉ *10901 County Rd. 117, 81601,* ☎ *970/945–7491.* ⏲ *Late-Nov.–early Apr.*

Shopping

Glenwood Springs Mall (✉ 51027 U.S. 6, at U.S. 24, ☎ 970/945–1200) offers everything from Kmart and JCPenney to factory outlets and specialty shops. The **Watersweeper and the Dwarf** (✉ 717 Grand Ave., ☎ 970/945–2000) sells handicrafts and Americana fashioned from silver, gold, clay, wood, glass, stone, wool, wax, and patience.

En Route At Carbondale, Route 82 splits and continues southeast, skirting the Roaring Fork River on its way to Aspen. Route 133 veers south on its way to Redstone.

Redstone

36 *29 mi from Glenwood Springs via Rte. 82 south and Rte. 133 south.*

Redstone is a charming artists' colony whose streets are lined with pretty galleries and boutiques, and whose boundaries are ringed by impressive sandstone cliffs from which the town draws its name. Its history dates back to the late 19th century when J. C. Osgood, director of the Colorado Fuel and Iron Company, built Cleveholm Manor, now known as **Redstone Castle** (✉ 58 Redstone Blvd.) to entertain the other titans of his day, such as John D. Rockefeller, J. P. Morgan, and Teddy Roosevelt. Among the home's embellishments are gold-leaf ceilings, maroon velvet walls, silk brocade upholstery, marble and mahogany fireplaces, Persian rugs, and Tiffany chandeliers. Today, the future of the hotel is uncertain. It closed to the public in 1999, but you can catch a glimpse of the baronial splendor if you drive past.

Dining and Lodging

$–$$ ✕🏨 **Redstone Inn.** The inn was originally designed as an elegant 35-room lodging for the company's bachelor employees. (Osgood's largesse extended to his employees, for whom he constructed one of the first planned communities, a utopian model in its day.) Eat in the poolside Grill or the more formal Redstone Room ($$–$$$). Specialties range from tortilla lasagna to duck ravioli to elk in phyllo with mushrooms, spinach, pine nuts, and goat cheese. The Sunday brunch is famous. You can also stay overnight at the cozy, relaxing inn, and enjoy the pool and health spa. ✉ *82 Redstone Blvd., 81623,* ☎ *970/963–2526. 35 rooms. AE, D, MC, V.*

Aspen/Snowmass

42 mi from Glenwood Springs via Rte. 82 south; 200 mi from Denver via I–70 west and Rte. 82 south; 165 mi from Denver via I–70 west, Rte. 91 south, and Rte. 82 west (summer only).

37 One of the world's fabled resorts, **Aspen** is practically a byword for glitz, glamour, and glorious skiing. To the uninitiated, Aspen and Vail are virtually synonymous. To residents, a rivalry exists, despite the current détente that led to the formation of the Aspen/Vail Premier Passport (an interchangeable ski pass that includes a one-way transfer). Comparisons are admittedly odious and at best superficial, though a few instructive generalizations can be made.

The most obvious distinction is the look: Vail is a faux-Bavarian development, Aspen is an authentic mining town. Vail is politicians–where Gerald Ford, Dan Quayle, and John Sununu fled to escape the cares of state. Aspen is recording stars and Hollywood—where Don Johnson and Melanie Griffith remarried (and divorced) and Barbra Streisand took a stand against controversial Amendment 2.

Aspen is a slave to fashion, so much so that the term "Aspen formal" was coined to describe a dinner jacket or evening gown with a ski hat and mittens. Aspen has always been a magnet for cultural and countercultural types. After all, bad-boy gonzo journalist Hunter S. Thompson is one of the more visible citizens of the nearby community of Woody Creek. One of Aspen's most beloved figures is unrepentant hippie John Bennett, who tools around in his "Ultimate Taxi" (it's plastered with 3-D glasses, crystal disco balls, and neon necklaces and is redolent of dry ice and incense). You'll find everyone from "social X rays" with Vogue exteriors and vague interiors to long-haired musicians in combat boots and fatigues. To be fair, most Aspenites couldn't care less: Theirs is a freewheeling, tolerant town that welcomes diversity of personal expression. It's all part of the Aspen mystique. Ultimately, it doesn't matter what you wear here, as long as you wear it with conviction.

Originally called Ute City (after its displaced former residents), Aspen was founded in the late 1870s during a silver rush. The silver market crashed in 1893, and Aspen's population dwindled from 15,000 to 250 people by the depression era. In the late 1930s, the region struck gold when Swiss mountaineer and ski consultant Andre Roche determined that Aspen Mountain would make a prime ski area. By 1941 it had already landed the U.S. Nationals, but Aspen was really put on the world map by Walter Paepcke, who developed the town as a cultural mecca. In 1949, he helped found the Aspen Institute for Humanistic Studies, and he organized an international celebration to mark Johann Wolfgang von Goethe's 200th birthday. This event paved the way for such renowned annual festivities as the Aspen Music Festival and the International Design Conference.

Downtown Aspen is easily explored on foot. It's best to wander without a planned itinerary, although the Aspen Historical Society puts out a walking-tour brochure. You can spend an afternoon admiring the sleek window displays and graceful Victorian mansions, many of which now house fine boutiques and restaurants.

The most prominent early citizen was Jerome Wheeler, who in 1889, at the height of Aspen's prosperity, opened two of Aspen's enduring landmarks. The ornate lobby, bar, and restaurant of the sturdily elegant redbrick **Jerome Hotel** (✉ 330 E. Main St., ☎ 970/920–1000) re-create fashionable turn-of-the-20th-century living. The elegant **Wheeler Opera House** (✉ 320 E. Hyman Ave., ☎ 970/920–5770) remains a concert venue today.

You can obtain great insight into Victorian high life at the **Wheeler-Stallard House Museum,** which displays period memorabilia collected by the Aspen Historical Society. ✉ *620 W. Bleeker St.,* ☎ *970/925–3721.* 🎫 *$3.* ⏲ *Jan.–Mar. and mid-June–mid-Sept., Tues.–Fri. 1–4.*

Your next stop should be the **Aspen Art Museum,** where top local and national artists are exhibited. The complimentary wine-and-cheese-session-cum-gallery-tour, held Thursday at 5, is a lot of fun. ✉ *590 N. Mill St.,* ☎ *970/925–8050.* 🎫 *$3.* ⏲ *Tues., Wed., Fri., Sat. 10–6, Thurs. noon–8, Sun. noon–6.*

Between galleries, museums, international conferences, and events, there's so much going on year-round that even in winter many people come to "do the scene," and don't even ski. Still, **Aspen Mountain** (also known as Ajax) is the standard by which many good skiers test themselves. Aspen is not for beginners (there are no green runs). A black diamond here might rank as a double diamond elsewhere. The narrow mountain is laid out as a series of steep unforgiving ridges with little room for error. Those wanting cruisers ski the ridge tops or valleys: Ruthie's Run, Buckhorn, and International are the classics. Bell Mountain provides some of the best bump skiing anywhere, followed by Walsh's Gulch, Hyrup's, and Kristi's. If you don't like catching air, or don't want your knees to get a workout, go elsewhere!

Southeast along Route 82 you'll see the turnoffs (Brush Creek or Owl
38 Creek roads) to **Snowmass,** one of four ski areas owned by the Aspen Skiing Company. Snowmass Village has its share of chic boutiques and eateries, but it's more affordable and down-to-earth than Aspen, and it predominantly caters to families. These differences apply equally to the development and to the mountain itself. Aspen Mountain is a rigorous ski experience. Snowmass is Aspen Skiing Company's family resort, with 52% of its 2,655 skiable acres designated intermediate, including the renowned classic cruiser runs off Big Burn lift, the stuff of ego massage. However, don't overlook that Snowmass is four times the size of Aspen Mountain, and has triple the black and double black diamond terrain of its famed sister, including several fearsomely precipitous gullies and Hanging Valley, accessible by a short hike. More and more skiers are discovering Snowmass's other personality, although Aspen Mountain remains the definitive test of skiing ability.

Buttermilk, accessed by West Buttermilk Road, is unfortunately known as Aspen's "learning" mountain. It's often dismissed as a beginner's area, but the Tiehack section on the east contains several advanced runs (though nothing truly expert), as well as sweeping views of Maroon Creek Valley. It also has superb powder, and deep snow sticks around longer because so few serious skiers realize what they're missing.

Aspen Highlands is reached off Maroon Creek Road. Until 1993, it was the only area not owned by the Aspen Skiing Company. This alone made the Highlands a favorite of antiestablishment types. Though it can no longer play on its independence by billing itself as the "maverick ski area," locals ski here for other reasons as well, including the best views among the four mountains, comparatively short lift lines, and some heart-pounding runs. Although not quite as hairy as Aspen Mountain, the Highlands offers thrilling descents at Steeplechase and Olympic Bowl, as well as a wide-open bowl called Thunder, where intermediates play. While you're here, enjoy Aspen Highlands' anything-goes spirit, evidenced by special events such as the freestyle contests every Friday, and the now-legendary Ski Patrol Jump, over the deck—and over startled skiers—at the Cloud Nine Picnic Hut. It's held every day at noon, weather permitting.

Aspen is equally popular in summer, with hiking and biking throughout the **White River National Forest.** A favorite jaunt through the forest is to the majestic **Maroon Bells,** twin peaks more than 14,000 ft high, so colorful, thanks to mineral streaking, you'd swear they were blanketed with primrose and Indian paintbrush. It's one of the most photographed spots in the state. Cars are allowed only partway, but Roaring Fork Transit provides shuttle buses that leave regularly in the summer from the Aspen Highlands parking lot.

Dining and Lodging

$$$$ ✕ **Ajax Tavern.** The brains behind Mustards Grill and Tra Vigne, two
★ of Napa Valley's finest eateries, have created this bright, pleasant restaurant with its mahogany paneling, diamond-pattern floors, leather banquettes, open kitchen, and an eager, unpretentious wait staff. Greg Topper's original, healthful dishes take advantage of the region's bountiful produce whenever possible. You might begin with the grilled spring asparagus with roasted pepper and Kalamata olive tapenade, followed with the braised short ribs with roasted garlic polenta or the grilled double-cut pork chop with sweet potato, parmesan, and thyme. Try the caramel-apple cobbler for dessert. The wine list, showcasing

Napa's best, is almost matched by the fine selection of microbrews. ✉ *685 E. Durant Ave., Aspen,* ☎ *970/920–9333. Reservations essential. AE, D, DC, MC, V.*

$$$$ ✕ **Cache Cache.** Chef Mike Barry is a practitioner of *cuisine minceur*—no butter or cream is used in his preparations. But the sunny flavors of Provence explode on the palate, thanks to the master's savvy use of garlic, tomato, eggplant, fennel, and rosemary. The lamb loin sandwiched between crisp, potato *galettes* (pancakes) on a bed of spinach is sublime; salads and rotisserie items are sensational. ✉ *205 S. Mill St., Aspen,* ☎ *970/925–3835. AE, MC, V.*

$$$$ ★ ✕ **Krabloonik.** Owner Dan MacEachen has a penchant for dogsled racing, and Krabloonik (Eskimo for "big eyebrows," and the name of his first lead dog) helps subsidize his expensive hobby. This cozy rustic-elegant cabin is on the slopes, but you can also drive there. You'll dine sumptuously on some of the best game in Colorado, perhaps carpaccio of smoked caribou with lingonberry vinaigrette; elk loin with marsala and sun-dried cherry glaze; pheasant breast with Gorgonzola; or wild boar medallions with morel cream sauce. The western decor features dogsled memorabilia and throw rugs. After lunch, you might get treated to a dogsled ride (the kennels are right next to the restaurant.) ✉ *4250 Divide Rd., Snowmass,* ☎ *970/923–3953. Reservations essential. AE, MC, V. No lunch in summer.*

$$$$ ✕ **Matsuhisa.** Renowned in New York, Los Angeles, London, and Tokyo, Matsuhisa brings its nouveau-Japanese cuisine to Aspen. The result: raves from locals and visitors alike. Mirrors hung about the downstairs dining area give a deceptive impression of space. Among the specialties are lobster with wasabi pepper, king crab claw tempura, or baby abalone with a light garlic sauce. While heavy on seafood, the menu also includes chicken and beef dishes, salads, and a variety of sashimi selections. ✉ *303 E. Main St.,* ☎ *970/544–6628. Reservations essential. AE, MC, V.*

$$$$ ★ ✕ **Renaissance.** The decor of this stunner is a coolly seductive, abstract rendition of a sultan's tent. Of course, this tent is unique—it boasts a knockout view of Aspen Mountain from the patio. Owner-chef Charles Dale apprenticed as chef saucier to his mentor, Daniel Boulud, at New York's trendiest mineral watering hole, Le Cirque, before opening Renaissance in 1990. Opt for his *menu degustation*—six courses matched with the appropriate glass of wine. The menu, as well as the style of preparation for many signature dishes, changes seasonally. Among his standouts are crispy Chilean sea bass with artichoke, shiitakes, and foie gras, and rack of lamb with an aromatic sauce. Upstairs, the Bistro offers a taste of the kitchen's splendors at down-to-earth prices. ✉ *304 E. Hopkins St., Aspen,* ☎ *970/925–2402. Reservations essential. AE, D, DC, MC, V. No lunch.*

$$$$ ★ ✕ **Syzygy.** Personable owner Walt Harris succeeds at providing a harmony of expressive cuisine, fine service, and elegant atmosphere (the name refers to the alignment of heavenly bodies) thanks to a sterling, unusually helpful wait staff and the assured, sublimely seasoned creations of chef Morton Oswald. His food is crisply flavored and sensuously textured, floating from French to Oriental to Southwestern influences without skipping a beat. Standouts include the Szechuan tempura lobster with grilled pineapple and Asian vegetable salad to start, followed by such main courses as elk tenderloin with sundried fig chutney and ancho chile aioli. The patient and knowledgeable will find a few good buys on the extensive wine list. ✉ *520 E. Hyman Ave., Aspen,* ☎ *970/925–3700. Reservations essential. AE, D, DC, MC, V. No lunch.*

$$$–$$$$ ★ ✕ **Farfalla.** The food is quite good at this Northern Italian winner. This slick, sleek L.A.-style eatery, well-lit and adorned with fine art, is one of the best spots in town. Specialties include tortellini with asparagus

and ham in walnut pesto, and deboned quail in vegetable sauce on a bed of polenta and beans. Reservations are accepted for parties of six or more, and lines form early. ✉ *415 E. Main St., Aspen,* ☎ *970/925–8222. AE, D, MC, V.*

$$$–$$$$ ✕ **Pine Creek Cookhouse.** You cross-country ski or board a horse-drawn sleigh (or hike during the summer) to this homey log cabin—Krabloonik's main competition—where the emphasis is also on game specialties, including quail, elk, and wild boar. ✉ *11399 Castle Creek, Aspen,* ☎ *970/925–1044. Reservations essential. AE, MC, V.*

$$$ ✕ **Kenichi.** This Asian restaurant gets the nod as much for its elegant spacious setting as for the delectable bamboo salmon and Oriental roast duck served Peking style with pancakes, cilantro, scallions, and hoisin sauce, with a side of melting asparagus tempura. Blackened sea bass is very popular, as is the seared ahi tuna with Cajun spices. ✉ *533 E. Hopkins Ave., Aspen,* ☎ *970/920–2212. AE, MC, V. No lunch.*

$$$ ✕ **L'Hostaria.** This latest entry vying for Aspen's Northern Italian restaurant-of-the-moment was started by the former manager of Farfalla (☞ *above*), Dante Medri. He and his wife Cristina brought over all of the furniture and fixtures from Italy, to create a sophisticated, yet rustic look with an open-beam farmhouse ceiling, sleek blond wood chairs, contemporary art, and a floor-to-ceiling glass wine cooler in the center of the room. The menu relies on simple, subtle flavors in specialties such as goat cheese flan on mixed greens, gnocchi with duck ragout, risotto with veal sauce, and a delectable veal Milanese. ✉ *620 W. Hyman Ave., Aspen,* ☎ *970/925–9022. AE, DC, MC, V.*

$$–$$$ ✕ **Il Poggio.** This spirited trattoria suits all moods, with a light lively café and a quieter, more romantic back room (for which reservations are advised). Try the dishes straight from the wood-burning oven, such as free-range chicken wrapped in pancetta and duck breast with polenta in honey grappa sauce. Fine pizzas and pasta are also served. ✉ *Elbert La., Snowmass,* ☎ *970/923–4292. MC, V. No lunch.*

$$ ✕ **Little Annie's Eating House.** Everything at this charming place is ultrasimple, from the wood paneling and red-and-white checked tablecloths to the fresh fish, barbecued ribs and chicken, and Colorado lamb. Annie's is a big favorite with locals who like the relaxed atmosphere, dependable food, and reasonable prices. ✉ *517 E. Hyman Ave., Aspen,* ☎ *970/925–1098. AE, MC, V.*

$$ ✕ **Main Street Bakery & Café.** Perfectly brewed coffee and hot breakfast buns and pastries are served at this café along with a full breakfast menu including eggs and homemade granola. During the late season when the sun is out, head out back to the deck for the mountain views. This is also a good spot for lunch and dinner. Try the Yankee pot roast, chicken potpie, and homemade soups. ✉ *201 E. Main St., Aspen,* ☎ *970/925–6446. AE, D, MC, V. No dinner Sun.–Mon.*

$$ ✕ **Rusty's Hickory House.** Tie on your bib and dig in. Rusty's hickory-smoked baby back ribs have won more than 40 national competitions. Enjoy the slow-smoked meats and chicken in a rustic Western atmosphere. You can get your hands and face covered in the secret sauce, and no one will mind. Rusty's is also known for homemade biscuits and gravy, salsa, and hand-cut onion rings. Don't miss the gooey, rich chocolate desserts. ✉ *730 W. Main St., Aspen,* ☎ *970/925–2313. AE, MC, V.*

$–$$ ✕ **Boogie's Diner.** This cheerful spot filled with diner memorabilia and an outrageous waitstaff resounds with rock-and-roll faves from the '50s and '60s. The menu has true diner range—from vegetarian specialties to grilled cheese and half-pound burgers (including turkey). Other items are excellent milk shakes, fresh soups, a monster chef salad, meat loaf and mashed potatoes, and a hot turkey sandwich. There's even a potato bar with one-pound taters and many topping choices. ✉ *534 E. Cooper Ave., Aspen,* ☎ *970/925–6610. AE, MC, V.*

$–$$ ✕ **La Cocina.** For good inexpensive eats, follow the locals. They'll lead you to this small Mexican restaurant, which they've been frequenting for more than 20 years. Almost every night the house is packed full. If the wait is too long, you'll likely cop a complimentary salsa dip or margarita for your trouble. ✉ *308 E. Hopkins Ave., Aspen,* ☎ *970/925–9714. No credit cards.*

$ ✕ **Flying Dog Brew Pub and Grille.** This local hangout, with exposed brick walls and wood beams, has a pleasant ambience. Cheap and cheery, Aspen's only brew pub has a good selection of outstanding beers. Try them one at a time or as a four-glass sampler. A substantial selection of pub grub is available, too, from ribs to sandwiches to burgers and other assorted finger foods. The solid pub grub is a bonus, but mostly customers howl for the home-brewed beers. Try the sweet and smooth Old Yeller, the gold-medal-winning Doggie-Style amber, or the malty Rin Tin Tin. ✉ *424 E. Cooper Ave., downstairs, Aspen,* ☎ *970/925–7464. AE, MC, V.*

$$$$ ★ **Aspen Club Lodge.** This refined, intimate ski-in hotel has a delightfully European flavor. The rooms are tastefully outfitted in rich mountain colors and desert pastels, with polished pine woodwork and beams, French doors opening onto the patio or balcony, down comforters, and minirefrigerators. The plush restaurant serves moderately priced American food. Guests may use a nearby health club. ✉ *709 E. Durant Ave., Aspen 81611,* ☎ *970/925–6760 or 800/882–2582,* FAX *970/925–6778. 84 rooms, 6 suites. Restaurant, bar, pool, hot tub, ski shop, airport shuttle. AE, MC, V.*

$$$$ **Hotel Lenado.** If the Sardy House is full, head down the block to this equally sumptuous property under the same management. The focal point of this dramatic B&B is a 28-ft stone and concrete fireplace. The smallish but quaint rooms contain either intricate carved apple-wood or Adirondack ironwood beds (*lenado* is Spanish for wood, and the motif appears throughout the hotel), antique armoires, even wood-burning stoves, in addition to modern amenities such as cable TV and tile baths. ✉ *200 S. Aspen St., Aspen 81611,* ☎ *970/925–6246 or 800/321–3457,* FAX *970/925–3840. 19 rooms. Breakfast room, lobby lounge, hot tub. AE, DC, MC, V.*

$$$$ ★ **Little Nell.** The Nell is the only truly ski-in/ski-out property in Aspen, and that alone is worth something. Belgian wool carpets and large, overstuffed down couches surround the massive lobby fireplace. The luxurious rooms have a fireplace, one king-size or two queen-size beds with down comforters, a plush down couch and chair, and a large marble bathroom. They are decorated in mountain colors and have every conceivable amenity and comfort, including patio, safe, cable TV, and minibar. Equally superior is the wait staff, who anticipate your every need. There's even a ski concierge to help guide your way. The restaurant, under new executive chef Brian Moscatello, is one of the best in town. ✉ *675 E. Durant Ave., Aspen 81611,* ☎ *970/920–4600 or 800/525–6200,* FAX *970/920–4670. 77 rooms, 15 suites. 2 restaurants, bar, in-room safes, minibars, room service, outdoor pool, hot tub, health club. AE, DC, MC, V.*

$$$$ ★ **The St. Regis Aspen.** The property is a memorable one, even by Aspen's exacting standards. The august reception area has elegant burnished hickory walls, crystal chandeliers, Colorado green-granite floors, and a $5 million art collection highlighted by commissioned sculptures and faux-18th-century landscapes and portraiture. The mostly peach-color rooms are more casual than the lobby, with cherry furnishings, luxuriant marble baths, and three phones. The property is ski-out, though not quite ski-in. ✉ *315 E. Dean St., Aspen 81611,* ☎ *970/920–3300 or 888/454–9005,* FAX *970/920–7353. 231 rooms, 26 suites. Restau-*

rant, bar, pool, beauty salon, indoor and outdoor hot tubs, sauna, steam room, health club, meeting rooms. AE, DC, MC, V.

$$$$ ★ 🏨 **Sardy House.** The tiny reception area opens onto an inviting parlor, with bay windows and dripping with chintz and lace. A narrow winding staircase with a magnificent oak balustrade leads to the precious rooms, decorated in aubergine, mauve, and rose, with Axminster carpets from Belfast, cherry armoires and beds, wicker furniture, and such welcome touches as Laura Ashley bedclothes and duvets, heated towel racks, and whirlpool tubs. The new wing scrupulously duplicates the authentic Victorian feel of the original house. The restaurant serves exquisite Continental cuisine. ✉ *128 E. Main St., Aspen 81611,* ☎ *970/920–2525 or 800/321–3457,* FAX *970/920–4478. 14 rooms, 6 suites. Restaurant, pool, hot tub, sauna. AE, DC, MC, V.*

$$$–$$$$ ★ 🏨 **Hotel Jerome.** One of the state's truly grand hotels since 1889, this is a treasure trove of Victoriana and froufrou. The sumptuous public rooms alone have five kinds of wallpaper, antler sconces, and more than $60,000 worth of rose damask curtains. Victorian grandeur oozes from a dazzling array of vintage furnishings, crystal chandeliers, intricate woodwork, and gold-laced floor tiling. All rooms are large, with high ceilings and such luxurious touches as oversize beds, antique armoires and chests, and huge bathtubs. Each room and suite is individually decorated in soft pastel hues with period furnishings, minibar, and cable TV. ✉ *330 E. Main St., Aspen 81611,* ☎ *970/920–1000 or 800/331–7213,* FAX *970/925–2784. 93 rooms, 16 suites. 2 restaurants, 2 bars, minibars, room service, pool, 2 hot tubs, fitness room, ski shop, meeting rooms, airport shuttle. AE, DC, MC, V.*

$$–$$$$ 🏨 **Hotel Aspen.** Considering its great location on Main Street, just a few minutes from the mall and the mountain, this hotel is a good find. The modern exterior is opened up with huge windows to take full advantage of the view; inside reveals a Southwestern influence. Most rooms have a balcony or terrace and are comfortable, if not luxurious. Four guest rooms have hot tubs. Continental breakfast is included in the room rate. ✉ *110 W. Main St., Aspen 81611,* ☎ *970/925–3441 or 800/527–7369,* FAX *970/920–1379. 45 rooms. Outdoor pool, 2 hot tubs. AE, D, DC, MC, V.*

$$–$$$$ 🏨 **Silvertree Hotel.** This ski-in/ski-out property, under the same management as the Wildwood Lodge next door, is actually built into Snowmass Mountain. It's sprawling, with virtually everything you need on-site. Rooms and suites feature subdued attractive decor, with all the expected amenities of a first-class hotel. Condominium units are also available, with full use of facilities. ✉ *Box 5009, Snowmass Village 81615,* ☎ *970/923–3520 or 800/525–9402,* FAX *970/923–5192. 627 rooms. 4 restaurants, bar, 3 pools, 2 hot tubs, spa, health club, ski shop, cabaret, meeting rooms. AE, D, DC, MC, V.*

$$$ ★ 🏨 **Snowmass Club.** These privately owned condos, decorated mostly in Southwestern style, are available for rental. The Ed Seay-designed 18-hole championship golf course doubles as a cross-country ski center in winter. Children stay here free, and there's also a fine day-care center. Sage's Bistro, featuring executive chef Mitch Liz's Colorado cuisine based on game and fresh fish, is a standout spot in the area. ✉ *Box G-2, Snowmass Village 81615,* ☎ *970/923–5600 or 800/525–0710,* FAX *970/923–6944. 67 suites. Restaurant, bar, 2 pools, hot tub, sauna, spa, steam room, 18-hole golf course, 9 tennis courts, health club, cross-country skiing, ski shop, meeting rooms, airport shuttle. AE, DC, MC, V.*

$$–$$$ 🏨 **Limelite Lodge.** In the early '50s this Aspen institution was a nightclub, but in 1958 it was converted to an inn by its present owners. Today it is a good value, particularly because of its prime location, just two blocks from the mall and three blocks from Lift 1A on Aspen Mountain. The guest rooms are furnished with brass or cherry-wood beds

and wooden furniture. All are accessible from the outside, motel style, which makes the lodge convenient for families. ✉ *228 E. Cooper St., Aspen 81611,* ☎ *970/925–3025 or 800/433–0832,* FAX *970/925–5120. 73 rooms, 3 suites. 2 outdoor pools, sauna, 2 outdoor hot tubs, ski storage. AE, D, DC, MC, V.*

$$–$$$ **Skier's Chalet.** One of Aspen's best bargains, Skier's Chalet has been under the same ownership for half a century. The location—100 ft from the ticket office and Chairlift 1A—can't be beat for the price. Basic but snug rooms all have cable TV, private bath, and phone, and the staff and fellow clientele are unfailingly congenial. A complimentary Continental breakfast is served every morning. ✉ *233 Gilbert St., Aspen 81611,* ☎ *970/920–2037 or 800/262–7736. 16 rooms. Restaurant, pool. MC, V. Closed late-Apr.–late-Nov.*

$$–$$$ **Snowflake Inn.** This is another property with wildly divergent accommodations, all quite comfortable and decorated mostly in tartans or bright colors. The rustic lobby with its stone fireplace and wood beams is a convivial gathering place for the complimentary Continental breakfast and afternoon tea. ✉ *221 E. Hyman Ave., Aspen 81611,* ☎ *970/925–3221 or 800/247–2069,* FAX *970/925–8740. 38 rooms. Pool, hot tub, sauna. AE, MC, V.*

$$ **Boomerang Lodge.** This comfortable, functional property offers a wide range of accommodations, from standard, somewhat drab hotel rooms to smartly appointed studios and deluxe rooms to three-bedroom apartments. There's even a log cabin. The nicest lodgings are the deluxe units, decorated in earth tones and with a Southwestern flair, each with a balcony, an enormous marble bath, a fireplace, and a wet bar. The staff is most hospitable. Continental breakfast is included in the rate. ✉ *500 W. Hopkins Ave., Aspen 81611,* ☎ *970/925–3416 or 800/992–8852,* FAX *970/925–3314. 38 rooms. Breakfast room, pool, hot tub, sauna. AE, MC, V.*

CONDOMINIUMS

Aspen Central Reservations (☎ 800/262–7736). **Coates, Reid & Waldron** (✉ 720 E. Hyman Ave., Aspen 81611, ☎ 970/925–1400 or 800/222–7736, FAX 970/920–3765). **Aspen Alps Condominium Association** (✉ 700 Ute Ave., Aspen 81611, ☎ 970/925–7820 or 800/228–7820, FAX 970/920–2528). **Frias Properties** (✉ 730 E. Durant Ave., Aspen 81611, ☎ 970/920–2010 or 800/633–0336, FAX 970/920–2020). **Destination Resort Management** (✉ 610 W. End St., Aspen 81611, ☎ 970/925–5000 or 800/345–1471, FAX 970/925–6891). **McCartney Property Management** (✉ 421-G Aspen Airport Business Center, Aspen 81611, ☎ 970/925–8717 or 800/433–8465, FAX 970/920–4770).

Snowmass Central Reservations (☎ 800/598–2004). **Snowmass Lodging Company** (✉ Box 6077, Snowmass Village 81615, ☎ 970/923–3232 or 800/365–0410, FAX 970/923–5740). **Village Property Management** (✉ Box 5009, Snowmass Village 81615, ☎ 970/923–4350 or 800/525–9402, FAX 970/923–5192).

Nightlife and the Arts

Aspen's **Wheeler Opera House** (☎ 970/925–2750) is the venue for big-name classical, jazz, and opera, especially in summer. The **Aspen Music Festival and School,** featuring chamber music to jazz, runs late-June–September. Aspen hosts a highly regarded **film festival** (☎ 970/925–6882) in late September.

BARS AND LOUNGES

Thirtysomethings who act like twentysomethings come to **Double Diamond** (✉ 450 S. Galena St., Aspen, ☎ 970/920–6905) for high-energy cruising and dancing with either live entertainment or a DJ. Whiskey is the claim to fame of **Eric's Bar** (✉ 315 E. Hyman Ave., Aspen,

☎ 970/920–6707), a curious little watering hole where you can also find a varied lineup of imported beers on tap.

Tourists now outnumber locals at the **'J' Bar** (✉ Hotel Jerome, 330 E. Main St., Aspen, ☎ 970/920–1000), but it's still a fun, lively spot and a necessary Aspen experience.

By its own admission, the **Woody Creek Tavern** (✉ Woody Creek Plaza, Woody Creek, ☎ 970/923–4585) "has no redeeming features." This may be true, except that it's is a great hangout, with a grungy atmosphere, assorted bar games, and notable visitors such as Don Johnson and Hunter S. Thompson.

The Tippler (✉ 535 E. Dean St., Aspen, ☎ 970/925–4977) has been affectionately nicknamed "The Crippler," because happy customers stagger out after such legendary occasions as Tuesday Disco nights, for which fans dress in their best polyester. The Tippler attracts a slightly older crowd looking to party without having the young bloods cut in on their action. Music, mayhem, and mid-life crises are all to be found on one packed deck.

The **Hard Rock Café** (✉ 210 S. Galena St., Aspen, ☎ 970/920–1666) is perfect for avid star seekers. **Planet Hollywood** (✉ 312 S. Galena St., Aspen, ☎ 970/920–7817), conveniently located a block from the Hard Rock, is of similar value.

CABARET

The **Crystal Palace** (✉ 300 E. Hyman Ave., Aspen, ☎ 970/925–1455) is an Aspen fixture, offering two seatings nightly with fine food and a fiercely funny up-to-the-minute satirical revue. The **Tower** (✉ Snowmass Mall, Snowmass, ☎ 970/923–4650) features hokey but hilarious magic and juggling acts.

MUSIC AND DANCE CLUBS

There's usually live **country music** and dancing at Cowboys (✉ Silvertree Hotel, Snowmass, ☎ 970/923–5249) and Shooters Saloon (✉ Galena and Hopkins Sts., Aspen, ☎ 970/925–4567). **Jazz** can be heard at Little Nell (✉ 675 E. Durant Ave., Aspen, ☎ 970/920–4600) and La Boheme (✉ Snowmass Village Mall, Snowmass, ☎ 970/923–6804). Club Soda (✉ 419 E. Hyman Ave., Aspen, ☎ 970/925–8154) is where the beautiful people and their admirers **dance** up a polite sweat.

Outdoor Activities and Sports

Aspen Center for Environmental Studies (✉ Hallam Lake Wildlife Sanctuary, 100 Puppy Smith St., Aspen, ☎ 970/925–5756) is a research center and wildlife sanctuary where children and adults alike can take refuge. The facility sponsors snowshoe walks with naturalist guides in winter, and backyard-wildlife workshops that teach children to create a minisanctuary in their own yard. In summer there are bird-watching hikes and Special Little Naturalist programs for four- to seven-year-olds, which include nature walks and arts and crafts.

Aspen Sports (✉ 303 E. Durant Ave., Aspen, ☎ 970/925–6332) runs fly-fishing tours of local waterways. **Pomeroy Sports** (✉ 614 E. Durant Ave., Aspen, ☎ 970/925–7875) also runs trips for anglers. For horseback riding, try **T Lazy Seven** (✉ Aspen, ☎ 970/925–4614), which offers snowmobiling in the winter. **Blazing Adventures** (✉ Aspen, ☎ 970/925–5651, 970/923–4544, or 800/282–7238) offers downhill bicycle tours through Aspen and the surrounding countryside. **The Hub of Aspen** (✉ 315 E. Hyman Ave., ☎ 970/925–7970) rents bicycles and hosts the annual Aspen Mountain Bike Festival. **Snowmass Club Golf Course** (✉ 239 Snowmass Village Circle, ☎ 970/923–

3148) is an 18-hole, 6,900-yard championship course designed by Arnold Palmer and Ed Seay.

FITNESS

Aspen Athletic Club (✉ 720 E. Hyman Ave., ☎ 970/925–2531) is fully equipped, and includes a steam room, tanning salon, and massage therapy. The **Aspen Club** (✉ 1450 Crystal Lake Rd., ☎ 970/925–8900) has weight-training and cardiovascular equipment, as well as indoor alpine skiing, squash, pools, basketball, and more. The **Snowmass Club** (✉ Snowmass Village, ☎ 970/923–5600) is a fully equipped health club open to guests.

HUT AND TRAIL SYSTEMS

Alfred A. Braun Hut System. This system explores the backcountry between Aspen and Crested Butte (✉ Box 7937, Aspen 81612, ☎ 970/925–6618), and is run by the U.S. Ski Association. This is an exhilarating but grueling trek—a perfect test of skiing expertise.

10th Mountain Hut and Trail System. During World War II a group of hardy soldiers camouflaged in white parkas practiced maneuvers in the stinging cold at Camp Hale, in the Elk Mountain Range between Aspen, Vail, and Leadville. That's where the U.S. Army 10th Mountain Division prepared for alpine fighting on hickory skis. Today, strong intermediates and experts can follow in their tracks on the 300 mi of trails crisscrossing the area. The surprisingly comfortable huts (accommodating up to 16 people in bunks; bring a sleeping bag) are solar-powered and have wood-burning stoves. Huts cost $22 per person per night and are usually booked well in advance. For details and reservations contact the **10th Mountain Trail Association** (✉ 1280 Ute Ave., Aspen 81611, ☎ 970/925–5775). The huts can be used by mountain bikers and hikers from July to September.

RAFTING

Aspen Whitewater/Colorado Riff Raft (☎ 970/925–1153, 970/925–5405, or 800/759–3939) operates mild to wild excursions on the Shoshone, Upper Roaring Fork, and lower Colorado. **Blazing Paddles/River Rats/Snowmass Whitewater** (☎ 970/923–4544 or 800/282–7238) runs trips to various rivers and canyons in the area and beyond.

SKIING

Aspen Highlands. Six lifts access 619 acres of terrain with a 3,635-ft vertical drop. *☎ 970/925–1220 or 800/525–6200. ⏲ Early Dec.–early Apr., 9–4.*

Aspen Mountain. Eight lifts, including a high-speed gondola, service the 631 acres of challenging terrain, spanning a vertical of 3,267 ft. *☎ 970/925–1220. ⏲ Late Nov.–mid-Apr., 9–4.*

Snowmass. This is a sprawling mountain, with five clearly defined skiing areas totalling 2,655 acres with a 4,206-ft vertical drop, and accessed by 20 lifts. As at Breckenridge, it's a good idea to plan your route carefully, especially if you're meeting someone on the mountain. *☎ 970/925–1220. ⏲ Late-Nov.–mid-Apr., 9–4.*

Buttermilk. This is often called Aspen's "learning" area, because it offers plenty of wide, gently rolling slopes for beginners and intermediates: more than 410 acres with 43 trails and a vertical of 2,030 ft. *✉ Off Rte. 82, ☎ 970/925–1220. ⏲ Late Nov.–early Apr., 9–4.*

For ski touring, **Aspen Alpine Guides** (☎ 970/925–6618) arranges customized multiday tours along the 10th Mountain Hut and Trail System connecting Aspen and Vail; and through the Alfred A. Braun Hut System connecting Aspen and Crested Butte (☞ Outdoor Activities and Sports *in* Aspen/Snowmass, *above*). **Paragon Guides** (✉ Edwards, ☎ 970/926–5299) also arranges tours along the hut systems. Or, you can contact the **10th Mountain Hut and Trail System** (☎ 970/925–5775) directly.

For cross-country, **Ashcroft Ski Touring** (✉ Aspen, ☎ 970/925–1971) features 40 km (25 mi) of groomed trails in the White River National Forest. **Aspen/Snowmass Nordic Trail System** (☎ 970/544–9246) contains 80 km (48 mi) of trails through the Roaring Fork Valley.

Shopping

Downtown Aspen is an eye-popping display of conspicuous consumption. Among the **malls** with ultra-chic stores are **Hyman Avenue Mall** (✉ Hyman Ave. between Mill and Galena Sts.), **Cooper Avenue Mall** (✉ Cooper Ave. between Mill and Galena Sts.), **Ute City Building** (✉ Hyman Ave. and Galena St.), and **Mill Street Mall** (✉ Hyman Ave. and Durant St.).

ANTIQUES

Fetzer Antiques (✉ 113 Aspen Airport Center, ☎ 970/925–5447) carries Aspen's finest antiques, and specializes in 18th- and 19th-century English and Continental goods. **Uriah Heep's** (✉ 112 S. Mill St., Aspen, ☎ 970/925–7456) purveys an amazing assortment of antique quilts, furnishings, and clothing, as well as exotic textiles, rugs, and folk art.

ART GALLERIES

Anderson Ranch Arts Center (✉ Snowmass Village, ☎ 970/923–3181) sells the work of resident artists. **Hill Gallery of Photography** (✉ 312 E. Hyman St., Aspen, ☎ 970/925–1836) captures nature's artistry in works by leading American photographers. **Joel Soroka Gallery** (✉ 400 E. Hyman Ave., Aspen, ☎ 970/920–3152) specializes in rare photos.

BOUTIQUES

In Aspen, **Boogie's** (✉ 534 E. Cooper Ave., ☎ 970/925–6111) sells kitschy clothes and jewelry; you can grab a bite in their diner, too. **Chepita's** (✉ 525 E. Cooper Ave., ☎ 970/925–2871) calls itself a "toy store for adults," and the whimsy continues with kinetic clothing and wood-carved sartorially resplendent pigs, to complement the standard designer watches and jewelry. **Funky Mountain Threads** (✉ 520 E. Durant Ave., ☎ 970/925–4665) offers just that: ethnic clothes, festive hats, extravagant beadwork, and imaginative jewelry. **Gracy's** (✉ 202 E. Main St., ☎ 970/925–5131) has first-class secondhand clothing. **Scandinavian Designs** (✉ 607 E. Cooper Ave., ☎ 970/925–7299) features some of Aspen's finest hand-knit sweaters, as well as everything Scandinavian from Swedish clogs to Norwegian trolls. **Limited Additions** (✉ 205 S. Mill St., ☎ 970/925–7112) features unique wearable art, handwoven or painted garments, and handcrafted jewelry.

CRAFTS

Aspen Potters (✉ 231 E. Main St., ☎ 970/925–8726) offers the latest designs from local artisans. **Geraniums 'n' Sunshine** (✉ 520 E. Durant Ave., Aspen, ☎ 970/925–6641) features Susan Eslick's colorful ceramics, as well as unique handcrafted toys and wearable art for children. **Quilts Unlimited** (✉ Silvertree Plaza Mall, 100 Elbert La., Snowmass, ☎ 970/923–5467) sells superb handmade antique and contemporary quilts, as well as various regional handicrafts. **Rachael Collection** (✉ 433 E. Cooper Ave., Aspen, ☎ 970/920–1313) exhibits more than 250 acclaimed American glass artists.

SPORTING GOODS

Aspen Sports (✉ 408 E. Cooper Ave., ☎ 970/925–6331; ✉ 303 E. Durant Ave., ☎ 970/925–6332; ✉ Snowmass Mall, ☎ 970/923–

6111; ✉ Snowmass Center, ☎ 970/923–3566; ✉ Silvertree Hotel, ☎ 970/923–6504) carries a full line of apparel and equipment.

I-70 and the High Rockies A to Z

Arriving and Departing

BY BUS

Greyhound Lines (☎ 800/231–2222) offers regular service from Denver to several towns along I–70.

BY CAR

If you're entering Colorado from the north or south, take I–25, which intersects with I–70 in Denver. If you're entering from the east or west, I–70 bisects the state. Idaho Springs, Summit Country, the Vail Valley, and Glenwood Springs are all on I–70. Winter Park is north of I–70, on U.S. 40, which has several hairpin turns. Leadville and Ski Cooper are south of I–70 along U.S. 24 or Route 91. Steamboat Springs is most easily reached via Route 131, north from I–70. Aspen/Snowmass can be reached via Route 82, south from I–70.

BY PLANE

Aspen Airport (☎ 970/920–5385) is served daily by United Express, America West Express/Mesa, Northwest Express/Mesaba, and has nonstop United service to Los Angeles, Dallas, and Chicago in ski season. American, Continental, Northwest, TWA, United, America West, Air Wisconsin, and United Express fly nonstop from various gateways during ski season to Steamboat Springs' **Yampa Valley Airport** (☎ 970/276–3669). The Vail Valley is served by **Eagle County Airport** (✉ Gypsum, ☎ 970/524–9490), 35 mi west of Vail. During ski season, Delta, United, and Northwest offer nonstop flights from several gateways. American flies here year-round, as do Continental and America West.

Most of the I–70 corridor, however, is served via Denver and its airports (☞ Arriving and Departing *in* Denver A to Z, *above*). This used to be the surer choice because flying into the smaller airports in winter was always iffy, but with jets making nonstop flights to many of those smaller airports now, the decision of which airport to use depends more on where you're coming from and which flights are convenient. There's an extensive list of Denver-based companies that specialize in transportation to the mountain resorts.

To and from Aspen/Snowmass: Roaring Fork Transit Agency (☎ 970/925–8484) provides bus service from Aspen Airport to the Ruby Park bus station in Aspen. **High Mountain Taxi** (☎ 970/925–8294 or 800/528–8294) runs trips to Denver, Glenwood Springs, and Vail. **Colorado Mountain Express** (☎ 970/949–4227 or 800/525–6353) runs trips to Vail and Aspen.

To and from Summit County (Breckenridge, Copper Mountain, Dillon, Frisco, Keystone): **Resort Express** (☎ 970/468–7600 or 800/334–7433) and **Colorado Mountain Express** (☎ 970/668–5466 or 800/525–6353) have regular service to and from Denver airports.

To and from Steamboat Springs: Alpine Taxi (☎ 970/879–2800) offers service from the airport, as well as special rates to Vail, Boulder, and Denver.

To and from Vail/Beaver Creek: Airport Transportation Service (☎ 970/476–7576). **Colorado Mountain Express** (☎ 970/949–4227 or 800/525–6353). **Vans to Vail** (☎ 970/476–4467 or 800/222–2212).

To and from Winter Park: Home James Transportation (☏ 970/726–5060 or 800/451–4844) offers service from Denver. **Greyhound Lines** (☏ 800/231–2222) runs from Denver to Winter Park.

BY TRAIN

Amtrak (☏ 970/726–5587 or 800/872–7245) offers service from Denver's Union Station to the Winter Park Ski Area station in nearby Fraser (where shuttles to the area are available). Glenwood Springs is on the *California Zephyr* route.

The nonstop **Ski Train** (☏ 303/296–4754) leaves Denver's Union Station every Sunday morning, chugging through 29 tunnels before depositing passengers only 50 yards from Winter Park's lifts.

Getting Around

BY BUS OR SHUTTLE

For intercity bus service try **Greyhound Lines.** Free shuttles serving the resorts are offered throughout the area.

Aspen/Snowmass: Within Snowmass there is free shuttle service; five colored flags denote the various routes. The **Roaring Fork Transit Agency** (☏ 970/925–8484) provides free shuttle service within Aspen and between Aspen and Snowmass.

Steamboat: Steamboat Springs Transit (☏ 970/879–5585) provides free transportation between the mountain and the town.

Summit County: Summit Stage (☏ 970/668–0999) links Breckenridge, Frisco, Copper Mountain, Dillon, Silverthorne, and Keystone for free. **Breckenridge Free Shuttle and Trolley** (☏ no phone) runs through town and up to the ski area, **Keystone Resort Shuttle Service** (☏ 970/468–2316) serves the extended Keystone area, and **KAB Express** (☏ 970/468–4200) serves Keystone/Arapahoe Basin and Breckenridge. **Resort Express** (☏ 970/468–7600) provides service between Keystone and Denver International Airport.

Vail Valley: Avon Beaver Creek Transit (☏ 970/949–6121) runs shuttles the length of the valley, daily, between 7 AM and 2:30 AM, every 20–30 minutes, for $2 each way.

Winter Park: The **Winter Park Lift** (☏ 970/726–4163) is the area's free shuttle service.

BY CAR

I–70 is a fast, convenient superhighway that is remarkably well maintained. All major sights in this tour are either on I–70 or on clearly marked side routes.

BY TAXI

Aspen/Snowmass: High Mountain Taxi (☏ 970/925–8294); **Steamboat Springs: Alpine Taxi** (☏ 970/879–2800). **Summit County: Rainbow Taxi** (☏ 970/453–8294). **Vail Valley: Vail Valley Taxi** (☏ 970/476–8294).

Contacts and Resources

DOCTORS AND DENTISTS

Aspen/Snowmass: Aspen Valley Hospital (✉ 0401 Castle Creek Rd., ☏ 970/925–1120). **Glenwood Springs: Valley View Hospital** (✉ 1906 Blake St., ☏ 970/945–6535). **Summit County: Summit Medical Center** (✉ Rte. 9 and School Rd., Frisco, ☏ 970/668–3300). **Vail Valley: Vail Valley Medical Center** (✉ 181 W. Meadow Dr., Vail, ☏ 970/476–2452). **Beaver Creek Village Medical Center** (✉ 1280 Village Rd., Beaver Creek, ☏ 970/949–0800).

GUIDED TOURS

A romantic way to orient yourself to Aspen is by taking the **T Lazy Seven Ranch** (☎ 970/925–4614) private sleigh ride. **Aspen Carriage Co.** (☎ 970/925–339) offers stagecoach tours. In summer, narrated bus tours from Aspen to the **Maroon Bells** are available (☎ 970/925–8484). The **Breckenridge Historical Society** (☎ 970/453–9022) offers lively 1½-hour tours of Colorado's largest National Historic District, Wednesday–Saturday at 11 AM. Several tour companies include Idaho Springs on their itineraries, and the **Idaho Springs Visitor Information Center** (✉ 2060 Miner St., ☎ 303/567–4660) can supply information. Steamboat's **Sweet Pea Tours** (☎ 970/879–5820) visits nearby hot springs. Vail's **Nova Guides** (☎ 970/949–4232) offers Jeep and ATV (all-terrain vehicle) tours, as well as rafting, fishing, snowmobiling, and hiking expeditions.

VISITOR INFORMATION

Aspen Chamber Resort Association (✉ 425 Rio Grande Pl., 81611, ☎ 970/925–1940 or 800/262–7736). **Breckenridge Resort Chamber** (✉ 309 N. Main St., 80424, ☎ 970/453–6018). **Glenwood Springs Chamber Resort Association** (✉ 806 Cooper Ave., 81601, ☎ 970/945–6589 or 800/221–0098). **Leadville Chamber of Commerce** (✉ 809 Harrison St., 80461, ☎ 719/486–3900). **Steamboat Springs Chamber Resort Association** (✉ 1255 S. Lincoln Ave., 80477, ☎ 970/879–0880 or 800/922–2722). **Summit County Chamber of Commerce** (✉ Main St., Frisco 80443, ☎ 970/668–5000 or 800/530–3099). **Vail Valley Tourism and Convention Bureau** (✉ 100 E. Meadow Dr., Vail 81658, ☎ 970/476–1000 or 800/824–5737). There are Tourist Information Centers in the Vail Village and Lionshead parking structures.

SOUTHWEST COLORADO

"Colorado" is a Spanish word meaning ruddy or colorful—adjectives that clearly describe many regions of the state, but particularly the Southwest. The terrain varies widely—from yawning black canyons and desolate monochrome moonscapes to pastel deserts and mesas, shimmering sapphire lakes, and 14,000-ft mountains. It's so rugged in the Southwest that a four-wheel-drive vehicle is necessary to explore the wild and beautiful backcountry. The mostly paved Alpine Loop Scenic Byway joins Lake City with Ouray and Silverton, shimmying through some stunning scenery.

The region's history and people are as colorful as the landscape, from the mysterious Anasazi (meaning "ancient ones"), who constructed impressive cliff dwellings in Mesa Verde National Park to such notorious outlaws as Butch Cassidy, who embarked on his storied career by robbing the Telluride Bank in 1889. Even today, the more ornery, independent locals, disgusted with the political system, periodically talk of seceding. They can be as rough as the country they inhabit.

Southwest Colorado offers such diversity that, depending on where you go, you can have radically different vacations, even during the same season. Visit the world-class resorts of Crested Butte, Purgatory, and Telluride for quality ski and golf holidays. Then move on to the Old West railroad town of Durango, followed by a pilgrimage to the Anasazi ruins that dot the area. Even for Colorado, the combination of recreational, historical, and cultural opportunities is diverse. This tour spirals from the towering peaks of the San Juan range to the plunging Black Canyon of the Gunnison, taking in alpine scenery along the way, as well as the eerie remains of old mining camps, before winding through striking desert landscapes, the superlative Anasazi ruins, and the Old West town of Durango.

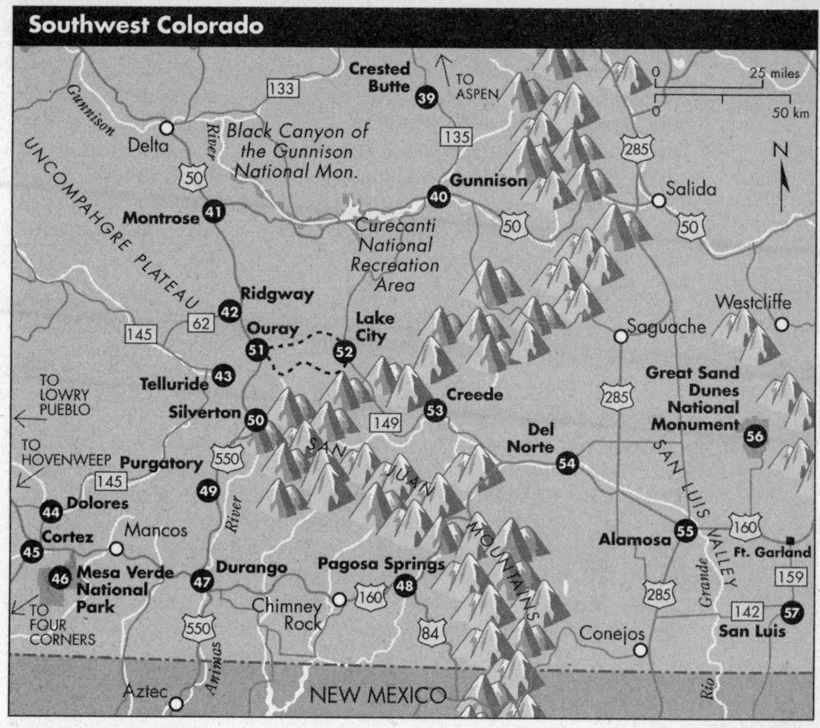

Crested Butte

39 *90 mi from Glenwood Springs via Rtes. 82 and 133 south and Rte. 135 east (gravel road over Kebler Pass, summer only); 110 mi from Aspen via Rte. 82 north, Rte. 133 south, and Rte. 135 (summer only); 190 mi from Glenwood Springs, south via Rtes. 82 and 133 south, Rte. 92 south, U.S. 50 west, and Rte. 135 north; 210 mi from Aspen via Rte. 82 north, south on Rte. 133 south, Rte. 92 south, U.S. 50 west, and Rte. 135 north.*

Crested Butte is literally just over the mountain from Aspen, but a 15-minute scenic flight or one-hour drive (or five-hour walk) in summer turns into a four-hour trek by car in winter, when Kebler Pass is closed. The town of Crested Butte has been declared a National Historic District and, like Aspen, it was once a quaint mining center whose exquisite, pastel, Victorian gingerbread-trim houses remain. Unlike Aspen, however, Crested Butte never became chic. A controversial ad campaign about its ski area (3 mi from town) touted it as: "Aspen like it used to be, and Vail like it never was."

That boast might make the locals seem crustier than they are; they're just proud and independent, with a puckish sense of humor. In a state that prides itself on hospitality, Crested Butte just may be the friendliest ski town of them all. A sense of warmth and whimsy pervades the area, most evident in the hot pink, magenta, and chartreuse facades of the buildings along Elk Avenue, the main drag. And for proof that nothing "em-bare-asses" the locals, check out the diehards streaking down the mountain nude on the last day of the season, or join the mavericks (for this event fully clothed) who hike up Snodgrass (slated for development as Crested Butte West) and bomb down every full moon.

Crested Butte Mountain Resort is a trailblazer and renegade in many respects: it initiated a daring—and wildly successful—venture in which everyone skis free the first four weeks of the season, and first-timers get free lessons. While many resorts are limiting their "out-of-bounds" terrain owing to increasing insurance costs and lawsuits, Crested Butte is thumbing its nose at the establishment by steadily increasing its extreme skiing terrain, which now speaks for 550 ungroomed acres. The Extreme Limits and The North Face should only be attempted by experts, but there are plenty of cruisable trails for recreational skiers. In the summer, mountain bikers challenge the hundreds of miles of trails surrounding the town, which are blanketed with columbine and Indian paintbrush.

Crested Butte is considered the quintessential ski bum's town: friendly, reasonably priced, cute as hell, great bars, impressive restaurants, and a gnarly mountain that remains far less crowded than its better-known neighbors.

Dining and Lodging

$$$$ ★ ✕ **Soupçon.** Soupçon ("soup's on," get it?) occupies two intimate rooms in a delightful log cabin—and a cozier place doesn't exist in this town. Chef Peter McCurrach brings innovative variations on classic bistro cuisine and changes his menu daily. His roast duckling, usually topped with an impeccably balanced Michigan cherry sauce, may be the best in the state, and the fish dishes are sublime. Try petrale sole lightly breaded in corn flour, glistening with black bean, ginger, and sake sauce. Desserts, however, really shine. Order the Jack Daniel's bread pudding, the hazelnut ice-cream cake, or any soufflé. ✉ *Just off 2nd St., behind the Forest Queen,* ☎ *970/349–5448. Reservations essential. AE, MC, V. No lunch.*

$$$–$$$$ ✕ **Timberline.** This handsome, cozy restaurant is set in a restored Victorian home. Among the top starters are fettuccine Alfredo with garden peas and goat-cheese terrine. Grilled salmon or herb-crusted veal rib chops might make a perfect second course. In the downstairs café, entrées start at $10. ✉ *21 Elk Ave.,* ☎ *970/349–9831. AE, MC, V. No lunch.*

$$$ ★ ✕ **Powerhouse.** This enormous barnlike structure has a delightful Gay '90s bar. The cuisine is haute Mexican, with scrumptious tacos and burritos and more exotic dishes, such as soft-shell crab in cornmeal and delectable mesquite-roasted *cabrito* (kid)—a true delicacy. The margaritas are the best in town, complemented by a knockout list of more than 70 tequilas by the glass. ✉ *130 Elk Ave.,* ☎ *970/349–5494. Reservations not accepted. AE, D, DC, MC, V. No lunch.*

$$$ ✕ **Swiss Chalet.** The owner duplicates the true Alpine experience, right down to the *Bierstube* (pub) with Paulaner on tap. The *Kalbsgeschnetzeltes* (veal loin sautéed with mushrooms and shallots in white-wine cream sauce), raclette, and fondue are luscious, as are such hard-to-find specialties as *Buendnerfleisch* (savory air-dried beef soaked in wine). ✉ *621 Gothic Rd., Mt. Crested Butte,* ☎ *970/349–5917. AE, MC, V. No lunch in summer.*

$ ✕ **Donita's Cantina.** This down-home Mexican restaurant is hard to miss: It's the one in the hot-pink building. The food isn't nearly as showy: simply good, solid standards such as fajitas and enchiladas, and a tangy salsa. It may be owing to either the bargain prices or the killer margaritas, but the crowds here are always jovial. ✉ *330 Elk Ave.,* ☎ *970/349–6674. Reservations not accepted. AE, D, MC, V. No lunch.*

$ ★ ✕ **Slogar.** Set in a lovingly renovated Victorian tavern awash in lace and stained glass, this restaurant—run by Mac Bailey—is just plain cozy. Slogar's turns out some of the plumpest, juiciest fried chicken west of the Mississippi. The fixings are just as sensational: flaky biscuits, creamy mashed potatoes swimming in hearty chicken gravy, and unique sweet-and-sour coleslaw from a Pennsylvania Dutch recipe that dates back nearly two centuries. You get all that and more, including homemade ice cream, for $12.95! ✉ *2nd and Whiterock Sts.,* ☎ *970/349–5765. MC, V. No lunch.*

$$–$$$ ★ 🏨 **Crested Butte Club.** This quaint, stylish inn is a Victorian dream: Each sumptuous, individually furnished room contains a brass or mahogany bed, Axminster carpets, and cherry-wood antiques or good-quality reproductions. All have spacious modern bathrooms and such little extras as footed copper and brass tubs or gas fireplaces. The downstairs bar is similarly delightful, but best of all is the full health club on the property, so you don't have to go far to soothe your weary muscles after a hard day's hiking or skiing. The Continental-plus breakfast is complimentary. ✉ *512 2nd St., 81224,* ☎ *970/349–6655 or 800/815–2582,* FAX *970/349–7580. 7 rooms. Bar, indoor lap pool, health club. D, MC, V.*

$$–$$$ 🏨 **Crested Butte Marriott.** This ski-in/ski-out property offers all the amenities and facilities of other luxury hotels at down-to-earth prices. Huge rooms are decorated in muted earth and pastel tones and feature wet bars, whirlpool tubs, and private balconies. The public spaces are dotted with towering plants, regional paintings and sculptures, and overstuffed armchairs and sofas. The Dugout, the resident sports bar, is a lively place to watch the Broncos. ✉ *500 Gothic Rd., Box 5006, Mt. Crested Butte 81225,* ☎ *970/349–7561 or 800/642–4422,* FAX *970/349–4466. 210 rooms, 52 suites. Restaurant, bar, indoor pool, outdoor hot tub, sauna, exercise room, recreation room, laundry service, meeting rooms. AE, D, DC, MC, V.*

$ 🏨 **Pioneer Guest Cabins.** Only 10 minutes out of town, on 7 acres of the Gunnison National Forest, this is a dream getaway. Rustic log cabins from the 1930s have been appointed with all new appliances, down comforters, and antique furnishings. You can hear and see the stream that runs through the property from every cabin. Each cabin has its own personality and comes with a fully equipped kitchen, as well as a fireplace or wood-burning stove. Cement Creek, ½-mi away, is a world-class fishing stream. A resident guide conducts mountain bike, snowshoe, and cross-country skiing tours. ✉ *Cement Creek Rd., 81224,* ☎ *970/349–5517,* FAX *970/349–5517. 8 cabins. Kitchenettes, hiking, cross-country skiing. MC, V.*

CONDOMINIUMS

Crested Butte Vacations (✉ Box A, Mt. Crested Butte 81225, ☎ 800/544–8448, FAX 970/349–2250) can make arrangements for all condominiums on the mountain.

Nightlife

Kochevar's (✉ 127 Elk Ave., ☎ 970/349–6745), a hand-hewn 1896 log cabin, is a classic pool hall–saloon. The other popular bar in town is the **Wooden Nickel** (✉ 222 Elk Ave., ☎ 970/349–6350), which has happy hours daily 3:30–6. **Rafters** (✉ Gothic Bldg., Ski Village, Mt. Crested Butte, ☎ 970/349–2298) is a big barn with cheap eats, strong drinks, and loud rock music (often live on weekends).

Outdoor Activities and Sports

CYCLING

The **Alpineer** bike shop (✉ 419 Sixth St., ☎ 970/349–5210) rents bikes and leads free guided mountain bike tours. **Fantasy Ranch** (✉ Box 236, Crested Butte 81224, ☎ 970/349–5425) provides horses for riding tours. **Alpine Outside** (✉ Crested Butte, ☎ 970/349–5011) runs fishing trips. **Three Rivers Outfitting** (✉ Box 339, Almont 81225, ☎ 970/641–1303) offers rafting trips and kayaking lessons. In the winter, for snowmobiling contact **Action Adventures** (✉ 15 Emmons St., Mt. Crested Butte, ☎ 970/349–5909 or 800/383–1974). **Alpine Expeditions** (✉ 315 Sixth St., ☎ 970/349–5011 or 800/833–8052) also outfits snowmobilers.

Crested Butte Country Club (✉ 385 Country Club Dr., ☎ 970/349–6127) is a ravishing 18-hole course designed by Robert Trent Jones, Jr., and although it belongs to the country club, it is open to the public. Crested Butte and Mt. Crested Butte Town parks have free public **tennis** courts.

SKIING

For some of the best extreme terrain in the country, as well as a good beginner area and remarkable "ski free" deals, head to **Crested Butte Mountain Resort,** with 85 trails, 14 lifts, 1,162 acres, and a 2,775-ft vertical drop. ✉ *Rte. 135,* ☎ *970/349–2222.* ⏲ *Late-Nov.–late Apr., daily 9–4.*

For cross-country, the **Crested Butte Nordic Center** (✉ 602 2nd St., ☎ 970/349–1707) has an 18-mi groomed track system and also offers guided tours into the backcountry.

For more information about skiing in this area, *see* Crested Butte *in* the Colorado section *of* Chapter 2.

Shopping

Creekside Pottery (✉ 126 Elk Ave., ☎ 970/349–6459) showcases local artist Mary Jursinovic's pottery and landscape lamps.

En Route The Route 135 scenic loop goes west from Crested Butte over Kebler Pass to Paonia, and south through banks of cottonwoods (which usually attract several swooping bald eagles).

Gunnison

40 *28 mi from Crested Butte via Rte. 135 south.*

At the confluence of the Gunnison River and Tomichi Creek, Gunnison has been a fishing and hunting community ever since the Utes adopted it as their summer hunting grounds. It provides economical lodging for those skiing Crested Butte and for backpackers, mountain bikers, and fishermen in summer.

The **Gunnison County Chamber of Commerce** (✉ 500 E. Tomichi Ave., ☎ 970/641–1501) issues an informative historical walking-tour brochure of downtown. Those interested in the region's history can also stop by the **Pioneer Museum,** a living history complex that includes several buildings and relics that date from the late 19th century. ✉ *U.S. 50 and S. Adams St.,* ☎ *970/641–4530.* 🎟 *$3.* ⏲ *Memorial Day–Labor Day, Mon.–Sat. 9–5, Sun. 1–5.*

Aside from its easy access to Crested Butte, Gunnison is recognized for two other things. Its **Western State College,** the local seat of higher learning, boasts a 320- by 420-ft whitewashed rock that's shaped like a W and is on Tenderfoot Mountain, just to the north of the campus. Ostensibly, this is the largest collegiate insignia in the world. Gunnison's other claim to fame is that the town has recorded some of the coldest temperatures ever reported in the continental United States.

Nine miles west of Gunnison on U.S. 50 is the **Curecanti National Recreation Area** (☎ 970/641–2337), set amid a striking eroded volcanic landscape and stretching for more than 60 mi. Dams built during the 1960s created three reservoirs, including Blue Mesa, the state's largest body of water. The reservoirs provide a wealth of aquatic recreational opportunities, as well as fine camping and hiking. At the western entrance to the recreation area, the Cimarron Visitor Center (✉ U.S. 50, ☎ 970/249–4074), open June–September, daily 8–4:30, displays vintage locomotives, an 1882 trestle listed on the National Register of Historic Places, and a reconstruction of a railroad stockyard.

Dining and Lodging

$–$$ ✕ **Garlic Mike's.** For upscale Italian, a nightly changing menu, and good seafood, give this spot a try. Try the homemade meat ravioli, pizzas, and eggplant Parmesan. The marinated sirloin steak carbonara wins as the house favorite. The menu is a welcome change of pace from the usual burger and fast-food joints that abound in the area. ✉ *2674 Hwy. 153,* ☎ *970/641–2493. AE, D, MC, V. No lunch.*

$$ **Mary Lawrence Inn.** This restored Victorian is an unexpected delight in Gunnison. The large rooms are furnished with tasteful antiques and Victorian touches such as lace curtains, stenciled walls, handmade quilts, vivid local art, and potpourri. A complimentary breakfast is offered each morning, along with a smile and advice for the day's adventures from helpful owners Beth and Doug Parker. ✉ *601 N. Taylor St., 81230,* ☎ *970/641–3343. 7 rooms. MC, V.*

Outdoor Activities and Sports

For fishing, the **Blue Mesa Reservoir** (✉ U.S. 50, ☎ 970/641–2337) in the Curecanti National Recreation Area outside Gunnison is a top choice. Also good is **Lake San Cristobal,** about 60 mi south of Gunnison on Route 149.

Water comes into play on 17 of the 18 holes at **Dos Rios Golf Club** (✉ County Rd. 33 off U.S. 50, 2 mi west of Gunnison, ☎ 970/641–1482).

Lazy F Bar Outfitters (✉ Box 383, 81230, ☎ 970/349–7593) provides horses for riding tours.

Shopping

Let's Go Country (✉ 234 N. Main St., ☎ 970/641–1638) is a good place to browse for crafts, CDs, and handmade lace. **The Corner Cupboard** (✉ 101 N. Main St., ☎ 970/641–0313) has a nifty selection of specialty food items.

Montrose

41 *65 mi from Gunnison via U.S. 50 west.*

The self-described "Home of the Black Canyon" sits amid glorious surroundings, but it's an otherwise nondescript town with little more than a collection of truck stops, trailer parks, and strip malls. However, Montrose is perfectly placed for exploring Curecanti and the Black Canyon to the east; the San Juans to the south; the world's largest flattop mountain, Grand Mesa (☞ Northwest Colorado, *below*) to the north; and the fertile Uncompahgre Plateau to the west.

If you're interested in learning more about the original residents of the area, stop by the excellent **Ute Indian Museum,** 3 mi south of town on U.S. 550. The museum contains several dioramas and the most comprehensive collection of Ute materials and artifacts in Colorado. ✉ *17253 Chipeta Dr.,* ☎ *970/249–3098.* *$2.* ⏲ *Mid-May–Sept., Mon.–Sat. 10–5, Sun. 1–5.*

The Gunnison River slices through one of the West's most awe-inspiring ★ sights, the **Black Canyon of the Gunnison National Monument,** a vivid testament to the powers of erosion. This 2,500-ft-deep gash in the earth's crust is 1,300 ft wide at its top and only 40 ft wide at the bottom. The canyon's name comes from the fact that so little sunlight penetrates its depths, and the eternal shadows permit scant plant growth on its steep walls. To reach the south rim of the canyon, take U.S. 50 east from Montrose (or west from Gunnison) and head north on Route 347. The fine visitor center has exhibits on the region's geology, history, and flora and fauna, and schedules nature walks to the canyon's forbidding rim. ✉ *Visitor center: Rte. 347, 6 mi east of Montrose,* ☎ *970/*

249–1915 or 970/249–7036. ⏲ *Apr.–Sept., daily 9–5. Park:* 🎫 *$4 per vehicle.* ⏲ *Apr.–Sept., daily 8–7.*

Dining and Lodging

$ ✕ **Sally's Café.** Gum-cracking waitresses serve up huge portions of gravy-laden food at Sally's Café. The menu has it all, from Mexi-burgers, patty melts, chicken-fried steak, and grilled PB&J sandwiches to Duncan Hines cakes and dull-as-dirty-dishwater coffee. The decor, too, reflects a quirky, local flavor, with a reindeer made out of an old clock that hangs on the wall, and Sally's own diverse collection of china ("I like my dishes," says Sally with typical understatement). ✉ *715 S. Townsend Ave.,* ☎ *970/249–6096. No credit cards. Closed Wed. and Thurs. No dinner.*

$ ✕ **The Whole Enchilada.** You'll get the whole enchilada and then some at this lively place. Portions are gargantuan, and the food goes down easily, especially the tasty chimichangas, blue-corn enchiladas, and homemade pies. The patio is a pleasant place to sit in summer. ✉ *44 S. Grand St.,* ☎ *970/249–1881. AE, MC, V.*

$$ 🏨 **Best Western Red Arrow Motor Inn.** This fully outfitted property is one of the nicest in the area, mainly because of the large, prettily appointed rooms adorned in greens and browns with handsome mahogany furnishings. The full baths include jetted whirlpool tubs. ✉ *1702 E. Main St., 81401,* ☎ *970/249–9641 or 800/468–9323,* FAX *970/249–8380. 60 rooms. Hot tub, exercise room, laundry service, meeting rooms. AE, D, DC, MC, V.*

$ 🏨 **Red Barn Motel.** This friendly property offers pleasing, fair-size rooms with all the usual motel amenities, as well as free Continental breakfast. Apart from the Red Arrow, the Red Barn boasts the most facilities in town, at a considerably lower rate than the competition. Children under 12 stay free in their parents' room. ✉ *1417 E. Main St., 81401,* ☎ *970/249–4507. 71 rooms. Restaurant, bar, pool, hot tub, sauna, exercise room, coin laundry. AE, D, DC, MC, V.*

Nightlife and the Arts

The **Montrose Pavilion** (✉ 1800 Pavilion Dr., ☎ 970/249–7015) includes a 602-seat auditorium where well-known musicians, comedians, dance companies, and regional orchestras often perform.

Outdoor Activities and Sports

For information on boating, camping, and fishing in the wilderness area of the San Juans and Sangre de Cristo, contact the **Curecanti National Recreation Area** (✉ Montrose, ☎ 970/641–2337) and the **Gunnison National Forest** (✉ Delta, ☎ 970/641–0471). For boating, you can also contact the **Elk Creek Marina** (✉ Montrose, ☎ 970/641–0707). For fishing, call the **Colorado Division of Wildlife** (✉ 2300 S. Townsend Ave., 81401, ☎ 970/249–3431). **Gunnison River Expeditions** (✉ Montrose, ☎ 970/249–4441) specializes in Gunnison River tours.

Shopping

Zappa Pottery (✉ 18800 T61 Trail, ☎ 970/249–6819) showcases the fine stoneware designs of Nick and Joan Zappa.

Ridgway

42 *26 mi from Montrose via U.S. 550 south.*

The 19th-century railroad town of Ridgway has been the setting for some classic Westerns, including *True Grit* and *How the West was Won.* It's also home to many swank ranches, including Ralph Lauren's.

Lodging

$$ ★ **Chipeta Sun Lodge.** Hosts Lyle and Shari Braund are happy to direct guests to their favorite hiking, mountain-biking, and cross-country ski trails. Their Southwestern-style adobe inn features rooms with handmade log beds, Mexican tiles, and stunning views. The hearty complimentary breakfast is served in a sunny solarium. ✉ *304 S. Lena St., 81432,* ☎ *970/626–3737 or 800/633–5868. 13 rooms. Hot tub. D, DC, MC, V.*

Nightlife

The Big Barn (✉ Trail Town, U.S. 550 and Rte. 62, ☎ 970/626–3600) is just that, offering a 1,000-square-ft dance floor, free video country dance lessons, and live music.

Shopping

Trail Town (✉ U.S. 550 and Rte. 62) is an entire mall devoted to the Western lifestyle, with restaurants, a dance hall, and clothing, furniture, and home-accessories stores. **Unicas Southwest** (✉ Ft. Smith Saloon Bldg., ☎ 970/626–5723) has clothing, folk art, and other Southwestern wares.

En Route U.S. 550 and Route 62 fan out from Ridgway to form one of the country's most stupendously scenic drives, the **San Juan Skyway,** which weaves through a series of "fourteeners" (a Rockies term for peaks reaching more than 14,000 ft) and picturesque mining towns. U.S. 550 continues through historic Ouray and Silverton to Durango. Route 62 and Route 145 reach Durango via the extraordinary Anasazi cliff dwellings of Mesa Verde National Park.

Telluride

43 *45 mi from Ridgway via Rte. 62 west and Rte. 145 east.*

Tucked like a jewel in a tiny valley caught between azure sky and gunmetal mountains is Telluride, once so inaccessible that it was a favorite hideout for desperadoes such as Butch Cassidy, who robbed his first bank here in 1889. The savage but beautiful terrain now attracts mountain people of a different sort—alpinists, snowboarders, freestylers, mountain bikers, and freewheeling four-wheelers—who attack any incline, up or down, and do so with abandon.

The ski area, too, is not for the faint of heart. Telluride poses the ultimate test for skiers, with one legendary challenging run after another. In particular, the terrain accessed by Chairlift Nine, including the famed Spiral Staircase and The Plunge, is for experts only (although one side of The Plunge is groomed for advanced skiers). Telluride has also expanded its "ultimate skiing" terrain to include more than 400 acres on Gold Hill. Forgotten in the excitement of all the challenge is that Telluride has a superb beginners' and learners' area. It's middle-of-the-road intermediates who may find themselves between a rock and a hard place.

The town's independent spirit is shaped not only by its mining legacy, but also by the social ferment of the '60s and early '70s. Before the ski area opened in 1971, Telluride had been as remote as it was back in Cassidy's day. It was even briefly included on the "Ghost Town Club of Colorado" itinerary, but that was before countercultural types moved in, seeking to lose themselves in the wilderness. By 1974 the town's orientation had changed so radically that the entire council was composed of hippies. Today there is one holdover—Councilman Rasta Stevie (he's white, but his waist-length dreadlocks might have made Bob Marley envious). Stevie defends an enduring Telluride tradition called the Freebox (✉ Pine St. and Colorado Ave.), where indigent residents can sort through and take whatever used clothing and appliances they need. (One memorable day, just after a fur shop had the temerity to open in town, surprised residents found a wide selection of minks, sables, and chinchillas at the Box. After the mysterious break-in, the furriers got the point and moved on.)

Despite such efforts at keeping such visible signs of wealth away, more and more locals are finding they can no longer afford to live here. Things were fine when the town was isolated, but thanks to the construction of the Telluride Regional Airport in the late 1980s, it has become quite accessible. Today Telluride is positioning itself as an upscale alternative to Vail and Aspen, and celebrities who need only be identified by their first names (Arnold and Oprah, for example) own homes here.

Telluride is chic—and not everyone's happy about it. Many townies deplore the mushrooming Telluride Mountain Village development at the base of the ski area, and some bitterly resent the Peaks at Telluride, a glamorous resort/spa. The ambivalence felt about the influx of wealth and new buildings brings into question whether development is inevitable, whether the pristine can be preserved in this fast-paced world. For better or worse, Telluride is gorgeous. The San Juans loom over town either menacingly or protectively, depending on the lighting.

The 425-ft liquid diamond **Bridal Veil Falls,** Colorado's highest cascade, tumbles lavishly just a short hike from the end of Colorado Avenue, the main street. The town itself offers one pastel Victorian residence or frontier trading post after another. The 1887 brick **San Miguel County Courthouse** (✉ Colorado Ave., between Fir and Aspen Sts.) was the county's first courthouse, and it still operates as one today. William Jennings Bryan spoke at the 1895 **New Sheridan Hotel and Opera House** (✉ 231 W. Colorado Ave., ☎ 970/728–4351) during his 1896 presidential campaign. The opera house, added in 1914 and completely redone in 1996, is now home to the thriving Sheridan Arts Foundation. *Telluride* magazine prints an excellent historic walking tour in its "Visitors' Guide" section. Today it's hard to believe that those lovingly restored shops and restaurants once housed gaming parlors and saloons known for the quality of their "waitressing."

That party-hearty spirit lives on, evidenced by the numerous annual events held here. Highly regarded wine and wild-mushroom festivals alternate with musical performances celebrating everything from bluegrass to jazz to chamber music. And the Telluride Film Festival is one of the world's leading showcases for the latest releases.

Dining and Lodging

$$$$ ★ ✕ **Campagna.** Vincent and Joline Esposito transport diners to a Tuscan farmhouse, from the decor (open kitchen, oak and terra-cotta floors, turn-of-the-20th-century photos of the Italian countryside, and Tuscan cookbooks) to the assured, classically simple food. Most everything is grilled or roasted with garlic, sage, or rosemary in olive oil, allowing the natural juices and flavors to emerge. Wild mushrooms (porcini or portobello) and wild boar chops are among the enticing possibilities. Finish your meal off with a letter-perfect tiramisu or hazelnut torte and a fiery house grappa. ✉ *435 W. Pacific Ave.,* ☎ *970/728–6190. Reservations essential. MC, V. No lunch.*

$$$$ ✕ **Cosmopolitan.** The Cosmopolitan restaurant, dormant for a century, has been revived. The original "Cosmo" was on Main Street next to the Bank of Telluride; the elegant new incarnation is in the sleek Hotel Columbia at the base of the gondola, overlooking the slopes. Chef Chad Scothorn, who cut his culinary teeth at Beano's Cabin in Beaver Creek,

has created a menu with a true cosmopolitan flair. Try the sesame-seared tuna with cucumber salad and mango-vanilla nori roll, the rack of New Zealand lamb, or the coriander-crusted yellowfin tuna. ✉ *300 W. San Juan Ave.,* ☎ *970/728–1292. Reservations essential. AE, MC, V.*

$$$$ ★ ✕ **La Marmotte.** This romantic bistro seems transplanted from Provence, with its brick walls, lace curtains, and baskets overflowing with flowers or garlic bulbs. The fish specials, such as grilled salmon with citrus risotto, are particularly splendid. The only drawback here is a surprisingly skimpy wine list with criminally high prices. ✉ *150 W. San Juan Ave.,* ☎ *970/728–6232. Reservations essential. AE, D, MC, V. No lunch.*

$$$$ ✕ **221 South Oak Bistro.** It had to happen that an ever more trendy Telluride would eventually have a "bistro." This one is very pretty, too, with high-tech, Southwestern decor, spot-lit peach walls, and a blond-wood bar. Soft music wafts through the casually elegant space. The menu sounds exciting but fails to deliver on its promise. Stick to New American dishes prepared by the new chef-owner John Helleberg, such as the veal loin chop with white beans, artichoke, and fennel; the sea scallops with cauliflower mousse; and the Mediterranean striped bass with saffron pasta. ✉ *221 S. Oak St.,* ☎ *970/728–9507. AE, MC, V.*

$$$–$$$$ ★ ✕ **The PowderHouse.** Tony Clinco (a former Golden Gloves winner who found another use for his hands) bills his food as "Rocky Mountain Cuisine." In reality, this is classic Italian married to wild game. Among the winners are pheasant ravioli; smoked buffalo sausage; and the game special—stuffed quail, venison chop, and marinated elk, each in its own sauce. ✉ *226 W. Colorado Ave.,* ☎ *970/728–3622. AE, MC, V.*

$$–$$$ ✕ **Floradora.** This Telluride institution is named for two turn-of-the-20th-century ladies of the evening (although locals call it Howie's, after the owner). The rafters are draped with pennants contributed by patrons over the years. The food is nothing special, but you come here for the ambience. Specials include applewood-smoked baby back ribs, chipotle-teriyaki-glazed salmon, and chicken and wild mushroom pasta. ✉ *103 W. Colorado Ave.,* ☎ *970/728–3888. AE, MC, V.*

$–$$ ✕ **Roma Bar and Café.** In operation since 1897, this restaurant offers good value and an incomparable air of history. The 1860 Brunswick bar, with 12-ft-high mirrors, has seen everything, including cowboys riding their mounts up to the stools. Flappers even brewed rotgut whiskey in the cellar during Prohibition. The pasta specials are terrific, as are the burgers. ✉ *133 E. Colorado Ave.,* ☎ *970/728–3669. AE, MC, V.*

$–$$ ✕ **South Park Café.** This ultracasual spot serves up heaping helpings of pastas, seafood, sandwiches, homemade soups and stews, and gourmet pizzas (choose from more than two dozen toppings). The excellent landscape photos that adorn the walls are for sale. ✉ *300 W. Colorado Ave.,* ☎ *970/728–5335. MC, V.*

$ ✕ **Fat Alley's BBQ.** A few family-style tables and benches, along with some old skis and ceiling fans fill this popular spot. Messy, mouth-watering ribs are complemented by delectable side dishes such as red beans and rice, baked sweet potatoes, snap-pea and feta salad, and coleslaw. A few beers and wines are available, in addition to homemade iced tea and pink lemonade. ✉ *122 S. Oak St.,* ☎ *970/728–3985. Reservations not accepted. AE, MC, V.*

$$$$ 🏨 **The Peaks at Telluride Resort and Spa.** The pastel-color, prisonlike exterior and lapses in service can be excused at this ski-in/ski-out, golf-in/golf-out luxury resort, thanks to its invigorating, revitalizing spa facilities, where more than 55 treatments are offered. The setting is glorious, dominated by fourteener Mt. Wilson (the peak on the Coors can). Rooms are sizable, if somewhat sterile, decorated in Norwegian wood and muted shades of green, with all amenities; many have balconies. So much money was sunk into the resort that it went into receivership during its first year, resulting in the continual turnover of staff (few of them locals) who, though eager, have difficulty answering the simplest questions about the area. The sports offerings here are vast. There's even an indoor climbing wall. ✉ *136 Country Club Dr., 81435,* ☎ *970/728–6800 or 800/789–2220,* FAX *970/728–6567. 145 rooms, 32 suites. 2 restaurants, bar, indoor-outdoor pool, beauty salon, hot tubs, sauna, spa, 5 tennis courts, exercise room, racquetball, squash, water slide. AE, DC, MC, V.*

$$–$$$$ **Pennington's Mountain Village Inn.** This secluded, exclusive inn features huge rooms in varying color schemes, with smashing mountain views from private decks, brass beds with cushy down comforters, handcrafted furniture, and stocked minirefrigerators. The pampering includes concierge service, breakfast, and afternoon hors d'oeuvres. ✉ *100 Pennington Ct., off Mountain Village Blvd., 81435,* ☎ *970/728–5337 or 800/543–1437. 9 rooms, 3 suites. Lobby lounge, refrigerators, hot tub, steam room, recreation room, laundry service. AE, MC, V.*

$$–$$$$ ★ **San Sophia B&B.** This is a Victorian-style inn, replete with turrets and gingerbread trim. Pristine mountain light streams into every room, warmly accented with whitewashed oak woodwork. Rooms have contemporary brass beds with handmade quilts, tables and nightstands handcrafted by Colorado artisans, stylish black-and-white landscape photographs, and stained-glass windows over the oversize tubs. The inn is known for its fabulous breakfasts and après-ski treats, and it offers supper nightly. Owners Alicia Bixby and Keith Hampton also run a promotion firm in town, put on the annual wine festival, and raise two young children, but they still find time to mingle with the guests. ✉ *330 W. Pacific St., 81435,* ☎ *970/728–3001 or 800/537–4781,* FAX *970/728–6226. 16 rooms. Hot tub. AE, MC, V.*

$$–$$$ **Ice House.** This property offers an appealing blend of Scandinavian and Southwestern decor: blond woods; jade carpets; fabrics in beiges, forest greens, and maroons; Native American tapestries; and polished wood ceilings. The spacious rooms feature cable TV, oversize tubs, balconies, and minibars. The hotel provides a free Continental breakfast and a place to store your skis. Best of all, the Oak Street lift is just a little more than a block away. ✉ *310 S. Fir St., 81435,* ☎ *970/728–6300 or 800/544–3436,* FAX *970/728–6358. 42 rooms, 16 condos. Minibars, pool, hot tub, steam room. AE, D, DC, MC, V.*

$$–$$$ **New Sheridan Hotel.** William Jennings Bryan delivered his rousing "Cross of Gold" speech here in 1896, garnering a presidential nomination in the process. Until 1994, when it was purchased by the Four Sisters Inns, the noted California chain, the New Sheridan seemed frozen in time. Now it's new indeed, albeit in tasteful period style. Decor favors exposed brick walls; old tintypes; marble-top dressing tables; faux Tiffany, crystal, or fringed lamps; and red velour love seats. Fortunately, the gorgeous Victorian bar, a local favorite, remains untouched. A complimentary breakfast and afternoon tea complete the picture of fin de siècle gracious living. ✉ *231 W. Colorado Ave., 81435,* ☎ *970/728–4351. 26 rooms, 16 with bath; 6 suites. Restaurant, bar, 2 hot tubs, exercise room, meeting room. AE, MC, V.*

CONDOMINIUMS

Telluride Central Reservations (☎ 800/525–3455) handles all properties at Telluride Mountain Village, and several in town. **Telluride Resort Accommodations** (✉ Box 100, 81435, ☎ 800/538–7754 or 800/538–7754) offers several top-notch accommodations in town.

Nightlife and the Arts

BARS AND LOUNGES

Leimgruber's Bierstube and Restaurant (✉ 573 W. Pacific Ave., ☎ 970/728–4663) is arguably Telluride's most popular après-ski hangout, thanks to gemütlich owner Christel Leimgruber; a Bavarian ambience enhanced by barmaids in dirndls; and a clientele that seems on the verge of launching into "The Drinking Song." Leimgruber's offers such traditional Alpine food as mixed German and wild-game sausage plates, mouth-puckering sauerbraten, and, of course, apple strudel. If you only want a brew, stop by to down a Paulaner or hoist a glass boot, which holds more than a liter of beer. The elegant turn-of-the-20th-century bar at the **New Sheridan Hotel** (✉ 231 W. Colorado Ave., ☎ 970/728–4351), the billiards parlor at **Swede-Finn Hall** (✉ 472 W. Pacific Ave., ☎ 970/728–2085), and the huge fireplaces at **Club Biota** (✉ 112 E. Colorado Ave., ☎ 970/728–6132) are the other popular **après-ski** nightspots.

The House (✉ 131 N. Fir St., ☎ 970/728–6207) is set in a building once dubbed "The Freak House" for the colorful characters who lived here during the '70s and '80s. These days the atmosphere is more refined—likened to a European pub by owner Tom Wirth—with fine ales on tap, along with cribbage, backgammon, Trivial Pursuit, and chess.

FESTIVALS

The **Telluride Film Festival** (☎ 603/643–1255) in September is considered one of the world's leading showcases of foreign and domestic films. Telluride offers numerous music festivals during the summer, including the monstrous jazz and bluegrass festivals (☞ Festivals and Seasonal Events *in* Chapter 1).

ROCK CLUBS

The **Fly Me To The Moon Saloon** (✉ 132 E. Colorado Ave., ☎ 970/728–6666) has live music—jazz, blues, funk, ska, rock, you name it—most nights, and the action gets wild on the spring-loaded dance floor. The **Last Dollar Saloon** (✉ 100 E. Colorado Ave., ☎ 970/728–4800) couldn't be less chic (and couldn't care less); when it's not a pool hall-saloon, it's the best venue for local rock bands. **Excelsior Café** (✉ 200 W. Colorado Ave., ☎ 970/728–4250) is the spot to hear the best in folk rock.

THEATER

The **Sheridan Arts Foundation** (☎ 970/728–6464) is a mentoring program that brings top actors to town to perform alongside budding young artists in the Sheridan Opera House. The **Telluride Repertory Theater Company** (☎ 970/728–4539), a year-round local resident artist group, also brings big names to town to perform in the Art Factory, a converted warehouse at the west end of town.

Outdoor Activities and Sports

Fantasy Ridge Alpinism (☎ 970/728–3546) is a climbing club in the region. **Telluride Whitewater** (☎ 970/728–3895) explores the Gunnison, Dolores, Colorado, and Animas rivers. **Telluride Outside** (✉ Box 685, 81435, ☎ 970/728–3895) provides horses for riding tours. Both **Telluride Angler** (☎ 970/728–0773) and **Telluride Outside** (☎ 970/728–3895) run fishing trips. For snowmobiling contact **Telluride Outside** (☎ 970/728–3895 or 800/831–6230).

Telluride Golf Club (✉ Telluride Mountain Village, ☎ 970/728–6900) boasts breathtaking views of Mt. Wilson and Mt. Sunshine, which dominate this 7,009-yard course. Free public tennis courts are offered at **Telluride Town Park** (☎ 970/728–3071).

SKIING

For downhill skiing, **Telluride** has 64 trails; 1 gondola, 9 chairs, and a Poma lift; 1,050 acres; and a 3,165-ft vertical drop (3,522-ft vertical if you hike to the highest ridge). ✉ *Rte. 145,* ☎ *970/728–6900 or 800/525–3455.* ⏲ *Late Nov.–early Apr., daily 9–4.*

Telluride Nordic Center (☎ 970/728–6911) provides 62 mi of pristine cross-country trails. The areas around Molas Divide and Mesa Verde National Park are also popular. **Telluride Helitrax** (☎ 970/728–4904) offers thrilling heli-skiing touring through the New Eastern Powder Circuit. For ski touring, the **San Juan Hut System** (✉ Telluride, ☎ 970/728–6935) connects Telluride with Ridgway. There are five huts equipped with beds, blankets, and stoves. Huts are about 7 mi apart. For more information about skiing in this area, *see* the Colorado section *in* Chapter 2.

Shopping

BOOKS

Between the Covers Bookstore and Coffee House (✉ 224 W. Colorado Ave., ☎ 970/728–4504) offers the perfect ambience for browsing through the latest titles while sipping a cappuccino. **Bookworks** (✉ 191 S. Pine St., ☎ 970/728–0700 or 800/371–1911) is an independent bookstore with a knowledgable owner.

BOUTIQUES

The **Bounty Hunter** (✉ 226 W. Colorado Ave., ☎ 970/728–0256) is the spot for leather, especially boots and vests. It also houses an astonishing selection of hats, among them Panama straw, beaver felt, Australian Outback, and just plain outrageous. **Wm. Donald** (✉ 220 E. Colorado Ave., ☎ 970/728–3489) offers stylish togs, including hand-tooled leather vests, one-of-a-kind hand-spun angora/mohair jackets, limited edition sweaters with such whimsical designs as chili peppers, as well as Coogis from Australia and Pendleton from Oregon.

CRAFT AND ART GALLERIES

Hellbent Leather and Silver (✉ 209 E. Colorado Ave., ☎ 970/728–6246) is a fine source for Native American arts and crafts. **The Potter's Wheel** (✉ 221 E. Colorado Ave., ☎ 970/728–4912) has decorative and functional pottery crafted by local artisans.

SPORTING GOODS

Telluride Sports (✉ 150 W. Colorado Ave., ☎ 970/728–4477) has equipment and clothing for all seasons.

Dolores

44 *75 mi from Telluride via Rte. 145 south.*

The enchanting **Galloping Goose Museum** (✉ 5th St. and Rte. 145, ☎ 970/882–4018) in Dolores is a replica of a Victorian train station that contains an original narrow-gauge locomotive. The gentle rising hump to the southwest of town is **Sleeping Ute Mountain,** which resembles the reclining silhouette of a Native American replete with headdress. The site is revered by the Ute Mountain tribe as a great warrior god who, mortally wounded in a titanic battle with the evil ones, lapsed into eternal sleep, his flowing blood turning into the life-giving Dolores and Animas rivers.

In 1968, construction of an irrigation dam on the Dolores River was authorized, forming the **McPhee Reservoir,** a haven for boaters and fishermen. An environmental-impact study was mandated by law, and it concluded that hundreds of potentially valuable archaeological sites would be flooded. This led to massive, federally funded excavations that uncovered the freestanding pueblos and cliff dwellings of the Anasazi. The mysterious and talented people who thrived until 1300 were probably the ancestors of present-day Pueblo tribes. No one knows for sure why they abandoned their homes, although most anthropologists surmise that a combination of drought and overfarming sent them off in search of greener pastures. One current school of thought is that they never really disappeared at all; rather they migrated, and actually still live on in the modern Pueblo Indians. Striking similarities between the artwork and customs of the two cultures seem to support this thinking.

★ The state-of-the-art **Anasazi Heritage Center** houses the finest artifacts culled from more than 1,500 excavations, as well as a theater, a library, a gift shop, and a full-scale replica of an Anasazi pit-house dwelling that illustrates how the Anasazi lived around 850. The complex is particularly notable for its Discovery Center, a series of hands-on, hologramlike interactive displays that enable visitors to weave on a Navajo loom, grind corn, and even generate an Anasazi village using a computer. ✉ *27501 Rte. 184, 3 mi west of Dolores,* ☎ *970/882–4811.* *$3.* *Daily 9–5.*

The first white explorers to stumble upon Anasazi ruins were the Spanish friars Dominguez and Escalante, who set out in 1776 from Santa Fe to find a safe overland route to Monterey, California. The two major ruins at the Anasazi Heritage Center are named for them. The Dominguez site, right next to the parking lot, is unimpressive, although it is of great archaeological interest because extremely rare evidence of a "high-status burial" was found here. The Escalante site, ½ mi away, is a 20-room masonry pueblo standing eerie guard over McPhee Reservoir.

OFF THE BEATEN PATH

LOWRY PUEBLO – The Lowry site has only eight kivas (Native American ceremonial structures, usually partly underground) and 40 rooms, and it may have been a "suburb" of larger communities in the area during its occupation from about 800 to 1110. Of particular note are the Great Kiva, one of the largest such structures ever discovered, and a painted kiva, which provides insight into Anasazi decorative techniques. A brochure, which details the self-guided tour, is available at the entrance to the site. ✉ *From Dolores, take Rte. 184 west to U.S. 666, and head west (follow signs) for 9 mi at Pleasant View,* ☎ *no phone.* *Free.* *Daily 9–5.*

Cortez

45 *10 mi from Dolores via Rte. 145 south and Rte. 160 west.*

The northern escarpment of Mesa Verde and the volcanic blisters of the La Plata mountains to the west dominate sprawling Cortez. A series of Days Inns, Dairy Queens, and Best Westerns, the town's architecture seems to have been determined by neon-sign and aluminum-siding salesmen of the '50s. Hidden among these, however, are fine galleries and a host of pawn shops that can yield surprising finds.

The exterior of the excellent **Cortez/Colorado University Center** has been painted to resemble the cliff dwellings of Mesa Verde. Exhibits focus on regional artists and artisans, the Ute Mountain branch of the Ute tribe, and various periods of Anasazi culture. Summer evenings include Native American dances; sandpainting, rug weaving, and pottery-making demonstrations; and storytelling events. ✉ *25 N. Market St.,* ☎ *970/565–1151.* *Free.* *June–Aug., weekdays 10–9, Sat. 1–9; May and Sept., Mon.–Sat. 10–6; Oct.–Apr., weekdays 10–5.*

The **Cultural Park** at the University Center (✉ 25 N. Market St., ☎ 970/565–1151) contains an authentic Navajo hogan and a Ute tepee. The park is open 9–5; admission is free. Visitor information is available at the **Colorado Welcome Center** (✉ Cortez City Park, 928 E. Main St., ☎ 970/565–3414 or 800/253–1616).

Dining and Lodging

$ ✕ **M&M Family Restaurant and Truck Stop.** Semis and RVs jammed into the parking lot attest that M&M is the real McCoy as truck stops go. If chicken-fried steak, enchiladas, and huge breakfasts (served 24 hours a day) are your fancy, you'll be thrilled to eat here. There are posher restaurants in town, but none better—certainly not for these prices. ✉ *7006 U.S. 160 S, ☎ 970/565–6511. Reservations not accepted. AE, MC.*

$ **Anasazi Motor Inn.** This is definitely the nicest hotel on the strip, mostly because its air-conditioned rooms are spacious and pleasantly decorated in Southwestern colors. Children under 18 stay free in their parents' room. ✉ *640 S. Broadway, 81312, ☎ 970/565–3773 or 800/972–6232, FAX 970/565–1027. 89 rooms. Restaurant, bar, pool, hot tub, meeting rooms, airport shuttle. AE, D, DC, MC, V.*

Nightlife

Colorado's first tribal gaming facility, offering limited-stakes gambling—slots, poker (video and live), bingo, and 21—is the **Ute Mountain Casino** (✉ 3 Weeminuche Dr., at Yellow Hat, Towaoc, ☎ 970/565–8800), 11 mi south of Cortez on U.S. 160/666.

Outdoor Activities and Sports

Conquistador Golf Course (✉ 2018 N. Dolores St., ☎ 970/565–9208) is an 18-hole public course with views of Mesa Verde and Sleeping Ute Mountain.

Shopping

Earth Song Haven (✉ 34 W. Main St., ☎ 970/565–9125) is a fine bookstore, with an espresso bar and tearoom in back. Cortez seems an unlikely spot for this European touch, but the café makes coffees, sandwiches, and high-calorie desserts such as peanut-butter cream pie. **Mesa Verde Pottery** (✉ 27601 Hwy. 160 E, ☎ 970/565–4492) offers a comprehensive sampling of ceramics from most Southwestern tribes. **Ute Mountain Pottery Plant** (✉ Rtes. 160 and 666, Towaoc, ☎ 970/565–8548) invites customers to watch the painstaking processes of molding, trimming, cleaning, painting, and glazing, before adjourning to the showroom to buy pieces straight from the source.

OFF THE BEATEN PATH

FOUR CORNERS MONUMENT – A stone slab marks the only spot where four states—Colorado, Arizona, Utah, and New Mexico—meet. This is photo-op country. Snacks and souvenirs are sold by Native Americans. To get here, travel south from Cortez on Route 160 for about 40 mi. You can't miss the signs. ✉ *Rte. 160 (follow signs).* *$2 per vehicle.* ⏲ *Daily 8–6.*

Mesa Verde National Park

46 *10 mi from Cortez via U.S. 160 east.*

Cortez is the gateway to Mesa Verde National Park, an 80-square-mi area that forms one of the nation's most riveting attractions. In 1888, two ranchers—Richard Wetherill and Charlie Mason—set off in search of stray cattle and stumbled upon the remarkable and perfectly preserved Cliff Palace, apartment-style cliff dwellings built into the canyon walls. By the next day's end they had discovered two more major sites: Spruce Tree House and Square Tower House. Excitement over their find culminated in the 1906 creation of the national park by Congress, making it the first park established to preserve the works of humankind.

Mesa Verde is one of Colorado's highlights, but consider either going off-season (though many of the ruins are closed) or overnighting in the park (after the tour buses have departed) to appreciate its full effect, without the crowds. You can pick up information on the park's attractions and accommodations at the entrance on U.S. 160. From here a 15-mi drive corkscrews up the mesa, skirting canyons and plateaus, to the Far View Visitor Center. ✉ *U.S. 160,* ☎ *970/529–4461 or 970/529–4465.* *Parking: $10 per vehicle.* ⏲ *Visitor center: May–Sept., daily 8–6; Oct.–Apr., daily 8–5.*

From the visitor center, you can head in one of two directions within the park. Your first option is to take the scenic route to **Wetherill Mesa,** open Memorial Day–Labor Day, which affords vistas of the Shiprock Formation in New Mexico and Monument Valley in Arizona and Utah. A minitram departs every half hour between 8:55 AM and 4:55 PM from the Wetherill parking lot, on a 4-mi loop to view the ruins; self-guided and ranger-led tours of Long House, the second-largest dwelling in the park, are also options. The other Far View route, **Ruins Road,** accesses the major sites on Chapin Mesa in two 6-mi loops. If you don't want to hike down into the canyons to view the ruins up close (which requires a free ticket available at the visitor center), this drive offers several strategic overlooks.

The first stop on the Ruins Road is the park's informative archaeological museum, which traces the development of Anasazi/Pueblo culture. It's a short walk from the museum to one of the most extraordinary sites, **Spruce Tree House,** the only ruin open year-round. Here you can climb down into an excavated kiva, symbolic of the womb of Mother Earth, for a better sense of how the Anasazis worshipped.

From the museum trailhead, one loop leads to the most famous ruin, **Cliff Palace,** the largest dwelling of its kind in the world (accessible by a moderately strenuous 15-minute hike), and to the more remote Balcony House (an arduous trek into the canyon below). Ranger-guided tours are available. The other loop accesses two major ruins, **Sun Temple** and **Square Tower House,** both involving a significant amount of walking and climbing.

Dining and Lodging

$$ ✕ **Millwood Junction.** Folks come from four states (no fooling) for the 25-item salad bar and phenomenal Friday-night seafood buffet. Steaks and seafood are featured in this upscale Red Lobster/Sizzler–style eatery. ✉ *U.S. 160 and Main St., Mancos,* ☎ *970/533–7338. MC, V. No lunch.*

$$ **Far View Lodge.** The rustic rooms at this lodge include private balconies with panoramas of Arizona, Utah, and New Mexico. Soothing Southwestern pastels predominate. Another draw here is the hotel's enthusiastic arrangement of guided tours. There are also nightly talks for guests by either a local Native American or an author, before a multimedia show on the Anasazi is shown. ✉ *Navajo Hill, 15 mi inside Mesa Verde National Park; Box 277, Mancos 81328,* ☎ *970/529–4421. 150 rooms. Restaurant. AE, D, MC, V. Closed mid-Oct.–mid-Apr.*

Outdoor Activities and Sports

Rimrock Outfitters (✉ Echo Basin, 1275 County Rd. 44, Mancos 81328, ☎ 970/533–7588) provides horses for riding tours, which range from one-hour walks to steak dinners to overnight excursions; rates begin at $18.

CAMPING

Campsites are available in Mesa Verde and Hovenweep; contact the **National Park Service** (✉ Mesa Verde National Park, Box 8, Mesa Verde, 81330, ☎ 970/529–4461).

OFF THE BEATEN PATH

HOVENWEEP NATIONAL MONUMENT – This site—whose literal translation from Ute means "deserted valley"—contains several major ruins, including imposing square, oval, and circular man-made towers such as Holly, Cajon, Hackberry, and Horseshoe, all of which are accessible only on foot. The most impressive ruin, called the Castle, underscores the site's uncanny resemblance to a medieval fiefdom. Hovenweep is approached via Route 160 west to County Road G (McElmo Canyon Rd.), which enters the red-walled McElmo Canyon along the way. ✉ *McElmo Canyon Rd.,* ☎ *970/749–0510.* *$6 per vehicle; camping entry fee $8.* *Daily sunrise–sunset.*

En Route Driving east on U.S. 160 from Mesa Verde will take you past an endearing bit of classic American kitsch, the **Mud Creek Hogan** (✉ U.S. 160, ☎ 970/533–7117). More than a dozen enormous arrows stuck in the ground mark the spot of this hokey trading post and museum (where you get the feeling that everything is for sale) adorned with tepees and a giant plastic horse. Beside the shop is a re-creation of a frontier town, replete with saloon, hotel, bank, jail, and livery station. Don't breathe too hard or you'll blow the town over: The "buildings" are only fronts. U.S. 160 continues through the lush Mancos Valley to the small and charming town of **Mancos,** where there are several excellent crafts shops, such as the **Bounty Hunter** (✉ 119 W. Grand Ave., ☎ 970/533–7215), that offer everything from saddles to 10-gallon hats, and a cute **Cowboy Museum** (✉ 100 Bauer St., ☎ 970/533–7741) in a restored mansion that also houses a B&B and the Old Mesa Verde Inn restaurant.

Durango

47 *45 mi from Cortez via U.S. 160 east.*

Will Rogers had this to say about Durango: "It's out of the way and glad of it." His crack is a bit unfair, considering that as a railroad town Durango has always been a cultural crossroads and melting pot (as well as a place to raise hell). It was founded in 1879 by General William Palmer (president of the all-powerful Denver & Rio Grande Railroad), when nearby Animas City haughtily refused to donate land for a depot; within a decade Durango had absorbed its rival completely. The booming town quickly became the region's main metropolis and a gateway to the Southwest. A walking tour of the historic downtown bears eloquent witness to Durango's prosperity during the late 19th century. The northern end of Main Avenue offers the usual assortment of cheap motels and fast-food outlets, all evidence of Durango's present status as the major hub for tourism in the area.

At 13th Avenue and Main Avenue (also known as Main Street)—the beginning of its **National Historic District**—the tenor changes dramatically, with old-fashioned gas lamps gracing the streets and a superlative collection of Victorians filled with chic galleries, restaurants, and brand-name outlet stores. The **1882 Train Depot** (✉ 4th St. and Main Ave.), the 1887 **Strater Hotel** (✉ 7th St. and Main Ave.), and the three-story sandstone **Newman Building** (✉ 8th St. and Main Ave.) are among the elegant edifices restored to their original grandeur. Stop into the Diamond Belle Saloon (in the Strater Hotel)—awash in velour and lace, with a player piano, gilt-and-mahogany bar, and scantily clad Gay '90s waitresses—for an authentic re-creation of an old-time honky-tonk.

The **Third Avenue National Historic District** (known simply as "The Boulevard"), two blocks east of Main Avenue, contains several Victorian residences, ranging from the imposing mansions of railroad and smelting executives to more modest variations erected by well-to-do merchants. The hodgepodge of styles veers from Greek Revival to Gothic Revival to Queen Anne to Spanish Colonial and Mission designs.

The most entertaining way to relive those halcyon days of the Old West is to take a ride on the **Durango & Silverton Narrow Gauge Railroad,** an eight-hour, round-trip journey along the 45-mi railway. You'll travel in comfort in restored 1882 parlor cars, and listen to the train's shrill whistle as the locomotive chugs along the fertile Animas River Valley and, at times, clings precariously to the hillside. ✉ *479 Main Ave.,* ☎ *970/247–2733.* *$53.* *Operates year-round except for late Oct.–late Nov., daily; times vary.*

Trimble Hot Springs (✉ County Rd. 203, off U.S. 550, 7 mi north of Durango, ☎ 970/247–0111) is a great place to soak your aching bones, especially if you've been doing some hiking.

Dining and Lodging

$$$ ✕ **The Red Snapper.** If you're in the mood for fresh fish, head to this congenial place, decorated with more than 200 gallons of saltwater aquariums. Try the oysters Durango, with jack cheese and salsa; salmon Wellington; or snapper Monterey with jack cheese and tarragon. Of course, delicious steaks and prime rib are also available. The salad bar includes more than 50 items. ✉ *144 E. 9th St.,* ☎ *970/259–3417. AE, MC, V. No lunch.*

$$–$$$ ✕ **Ariano's.** This popular Northern Italian restaurant occupies a dimly lit room plastered with local art. It offers pastas made fresh daily and a sure touch with meats. Try the veal scallopini with fresh sage and garlic. Next door, under the same ownership, is Pronto, a bright and noisy trattoria where you can get the same pastas (at a lower price) as well as pizza. ✉ *150 E. College Dr.,* ☎ *970/247–8146. AE, D, DC, MC, V. No lunch.*

$$–$$$ ✕ **Ore House.** Durango is a meat-and-potatoes kind of town, and this is Durango's idea of a steak house, where the aroma of beef smacks you in the face as you walk past. This classic eatery offers enormous slabs of aged Angus—cholesterol heaven hand-cut daily. ✉ *147 E. College Dr.,* ☎ *970/247–5707. AE, D, DC, MC, V.*

$ ✕ **Carver's Bakery and Brew Pub.** This microbrewery run by the "Brews Brothers," Bill and Jim Carver, offers about eight beers at any given time, including such flavors as Raspberry Wheat Ale (which brew-master Chris Tough nicknames "Seduction Ale"), Jackrabbit Pale Ale, and Colorado Trail Nut Brown Ale. There's a patio out back. From breakfast to the wee hours, the place is always hopping. Try the acclaimed baby-back ribs, or the bread bowls filled with either soup or salad. ✉ *1022 Main Ave.,* ☎ *970/259–2545. Reservations not accepted. AE, MC, V.*

$ ✕ **Olde Tymer's Café.** Locals flock to this former drugstore, which still drips with atmosphere from days gone by. The balcony, pressed-tin ceiling, and walls plastered with artifacts and locals' photos lend a '20s dance-hall look to the place. You can get cheap draft beer and great burgers. ✉ *1000 Main Ave.,* ☎ *970/259–2990. Reservations not accepted. AE, MC, V.*

$$–$$$ ★ **New Rochester Hotel.** Mother-and-son team Diane and Kirk Komick restored both hotels. The Rochester had served as a flophouse, and the Komicks rescued some of the original furniture, creating an atmosphere of funky chic. Steamer trunks, hand-painted settees, wagon-wheel chandeliers, and quilts contribute to the authentic feel. Denver and Rio Grande train windows convert the back porch into a parlor car, and gas lamps under towering maple trees grace the courtyard. The nearby **Leland House,** with the same owners, utilizes Southwestern pastel fabrics to create a Western effect, too. The Leland House has a complimentary full breakfast, while the Rochester's is Continental. ✉ *726 E. 2nd Ave., 81301,* ☎ *970/385–1920 or 800/664–1920,* FAX *970/385–1967. New Rochester: 17 rooms, 8 suites; Leland House: 10 rooms. Restaurant, kitchenettes, massage. MC, V.*

$$–$$$ ★ **Strater Hotel.** This Victorian beauty originally opened in 1887 and has been lovingly restored. Inside, Henry's restaurant and the Diamond Belle Saloon sport crystal chandeliers, beveled windows, original oak beams, flocked wallpaper, and plush velour curtains. The individually decorated rooms are swooningly exquisite: After all, the hotel owns the largest collection of Victorian walnut antiques in the country and even has its own wood-carving shop on site to create exact period reproductions. Your room might have entertained Butch Cassidy, Gerald Ford, Francis Ford Coppola, Louis L'Amour (he wrote *The Sacketts* here), JFK, or Marilyn Monroe (the latter two at separate times). ✉ *699 Main Ave., 81301,* ☎ *970/247–4431 or 800/247–4431,* FAX *970/259–2208. 93 rooms. Restaurant, bar, hot tub. AE, D, DC, MC, V.*

$$ ★ **Apple Orchard Inn.** Tucked into the lush Animas Valley, 8 mi from downtown Durango, is this gem of a country inn on 5 acres. The main house and six cottages surround a flower-bedecked pond, complete with friendly geese. There are cherry-wood antiques, feather beds, and handcrafted armoires in the handsome rooms. In the evening, relax on your cottage swing, enjoying views of the surrounding cliffs. The owners' experience at European cooking schools is evident in the breakfasts—and in the "train cookies" sometimes sent along with guests who take the train to Silverton. ✉ *7758 County Rd. 203, 81301,* ☎ *970/247–0751 or 800/426–0751,* FAX *970/385–6976. 10 rooms. Hot tub. D, MC, V.*

$–$$ **Comfort Inn.** This is one of the nicer properties along Durango's strip, because it's clean, comfortable, and has sizable rooms decorated in subdued teals and maroons. ✉ *2930 N. Main St., 81301,* ☎ *970/259–5373. 48 rooms. Pool, 2 hot tubs. AE, D, DC, MC, V.*

Nightlife and the Arts

BARS AND CLUBS

The hot spot is the **Diamond Belle Saloon** (✉ Strater Hotel, 699 Main Ave., ☎ 970/247–4431), whose antique, gold-leaf filigree bar, honky-tonk piano player, and waitresses dressed as 1880s saloon girls pack them in. **Lady Falconburgh's Barley Exchange** (✉ 640 Main Ave., ☎ 970/382–9664) is a favorite local pub with more than 140 beers available.

CASINOS

The **Sky Ute Lodge and Casino** (✉ Ignacio, ☎ 800/876–7017), 25 mi southeast of Durango on Route 172, offers limited-stakes gambling.

DINNER SHOWS

Bar D Chuckwagon (✉ 8080 County Rd. 250, East Animas Valley, 9 mi from Durango, ☎ 970/247–5753) serves barbecued beef, beans, and biscuits, along with a heaping helping of their Bar D Wranglers singing group.

THEATER

The **Diamond Circle Theater** (✉ 699 Main Ave., ☎ 970/247–4431) stages rip-roaring melodramas in summer. The **Durango Lively Arts Co.** (✉ Durango Arts Center, 802 2nd Ave., ☎ 970/259–2606) presents fine community theater productions.

Outdoor Activities and Sports

Two good **sources for information** about local camping, cycling, fishing, and hiking are the Bureau of Land Management (☎ 970/947–2800) and the San Juan National Forest (☎ 970/247–4874).

Mountain Bike Specialists (✉ 949 Main Ave., ☎ 970/259–6661) rents bikes. **Mountain Marina** (☎ 970/884–9450) rents canoes on Vallecito Lake, northeast of Durango on County Road 501. For information on climbing, contact **SouthWest Adventures** (✉ Durango, ☎ 970/259–0370). **Duranglers** (☎ 970/385–4081) runs trips to fishing spots in the area. **Southfork Stables** (✉ 28481 U.S. 160, ☎ 970/259–4871) provides horses for riding tours. **Durango Rivertrippers** (☎ 970/259–0289) runs expeditions down the Animas River.

GOLF

Dalton Ranch and Golf Club (✉ U.S. 550, 7 mi north of Durango, ☎ 970/247–7921) is a Ken Dye–designed 18-hole championship course with inspiring panoramas of red-rock cliffs. The restaurant has become a popular hangout for both duffers and skiers, who enjoy watching the resident elk herd on its afternoon stroll.

Hillcrest Golf Course (✉ 2300 Rim Dr., ☎ 970/247–1499) is an 18-hole public course perched on a mesa. **Durango City Park** (☎ 970/385–2950) has free public tennis courts. Reservations are advised.

Shopping

BOOKS

Maria's Books (✉ 960 Main Ave., ☎ 970/247–1438) specializes in regional literature and nonfiction.

BOUTIQUES

Appaloosa Trading Co. (✉ 501 Main Ave., ☎ 970/259–1994) is one of the best venues for all things leather, from purses to saddles, hats to boots, as well as jewelry, weaving, and other crafts. **O'Farrell Hat Company** (✉ 563 Main Ave., ☎ 970/259–2517) form-fits hats with a "customizer" machine; heads they've fitted include former presidents Bush and Reagan. **Shirt Off My Back** (✉ 680 Main Ave., ☎ 970/247–9644) sells silk-screened T-shirts (choose from more than 60 images or create your own).

CRAFT AND ART GALLERIES

Artesanos (✉ 115 W. 9th St., ☎ 970/259–5755) carries a selection of eclectic furnishings from around the world (the Mexican crafts are remarkably fine). **Dietz Market** (26345 U.S. 160, ☎ 970/259–5811 or 800/321–6069) carries pottery, metalwork, candles, weavings, and foodstuffs, all celebrating the region. **Hellbent Leather and Silver** (✉ 741 Main Ave., ☎ 970/247–9088) carries Native American arts and crafts.

Toh-Atin Gallery (✉ 145 W. 9th St., ☎ 970/247–8277) and the related Toh-Atin's Art on Main (✉ 865 Main Ave., ☎ 970/247–4540) around the corner make up perhaps the best Western, Native American, and Southwestern art gallery in Colorado, offering a wide-ranging selection of paintings, pottery, prints, records, foodstuffs, clothing, and jewelry.

En Route At the junction of U.S. 550 and U.S. 160 you have two options: Pick up U.S. 550 north toward Purgatory (☞ *below*), or follow U.S. 160 east toward Pagosa Springs. Thirty-five miles from Durango is **Chimney Rock,** so-named for the distinctive, twin-rock spires that architecturally are more closely related to the Chaco Canyon Anasazi sites in New Mexico than to those in Mesa Verde. Anthropologists debate whether the rocks served as a trading post or as an astronomical observatory of great religious significance. Whatever the origin, many believe that the mystical ruins retain their power and resonance. Access to the site is only possible with a Forest Service guide; reservations are mandatory for the free tour. For information contact the Pagosa Springs Forest Ranger District (☎ 970/264–2268).

Pagosa Springs

48 *62 mi from Durango via U.S. 160 east.*

Although not a large town, Pagosa Springs, 17 mi east of Chimney Rock, is a major outdoor sports center, where hiking, fishing, and cross-country-skiing opportunities abound not far from an excellent but under-used ski area, Wolf Creek. A bonus is the hot mineral baths right in town, where recreationalists can soak sore muscles.

Dining and Lodging

$-$$ ✕ **Elkhorn Café.** Filling and fiery Mexican fare (try the stuffed sopaipillas), as well as robust American standards such as meat loaf and pot roast, draws people from miles around. Fill up on a breakfast burrito before attacking the Wolf Creek bowls. ✉ *438 Main St.,* ☎ *970/264–2146. AE, D, MC, V.*

$-$$ 🏨 **Davidson's Country Inn B&B.** This three-story log cabin is on a 32-acre working ranch in the middle of Colorado's San Juan mountains, just north of Pagosa Springs. The location is perfect, just 20 minutes from Wolf Creek Ski Area (which has no lodging of its own). Rooms are comfortable and crammed with family heirlooms and antiques. A complimentary full breakfast is served. ✉ *2763 U.S. 160 E, 81147,* ☎ *970/264–5863,* FAX *970/264–5492. 9 rooms, 4 with shared bath. Recreation room. AE, D, MC, V.*

Outdoor Activities and Sports

For information on the area's fishing and hiking opportunities, contact the **Bureau of Land Management** (☎ 970/947–2800) or the **San Juan National Forest** (☎ 970/247–4874). **Fairfield Pagosa Resort** (✉ U.S. 160, 3 mi west of Pagosa Springs, ☎ 970/731–4123) offers both an 18-hole and a 9-hole course.

SKIING

With five lifts, 800 acres, and a 1,425-ft vertical drop, **Wolf Creek** is one of Colorado's best-kept secrets and a powder hound's dream: It's uncrowded with no lift lines, and it gets phenomenal snow (averaging more than 450 inches a year). The 50 trails run the gamut from wide-open bowls to steep glade skiing. ✉ *U.S. 160, at the top of Wolf Creek Pass,* ☎ *970/264–5629.* ⊙ *Early Nov.–mid-Apr., daily 9–4.*

En Route Double back along U.S. 160 to Durango to continue on to Purgatory. U.S. 550 North from Durango along the section of the San Juan Skyway is also known as the **Million Dollar Highway.** Depending on whom you ask, the name refers to either the million dollars worth of gold and silver mined each mile along the stretch, the low-grade ore from mining residue that was used to pave the road, the cost of the road's construction, or the million-dollar views it offers.

Purgatory

49 *25 mi from Durango via U.S. 550 north.*

North of the U.S. 160 and U.S. 550 junction are two famous recreational playgrounds: the ravishing golf course and development at Tamarron (☞ Dining and Lodging, *below*) and the Purgatory Ski Area. Purgatory is about as down-home as ski resorts get, with a clientele that runs toward families, cowboys, and college kids on break.

What's unique about Purgatory is its stepped terrain: lots of humps and dips, and steep pitches followed by virtual flats. This profile makes it difficult for skiers to lose control. There are some great powder days on the mountain's back side that will convince anyone that Purgatory isn't just "Pleasant Ridge," as it's derisively known in Crested Butte and Telluride.

Dining and Lodging

$$$$ ✕ **Café Cascade.** Many locals' choice for the best restaurant on the mountain, if not in the region, this intimate split-level eatery features the Southwestern stylings of chef Roy Griffiths. The menu has been made more affordable in recent years. Try roast Colorado lamb with grilled Anasazi

beans or grilled elk tenderloin over wild mushrooms in a lingonberry-merlot demiglaze. Rabbit satay with peanut sauce is a sterling appetizer. ✉ *50827 U.S. 550 N (1 mi north of Purgatory), Cascade Village,* ☎ *970/259–3500. AE, D, DC, MC, V. No lunch.*

$$$ ★ ✕ **Sow's Ear.** It's a toss-up between the Ore House (☞ Durango, *above*) and this Purgatory watering hole for the "Best Steak House" award. The Sow's Ear gets the edge, though, for its great views of the mountain and show kitchen in the dining area where you can view your meal as it's prepared. The mouthwatering, fresh-baked jalapeño-cheese rolls and honey-wheat rolls, and creative preparations such as blackened filet mignon and the daunting "hodgeebaba"—an 18-ounce rib eye smothered with sautéed mushrooms and onions—are a few more reasons Sow's Ear leads the pack. ✉ *Silver Pick Resort, 48475 U.S. 550,* ☎ *970/247–3527. MC, V. No lunch.*

$$–$$$ ★ **Tamarron.** This handsome development, on 750 acres surrounded by the San Juan National Forest, harmonizes beautifully with the environment. The main lodge seems an extension of the surrounding cliffs. Units are a blend of frontier architecture and Southwestern decor, and nearly all feature a fireplace, a full kitchen, and a terrace. Tamarron is famed for one of the country's most ravishing championship golf courses, and tennis and horseback riding (and condominium rentals) are also available. ✉ *18 mi north of Durango on U.S. 550; Drawer 3131, 81302,* ☎ *970/259–2000 or 800/678–1000,* FAX *970/259–0745. 300 rooms. 2 restaurants, bar, indoor-outdoor pool, hot tub, spa, 18-hole golf course, 3 tennis courts, horseback riding, children's programs (ages 4–12). AE, D, DC, MC, V.*

$$ ★ **Purgatory Village Hotel.** This luxurious ski-in/ski-out property offers both hotel rooms and condos, all decorated with Southwestern flair, including Native American rugs and prints. The condos include full kitchen, private balcony, washer/dryer, whirlpool bath, and wood-burning fireplace. ✉ *5 Skier Pl., Box 2062, 81302,* ☎ *970/385–2100,* FAX *970/382–2248. 133 rooms. 2 restaurants, bar, pool, 3 hot tubs. AE, D, DC, MC, V.*

CONDOMINIUMS

There are fine condo units at **Cascade Village** (✉ 50827 U.S. 550 N, 81301, ☎ 970/259–3500 or 800/525–0896).

Nightlife

Check out **Farquahrt's** at Purgatory Mountain Village (☎ 970/247–9000, ext. 3123), which attracts a lively, youthful crowd and hosts bands on weekends.

Outdoor Activities and Sports

Tamarron Resort (✉ 40292 U.S. 550 N, ☎ 970/259–2000) is an 18-hole, 6,885-yard course, frequently ranked among *Golf Digest's* top 75 resort courses.

For snowmobiling, contact **Snowmobile Adventure Tours** (✉ Purgatory, ☎ 970/247–9000).

SKIING

Purgatory-Durango has 75 trails, 9 chairs, 1,200 acres, and a 2,029-ft vertical drop—with a lot of intermediate runs and glade and tree skiing. For cross-country, there are 26 mi of machine-groomed scenic trails just outside the ski area. ✉ *U.S. 550,* ☎ *970/247–9000 or 800/525–0892.* ⏲ *Late Nov.–early Apr., daily 9–4.*

Shopping

Honeyville Station (✉ 33633 U.S. 550 N, Hermosa, ☎ 800/676–7690) south of Purgatory sells jams, jellies (try the chokecherry), condiments, and, of course, honey. You can watch how the bees make honey

Close-Up

PIONEERS OF COLORADO'S WILD WEST

EXPLORERS, SOLDIERS, immigrants, travelers, and exploiters of the wealth of the land all found their way to Colorado during pioneer days. Opportunists of every variety found unlimited opportunity here in the 19th century. Rocky Mountain country made them or broke them. Sometimes it did both. Those history remembers stand out as audacious giants, outlaws, showmen, stubborn fools, and lucky sons of guns.

While evidence of Colorado habitation goes back at least as far as the Basketmaker culture of 325 BC, early European contact came in 1776, with the Dominguez-Escalante Expedition that mapped the region. At the time, Colorado was home and hunting grounds of Utes, Comanches, Arapaho, and Cheyenne. With the signing of the Louisiana Purchase in 1803, Colorado territory became part of the United States, opening the way for the fur traders, mountain men, miners, cattlemen, and homesteaders who followed and drove out the original inhabitants.

The names of early Colorado explorers are as much legend as they are history. Zebulon Pike entered Colorado in 1806. He was followed almost immediately by fur trader John Jacob Astor in 1808. Major Stephen H. Long's expedition up the South Platte River and along the Front Range opened the way for traders to follow. William Becknell, forger of the Santa Fe Trail in 1821, "destined to the westward for the purpose of trading for Horses and Mules, and catching wild animals of every description." Traders Charles Bent and Cerain St. Vrain formed a partnership; Bent's Fort on the bank of the Arkansas near La Junta in eastern Colorado became the major trading center along the Santa Fe Trail. Indian scout Kit Carson; Uncle Dick Wooten, master of the tollgate over Raton Pass; and later, Buffalo Bill Cody with his Wild West Show, all left their mark.

Following the mountain men came the '59ers in a stampede to the Cherry Creek gold rush. As it turned out, there wasn't much gold in Auraria, or Denver, to be found, but there was plenty higher up, and silver, too, in the San Juans and other seemingly inaccessible high mountains. In 1861, Colorado officially became a territory of the United States, and in 1864, the massacre of the Cheyenne at Sand Creek, led by Colonel John Chivington, was a clear indication where the country was heading, and how it would get there.

Otto Mears, an immigrant Russian orphan, engineered the high mountain roads and railroads necessary to bring out the gold. Baby Doe Tabor, the second wife of Leadville silver king Horace Tabor, became the first woman to run a mine. Richard Wetherill and his brothers, of Mancos, encountered the remains of Anasazi civilization when they came upon the Cliff Palace ruins at Mesa Verde.

The pattern of boom and bust prevailed throughout the 19th century and into the 20th. Towns sprang up, then were deserted, as fortunes were made, then lost. Life was hard work.

Isabella Bird, the Victorian Englishwoman who rode horseback 200 mi through the Front Range to Estes Park in 1873 wrote in *A Lady's Life in the Rocky Mountains*: "This scenery satisfies my soul. Now, the Rocky Mountains realize—nay, exceed—the dream of my childhood. It is magnificent and the air is life giving. I should like to spend some time in these higher regions."

More than a century later, Colorado continues to draw us, just as it drew the earlier pioneers.

—Sharon Niederman

(in glass hives), and you may be treated to a lecture by a fully garbed beekeeper.

En Route The tortuous northern route from Purgatory to Silverton begins a dizzying series of switchbacks as it climbs over the Molas Pass, yielding splendid vistas of the Grand Turks, the Needles Range, and Crater Lake. This is prime mountain biking and four-wheeler territory. On the other side of the pass you'll reach the town of Silverton.

Silverton

50 *20 mi from Purgatory via U.S. 550 north.*

Glorious peaks ring Silverton, an isolated, unspoiled old mining community. It reputedly got its name when a miner exclaimed, "We ain't got much gold but we got a ton of silver!" The entire town is a National Historic Landmark District. The chamber of commerce (✉ 414 Greene St., ☎ 970/387–5654 or 800/752–4494) has issued a fact-filled walking-tour brochure that describes—among other things—the most impressive buildings lining Greene Street: **Miners' Union Hall,** the **Teller House, Town Hall, San Juan County Courthouse** (site of the county historical museum), and the **Grand Imperial Hotel.** These structures hold historical significance, but more history was probably made in the raucous red-light district along Blair Street.

Silverton has always been a rowdy town with a hardy populace, and that spirit remains. Every summer evening at 5:30, gunfights are staged at the corner of Blair and 12th streets. But the lawlessness evoked by such events is only part of the heritage that the town wishes to commemorate. If you look north toward Anvil Mountain, you'll see the community's touching tribute to miners—the **Christ of the Mines Shrine**—built in the '50s out of Carrara marble.

Dining and Lodging

$$ ✕ **Handlebars.** As much a museum as an eatery, the restaurant is crammed with mining artifacts, antiques, and animal mounts—including a full-size elk. Baby-back ribs are the specialty, basted with the restaurant's own barbecue sauce (bottled to go). The hearty menu also includes steaks, hamburgers, mashed potatoes, and the like. On weekends, the action heats up on the dance floor with live country and western and rock bands. ✉ *117 13th St.,* ☎ *970/387–5395. D, MC, V. Closed Nov.–Apr.*

$$–$$$ 🏨 **Wyman Hotel & Inn.** This wonderful 1902 red-sandstone building has 24-inch-thick walls, cathedral ceilings, and arched windows. The building is listed on the National Register of Historic Places. The attractive rooms all contain period antiques and pretty wallpapers, brass lamps, and VCRs. Three rooms have whirlpool tubs. A full breakfast and afternoon tea are included. The inn is entirely no-smoking. ✉ *1371 Greene St., 81433,* ☎ *970/387–5372 or 800/609–7845,* FAX *970/387–5745. 17 rooms, 1 suite. AE, D, MC, V.*

$ 🏨 **Wingate House Bed & Breakfast.** Owner Judy Graham, a prominent landscape artist, adorns the walls of the inn with her and her friends' works and family photos dating from the Civil War; the entire effect is both sophisticated and homey. The breezy front porch overlooks a majestic "thirteener" (mountain higher than 13,000 ft). Large sunny rooms are filled with antiques and have down pillows, comforters, and an eclectic library culled from Judy's journeys. A complimentary breakfast is served. ✉ *1045 Snowden St., 81433,* ☎ FAX *970/387–5520. 5 rooms, 3 with bath. Hot tub. MC, V.*

Nightlife and the Arts

A Theatre Group (✉ Miners Union Theatre, Greene St., ☎ 970/387–5337) presents a varied repertory season.

Shopping

Blair Street Emporium (✉ 747 Blair St., ☎ 970/387–5323) specializes in all manner of Christmas ornaments, lights, and decorations. **My Favorite Things** (✉ 1145 Greene St., ☎ 970/387–5643) is a Victorian gift shop with porcelain dolls; potpourri; antique jewelry; and romantic, lacy wearables.

Ouray

51 *23 mi from Silverton via U.S. 550 north.*

The town of Ouray is trapped in a narrow, steep-wall valley in the bullying shadow cast by rugged peaks of the San Juan Mountains. It was named for the great Southern Ute chief Ouray, labeled a visionary by the U.S. Army and branded a traitor by his people because he attempted to assimilate the Utes into white society. The mining town is yet another National Historic Landmark District, with a glittering array of lavish old hotels and residences. More than 25 classic edifices are included in the historic walking-tour brochure issued by the chamber of commerce (✉ 1222 Main St., ☎ 970/325–4746); among the points of interest are the grandiose **Wright's Opera House;** the **Beaumont, Western,** and **St. Elmo hotels;** and the **Elks Lodge.**

Ouray's architecture is notable, but the town's ultimate glory lies in its surroundings, and it has become an increasingly popular destination for climbers (both mountain and ice varieties), fat-tire fanatics, and hikers. One particularly gorgeous jaunt is to **Box Canyon Falls and Park,** just south of town, off U.S. 550. The turbulent waters of Clear Creek (part of the falls) thunder 285 ft down a narrow gorge. A steel suspension bridge and various well-marked trails afford breathtaking panoramic vistas.

More opportunities to immerse yourself in nature present themselves at the various hot springs in the area. It's hard to tell which is more revivifying: the 104-degree waters or the views of surrounding peaks at the **Ouray Hot Springs Pool.** ✉ *U.S. 550 at the north end of town,* ☎ *970/325–4638.* 🎫 *$6.* ⏲ *Weekdays 1–9, weekends noon–9.*

For a trip to the springs' source, visit the **Wiesbaden Vapor Cave,** an underground chamber where you can soak in the pools and breathe in the hot vapors. Massage and mud wraps are offered at the spa here. ✉ *625 5th St.,* ☎ *970/325–4347.* 🎫 *$9 for vapor cave and pool.* ⏲ *Daily 8 AM–9:45 PM.*

Lodging

$–$$$ ★ **China Clipper Inn.** A welcome relief from the typical Western- or Victorian-style inns in this area, the China Clipper is tastefully decorated with Oriental and nautical antiques. Most rooms open onto a charming garden patio and hot tub. The inn was built almost entirely, with great attention to detail, by a retired Navy commander from Louisville, Kentucky. He is warm and interesting without being overly ingratiating. ✉ *525 2nd St., 81427,* ☎ *970/325–0565 or 800/315–0565,* FAX *970/325–4190. 11 rooms. Hot tub. AE, D, MC, V.*

$–$$ **Box Canyon Lodge and Hot Springs.** The private mineral spring here was used first by the Ute, then by the Cogar Sanitarium (formerly on site). Soak away your cares in four redwood tubs full of steaming 103-degree to 107-degree water, with mountain views around you. The rooms are nondescript, but modern and comfortable, with all amenities. ✉ *45 3rd Ave., 81427, ☎ 970/325–4981 or 800/327–5080. 38 rooms. Hot springs. AE, D, DC, MC, V.*

$–$$ ★ **St. Elmo Hotel.** This tiny 1898 hostelry was originally a haven for "miners down on their luck," or so the story goes, thanks to its original owner Kitty Heit, who couldn't resist a sob story. Her son's ghost reputedly hovers about protectively. The rooms are awash with polished wood, stained glass, brass or mahogany beds, marble-top armoires, and other antiques. A complimentary breakfast buffet is served in a sunny parlor. The Bon Ton restaurant, Ouray's best, serves fine Continental cuisine with an Italian flair. ✉ *426 Main St., 81427, ☎ 970/325–4951, FAX 970/325–0348. 7 rooms, 2 suites. Restaurant, hot tub, sauna. AE, D, DC, MC, V.*

Outdoor Activities and Sports

Ouray has some of the best **four-wheel-drive roads** in the country (they lead to ghost towns high in the San Juans), but you should be an experienced off-roader to explore them solo. **Switzerland of America Tours** (☎ 970/325–4484) leads guided tours in open-air, six-passenger Jeeps.

San Juan Skyway Marina (☎ 970/626–5094 or 970/626–5538 off-season) rents canoes and boats at the Ridgway State Recreation Area (✉ U.S. 550, 12 mi north of town). Free public tennis courts can be found at **Ouray Hot Springs Pool** (✉ 1220 Main St., ☎ 970/325–4638).

Ouray is gaining fame in ice-climbing circles, with its abundance of frozen waterfalls. **Mountain Ouray Sports** (☎ 970/325–4284) arranges lessons and guided tours.

Shopping

Buckskin Trading Co. (✉ 636 Main St., ☎ 970/325–4044) sports an array of mining, railroading, Native American, and cowboy antiques and collectibles. **Images Gift Shoppe** (✉ 541 Main St., ☎ 970/325–7378) glories in tchotchkes and caters to a broad clientele, with items ranging from pottery to potpourri. **Circumstance Leatherworks** (✉ 306 6th Ave., ☎ 970/325–7360) sells belts, purses, and backpacks crafted by Robert Holmes.

Lake City

52 *45 mi from Ouray via the Alpine Loop Scenic Byway (summer only); 55 mi from Gunnison via U.S. 50 south and Rte. 149 north; 49 mi from Creede via Rte. 149 north.*

Lake City is noted for the superb hiking and fishing in Uncompahgre National Forest, especially at Lake San Cristobal. The town—with its collection of lacy gingerbread-trim houses and false-front Victorians—also has the largest National Historic Landmark District in Colorado. But Lake City is best known for the lurid history surrounding a notorious gentleman named Alfred Packer. Packer was a member of a party of six prospectors who camped near Lake San Cristobal during the winter of 1874. That spring, only Packer emerged from the mountains, claiming to have been deserted, and to have subsisted on roots and rabbits. Soon after, a Ute came across a grisly scene: strips of human flesh and crushed skulls. Packer protested his innocence and fled, but a manhunt ensued; Packer was finally caught nine years later, tried, and sentenced to life (he was convicted of manslaughter because of a technicality). To this day the event is commemorated by an Alferd Packer Barbecue, held annually in June.

The inspiring **Alpine Loop Scenic Byway** joins Lake City with Ouray and Silverton. This circle is only open in summer and is not paved over

Cinnamon and Engineer passes. However, this is four-wheel heaven, dizzily spiraling from 12,800-ft passes to gaping valleys.

Lodging

$$ **Old Carson Inn.** This peaceful log cabin nestled among stands of towering aspen and spruce has seven rooms brimming with rustic charm and nicely appointed with down comforters and private baths. The complimentary country breakfast, served family style, should get you off to a good start. ✉ *Box 144, County Rd. 30, 81235,* ☎ *970/944–2511. 7 rooms. Hot tub. AE, D, MC, V.*

Southwest Colorado A to Z

Arriving and Departing

BY BUS

Greyhound Lines (☎ 800/231–2222) serves most of the major towns in the region via Salt Lake City, Denver, or Albuquerque/Santa Fe.

BY CAR

If you're entering Colorado from the south, U.S. 550, U.S. 160, and U.S. 666 lead to the Four Corners region. From the east or west, I–70 (U.S. 6) intersects U.S. 50 in Grand Junction; U.S. 50 runs south to the San Juans and Four Corners area. From the north, take I–25 to I–70 in Denver, for a long drive west to U.S. 50.

BY PLANE

The **Durango-La Plata Airport** (☎ 970/247–8143) receives daily flights from American, America West Express, and United Express. **Gunnison County Airport** (☎ 970/641–0526), which also serves Crested Butte, has flights by United Express. **Montrose Airport** (☎ 970/249–3203) is served by America West and United Express. **Telluride Regional Airport** (☎ 970/728–5313) welcomes flights from America West and United Express (☞ Air Travel *in* Smart Travel Tips A to Z).

Several companies offer transportation between the airports and the resorts. Shuttles average $15–$20 per person. **Crested Butte: Alpine Express** (☎ 970/641–5074 or 800/822–4844). **Durango: Durango Transportation** (☎ 970/247–4161 or 800/626–2066). **Montrose: Western Express Taxi** (☎ 970/249–8880). **Telluride: Shuttle and Taxi** (☎ 970/728–6667) and **Telluride Transit** (☎ 970/728–6000).

Getting Around

BY CAR

The main roads are Route 135 between Crested Butte and Gunnison; U.S. 50 linking Poncha Springs, Gunnison, Montrose, and Delta; Route 149 between Gunnison, Lake City, and Creede; U.S. 550 from Montrose to Ridgway; Route 62 and Route 145 linking Ridgway with Telluride, Dolores, and Cortez; Route 110 running from Ridgway through Ouray and Silverton to Durango; and U.S. 160, the closest thing to a major highway in the area, from Cortez to Durango via the Mesa Verde National Park north entrance.

BY BUS OR SHUTTLE

The **Crested Butte Mountain Express** (☎ 970/349–5616) runs regularly between the town and the ski area. **Durango Lift** (☎ 970/259–5438) has regular bus service up and down Main Street, as well as to Purgatory Ski Area during ski season. **The Tellu-Ride** (☎ 970/728–5700) provides an in-town loop, while the new gondola connects the town of Telluride with the Mountain Village for free, 7 AM–11 PM.

BY TAXI

In most cases you'll need to call for a cab; taxis are plentiful and the wait is only about 15 minutes. **Crested Butte Town Taxi** (☎ 970/349–

5543). **Durango Transportation** (☒ ☎ 970/259–4818). **Montrose Taxi** (☒ ☎ 970/249–8880). **Telluride Shuttle and Taxi** (☒ ☎ 970/728–6667). **Telluride Transit** (☒ ☎ 970/728–6000).

Contacts and Resources

DOCTORS AND DENTISTS

Southwest Memorial Hospital (☒ 1311 N. Mildred St., Cortez, ☎ 970/565–6666). **Mercy Medical Center** (☒ 375 E. Park Ave., Durango, ☎ 970/247–4311). **Gunnison Valley Hospital** (☒ 214 E. Denver Ave., Gunnison, ☎ 970/641–1456). **Montrose Memorial Hospital** (☒ 800 S. 3rd St., Montrose, ☎ 970/249–2211). **Telluride Medical Center** (☒ 500 W. Pacific Ave., Telluride, ☎ 970/728–3848).

GUIDED TOURS

Adventures to the Edge (☒ Crested Butte, ☎ 970/349–5219) creates customized treks, ski tours, and alpine ascents in the Crested Butte area. **ARA Mesa Verde Company** (☒ Mancos, ☎ 970/529–4421) runs three- and six-hour tours into Mesa Verde National Park. **Durango Transportation** (☎ 970/259–4818) arranges tours of Mesa Verde, Chaco Canyon (in New Mexico), and the San Juan Skyway.

Historic Tours of Telluride (☎ 970/728–6639) provides humorous walking tours of this historic town, enlivening them with stories of famed figures such as Butch Cassidy and Jack Dempsey.

Crow Canyon Archaeological Center (☒ 23390 County Rd. K, Cortez 81321, ☎ 970/565–8975 or 800/422–8975) promotes understanding and appreciation of Anasazi culture by guiding visitors through excavations and botanical studies in the region. Also included in the week-long programs are day trips to isolated canyon sites and hands-on lessons in weaving and pottery-making with Native American artisans. Day programs are available on a reservation-only basis to families and groups. Native American guides at **Ute Mountain Tribal Park** (☒ Towaoc 81334, ☎ 970/565–3751, ext. 282) lead grueling hikes into this dazzling primitive repository of Anasazi ruins, including the majestic Tree House cliff dwelling and enchanting Eagle's Nest petroglyphs. Tours usually start at the Ute Mountain Pottery Plant, 15 mi south of Cortez, on U.S. 666. Overnight camping can also be arranged.

HIKING

For general information about hiking in southwest Colorado, contact the **San Juan National Forest Ranger District** (☒ 100 N. 6th St., Dolores 81323, ☎ 970/882–7296).

VISITOR INFORMATION

Cortez Area Chamber of Commerce (☒ 928 E. Main St., 81321, ☎ 970/565–3414). **Crested Butte–Mt. Crested Butte Chamber of Commerce** (☒ 7 Emmons Loop, 81321, ☎ 970/349–6438 or 800/545–4505). **Durango Chamber Resort Association** (☒ 111 S. Camino del Rio, 81302, ☎ 970/247–0312 or 800/525–8855). **Gunnison County Chamber of Commerce** (☒ 500 E. Tomichi Ave., 81230, ☎ 970/641–1501 or 800/274–7580). **Lake City Chamber of Commerce** (☒ 306 N. Silver St., 81235, ☎ 970/944–2527). **Mesa Verde National Park** (☒ Box 8, Supt., Mesa Verde Park 81330, ☎ 970/529–4465). **Mesa Verde Country** (☒ Box HH, Cortez 81321, ☎ 800/253–1616). **Montrose Chamber of Commerce** (☒ 1519 E. Main St., 81401, ☎ 800/923–5515) and **Visitor Information Center** (☒ 550 S. Chipeta Rd., 81401, ☎ 970/249–1726). **Ouray County Chamber** (☒ 1222 Main St., 81427, ☎ 970/325–4746 or 800/228–1876). **Pagosa Springs Chamber of Commerce** (☒ 402 San Juan St., 81147, ☎ 303/264–2360 or 800/252–2204). **San Juan National Forest Ranger District** (☒ 100 N. 6th St., Dolores 81323, ☎ 970/533–7716). **Silverton Chamber of Commerce** (☒ 414 Greene St., 81433,

☎ 970/387–5654 or 800/752–4494). **Southwest Colorado Travel Region** (☎ 800/933–4340). **Telluride Chamber Resort Association** (✉ 666 W. Colorado Ave., 81435, ☎ 970/728–3041).

THE SAN LUIS VALLEY

At 8,000 square mi, the San Luis Valley is the world's largest alpine valley, nestled between the San Juan Mountains to the west and the Sangre de Cristo range to the east. Despite its average altitude of 7,500 ft, its sheltering peaks help to create a relatively mild climate. The valley is one of Colorado's major agricultural producers, with huge annual crops of potatoes, carrots, canola, barley, and lettuce. It's so self-sufficient that local businessmen threatened to secede in the '50s to prove that the state couldn't get along without the valley and its valuable produce.

Watered by the mighty Rio Grande and its tributaries, the San Luis Valley also supports a magnificent array of wildlife, including flocks of sandhill cranes and even whooping cranes. The range of terrain is equally impressive, from the soaring fourteener, Mt. Blanca, to the stark moonscape of the Wheeler Geologic Area, to the tawny, undulating Great Sand Dunes National Monument.

The area was settled first by the Ute, then by the Spanish, who left their indelible imprint in the town names and local architecture. The oldest town (San Luis), the oldest military post (Ft. Garland), and the oldest church (Our Lady of Guadalupe in Conejos) in the state are in this valley. It's no surprise that this is a highly religious, traditional area. The natural beauty is simply awe-inspiring.

World-class climbing can be found outside Del Norte in the Penitente Canyon and in the Wheeler Geologic Area outside Creede. The Great Sand Dunes are a favorite hike. The Rio Grande National Forest offers more than a million acres of pristine wilderness. River tours, with trips down the Arkansas, Taylor, and Gunnison, can last for an afternoon or for 10 days, depending on the arrangements.

Numbers in the margin and in the text in the section below refer to bullets on the Southwest Colorado map.

Creede

53 *105 mi from Gunnison via U.S. 50 west and Rte. 149 south; 49 mi from Lake City via Rte. 149 south.*

Creede once earned a reputation as Colorado's rowdiest mining camp and was immortalized in an evocative poem by the local newspaper editor, Cy Warman: "It's day all day in daytime, and there is no night in Creede." Every other building was a saloon or bordello. Bob Ford, who killed Jesse James, was himself gunned down here; other notorious residents included Calamity Jane and Bat Masterson. As delightful as the town is, its location is even more glorious, with the pristine Weminuche Wilderness 30 mi to the south and the Wheeler Geological Area 20 mi to the west, where the unusual rock formations resemble playful abstract sculptures or an M. C. Escher creation.

The **Creede Museum,** occupying the original Denver & Rio Grande Railroad Depot, paints a vivid portrait of those rough-and-tumble days. Highlights include an underground firehouse and mining museum. ✉ *6th and San Luis Sts.,* ☎ *719/658–2374.* 🎟 *Free.* ⏲ *Memorial Day–Labor Day, Mon.–Sat. 10–4.*

Lodging

$–$$ **Creede Hotel.** A relic of the silver days, this charming 1890s structure has been fully restored, and the rooms offer the usual Victoriana. The gracious dining room serves excellent meals in addition to the complimentary breakfast. There are four rooms in the hotel and another three in a restored house nearby, along with a separate two-bedroom cabin. *✉ 120 Main St., 81130, ☎ 719/658–2608, FAX 719/658–0725. 8 rooms. Restaurant. AE, D, MC, V. Closed Nov.–Mar.*

En Route Continue along Route 149—declared the Silver Thread National Scenic Byway—on its impossibly beautiful journey east through South Fork (where Route 149 joins U.S. 160) and the **Rio Grande National Forest.** The route flirts with the Rio Grande, passes near the majestic North Clear Creek Falls, and ambles through numerous ghost towns along the way.

Del Norte

54 *38 mi from Creede via Rte. 149 south and U.S. 160 east.*

In and around Del Norte are several historic sites, one of which is an original 1870s station on the Barlow-Sanderson Stagecoach Line. The **Rio Grande County Museum and Cultural Center** celebrates the region's multicultural heritage with displays of petroglyphs, mining artifacts, early Spanish relics, and rotating shows of contemporary art. *✉ 580 Oak St., ☎ 719/657–2847. $1. May–Sept., weekdays 10–5, Sat. 1–5; Oct.–Apr., weekdays 11–4.*

Just west of town is the gaping **Penitente Canyon,** which is usually crawling with rock climbers. Several miles north of town, off Route 112, near La Garita, is another marvel—the towering rock formation **La Ventana Natural Arch.**

The Rio Grande River—between Del Norte and South Fork—teems with rainbows and lunker browns. Gold Medal waters, where special restrictions control the size and type of fish you can hook, abound in the area.

Shopping

Casa de Madera (✉ 680 Grand St., ☎ 719/657–2336) sells regional wood carvings. **Haefeli's Honey Farms** (✉ 0041 South Rd. 1, Monte Vista, ☎ 719/852–2301), on the way to Alamosa in Monte Vista, sells delectable mountain-bloom honeys.

Alamosa

55 *34 mi from Del Norte via U.S. 160 east.*

The San Luis Valley's major city is best known as the Olympic high-altitude training center for long-distance runners. Just outside town is the **Alamosa National Vista Wildlife Refuge.** These natural and man-made wetlands—an anomaly amid the arid surroundings—are an important sanctuary for the nearly extinct whooping crane and its cousin, the sandhill. *✉ 9383 El Rancho La., ☎ 719/589–4021. Free. Daily sunrise–sunset.*

The **Adams State College** complex (in town, along Main Street) contains several superlative examples of 1930s, WPA-commissioned murals in its administrative building. The college's **Luther Bean Museum and Art Gallery** displays European porcelain and furniture collections in a handsome, wood-paneled 19th-century drawing room, and changing exhibits of regional arts and crafts. *✉ Richardson Hall, Richardson and Third Sts., ☎ 719/589–7121. Free. Weekdays 1–4:30.*

Dining and Lodging

$–$$ ✕ **True Grits.** At this noisy steak house the cuts are predictably good, but that's not the real draw: As the name implies, the restaurant is really a shrine to John Wayne. His portraits hang everywhere: the Duke in action; the Duke in repose; the Duke lost in thought. ✉ *Jct. U.S. 160 and Rte. 17,* ☎ *719/589–9954. MC, V.*

$$ **Conejos River Guest Ranch.** On the Conejos River, this peaceful, family-friendly retreat 14 mi south of Alamosa offers private fishing. The six recently remodeled cabins—all fully equipped—and seven guest rooms are pleasantly outfitted with ranch-style decor, including lodgepole pine furnishings. Breakfast is complimentary. ✉ *25390 Rte. 17, Antonito, 81120,* ☎ *719/376–2464. 7 rooms, 6 cabins. Restaurant, horseback riding, fishing. D, MC, V.*

$–$$ ★ **Cottonwood Inn B&B.** This pretty cranberry-and-azure house was built in 1908 and lovingly refurbished by an Adams State professor and his wife. Public rooms feature both original and reproduction Stickley woodwork and furnishings; regional photographs and watercolors (most of them for sale) grace the walls. In the five sunny rooms with country-French washed walls, there are hand-painted florets, framed knits, weavings, dried flowers, lace curtains, and predominantly wicker furnishings. There are also four suites, two with oak floors and all with claw-foot tubs. A complimentary breakfast is provided. Cooking and writing workshops are offered from time to time. ✉ *123 San Juan Ave., 81101,* ☎ *719/589–3882 or 800/955–2623,* FAX *719/589–6437. 5 rooms, 4 suites. AE, DC, MC, V.*

$ **Best Western Alamosa Inn.** This sprawling, well-maintained complex, scattered over several blocks, is the best hotel bet in town. Rooms are spacious and offer the standard amenities. ✉ *1919 Main St., 81101,* ☎ *719/589–4943. 121 rooms. Restaurant, bar, indoor pool. AE, D, DC, MC, V.*

Outdoor Activities and Sports

Alamosa Golf Course (✉ 6678 River Rd., ☎ 719/589–5330) is an 18-hole championship course. **Cattails Golf Course** (✉ 6615 N. River Rd., ☎ 719/589–9515), also in Alamosa, is an 18-hole, par-72 course that wraps scenically around the Rio Grande.

Shopping

CRAFT AND ART GALLERIES

Firedworks Gallery (✉ 608 Main St., ☎ 719/589–6064) sells fine art, collectibles, jewelry, weavings and prints. **The Turquoise Shop** (✉ 423 San Juan Ave., ☎ 719/589–2631) sells sterling silver and turquoise jewelry and various arts and crafts.

FOOD

The San Luis Valley is noted for its produce. Mycophiles should stop by the **Rakhra Mushroom Farm** (✉ 10719 Rd. 5 S, ☎ 719/589–5882).

OFF THE BEATEN PATH

JACK DEMPSEY MUSEUM – Jack Dempsey (known as the Manassa Mauler), one of the greatest heavyweight boxing champions of all time, is honored at a hometown museum (✉ 401 Main St., ☎ 719/843–5207), open summers Monday–Saturday, 9–5. Also in Manassa, **Something Pewter** (✉ 419 Main St., ☎ 719/843–5702) fashions seemingly everything, from bolos to belts, charms to figurines—all in pewter. The town is 23 mi from Alamosa, south on U.S. 285 and east on Route 142, or 10 mi from Antonito, north on U.S. 285 and east on Route 142.

Great Sand Dunes National Monument

56 *35 mi from Alamosa via U.S. 160 east and Rte. 150 north.*

Created by windswept grains from the Rio Grande floor, the sand dunes—which rise up to 700 ft in height—are an improbable, unforgettable sight silhouetted against the sagebrush plains and looming forest slopes of the San Juans. The dunes, as curvaceous as Rubens' nudes, stretch for 55 square mi and are painted with light and shadow that shift through the day. Their very existence seems tenuous, as if they might blow away before your eyes, yet they're solid enough to withstand the stress of hikers and skiers. The sand is as fine and feathery as you'll find anywhere. It's a place for contemplation and repose, the silence broken only by passing birds and the faint rush of water from the Medano Creek. The park is open 24 hours; the visitor center is open daily from 9 to 6. ⊠ *11500 Rte. 150, Mosca,* ☎ *719/378–2312.* 🎟 *$3.* ⏲ *Daily.*

Just outside the national monument is the **Great Sand Dunes Oases** (⊠ 5400 Rte. 150, Mosca 81146, ☎ 719/378–2222), with restaurant, gift shop, motel rooms, campground—and the concession for tours of the sand dunes. The two-hour tours are in four-wheel-drive, open-air, sun-shaded, converted trucks and cost $14.

Outdoor Activities and Sports

Great Sand Dunes Country Club (⊠ 5303 Rte. 150, Mosca, ☎ 719/378–2357) is an 18-hole course with the billowing dunes as a backdrop.

San Luis

57 *46 mi from Alamosa via U.S. 160 east and Rte. 159 south; 32 mi from Manassa, via Rte. 142 east.*

San Luis, founded in 1851, is the oldest incorporated town in Colorado. Its Hispanic heritage is celebrated in the **San Luis Museum and Cultural Center,** with its extensive collection of santos (decorated figures of saints used for household devotions), *retablos* (paintings on wood), and *bultos* (carved religious figures). Murals depicting famous stories and legends of the area adorn the town's gracious tree-lined streets. A latter-day masterpiece is the *Stations of the Cross Shrine,* created by renowned local sculptor Huberto Maestas. Perched above town on a mesa called La Mesa de la Piedad y de la Misericordia (Hill of Piety and Mercy), its 15 figures illustrate the last hours of Christ's life. The trail culminates in a tranquil grotto dedicated to the Virgin Mary. ⊠ *401 Church Pl.,* ☎ *719/672–3611.* 🎟 *$2.* ⏲ *Memorial Day–Labor Day, weekdays 8–4:30, weekends 10–3.*

OFF THE BEATEN PATH

FT. GARLAND – Colorado's first military post, established in 1856 to protect settlers, lies in the Sangre de Cristos (Blood of Christ, after the ruddy color of the peaks at dawn). The legendary Kit Carson commanded the outfit, and the six original adobe structures are still around, composing the **Ft. Garland State Museum**. The venue features a re-creation of the commandant's quarters, various period military displays, and a rotating local folk-art exhibit. ⊠ *South of intersection of U.S. 160 and 159, 16 mi north of San Luis via Rte. 159, 24 mi east of Alamosa via U.S. 160,* ☎ *719/379–3512.* 🎟 *$3.* ⏲ *Memorial Day–Labor Day, Thurs.–Mon. 8–4.*

San Luis Valley A to Z

Arriving and Departing

San Luis Valley can be reached by car via U.S. 160 from both the west (direct from Durango) and the east (via I–25 south to U.S. 160), or via U.S. 285 from New Mexico.

Contacts and Resources

DOCTORS AND DENTISTS

San Luis Valley Regional Medical Center (✉ 106 Blanca Ave., Alamosa, ☎ 719/589–2511).

VISITOR INFORMATION

San Luis Valley Information Center (✉ Box 165, 947 First Ave., Monte Vista 81144, ☎ 719/852–0660 or 800/835–7254).

COLORADO SPRINGS AND VICINITY

The contented residents of the Colorado Springs area believe they live in an ideal location, and it's hard to argue with them. To the west, the Rockies form a majestic backdrop. To the east, the plains stretch for miles. Taken together, the setting ensures a mild, sunny climate year-round, and makes skiing and golfing on the same day feasible with no more than a two- or three-hour drive. This easy access to diverse outdoor activities attracts tourists seeking a varied vacation: They can climb the Collegiate Peaks one day, and go white-water rafting on the Arkansas River the next.

Colorado Springs is among the most contemporary cities in the West, with its sleek, shining arts and convention center. The region abounds in natural and man-made wonders, from the eerie sandstone formations of the Garden of the Gods to the space-age architecture of the U.S. Air Force Academy. However, the most indelible landmark is unquestionably Pikes Peak, from whose vantage point Katharine Lee Bates penned "America the Beautiful." The song's lyrics remain an accurate description of south central Colorado's many glories.

Colorado Springs

Colorado Springs, the state's second-largest city, unfortunately made headlines in 1992 when it was identified as the headquarters for several right-wing groups behind the controversial Amendment 2, which outlawed antidiscrimination legislation that gave protection to the gay and lesbian community. With active and retired military personnel and their families making up nearly a third of the population, it's no surprise that the Springs is staunchly conservative. Although for a brief time a state boycott was called and the Springs continues to be seen as the place where the controversy snowballed, the political situation hasn't affected tourism significantly. The Springs, after all, has a dazzling array of tourist attractions. Pikes Peak, for instance, is the state's most famous landmark, but only one of the city's many natural and man-made wonders. Other tourist draws include the Cave of the Winds, the Garden of the Gods, and historic neighborhoods such as Manitou Springs and Old Colorado City.

Colorado Springs was created by General William Palmer, president of the Denver & Rio Grande Railroad, as a utopian vision of fine living in the 1870s. The original broad, tree-lined boulevards still grace the southwest quadrant of the city. With the discovery of hot springs in the area, the well-to-do descended on the bustling resort town to take the waters and to enjoy the mild climate and fresh air. It soon earned the monikers "Saratoga of the West" and "Little London," the latter for the snob appeal of its considerable resident and visiting English population. The discovery of gold at nearby Cripple Creek toward the end of the century signaled another boom for the Springs. In the early part of the 1900s, until the mines petered out just before World War I, the residents' per-capita wealth was the highest in the nation.

Broadmoor, **61**
Cave of the Winds, **74**
Cheyenne Zoo, **62**
Cliff Dwellings Museum, **73**
Fine Arts Center, **66**
Garden of the Gods, **72**
Ghost Town, **68**
Glen Eyrie, **71**
Manitou Spr., **75**
Miramont Castle, **76**
Old CO City, **70**
Olympic Training Center, **67**
Pikes Peak Cog Railway, **77**
Pioneers Museum, **65**
Pro Rodeo Hall of Fame, **60**
Seven Falls, **64**
USAF Academy, **58**
Van Briggle, **69**
Western Museum, **59**
Will Rogers Shrine of the Sun, **63**

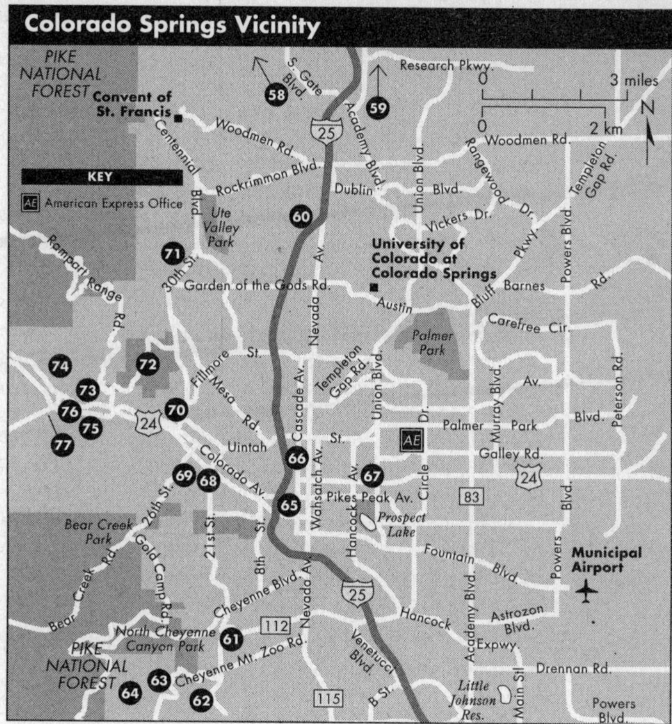

After World War II, the city fathers invited the military to move in, and the city's personality changed drastically. Today, a large portion of the local economy is derived from Department of Defense contracts, directly or indirectly, from the army's Fort Carson (Colorado's largest military base, just south of downtown Colorado Springs) and the Peterson Air Force Complex.

A Good Tour

Begin at the **U.S. Air Force Academy** (58). Directly across I–25 from the north gate of the academy is the **Western Museum of Mining and Industry** (59). Continue along I–25 South toward downtown and get off at Exit 147. A bronze rodeo bull lures visitors to the **Pro Rodeo Hall of Fame and Museum of the American Cowboy** (60). Now take I–25 or Nevada Avenue to the southern end of the city for a glimpse of its posher neighborhoods, where the **Broadmoor** (61) stands. From the Broadmoor, make a left onto Mesa Avenue, and then turn right onto Evans. Continue along Evans, and then take the Cheyenne Mountain Zoo Road to begin the ascent of Cheyenne Mountain. Aside from panoramic views of the city and Pikes Peak in the distance, the road also offers two major attractions. First up is the **Cheyenne Mountain Zoo** (62). Continue up the spiraling road to the **Will Rogers Shrine of the Sun** (63), the other big attraction off the zoo road. At the base of the mountain, turn west on Cheyenne Road and follow the signs to **Seven Falls** (64). Take Cheyenne Mountain Zoo Road back into town and turn north on Nevada Avenue. Colorado Springs' handsome downtown contains many historically significant buildings, including the **Pioneers Museum** (65). A few blocks north is the **Colorado Springs Fine Arts Center** (66). Take Nevada Avenue south and Boulder east to the **Olympic Training Center** (67). Cross under I–25 to Colorado Avenue and take it west, turning left on 21st Street, which you'll follow to **Ghost Town** (68) and the **Van Briggle Art Pottery Factory and Showroom** (69). Back on Colorado Avenue you'll find yourself in **Old Colorado City** ⑩, once a separate, rowdier town where miners caroused, today it's a National Historic Landmark District whose restored buildings house the city's choicest galleries and boutiques.

TIMING

You'll need a car, as these attractions are fairly spread out. It takes at least an hour to tour the Air Force Academy. The Olympic Training Center tours last an hour. Save some time to wander around the Broadmoor, and while you're in the neighborhood, at least drive through Seven Falls. The Fine Arts Center also merits at least 45 minutes. All of these attractions are open daily, year-round, except the Fine Arts Center (closed Mon.).

Sights to See

61 **Broadmoor.** The pink-stucco, Italianate complex, built in 1918, still stands as one of the world's great luxury resorts (☞ Dining and Lodging, *below*), a tribute to the foresight of its original owner, the enterprising Spencer Penrose, one of Colorado Springs' wealthiest (and most conspicuously consuming) philanthropists. Having constructed the zoo, the Cheyenne Mountain Highway, and Pikes Peak Cog Railway, Penrose is credited with making the town the tourist mecca it is today. The free **Carriage House Museum** (☎ 719/634–7711, ext. 5353) at the Broadmoor displays Penrose's prodigious carriage collection, from broughams (closed carriages with driver outside) to opera buses. It's open Tuesday–Saturday 10–noon and 1–5; Sunday 1–5.

62 **Cheyenne Mountain Zoo.** America's highest zoo, at 6,800 ft, has more than 800 animals amid mossy boulders and ponderosa pines. ✉ *425 Cheyenne Mt. Zoo Rd.,* ☎ *719/633–9925.* 🎫 *$7.50.* ⏲ *June–Sept., daily 9–6; Oct.–May, daily 9–5.*

★ 66 **Colorado Springs Fine Arts Center.** This pueblo-style space includes a performing-arts theater, an art school, and a room devoted to the work and life of famed Western artist Charles Russell. Also at the center are a handsome sculpture garden, a surprisingly fine permanent collection of modern art, and rotating exhibits that highlight the cultural contributions of the area's diverse ethnic groups. ✉ *30 W. Dale St.,* ☎ *719/634–5581.* 🎫 *$4.* ⏲ *Tues.–Fri. 9–5, Sat. 10–5, Sun. 1–5.*

68 **Ghost Town.** You can play a real player piano and nickelodeon at this complete, authentic Western town with a sheriff's office, general store, saloon, and blacksmith. ✉ *400 S. 21st St.,* ☎ *719/634–0696.* 🎫 *$4.50.* ⏲ *May–Labor Day, Mon.–Sat. 9–6, Sun. noon–6; Labor Day–Apr., Mon.–Sat. 10–5, Sun. noon–5.*

70 **Old Colorado City.** Once a separate, rowdier town where miners caroused, today it's a National Historic Landmark District whose restored buildings house the city's choicest galleries and boutiques.

67 **Olympic Training Center.** This is where America's hopefuls come to train and be tested, and depending on which teams are in residence at the time, you might catch a glimpse of some future Wheaties-box material. The guided tours every hour begin with a stirring half-hour movie, then take you on a half-hour walk around the facilities. A highlight is the flume—a kind of water treadmill, where swimmers can have every aspect of their stroke analyzed. ✉ *1 Olympic Plaza, Boulder St.,* ☎ *719/578–4500.* 🎫 *Free.* ⏲ *Mon.–Sat. 9–4, Sun. noon–4.*

65 **Pioneers Museum.** Once the Old El Paso Courthouse, this repository of artifacts relating to the entire Pikes Peak area is most notable for the special exhibits it mounts (or are loaned on tour from institutions such as the Smithsonian), such as a quilt competition commemorating the 100th anniversary of the song "America the Beautiful." ✉ *215*

S. Tejon St., ☎ *719/578–6650.* 🎟 *Free.* ⏲ *May–Oct., Tues.–Sat. 10–5, Sun. 1–5; Nov.–Apr., Tues.–Sat. 10–5.*

60 **Pro Rodeo Hall of Fame and Museum of the American Cowboy.** Even a tenderfoot would get a kick out of this museum, which includes changing displays of Western art; permanent photo exhibits that capture both the excitement of bronco-bustin' and the lonely life of the cowpoke; gorgeous saddles and belt buckles; and multimedia tributes to rodeo's greatest competitors. ⊠ *101 Pro Rodeo Dr. (Exit 147 off I–25),* ☎ *719/528–4764.* 🎟 *$6.* ⏲ *Daily 9–5.*

★ 64 **Seven Falls.** The road up to this transcendent series of seven cascades is touted as the "grandest mile of scenery in Colorado." Considering the state's splendors, that may be an exaggeration, but the red-rock canyon *is* amazing—though no more so than the falls themselves, plummeting into a tiny emerald pool. A set of 224 steep steps leads to the top, but there is an elevator for those who don't wish to walk. ⊠ *Cheyenne Blvd.,* ☎ *719/632–0765.* 🎟 *$6.50.* ⏲ *May–Sept., daily 8 AM–11 PM; Oct.–Apr., daily 9–4.*

58 **U.S. Air Force Academy.** The academy, which set up camp in 1954, has become one of Colorado's largest tourist attractions. It's partly notable for its striking futuristic design, but even more extraordinary are the 18,000 beautiful acres of land that have been dedicated as a game reserve and sprinkled with antique and historic aircraft. Most of the campus is off-limits to civilians, but there is a ⅓-mi self-guided tour. At the visitors' center you'll find photo exhibits, a model of a cadet's room, a gift shop, a snack bar, and a 14-minute film designed to make you want to run out and join up. Other tour attractions include a B-52 display, sports facilities, a planetarium, a parade ground (the impressive cadet review takes place daily at noon; other times of day, watch the freshmen square off their corners), and the chapel. The Air Force chapel is easily recognized by its unconventional design, which features 17 spires that resemble sharks' teeth or billowing sails. Catholic, Jewish, and Protestant services can be held simultaneously, without the congregations disturbing one another. ⊠ *Exit 156B, off I–25 N,* ☎ *719/472–0102.* 🎟 *Free.* ⏲ *Daily 9–5.*

69 **Van Briggle Art Pottery Factory and Showroom.** The Van Briggle factory has been in operation since the turn of the 20th century, and its ceramic work is admired for its graceful lines and pure, vibrant glazes. A free tour of the facility is offered, culminating—naturally—in the mind-boggling showroom. ⊠ *600 S. 21st St.,* ☎ *719/633–7729.* 🎟 *Free.* ⏲ *Mon.–Sat. 8:30–4:30.*

59 **Western Museum of Mining and Industry.** The rich history of mining is represented through comprehensive exhibits of equipment and techniques and hands-on demonstrations, including gold panning. The 27-acre mountain site has several outdoor exhibits, and is a great spot for a picnic. ⊠ *Exit 156A off I–25 N,* ☎ *719/488–0880.* 🎟 *$6.* ⏲ *June–Sept., Mon.–Sat. 9–4, Sun. noon–4; call for winter hrs.*

63 **Will Rogers Shrine of the Sun.** This tower guarded by two carved Chinese dogs was dedicated in 1937 after the tragic plane crash that claimed Rogers's life. Its interior is painted with all manner of Western scenes (in which Rogers and Spencer Penrose figure prominently) and is plastered with photos and the homespun sayings of America's favorite cowboy. ⊠ *Cheyenne Mt. Zoo Rd.,* ☎ *no phone.* 🎟 *Free with zoo ticket.* ⏲ *Memorial Day–Labor Day, daily 9–5:30; Labor Day–Memorial Day, daily 9–4:30.*

Manitou Springs and Environs

The home of Manitou Springs mineral water is set in this quaint National Historic Landmark District, which exudes a slightly shabby, but genteel charm. The chamber of commerce (☞ Visitor Information *in* Colorado Springs and Vicinity A to Z, *below*) offers free walking tours of the springs. The springs are all naturally effervescent; you might stop by Soda Springs for an after-dinner spritz (it tastes and acts just like Alka-Seltzer), or Twin Springs, sweet-tasting and loaded with lithium (which, say residents, is why they're always calm and smiling). Antique trolleys ply the streets in summer. Manitou has a growing artist population; the Manitou Art Project sponsors a year-round public exhibition, and the galleries offer a delightful ArtWalk Thursday evening in summer.

A Good Tour

Take U.S. 24 west from I–25 and 30th Street north to reach the **Glen Eyrie** (71) estate. Double back on 30th Street to the **Garden of the Gods** (72) visitor center. Drive through Garden of the Gods and back onto U.S. 24 west to the **Cliff Dwellings Museum** (73) and the **Cave of the Winds** (74). On the left of U.S. 24 headed west is **Manitou Springs** (75), home of the mineral water. Off Ruxton Avenue, just past downtown is the **Miramont Castle Museum** (76). Continue down Ruxton Avenue to the **Pikes Peak Cog Railway** (77).

TIMING

Most of Manitou Springs' attractions are clustered in a fairly small area; you should be able to cover them on foot in an hour. The exceptions are the Garden of the Gods and the Glen Eyrie estate, which you'll need to drive to. The Cave of the Winds tours take 45 minutes; the Glen Eyrie estate tours take about the same. Most of these attractions are open daily, year-round, except for the Miramont Castle, which is closed Wednesday and Thursday in the off-season. Save some time to hike in the Garden of the Gods and browse in Manitou Springs' downtown.

Sights to See

74 **Cave of the Winds.** Discovered by two boys in 1880, the cave has been exploited as a tourist sensation ever since. The entrance is through the requisite "trading post," but once inside the cave you'll forget the hype and commercialism. You'll pass through grand chambers with such names as the Crystal Palace, Oriental Garden, the Old Curiosity Shop, the Temple of Silence, and the Valley of Dreams. The cave contains examples of every major sort of limestone formation, from stalactites and stalagmites to delicate cave flowers, rare anthracite crystals, flowstone (rather like candle wax), and cave coral. Enthusiastic guides, most of them members of the Grotto Club (a spelunking group), also run more adventurous cave expeditions, called Wild Tours. The entrance to the cave is via **Williams Canyon,** off the highway. Summer evenings, a laser show transforms the canyon into an unsurpassed sound-and-light show of massively corny, yet undeniably effective, proportions. ✉ *U.S. 24,* ☎ *719/685–5444.* 🎟 *$12.* ⏲ *May–Sept., daily 9–9; 45-minute tours conducted continuously.*

73 **Cliff Dwellings Museum.** You can see 40 rooms of prehistoric ruins, featuring Anasazi cliff dwelling ruins dated to AD 1100. Two rooms of artifacts offer information on the history of the dwellings. Native American dancing takes place several times a day during the summer in front of the cliff dwellings. ✉ *U.S. 24,* ☎ *719/685–5242.* 🎟 *$5.* ⏲ *June–Aug., daily 9–8; May and Sept., daily 9–6; Oct.–Apr., daily 9–5.*

72 **Garden of the Gods.** These magnificent, eroded red-sandstone formations—from gnarled jutting spires to sensuously abstract monoliths—were sculpted more than 300 million years ago. The visitor center has

several geologic, historic, and hands-on displays. Follow the road as it loops through the Garden of the Gods, past such oddities as the Three Graces, the Siamese Twins, and the Kissing Camels. High Point, near the south entrance, provides camera hounds with the ultimate photo-op: the jagged formations framing Pikes Peak. ✉ *30th St.,* ☎ *719/634–6666.* 🎟 *Free.* ⏲ *June–Aug., daily 8–8; Sept.–May, daily 9–5.*

71 **Glen Eyrie.** William Packer's grandiose estate is maintained by a nondenominational fundamentalist sect called the Navigators, which publishes various religious literary works. The original gas lamps and sandstone structures remain, many of whose rocks were hewn with the moss still clinging, to give them an aged look. Try to come here for high tea, or during the Christmas season, when there's an extravagant drive-through nativity scene. ✉ *North of Garden of the Gods, 3820 30th St.,* ☎ *719/598–1212.* 🎟 *$5.* ⏲ *Tours June–Aug., 3 times daily; Sept.–May at 1 PM.*

75 **Manitou Springs.** The town grew around the springs, so all nine of them are smack in the middle of downtown. Competitions to design the fountains that bring the spring water to the public ensure that each fountain design is unique. The Chamber of Commerce publishes a free guide to the springs. ☎ *719/685–5089.* 🎟 *Free.* ⏲ *Daily.*

76 **Miramont Castle Museum.** This Byzantine extravaganza was commissioned in 1895 as the private home of French priest Jean-Baptiste Francolon. The museum is a mad medley of exhibits, with 46 rooms offering a wide variety of displays, from original furnishings to antique doll and railroad collections. ✉ *9 Capitol Hill Ave.,* ☎ *719/685–1011.* 🎟 *$4.* ⏲ *June–Aug., daily 10–5; Sept.–May, daily 11–4.*

77 **Pikes Peak Cog Railway.** The world's highest cog railway departs from Manitou and follows a frolicking stream up a steep canyon, through copses of quaking aspen and towering lodgepole pines, before reaching the timberline and the 14,100-ft summit. ✉ *Ruxton Ave. (depot),* ☎ *719/685–5401.* 🎟 *Round-trip fare: $23.* ⏲ *Runs May–Oct., daily 9–5.*

OFF THE BEATEN PATH

PIKES PEAK HIGHWAY – You can drive the 19-mi Pikes Peak Highway, which rises nearly 7,000 ft in its precipitous, dizzying climb to the Summit House, a pit-stop café and trading post, in approximately three hours, round trip. This is the same route that leading race-car drivers follow every July in the famed "Race to the Clouds," at 100 mi an hour. ✉ *Hwy. 24 west to Cascade (4 mi from Manitou Springs),* ☎ *719/684–9383.* 🎟 *$8.* ⏲ *Summit House: May–Oct., daily, 7–7; Nov.–Apr., daily 9–3.*

Dining and Lodging

$$$$ ★ ✕ **Craftwood Inn.** This intimate, restful restaurant regularly hosted such luminaries as Cary Grant, Bing Crosby, and Liberace. The inn is more than 50 years old, with a delightful Old English feel, with wrought-iron chandeliers, stained glass partitions, heavy wood beams, and a majestic stone-and-copper fireplace. To start, try the crab and artichoke bisque, smoked duck ravioli, or warm spinach salad with wild boar bacon. The mixed game bird and wild grill are particularly memorable entrées, especially when accompanied by a selection from the well-considered and fairly priced wine list. ✉ *404 El Paso Blvd., Manitou Springs,* ☎ *719/685–9000. AE, D, DC, MC, V. No lunch.*

$$$$ ✕ **La Petite Maison.** This pretty Victorian abode has been divided into several romantic dining rooms. Pale pink walls, floral tracery, Parisian gallery posters, and pots overflowing with flowers create the atmosphere of a French country home. The menu offers an expert balance of old-fashioned standards and newfangled Southwestern fare. Recommended appetizers include curried shrimp crepe with banana chutney, and mushroom and herb goat-cheese streudel. Top-notch main courses range from pork chop with Spanish apple liqueur to sautéed ocean shrimp with orange and sweet soy glaze. ✉ *1015 W. Colorado Ave.,* ☎ *719/632–4887. Reservations essential. AE, D, DC, MC, V. Closed Sun. and Mon.*

$$$ ★ ✕ **Briarhurst Manor.** The symphony of cherry wainscoting, balustrades, and furnishings; Van Briggle wood-and-ceramic fireplaces; tapestries; chinoiserie; and hand-painted glass make this one of the most exquisitely romantic restaurants in Colorado. There are several dining rooms, each with its own look and mood. Classical quartets play on the patio in summer. Chef-owner Sigi Krauss literally rescued this gorgeous old Victorian from the wrecker's ball, to the delight of his international clientele. Start with the house-smoked Rocky Mountain trout mousse or alligator pear (avocado stuffed with seafood, topped with both hollandaise and bordelaise sauces), then try the perfectly prepared rack of Colorado lamb or chateaubriand. ✉ *404 Manitou Ave.,* ☎ *719/685–1864. AE, MC, V. Closed Sun. No lunch.*

$$$ ★ ✕ **Corbett's.** Findlay Reed presides over this posh eatery, the hot spot among Manitou Springs elite. The high-tech space—halogen lamps, modern art, black tables and chairs—is matched by an equally contemporary menu (light and health-conscious). Appetizers are particularly sensational: try Parmesan-crusted Chilean sea bass; grilled calamari with crab stuffing and dill aioli; or seared beef roulade with an antipasto platter. The wine list is extensive and reasonably priced. ✉ *817 W. Colorado Ave.,* ☎ *719/471–0004. Reservations essential. AE, D, DC, MC, V. Closed Sun. No lunch in winter.*

$$$ ✕ **Margarita.** Plants, adobe walls, terra-cotta tile, and mosaic tables lend an air of refinement to this fine eatery, whose constantly changing menu is an intriguing hybrid of Mexican and Continental influences. ✉ *7350 Pine Creek Rd.,* ☎ *719/598–8667. AE, MC, V. Closed Mon. No lunch weekends.*

$$$ ✕ **Pepper Tree.** From its hilltop position the Pepper Tree enjoys smashing views of the city that enhance the restaurant's aura of quiet sophistication. Interior decor features a pink-and-maroon color scheme and a mirror wall. Table-side preparations (including the inevitable and delectable pepper steak) are its stock-in-trade, though the chef will go out on a limb with such daily specials as calamari stuffed with crabmeat and bacon. Still, this is one of those old-fashioned places where flambé is considered the height of both elegance and decadence. ✉ *888 W. Moreno Ave.,* ☎ *719/471–4888. Reservations essential. Jacket and tie. AE, MC, V. Closed Sun. No lunch.*

$ ✕ **Adam's Mountain Café.** With whirring ceiling fans, hanging plants, floral wallpaper, and old-fashioned hardwood tables and chairs, this cozy eatery is reminiscent of someone's great-grandmother's parlor. Come here for smashing breakfasts (wondrous muffins and organic juices); fine pastas (try the orzo Mediterranean, with sun-dried tomatoes, broccoli, onions, walnuts, and peppers sautéed in olive oil with feta, lemon, and tomato); great sandwiches (red-chili-rubbed free-range chicken on grilled polenta with cilantro pesto and lime sour cream); and yummy desserts. ✉ *110 Cañon Ave.,* ☎ *719/685–1430. Reservations not accepted. MC, V. No dinner Sun.–Mon.*

$ ★ ✕ **El Tesoro.** At the turn of the 20th century, this building served as a brothel, and then for many years it was an atelier for various artists. Today, it's a restaurant that doubles as an art gallery. The adobe and exposed brick walls and the tile work are original; rugs, textiles, and the ubiquitous garlands of chili add color. The sterling northern New Mexican food is the real thing—a savvy, savory blend of Native American, Spanish, and Anglo-American influences. The *posole* (hominy with pork and red chili) is magical, the green chili heavenly, and innovative originals such as mango quesadillas (a brilliant pairing of sweet and spicy elements) are simply genius. ✉ *10 N. Sierra Madre St.,* ☎ *719/471–0106. AE, D, MC, V. Closed Sun. No dinner Mon.; no lunch Sat.*

$ ✕ **King's Chef.** This original Valentine diner is scarcely recognizable as such, with the pink and purple turrets that have been added to make it resemble a castle. If you finish your order, consisting of a massive mound of real home fries or hash browns, served alongside an omelette or a red-chile cheeseburger, you'll receive a sticker that denotes you've won the "clean plate" award to mark your achievement. For breakfast all day, humor from behind the counter, and rubbing elbows at the counter with all kinds of locals, check this place out. The food is far from gourmet, but it's substantial and worth the experience. ✉ *10 E. Costilla Ave.,* ☎ *719/634–9135. No credit cards.*

$ ✕ **Old Chicago.** One of many "concept restaurants" popular throughout Colorado, this one features a sports bar in front and a pleasant enclosed atrium and outdoor patio in back. It's a pizza, pasta, and beer (110 varieties) joint, and it scores on all counts. ✉ *7115 Commerce Center Dr.,* ☎ *719/593–7678. AE, MC, V.*

$$$$ ★ **The Broadmoor.** One of America's truly great hotels, the Broadmoor celebrated 75 years of deluxe service in 1993, and it maintains its exalted status through continual upgrading and refurbishment. Completely self-contained, its 30 buildings sprawl majestically across 3,500 acres. The pink-and-ocher main building, crowned by Mediterranean-style towers, serenely commands a private lake. Rooms in this building are the loveliest, with period furnishings; others are more contemporary in style. The resort is renowned for its three world-class championship golf courses and former Davis Cup coach Dennis Ralston's tennis camps. Three of the nine restaurants (the Tavern, the Penrose Room, and the Charles Court) rank among the state's finest. ✉ *Lake Circle, Box 1439, 80906,* ☎ *719/634–7711 or 800/634–7711,* FAX *719/577–5700. 483 rooms, 217 suites. 9 restaurants, 3 bars, 3 pools, beauty salon, spa, 3 18-hole golf courses, 12 tennis courts, health club, horseback riding, squash, fishing, cinema, children's programs (ages 3–12), meeting rooms, car rental. AE, D, DC, MC, V.*

$$–$$$ ★ **Antlers Adams Mark.** Two previous incarnations of this hotel competed with the Broadmoor for the rich and famous, thanks to its superb, historic location downtown. This third Antlers was completely renovated and expanded in 1991. The large airy lobby strikes an immediate note of class when you enter, and the handsome rooms greet you with hunting-lodge decor. ✉ *4 S. Cascade Ave., 80903,* ☎ *719/473–5600 or 800/444–2326,* FAX *719/444–0417. 277 rooms, 13 suites. 2 restaurants, bar, room service, indoor pool, indoor hot tub, health club, meeting rooms. AE, D, DC, MC, V.*

$$ **Embassy Suites.** This is one of the original properties in this chain, and it's among the best. The airy atrium lobby, crawling with plants, has a stream running through it, stocked with koi fish. To complete the tropical motif, a waterfall tumbles lavishly into it. Suites are comfortable, favoring teal and dusty rose. The pool deck offers a view of Pikes Peak; jazz groups play here every Thursday night in season. A complimentary breakfast is offered to all guests. ✉ *7290 Commerce Center Dr., 80919,* ☎ *719/599–9100 or 800/362–2779,* FAX *719/599–4644. 207 suites. Restaurant, bar, indoor pool, hot tub, sauna, exercise room, meeting rooms. AE, D, DC, MC, V.*

$$ **Holden House.** Innkeepers Sallie and Welling Clark realized their dream when they lovingly restored this 1902 Victorian home and transformed it into a B&B. Two rooms in the main house, two in the adjacent carriage house, and one in the Victorian next door are filled to the brim with family heirlooms and antiques. Fireplaces, oversize

or claw-foot tubs in the private baths, and down pillows and quilts make guest rooms cozy. ✉ *1102 W. Pikes Peak Ave., 80904,* ☎ *719/471–3980. 5 rooms. AE, D, DC, MC, V.*

$$ **Red Stone Castle.** From the Castle, located on a private 20-acre estate overlooking Manitou Springs, you'll have views of the Garden of the Gods and Colorado Springs. The Castle was built in the 1890s, and a stay here is a fantasy adventure, where you can have a turret of your own. A full breakfast in included. ✉ *601 South Side Rd., 80829,* ☎ *719/685–5070. 2 suites. AE, D, MC, V.*

$$ **Victoria's Keep.** Proud owners Gerry and Donna Anderson preside over this turreted 1891 Queen Anne B&B. The parlor verges on the Dickensian, with its slightly fussy, Victorian clutter. There are carved tile ceilings and intricate tracery. Each room has its own fireplace and some distinguishing feature—a Jacuzzi or a claw-foot tub, stained-glass windows, or thrilling views of Miramont Castle. The decor is similarly eclectic, from ultramodern wicker furnishings to Victorian antiques. Full breakfasts and evening cheese and wine tastings add to the more-than-pleasant guest experience. ✉ *202 Ruxton Ave., 80829,* ☎ *719/685–5354 or 800/905–5337,* FAX *719/685–5913. 6 rooms. Hot tub, mountain bikes. AE, D, MC, V.*

Nightlife and the Arts

Colorado Springs' **Pikes Peak Center** (✉ 190 S. Cascade Ave., ☎ 719/520–7469) presents the **Colorado Springs Symphony,** as well as touring theater and dance companies.

BARS AND LOUNGES

The **Golden Bee** (✉ International Center at the Broadmoor, ☎ 719/634–7711) is an institution. The gloriously old-fashioned bar, with pressed-tin ceilings and magnificent woodwork, features a piano player leading sing-alongs. **Judge Baldwin's** (✉ Antlers Adams Mark, 4 S. Cascade Ave., ☎ 719/473–5600) is a lively brew pub. The singles head to **Old Chicago** (✉ 118 N. Tejon Ave., ☎ 719/634–8812). **Phantom Canyon Brewing Co.** (✉ 2 E. Pikes Peak Ave., ☎ 719/635–2800), in a turn-of-the-20th-century warehouse, has colorful rotating art exhibits and great pub grub (try the pizzas, barbecued shrimp braised in India Pale Ale, or the sinful black-and-tan cheesecake brownie).

COMEDY CLUBS

Laffs Comedy Corner (✉ 1305 N. Academy Blvd., ☎ 719/591–0707) showcases live stand-up comedy; some of the performers here are nationally known.

DINNER SHOWS

The **Flying W Ranch** (✉ 3300 Chuckwagon Rd., ☎ 719/598–4000), open mid-May–October, and weekends during the winter, ropes them in for the sensational Western stage show and chuck-wagon dinner. The **Iron Springs Chateau** (✉ across from Pikes Peak Cog Railway, ☎ 719/685–5104) offers stagings of comedy melodramas along with dinner.

MUSIC AND DANCE CLUBS

Cowboys (✉ 3910 Palmer Park Blvd., ☎ 719/596–1212) is for hard-core two-steppers. **Rodeo** (✉ 3506 N. Academy Blvd., ☎ 719/597–6121) tends to have a young, professional crowd. You can dance part of the night away at the Broadmoor's **Stars** (✉ 1 Lake Ave., ☎ 719/634–7711), a sleek, intimate boîte with a striking black granite bar, a black marble floor inlaid with gold stars, and walls covered with photos of celebrities who have stayed at the Broadmoor over the years. There is usually live jazz at the Broadmoor's (☞ Dining and Lodging, *above*) **Charles Court** several nights weekly.

Outdoor Activities and Sports

The **Garden of the Gods** is a popular place to test your climbing skills, thanks to its stark spires and cliffs. Register with the visitor center at the entrance. There are also popular in-line skating routes here, and the **Academy Riding Stables**(✉ Colorado Springs, ☎ 719/633–5667) offers trail rides on horseback.

GOLF

The Broadmoor (✉ Lake Circle, ☎ 719/634–7711) offers 54 splendid holes to guests and members. **Colorado Springs Country Club** (✉ 3333 Templeton Gap Rd., ☎ 719/473–1782) is another fine 18-hole course. The public **Pine Creek Golf Course** (✉ 9850 Divot Terr., ☎ 719/594–9999) has 18 holes.

HIKING

There are numerous trails in the Pikes Peak area, including Barr Trail up the mountain and North Cheyenne Canyon Trail. The Garden of the Gods, outside Colorado Springs, is also popular. Call the **El Paso County Parks Department** (☎ 719/520–6375) for further information about facilities in the Colorado Springs/Pikes Peak area.

Shopping

In Colorado Springs, the areas to shop are Old Colorado City, with numerous charming boutiques and galleries; **The Citadel** (✉ N. Academy Blvd., at E. Platte Ave.), which counts JCPenney and Dillard's among its more than 175 stores; and the very upscale Broadmoor One Lake Avenue Shopping Arcade. The streets of Manitou Springs and Cripple Creek offer one souvenir shop and gallery after another.

BOUTIQUES

Bandera Ranch Co. (✉ 2501 W. Colorado Ave., Colorado Springs, ☎ 719/635–1310) has stylish Western wear. **Helstrom Studios** (✉ 330 N. Institute St., Colorado Springs, ☎ 719/473–3620) showcases beads, textiles, silks, and batiks. **The Rhinestone Parrot** (✉ 725 Manitou Ave., Manitou Springs, ☎ 719/685–5333) sells dyed leather; brocaded and appliquéd purses, vests, and jackets; and antique costume jewelry.

CRAFT AND ART GALLERIES

Commonwheel Artists Co-Op (✉ 102 Cañon Ave., Manitou Springs, ☎ 719/685–1008) celebrates the diversity of art in the region, exhibiting jewelry and fiber, clay, and glass art. **The Flute Player Gallery** (✉ 2511 W. Colorado Ave., Colorado Springs, ☎ 719/632–7702) carries southwest Native American art. **Michael Garman Gallery** (✉ 2418 W. Colorado Ave., Colorado Springs, ☎ 719/471–1600) showcases Western-style paintings and unusual figurines and dioramas.

The **Dulcimer Shop** (✉ 740 Manitou Ave., Manitou Springs, ☎ 719/685–9655) sells these instruments. **Simpich Character Dolls** (✉ 2413 W. Colorado Ave., Colorado Springs, ☎ 719/636–3272) fashions detailed ceramic figurines and fabric dolls, including extraordinary marionettes. **Van Briggle Art Pottery and Showroom** (✉ 600 S. 21st St., Colorado Springs, ☎ 719/633–7729) offers free tours of its world-famous facility that end with a visit to their showroom. Woodcarver Sophie Cowman's evocative pieces—from spoons to sculpture, made out of scrub oak, fragrant cedar, and cottonwood—are for sale at the **Wood Studio** (✉ 725 Manitou Ave., Manitou Springs, ☎ no phone).

FOOD

Rocky Mountain Chocolates (✉ 2431 W. Colorado Ave., Colorado Springs, ☎ 719/635–4131) tempts with chocolates of every variety, in delightful seasonal and holiday arrangements. **Patsy's Candies** (✉

1540 S. 21st St., Colorado Springs, ☎ 719/633–7215) is renowned for its saltwater taffy and chocolate. **Pikes Peak Vineyards** (✉ 3901 Janitell Rd., Colorado Springs, ☎ 719/576–0075) offers tastings of its surprisingly fine wines, including merlots and chardonnays.

Colorado Springs and Vicinity A to Z

Arriving and Departing

BY BUS

Greyhound Lines (☎ 800/231–2222) and **TNM&O Coaches** (☎ 719/543–2775) both serve Colorado Springs.

BY CAR

I–25, which bisects Colorado and runs north–south from New Mexico to Wyoming, is the major artery giving access to the area. Colorado Springs is 68 mi south of Denver along I–25.

BY PLANE

Colorado Springs Airport (☎ 719/550–1900) is served by American, America West, TWA, and United.

Ground Transportation (☎ 719/597–4682) offers service from the Colorado Springs airport and downtown. For taxi service, try **Yellow Cab** (☎ 719/634–5000).

Getting Around

BY BUS

Colorado Springs Transit (☎ 719/385–7433) serves most of the Colorado Springs metropolitan area, including Manitou Springs.

Contacts and Resources

CAMPING

The Painted Rocks, South Meadows, and Colorado campgrounds are in the ponderosa forests; there are also campgrounds on the Ramparts Reservoir, where boating and fishing are allowed. The **Forest Service** (☎ 719/636–1602) can provide information.

DOCTORS AND DENTISTS

Colorado Springs Memorial Hospital (✉ 1400 E. Boulder Ave., Colorado Springs, ☎ 719/365–5000).

GUIDED TOURS

Orientation: Gray Line (☎ 719/633–1181) offers tours of the Colorado Springs area, including Pikes Peak and Manitou Springs, as well as jaunts to Cripple Creek.

VISITOR INFORMATION

Colorado Springs Convention and Visitors Bureau (✉ 104 S. Cascade Ave., Suite 104, 80903, ☎ 719/635–7506 or 800/368–4748). **Manitou Springs Chamber of Commerce** (✉ 354 Manitou Ave., 80829, ☎ 719/685–5089 or 800/642–2567).

SOUTH CENTRAL COLORADO

For those who enjoy history, south central Colorado has plenty to offer, its territory scouted and explored by the likes of Kit Carson and Zebulon Pike. The haunting remains of the Santa Fe Trail, which guided pioneers westward, weave through the southeastern section of the region. Towns such as Cripple Creek and Trinidad are living history. In fact, residents are so proud of their mining heritage that, despite economic hard times, they've earmarked tax revenues to preserve local landmarks.

South central Colorado has both alpine and desert scenery, and it holds such thrilling natural attractions as the Florissant Fossil Beds and

South Central Colorado

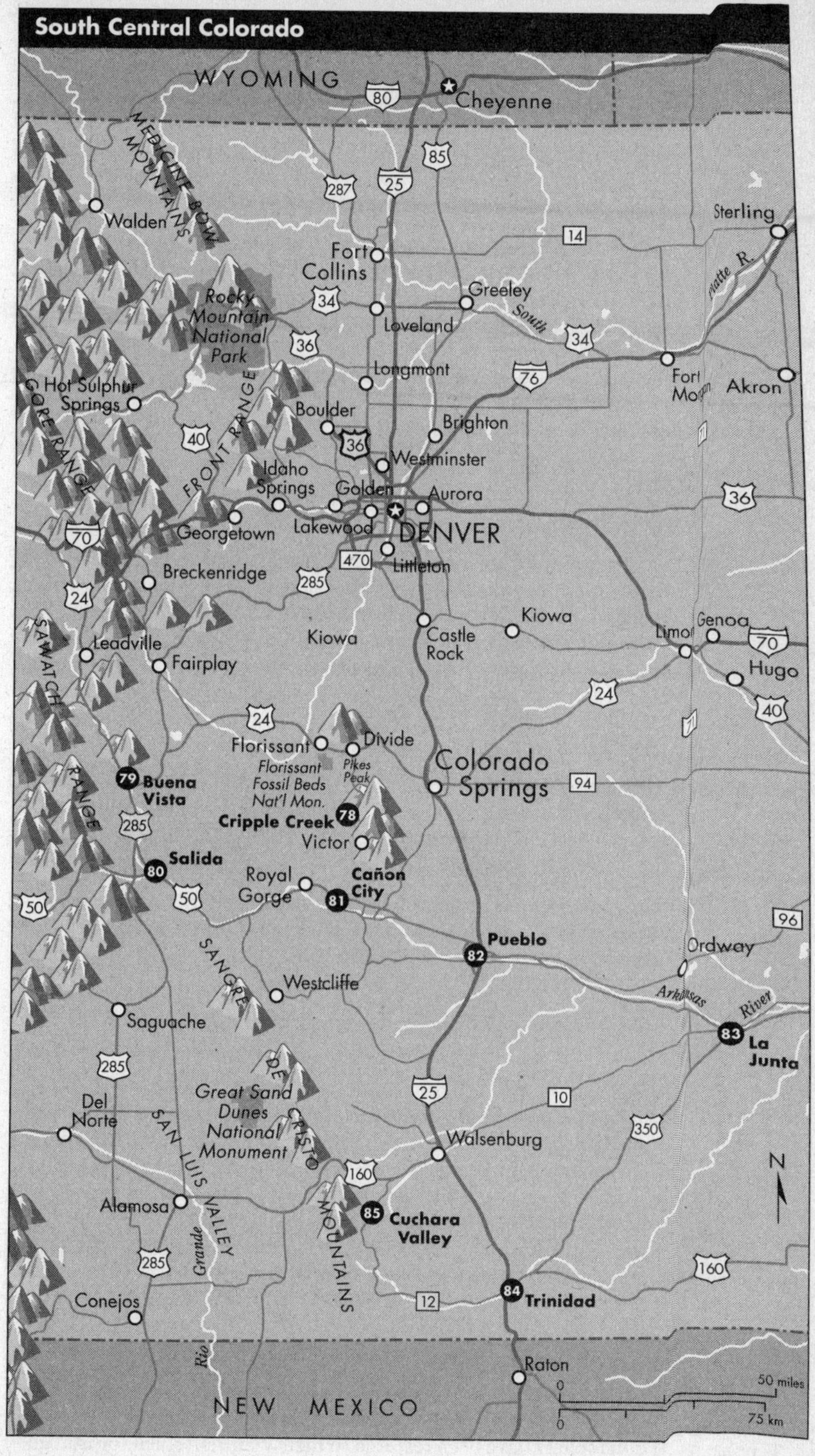

Royal Gorge. Outdoorsy types love the area: camping is superb in the San Isabel and Pike national forests. For climbers, Collegiate Peaks around Buena Vista and Salida offers a variety of ascents from moderate to difficult. The Royal Gorge, Redrocks Park, and Garden Park outside Cañon City are alive with intrepid clamberers. Pike, bass, and trout are plentiful in this region: favorite fishing spots include Trinidad Lake, Spinney Mountain Reservoir (between Florissant and Buena Vista), and the Arkansas and South Platte rivers.

The most direct route from Colorado Springs to the state's southern border is I–25, but it's certainly not the most interesting. Instead, make a loop to the west, starting in Cripple Creek and taking in Florissant Fossil Beds, Buena Vista, Salida, and Cañon City, and ending up in Pueblo, to hook up with I–25 again. From here, you can detour to the east to La Junta, and then rejoin I–25 in Trinidad. Finally, travel west to the lovely Cuchara Valley, and you will have experienced most of south-central Colorado's charms.

Cripple Creek

78 *46 mi from Colorado Springs via Rte. 24 west and Rte. 67 south.*

Colorado's third legalized gambling town, Cripple Creek once had the most lucrative mines in the state—and 10,000 boozing, brawling, bawdy citizens. Today, its old mining structures and the stupendous curtain of the Collegiate Peaks are marred by slag heaps and parking lots. Although the town isn't as picturesque as Central City or Black Hawk (☞ Side Trips West of Denver *in* Denver, *above*), the other gambling hot spots, Cripple Creek—a little rougher and dustier than the others—feels more authentic.

There are a few worthwhile attractions here: The **Cripple Creek District Museum** provides a glimpse into mining life at the turn of the 20th century. ⊠ *East end of Bennett Ave.,* ☎ *719/689–2634.* *$2.50.* ⊙ *Late-May–mid-Oct., daily 10–5; mid-Oct.–late-May, weekends noon–4.*

The **Mollie Kathleen Mine Tour** descends 1,000 ft into the bowels of the earth in a mine that operated continuously from 1892 to 1961. ⊠ *Rte. 67, north of town,* ☎ *719/689–2466.* *$10.* ⊙ *April–Oct., daily 9–5.*

Imperial Hotel and Casino offers a peek into the era's high life and a chance spin on the wheel of fortune. ⊠ *123 N. 3rd St.,* ☎ *719/689–7777.*

The **Cripple Creek and Victor Narrow Gauge Railroad** weaves past abandoned mines to Cripple Creek's former rival, Victor, 6 mi to the south. In bygone days, more than 50 ore-laden trains made this run daily. Today, however, Victor is a sad town, virtually a ghost of its former self; walking the streets—past several abandoned or partially restored buildings—is an eerie experience that does far more to evoke the mining (and post-mining) days than its tarted-up neighbor. ⊠ *Depot at Cripple Creek District Museum,* ☎ *719/689–2640.* *$8.* ⊙ *Memorial Day–Oct., daily 10–5, departs every 45 min.*

Dining and Lodging

$$ ✕ **Victor Hotel.** Listed on the National Register of Historic Places, the Victor Hotel is the nicest place to stay in the Cripple Creek area. Public spaces have been restored to their Victorian splendor, and guest rooms have mountain views. Unfortunately, aside from the original open brickwork and a few old-fashioned tubs and radiators, the decor and furnishings in the rooms are prosaically modern, and bathrooms are tiny. Adeline's Restaurant (open May–Sept.) serves steak and seafood

in an atmosphere of Victorian elegance. ✉ *4th and Victor Sts., Victor 80860,* ☎ *719/689–3553. 30 rooms. Restaurant. AE, D, MC, V.*

Outdoor Activities and Sports

Cripple Creek Horse Company (☎ 719/689–3051) offers rides into the Rockies.

Shopping

Victor Trading Co. & Manufacturing Works (✉ 114 S. 3rd St., Victor, ☎ 719/689–2346) has everything from beeswax candles to 43 styles of handmade brooms.

OFF THE BEATEN PATH

FLORISSANT FOSSIL BEDS NATIONAL MONUMENT – A primeval rain forest was perfectly preserved by volcanic ash 35–40 million years ago, making this little-known site a treasure trove for paleontologists. The visitor center offers guided walks into the monument, or you can follow the well-marked hiking trails and lose yourself in the Oligocene epoch, among 300-ft petrified redwoods. ✉ *26 mi north of Cripple Creek via Rte. 67 and U.S. 24 (east); 3 mi south of Florissant, off U.S. 24, follow signs,* ☎ *719/748–3253.* 🎫 *$2.* ⏲ *May–Sept., daily 8–7; Oct.–Apr., daily 8–4:30.*

Buena Vista

79 *112 mi from Cripple Creek via Rte. 67 north and U.S. 24 west.*

Sky-scraping mountains, the most impressive being the Collegiate Peaks, ring Buena Vista (or as locals pronounce it, *byoo*-na *vis*-ta). The 14,000-ft giants were first climbed by alumni from Yale, Princeton, Harvard, and Columbia, who named them for their alma maters. A small mining town turned resort community, Buena Vista offers the usual historic buildings alternating with motels.

The most compelling reason to visit this area is for the almost unequaled variety of recreational activities. Hiking, biking, and climbing in the **Collegiate Peaks Wilderness Area** are among the favorite jaunts. Also, Buena Vista bills itself as "The White-water Rafting Capital of the World" and offers numerous excursions down the Arkansas River.

After a full day of activities, check out the **Mt. Princeton Hot Springs** for a restorative soak. The springs have three swimming pools and several "hot spots in the creek." ✉ *5 mi west of Nathrop, County Rd. 162,* ☎ *719/395–2447.*

Before leaving downtown Buena Vista, meander through the four rooms of the **Buena Vista Heritage Museum.** Each is devoted to a different aspect of regional history: one to mining equipment and minerals, another to fashions and household utensils, a third to working models of the three railroads that serviced the area in its heyday, and the last to historical photos. ✉ *E. Main St.,* ☎ *719/395–8458 or 719/395–8453.* 🎫 *$2.* ⏲ *Memorial Day–Labor Day, daily 9–5.*

Lodging

$ **Adobe Inn.** This adobe hacienda has five charming rooms, each named for its predominant decorative motif: antique, Mexican, Native American, Mediterranean, and wicker. Some rooms have a fireplace. The airy solarium is dominated by a magnificent kiva. A complimentary breakfast is offered to guests. The owners—Marjorie, Paul, and Michael Knox—also run the charming Casa del Sol Mexican restaurant next door and can make arrangements for guests to dine there. ✉ *303 U.S. 24 N, 81211,* ☎ *719/395–6340. 5 rooms. Hot tub. MC, V.*

Nightlife

Head to the **Green Parrot** (✉ 304 Main St., ☎ 719/395–8985), which has live music weekends.

Outdoor Activities and Sports

CYCLING

Cycling is popular in the **Collegiate Peaks Wilderness Area,** around Buena Vista and Salida. **American Adventure Expeditions** (✉ 228 N. F St., Salida, ☎ 719/395–2409) provides mountain-bike rentals and tours.

RAFTING

The rafting and kayaking on the **Arkansas River** can be the most challenging in the state, ranging from Class II to V, depending on the season. Contact **American Adventure Expeditions** (☎ 719/395–2409) or **Dvorak Kayak & Rafting Expeditions** (☎ 800/824–3795).

Salida

80 *25 mi from Buena Vista via U.S. 24 and 285 and Rte. 291 south.*

Imposing peaks, including 14,000-plus-ft **Mt. Shavano,** dominate the town of Salida, which is situated along the Arkansas River. Salida draws some of the musicians from the Aspen Music Festival during the summer—classical pianists, brass ensembles, and the like—for its Salida-Aspen Series Concerts, July–August. The town's other big event is the annual (more than 40 years old) kayak and rafting white-water rodeo in June, on a section of river that cuts right through downtown.

Dining and Lodging

$–$$ ✕ **First Street Café.** Occupying a late-19th-century building in the historic district is this café serving creative heart-healthy and vegetarian specials, in addition to the expected robust Mexican-American fare. Breakfast is available, as are lunch and dinner. ✉ *137 E. 1st St.,* ☎ *719/539–4759. AE, D, MC, V.*

$ **River Run Inn.** On the Arkansas River, this gracious Victorian home has breathtaking mountain prospects. Rooms are filled with antiques and family memorabilia, and a complimentary breakfast is provided to guests. A coed dorm sleeps eight. ✉ *8495 County Rd. 160, 81201,* ☎ *719/539–3818 or 800/385–6925. 8 rooms, 4 with bath. AE, MC, V.*

Outdoor Activities and Sports

RAFTING

For rafting and kayaking on the Arkansas River, contact **River Runners** (☎ 800/525–2081) or **Canyon Marine Expeditions** (☎ 719/539–7476 or 800/643–0707).

SKIING

Monarch has 4 chairlifts, 54 trails, 677 acres, and a 1,160-ft vertical drop. The service is exceptional. Lift lines and lift ticket prices are nominal by most comparative standards. ✉ *U.S. 50 (18 mi west of Salida),* ☎ *719/539–3573.* ⏲ *Mid-Nov.–mid-Apr., daily 9–4.*

Shopping

Art Gallery of the Rockies (✉ 5051 N. Academy Blvd., ☎ 719/260-1873) showcases limited-edition prints and does custom framing.

Cañon City

81 *50 mi from Salida via U.S. 50 east.*

Cañon City is an undeniably quirky town—and proud of it. Where else would you find a shop entitled "Fluff 'em, Buff 'em, Stuff 'em"? Would you have guessed the services it provides: hairstyling, car waxing, and taxidermy? From its aggressive, even tacky, strip-mall veneer (softened,

fortunately, by some handsome old buildings) you'd think Cañon City existed solely for tourism. Nothing could be further from the truth. Cañon City's livelihood stems from its lordly position as "Colorado's Prison Capital." There are 10 prisons in the vicinity, all of which the citizens lobbied to get! It might seem a perverse source of income to court, but consider that the prisons have pumped nearly $200 million into the local economy, and, as an affable former mayor states, "You got these people walking around Denver and the Springs; here at least they're locked up." To be fair, Cañon City is also called the "Climate Capital of Colorado," for its temperate year-round conditions that attract retirees in droves.

Morbid curiosity seekers and sensationalists will revel in the **Colorado Territorial Prison Museum,** which formerly housed the Women's State Correctional Facility. Now it exhaustively documents prison life in Colorado, through old photos and newspaper accounts, as well as with inmates' confiscated weapons, contraband, and one warden's china set. The individual cell exhibits were funded by local businesses and civic organizations. There's also a video room where you can view titles such as "Prisons Ain't What They Used to Be" and "Drug Avengers." The original gas chamber sits in the courtyard. This museum is grim, grisly, gruesome, and fascinating. ✉ *1st and Macon Sts.,* ☎ *719/269–3015.* 🎫 *$4.* ⏲ *May–Oct., daily 8:30–6; Nov.–Apr., Fri.–Sun., 10–5.*

Not only is **Buckskin Joe Park and Railway** the largest Western-style theme park in the region, but it's also actually an authentic ghost town that was literally moved here from its original site 100 mi away. Such famous films as *True Grit* and *Cat Ballou* were shot in this place, which vividly evokes the Old West, especially during the re-created gunfights and hangings that occur daily. Children love the horse-drawn trolley rides, horseback rides, and gold panning, while adults appreciate live entertainment in the Crystal Palace and Saloon. The complex includes its own scenic railway that travels to the rim of Royal Gorge. ✉ *Cañon City, off U.S. 50,* ☎ *719/275–5149.* 🎫 *Combination ticket for all attractions: $12.* ⏲ *May–Sept., daily 9–6.*

Cañon City is also the gateway to the 1,053-ft-deep **Royal Gorge,** often called "The Grand Canyon of Colorado," which was carved by the Arkansas River more than 3 million years ago.

The gorge is spanned by the world's highest **suspension bridge.** Near the bridge, hubristic signs trumpet, "Who says you can't improve on Nature?" Never intended for traffic, it was originally constructed in 1929 as a commercial tourist enterprise. It now attracts more than half a million visitors annually, causing a fair amount of exploitation to the area. Families love crossing the bridge, particularly on gusty afternoons when it sways, adding to the thrill.

Other activities at the gorge are: riding the astonishing aerial tram (2,200 ft long and 1,178 ft above the canyon floor) and descending the **Scenic Railway** (the world's steepest-incline rail line) to stare at the bridge 1,000 ft above. Also on hand are a theater that presents a 25-minute multimedia show, outdoor musical entertainment in summer, and the usual assortment of food concessions and gift shops. ✉ *Royal Gorge Complex,* ☎ *719/275–7507.* 🎫 *$12.* ⏲ *Daily 8:30–dusk.*

This site has its share of history, too: The famed Royal Gorge War between the Denver & Rio Grande and Santa Fe railroads occurred here in 1877. The battle was over the right-of-way through the canyon, which could only accommodate one rail line. Rival crews would lay tracks during the day and dynamite each other's work at night. The dispute was finally settled in court—the Denver & Rio Grande won.

Dining and Lodging

$$ ✕ **Merlino's Belvedere.** This Italian standby has ritzy coffee-shop decor, with floral banquettes, centerpieces, and a "running water rock grotto." Locals swear by the top-notch steaks, seafood, and pasta. It's the usual choice for a big evening out. ✉ *1330 Elm Ave.,* ☎ *719/275–5558. AE, D, DC, MC, V.*

$ ★ ✕ **Janey's Chile Wagon.** Owner Janey Workman is a former New Yorker who fled the big city. *The National Enquirer* did a feature on her: "Waitress Builds Diner into $350,000 Restaurant!" Her food is haute greasy spoon, with huge portions of delicious burritos and the like, smothered in "green chili that won't stay with you all night, hon." The decor favors neon parrots, velvet paintings, and other tchotchkes, but nothing is as colorful as Janey herself. ✉ *807 Cyanide Ave.,* ☎ *719/275–4885. No credit cards. Closed Sun. and Mon.*

$–$$ **Cañon Inn.** Some of the famous people who have stayed here—John Belushi, Tom Selleck, Jane Fonda, John Wayne, Glenn Ford, and Goldie Hawn among them—now have their names emblazoned on the door of a hotel room here in their honor. Spacious and ultracomfortable accommodations are offered in two wings. All the rooms are decorated in muted pastels and earth tones. ✉ *U.S. 50 and Dozier St., 81212,* ☎ *719/275–8676,* FAX *719/275–8675. 152 rooms. 2 restaurants, bar, pool, 6 hot tubs. AE, D, DC, MC, V.*

Outdoor Activities and Sports

Cañon City–owned **Redrocks Park,** 12 mi north of town, offers splendid hiking among the sandstone spires.

RAFTING

Rafting through the **Royal Gorge** is not an experience for the faint of heart, as you pass between narrow canyon walls through rolling class IV and V waves, with hordes of tourists watching from the suspension bridge above. **Arkansas River Tours** (✉ Cotopaxi, ☎ 800/321–4352), **Buffalo Joe River Trips** (✉ Royal Gorge, ☎ 719/395–8757 or 800/356–7984), and **Echo Canyon River Expeditions** (✉ Cañon City, ☎ 719/275–3154 or 800/748–2953) are but a few of the reliable outfits that line U.S. 50, between Cañon City and the Royal Gorge.

Pueblo

82 *40 mi from Cañon City via U.S. 50 east; 42 mi from Colorado Springs via I–25 south.*

Pueblo is a city divided: It can't make up its mind whether to promote its historic origins or the active lifestyle it offers, with biking in the mountains and golfing in the desert. A working-class, multiethnic steel town, Pueblo lacks some of the traditional glamour of such towns as Aspen, whose growth mushroomed from gold and silver. Though sizable, it remains in the shadow of Colorado Springs to the north.

Civic leaders have embarked on an ambitious beautification plan, encouraging citizens to volunteer their time and talents. This has especially paid dividends in the extraordinary ongoing **Pueblo Levee Project,** the largest mural in the world. The grass-roots movement began with a lone artist's whimsical "statement," and now includes all manner of witty graffiti and illustrations gracing the levee along the Arkansas River. In addition, Pueblo businesses have banded together to sponsor sculptors whose works now adorn the ramps of I–25.

This civic-mindedness extends to the historical neighborhoods of Pueblo, which have many Victorian homes. The **Union Avenue Historic District,** including the glorious 1889 sandstone-and-brick Union Avenue Depot, is a repository of century-old stores and warehouses, now a fashionable commercial district. Among the landmarks are Mesa Junction, which celebrates Pueblo as a crossroads, at the point where two trolleys met; and Pitkin Avenue, lined with fabulous gabled and turreted mansions attesting to the town's more prosperous times. Walking-tour brochures of each district are available at the Chamber of Commerce (✉ 302 N. Santa Fe Ave., ☎ 719/542–1704). Pueblo's rich history is also on display in several superlative museums.

The **El Pueblo Museum** is ostensibly a holding place for the city's history, but it extends its scope to chronicle life on the plains from the prehistoric era onward, as well as Pueblo's role as a cultural and geographic crossroads, beginning when it was a trading post in the 1840s. ✉ *324 W. 1st St.,* ☎ *719/583–0453.* *$2.50.* *Mon.–Sat. 10–4:30, Sun. noon–3.*

At the airport, the **Fred E. Weisbrod Aircraft Museum** traces the development of American military aviation, with its more than two dozen aircraft in mint condition, ranging from a Lockheed F-80 fighter plane to a Boeing B-29 Super Fortress of atomic bomb fame. ✉ *31001 Magnuson, Pueblo Memorial Airport,* ☎ *719/948–9219.* *Free.* *Weekdays 10–4, Sat. 10–2, Sun. 1–4.*

Unquestionably, the glory of Pueblo is the **Rosemount Victorian Museum,** one of Colorado's finest historical institutions. This splendid 24,000-square-ft, 37-room mansion, showplace of the wealthy Thatcher family, features exquisite maple, oak, and mahogany woodwork throughout, with ivory glaze and gold-leaf trim. Italian marble fireplaces, Tiffany-glass fixtures, and frescoed ceilings complete the expensive look. This museum is the height of opulence, and the rooms seem virtually intact. The top floor—originally the servants' quarters—features the odd Andrew McClelland Collection: objects of curiosity this eccentric philanthropist garnered on his worldwide travels, including an Egyptian mummy. ✉ *419 W. 14th St.,* ☎ *719/545–5290.* *$5.* *Tours offered daily, but times vary so call ahead.*

Pueblo's equally vital concern with the present is documented in the gleaming **Sangre de Cristo Arts Center,** where several rotating exhibits in a well-thought-out space celebrate regional arts and crafts. The center also houses the superb, permanent Western art collection donated by Francis King; a performing arts theater; and PAWS Children's Museum, which offers fun, interactive audio-visual experiences. ✉ *210 N. Santa Fe Ave.,* ☎ *719/543–0130.* *Free.* *Mon.–Sat. 11–4.*

The more than 110 parks, in addition to hiking and biking trails, help to define Pueblo as a sports and recreation center. The **Greenway and Nature Center** (✉ off 11th St., ☎ 719/549–2414), on the Arkansas River, offers fine cycling, hiking, and canoeing. A small interpretive center describes the flora and fauna unique to the area, while a **Raptor Rehabilitation Center,** part of the nature center, cares for injured birds of prey.

Pueblo also has an uncommonly fine **City Park** (✉ 3455 Nuckolls Ave., ☎ 719/561–9664), which has fishing lakes, playgrounds, kiddie rides, tennis courts, a swimming pool, and the excellent **Pueblo Zoo**—a Biopark that includes an Ecocenter with a tropical rain forest and black-footed penguins.

Lake Pueblo State Recreation Area, off U.S. 50 west, offers more than 60 mi of shoreline and a full complement of water sports, as well as a beach.

Dining and Lodging

$$$ ✕ **Café del Rio.** This adobe café has a sunny outdoor patio on the Arkansas River and a festive dining room. The kitchen turns out Southwestern and Continental fare for lunch, afternoon "trail snacks," and early dinner (closing is at 9). Three-course prix-fixe dinners are served nightly, with dishes such as fresh grilled salmon and trout. The menu is fairly standard, but the setting on a summer evening makes it worth a stop. ✉ *5200 Nature Center Blvd.,* ☎ *719/549–2009. AE, D, MC, V. Closed Mon.*

$$ ✕ **La Renaissance.** This converted church and parsonage is the most imposing and elegant space in town, and the impeccably attired, unfailingly courteous wait staff completes the picture. The kitchen is stylish as well, offering such Continental standbys as filet mignon in mushroom sauce, superb baby-back ribs, and New Zealand deep sea bass fillet. Desserts are sinful enough to be sacrilegious, considering the restaurant's origins. The dinner price includes appetizer, soup, salad, and dessert. ✉ *217 E. Routt Ave.,* ☎ *719/543–6367. AE, D, DC, MC, V. Closed Sun. No lunch Sat.*

$–$$ ★ ✕ **Irish Brew Pub & Grill.** This bustling, consistently jam-packed hot spot is a bar and grill with a difference: It has a good kitchen. The owner *loves* food, and he has elevated pub grub to an art form. Even the house salad—field greens studded with pine nuts and blue cheese—is imaginative. Among the mouthwatering appetizers is a grilled smoked-duck sausage with goat cheese, topped with a honey-mustard sauce. Sandwiches are equally creative; try the buffalo burger or beaver (yes, beaver) sandwich. The range of entrées, many of them heart-healthy, is astonishing: from a dazzling prime rib to a lip-smacking, "border grill" turkey breast lightly dusted in flour, grilled, and then poached in chicken broth and raspberry vinaigrette. And of course, they brew their own beer—nine varieties. ✉ *108 W. 3rd St.,* ☎ *719/542–9974. AE, D, DC, MC, V. Closed Sun.*

$ ✕ **Grand Prix.** A neon sign announces the location of this authentic Mexican restaurant run by the Montoya family. Red neon lights and a painted false ceiling relieve the otherwise spartan decor. The food is classic: pork and avocado, chorizo, burritos, and Mexican steak, utilizing the flavorful local Pueblo chili and served with heaping helpings of rice and beans. ✉ *615 E. Mesa St.,* ☎ *719/542–9825. MC, V. Closed Sun. and Mon. No lunch Sat.*

$ ✕ **La Tronica's.** Although it's dressed like a saloon, with mirror beer signs and Christmas lights draping the bar, this 50-year-old restaurant is real "Mamma Mia" Italian. Waitresses, who invariably call you "sweetheart," have been here for as long as anyone can remember, and you may notice them watching approvingly as you take your first bite. Steak, seafood, scrumptious fried chicken (second-best in the Rockies, next to Slogar's in Crested Butte), and homemade pastas are the lure. ✉ *1143 E. Abriendo Ave.,* ☎ *719/542–1113. AE, MC, V. Closed Sun. and Mon. No lunch.*

$–$$ ★ 🏨 **Abriendo Inn.** This exquisite 1906 home, listed on the National Register of Historic Places, overflows with character. Gracious owners Kerrelyn and Chuck Trent did most of the painting, papering, and refurbishing themselves. The house now gleams with its original, lovingly restored parquet floors, stained glass, and Minnequa oak wainscoting. The 10 no-smoking rooms are richly appointed with antiques, oak armoires, quilts, crocheted bedspreads, and either brass or four-poster beds. Fresh fruit and cookies are left out for guests, and gourmet breakfasts are included in the rate. ✉ *300 W. Abriendo Ave., 81004,* ☎ *719/544–2703,* FAX *719/542–6544. 10 rooms. AE, DC, MC, V.*

$ 🏨 **Inn at Pueblo West Best Western.** This handsome, sprawling resort is a notch above most Best Westerns. Although it's out of the way for those who want to be close to town (about 15 minutes away by car), the golf course and activities on nearby Lake Pueblo keep guests busy. Large rooms in dark mountain colors, with terraces, have an elegant, woodsy feel. ✉ *201 S. McCulloch Blvd., 81007,* ☎ *719/547–2111 or 800/448–1972. 80 rooms. Restaurant, pool, 4 tennis courts. AE, D, DC, MC, V.*

Nightlife and the Arts

Gus' Place ✉ Elm and Mesa Sts., ☎ 719/542–0756) is a big Yuppie hangout that once held the record for the most kegs emptied in an evening. **Peppers** (✉ 4109 Club Manor Dr., ☎ 719/542–8629) has something going on every evening, from oldies nights to stand-up comedy. The **Irish Brew Pub & Grill** (✉ 108 W. 3rd St., ☎ 719/542–9974) is always hopping after work hours. **The Chief** (✉ 611 N. Main St., ☎ 719/546–1246) is a classic honky-tonk that has live bands most evenings.

The **Pueblo Symphony** (✉ 503 N. Main St., Suite 414, ☎ 719/549–2385) offers music, from cowboy to classical, throughout the year. **Broadway Theatre League** (✉ Memorial Hall, ☎ 719/545–4721) presents touring shows and specialty acts. The **Sangre de Cristo Arts and Conference Center** (✉ 210 N. Santa Fe Ave., ☎ 719/542–1211) presents various local and road shows.

Outdoor Activities and Sports

There is excellent camping and fishing at **Lake Pueblo State Park** (☎ 719/561–9320). Two marinas (✉ North Shore, ☎ 719/547–3880; ✉ South Shore, ☎ 719/564–1043) offer rental boats. You can hike in relative solitude in **San Isabel National Forest** (☎ 719/545–8737), 20 mi southwest of Pueblo.

CYCLING

Pueblo has an extensive **Bike Trail System,** which loops the city, following the Arkansas River part way, then goes out to the reservoir. There are popular in-line skating routes along these trails, too. The Pueblo Parks and Recreation Department (☎ 719/566–1745) can provide information.

GOLF

Pueblo City Golf Course (✉ City Park, ☎ 719/561–4946) is a handsome, highly rated 18-hole course. **Pueblo West Golf Course** (✉ Pueblo West Development, 8 mi west of town on U.S. 50, ☎ 719/547–2280) is an 18-hole championship course. **Walking Stick Golf Course** (✉ 4301 Walking Stick Blvd., ☎ 719/584–3400), an 18-hole course, is perennially ranked in the top 50 courses by *Golf Digest.*

Shopping

Pueblo's beautifully restored and renovated **Union Avenue Historic District** and **Mesa Junction** contain several fine antiques shops and boutiques. The **Pueblo Mall** (✉ 3429 Dillon Dr.) offers the usual assortment of fast-food outlets, video arcades, and franchises, including JCPenney. The **Midtown Center** (✉ 1000 W. 6th St.) mall includes chains such as Sears. There is a flea market every weekend at the **Pueblo Fairgrounds.**

ANTIQUES AND COLLECTIBLES

Tivoli's Antique Gallery (✉ 325 S. Union Ave., ☎ 719/545–1448) sells antique furniture. Numerous other antiques shops are to be found in the Union Avenue district.

BOUTIQUES

Gotcha Covered (✉ 111 W. B St., ☎ 719/544–6833) sells unique clothing from around the world. **Razmataz** (✉ 335 S. Union Ave., ☎ 719/544–3721) has creative clothing by local artists. **Back at the Ranch** (✉ 333 S. Union Ave., ☎ 719/544–7319) provides Western wear for dudettes.

CRAFT AND ART GALLERIES

John Deaux Art Gallery (✉ 221 S. Union Ave., ☎ 719/545–8407) specializes in contemporary art by southern Colorado artists. **Pueblo Pottery** (✉ 229 Midway St., ☎ 719/543–0720) features the designs of Tom and Jean Latka.

FOOD

Seabel's Baskets and Gifts (✉ 105 W. C St., ☎ 719/543–2400) offers fine cookware and delicacies.

OFF THE BEATEN PATH

BISHOP'S CASTLE – An elaborate re-creation of a medieval castle replete with turrets, buttresses, and ornamental iron is the prodigious (some might say monomaniacal) one-man undertaking of Jim Bishop, who began construction in 1969 and has hauled nearly 50,000 tons of rock used for the construction. Not yet complete, it soars three stories and nearly 75 ft, and Bishop has plans to build a drawbridge and moat. Bishop finances this enormous endeavor through donations and a gift shop. Anyone can stop by at any time; if you're lucky he'll be there, railing against the establishment (numerous posted signs graphically express his sentiments). To get there take I–25 south from Pueblo, turn west on Route 165 (Exit 74) and follow the signs. ✉ *Rte. 75,* ☎ *719/564–4366.* *Free.* *Daily, but hours vary.*

En Route If you head east on U.S. 50, leaving the Rockies far behind, you'll be traveling toward the eastern plains, where rolling prairies of the northeast give way to hardier desert blooms and the land is stubbled with sage and stunted piñons. One fertile spot—50 mi along the highway—is the town of **Rocky Ford,** dubbed the "Melon Capital of the World" for the famously succulent cantaloupes grown here.

La Junta

83 *65 mi from Pueblo via U.S. 50 east.*

Wholesome La Junta was founded as a trading post in the mid-19th century. The town is notable for its **Koshare Indian Museum,** which contains extensive holdings of Native American artifacts and crafts (Navajo silver, Zuni pottery, Shoshone buckskin clothing), as well as pieces from Anglo artists such as Remington, known for their depictions of Native Americans. The Koshare Indian Dancers (actually a local Boy Scout troop) perform regularly, keeping their precious traditions alive. ✉ *115 W. 18th St.,* ☎ *719/384–4411.* *$2.* *Daily 10–5.*

The splendid **Bent's Old Fort National Historic Site** is a perfect example of a living museum, with its painstaking re-creation of the original adobe fort, which burned down. Founded in 1833 by savvy trader William Bent, one of the region's historical giants, the fort anchored the commercially vital Santa Fe Trail, providing both protection and a meeting place for the military, trappers, and traders of the era. The museum's interior includes a smithy and soldiers' and trappers' barracks. The guided tour is most informative. ✉ *35110 Rte. 194 E,* ☎ *719/383–5010.* *$2.* *Daily 9–4.*

OFF THE BEATEN PATH

SANTA FE TRAIL'S MOUNTAIN BRANCH – This area of Colorado played a major role in opening up the West, through the Mountain Branch of the Santa Fe Trail. Bent's Fort was the most important stop between the route's origin in Independence, Missouri, and its terminus in Santa Fe, New Mexico. U.S. 50 roughly follows its faded tracks from the Kansas border through the pioneer towns of Lamar and Las Animas to La Junta, where U.S. 350 picks up the trail, traveling southwest to Trinidad. If you detour onto the quiet county roads, you can still discern its faint outline over the gentle hump of swales and the dip of arroyos. Here, amid the magpies and prairie dogs, it takes little imagination to conjure visions of the pioneers, struggling to travel just 10 mi a day by oxcart over vast stretches of territory.

Trinidad

84 *80 mi from La Junta via U.S. 350 southwest.*

Initially founded as a rest-and-repair station along the Santa Fe Trail, Trinidad boomed with the discovery of coal in the area, followed inevitably by the construction of the railroad. The period from 1880 to 1910 saw major building and expansion. The advent of natural gas, coupled with the Depression, ushered in a gradual decline in population, but not of spirit. Trinidad's citizens willingly contribute 1% of a 4% sales tax to the upkeep of the city's rich architectural heritage. That civic pride is clearly demonstrated in the town's four superb museums, a remarkably large number for a town its size.

Downtown, called the Corazon de Trinidad, is a National Historic Landmark District containing splendid Victorian mansions, churches, and the glorious, bright red domes and turrets of the Aaron House Synagogue. The Chamber of Commerce (⊠ 309 Nevada St., ☎ 719/846–9285) publishes an excellent walking tour of the neighborhood, which even retains its original paved brick streets.

With all the new people moving into town, Trinidad is coming to life, with restaurants, cafés, and galleries opening downtown. Local boosters like to think of it as "the next Durango."

Start at the **Baca House/Bloom House/Pioneer Museum Complex.** Visited together, this facility represents the most significant aspects of Trinidad's history. Felipe Baca was a prominent Hispanic trader whose 1870 residence—**Baca House**—is replete with original furnishings in the parlor, sitting room, kitchen, dining room, and bedrooms. The displays convey a mix of Anglo (clothes, furniture) and local Hispanic (santos, rosaries, textiles) influences. Next door, **Bloom House** provides an effective contrast to the Baca House. Frank Bloom made his money through ranching, banking, and the railroad, and although he was no wealthier than Baca, his mansion (built in the 1880s) reveals a very different lifestyle. The railroad enabled him to fill his ornate Second Empire–style Victorian (with mansard roof and elaborate wrought ironwork) with fine furnishings and fabrics brought from New York and imported from Europe. The adjacent **Santa Fe Trail Museum** is dedicated to the effect of the Santa Fe Trail on the community. Inside the museum are new exhibits from the days of Trinidad's heyday as a commercial and cultural center until the 1920s. Finish up with a stop at the **Historic Gardens,** a fine example of Southwest vegetable and herb gardens, as tended by the pioneers, with native plants and heirloom, century-old grapevines. ⊠ *Complex: 300 E. Main St.,* ☎ *719/846–7217.* *$5.* *May–Sept., daily 10–4.*

The **A. R. Mitchell Memorial Museum and Gallery** celebrates the life and work of the famous Western illustrator, whose distinctive oils, charcoal drawings, and watercolors graced the pages of pulp magazines and ranch romances. The museum also has his personal collection of other masters of the genre, such as Larry Heller and Harvey Dunn, as well as a re-creation of his atelier. The community holds Mitchell in great esteem: He was responsible for saving the Baca and Bloom houses from demolition, and he spearheaded numerous campaigns to restore the historic downtown. For a further glimpse into Trinidad history, be sure to see the **Aultman Collection of Photography** in the Memorial Museum Gallery. On display are photos by the Aultman family dating back to 1889; they offer a unique visual record of Trinidad. ✉ *150 E. Main St.,* ☎ *719/846–4224.* *Free.* ⊙ *Mid-Apr.–Sept., Mon.–Sat. 10–4.*

On the other side of the Purgatoire River, the **Louden-Henritze Archaeology Museum** takes viewers back millions of years to document the true origins of the region, including early geologic formations, plant and marine animal fossils, and prehistoric artifacts. ✉ *Trinidad State Junior College,* ☎ *719/846–5508.* *Free.* ⊙ *Jan.–Nov., weekdays 10–4.*

The **Trinidad Children's Museum** is located in the delightful Old Firehouse Number 1, and it displays fire-fighting memorabilia, such as a 1936 American LaFrance fire truck (children love clanging the loud bell) and the city's original fire alarm system. Upstairs is a fine re-creation of a Victorian schoolroom. ✉ *314 N. Commercial St.,* ☎ *719/846–8220.* *Free.* ⊙ *Summer, weekdays 1–4.*

Dining and Lodging

$$ ✕ **Elm Street Station.** Housed in a restored Burlington Northern passenger train depot, this restaurant is a must for train buffs. Food-lovers will appreciate executive chef Chris Eissler's creative touch, too. (He used to cook for the stars in Las Vegas.) He favors Italian recipes, with dishes such as *zuppa de pesce* (seafood soup), deep-fried Italian bread with fresh mozzarella and marinara sauce, and veal marsala. But you'll also find prime rib and green-chile chicken Alfredo on the menu. Don't miss the dark, triple chocolate spoon cake for dessert. The wine list holds hidden treasures. *516 Elm Street,* ☎ *719/846–1400. AE, D, DC, MC, V. Dinner only. Closed Mon.–Tues.*

$ ✕ **Main Street Bakery.** In a century-old building decorated with sunny interior murals, this homey café serves fresh-baked breads and desserts, a famous potpie, and splendid roast beef dinners. At breakfast, try the blueberry pancakes. The Oriental chicken salad is a thing of beauty, and ample enough for a full meal. Try the Branding Iron sandwich, roast beef and melted brie on foccacia, or the Michiganer, turkey breast salad mixed with dried cherries. This spot is usually very crowded with locals and visitors. Don't want a meal? Drop in for a pastry and a cup of strong coffee. ✉ *121 West Main St.,* ☎ *719/846–8779. AE, MC, V. No dinner Sun.–Wed.*

$ ✕ **Nana and Nano's Pasta House.** This homey, classic Neapolitan eatery, with red-and-white check tablecloths, red curtains, and posters of Italy, is always saturated with the tempting aroma of garlic and tomato sauce. Pastas are uniformly excellent, with standards such as fettuccine Alfredo, gnocchi Bolognese, and spaghetti *al sugo* (with gravy) among the standouts. If you don't have time for a sit-down lunch, stop in their deli next door for smashing heros and gourmet sandwiches. On Saturday morning, a good portion of the town turns out to stock up for the weekend on imported meats and cheeses. But don't ask for a glass of Chianti; alcohol is not served. Fran Monteleone is your amiable host. ✉ *415 University St.,* ☎ *719/846–2696. AE, DC, MC, V.* ⊙ *Closed Sun. and Mon.*

$ **Best Western Country Club Inn.** To apply the term "country club" is exaggerating this lodging's amenities. Still, rooms are clean and comfortable and are decorated in warm earth tones. ✉ *Exit 13A off I–25, 900 W. Adams St., 81082,* ☎ *719/846–2215. 55 rooms. Restaurant, bar, pool, hot tub, exercise room, coin laundry. AE, D, DC, MC, V.*

Nightlife and the Arts

The Other Place (✉ 466 W. Main St., ☎ 719/846–9012) hires top local rock bands on weekends to play its intimate classy space.

Outdoor Activities and Sports

There is swimming, hiking, fishing, horseback riding, and camping in the North Fork River valley at the **Trinidad Lake State Recreation Area** (☎ 719/846–6951), 3 mi west of Trinidad on Route 12.

Cuchara Valley

85 *55 mi from Trinidad (to town of Cuchara) via Rte. 12 northwest.*

From Trinidad, Route 12—the scenic **Highway of Legends**—curls north through the Cuchara Valley. As it starts its climb, you'll pass a series of company towns built to house coal miners. **Cokedale** is nestled in Reilly Canyon. The entire town is a National Historic Landmark District, and it is the most significant example of a turn-of-the-20th-century coal/coke camp in Colorado. As you drive through the area note the telltale streaks of black in the sandstone and granite bluffs fronting the Purgatoire River and its tributaries, the unsightly slag heaps, and the spooky abandoned mining camps dotting the hillsides. The impressive **Stonewall Gap,** a monumental gate of rock, roughly marks the end of the mining district.

As you approach Cuchara Pass, several switchbacks snake through rolling grasslands and dance in and out of spruce stands whose clearings afford views of Monument Lake, as you approach Cuchara Pass. There is camping, hiking, and fishing throughout this tranquil part of the **San Isabel National Forest,** emblazoned with a color wheel of wildflowers in spring and summer. Four corkscrewing miles later, you'll reach a dirt road that leads to the twin sapphires of **Bear and Blue lakes** and the resort town of **Cuchara.** Nestled in a spoon valley ("cuchara" means spoon), the area become popular as a turn-of-the-20th-century camping getaway for Texans and Oklahomans because of its cool temperatures and stunning scenery. Today it is becoming known as one of the undiscovered gems of the Rockies for its outdoor recreational opportunities and unspoiled feel. The quaint Western town consists of one main street lined with boardwalks and shops, bars, and restaurants, mostly open in summer only.

You'll begin to see fantastic rock formations with equally fanciful names, such as Profile Rock, Devil's Staircase, and Giant's Spoon. With a little imagination you can devise your own legends about the names' origins. There are more than 400 of these upthrusts, which radiate like the spokes of a wheel from the valley's dominating landmark, the **Spanish Peaks.** In Spanish they are known as *Dos Hermanos,* or "Two Brothers"; in Ute, their name *Huajatolla* means "breasts of the world." The haunting formations are considered to be a unique geologic phenomenon for their sheer abundance and variety of rock types.

The Highway of Legends passes through the charming, laid-back resort town of **La Veta** before reaching its junction with I–25 at Walsenburg, another city built on coal, and the largest town between Pueblo and Trinidad. Colorado Springs is 90 mi north on I–25.

Dining

$$$ ✕ **Silver Spoon.** On the banks of the Cuchara River, this elegant restaurant is one of Cuchara's charms. In winter, the candlelit dining room is warmed by a stone fireplace, with rustic sleds and skis completing the decor; in summer, dine outdoors by the river and wander across a small bridge to an island gazebo. The menu includes grilled bacon-wrapped shrimp, French-sauce preparations such as pepper steak with a raspberry and blackberry brandy cream sauce, and chicken with blue-cheese pepper sauce. Save room for the homemade desserts, especially the pumpkin praline torte with pecan glaze or lemon torte with rasp-

berry melba sauce. ✉ *16984 Hwy. 12, Cuchara,* ☎ *719/742–3764. Reservations essential in summer. AE, D, MC, V. No lunch weekdays, Nov.–Apr.*

South Central Colorado A to Z

Arriving and Departing

BY BUS

Greyhound Lines (☎ 800/231–2222) and **TNM&O Coaches** (☎ 719/544–6295) serve most of the major towns in the region.

BY CAR

See Colorado Springs and Vicinity A to Z, *above*

BY PLANE

The area is served by Colorado Springs (☞ Colorado Springs and Vicinity A to Z, *above*) and **Pueblo Memorial Airport** (☎ 719/948–3355), which welcomes flights from United Express. To summon a taxi from the Pueblo airport, call **City Cab** (☎ 719/543–2525).

BY TRAIN

Amtrak (☎ 800/872–7245) stops in Trinidad and La Junta.

Getting Around

BY BUS

Pueblo Transit (☎ 719/542–4306) services Pueblo and outlying areas. The **Trinidad Trolley** (summer only) stops at parks and historical sites, departing from the parking lot next to City Hall (for information, call the Chamber of Commerce, ☎ 719/846–9285).

BY CAR

Pueblo is on I–25. Florissant and Buena Vista are reached via U.S. 24 off I–25; Cañon City and the Royal Gorge via U.S. 50. Salida can be reached via CO 291 from either U.S. 24 or U.S. 50. La Junta can be reached via U.S. 50 from Pueblo or U.S. 350 from Trinidad.

BY TAXI

Pueblo: City Cab (☎ 719/543–2525). **Trinidad: City Cab** (☎ 719/846–2237).

Contacts and Resources

CAMPING

The **U.S. Forest Service** (☎ 719/636–1602) operates many campsites in the area.

DOCTORS AND DENTISTS

Arkansas Valley Regional Medical Center (✉ 1100 Carson Ave., La Junta, ☎ 719/384–5412). **Heart of the Rockies Regional Medical Center** (✉ 448 E. 1st St., Salida, ☎ 719/539–6661). **Mt. San Rafael Hospital** (✉ 410 Benedicta St., Trinidad, ☎ 719/846–9213). **Parkview Episcopal Medical Center** (✉ 400 W. 16th St., Pueblo, ☎ 719/584–4000). **St. Thomas More Hospital** (✉ 1338 Phay Ave., Cañon City, ☎ 719/269–2000).

FISHING

For fishing information, call the **Colorado Division of Wildlife Southeast Region** (☎ 719/473–2945).

VISITOR INFORMATION

Buena Vista Chamber of Commerce (✉ U.S. 24, Buena Vista 81211, ☎ 719/395–6612). **Cañon City Chamber of Commerce** (✉ Bin 749, 403 Royal Gorge Blvd., Cañon City 81212, ☎ 719/275–2331). **Heart of the Rockies Chamber of Commerce** (✉ 406 W. Rainbow Blvd., Salida 81201, ☎ 719/539–2068). **Huerfano County Chamber of Commerce** (✉ 400 Main St., Walsenburg 81089, ☎ 719/738–1065). **La Junta Chamber of Com-**

merce (✉ 110 Santa Fe Ave., La Junta 81050, ☎ 719/384–7411). **La Veta/Cuchara Chamber of Commerce** (✉ Box 32, La Veta 81055, ☎ 719/742–3676). **Lamar Chamber of Commerce** (✉ Box 860, Lamar 81052, ☎ 719/336–4379). **Pueblo Chamber of Commerce and Convention & Visitors Bureau** (✉ 302 N. Santa Fe Ave., Pueblo 81003, ☎ 719/542–1704 or 800/233–3446). **Trinidad/Las Animas Chamber of Commerce** (✉ 309 Nevada St., Trinidad 81082, ☎ 719/846–9285).

NORTHWEST COLORADO

As you drive through northwest Colorado, its largely barren terrain sculpted by eons of erosion, it may be difficult to imagine the region as a primeval rain forest. Yet millions of years ago much of Colorado was submerged under a roiling sea. That period left a vivid legacy in three equally precious resources: vast oil reserves, abundant uranium deposits, and one of the world's largest collections of dinosaur remains. Throughout the area the evidence of these buried treasures is made obvious by unsightly uranium tailings, abandoned oil derricks, and the huge mounds of dirt left from unearthing valuable fossils. Some of the important paleontological finds made here have radically changed the fossil record and the way we look at our reptilian ancestors. These discoveries even fueled the imagination of *Jurassic Park* author Michael Crichton: the book's fierce and ferocious predator, velociraptor, was first uncovered here.

Grand Junction makes the ideal hub for exploring the region: The starkly beautiful rock formations of the Colorado National Monument; the important petroglyphs of Canyon Pintado; the forest and lakes of Grand Mesa, the world's largest flattop mountain; and the surprising orchards and vineyards of Palisade and Delta to the south and east. Most of the sights covered in this section are less than a two-hour drive in various directions. Beginning at Grand Junction, you can make the loop from Palisade to Grand Mesa and Cedaredge to Delta easily in a day. If you want to break up the trip, stop in the lovely town of Cedaredge overnight. The loop in the opposite direction—including Rifle, Craig, Dinosaur National Monument, and Colorado National Monument—is quite a bit longer, but there is decent lodging in any of the stops along the way, with the exception of Dinosaur National Monument (unless you're prepared to camp.)

Grand Junction

86 *255 mi from Denver via I–70 west.*

Grand Junction sits between the gunmetal Grand Mesa to the south and the multihued Bookcliffs to the north. As the largest city between Denver and Salt Lake City, it provides a variety of services and facilities to the surrounding populace and offers a fair amount of cosmopolitan sophistication for a comparatively small town.

Grand Junction's cultural sophistication is readily apparent in the Art on the Corner exhibit, a year-round event showcasing leading regional sculptors whose latest works are installed on the Main Street Mall. Each year the community selects and purchases its favorites for permanent display. Art on the Corner is organized by the **Western Colorado Center for the Arts,** which rotates its fine permanent collection of Native American tapestries and Western contemporary art, including the only complete series of lithographs by noted printmaker Paul Pletka. The fantastically carved doors—done by a WPA artist in the '30s—alone are worth the visit. Take time to enjoy the elegant historic homes along

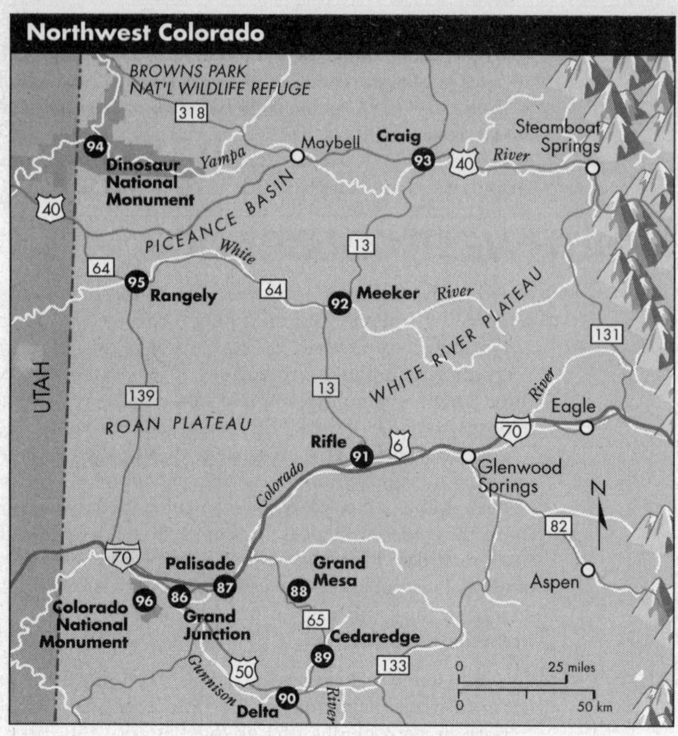

North 7th Street afterward. ✉ *1803 N. 7th St.,* ☎ *970/243–7337.* 🎫 *$2.* ⏲ *Tues.–Sat. 9–4.*

The **Museum of Western Colorado** relates the history of the area dating from the 1880s, with an 11-decade time line, a firearms display, and two gorgeous parlor organs. It also runs the Cross Orchards Living History Farm and the Dinosaur Valley Museum (☞ *below*) and oversees paleontological excavations. ✉ *248 S. 4th St.,* ☎ *970/242–0971.* 🎫 *$2. Mon.–Sat. 8–4.*

The **Cross Orchards Living History Farm** re-creates a historic agricultural community of the early 20th century on its 24½-acre site, listed on the National Register of Historic Places. A workers' bunkhouse, blacksmith shop, country store, and an extensive collection of vintage farming and road-building equipment are among the exhibits to be seen on the 1½–2 hour tours. ✉ *3079 F Rd.,* ☎ *970/434–9814.* 🎫 *$3.* ⏲ *Apr.–Sept., Mon.–Sat. 9–5, Sun. noon–4; Oct.–Dec., Tues.–Sat. 10–4. Tours run mid-May–Nov. 1.*

The entertaining and instructive **Dinosaur Valley Museum** has half-size, moving, roaring replicas of the dinos found in the region. The museum is designed for children and adults alike with numerous hands-on exhibits that emphasize understanding the wealth of the local fossil record. You can handle real fossils in the open storage displays, look into a working laboratory, and talk with the volunteers preparing and cataloguing the latest excavated specimens. Three working sites run by the museum are open to the public: **Riggs Hill, Dinosaur Hill,** and the **Rabbit Valley Trail Through Time.** Each is a self-guided tour that will increase your knowledge and appreciation of paleontology. ✉ *4th and Main Sts.,* ☎ *970/241–9210.* 🎫 *$4.* ⏲ *Apr.–Sept., Mon.–Sat. 9–5, Sun. 9–4; Oct.–Mar., Tues.–Sat. 10–4.*

Rim Rock Adventures offers a variety of rafting and horseback-riding expeditions, as well as a petting zoo, a deer park, and a somewhat hoary wildlife museum. ✉ *Rte. 340, Exit 19, Fruita,* ☎ *970/858–9555.* *$3.50.* *May–Sept., daily 8:30–5:30.*

Dining and Lodging

The Grand Junction dining scene is fairly sophisticated, compared with other towns in the region, though it's hardly fancy or exotic. There's a lot of standard beef and burritos. Grand Junction offers the widest selection of accommodations; outside the town, expect motels and fairly rustic guest ranches.

$$ ✕ **Dolce Vita.** Chef-owner Massimiliano Perucchini is a fourth-generation chef who hails from Verona. His Northern Italian restaurant with its outdoor patio fronting on Main Street provides consistently wonderful cooking. Try the Portobello mushroom marinated in Chianti and served on polenta with red onions and pancetta; the veal picatta; and the chicken with mushrooms, capers, artichoke hearts, and lemon butter on angel-hair pasta. It's a tough call between the homemade cannoli and tiramisu—you may need to try them both. ✉ *336 Main St.,* ☎ *970/242–8482. AE, D, DC, MC, V. Closed Sun.*

$$ ✕ **The Winery.** This is *the* place for the big night out and special occasions. It's very pretty, awash in stained glass, wood beams, exposed brick, and hanging plants. The menu isn't terribly adventuresome, but it does turn out top-notch steak, chicken, prime rib, and shrimp in simple, flavorful sauces and fresh fish specials. ✉ *642 Main St.,* ☎ *970/242–4100. AE, D, DC, MC, V. No lunch.*

$ ✕ **Crystal Café & Bake Shop.** Locals flock to this European-style café for its apple pancakes and homemade granola at breakfast. They rave about the fresh soups such as carrot-peanut, cream of mushroom, and chicken with wild rice. The Oriental chicken salad and grilled vegetable sandwiches are also favorites. ✉ *314 Main St.,* ☎ *970/242–8843. No credit cards. No dinner.*

$ ✕ **G. B. Gladstone's.** This local hangout boasts of its own style of turn-of-the-20th-century decor: stained-glass windows, faux-Victorian gas lamps, and antique skis and kayaks on the walls. It's particularly lively on Friday night, but whatever the day, you can enjoy such savory starters as jumpin' jacks (fried jack cheese and cheddar rolls stuffed with jalapeños) and Frankie's hot steak strips, as well as the freshest fish in town (try the blackened sea bass if it's a daily special). The meat and poultry specials are good too, especially the fine prime rib; teriyaki steak; and Thai pesto linguine with broiled chicken strips, basil, garlic, and chilies. ✉ *2531 N. 12th St.,* ☎ *970/241–6000. AE, D, DC, MC, V.*

$$–$$$ **Los Altos Bed & Breakfast.** Perched on a hill, this B&B offers a 360-degree view; you can see clear to Utah. This cozy lodging—a Victorian inn—feels timeless. Guests enjoy relaxing in the third-floor observatory room or stepping out onto the wraparound deck. Several rooms have French doors leading to private decks. Breakfast includes home-baked muffins, coffee cakes, and multigrain pancakes. Tea is served in the winter. ✉ *375 Hillview Dr., 81503,* ☎ *970/256–0964 or 888/774–0982. 7 rooms, 3 suites. Breakfast room. AE, D, MC, V.*

$$ ★ **Adams Mark Grand Junction.** By far the premier property in the area, the Adams Mark offers quiet pampering at affordable rates, although some of the units could use refurbishing. Rooms are large and have welcome extras, such as a phone *and* TV in the bathroom. The bar and nightclub are longtime local favorites. ✉ *743 Horizon Dr., 81506,* ☎ *970/241–8888,* FAX *970/242–7266. 246 rooms, 14 suites. 2 restaurants, 2 bars, pool, hot tub, 3 tennis courts, exercise room, recreation room, airport shuttle. AE, D, DC, MC, V.*

$$ ★ **Grand Vista Hotel.** Management does its utmost to create a warm, inviting ambience, and it succeeds, with plush high-back chairs in the welcoming lobby and a private library/club look in the main restaurant, Oliver's. Old-fashioned charm and dark mountain colors characterize the rooms. ✉ *2790 Crossroads Blvd., 81506,* ☎ *970/241–8411,* FAX *970/241–1077. 158 rooms. Restaurant, bar, patisserie, indoor pool, hot tub, health club privileges, nightclub, meeting rooms, airport shuttle. AE, D, DC, MC, V.*

$ **Budget Host.** The owner continually refurbishes this property (you can occasionally catch him scrubbing the floors), whose gray-and-white exterior seems more country inn than motor lodge. Care is also lavished on the smart, fresh rooms, which have an early-American look with Stanley cherry furniture, burgundy carpets, and floral spreads. ✉ *721 Horizon Dr., 81506,* ☎ *970/243–6050 or 800/888–5736. 55 rooms. Outdoor pool. AE, D, DC, MC, V.*

$ **The Historic Melrose House.** This funky 100-year-old, brick-red-and-forest-green building functions as both a full-service hotel and a hostel. Most of the hotel rooms are bright and airy, with a smattering of antiques and feature cable TV, air-conditioning, sink (some have a private shower), and the original woodwork. This is a great place to connect with students from around the world. The hosts couldn't be more friendly and helpful, full of tips on how to save money in the area. Hostelers enjoy a pleasant common room. Morning coffee and Danish pastry is complimentary. ✉ *337 Colorado St., 81501,* ☎ *970/242–9636. 21 hotel rooms, 6 with private bath, 2 dorms. AE, D, DC, MC, V.*

$ **Peachtree Inn.** This pleasant property—with pool and restaurant—offers more amenities and facilities than most "strip" motels. The appealing room decor includes gray carpeting and a mauve and light-blue color scheme. ✉ *1600 North Ave., 81501,* ☎ *970/245–5770 or 800/525–0030. 75 rooms. Restaurant, bar, pool. AE, D, MC, V.*

Nightlife and the Arts

Country Jam (Grand Junction Visitor and Convention Bureau, ☎ 970/244–1480 or 800/530–3020), held annually in June, attracts the biggest name acts, such as Garth Brooks and Willie Nelson. The 65-piece **Grand Junction Symphony** (☎ 970/243–6787) is highly regarded.

BARS AND LOUNGES

River City (✉ 748 North Ave., ☎ 970/245–8040). The Adams Mark Grand Junction's (☞ Dining and Lodging, *above*) **Observatory Lounge. G. B. Gladstone's** (☞ Dining and Lodging, *above*). The **Rockslide Brewery** (✉ 401 Main St., ☎ 970/245–2111) has won awards for its ales, porters, and stouts.

COFFEEHOUSE

At **Mountain Roasted** (✉ 620 Main St., ☎ 970/242–5282) biscotti, homemade muffins, and pastries are served with gourmet coffees in an arty atmosphere. The local art gracing the walls is also for sale, and live music is offered several evenings a week.

MUSIC AND DANCE CLUBS

Cahoots Crossing (✉ 490 28¼ Rd., ☎ 970/241–2282) features live bands several nights weekly. Grand Junction kicks up its heels at the **Branding Iron Lounge** (✉ 2701 U.S. 50, ☎ 970/242–9897). **Cinnamon's** (✉ Holiday Inn, 755 Horizon Dr., ☎ 970/243–6790) has a dance floor and live music. For a more Western atmosphere, try the **Cancun Saloon** (✉ Adams Mark Grand Junction, (☞ Dining and Lodging, *above*).

Outdoor Activities and Sports

Vertical Horizons Rock Guides (☎ 970/245–8513) offers guided climbs and lessons in the area. **Adventure Bound River Expeditions** (☎ 970/245–

5428) runs trips on the Colorado and Green rivers (the latter through the canyons of Dinosaur National Monument). For cyclists, **Kokopelli's Trail** links Grand Junction with the famed **Slickrock Trail** outside Moab, Utah. The 128-mi stretch winds through high desert and the Colorado River valley before climbing the La Sal Mountains. Those interested in bike tours should get in touch with the **Colorado Plateau Mountain Bike Trail Association** (☎ 970/249–8055). **Rim Rock Deer Park** (✉ 927 17 Rd., Fruita, ☎ 970/858–9555) offers everything from one-hour horseback rides into Colorado National Monument to overnight pack rides.

Tiara Rado Golf Course (✉ 2063 S. Broadway, ☎ 970/245–8085) is an 18-hole championship course set at the foot of the Colorado National Monument.

Shopping

ANTIQUES

A Haggle of Vendors Emporium (✉ 510 Main St., ☎ no phone) is just what it says. It's as if every attic you'd ever seen had emptied its contents here.

CRAFT AND ART GALLERIES

Frameworks (✉ 309 Main St., ☎ 970/243–7074) specializes in local artist's works and carries serigraphs, sculpture, oils, watercolors, etchings and photos. **Sunlit Glass** (✉ 2493 U.S. 6, ☎ 970/434–4600) specializes in stained glass. **Terry Shepherd** (✉ 825 N. 7th St., Grand Junction, ☎ 970/243–4282) sells his own stoneware and salt-vapor designs, where the salt forms trails on the pottery.

FOOD

Enstrom's (✉ 200 S. 7th St., ☎ 970/242–1655) makes scrumptious candy and is world-renowned for their toffee.

WESTERN PARAPHERNALIA

Champion Boots and Saddlery (✉ 545 Main St., ☎ 970/242–2465), in business since 1936, is the best place in the area for the likes of Tony Lama boots or Minnetonka moccasins.

OFF THE BEATEN PATH

TABEGUACHE/UNAWEEP SCENIC BYWAY – This 150-mi stretch of savage scenery (Route 141) sweeps south from Grand Junction, arcing almost to the Utah border before curling over to Naturita, where you can pick up Route 145 to Telluride. It slices through the Uncompahgre Plateau, an area of great geologic interest. Unaweep means "Canyon with Two Mouths," and the piddling streams seem insufficient to have carved these harsh gashes. Along the way you'll see an engineering marvel: the 7-mi long Hanging Flume, used to transport water, virtually defies gravity by clinging to the sheer cliff. One of Colorado's oddest communities, Nucla, also lies along this route, 3 mi north of Naturita on Route 97. Founded as an early experiment in communal living (though the current conservative residents could hardly be called hippies), Nucla today is famous for one thing: The Top Dog World Prairie Dog Shootout, held every June. Residents justify the carnage by insisting that prairie dogs are only pests and that they run roughshod over the grazing lands.

Palisade

87 *12 mi from Grand Junction via Rte. 65 east.*

Palisade is nestled between the wintry Grand Mesa (10,000 ft high and mostly snow-covered year-round) and semiarid terrain. The surprisingly temperate microclimate produces delectable Elberta peaches, apples, plums, pears, and cherries, making Palisade the center of Colorado's orchard and vineyard territory. Plucky wine makers have been experimenting with several varietals since the early '80s, and the results have been encouraging. There are fewer than 20 vineyards in the state; the best are located right here in the Grand Valley.

You can find all the great European grapes here: Riesling, chardonnay, pinot noir, cabernet, merlot. So far, the top results have been obtained with merlot and chardonnay. Wine lovers will appreciate the heady, uncomplicated varietal bouquet and surprising depth and complexity of some of the vintages. Four vineyards are open to the public, offering tours, tastings, and the opportunity to meet wine makers and discuss their craft. The oldest, largest, and most commercially successful (to date) is **Colorado Cellars** (✉ 3553 E Rd., ☎ 970/464–7921). **Carlson Vineyards** (✉ 461 35 Rd., ☎ 970/464–5554) produces wines with names such as Tyrannosaurus Red and Prairie Dog. Probably the best wines to buy here are those made from fruit (such as the peach pearadactyl). One of the most promising in quality is undoubtedly **Plum Creek Cellars** (✉ 3708 G Rd., ☎ 970/464–7586). **Grande River Vineyards** (✉ 787 Elberta Ave., ☎ 970/464–5867) is experimenting with Rhone varietals (Syrah and Viognier).

Shopping

Harold and Nola Voorhees (✉ 3702 G 7/10 Rd., ☎ 970/464–7220) sells a range of dried fruits, including cherries, pears, apricots, and peaches. **Slice-O-Life Bakery** (✉ 105 W. 3rd St., ☎ 970/464–0577) is run by two of the zaniest bakers in Colorado, Mary and Tim Lincoln. All the savory, aromatic goodies are baked with whole grains and fresh local fruits. Buy your favorites, grab a bottle of wine at one of the nearby wineries, add in some fresh fruit from an orchard, and you have the makings of a picnic.

Grand Mesa

88 *32 mi from Palisade or 44 mi from Grand Junction via Rte. 65 east and south.*

The world's largest flattop mountain towers 10,000 ft above the surrounding terrain and sprawls an astounding 50 square mi. Grand Mesa's landscape is dotted with more than 200 sparkling lakes—a fisherman's paradise in summer. According to Ute legend, a great eagle carried off a Native American child, and in retaliation the father hurled its eaglets to the base of the mesa, where they were devoured by a serpent. The enraged eagle seized the serpent and tore it into hundreds of pieces, which formed deep pits upon hitting the earth. The eagle's ire caused the mesa to rattle with thunder, and torrents of rain filled the pits, creating lakes.

The stands of golden quakies (aspens) blanketing the mesa are glorious in autumn. Even on brilliantly sunny days, wispy clouds seem to catch and reflect the sun's rays, draping the summit in prismatic light. The views of the Grand Valley and the Bookcliffs (escarpments) are absolutely ravishing here, and an excellent little ski area, **Powderhorn,** takes full advantage of them. The slopes intriguingly follow the fall line of the mesa, carving out natural bowls, those on the western side being steeper than they first appear.

Outdoor Activities and Sports

The **Grand Mesa Lakes** provide some of the best angling opportunities in Colorado. For information, contact the Grand Mesa National Forest (☎ 970/242–8211) or the U.S. Forest Service (☎ 970/242–8211). The **Crag Crest Trail** on top of Grand Mesa affords hikers breathtaking views of the canyons and cliffs below.

SKIING

Powderhorn has 20 trails, 4 lifts, 240 acres, and a 1,650-ft vertical drop. ✉ *Rte. 65,* ☎ *970/268–5700.* ⏲ *Nov.–mid-Apr., 9–4.*

For **cross-country skiing,** the acres of untracked powder amid stands of aspen and spruce on Grand Mesa are a Nordic nirvana. For information, contact the Grand Mesa National Forest (*above*) or the Grand Mesa Nordic Council (☎ 970/434–9753).

Cedaredge

89 *15 mi from Grand Mesa or 59 mi from Grand Junction via Rte. 65 south.*

The **Grand Mesa Scenic Byway** runs from Grand Junction to Cedaredge along this route (I–70 and Rte. 65). Cedaredge is an exceptionally pretty town in the shadow of the Grand Mesa and is complemented by the silvery San Juans shimmering to the south. Among its attractions is **Pioneer Town,** a cluster of 23 authentic buildings that re-create turn-of-the-20th-century life. ✉ *Rte. 65,* ☎ *970/856–7554.* *$3.* ⏲ *June–Sept., daily 10–4.*

Lodging

$–$$ **Cedars' Edge Llamas B&B.** The pretty cedar house and guest cottage offer four neatly appointed rooms. Breakfast is on a private deck or in the sunroom, which affords astonishing 100-mi views. The best part about staying at Ray and Gail Record's retreat, however, is the llama herd (yes, they accompany guests on picnics). ✉ *2169 Hwy. 65, 81413,* ☎ *970/856–6836. 4 rooms. AE, MC, V.*

Shopping

The Apple Shed (✉ 250 S. Grand Mesa Dr., ☎ 970/856–7007) is a group of galleries that sell an impressive array of Colorado crafts.

Delta

90 *15 mi from Cedaredge via Rte. 65 south; 46 mi from Grand Junction via Rte. 50 south.*

Delta is the headquarters of the Grand Mesa, Gunnison, and Uncompahgre national forests. The town is ideally located for exploring the region's natural wonders and also has an interesting attraction that has earned Delta the accolade, "The City of Murals." Seven murals, most of them lining Main Street, were painted by local artists in the late 1980s and celebrate various aspects of life in the area, from wildlife in "Delta County Ark" and ranching in "High Country Roundup," to agriculture in both "A Tribute to Agriculture" and "Labels of Delta County."

There are also museums of interest in Delta. At **Ft. Uncompahgre,** docents in period attire guide visitors through this 1826 fur-trading post. ✉ *Confluence Park,* ☎ *970/874–8349.* *$3.50.* ⏲ *Mar.–Dec., Tues.–Sat. 10–4. Also Sun. 10–5 in summer.*

The **Delta County Museum** has an eclectic display that includes local dinosaur finds, an 1886 jail, a butterfly collection, and a collection of large bells. ✉ *251 Meeker St.,* ☎ *970/874–8721.* *$2.* ⏲ *May–Sept., Tues.–Sat. 10–4; Oct.–Apr., Wed. and Sat. 10–4.*

Shopping

Windfeather Designs (✉ 1204 Bluff St., ☎ no phone) offers Jean Madole's extraordinary weaving, a reinterpretation of designs from extinct cultures such as the Mimbre.

Rifle

91 *58 mi from Grand Junction via I–70 east.*

This unassuming community (which lives up to its name with gun racks outnumbering ski racks on cars) is developing quite a reputation among mountain bikers for the series of high-quality trails along the Roan Cliffs, and with ice climbers for the frozen waterfalls and ice caves in the Rifle Gap State Recreation Area. Rifle boasts a variety of terrain that veers from semiarid to subalpine and invites hikers, bikers, and climbers.

Take Route 325 north out of town to the **Rifle Gap State Recreation Area** ($3 admission), passing Rifle Gap on the way. As you gaze at the huge rock window, try to imagine a huge, orange nylon curtain billowing between the steep walls. Famed installation artist Christo did; two of his efforts were foiled due to wind, save for one amazing day when his *Valley Curtain* piece was gloriously unfolded for a brief few hours. The road wraps around a tiny reservoir before reaching **Rifle Falls,** a triple flume cascading down moss-covered cliffs. Farther on out Route 325, are the **Rifle Fish Hatchery,** with huge schools of trout, including an intriguing iridescent blue hybrid, and **Rifle Mountain Park.**

Dining and Lodging

$$ ✕ **Fireside Inn.** This dining spot has an enormous stone fireplace as its centerpiece. The owner is Italian, and along with Continental favorites such as veal marsala and prime rib au jus, he offers tasty homemade ravioli and chicken Alfredo. The Fireside Inn serves Sunday brunch, as well as lunch and dinner. ✉ *1214 Access Rd.,* ☎ *970/625–2233. AE, D, MC, V. No lunch Sat. Closed Mon.*

$ **Rusty Cannon Motel.** This motor lodge offers spacious accommodations and is plain but clean and comfortable. ✉ *701 Taughenbaugh Blvd., 81650,* ☎ *970/625–4004. 89 rooms. Pool, sauna. AE, D, DC, MC, V.*

Outdoor Activities and Sports

The **Rifle Gap Reservoir** (☎ 970/625–1607) is plentifully stocked with rainbow trout and walleye pike. **Battlement Mesa Golf Course** (✉ 3930 N. Battlement Mesa Pkwy., Battlement Mesa, ☎ 970/285–7274) is an 18-hole championship course with ravishing views of the Grand Valley and Grand Mesa in the distance. **Battlement Mesa,** outside Rifle, also offers rugged hiking trails.

CLIMBING

The rock faces and ice caves of the **Rifle Mountain Park** (✉ Rte. 325, ☎ 970/625–2121) are a magnet for rock and ice climbers, depending on the season.

CYCLING

The biking around Rifle is gaining momentum among aficionados for the variety of trails around the Roan Cliffs, through shale, sagebrush, and piñon, punctuated by panoramic views. Call the **Rifle Chamber of Commerce** (☎ 970/625–2085) for maps and details.

Meeker

92 *43 mi from Rifle or 101 mi from Grand Junction via I–70 east and Rte. 13 north.*

Back on I–70, turn north on scenic Route 13 to Meeker, named for Nathan Meeker, who attempted to "civilize" the Utes with little success. When Meeker began to fear that the Utes resented his arrogant disregard for their land rights, he sent for the cavalry. The Utes became further enraged and ambushed the troops in the 1879 Meeker Massacre, which ushered in yet another period of intransigence on the part of the U.S. government. The town is predominantly known as an outdoorsy place, but its handsome historical buildings include the still-operating Meeker Hotel on Main Street and the worthy **White River Museum,** which features pioneer artifacts and historical photos. ✉ *565 Park St.,* ☎ *970/878–9982.* 🎟 *Free.* ⏲ *Mid-Apr.–Nov., weekdays 9–5; Nov.–Apr., weekdays 11–3.*

East of Meeker is the **Flattops Scenic Byway,** an 82-mi gravel road from Meeker to Yampa, through an area shaped by molten lava flows and glaciers that gouged tiny jewel-like lakes in the folds of the mountains.

Dining and Lodging

$–$$ ★ ✕🏨 **Sleepy Cat Lodge and Restaurant.** The original lodge burned down in 1991, but the new Sleepy Cat (owned by the same family since 1964) rose like a phoenix, and it's even better than before. The huge log structure is filled with gorgeous beveled glass and the requisite trophies and bearskins mounted on the walls. Soup and salad bar accompany full and filling dinners; ribs, huge cuts of steak, teriyaki chicken, and pan-fried trout are among the top choices. There are several cozy cabins for rent as well. ✉ *County Rd. 8, 16 mi east of Meeker, 81641,* ☎ *970/878–4413. 27 cabins. Restaurant. D, MC, V. Restaurant hrs vary; call ahead.*

Craig

93 *48 mi from Meeker via Rte. 13 north; 149 mi from Grand Junction via I–70 east and Rte. 13 north.*

Craig is a growing cow town, made newly prosperous by coal and oil (you'll see billowing white plumes belch from Colorado's largest coal-processing plant, the Colorado-Ute Power Station), but it's also set in pristine wilderness, teeming with wildlife. The **Sandstone Hiking Trail,** an easy ½-mi walk beginning in town along Alta Vista Drive, is a splendid vantage point for viewing the local elk and deer herds, as well as ancient Native American petroglyphs carved on the cliff.

In town is the **Museum of Northwest Colorado,** with its eclectic collection of everything from arrowheads to a fire truck. The upstairs of this restored county courthouse is devoted to one man's obsession: Bill Mackin, one of the leading traders in cowboy collectibles, has spent a lifetime gathering guns, bits, saddles, bootjacks, holsters, and spurs of all descriptions. It's the largest privately owned collection of working cowboy artifacts in the world. ✉ *590 Yampa Ave.,* ☎ *970/824–6360.* 🎟 *Free (donations accepted).* ⏲ *Mon.–Sat. 10–5.*

Dining and Lodging

$–$$ ✕ **Golden Cavvy.** A "cavvy" is the pick of a team of horses, and this restaurant is certainly the selection in town, for the price. It's a standard coffee shop enlivened by mirrors, hanging plants, faux-antique chandeliers, and the incredible masonry of the original 1900s fireplace of the Baker Hotel (which burned down on this spot). Hearty breakfasts, homemade pies and ice cream, pork chops, and anything deep-fried (try the mesquite-fried chicken) are your best bets. ✉ *538 Yampa Ave.,* ☎ *970/824–6038. MC, V.*

$–$$ 🏨 **Holiday Inn.** This property is pleasant enough for a remote Holiday Inn. It boasts the usual "holidome" with pool, and rooms are a good size; they're decorated in teal and floral fabrics. ✉ *300 Rte. 13 S, 81625,* ☎ *970/824–4000,* FAX *970/824–3950. 152 rooms. Restaurant, bar, indoor pool, hot tub, exercise room, nightclub, recreation room. AE, D, DC, MC, V.*

Outdoor Activities and Sports

Around Craig and Meeker, the **Yampa** and **Green rivers, Trappers Lake, Lake Avery,** and **Elkhead Reservoir** are known for pike and trout; contact the Craig **Sportsman's Center** (☎ 970/824–3046) for information.

Yampa Valley Golf Course (✉ County Rd. 394, ☎ 970/824–3673) is an 18-hole course dotted with copses of willow and cottonwood by the Yampa River.

En Route Outside Craig, U.S. 40 gradually shifts into hillier sagebrush country. This is ideal land for raising cattle, which are about all you'll see for miles on this desolate stretch of highway. The route winds through increasingly minuscule towns every 15 mi or so, including Maybell, Elk Springs, Massadona, Blue Mountain—some not even on the map.

OFF THE BEATEN PATH **BROWNS PARK WILDLIFE REFUGE** – At Maybell, the road forks. If you follow Route 318 northwest for about 60 mi you'll reach the refuge, with lacy waterfalls and canyons carved by the Green River and straddled by a swinging bridge. The area was a notorious hideaway for the likes of Butch Cassidy and the Sundance Kid, Tom Horn, and John Bennett. This is an unspoiled, almost primitive spot, ideal for watching antelope and bighorn sheep, as well as nesting waterfowl such as mallards, redheads, and teal. You might also see elk, pronghorn, and various songbirds. The route here is complicated, so call first for directions. ✉ *1318 Rte. 318,* ☎ *970/365–3613.* *Free.* ⏲ *7:30 AM–sunset.*

Dinosaur National Monument

94 *90 mi from Craig via U.S. 40 west; 106 mi from Grand Junction via I–70 west, Rte. 139 north, Rte. 64 north, and U.S. 40 east (to national monument headquarters).*

As you continue west along U.S. 40, you'll note that the earth becomes increasingly creased and furrowed, divided by arroyos and broken by the mauve- and rose-streaked cliffs of Dinosaur National Monument (Park Headquarters, ✉ 4545 U.S. 40, Dinosaur, 81610, 25 mi from the park, ☎ 970/374–3000). The Dinosaur Quarry is actually located on the Utah side of the monument, but the Colorado section offers some of the finest hiking in the West, along the **Harpers Corner/Echo Park Drive** and the ominous-sounding **Canyon of Lodore** (where rafting is available along the rapids of the Green River). The drive is only accessible in summer—even then, four-wheel drive is preferable—and some of the most breathtaking overlooks are well off the beaten track. Still, the 62-mi-round-trip paved Harpers Corner Drive will take you past looming buttes and yawning sunbaked gorges etched by the Green and Yampa rivers. The dirt Echo Park Road is dotted with angular rock formations stippled with petroglyphs; the route skirts the rim of narrow 3,000-ft-deep crevasses that ripple from beige to black depending on the angle of the sun. Wherever you go, remember this austerely beautiful park is fragile: Avoid the rich black soil, which contains actual cryptogams—one-celled creatures that are the building blocks of life in the desert; and don't touch the petroglyphs.

Dinosaur, a few miles west of the monument's headquarters, is a sad little town whose streets are named for the giant reptiles. It offers little more than pit stops and dinky motels. If you've traveled this far, though, you're almost better off camping in the park, which is first-come, first-served.

Dining

$ ✕ **B&B Family Restaurant.** Capitalizing on its location, this restaurant has a dino emblazoned on the side of the building. The decor is simple:

one wall is papered with potato sacks and another is adorned with cheesy wildlife art; there are also still surprisingly beautiful remnants of an old bar with intricate carving and mirrors. The menu is cute and unusual: Where else can you get Brontoburgers, Stegosaurus rib-eyes, and Plateosaurus rib-eyes? ✉ *Ceratosaurus St. and U.S. 40,* ☎ *970/374–2744.*

Outdoor Activities and Sports

CAMPING

Pristine **campsites** are available at **Gates of Lodore** (✉ Rte. 318, 68 mi from Maybell), **Deerlodge Park** (✉ off U.S. 40, between Elk Springs and Maybell), and **Echo Park** (✉ off Harper's Corner Rd., 13 mi from national monument headquarters). Call Dinosaur National Monument (☞ *above*) for information. Most sites are available on a first-come, first-served basis.

Rangely

95 *19 mi from Dinosaur via Rte. 64 south; 96 mi from Grand Junction via I–70 west and Rte. 139 north.*

Rangely proudly touts itself as the "Oil Capital of Colorado." It's also nicknamed Strangely: A perverse sense of humor is required to live in this desolate neck of the woods. The life of oil riggers and uranium miners is a hard one, after all.

Rangely's most compelling sights are the superb Fremont petroglyphs—dating from between 600 and 1300—in Douglas Creek Canyon, south of town along Route 139. This stretch is known as the **Canyon Pintado Historic District,** and the examples of rock art are among the best-preserved in the West. A brochure listing the sites is available; half the fun is clambering up the rocks to find them.

Colorado National Monument

96 *78 mi from Rangely via Rte. 139 south and I–70 east; 23 mi from Grand Junction via Rte. 340 west.*

Route 139 meets up with I–70 a few miles east of the Utah border. Turn east onto the highway and you'll shortly reach the western entrance of the Colorado National Monument. The 23-mi Rim Rock Drive climbs this colorful plateau that's been nearly 1 billion years in the making, yielding sterling views of the gaping canyons and gnarled knobby monoliths below. This is dramatic, rugged country, stubbled with stunted piñon trees and junipers; populated by mule deer, gray foxes, and bobcats; and perpetually swept by ravens, swifts, and golden eagles. The starkly beautiful sandstone and shale formations include Balanced Rock, Independence Monument, and the slender, willowy sculptures of the Kissing Couple and Praying Hands. Backcountry camping is permitted. An eccentric visionary named John Otto was instrumental in having the park declared a national monument in 1911. To get his way, the headstrong Otto frequently threatened members of Congress with everything from blackmail to beatings, acts that caused him to be institutionalized on three occasions. But as locals observed, "He's the sanest man in town 'cause he's got the papers to prove it." ✉ *Fruita,* ☎ *970/858–3617.* *$5 per car for 7-day pass.* ⏲ *Park: daily, 24 hours; visitor center: daily, hours vary.*

West of the monument, it's a treacherous 7-mi hike into **Rattlesnake Canyon** (☎ 970/244–3000). The intrepid will be rewarded with thrilling natural arches and spires. The canyon can be reached in summer from the upper end of Rim Rock Drive with four-wheel-drive vehicles.

Just opposite the western entrance to the monument is **Devil's Canyon Science and Learning Center.** This sparkling facility for children of all ages was created by the Dinamation International Society, the folks who fabricate robotic dinos. The society's Dr. Robert Bakker advises, "Don't think of T. rex as a 'tyrant lizard,' but as a 10,000-pound roadrunner that could eat a school bus." In addition to the amazingly lifelike robotics (including a hatching egg), there are more than 20 interactive displays. Children can stand in an earthquake simulator, dig up "fossils" in a mock quarry, or make dino prints in dirt (along with reptile and bird tracks for comparison). Kids get a special passport that's stamped as they visit each dinosaur exhibit, and they have the chance to watch local volunteers at work cleaning and preparing fossils for study. ✉ *Exit 19 off I–70, 550 Jurassic Ct., Fruita,* ☎ *970/858–7282 or 800/344–3466.* 🎟 *$5.50.* ⏲ *Daily 9–5.*

Northwest Colorado A to Z

Arriving and Departing

BY BUS

Greyhound Lines (☎ 800/231–2222) serves most of the major towns in the region.

BY CAR

I–70 bisects Colorado running east–west; it's the easiest way to approach the region.

BY PLANE

Walker Field Airport (✉ Grand Junction, ☎ 970/244–9100), the only major airport in the region, is served by America West Express, Sky West, and United Express.

BY TRAIN

Amtrak (☎ 800/872–7245) stops in Grand Junction.

Getting Around

BY CAR

I–70 (U.S. 6) is the major thoroughfare, accessing Grand Junction, Rifle, and Grand Mesa (via Rte. 65, which runs to Delta). Meeker is reached from Rifle via Route 13 and Rangely/Dinosaur via Route 64. U.S. 40 east from Utah is the best way to reach Dinosaur National Monument and Craig.

BY TAXI

Sunshine Taxi (☎ 970/245–8294) serves Grand Junction. **A Touch of Class** (☎ 970/245–5466) has regular service into Grand Junction and outlying communities from Walker Field.

Contacts and Resources

DOCTORS AND DENTISTS

Craig Memorial Hospital (✉ 785 Russell Ave., Craig, ☎ 970/824–9411). **Grand Junction Community Hospital** (✉ 2021 N. 12th St., Grand Junction, ☎ 970/242–0920). **Pioneers Hospital** (✉ 345 Cleveland St., Meeker, ☎ 970/878–5047). **St. Mary's Hospital** (✉ 2635 N. 7th St., Grand Junction, ☎ 970/244–2273).

GUIDED TOURS

Orientation: Coopertours (✉ Grand Junction, ☎ 970/434–0224) specializes in tours for artists and photographers. Eagle Tree Tours (✉ Grand Junction, ☎ 970/241–4792) offers tours of Colorado National Monument and the Grand Junction area, including some with four-wheel-drive vehicles, hiking, or biking.

Special-Interest: Dinamation: Dinosaur Discovery (✉ 550 Jurassic Ct., Fruita 81521, ☎ 970/858–7282 or 800/344–3466) runs five- to six-day paleontological treks that include work in a dinosaur quarry.

Meander Tours (✉ 209 Main St., Collbran 81624, ☎ 970/487–3402) offers scenic and Western-theme adventures.

VISITOR INFORMATION

Battlement Mesa, Inc. (✉ Box 6000, Battlement Mesa 81636, ☎ 970/285–9700 or 800/545–6372). **Cedaredge Chamber of Commerce** (✉ Box 278, Cedaredge 81413, ☎ 970/856–6961). **Delta Chamber of Commerce and Visitors Center** (✉ 3rd and Main Sts., Delta 81646, ☎ 970/874–8616 or 800/436–3041). **Dinosaur Chamber of Commerce** (✉ Box 102, Dinosaur 81610, ☎ no phone). **Greater Craig Chamber of Commerce** (✉ 360 E. Victory Way, Craig 81625, ☎ 970/824–5689). **Grand Junction Area Chamber of Commerce** (✉ 740 Horizon Dr., Grand Junction 81501, ☎ 970/244–1480 or 800/962–2547). **Meeker Chamber of Commerce** (✉ Box 869, Meeker 81641, ☎ 970/878–5510). **Nucla/Naturita Area Chamber of Commerce** (✉ 230 W. Main St., Naturita 81422, ☎ 970/865–2350). **Palisade Chamber of Commerce** (✉ Box 729, Palisade 81526, ☎ 970/464–7458). **Plateau Valley Chamber of Commerce** (✉ 209 Main St., Collbran 81624, ☎ 970/487–3402). **Rangely Chamber of Commerce** (✉ 209 E. Main St., Rangely 81646, ☎ 970/675–5290). **Rifle Area Chamber of Commerce** (✉ 200 Lions Park Circle, Rifle 81650, ☎ 970/625–2085).

THE EASTERN PLAINS

One-third of Colorado is prairie land—vast stretches of hypnotically rolling corn and wheat fields, Russian thistle, and tall grasses coppered by the sun. This is middle America, where families have been ranching and farming the same plot of land for generations; where county fairs, livestock shows, and high-school football games are the main forms of entertainment; where the Corn and Bible belts stoically tighten a notch in times of adversity.

If you want to get in touch with America's roots, here is a good place to begin. The small one-horse towns such as Heartstrong and Last Chance—names redolent of the heartland—tell an old story, that of the first pioneers who struggled across the continent in search of a better life. The Pony Express and Overland trails cut right through northeast Colorado (James Michener set his epic historical novel *Centennial* in this territory), where even today you'll find weathered trading posts, lone buttes that guided the weary homesteaders westward, and down-home friendly people who take enormous pride in their land and their heritage.

In this tour, the towns are arranged as you would pass through them if driving east from Denver on I–70 or I–76. If time allows, occasionally get off the interstate highway and drive the two-lane byways to get a real sense of this region's communities and slower pace of life.

Fort Morgan

68 mi from Denver via I–76 east.

Fort Morgan, the seat of Morgan County, is a major agricultural center for corn, wheat, and sugar beets, the big cash crops in these parts. But its true claim to fame is as bandleader Glenn Miller's birthplace.

The **Fort Morgan Museum** is a repository of local history that describes the town's origins in 1864 as a military fort constructed to protect gold miners, and displays Miller memorabilia. Items exhibited include artifacts from the Koehler Site, an excavated landfill nearby that revealed a prehistoric campsite, a recreation of an old fort, and classic Americana such as a 1920s soda fountain from an old drugstore. On your way out, pick up a historical downtown walking-tour brochure to tell you about some of the handsome homes lining Main Street. ✉ *414 Main St.,* ☎ *970/867–6331.* 🎫 *Free.* ⏲ *Weekdays 10–5, Sat. 11–5.*

Dining and Lodging

$$ ✕ **Country Steak-Out.** Fort Morgan's first steak house—a combination between a diner and a barn—looks as if it hasn't changed since the Dust Bowl era. After a long day of following behind pickup trucks with bumper stickers that admonish you to "Eat beef," you might as well succumb to the succulent steaks served here. ✉ *19592 E. 8th Ave.,* ☎ *970/867–7887. AE, MC, V. Closed Mon. No dinner Sun.*

$ 🏨 **Best Western Park Terrace.** Clean, pleasant rooms with cable TV are what you'll find in this perfectly comfortable, typical motel. ✉ *725 Main St., 80701,* ☎ *970/867–8256. 24 rooms. Restaurant, pool. AE, D, DC, MC, V.*

Sterling

46 mi from Fort Morgan via I–76 east.

Peaceful, prosperous Sterling is a town of graceful whitewashed houses with porch swings and shady trees that fringe neighborhood streets. Sterling bills itself as "The City of Living Trees," a tribute to local artist Brad Rhea, who has chiseled living trees into fanciful works of art: towering giraffes, festive clowns, golfers (at the country club), and minutemen (at the National Armory). Several downtown buildings, listed on the National Register of Historic Places, are supreme examples of turn-of-the-20th-century pioneer architecture; among them is Logan County Courthouse.

The **Overland Trail Museum,** a replica of a classic old fort carved out of rock, offers displays of homesteading life, with painstaking re-creations of a typical blacksmith shop and schoolhouse, as well as exhibits of Plains Natives and pioneer clothing and utensils. ✉ *Jct. of U.S. 6 and I–76,* ☎ *970/522–3895.* 🎫 *Free.* ⏲ *Nov.–Mar., Tues.–Sat. 10–4; Apr.–Oct., Mon.–Sat. 9–5, Sun. and holidays 10–5.*

Dining and Lodging

$ ✕ **Fergie's West Inn Pub.** This small, simple restaurant-bar serves up sensational soups and sandwiches, including predictably mouthwatering barbecued beef. ✉ *324 W. Main St.,* ☎ *970/522–4220. MC, V. Closed Sun.*

$$ 🏨 **Best Western Sundowner.** This property is a notch above the usual chain motel, with spacious, tasteful rooms, and several amenities. Continental breakfast is included in the room rate. ✉ *Overland Trail St., 80751,* ☎ *970/522–6265. 29 rooms. Pool, hot tub, exercise room, coin laundry. AE, D, DC, MC, V.*

$ 🏨 **Crest Motel.** You'll receive friendly, thoughtful treatment in this small, decently outfitted motel. ✉ *516 Division Ave., 80751,* ☎ *970/522–3753. 8 rooms. AE, D, DC, MC, V.*

OFF THE BEATEN PATH

FT. SEDGWICK DEPOT MUSEUM – Mark Twain once called Julesburg "the wickedest city in the West," though today it's hard to picture the sleepy town as Sodom and Gomorrah rolled into one. Julesburg, 54 mi northeast of Sterling on I–76, is the proud site of the only Pony Express station in Colorado, duly celebrated at the local museum, with assorted paraphernalia, from mail patches to saddles. ✉ *202 W. 1st St., Julesburg,* ☎ *970/474–2264.* 🎫 *$1.* ⏲ *June–Sept., Mon.–Sat. 9–5, Sun. 1–5.*

Genoa

98 mi from Denver via I–70 east.

A ferocious twister leveled Limon in 1990 (which you'll pass 10 mi before reaching Genoa if you're traveling east of Denver on I–70), but its residents banded together and today there are few apparent signs of the devastation. The town's rich past is displayed at the **Limon Heritage Museum,** offering collections of saddles and arrowheads, a restored 1912 railroad diner, a Union Railroad caboose, and changing photo and graphics exhibits, housed in the original Limon Depot. ✉ *E. Ave. and 1st St.,* ☎ *719/775–2373.* *Free; donations accepted.* ⏲ *June–Aug., Mon.–Sat. 1–8.*

The intriguing **Genoa Tower Museum** bills itself as the "highest point between the Rockies and the Mississippi." Aside from providing splendid vistas of the plains—the view of six states was proved by Ripley—the tower houses an eclectic collection of Native American artifacts, fossils, weird tools, and Elvis Presley memorabilia. Owner Jerry Chubbock says, "If it ain't here, it don't exist." The Ripleyesque display of animal monstrosities seems to support his boast. ✉ *Exit 371, off I–70 (follow signs from exit),* ☎ *719/763–2309.* *$1.* ⏲ *Daily 8–8; call first to check.*

Burlington

63 mi from Genoa via I–70 east.

Folks in Burlington, 12 mi from the Kansas border, take their history seriously. Exhibit A is **Old Town,** a lovingly authentic re-creation of a 1900s Old West village, with more than 20 restored turn-of-the-20th-century buildings complete with antique frontier memorabilia. Daily cancans and weekend gunfights take place in the Longhorn Saloon throughout the summer, as well as rip-roaring melodramas and madam shows (with the occasional catfight). It's a hoot and a half. ✉ *I–70 Exit 437,* ☎ *719/346–7382.* *$6.* ⏲ *June–Sept., daily 8:30–7; Oct.–May, daily 9–6.*

Burlington's other main attraction was designated one of Colorado's 13 National Historic Landmarks. The **Kit Carson County Carousel** is a fully restored and operational carousel hand-carved by the Philadelphia Toboggan Company in 1905. It's one of fewer than 170 carousels to retain its original paint. Forty-six exquisitely detailed creatures bob and weave to the jaunty accompaniment of a 1909 Wurlitzer Monster Military Band Organ. Among the residents here are richly caparisoned camels, fiercely toothsome tigers, and gamboling goats. ✉ *Burlington Fairgrounds, 15th St. at Colorado Ave.,* ☎ *719/346–8070.* ⏲ *June–Sept., daily 1–8.*

Dining and Lodging

$ ✕ **Mitten's Interstate House.** Locals swear by this glorified truck stop, off I–70. The humongous portions and daily specials define economical. Try the chicken fried steak, biscuits and gravy, or green chili. ✉ *415 S. Lincoln St.,* ☎ *719/346–7041. AE, D, DC, MC, V.*

$ **Chaparral Budget Host.** This serviceable motor lodge is perfectly located right near Old Town, and it offers the usual amenities, such as cable TV. ✉ *I–70 Exit 437, 80807,* ☎ *719/346–5361. 39 rooms. Pool, hot tub. AE, D, DC, MC, V.*

Shopping

For the best (if hokiest) selection of souvenirs, head for the **Old Town Emporium** (✉ I–70 Exit 437, ☎ 719/346–7382).

The Eastern Plains A to Z

Getting Around

I–70 cuts through the center of Colorado into Kansas, and I–76 angles northeast into Nebraska. If you're driving to Denver from the north or east, follow the itinerary in reverse. **Greyhound Lines** (☎ 800/231–2222) offers service to several towns throughout the region, including Fort Morgan, Sterling, Limon, and Burlington.

Contacts and Resources

DOCTORS AND DENTISTS

Fort Morgan: Colorado Plains Medical Center (✉ 1000 Lincoln St., ☎ 970/867–3391). **Sterling: Sterling Regional Medical Center** (✉ 615 Fairhurst St., ☎ 970/522–0122). **Burlington: Kit Carson County Memorial Hospital** (✉ 286 16th St., ☎ 719/346–5311).

VISITOR INFORMATION

Burlington Chamber of Commerce (✉ 415 15th St., Burlington 80807, ☎ 719/346–8070). **Colorado Welcome Center** (✉ 48265 I–70, Burlington 80807, ☎ 719/346–5554). **Fort Morgan Area Chamber of Commerce** (✉ 300 Main St., Fort Morgan 80701, ☎ 970/867–6702 or 800/354–8660). **Logan County Chamber of Commerce** (✉ Box 1683, Main and Front Sts., Sterling 80751, ☎ 970/522–5070). **Northeast Colorado Travel Region** (✉ 215 S. Main St., Yuma 80759, ☎ 800/777–9075).

COLORADO A TO Z

Getting Around

By Bus

Greyhound Lines (☎ 800/231–2222) operates regular intercity routes with connections from Denver. Smaller bus companies provide service within local areas. One such line is **Springs Transit Management** (☎ 719/385–7433) in Colorado Springs.

By Car

The U.S. interstate highway network provides quick, easy access to Colorado despite imposing mountain barriers. Denver is served by I–25, running north–south through Colorado Springs and Pueblo; I–70, running east–west via Vail, Glenwood Springs, and Grand Junction; and I–76 running northeast from Denver via Fort Morgan into Wyoming. U.S. 666 flirts with the southwest corner of the state. U.S. 160 traverses southern Colorado, while U.S. 40 accesses the northwest section.

Right turns on red lights (after making a stop) are legal in Colorado.

By Plane

Regional carriers include Mesa, Midwest Express, Delta/SkyWest, and United Express and Western Pacific.

By Train

Amtrak (☎ 800/872–7245), the U.S. passenger rail system, has daily service to Denver's Union Station. The railroad, of course, helped to shape and develop the American West, and it's still a way to see the state at leisure. The westbound route to California cuts through the Glenwood Canyon.

Contacts and Resources

Emergencies

Ambulance (☎ 911). **Fire** (☎ 911). **Police** (☎ 911). For hospitals and referral services, *see* the individual A to Z sections, *above*.

Fishing

Fishing is legal year-round (though several restrictions apply in Rocky Mountain National Park), but you must obtain a license. Fees for nonresidents are $40.25 annually, $18.25 for a five-day period, and $5.25 for a single day. For more information, including the "Fishing Hotspots" and "Watchable Wildlife" booklets, contact the **Colorado Division of Wildlife** (✉ 6060 Broadway, Denver 80216, ☎ 303/297–1192).

Golf

Colorado Golf Association (✉ 5655 S. Yosemite, Suite 101, Englewood 80111, ☎ 303/366–4653). ***Colorado Golf*** **magazine** (✉ 559 E. 2nd Ave., Castle Rock 80104, ☎ 303/688–8262). **Colorado Golf Resort Association** (✉ 2110 S. Ash St., Denver 80222, ☎ 303/699–4653).

Guided Tours

Gray Line of Denver (✉ Box 17646, Denver 80217, ☎ 303/289–2841 or 800/348–6877) offers two- to five-day tours of the surrounding areas. **Maupintour** (✉ Box 807, Lawrence, KS 66044, ☎ 785/843–1211 or 800/255–4266) offers a nine-day rail tour that takes in Colorado and parts of New Mexico. **Tauck Tours** (✉ 276 Post Rd. W, Westport, CT 06880, ☎ 203/226–6911 or 800/468–2825) offers an eight-day tour of the state. If your time is limited or if the entire itinerary doesn't appeal to you, you can take only part of the tour (at least 50%) for a slight surcharge.

Hiking and Backpacking

Bureau of Land Management (☎ 970/947–2800) has information on Colorado's sterling trekking opportunities. The **U.S. Forest Service** (✉ Box 25127, Lakewood 80225, ☎ 303/275–5350; ✉ Arapahoe, ☎ 970/498–1100; ✉ Medicine Bow/Routt, ☎ 970/879–1722; ✉ White River, ☎ 970/945–2521) is another good source of information. The 500-mi Colorado Trail winds its way from Durango to Denver and is popular with both bikers and hikers. For more information, contact the **Colorado Trail** (✉ Box 260876, Lakewood 80226, ☎ 303/526–0809).

Mountain Biking

For a free trail map, send a SASE to **Colorado Plateau Mountain Bike Trail Association** (✉ Box 4602, Grand Junction 81502, ☎ 970/249–8055). You can also obtain brochures and maps from the **Colorado State Office of the U.S. Bureau of Land Management** (✉ Dept. of the Interior, 2850 Youngfield St., Lakewood 80215, ☎ 303/239–3600). For general information on mountain biking, contact the **International Mountain Bike Association** (✉ 1121 Broadway, Suite 202, Boulder 80304, ☎ 303/545–9011).

Rafting

Rivers such as the Colorado, Arkansas, and Animas abound in Level IV and V rapids, as well as gentler stretches for beginners. For more information, contact the **Colorado River Outfitters Association** (✉ 730 Burbank St., Broomfield 80020-1658, ☎ 303/280–2554).

Skiing

For complete information on more than 30 ski areas in Colorado—from the large, world-famous resorts to the "Gems of Colorado" (smaller resorts that would be considered quite large elsewhere)—contact **Colorado Ski Country USA** (✉ 1560 Broadway, Suite 2000, Denver 80202, ☎ 303/837–0793). More adventuresome types may want to contact **Heli-Trax** (✉ Box 1560, Telluride 81435, ☎ 970/728–6990).

Snowmobiling

Colorado Snowmobile Association (✉ Box 1260, Grand Lake 80447, ☎ 800/235–4480).

Water Sports

Canoeing, kayaking, windsurfing, and sailing are available on many lakes and reservoirs, most notably **Dillon** (✉ Dillon Marina, ☎ 970/468–5100.

Visitor Information

Contact the **Colorado State Tourist Office** (☎ 800/433–2656, www.colorado.com) to receive a vacation planner. **TravelBank Colorado** (✉ Box 200594, Denver 80220, ☎ FAX 303/320–8550) will provide information via modem. In Canada, call the **U.S. Travel and Tourism Office** (✉ 480 University Ave., Suite 602, Toronto, Ontario M5G IV2, ☎ 416/595–0335, FAX 416/595–5211).

5 IDAHO

Utter the word *Idaho* and inevitably the starchy tuber, a staple of the American dinner table, comes to mind. The potato fields spread out along southeastern Idaho's fertile Snake River plain support the state's largest cash crop. But across the state in the Boise basin it's chips of a different (micro) kind that yield a technological cash crop. And deep in the heart of the Gem State is a vast wilderness area (the largest in the lower 48 states) that nurtures the popular notion that Idaho is the last true vestige of frontier wilderness.

Revised and updated by Kristin Rodine

WHEN PEOPLE TALK ABOUT IDAHO, they talk about escaping cities for the simple life. They talk about mountain biking in summer on mountains they ski on during winter. They talk about fishing the Salmon and Snake rivers and about rafting the white water through tremendous chunks of wilderness. Outdoor recreation is the unofficial state religion, and it has been embraced by thousands of new immigrants from California, Washington, New York, and elsewhere. It's why they say that if God doesn't live in Idaho, He at least has a vacation home here.

This popularity was a long time coming, however. Until the 1980s, Idaho may well have qualified as the most ignored state in the Union. Such Native American tribes as Nez Percé, the Coeur d'Alene, and the Shoshone-Bannock settled here because they found the rivers full of fish, the land fertile, and the game abundant. But, despite Lewis and Clark's trip through the state in 1805, white folks didn't show up in significant numbers until the 1840s, when pioneers on the Oregon Trail came, saw, and kept heading west. It wasn't until 1860, when a few Mormons came up from Utah at the direction of Brigham Young and settled in Franklin, that a true Anglo settlement was established.

Beginning in the 1940s J. R. Simplot, patriarch of the potato industry and now a billionaire who lives atop a hill in Boise, masterminded ways to add value to the simple potato by freezing, frying, and drying. Simplot hit pay dirt and transformed the common spud into Idaho's Famous Potatoes, an industry that earns $526 million annually. The savvy Simplot (license plate: Mr. Spud) also sunk his roots into another major Idaho industry, helping found computer- and microchip-giant Micron. Boise, the state's capital and largest city, anchors the southwestern corner of the state with a rapidly growing technology industry. Venture beyond the potato fields and the tech basin of Boise and another Idaho takes shape.

Deep in the heart of Idaho, the 2-million-acre Frank Church–River of No Return Wilderness Area (the largest such area in the lower 48 states) extends across much of the state's midsection. Here is a rugged wilderness of mountain, forest, and stream so impenetrable that even Lewis and Clark scouts, after catching an eyeful of the frothy, unforgiving Salmon River, turned back and sought a kinder, gentler route over the Continental Divide. At first glance Idaho *is* an inhospitable place. The Snake River plain in southern Idaho is high-plateau desert, a thin layer of soil over the ancient lava flows, and it's *hot* in summer. The Sawtooth Mountains, with peaks as high as 11,800 ft, loom to the north, and there it gets mighty *cold*. Northern Idaho is cloaked in dense forest and glacier-carved lakes that are revealed like jewels when the heavy winter snow melts.

These days, though, we have Gore-Tex and down and waterproofing, and what looked like misery to pioneers looks like fun to us. So, despite the cries of native Idahoans about all the newcomers arriving in their Volvos and bringing their espresso shops with them, people keep coming. Still, Idaho has just over 1 million people spread over its 82,413 square mi. That's 12 people per square mile. Considering that 400,000 Idahoans live in just 10 towns—135,000 in Boise alone—there's a lot of land out there with nobody on it. Only 0.4% of the state (215,000 acres) is considered urban, and virtually the entire eastern two-thirds is wilderness or national forest. Point all this out to Idahoans, and they'll shoot back that the population increased by 62,000 from 1980 to 1990 and that you're not from around here, or else you'd feel how crowded it's gotten.

The fact is, Idahoans do feel some pressure. They lived a certain way for nearly 150 years: They fished, hunted, did a little skiing, trapped furbearing animals, mined the hills, and cut down trees. Now people, including many newcomers, are telling them that their way of life is all wrong. There is a palpable cultural rift between new arrivals and old-timers. For now, though—aside from celebrity-filled Sun Valley, which some Idahoans look upon as a different planet—this is a meat-and-potatoes, cowboys and fishermen, back-to-basics kind of place. It is a conservative agricultural state despite the growth of manufacturing. There are the famous potatoes, of course, but also barley, sugar beets, hops, beans, and a burgeoning wine industry. Surprisingly, Idaho raises 70% of the nation's trout, and the dollar value of cattle outstrips even that of potatoes. Lumber, too, is still a tremendous industry in Idaho.

Things still operate very informally here. Unless you are conducting business, it is possible to go into any restaurant sans coat and tie and feel completely at home. This is a state where the lieutenant governor could enter a local tight jeans contest, win it, travel out of town to the national finals, and hear little more from his constituents than a chuckle.

Pleasures and Pastimes

Dining

It is virtually impossible to go hungry in Idaho, especially if you like basic American cooking. What restaurants lack in Continental flair, they make up for in volume. Meals are often served on platters big enough to be mistaken for UFOs. But what Idaho does, it does well: A good steak and a hearty breakfast can be found most anywhere. There are a few standouts in places such as Boise, Coeur d'Alene, Sandpoint, and, of course, Sun Valley, where it's possible to find food prepared with as much sophistication as you'd find in any U.S. city. Dress is predominantly casual.

CATEGORY	COST*
$$$	over $20
$$	$10–$20
$	under $10

**per person, excluding drinks, service, and 5% state sales tax*

Lodging

Although there are bed-and-breakfasts and lodge-style accommodations, particularly in resort areas, most of the lodging in southern Idaho is in Best Westerns, AmeriTels, Shilo Inns, and other national and regional motel chains on I–84 from Boise to south central Idaho and along I–86 and I–15 in the southeastern and eastern regions of the state. Boise has more than 3,000 motel rooms, and from the capital north, lodging becomes more diverse: B&Bs, guest ranches, grand old hotels, and resort lodges. Short- and long-term condominium, apartment, and home rentals are available in the Ketchum/Sun Valley area and in many of the other resort areas. Guest and dude ranches near wilderness areas offer complete vacation packages, including horseback riding, rodeos, and even cattle herding. Information on dude and guest ranches, farm vacations, and similar accommodations is available from several sources, including the Idaho Guest and Dude Ranch Association (✉ c/o John Muir, 7600 E. Blue Lake Rd., Harrison, ID 83833); and the Idaho Department of Agriculture, (✉ Division of Marketing and Development, Box 790, Boise, ID 83701, ☎ 208/334–2227) which publishes a farm and ranch recreation guide. The *Idaho Official Travel Guide* is available from the Idaho Division of Tourism Development (☞ Visitor Information *in* Idaho A to Z, *below*), and it lists accommodations across the state. Unless otherwise noted in the reviews, rooms have private baths.

CATEGORY	COST*
$$$	over $95
$$	$50–$95
$	under $50

**All prices are for a standard double room.*

Outdoor Activities and Sports

CANOEING, KAYAKING, AND RAFTING

Aficionados will tell you there is no better state for white-water kayaking, canoeing, and rafting, with the possible exception of Alaska. Canoe and raft trips range from placid to truly dangerous, and because the state is so outdoor-conscious, the public has access to virtually every body of water. The Middle Fork of the Salmon and the Payette, Selway, and Lochsa rivers are among the top white-water rafting choices. Be sure to book rafting and boating trips well in advance (☞ Guided Tours *in* Idaho A to Z, *below*); July through September are by far the most popular months.

FISHING

There's a reason Hemingway liked Idaho so much. It has some of the best fly-fishing in the world and is known for its steelhead and sturgeon. (Unfortunately, sockeye salmon have been dammed out of existence, and chinook are barely hanging on.) Locals will tell you the fishing is always good in Idaho. Maybe, but some spots are better than others. An excellent publication, *The Official Guide to Fishing in Idaho,* details boat ramp locations, regulations (taking undersize fish or not releasing in a catch-and-release area isn't just frowned upon, it's illegal), the best spots for various species, and even filleting instructions. It's available from the Idaho Department of Fish and Game, and information on guided fishing adventures is available from the Idaho Outfitters and Guides Association (☞ Fishing *in* Idaho A to Z, *below*).

By early July most years, river levels fall and the water clears, making the conditions just about right for fly fishing. With 80,000 river miles crisscrossing the state, the fishing opportunities are endless. Two prime spots to put on the must-fish list are the high-desert, cold-spring-fed Silver Creek Preserve south of Sun Valley, and Henry's Fork in Idaho's Yellowstone/Teton territory. The northern Panhandle has spun its share of big fish stories with Lake Pend Oreille's famed kamloops (large rainbows) and bull trout tipping the scales at 30 pounds (☞ Northern Idaho, *below*).

SKIING

Because the state falls in the Northwest's weather pattern, it receives plenty of winter precipitation. But as elsewhere in the West, the snow is often dry and powdery. For skiers, it's the best of both worlds. Idaho, especially Sun Valley, is known for alpine skiing. The popularity of Nordic skiing has soared, however, and many alpine resorts now offer groomed cross-country tracks at their hill's base or near the principal lodge. There are trails in many state parks. Snowshoeing is also rapidly gaining in popularity, and most cross-country areas now offer groomed snowshoe trails and equipment rentals.

Fortunately, the major downhill ski resorts now reach out to both skiers and non-skiers with a full list of activities including snowshoeing, spa and fitness programs, indoor tennis, swimming, and just plain rest and relaxation. Many areas also offer heli and Sno-Cat skiing. Check with the local U.S. Forest Service office or the chamber of commerce and the regional travel association about backcountry yurt-to-yurt ski treks. There are yurt systems in the Sawtooth National Recreation Area north of Sun Valley and the U.S. National Forest systems near Lava Hot Springs in southeastern Idaho. For the most part, though, there is plenty to do within the immediate vicinity of the ski resorts.

Exploring Idaho

Like a crazy quilt, the terrain of Idaho is a colorful patchwork of patterns, textures, and shapes. High desert plateaus, sugary sand dunes, miles of ink-black lava flows, deep river canyons, and sheer mountain wilderness are all stitched together by a lacy web of rivers and streams. In the eastern and southeastern corners of the state, Native Americans', emigrants', and explorers' trails enter the state and fan out westward. Ruts from wagons on the Oregon Trail and historic sites give testament to the frontier spirit that helped shape the face of Idaho. Dipping down and traveling near the state's southern border, the 1,000-mi-long Snake River carves a steady course as it provides the lifeblood to Idaho's famous potato fields. Along the way, waterfalls higher than Niagara Falls, springs gushing from canyon walls, and a gorge deeper than the Grand Canyon remind travelers of the humbling power behind the mighty Snake.

Roughly in the middle of the state, desert and alpine climes converge. Here, on the upper reaches of the Snake River Plain, a highly unusual mix of geologic phenomena occur. A great volcanic rift zone ripples across the state leaving in its wake spatter cones, calderas, and a blackened landscape as far as the eye can see. Then, traveling north like a living brick wall, the 2-million-acre Frank Church–River of No Return Wilderness Area holds its ground. In the thick of this dense wilderness mosaic is the nation's longest wild river, the Salmon, and its Middle Fork of white-water fame. Here is a mountain-and-forest landscape so impenetrable that even cartographers are hard-pressed to sketch roadways across much of it. Fortunately, under the expert guidance of Sacajawea, a Nez Percé guide, the Lewis and Clark expedition eventually charted a course across the lower end of Idaho's Panhandle. At the upper end of the Panhandle, mankind has managed to tame much of the lake district, transforming it into a huge watery playground.

This chapter is organized around these three geographical sections of the state: the Boise–Sun Valley loop, where desert and mountain alpine terrain meet to spectacular effect, and Boise and Sun Valley lure travelers; the East–Southeastern Triangle, east and west of the Snake River and extending to the Utah and Wyoming borders; and Northern Idaho, a deeply forested terrain claiming many of the nation's top "natural" honors, such as North America's deepest gorge—the Hells Canyon of the Snake River—and the nation's longest wild river, the Salmon.

Numbers in the text correspond to numbers in the margin and on the Idaho map.

Great Itineraries

IF YOU HAVE 3 DAYS

The giant loop tour connecting Boise to Sun Valley/Ketchum takes in an amazingly diverse mix of terrain, from stretches of arid high desert to pristine alpine mountain settings. On day one, strike out from **Boise** ① on I–84 for the two-hour drive to **Twin Falls** ③. Check out Shoshone Falls (higher than Niagara), and enjoy lunch in the town's charmingly retro downtown area. From there, head north on scenic Route 75 to Ketchum and **Sun Valley** ④. Depending on your interests and energy level, prowl the Sun Valley Resort's pedestrian mall, browse the shops and galleries along Ketchum's trendy main street, or bask in the

Idaho

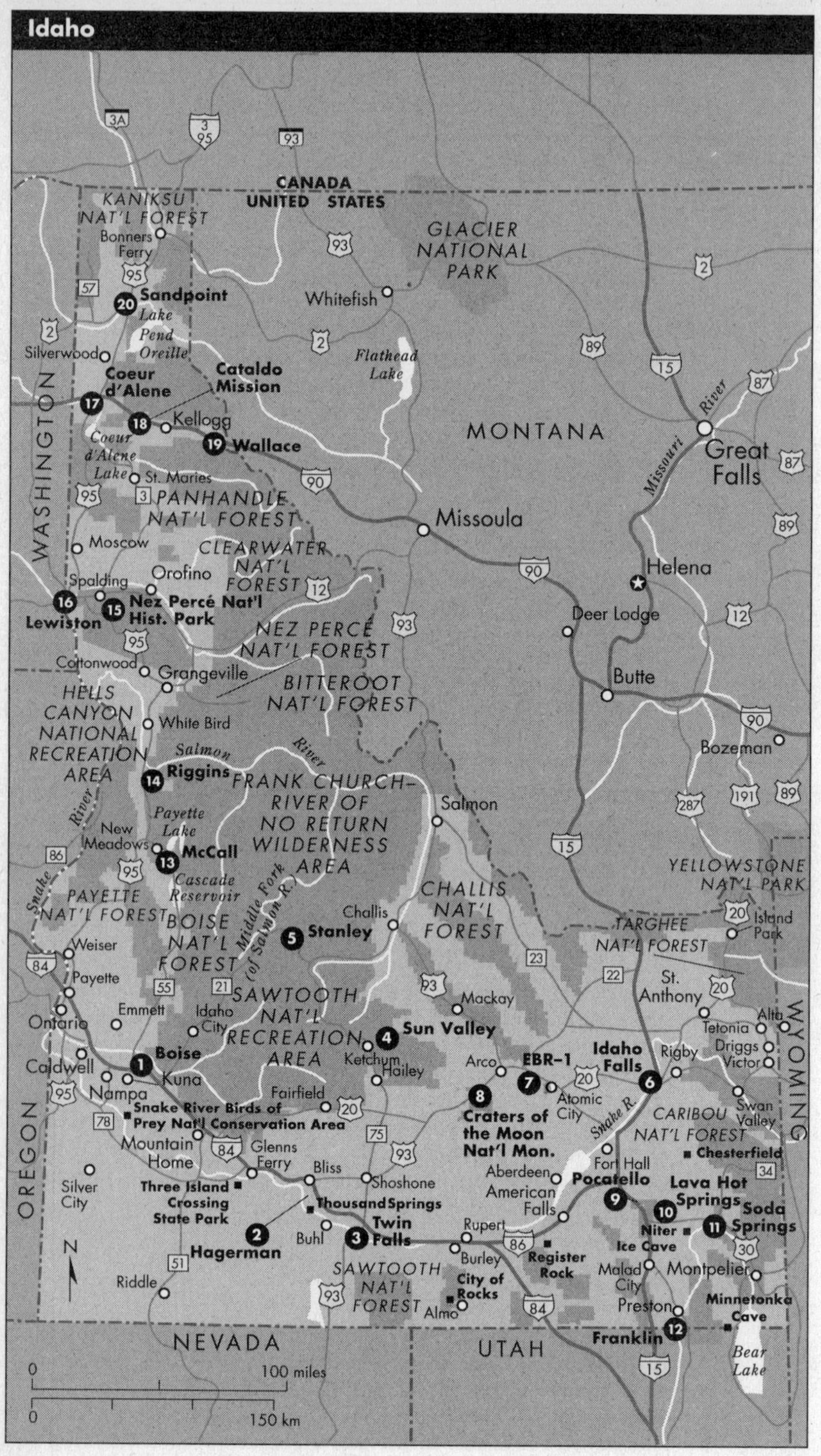

CANADA
UNITED STATES
KANIKSU NAT'L FOREST
Bonners Ferry
GLACIER NATIONAL PARK
Whitefish
20 Sandpoint
Lake Pend Oreille
Flathead Lake
Silverwood
Coeur d'Alene
Cataldo Mission
17
18 Kellogg
19 Wallace
MONTANA
Great Falls
Missouri River
Coeur d'Alene Lake
St. Maries
PANHANDLE NAT'L FOREST
WASHINGTON
Missoula
Moscow
CLEARWATER NAT'L FOREST
Helena
Spalding
Orofino
16 Lewiston
15 Nez Percé Nat'l Hist. Park
Deer Lodge
NEZ PERCÉ NAT'L FOREST
Cottonwood
Grangeville
Butte
HELLS CANYON NATIONAL RECREATION AREA
BITTEROOT NAT'L FOREST
White Bird
Salmon River
Bozeman
14 Riggins
FRANK CHURCH–RIVER OF NO RETURN WILDERNESS AREA
Salmon
Payette Lake
New Meadows
13 McCall
Cascade Reservoir
Middle Fork (of Salmon R.)
YELLOWSTONE NAT'L PARK
Snake River
PAYETTE NAT'L FOREST
BOISE NAT'L FOREST
CHALLIS NAT'L FOREST
Challis
5 Stanley
TARGHEE NAT'L FOREST
Island Park
Weiser
Payette
SAWTOOTH NAT'L RECREATION AREA
Mackay
St. Anthony
Emmett
Idaho City
Ontario
4 Sun Valley
Tetonia
Alta
WYOMING
Caldwell
1 Boise
Ketchum
Hailey
Arco
EBR-1
Idaho Falls
Rigby
Driggs
Victor
Kuna
Nampa
7
Atomic City
6
Fairfield
8 Craters of the Moon Nat'l Mon.
Snake R.
Swan Valley
Snake River Birds of Prey Nat'l Conservation Area
CARIBOU NAT'L FOREST
Mountain Home
Glenns Ferry
Fort Hall
Chesterfield
OREGON
Bliss
Shoshone
Aberdeen
Pocatello
Silver City
Three Island Crossing State Park
Thousand Springs
American Falls
9
Lava Hot Springs
10
Soda Springs
Twin Falls
3
Rupert
Niter Ice Cave
11
2 Hagerman
Buhl
Burley
Register Rock
N
SAWTOOTH NAT'L FOREST
City of Rocks
Malad City
Montpelier
Riddle
Almo
Preston
Minnetonka Cave
12 Franklin
NEVADA
UTAH
Bear Lake
0 100 miles
0 150 km

scenery along the Wood River Trails, an 18-mi network of paved trails for cycling, in-line skating, and walking. Take advantage of one of the area's fine restaurants, then sample the nightlife in Ketchum.

On day two, head into town for breakfast, then catch the sights you missed the day before. Drive north on Route 75 about 25 mi to the Galena Pass, overlooking the southern terminus of the Sawtooth range—worthy of the nickname "America's Alps"—and the beginnings of the Salmon River. All along Route 75 in the Sawtooth/White Cloud valley, which is about at the center of the Sawtooth National Recreation Area, gravel roads lead to trailheads and lakes in the Sawtooths and to the White Cloud range on the eastern side of the valley. Spend the afternoon hiking, cycling, or boating. End the day in the rough-and-tumble town of **Stanley** ⑤, with its awe-inspiring mountain backdrop.

On day three, head out on yet another gorgeous mountain road, Route 21, through the former gold mining town of Idaho City to Boise. The trip takes about three hours, leaving you plenty of time to sample some of the capital city's offerings, including the Old Idaho Penitentiary and the Morrison-Knudsen Nature Center, a capsulized tour of the area's ecosystems.

IF YOU HAVE 7 DAYS

There are many ways to spend a week in Idaho; we make two suggestions:

South Idaho: From spuds to waterfalls, lava flows to alpine peaks, this trip offers a whirlwind tour of southern Idaho's offerings. Spend your first two days in **Boise** ①. Check out the city's sights, venture out to the World Center for Birds of Prey, then sample the hands-on science displays of the Discovery Center. On day three, strike out for **Twin Falls** ③, detouring at Gooding for the Thousand Springs Scenic Route, where water gushes from the canyon walls. After checking out the town's namesake falls and charming downtown area, continue on I–84 to **Pocatello** ⑨ for the night. On day four, continue east on the freeway to Blackfoot, where you can check out the World Potato Exposition and benefit from its "free taters for out-of-staters" policy. Then take U.S. 23 north toward Arco and the land of lava and nuclear energy. From there, turn southwest on U.S. 93 toward the eerie landscape of **Craters of the Moon National Monument** ⑧. Spend a few hours exploring lava caves, learning about *pahoe* and *aa* (types of lava) and other geologic oddities and quirks of the volcanic lexicon. Then head to **Sun Valley** ④ via U.S. 93 south to U.S. 20 west and Route 75 north. Sit back, relax, and enjoy dinner outdoors at one of Ketchum's trendy bistros.

Explore the shops and trails of Ketchum/Sun Valley on day five before heading north to the stunning Sawtooth Range and **Stanley** ⑤. Spend the sixth day in this rugged mountain town doing outdoorsy things. Options include a Salmon River raft trip or a hiking, horseback, or fishing excursion in the Sawtooths or White Cloud Mountains. The award for the best short trail (under 5 mi round trip) with a view might go to the Fishhook Trail in the Redfish Lake area of the Sawtooths, which takes hikers on a gentle cruise along Fishhook Creek to a panorama of beaver ponds, a wildflower meadow, and snowcapped peaks. On day seven, head southwest on scenic Route 21 to return to Boise. At the end of this trip, travelers of this alpine-lava jaunt may feel that they have been to the moon and back.

Northern Idaho: A second seven-day trip encompasses the chasm dubbed Hell's Canyon as well as three of the state's most scenic lakes—Payette, Coeur d'Alene, and Pend Oreille—each accompanied by a charming resort town. Most of the trip follows U.S. 95. Start in **McCall** ⑬, about 108 mi north of Boise via scenic Route 55. Walk the white sand beaches of Payette Lake, play a round of golf, watch other tourists from a sidewalk café or enjoy one of the many hiking trails in the surrounding forest. On day two, continue north on Route 55 and U.S. 95 to **Riggins** ⑭, a tiny town with big recreational options. On the third day, use Riggins as your base for a raft trip on the Salmon or a jet boat or float trip in Hells Canyon National Recreation Area.

On day four, climb north on U.S. 95 over White Bird Summit, overlooking the valley where the Nez Percé War began. From there, the highway plunges rapidly into the Camas Prairie. At **Spalding,** tour the visitor center at the **Nez Percé National Historical Park** ⑮ to learn more about the tribe's history. Continue on to **Lewiston** ⑯, the nation's largest inland port. Or head straight for **Moscow,** a college town with a charming downtown historic district. End the day in **Coeur d'Alene** ⑰, where you can spend the next two nights.

Start the fifth day with an early deck-side breakfast along the waterfront. Spend the day exploring the Coeur d'Alene area: Stroll the world's longest floating boardwalk, take a boat ride on the lovely lake, check out the town's many shops and galleries, or pedal along the paved Centennial Trail. Make the sixth day a "play day" at **Silverwood Amusement Park,** Idaho's one and only such facility, located in Athol 14 mi north of Coeur d'Alene. The park has not only the requisite eight-story roller coaster, but a perfectly reconstructed turn-of-the-20th-century mining town and rides on a narrow-gauge steam train. Wrap up your visit by mid-afternoon, visit nearby **Cataldo Mission** ⑱, and drive north on U.S. 95 to spend the night in **Sandpoint** ⑳, nestled next to Lake Pend Oreille.

On day seven, you can take a chairlift ride to the top of the ski mountain at Schweitzer Mountain Ski Resort—11 mi northwest of Sandpoint—shop in Sandpoint, and end the day with a quiet, relaxing dinner there.

When to Tour Idaho

The best time to visit Idaho and be assured of easy access to most parts of the state is during the summer and fall months. This is when many of the state's premier festivals and special events take place. Some of the top picks are the Boise River Festival in late June, the Old-Time Fiddlers' Contest in Weiser in June, the Teton Valley Hot Air Balloon Festival around July 4 in Driggs, and the Sun Valley outdoor ice shows with former Olympians and professional figure skaters carving the ice from June through September. With the largest concentration of Basques in the United States calling southern Idaho home since the 1800s, the small town of Gooding celebrates Basque heritage with music, dancing, and food during July. Shelley, in Southeastern Idaho, marks Idaho Spud Day in September. In Idaho's north-central lake district, the wild rice harvest takes place at Heyburn State Park near St. Maries in the fall.

Summer and fall are also opportune times to take advantage of some of the best outdoor diversions that the state has to offer—blue-ribbon fishing and white-water rafting. To be assured of milder weather, the safest bet is to schedule hiking, backpacking, and white-water rafting after July 4. By this date, the snow covering mountain hiking trails is melting and trails are relatively dry underfoot. The water warms up by mid-July as well, making rafting, kayaking, sailing, and other water activities more comfortable.

There are a few exceptions to the summer-fall rule for visiting Idaho. In the arid lava-flow, desert, and Snake River Plain areas, summer heats up. So, the best time to visit is late spring to early summer. In August at the volcanic rift zone of Craters of the Moon National Monument, daytime temperatures percolate in the 90s and feel hotter reflecting off the pitch-black lava. Similar mid-summer heat is found in the south-central and Owyhee uplands area in the southwestern corner of the state.

Many travelers are lured to Idaho by the powdery snow brought by winter storms. As a rule, if you come in the winter, be prepared to stay put: Sudden snowstorms can close mountain passes and make tire chains a mandatory automotive accessory. Winter offers some notable indoor attractions as well, including Moscow's Lionel Hampton Jazz Festival in February and the McCall Winter Carnival, which fills the resort town with world-class ice sculptures in late January.

When planning an itinerary, also take into consideration seasonal phenomena. For diehard anglers, when the snow flies, it means winter runs and prime fishing for steelhead trout in the Middle Fork of the Salmon River, and Bear Lake sardines, known as Bonneville Cisco. Dubbed "Niagara of the West," the 212-ft Shoshone Falls in south-central Idaho is at its peak in March and April, before the summer growing season kicks in and irrigation diverts much of the water. Bird-watchers flock to Harriman State Park during the winter, when some 300–400 Rocky Mountain Trumpeter swans make a layover there.

BOISE–SUN VALLEY LOOP

Most Idaho travelers' paths lead to Boise. It's the state's capital, its largest city, corporate headquarters, and cultural center. And it boasts outstanding natural amenities and variety, with a river flowing through it, a ski area just 16 mi away, and cool forests and desert sand dunes each within a short drive. Boise also offers two scenic routes to southern Idaho's other top draw, Sun Valley.

South central Idaho was a sleepy backwater, home to a few ranchers and Basque shepherds until 1935, when Union Pacific Railroad chief W. Averell Harriman realized he needed more riders for his trains. He hired a European count, who presumably understood what makes for a good ski area, to scout the West and come up with a site for a resort. The chosen spot was Ketchum, Idaho, and the result was Sun Valley. Although Twin Falls and the Magic Valley around it are still largely agricultural, growing beans and hops, there is considerable tourism, spurred by Sun Valley's presence 80 mi north. And the Oregon Trail and scenic Thousand Springs area in the Snake River Valley are interesting stops in their own right.

The Boise–Sun Valley Loop tour begins in the state's capital, then follows the course of the Snake River east to Twin Falls before veering north to the Wood River Valley, where Sun Valley and Ketchum mark the southernmost reaches of the region's alpine terrain. Stanley, in the Sawtooth Range, marks the northernmost stop on the tour and offers a scenic route back to Boise.

Boise

❶ *108 mi south from McCall via Route 55; 131 mi from Twin Falls via I–84 west; 157 mi from Ketchum/Sun Valley via Route 77 south, U.S. 26 west, and I–84 west; 43 mi from the Oregon border via I–84 east.*

"It's tough to be the object of so much swooning, so much rosy wooing . . . ," wrote *Idaho Statesman* reporter Marianne Flagg in 1992. "Now please stop writing about us." Nestled against foothills and riverbanks, with a desert to the south and alpine forests to the north, Boise is worried that its "discovery" will bring an end to its old (and pretty good) quality of life. A number of major corporate headquarters, including Boise Cascade and Micron Technology, are here, and things have been moving along swimmingly for a number of years.

Make no mistake, though: Even with 135,000 people and a university, Boise still functions as a small town. People know one another and exchange waves as they whiz by on their in-line skates or mountain bikes. A murder, a very rare event, is shattering news. As the state's capital and largest city, it boasts cultural attractions and dining variety found in few communities of its size.

The best place to start your exploration of Boise is at the **state capitol** (Capitol Blvd. and Jefferson St.), which is a scale replica of the Capitol in Washington, D.C. You can walk in the main rotunda during business hours. The rest of the city fans out from the capitol steps. From here, walk northwest to 8th Street, the heart of downtown. Streets on both sides of 8th are lined with cafés, businesses, and shops (☞ Shopping, *below*). After exploring the capitol area, head east on Warm Springs Avenue past mansions heated by underground hot springs.

Warm Springs Avenue leads to the **Old Idaho Penitentiary,** one of only three territorial prisons still standing. Built in 1870, the prison was used until 1974 without much improvement in conditions. Things became so intolerable that prisoners staged a series of rebellions starting in the 1960s. The final revolt, in 1973, prompted the move to a more modern facility. The cell blocks have been left exactly as they were after the riot. Scorched stone walls, tiny cells with calendars still in place, and metal bunks evoke the spirit of the place. A self-guided tour takes at least 90 minutes. The Idaho Botanical Gardens next door offer an attractive change of scenery. ✉ *2445 Old Penitentiary Rd., off Warm Springs Ave.,* ☎ *208/368–6080 or 208/334–2844.* 🎫 *$4.* ⏲ *Sept.–May, daily noon–5; Memorial Day–Labor Day, daily 10–5.*

The **Morrison-Knudsen Nature Center** behind the state's Department of Fish and Game headquarters features a man-made Idaho stream in a kind of outdoor natural museum. The stream has been constructed so that viewers can look from above and below the water's surface to see fish swimming, laying eggs, and doing what fish do. Walking trails pass a sampling of local ecosystems, from a wetlands pond to a high desert plain. ✉ *600 S. Walnut Ave., off Warm Springs Ave.,* ☎ *208/334–2225.* 🎫 *Donations accepted.* ⏲ *Daily sunrise–sunset.*

The **Idaho Historical Museum** surveys Idaho's past and includes very detailed reconstructions of building interiors that make accompanying text about the pioneer days come to life; a working wood shop is open Saturday from 11 to 3. ✉ *Julia Davis Park, 610 Julia Davis Dr., off Capitol Blvd.,* ☎ *208/334–2120.* 🎫 *Free.* ⏲ *Mon.–Sat. 9–5, Sun. 1–5.*

Julia Davis Park is also the spot to catch the Boise Tours train (☞ Guided Tours *in* Boise–Sun Valley Loop A to Z, *below*), but perhaps it's most notable as a key gateway to the renowned **Boise River Greenbelt,** which runs along both banks of the river. In all, there are about 19 mi of paved pathways linking parks and attractions. The trails are also favorites of in-line skaters, bicyclists, walkers, and joggers.

Located on the northern edge of Julia Davis Park, the **Discovery Center of Idaho** is a hands-on science museums for children (and adults who act like children). Almost every exhibit moves, talks, or otherwise acts up in response to a visitor's interaction with it. ✉ *131 Myrtle St.,* ☎ *208/343–9895.* 🎫 *$4.* ⏲ *Tues.–Sat. 10–5, Sun. noon–5.*

OFF THE BEATEN PATH

CHATEAU STE. CHAPELLE – Idaho's largest winery, and the oldest of the local grape-growing operations, is about 30 mi west of Boise in the fertile Sunny Slope region. Best known for its Rieslings, the winery also has award-winning cabernet and merlot. Its hilltop tasting room offers lovely views, a gift shop, and a free sampling of white and red wines. A grassy amphitheater is the scene of jazz concerts each summer Saturday. ✉ *19348 Lowell Rd., Caldwell; From I–84 west of Boise, take the Nampa Blvd. exit and follow signs to Hwy. 55 west; continue 12 mi to Lowell Rd.,* ☎ *208/459–7222.* ⏲ *Mon.–Sat. 10–6, Sun. noon–5.*

Dining and Lodging

$$–$$$ ✕ **Peter Schott's New American Cuisine.** The dining room in the Sun Valley Resort might argue the point, but this casually elegant restaurant is generally regarded as the best restaurant in Idaho. Its light walls, fireplace, and bookshelves create an intimate feel. Schott ran the restaurants at Sun Valley Resort after immigrating from Austria. Now a local celebrity with his own two-minute cooking show, Schott calls his food New American cuisine, but he also throws in a little Northern Italian. Fresh fish dominates the menu, and the wine list is complete (155 selections) but not extravagant. It's possible for two people to have dinner and a bottle of wine for $70 (not including tip). The restaurant is closed for renovations until September 2000. ✉ *928 Main St.,* ☎ *208/336–9100. AE, D, DC, MC, V. Closed Sun. No lunch.*

$$–$$$ ✕ **Sandpiper.** Candlelight, high ceilings, oak tables, and live music on weekends make this a popular gathering place for fine dining. Steaks, seafood, and prime rib are the specialties. ✉ *1100 W. Jefferson St.,* ☎ *208/344–8911. AE, D, DC, MC, V. No lunch Sun.*

$–$$$ ✕ **Doughty's Bistro.** This downtown restaurant's marble entry and high ceiling betray its history as a bank. The muted colors and ample space between tables provide a fine atmosphere for casual, intimate dining. Beautifully prepared dishes offer innovative ingredients and stylish presentations without ever lapsing into pretentiousness. Dishes draw on influences from all over the globe, from Tex-Mex to Asia. ✉ *199 N. 8th St.,* ☎ *208/366–7897. MC, V.*

$–$$ ✕ **Bar Gernika Basque Pub & Eatery.** This popular bar and café is a convenient downtown window on Idaho's long history of Basque culture. Many people come for the exotic Basque food, which features spicy meats, but burgers are also served, as are specialty coffees. You may have to squeeze yourself into this narrow, redbrick, corner café if you go on a weekend night. ✉ *202 S. Capitol Blvd., at Grove St.,* ☎ *208/244–2175. AE, MC, V. Closed Sun.*

$–$$ ✕ **Harrison Hollow Brewhouse.** This brew pub is a favorite stop for skiers heading to or returning from Bogus Basin. The building's massive timbers are echoed by huge portions of tasty food, from overstuffed sandwiches to red beans and rice. A central fireplace adds to the ski-lodge atmosphere. Speakers pour forth blues and R&B because an owner loves them. ✉ *24555 Harrison Hollow Rd.,* ☎ *208/343–6820. AE, MC, V.*

$–$$ ✕ **Tablerock Brew Pub and Grill.** This microbrewery makes some of the best beer in Idaho, and it has managed to turn that skill into a happening restaurant, especially on weekend nights. Neon lights, long, high tables, an energetic staff and loud pop music create a kinetic atmosphere. Food is basic—onion rings, chili, salads, and burgers—but it is served in great heaps. ✉ *705 Fulton St.,* ☎ *208/342–0944. AE, D, DC, MC, V.*

$$–$$$ ★ **Idaho Heritage Inn.** Tom and Phyllis Lupher operate this B&B in a former governor's mansion about 1 mi east of downtown. Each room is very different, but all have names with political themes. Antiques, wallpaper, and old-style bed frames retain an early 1900s feel. The top-floor room, carved out of the attic, is very private. A full breakfast is included. ✉ *109 W. Idaho St., 83702,* ☎ *208/342–8066. 6 rooms. Dining room. AE, D, MC, V.*

$$–$$$ **Owyhee Plaza.** Several Hawaiians got lost in the Idaho wilderness in the 1800s and became local legend. Idahoans, not knowing how to spell Hawaii, settled on Owyhee, now the name of a county and this hotel, built in 1910. Refurbished during the 1950s, the building lost a little of its charm, but its old glory can still be seen in its giant light fixtures and dark wood paneling. ✉ *1109 Main St., 83702,* ☎ *208/343–4611 or 800/233–4611,* FAX *208/381–0695. 100 rooms. 2 restaurants, bar, pool, beauty salon, meeting rooms. AE, MC, V.*

Nightlife and the Arts

The **Morrison Center for the Performing Arts** (✉ 2101 Campus La., ☎ 208/385–1609) offers one of the most extensive arts programs in any city this size. The Boise Opera Company, Ballet Idaho, the Boise Philharmonic, and the Boise Master Chorale all have full season programs, and touring Broadway productions make frequent stops here. In summer, a riverside amphitheater hosts nationally acclaimed productions of the **Idaho Shakespeare Festival** (✉ 5657 Warm Springs Ave., ☎ 208/336–9221).

In addition to the lively brew pubs Harrison Hollow and Tablerock (☞ Dining and Lodging, *above*), there are several bars that offer live jazz and pop on weekends in the neighborhood around 6th and West Idaho streets, and in the 8th Street Marketplace area downtown.

The **Blues Bouquet** (✉ 1010 W. Main St., ☎ 208/345–6605) features a beautiful mahogany bar, a small dance floor, and a diverse sampling of national and local blues artists, from Taj Mahal to Mitch Ryder. **The Interlude** (✉ 213 N. 8th St., ☎ 208/342–9593) is a Capitol hangout affectionately known as "the Tube." One step inside this long, narrow bar will tell you why. This spot draws lawyers, legislators, and other locals to discuss the issues of the day and watch sports on TV.

Outdoor Activities and Sports

CYCLING

The Greenbelt is a great place to cycle. Mountain biking is popular on the hills just outside central Boise. Trails include the 8th Street Extension (north on 8th St. to where the pavement ends) and Cartwright Road (Harrison Blvd. north to Hill Rd., to Bogus Basin Rd., then left on Cartwright Rd.). **Idaho Tandem Cyclery** (✉ 3139 N. Cole Rd., ☎ 208/375–1107) offers bicycles built for two or more. **Wheels R Fun** (✉ 831 S. 13th St., at Shoreline Park, ☎ 208/343–8228) rents bicycles.

GOLF

Quail Hollow (✉ 4520 N. 36th St., ☎ 208/344–7807), **Shadow Valley** (✉ 15711 Rte. 55, ☎ 208/939–6699), and **Warm Springs** (✉ 2495 Warm Springs Ave., ☎ 208/343–5661) all have 18-hole courses.

SKIING

Only 16 mi north of town, **Bogus Basin** (✉ 2405 Bogus Basin Rd., 83702, ☎ 208/332–5151 or 800/367–4397) is Boise's winter backyard playground. It's known for night skiing, which leads suit-clad executives to climb into their 4×4s and change into ski gear on the way. There are some serious black diamond runs as well as a healthy proportion of tame beginner trails. The vertical drop is 1,800 ft; six double chairs and four rope tows serve 48 runs, 17 of which are lighted.

TUBING

In summer, thousands of people go tubing—sitting in an inner tube and floating down the river. A special bus service from **Ann Morrison Park** (✉ Americana Blvd. between Owyhee St. and Capitol Blvd.) carries tubers to Barber Park, about 6 mi to the east across the Ada County line. From there, floaters drift back to Ann Morrison Park. Across from the park, Wheels R Fun (☞ Cycling, *above*) rents inner tubes.

Shopping

SHOPPING MALLS/DISTRICTS

A rich selection of stores lines 8th Street downtown. The **8th Street Shops** (✉ 8th St., between Grove and Broad Sts.) make up a restored turn-of-the-century block with specialty shops and small restaurants. The **8th Street Marketplace** (✉ Capitol Blvd. and Front St.), a brick warehouse converted into more than 30 stores, sits on the east side of 8th Street across from the convention center. In the same vicinity, **Capitol Terrace** (✉ Idaho and Main Sts., ☎ 208/384–3901) resembles a New Orleans French Quarter building with a balcony level of shops. On the west side of town, **Boise Towne Square** (✉ Franklin and Cole Rds., off I–84, Exits 49 or 50, ☎ 208/336–2631), a conventional 185-store mall, has the usual lineup of retailers and Pendleton (☎ 800/743–9606), the Northwest's maker of sought-after woolens. **Boise Factory Outlets** (✉ Gowen Rd., off I–84, Exit 57, ☎ 208/331–5000) is stretched out along the interstate in southeast Boise.

In Hyde Park, around the intersection of 13th and Eastman streets, just northwest of the state capitol, antiques shops abound, and several cafés and specialty stores with classic awnings and decorated windows vie for your attention.

SPECIALTY SHOPS

The **Book Shop** (✉ 906 W. Main St., ☎ 208/342–2659) has a huge selection of books, including the best array of books about Idaho in the state.

The **Idaho Angler** (✉ 1033 W. Bannock St., ☎ 208/389–9957) boasts the state's largest selection of fly-fishing equipment, including a broad range of gear to rent. Well-informed staff offer classes, personal instruction, and guided fishing trips.

OFF THE BEATEN PATH

WORLD CENTER FOR BIRDS OF PREY – The center, headquarters for a conservation project and educational program run by the Peregrine Fund, has species such as the harpy eagle and peregrine falcon on view. Guided 90-minute tours leave from the visitors' center throughout the day. Take Exit 50 off I–84, head south for 6 mi on South Cole Road, and follow the signs. ✉ *5666 W. Flying Hawk La.,* ☎ *208/362–8687.* 💳 *$4.* ⏲ *Mar.–Oct., daily 9–5; Nov.–Feb., daily 10–4.*

To see falcons and eagles in their wild habitat, drive another 24 mi south to the **Snake River Birds of Prey Natural Conservation Area,** 482,640 acres administered by the Bureau of Land Management (☎ 208/384–3056), where many kinds of eagles, ospreys, hawks, and falcons nest and soar. Take I–84 west to Route 69 south; past Kuna, the road is unimproved. Although not easily accessible, the conservation area has become a key stop for those fascinated by North American raptors. You can get a closer look at falcons and eagles, their nests, and Native American petroglyphs on two-hour to four-day tours offered by

Whitewater Shop River Tours (✉ 252 N. Meridian Rd., Kuna 83634, ☎ 208/922–5285). Some tours are by river, some by land, some both; fares run from $40 to $100.

Hagerman

❷ *91 mi from Boise via I–84 east.*

Hagerman is home of the "world-famous" Idaho state fossil, a complete skeleton of a small Ice Age horse. On the way, look for large, round boulders scattered over the landscape. These "melon rocks" were eroded into that shape and dumped here by the Bonneville flood.

The **Idaho State Bank building** (✉ State and Hagerman Sts.) dates from 1887 and has served as a general store between stints as a bank. The teller area has been restored to a wooden and brass showplace, just the way a bank would have looked in the 1880s, so it's worth stopping in just to look around or to transact some business.

The **Hagerman Fossil Beds National Monument** covers 4,000 acres and offers a look at fossil beds along the west side of the Snake River canyon. The visitor center, on U.S. 30 across from Hagerman High Schol, houses more than 150 fossils of the famous Hagerman horse, *Equus simplicidens,* along with fossils from 90 other distinct species, from camels to turtles. Guided tours of the Pliocene Age (3.4 million years old) fossil beds are available. ✉ *221 N. State St.,* ☎ *208/837–4793.* 🎫 *Free.* 🕑 *Visitor center: Weekdays 8–5.*

Frank Lloyd Wright, perhaps the greatest architect of the 20th century, believed that buildings should harmonize with their sites. An excellent example of this philosophy, Idaho's only **Frank Lloyd Wright house,** is a private residence about 2½ mi west of Hagerman off U.S. 30. At the Snake River Pottery sign, just west of the Malad River Bridge, turn left and go 1½ mi. It's to the left, a stone masterpiece built into the hillside overlooking the Snake River and its magnificent canyon. For the best view, go as far as the driveway of Snake River Pottery (the oldest producer of pottery in Idaho), then head back up the road. (The house can also be seen from an overlook 1 mi farther uphill on U.S. 30.) Since it's a private home, please don't disturb the occupants.

En Route From Hagerman, take U.S. 30 east; the road gradually tumbles into the Snake River canyon until it is nearly level with the river at the Thousand Springs area. Here, dozens of springs literally pour out of the north canyon wall. Geologists think the water comes from mountains to the north and that it may take up to 100 years for it to make the underground journey to the Snake. It's possible to tour the area by boat on 1½-hour excursions offered by **Thousand Springs Tours** (✉ Box 449, Hagerman 83332, ☎ 208/837–9006 or 800/838–1096) several times daily, mid-April–September. Reservations are strongly recommended and necessary off-season; the fare is $24. Boats leave from **Sligar's Thousand Springs Resort** (✉ 18734 U.S. 30, ☎ 208/837–4987)—near where several swimming-pool operators have set up hot-springs pools and river-swimming areas—and motor about 5 mi up the Snake. They stop at various points, including eddies in which the water is a clear green, a favorite spot for scuba divers.

Twin Falls

❸ *35 mi from Hagerman via U.S. 30 east.*

Driving into Twin Falls feels like putting on a comfortable sweater. It is perhaps as all-American a city as you'll find anywhere. After a shopping mall was built just on the town side of the Perrine Bridge, downtown merchants banded together to take on the new competition. The result is a downtown straight out of the 1950s, with neon signs, a score of small shops, and some new eateries and bars. The massive Greek Revival **courthouse** (✉ 425 Shoshone St. N) faces a band shell in the park across the street, home to summertime concerts. The downtown's only drawback is its maddening adherence to the classic Mormon street grid. There are, for example, four 3rd avenues, one for each point on the compass.

Twin Falls used to be famous as the site of two **falls:** Shoshone Falls, 52 ft higher than Niagara, and the Twin Falls. Snake River dams have greatly reduced the flow over these once-majestic attractions, but in the spring, during the height of the snowmelt, the falls regain their former glory. Traveling on U.S. 93 south, cross the Snake on the I. B. Perrine Bridge; just after the river look for signs to the right (or west) and follow Canyon Springs Road about ½ mi west to a turnoff for the **Centennial Waterfront Park** (☏ 208/733–3974). The park, open from sunrise to sunset, offers the only river access from this area. It provides access to the bridge's pedestrian walkway, which offers outstanding views of the Snake River Gorge. To view Shoshone Falls, after the Perrine Bridge travel about 1 mi south to Falls Avenue. Turn left (east) and travel another 2 mi to 3300 East Road, which leads to **Shoshone Falls Park,** a prime falls-viewing area along the southern rim. Entry costs $3 per vehicle. Another 3 mi east on Falls Avenue and off 3500 East Road, Idaho Power Company maintains a viewing area of Twin Falls, **Twin Falls Park** (☏ 208/773–3974).

Dining and Lodging

$$–$$$ ✕ **Rock Creek.** This steak, prime rib, and seafood house west of downtown is a throwback to the days when cholesterol and red meat reigned. With a dark red interior, thick booths, and a massive salad bar, it's known for its wide selection of single-malt whiskeys and vintage ports and for the most comprehensive wine list in town. ✉ *200 Addison Ave. W,* ☏ *208/734–4154. AE, D, MC, V. No lunch.*

$–$$ ✕ **A'roma.** Opened by Mark and Dawn Makin in 1985, when downtown Twin Falls was struggling, this small Italian restaurant has become a local favorite by serving such fresh, zesty standards as lasagna, ravioli, and pizza. Tablecloths are plastic and the decor simple, but service is friendly and the food reliable. ✉ *147 Shoshone St. N,* ☏ *208/733–0167. D, MC, V. Closed Sun.*

$ ★ ✕ **Buffalo Café.** Ask anybody in town where to go for breakfast, and you'll get the same answer. This tiny café, with a twin in Sun Valley, is squeezed next to a tire store, across from a truck lot surrounded by barbed wire. You can sit at the counter or at one of 10 tables, but if you go on Sunday, expect to wait. The house specialty is the Buffalo Chip, a concoction of eggs, fried potatoes, cheese, bacon, peppers, and onion. (The brave can ask for a Mexi-chip, made with spicy chorizo sausage.) A half order should fill most stomachs. ✉ *218 4th Ave. W,* ☏ *208/734–0271. No credit cards. No dinner.*

$$ 🏨 **AmeriTel Inn–Twin Falls.** Built in 1993 and expanded in 1995, this motel offers large rooms with dark wood furnishings and a color scheme of blue-green florals and mauves. Some units feature whirlpool tubs. Fresh-baked cookies are served in the evening and a generous Continental breakfast in the morning. ✉ *1377 Blue Lakes Blvd. N, 83301,* ☏ *208/736–8000 or 800/822–8946,* FAX *208/734–7777. 118 rooms. Kitchenettes, indoor pool, hot tub, exercise room, meeting room. AE, D, DC, MC, V.*

$$ 🏨 **Best Western Springs Park Hotel.** This property boasts very well-kept rooms that are larger than those at most other motels. Some units

have a balcony with a pool view. ✉ *1357 Blue Lakes Blvd. N, 83301,* ☎ *208/734–5000 or 800/727–5003,* FAX *208/734–5000. 112 rooms. Restaurant, bar, pool. AE, D, DC, MC, V.*

$ **Best Western–Apollo Motor Inn.** This smaller motel offers clean, reliable rooms but no restaurant or lounge. A Continental breakfast is served in the lobby, and restaurants are a short walk away. ✉ *296 Addison Ave. W, 83301,* ☎ *208/733–2010 or 800/528–1234. 50 rooms. Hot tub. AE, D, DC, MC, V.*

Nightlife and the Arts

Dunken's (✉ 102 Main Ave., ☎ 208/733–8114), Tim Jones's homage to microbreweries, has become a regular stop for downtown workers. There are 19 taps, covering most of the better Northwest brews. Many regulars come for a beer, some good conversation, and a few games of cribbage, dominoes, or chess. If you bring an out-of-town newspaper, Jones will be your friend for life.

Outdoor Activities and Sports

Canyon Springs (✉ Canyon Springs Rd., ☎ 208/734–7609) sits on the south rim of the Snake River canyon with a breathtaking view and 18 holes.

The **City of Rocks National Reserve** (☎ 208/824–5519), 77 mi southeast of Twin Falls via I–84 and Route 27, draws European and American rock climbers to its sheer faces. The rock formations, reaching 100–300 ft, tower out of the desert floor and are considered some of the most challenging in the American West.

Shopping

Downtown Twin Falls has a variety of small stores. Shopping along Main Avenue around the intersection with Shoshone Street is much the way shopping in small American towns used to be before malls arrived. If you're hankering for a mall, the **Magic Valley Mall** (✉ 1485 Pole Line Rd., ☎ 208/733–3000) is near the Perrine Bridge.

En Route U.S. 93 crosses the Perrine Bridge just north of Twin Falls. Unsuspecting travelers may feel a sudden sense of vertigo as they cross the massive Snake River canyon, justly known for its drama. (A similar effect occurs to travelers over the Hansen Memorial Bridge, by which U.S. 50 crosses the valley a few miles east of town via I–84.) The flat plain to the north simply falls away into the chasm below. About 15,000 years ago, a massive inland sea, Lake Bonneville (the remnant of which is the Great Salt Lake), crashed through its natural dikes in southeast Idaho and poured into the Snake. For about six weeks, a volume of water many times greater than the flow of the Amazon acted like a giant plow as it thundered down the Snake and carved the canyon.

Sun Valley/Ketchum

❹ *82 mi north from Twin Falls via Route 75 and U.S. 93.*

Since the late 1930s and especially after World War II, Sun Valley has been one of the premier ski destinations in the country. The precursor of later resorts, it helped to create the idea that the slopes used for skiing in the winter could also draw visitors for summer activities. Today Sun Valley and its neighbor, Ketchum, are gold-plated resort towns with a gentrified Western feel. The nearby Wood River is also a haven for outdoor activities, which residents pursue with manic energy.

Sightseeing in the area is largely limited to mountain vistas, visiting movie stars, and **Hemingway's grave site** in the Ketchum cemetery (✉ off Rte. 75 near 10th St.), a small memorial to him just north of the Sun Valley resort up Sun Valley Road.

Dining and Lodging

$$$ ✕ **Michel's Christiania.** This is as old-line as Sun Valley gets. Hemingway had cocktails here during his final months. Michel Rudigoz, a former U.S. ski-team coach, took over the chalet-style restaurant in 1994, reinvigorating the menu with traditional French cuisine. The atmosphere blends white-linen elegance with old timbers and gigantic wrought-iron chandeliers. Idaho ruby-red trout is sautéed then drizzled with cream and dusted with toasted hazelnuts. Elk, duckling, and fresh seafood also receive dramatic presentations. ✉ *303 Walnut Ave., Ketchum,* ☎ *208/726–3388. AE, D, MC, V.*

$$$ ✕ **A Winter's Feast.** No doubt about it, this is different. The owner calls it gourmet yurt dining. Okay, well, this is Sun Valley. The idea here is to cross-country ski or hike along an easy trail for about ½ mi, take the skis off, enter an authentic Mongolian yurt, and indulge in a five-course gourmet meal. You're supposed to feel as if you're eating in the wilds, but the lights shining from million-dollar homes on the hill detract from the intended ruggedness. The food is expertly created by Colleen Crain. Entrées include home-smoked salmon, beef tenderloin, and rack of lamb. ✉ *Warm Springs Golf Course, Warm Springs Rd., 1 mi west of Ketchum, Ketchum,* ☎ *208/788–7655. Reservations essential. MC, V.*

$$–$$$ ✕ **Globus.** The menu borrows from Asia with inventive fare spanning the culinary corridor from Thailand and China to India. Diners dive into huge white porcelain bowls mounded with steaming Hunan chili beef, sizzling twice-cooked pork, and pungent vegetarian Thai green curry. Homemade desserts such as five-spice ice cream cool down the palate. ✉ *291 6th St., Ketchum,* ☎ *208/726–1301. AE, D, MC, V. No lunch.*

$–$$ ✕ **Desperado's.** For well-prepared fresh Mexican food head to this informal restaurant in the heart of Ketchum. Huge fish burritos, black beans, and four kinds of salsa headline the menu, which offers low-fat options. The restaurant also has a steady carry-out business. ✉ *4th St. and Washington Ave.,* ☎ *208/726–3068. AE, D, MC, V.*

$–$$ ✕ **Gretchen's.** This rustic, cozy restaurant offers breakfast, lunch, and dinner overlooking the ice rink inside the Sun Valley Lodge. The menu features well-prepared entrées such as fresh salmon, trout, and zesty pasta dishes, as well as more casual sandwich-and-salad fare. The hamburgers are enormous, and the young staff is very enthusiastic. ✉ *Lodge, Sun Valley Village,* ☎ *208/622–2144. AE, MC, V.*

$ ✕ **Perry's.** The Belgian waffles in this café are favorites of local skiers who want a carbohydrate and sugar rush. Hot oatmeal, cereal, yogurt parfaits, and legendary cakelike muffins round out the breakfast menu. Hot and cold sandwiches, soups, and a selection of salads are offered for lunch, which lasts until 5:30 PM. Take-out service is available. ✉ *131 W. 4th St., Ketchum,* ☎ *208/726–7703. MC, V. No dinner.*

$$$ ✕🏨 **Knob Hill Inn.** With lots of wood and log furnishings, the interior of this exclusive inn suits Ketchum's Western character, but since this is a new building, everything that should be modern is. All rooms have large tubs, wet bars, and balconies with mountain views. Intermediate rooms, suites, and penthouse suites have fireplaces. The intimate Felix at the Knob Hill Inn restaurant has exquisitely prepared Continental cuisine with Mediterranean flair. Specialities include marinated lamb shanks, paella, and Wiener schnitzel with spaetzle. A full breakfast, afternoon refreshments, and fresh baked goods are included. ✉ *960 N. Main St., Box 800, Ketchum 83340,* ☎ *208/726–8010 or 800/526–8010,* FAX *208/726–2712. 20 rooms, 4 suites. 2 restaurants, indoor-outdoor pool, sauna, exercise room. AE, MC, V.*

$$$ ✕🏨 **Sun Valley Resort.** Since 1936 this has been the most complete year-round vacation option in Idaho. The "mall" between the lodge and the inn is patterned after an Austrian village, with a lawn and ponds where white swans quietly troll the waters. In winter, with a thick frosting of snow, the place takes on the look of a toy town. The lodge's poured-concrete exterior is almost indistinguishable from wood (from a slight distance), while the interior has a country European feel. Inspired by European traditions, the Lodge Dining Room, a dramatic, circular, two-level room, serves old standards, fresh fish, and a standout Caesar salad prepared tableside. The resort has five restaurants on site and three on the mountain. ✉ *Sun Valley Rd., Sun Valley 83353,* ☎ *800/786–8259,* FAX *208/622–3700. 234 rooms, 301 suites. 8 restaurants, 3 pools, sauna, 18 tennis courts, bowling, horseback riding, ice-skating, cross-country skiing, downhill and Nordic school, downhill skiing, cinema, nightclub. AE, D, DC, MC, V.*

$$$ **Idaho Country Inn.** This quiet inn in a residential neighborhood looks like a tremendous log home with a river-rock foundation. Inside, the wood accents continue. Four-poster beds made of local wood, such as pine or willow, furnish the spacious, rustic rooms. The building is new, however, so the works are modern. The river-rock fireplace in the sitting room is tempting, as is the plate of homemade chocolate chip cookies kept at fireside. Breakfast is included. ✉ *134 Latigo La., Box 2355, Sun Valley 83353,* ☎ *208/727–4000 or 800/635–4444,* FAX *208/726–2712. 11 rooms. AE, MC, V.*

$$–$$$ **Elkhorn Resort & Golf Club.** This is Sun Valley's "other" resort, a large hotel and restaurant complex nestled next to a sage-covered mountainside and surrounded by condominiums. The resort is just over the mountain from the Sun Valley Resort. Elkhorn's hotel has fully appointed rooms with modern decor and refrigerators. Upgraded rooms have fireplaces, kitchens, and Jacuzzis. The resort offers a variety of year-round activities, including jazz concerts under the stars on the complex's center terrace and surrounding lawn area. The Robert Trent Jones–designed golf course challenges even the best golfers. ✉ *Elkhorn Rd., Box 6009, Sun Valley 83353,* ☎ *208/622–4511 or 800/333–3333,* FAX *208/622–3261. 131 rooms. 3 restaurants, bar, pool, 18-hole golf course, 18 tennis courts, nightclub. AE, D, MC, V.*

$$–$$$ **Heidelberg Inn.** This friendly motel offers spacious, attractive rooms with kitchenettes; some rooms have fireplaces. The complimentary Continental breakfast is skimpy, but it is delivered to your room. ✉ *1908 Warm Springs Rd., Ketchum 83340,* ☎ *208/726–5361 or 800/284–4863,* FAX *208/726–2084. 30 rooms. Kitchenettes, pool. AE, D, MC, V.*

$–$$ **Lift Tower Lodge.** Don't let the genuine lift tower and chair outside the front door (just for show—think of it as Western-style lawn art) put you off. Remodeled in 1995, rooms feature remote cable TVs. There is a free Continental breakfast. Half the rooms look toward the ski mountain, the other seven face Route 75 (also known as Ketchum's Main Street). ✉ *703 S. Main St., Box 185, Ketchum 83340,* ☎ *208/726–5163 or 800/462–8646,* FAX *208/726–2614. 14 rooms. Refrigerators, outdoor hot tub. AE, D, DC, MC, V.*

CONDOMINIUMS

Premier Resorts at Sun Valley offers a collection of condominiums and homes throughout the Wood River Valley in the $$–$$$ range for short- and long-term stays. Premier prides itself in representing top-notch properties, from in-town condominiums for families to ski-to-your-door luxury homes at the base of the ski mountain, coupled with special touches and services that make lodgers feel at home during their stays. ✉ *Box 659, Sun Valley 83353,* ☎ *208/727–4000 or 800/635–4444,* FAX *208/727–4040. AE, MC, V.*

Nightlife and the Arts

The nightspot for a decade has been **Whiskey Jacques** (✉ Main St. and Sun Valley Rd., Ketchum, ☎ 208/726–3200). It's a cross between a nightclub and a cowboy bar. Live music, Western dancing, and lots of drinking help to create a rowdy crowd and a few red eyes on ski slopes the next day. The food is popular, too—everything from burgers to hand-thrown pizzas. The Sun Valley Resort's **Duchin Lounge** (☏ 208/622–2145) is more subdued and features live jazz trios and elegant appetizers.

Outdoor Activities and Sports

A public biking/in-line skating/walking trail runs most of the length of the Wood River Valley in the Sun Valley area. It's possible to take the trail all the way from Hailey to a point about 2 mi north of the Sun Valley Resort, a distance of about 18 mi. Maps are available from the **Blaine County Recreation District** (✉ Box 297, Hailey 83333, ☏ 208/726–6662). **Pete Lane's** (✉ Sun Valley Mall, ☏ 208/622–2276) has bike, ski, and skate rentals by the hour or the day, as do other outdoor recreation shops in Ketchum.

FISHING

Right in Ketchum and Sun Valley's backyard is excellent trout fishing. Most of the streams in the **Wood River Valley** have 10- to 15-ft easements for fishing along the banks, or they are conducive to wading. Trout are plentiful in all the valley fisheries, including the East Fork of the Big Wood River and Trail and Warm Springs creeks. Various streams have specific rules as to bait, catch-and-release fishing, and trout limits, so it's best to check first and get a fishing map before throwing out a lure. Contact the Blaine County Recreation District (✉ 308 N. Main St., Hailey, ☏ 208/788–2117) for more information. The Sun Valley area on the Wood River (also known as the Big Wood, not to be confused with the Little Wood) and Silver Creek are known worldwide for dry fly-fishing. The high-desert, cold-spring-fed **Silver Creek Preserve,** about 30 mi south of Sun Valley, (✉ Silver Creek Preserve Rd., Box 624, Picabo, ☏ 208/788–2203), is a slow-moving, easy-to-wade, yet extremely challenging fishery with huge browns and native rainbows.

Bill Mason Outfitters (✉ Sun Valley Mall, Box 127, Sun Valley, ☏ 208/622–9305) boasts that its classes can teach even a novice to fly-fish in just 15 minutes, and it's true. You may not be a champion, but you'll be able to cast and even catch fish. Classes for children (morning and afternoon sessions daily) include equipment, instruction, transportation, and fishing on a private, stocked pond. Reservations are required. The **Lost River Outfitters** (✉ 171 N. Main St., Ketchum, ☏ 208/726–1706) staff practice what they preach. Each an avid angler, they can point customers to just-fished hot spots in the Lost River Mountains and Copper Basin area, Silver Creek, and the Wood River drainage, where rainbows and brookies are rising and—given the right bug presented properly—might be caught. After all, Lost River is quick to point out that with fly-fishing, presentation is everything.

GOLF

Without question, two of Idaho's three premier golf courses are at the **Elkhorn Resort & Golf Club** and **Sun Valley Resort** (see Dining and Lodging, *above*) They are both expensive (more than $90). **Bigwood Golf Course** (✉ Saddle Rd. and Rte. 75, 1 mi north of Ketchum, ☏ 208/726–4024) and **Warm Springs Golf Course** (✉ Warm Springs Rd., 1 mi southwest of Ketchum, ☏ 208/726–3715) are reasonably priced nine-hole courses on the outskirts of Ketchum.

SKIING

For cross-country skiing, the **Sun Valley Resort** has trails evenly divided among beginner, intermediate, and advanced. Most trails run along the golf course, and classical and skating lanes are groomed into the tracks. (For information on the condition of other trails throughout the valley, call ☎ 208/762–6662.) You can rent cross-country skis at **Sun Valley Nordic Center** (✉ Sun Valley Resort golf course, ☎ 208/622–2251); the **Elephant's Perch** (✉ 280 N. East Ave., ☎ 208/726–3497), and **Backwoods Sports** (✉ 711 N. Main St., ☎ 208/726–8818).

The **Blaine County Recreation District** (☎ 208/726–6662) handles grooming of more than 80 mi of trails in the immediate area and at Galena, 22 mi north of Ketchum. Galena is ideal for a daylong ski with rest breaks at **Galena Lodge** (☎ 208/726–4010), a roomy, log day lodge with a huge fireplace, a ski shop with rentals, lessons, tasty lunches, and snacks. Designated trails in the system allow dogs.

For **downhill skiing**, there's no doubt that **Sun Valley** (☎ 800/635–8261; ☞ Chapter 2) is one of the best ski resorts in the country. Bald Mountain, primarily an intermediate and advanced hill, has one small area, Seattle Ridge, that's essentially for beginners. However, because of the mountain's steep, 3,400-ft vertical drop, an intermediate run here might earn a black diamond elsewhere. Dollar, a much smaller teaching hill near the Radisson Elkhorn, is almost completely beginner terrain. Together they have 75 runs serviced by three quads, five double chairs, and seven T-bars. On-hill facilities include three restaurants, and the children's program is among the most comprehensive of any ski resort. Some purists might find Baldy a little crowded with glittery lodge sitters, but they add color and lend a festive atmosphere to the day.

For cross-country and downhill skiing and racing information, contact the **Sun Valley Ski Association** (✉ Box 2420, Sun Valley 83353, ☎ 208/622–3003).

Shopping

SHOPPING DISTRICTS/MALLS

Central Ketchum is packed with small shops, art galleries, and cafés. Everything from Ralph Lauren designs to Native American beadwork beckons from shop windows. **Sun Valley Village,** in Sun Valley Resort's pedestrian mall, offers 13 mostly upscale specialty shops ranging from Bill Mason Outfitters to Towne and Park Jewelers.

GALLERIES

There are no fewer than 20 art galleries in central Ketchum, featuring a range of art from the wildly esoteric to traditional Western. For more information on gallery tours, or a map, contact **Sun Valley Gallery Association** (✉ Box 1241, Sun Valley 83353, ☎ 208/726–2602).

Stanley

❺ *61 mi from Ketchum via Rte. 75 north.*

Deep in the heart of south central Idaho, the Sawtooth range gathers together more than 40 gray needlelike spires reaching more than 10,000 ft and marches across the Sawtooth/White Cloud valley floor for more than 35 mi. The 8,700-ft Galena Pass overlook, about 25 mi north of Ketchum on Route 75, marks the southern end of the Sawtooths and the White Cloud Range, which faces the Sawtooths on the east side of the valley. From the turnout at the pass, the headwaters of the Salmon River looks like a squiggly dribble. But by the time the Salmon River reaches the town of Stanley, a straight shot about 30 mi north on U.S. 75, the lapping dark-blue waters are some 25 ft wide. In the summer, Stanley hosts a swarm of rafters and kayakers who put in at this point and make the white-water journey down the famed stream. With the jagged Sawtooths as a backdrop, the usually subdued dirt-road town lights up on weekend nights when cowboys and river guides return to saloons in town to unwind doing the "Stanley Stomp," a version of two-steppin'.

Following U.S. 75 east and north from Stanley to Challis, 38 mi away, the roadway mirrors the Salmon River corridor, offering mesmerizing views and earning this stretch of asphalt the title of Salmon River Scenic Byway. U.S. 93 continues the scenic drive along the river north past the town of Salmon, although many travelers may choose to take U.S. 93 south to loop back to the Sun Valley/Ketchum area or head on to Twin Falls.

Lodging

$$$ 🏨 **Idaho Rocky Mountain Ranch.** Constructed in the 1930s by a New York businessman as an invitation-only guest ranch, the 8,000-square-ft lodge with its massive rock fireplace remains much the same, with period photographs on the walls, animal trophies, and even the original monogrammed white china. Lodge rooms and most of the surrounding duplex cabins have Oakley stone showers and handcrafted log furniture. A natural hot-springs pool is a short walk from the lodge and cabins. At weekend barbecue dinners on the wide front porch, musicians entertain with toe-tapping acoustic Western music and spin yarns about Idaho cowboys and Sawtooth ghosts. All meals are included. ✉ *Off U.S. 75, 9 mi south of Stanley; HC 64, Box 9934, Stanley 83278,* ☎ *208/774–3544,* FAX *208/774–3477. 2 lodge rooms, 8 duplex cabins. Dining room, hot-springs pool, hiking, horseback riding, horseshoes, volleyball. D, MC, V. Closed May and Oct.*

$$$ 🏨 **Twin Peaks Ranch.** One of America's first authentic dude guest ranches, Twin Peaks was homesteaded in 1923 and then established as a dude ranch by the E. DuPont family in the mid-1900s. The 2,300-acre ranch is nestled in a mile-high valley between the Salmon River and the Frank Church–River of No Return Wilderness Area. A stately lodge, cabins, the original ranch house, and an apple orchard are set on several acres of lawn. Learn horsemanship from experienced wranglers in the full-size rodeo arena, then venture out for a guided day ride or an overnight pack trip. Stocked trout ponds attract anglers, and guided fishing and white-water rafting trips can be arranged. Rates include meals and all activities. ✉ *Off U.S. 93, 18 mi south of Salmon; Box 774, Salmon 83467,* ☎ *208/894–2290 or 800/659–4899,* FAX *208/894–2429. 13 cabins. Dining room, pool, hot tub. MC, V. Closed Jan.–Apr.*

$–$$ 🏨 **Jerry's Country Store and Motel.** This pleasant, easy-going motel offers clean, affordable rooms and an excellent view of the Sawtooths. Rooms have VCRs, and movies can be rented. ✉ *1 mi north of Stanley on U.S. 75; HC 67, Box 300, Stanley 83278,* ☎ *208/774–3566,* FAX *208/774–3518. 9 rooms. Kitchenettes. AE, D, MC, V.*

Outdoor Activities and Sports

The Sawtooth Mountains and Salmon River offer plenty of opportunities for all types of outdoor sports and recreation. Most lodging services can also arrange for guided adventures or coordinate with specific outfitters or guides for fishing, hiking, pack-horse, mountain-biking, and river trips. Horse-pack trips can combine other activities such as fishing and hiking. **Sawtooth Wilderness Outfitters** (✉ Box 8ITG, Garden Valley 83622, ☎ 208/462–3416 or 208/259–3408) organizes and leads horse-pack trips in the Sawtooths, ranging from 1 to 10 days.

HIKING

Fishhook Trail in the Sawtooths is gentle and less than 5 mi round trip (hikers can get by comfortably with just sturdy running shoes) along Fishhook Creek, with spectacular views of meadows and snowcapped peaks. The trailhead parking area is near Redfish Lake, about 2 mi south of Stanley on Route 75.

OFF THE BEATEN PATH

CUSTER MOTORWAY ADVENTURE ROAD – The 35-mi driving tour takes about three hours and follows Forest Service Road 070, from the Sunbeam Dam on U.S. 75, 10 mi east of Stanley. The motorway continues east, terminating in Challis. The narrow dirt road is suitable for high-clearance and four-wheel-drive vehicles. The route had its start a little more than a century ago as miners rushed to the Yankee Fork gold mines in the 1870s. By 1879, Alex Toponce, an enterprising freighter, had built a toll road from Challis to Bonanza. Town sites, mines, and several "stations" serving those venturing the rugged back road with accommodations and supplies sprang up along the way. (Back then, the trip from the Yankee Fork mines to Challis took nine hours and cost $8.) Because of the popularity of the Yankee Fork mining district, the old road was reconstructed by the Civilian Conservation Corps (CCC) in 1933 and designated the Custer Motorway. Today, the Motorway retraces the historic mining route, with remains of a tollgate station; the Custer ghost town site and museum; and the mammoth, 112-ft-long, 988-ton Yankee Fork dredge, which was used for digging into the valley to recover gold. A brochure with a map and description of numbered interpretive sights on the motorway is available from the South Central Idaho Travel Association (☞ Visitor Information *in* Boise–Sun Valley Loop A to Z, *below*), Idaho Department of Parks and Recreation (☞ Camping *in* Idaho A to Z, *below*), Yankee Fork Ranger District (✉ HC 67, Box 650, Clayton 83227, ☏ 208/838–2201), or Challis Ranger District (✉ HC 63, Box 1669, Challis 83227, ☏ 208/879–4321).

Boise–Sun Valley Loop A to Z

Arriving and Departing

BY BUS

Boise–Winnemucca Stages (☏ 208/336–3300) serves the U.S. 95 corridor from Nevada to Boise, with stops in towns around Boise. **Greyhound Lines** has service to the Boise Bus Depot (✉ 1212 W. Bannock St., ☏ 208/343–3681), as well as service into Twin Falls from Boise or Idaho Falls.

BY CAR

Twin Falls and Boise are both on I–84. From the north, enter the region on Route 55. From the south, you may find it easier to take U.S. 93 through Jackpot, Nevada, which joins U.S. 30 near Twin Falls, rather than taking the smaller and twisting Routes 225 (Nevada) and 51 (Idaho).

BY PLANE

Jet service into **Boise Municipal Airport** (☏ 208/383–3110) is provided by American, Delta, Northwest, Southwest, and United. Most flights originate in Salt Lake City, although United flies direct from Chicago and Denver. The commuter carriers Horizon and SkyWest also serve Boise.

Twin Falls and Sun Valley are served by Horizon and SkyWest. Because the Sun Valley airport—actually in Hailey, south of Ketchum—is at a high elevation, be prepared for delays or diversions. In winter, the same snow that attracts skiers can also close the airport. An alternative route is to land in Twin Falls or Boise and rent a car. Sun Valley hotels often offer guests free shuttle service from Hailey. Ask when making reservations.

Getting Around

BY BUS

In Boise, **Boise Urban Stages** (☏ 208/336–1010), called simply "the Bus," runs frequently from the airport to major points around the city. The cost is approximately 75¢ to downtown.

Sun Valley and Ketchum offer free service on **KART** (Ketchum Area Rapid Transit, ☎ 208/726–7140) to most major lodgings, downtown Ketchum, and the River Run and Warm Springs ski lifts. Buses run about every 20 minutes from Sun Valley and Elkhorn resorts and about every hour from central Ketchum.

BY CAR

The region's main highway, I–84, stretches from Boise in the west through Twin Falls, and then east and south into Utah. However, a much more scenic route from Boise to Twin Falls is U.S. 30, which turns off at Bliss and follows the Snake River canyon. From Boise to Sun Valley, there are several options. In summer, Routes 21 and 75 through Stanley and the Sawtooth National Recreation Area make for a long but very beautiful drive. In winter, the road is often closed, so be sure to check road conditions. The shortest route from Boise is to head east on I–84 to Mountain Home and then take U.S. 20 east to U.S. 75 north. From Twin Falls or points farther east along I–84, take U.S. 93 and U.S. 75 north. For the most part, this is the high-desert lava-field area. If there is snow it is cleared or melts quickly.

BY TAXI

Boise: Blue Line (☎ 208/384–1111), **Boise City Taxi** (☎ 208/377–3333), **Metro Cab** (☎ 208/866–0633). **Ketchum and Sun Valley: A-1 Taxi** (☎ 208/726–9351).

Contacts and Resources

DOCTORS AND DENTISTS

St. Alphonsus Regional Medical Center (☒ 1055 N. Curtis Rd., Boise, ☎ 208/378–2121, emergency room 208/378–2121). **St. Luke's Regional Medical Center** (☒ 190 E. Bannock St., Boise, ☎ 208/381–2222, emergency room 208/386–2344). **Wood River Medical Center** (☒ Sun Valley, adjacent to the east end of Sun Valley Village, near the Inn and resort golf course, ☎ 208/622–3333). **Magic Valley Regional Medical Center** (☒ 650 Addison Ave. W, Twin Falls, ☎ 208/737–2000, TTY 208/737–2114).

GUIDED TOURS

Boise Tours (☒ Julia Davis Park, ☎ 208/342–4796 or 800/999–5993) uses a tour train or trolley to take sightseers on a tour of Boise for $5.50, May–October. **Sun Valley Stages** (☒ 119 S. Park Ave. W, Twin Falls, ☎ 208/622–4200) can arrange tours or charters of the Sun Valley area.

Idaho has a rapidly growing wine industry, which proud locals say is catching up to Oregon's and Washington State's, especially in the white varietals. You can see for yourself how successful the wineries have become by visiting them; 5 of the 12 are west of Boise in Nampa and Caldwell, and one is in Hagerman. Entry to all wineries is free. For a map, contact **Idaho Grape Growers and Wine Producers Commission** (☒ Box 790, Boise, ☎ 208/334–2227).

VISITOR INFORMATION

Boise Convention and Visitors Bureau (☒ 168 N. 9th St., Suite 200, 83702, ☎ 208/344–7777 or 800/635–5240). **South Central Idaho Travel Association** (☒ Twin Falls Chamber of Commerce, 858 Blue Lakes Blvd. N, Twin Falls 83301, ☎ 800/255–8946). **Southwest Idaho Travel Association** (☒ Boise Convention and Visitors Bureau, Box 2106, 168 N. 9th St., Boise 83702, ☎ 800/635–5240). **Stanley-Sawtooth Chamber of Commerce** (☒ Box 8, Stanley 83278, ☎ 208/774–3411 or 800/848–7950).

EAST–SOUTHEASTERN TRIANGLE

During the 1840s, westbound pioneers on the Oregon Trail seemed to lose their way in southeastern Idaho. They tried several routes, the remnants of which now crisscross the region, attempting to find the best way out. Now if you tell people in Boise, for example, that you plan to spend time in this area, they'll look at you cross-eyed and ask why. What's here is a kind of time capsule. Those living in cities may have forgotten what it's like in hamlets of 230 or 407 or even 103, but such villages still exist in southeast Idaho. Here women drive pickups with bumper stickers declaring WRANGLER BUTTS DRIVE ME NUTS. One village is locally renowned for its automatic car wash. The towns, collectively known as "Pioneer Country," were usually founded by hardy souls from Utah who trapped or hunted or farmed. Today they are almost unchanged since the days when folks such as Pegleg Smith opened trading posts. Often the only modern building is the local Mormon church.

Henry's Fork, Bear Lake, and other waters attract anglers to the area for blue-ribbon fishing. Hot springs, a geyser, and caves are among the geologic phenomena luring visitors to Lava Hot Springs, Soda Springs, and other small towns tucked in the southeastern corner of Idaho.

Our tour of east–southeastern Idaho traces the Snake River Valley and the frontier towns along the way, beginning with Idaho Falls. Then it ventures to points east and west of the river valley. To the east, deep in the heart of the forest-and-mountain terrain, tiny towns that are nothing more than crossroads are chock-full of history, legends, and lore. To the west the tour glimpses eerie sights such as spatter cones, lava flows, and other volcanic features that pockmark the arid Snake River plateau.

If you're coming from Wyoming or you just want to see some beautiful countryside, a good place to start a tour of Pioneer Country is on U.S. 20 in West Yellowstone, Montana, which dips down to Island Park, Idaho. Pristine Lower and Upper Mesa Falls are the main attractions along the Mesa Falls Scenic Byway, Route 47. Continue south and turn on Route 32 (Teton Scenic Byway) to Route 31 through Tetonia, Driggs, and Victor. Strictly farming and ranching towns until the Grand Targhee ski resort was built just across the Wyoming border in 1969, they're now part western ski town, part ranching community. Continue south on Route 31 through the Snake River Valley, one of the state's most beautiful drives in any season. In winter, hoofprints of elk, deer, and smaller animals zigzag across the hills, and in spring and summer, wildflowers coat the mountains. At Swan Valley, you'll meet up with U.S. 26, which crosses the Snake River and continues into Idaho Falls.

Idaho Falls

❻ *107 mi from Jackson, Wyoming, via U.S. 191 south, U.S. 26/89 west, and U.S. 91 south; 208 mi from Butte, Montana, via I–15 south; 210 mi from Salt Lake City via I–84 and I–15 north.*

Idaho Falls sits at the edge of the Snake River plain, which arcs across southern Idaho. This town of 50,000 people sprouted when an industrious stagecoach worker figured a bridge across a narrow section of the Snake would be much faster for overland stages than the ferry used upstream. He completed the bridge in 1866, and a community, dubbed Eagle Rock, developed at the site. Later the name was changed to Idaho Falls, despite the lack of natural falls. In 1911 a weir was built in the river to generate power, lending some legitimacy to the name.

The **Bonneville Museum,** housed in a 1916 Andrew Carnegie Library building, is small but more impressive than most small-town museums. Somehow the volunteer historical society that operates it has managed to re-create early Eagle Rock in the basement. The faux street is complete with a dentist's office, dry-goods store, and other facades. Upstairs, displays include objects and photos from the early days of Bonneville County, including an extensive selection of Shoshone-Bannock artifacts. ✉ *200 N. Eastern Ave.,* ☎ *208/522–1400.* 🎫 *$1.* ⏲ *Weekdays 10–5, Sat. 1–5 (winter hrs slightly irregular).*

The Idaho Falls Parks and Recreation Department manages more than 50 parks with 1,400 acres of grounds in the area. If the weather is warm and the skies are blue, take a break on the 2⅓-mi pathway that encircles Greenbelt Park, spread along both sides of the Snake River between the Broadway Bridge and the John's Hole Bridge. Locals take lunch breaks and bike, walk, or in-line skate along the paved paths, and picnic tables are set up at intervals.

With 222 square mi, **Hell's Half Acre Lava Flows** is a smaller version of Craters of the Moon National Monument (☞ *below*), about 25 mi south of Idaho Falls on I–15. The centerpiece is a vent reaching 5,350 ft and measuring up to 200 ft wide and 730 ft long with 13 pit craters. The area includes a rest stop on the interstate and an interpretive sign.

Dining and Lodging

$$–$$$ ✕ **Sandpiper.** Although the nautical theme may have gone a little overboard (pun intended), this seafood and steak establishment is one of the better dining spots in town. Because it sits on the bank of the Snake River, there are lovely views from the back windows. ✉ *750 Lindsay Blvd.,* ☎ *208/524–3344. AE, D, DC, MC, V.*

$–$$ ✕ **Snakebite.** This lively, casual eatery offers gourmet burgers, vegetarian burgers, steaks, and pasta in at atmosphere that the manager dubs Southwestern eclectic. Snakebite has the city's widest selection of microbrewery beers. ✉ *425 River Pkwy.,* ☎ *208/525–2522. MC, V. Closed Sun., no dinner Mon.*

$ ✕ **Mama Inez.** Located downtown, the Idaho Falls outpost of this popular Mexican restaurant chain is regarded as the best south-of-the-border home-style food in town. ✉ *344 Park Ave.,* ☎ *208/525–8968. MC, V.*

$ ✕ **Smitty's Pancake House Restaurant.** The waitresses still call you "honey" in this cross between a Big Boy and a roadhouse. The pancakes are meals in themselves, and if you don't want it fancy, the burgers, steaks, and chicken are reliable. Breakfast is served all day in this friendly, bustling eatery. ✉ *645 W. Broadway,* ☎ *208/523–6450. MC, V.*

$$$ 🏨 **AmeriTel Inn.** The newest motel in town, this immediately became a top-choice business destination. Guest rooms are handsomely decorated in deep hunter green, burgundy, and cream with coordinating print bedspreads; oak armoires hide TVs. Some units feature whirlpool tubs, fireplaces, and kitchen suites. There is a comfortable lounge with plump sofas and a big-screen TV, fitness equipment, and such business amenities as fax and copy facilities, in-room data ports, and two-line speakerphones. A Continental breakfast and fresh-baked cookies in the evening are included in the room charges. ✉ *645 Lindsay Blvd., 83402,* ☎ *208/523–1400 or 800/528–1234,* FAX *208/523–0004. 126 rooms. In-room data ports, indoor pool, hot tub, exercise room, business services, meeting rooms. AE, D, DC, MC, V.*

$$$ 🏨 **Teton Ridge Ranch.** Built in 1984 of lodgepole pine, this secluded, luxuriously rustic ranch lodge (83 mi from Idaho Falls via U.S. 26 east and Rtes. 31 and 33 north) accommodates just 14 guests seeking the utmost in comfort and service. All meals are included in the lodging price. Both the lodge (with cathedral-beam ceilings, stone fireplaces, and comfy sofas in the library) and the guest suites offer majestic views of the Tetons. Suites are equipped with woodstoves, hot tubs, and steam showers. More than 4,000 acres offer plenty of room to wander in. Activities include hiking on 14 mi of marked trails, riding with an experienced wrangler, fishing at two spring-fed stocked ponds, cycling, and shooting at two sporting clay courses. ✉ *200 Valley View Rd., Tetonia 83452,* ☎ *208/456–2650,* FAX *208/456–2218. 7 suites. Dining room, hiking, horseback riding, fishing, library. No credit cards. Closed Nov.–Dec. 25, Apr.–May.*

$–$$ **Best Western Driftwood Inn.** Remodeled in 1994, guest rooms on two levels are dressed in traditional light-pine furnishings, with soft floral bedspreads and curtains. Rooms have coffeemakers, microwaves, and refrigerators. Picture windows look out across the lawn, the Snake River, and the falls, which lie just 74 steps away. The grounds feature a lush garden overflowing in blooms and plenty of benches and chairs for relaxing. The Driftwood sits between the Greenbelt and the Lindsay Boulevard motel strip. ✉ *575 River Pkwy., 83402,* ☎ *208/523–2242 or 800/528–1234,* FAX *208/523–0316. 74 rooms. Refrigerators, coin laundry. AE, D, MC, V.*

Nightlife and the Arts

The **Idaho Falls Symphony** (☎ 208/529–1080) presents a five-concert series each year, often with renowned special guests. Each August the **Shoshone-Bannock Indian Festival,** south of Idaho Falls in Fort Hall, celebrates the culture of the region's original inhabitants; for information, contact the Idaho Falls Arts Council (☎ 208/522–0471) or the Southeastern Idaho Travel Council (☎ 208/776–5273 or 800/423–8597).

Outdoor Activities and Sports

BIRD-WATCHING

Bird-watchers should flock to **Harriman State Park,** about 80 mi north of Idaho Falls and 33 mi southwest of West Yellowstone, Montana. In this 16,000-acre wildlife refuge you'll glimpse Canada geese, osprey, bald eagles, and waterfowl year round. In winter, a large number (some 300–400) of Rocky Mountain trumpeter swans (the world's heaviest flying bird) make a layover here. ✉ *HC 66, Box 500, Island Park 83429,* ☎ *208/558–7368.*

CYCLING

The greenbelt in Idaho Falls is an excellent place to pedal. For information on bike rentals, call **Idaho Falls City Parks** (☎ 208/529–1480).

FISHING

Idaho Falls is the drift-boat manufacturing capital of the world. (A drift boat resembles a banana-shape rowboat.) So it's only natural that drift-boat and bank fishing are the favored modes of fishing Henry's Fork of the Snake River and other local waterways. Area fisheries produce abundant populations of rainbow, brown, and cutthroat trout, Kokanee salmon, and whitefish. The Eastern Idaho Yellowstone/Teton Territory Visitor Information Center (☞ Visitor Information *in* East–Southeastern Triangle A to Z, *below*) can provide information on local fishing.

GOLF

Eighteen-hole courses include **Pine Crest** (✉ 701 E. Elva St., ☎ 208/529–1485), **Sage Lakes** (✉ 100 E. 65 N, ☎ 208/528–5535), and **Sandcreek** (✉ 5230 Hackman Rd., ☎ 208/529–1115).

Shopping

Grand Teton Mall (✉ 2300 E. 17th St., 3 mi east of central Idaho Falls, ☎ 208/525–8300 or 208/525–8301) has a variety of specialty and department stores, including JCPenney, ZCMI, and Made in Idaho, which lives up to its name with a bevy of products from the spud state.

Atomic City

35 mi from Idaho Falls via U.S. 20 west.

Today Idaho Falls derives most of its income from the **Idaho National Engineering and Environmental Laboratory** (INEEL), on 890 square mi of sage desert northwest of Idaho Springs. When you're driving on U.S. 20 to the site, near the aptly named Atomic City, it's easy to see why makers of B movies thought odd things might crawl out of the desert around nuclear facilities. Here, back in 1951, when the atom
7 was our friend, **EBR-1** became the nation's first nuclear reactor to generate usable amounts of electricity. It is now the site of more nuclear reactors (52) than anywhere else on earth. Here, research is conducted on subjects ranging from nuclear-powered naval vessels to radioactive-waste management. EBR-1 is now a National Historic Landmark. Tours can be arranged through INEEL Public Affairs. ✉ *785 DOE Pl., MS 3516, 83401,* ☎ *208/526–0050.* 🎫 *Free.* ⏲ *Memorial Day–Labor Day, daily 8–4.*

Craters of the Moon National Monument

8 *45 mi from Atomic City via U.S. 93 and U.S. 26 west.*

In case movie directors need more inspiration about what the world might look like after a nuclear war, they could travel farther west to Craters of the Moon National Monument. Just 15,000 years ago, the earth opened up north of here and poured molten rock over the landscape. The flows pushed the Snake River south and left this part of the Snake River Valley a ghostly plain punctuated by lava tubes and mysterious-looking formations. The visitor center, just off the highway 18 mi west of Arco, provides an introduction to the area, but those who want to learn and see more can drive a 7-mi loop self-guided tour beginning at the visitor center. ✉ *Box 29, Arco 83213,* ☎ *208/527–3257.* 🎫 *Loop: $4 per vehicle.* ⏲ *Visitor center: June 15–Labor Day, daily 8–6; Labor Day–June 14, daily 8–4:30. Loop road closed to cars Nov. 1–Apr. 15 (approximately).*

Pocatello

9 *51 mi from Idaho Falls via I–15 south.*

Trains, trails, and travelers have all figured in Pocatello's history. Spread out along the Snake River in a fertile valley ringed by softly sculpted mountains, Pocatello was once the largest rail center west of the Mississippi, earning it the name "Gate City." Now the state's second-largest city, with a population of about 52,000, it is still a gateway to the Teton Territory/Yellowstone area, Sun Valley, and the rest of the Idaho/Montana/Utah/Wyoming universe. Stroll the shady streets of Old Town Pocatello, a renovated shopping and commercial district, and glimpse the historic Oregon Short Line Depot and turn-of-the-20th-century houses trimmed with turrets and lovely brick and stone work. On the eastern edge of downtown, coeds scurry across the campus of the 11,000-student Idaho State University.

The **Idaho Museum of Natural History,** on the campus of Idaho State University, has a fine collection of more than 400,000 artifacts and Ice Age fossil specimens of mammoths, mastodons, and other previous residents of what is now Idaho. The Discovery Room gives kids hands-on encounters with fossils and computers. From I–15, take U.S. 91 to Yellowstone Avenue and follow the signs to the campus. ✉ *S. 5th Ave. and E. Dillon St., Box 8096,* ☎ *208/236–3168 or 208/236–3317.* 🎫 *Free.* ⏲ *Mon.–Sat. 10–4.*

Fort Hall was a major pioneer outpost northeast of Pocatello and it is now within the ½-million acre Fort Hall Indian Reservation. Massive wooden gates open to a museum complex, the **Fort Hall Replica,** representing an historic trading post once located on the Portneuf River and serving as an important stop along the Oregon Trail. ✉ *Upper Ross Park, Ave. of the Chiefs, off 4th St.,* ☎ *208/234–1795.* 🎫 *$2.25.* ⏲ *Apr.–May, Tues.–Sat. 10–2; June–Sept. 1, daily 9–7; Sept. 2–30, Tues.–Sat., 10–2.*

Dining and Lodging

$–$$ ✕ **Buddy's** This bustling family-owned restaurant has been packing 'em in for 30 years with tasty, affordable Italian food. Takeout is available. ✉ *626 E. Lewis St.,* ☎ *208/333–1172. MC, V.*

$–$$ ✕ **Frontier Pies Restaurant and Bakery.** Tender cornbread and honey comes with breakfast, lunch, and dinner at this Old West-theme family restaurant. High-back booths and home-style cooking keep the crowds coming. ✉ *1205 Yellowstone Ave.,* ☎ *208/237–7159. D, DC, MC, V.*

$$ 🏨 **Best Western Cotton Tree Inn.** This motel is conveniently located off I–15 at Exit 71 (Pocatello Creek Road exit). Rooms were recently remodeled; some have whirlpool tubs and kitchenettes. ✉ *1415 Bench Rd., 83201,* ☎ *208/237–7650 or 800/662–6886,* FAX *208/238–1355. 149 rooms. Restaurant, bar, hot tub, racquetball, coin laundry. AE, D, DC, MC, V.*

OFF THE BEATEN PATH

REGISTER ROCK – Wagons on their way west often stopped to camp here, just a few miles from what is now Massacre Rocks State Park (☎ 208/548–2672). During the night, pioneers left proof of their passage by painting or carving their names into the stone. Some of their markings date back to the 1860s. The 20-ft-high rock is now protected by a roofed and fenced enclosure. Take I–86 west from Pocatello 8 mi past its junction with Route 37, at which point signs lead you to the rock and surrounding picnic area. A $2 day-use fee is collected on the honor system in a box near the entrance.

Lava Hot Springs

⑩ *35 mi from Pocatello via I–15 and U.S. 30 east.*

Lava Hot Springs, population 400, is one of the funkiest little towns in Idaho. It has one main street, turn-of-the-century brick buildings, and some of the most desirable **hot springs** in the United States. The springs passed from Native American hands to the U.S. Army to the state of Idaho and are now operated by a state foundation, which has turned the pools into a garden spot. The springs have almost no sulfur or chlorine but are rich in other minerals. This attracts people who believe in the powers of mineral springs or simply relish a good, hot soak. ✉ *430 E. Main St.,* ☎ *208/776–5221 or 800/423–8597.* 🎫 *$4.* ⏲ *Apr.–Sept., daily 8 AM–11 PM; Oct.–Mar., daily 9 AM–10 PM.*

The **World Famous Hot Pools** and **Olympic Swimming Complex** offers five **hot pools** with temperatures ranging from 104°F to 112°F. Two swimming pools, one with ⅓ acre of water surface, are located on each end of the 25-acre landscaped property. Suits, towels, and lockers are available. 🎫 *Hot pools or swimming pools $4; both $7.* ⏲ *Hot pools: Apr.–Sept., daily 8 AM–11 PM; Oct.–Mar., daily 9 AM–10 PM. Swimming pools: Sun.–Fri. 11–8, Sat. 10–8.*

Dining and Lodging

$–$$ ✕ **Johnny's.** This pleasant, informal place has a burgundy-and-cream color scheme. Offerings include burgers, steaks, and seafood. ✉ *78 E. Main St.,* ☎ *208/776–5562. AE, D, MC, V.*

$$–$$$ ✕ **Royal Hotel Bed & Breakfast.** Lisa Toly fell into innkeeping by accident, but has since managed to take an old miners' rooming house and turn it into a cozy B&B. Renovated in 1993, the interior is decorated in turn-of-the-20th-century colors and furnishings. Rooms are small, but the second floor has a place especially for guests to make snacks in, and the honeymoon suite has a whirlpool tub. The full breakfast, including Toly's home-baked apple turnovers and frittata, is the best in town. If you're in time for lunch—and especially if you've got a hungry brood—stop in for pizza, a specialty. As improbable as it sounds, Toly makes pizza that would even make a New Yorker smile. ✉ *11 E. Main St., Box 476, 83246,* ☎ *208/776–5216. 3 rooms, 1 suite. Dining room. AE, D, MC, V.*

$$–$$$ **Lava Hot Springs Inn.** This grand old building was a hospital, a retirement/nursing-home facility, and now, after a complete renovation in the late 1980s, a European-style B&B. (A buffet breakfast is included.) The interior is done in pink-and-black art deco, and the rooms are neat and well appointed. Five suites have private baths with whirlpool tubs; a hot mineral pool, just steps away from the back door, overlooks the Portneuf River. ✉ *5 Portneuf Ave., Box 670, 83246,* ☎ *208/776–5830. 19 rooms, 2 with bath; 5 suites with bath. Dining room, hot springs, library. AE, D, MC, V.*

Outdoor Activities and Sports

Thunder Canyon (✉ 9898 E. Merrick Rd., Lava Hot Springs, ☎ 208/776–5048) is a nine-hole golf course.

OFF THE BEATEN PATH

CHESTERFIELD – Virtually a ghost town now, Chesterfield was founded in 1880 by Mormons, complete with the Mormon grid system for streets. Many of the original buildings still stand as if waiting for the inhabitants to return. Chesterfield, 20 mi from Lava Hot Springs via U.S. 30 east to Bancroft and Chesterfield Road north, is listed on the National Register of Historic Places.

Soda Springs

⓫ *20 mi from Lava Hot Springs via U.S. 30 east.*

Soda Springs is home to another regional landmark. No, not the Monsanto slag pour, which the town lists as a tourist attraction, but the only **man-made geyser** on earth, a sight that's more reputation than reality. It seems the town fathers were drilling for a swimming pool when they hit carbon dioxide, a gas that permeates this region. The carbon dioxide mixed with groundwater under pressure and started shooting out of the ground. Local boosters capped the geyser with a valve. Now, every hour during daylight, they turn Captive Geyser on—unless the wind is coming from the west, which would douse the parking lot. From U.S. 30, turn left onto Main Street; the geyser is right behind the Statesman's Lounge and Enders Café on the left side of the street.

OFF THE BEATEN PATH

MINNETONKA CAVE – Adventurous travelers may want to take a side trip on U.S. 30 east to Montpelier (31 mi), another interesting pioneer town, and then take U.S. 89 south to St. Charles (18 mi). Just west of St. Charles, first on a county highway and then on a U.S. Forest Service road (both numbered 30012), lies the Minnetonka Cave, a classic nine-room limestone cavern dotted with stalactites and stalagmites. The forest service gives 90-minute tours throughout the summer. Take a jacket. The cavern is naturally a constant 40°F. Nearby Bear Lake, famous for its odd turquoise color, is a local favorite with campers and anglers looking for cutthroat trout. ✉ *1¼ mi west of St. Charles,* ☎ *208/847–2407.*

$4. ⏲ Tours mid-June–Labor Day (approximately, depending on weather), daily 10:30–5, every ½ hr.

En Route U.S. 30 heads west from Soda Springs to Route 34. As you head south on Route 34, there's a small sign 3 mi past the town of Grace that points the way (left onto Ice Cave Road for a very short distance) to **Niter Ice Cave.** This may look like a small hole in the ground, but the cave, used by pioneers to keep food cold, is nearly ½ mi long. You can climb in if you want, but be sure to have a flashlight and be prepared to get dirty. Route 34 continues south through rolling ranch lands that were the object of range wars between farmers, who wanted to put up fences, and shepherds and cattlemen, who wanted an open range.

Franklin

⓬ *43 mi from Soda Springs via U.S. 30 west, Rte. 34 south, and U.S. 91 south (at Preston).*

The oldest town in Idaho was established on April 14, 1860, by order of Brigham Young, who sent settlers north from Utah. At first the pioneers struggled, but eventually a sawmill was installed and more cash flowed in. Today the town, population 478, contains the **Franklin Historic District** along Main Street. Turn left off U.S. 91; the **village hall,** built in 1904, is on the right. Across the street, the **Lorenzo Hatch** house (1870) is a fine example of Greek Revival architecture, popular in many Western pioneer towns. The exterior masonry is a marvel, considering how primitive the town was in 1870. Nearby stands the **Franklin Cooperative Mercantile Institution,** a great stone structure; it was built to house the local cooperative store and now contains a museum.

Continue south out of town on U.S. 91, and just before the Utah border you'll see the **town cemetery.** Many grave sites are more than 100 years old.

En Route From here, there is another, more scenic, route to Register Rock (☞ Pocatello, *above*). A nice drive dips into Utah, then loops back toward I–86 and Register Rock. Cross into Utah, take Route 61 to Cornish, and drive north on Route 23 toward Weston, where you pick up Route 36 to Malad City. If the weather is good and all roads are open, head south on I–15 to Route 38 west, follow it to Holbrook, and turn north on Route 37. This road winds through the Curlew National Grasslands and past abandoned homestead cabins sitting lonely on the rolling hills. When Route 37 meets I–86, drive west.

East–Southeastern Triangle A to Z

Arriving and Departing

BY BUS

Greyhound Lines (✉ 215 W. Bonneville St., Idaho Falls, ☎ 208/232–5365 or 800/231–2222) has regular service along the Boise–Idaho Falls corridor. To the east, buses run to Rexburg and West Yellowstone, Montana.

BY CAR

From the south, I–15 connects Salt Lake and other Utah cities to southeastern Idaho; from the north, it comes from western Montana. In Idaho, I–15 runs through Idaho Falls and Pocatello, where it intersects I–86 (the main route west), and along the edge of the pioneer towns in the southeast corner. From the east, the most scenic route into the region descends from Wyoming's Teton Pass and connects with Idaho's Routes 33 and 31 at Victor in the Targhee National Forest. Route 31 runs to Swan Valley and U.S. 26, which goes to Idaho Falls.

BY PLANE

The commuter carriers Horizon and SkyWest have service to Idaho Falls and Pocatello. American and Delta fly to Idaho Falls.

Getting Around

BY BUS

Pocatello has an urban bus service, **Pocatello Urban Transit** (☎ 208/254–2287). Schedules can be obtained from the Chamber of Commerce (☎ 208/233–1525).

BY CAR

A car is the only way to see most of the region. There is an abundance of car-rental companies with booths at the Pocatello and Idaho Falls airports. Be aware, however, that rentals in Idaho, especially during ski season, can be pricey.

Contacts and Resources

DOCTORS AND DENTISTS

Eastern Regional Medical Center (✉ 3100 Channing Way, Idaho Falls, ☎ 208/529–6111). **Pocatello Regional Medical Center** (✉ 777 Hospital Way, Pocatello, ☎ 208/234–0777).

EMERGENCIES

In an emergency, dial **911** except in Franklin County, where you should call ☎ 208/852–1234.

VISITOR INFORMATION

Eastern Idaho Yellowstone/Teton Territory Visitor Information Center (✉ 505 Lindsay Blvd., Box 50498, Idaho Falls 83402, ☎ 208/523–1010 or 800/634–3246). **Southeastern Idaho Travel Association** (✉ C/o Lava Hot Springs Foundation, Box 498, Lava Hot Springs 83246, ☎ 208/776–5500 or 800/423–8597).

NORTHERN IDAHO

Most Idahoans consider the Salmon River the unofficial boundary between north and south, since it bisects the state almost perfectly and separates the Pacific and Mountain time zones. The Salmon River is also one of the state's great scenic attractions. It is the longest wild river left in the United States, outside of Alaska, and the Middle Fork, which begins as runoff from the Sawtooths and flows through the Frank Church–River of No Return Wilderness Area, is recognized around the world for one of the wildest, most gorgeous river-raft trips on earth. The river system is a magnet for anglers, too. Riggins, near its western end; Stanley (☞ Boise–Sun Valley Loop, *above*), high in the Sawtooths near the Middle Fork; and Salmon, to the east near Montana, are the gateways to the Salmon River and its wilderness.

North of White Bird Summit, Idaho begins to feel more like the Northwest than the West. Lewiston, for example, is an inland port whose traffic comes from the Columbia River; it's also a portal to Hells Canyon, a natural wonder that forms the border between Oregon and Idaho.

The Panhandle of Idaho is a logging region that has been "discovered" by refugees from larger cities in California, Washington State, and elsewhere. The resort towns of Coeur d'Alene and Sandpoint are just the sort of places that drive visitors to look up the words "Real Estate" in the Yellow Pages.

The tour of northern Idaho meanders steadfastly northward via U.S. 95 through the Panhandle and on to the Canadian border. Most of the sights, towns, lakes, and waterways along the way stick close to the well-trod route.

Fishing

Despite the Salmon River's name, don't look for many salmon. Most runs have been dammed away, and a total of two sockeye made it back up the Salmon River to Red Fish Lake near Stanley in 1991. Coeur d'Alene Lake was successfully stocked with chinook a number of years ago, and people have been pulling out some large fish there.

Lake Pend Oreille is renowned for kamloops, a large variety of rainbow trout, and the Middle Fork of the Salmon River is known for cutthroat trout. Significant populations of steelhead, one of the state's largest trophy fish, are found in the Clearwater and northern sections of the Snake River. The Snake and Kootenai rivers are famous for sturgeon, an ancient species that can grow to well over 6 ft; however, sturgeon may not be removed from the water, even for weighing.

Rafting

The three premier raft trips in Idaho are on the Selway River, the Lochsa River, and the Middle Fork of the Salmon River. Rafting these rivers should not be undertaken casually. The Lochsa parallels U.S. 12, but the Selway and the Middle Fork run ferociously through true wilderness. Unless you are an expert, it's a good idea to pick a recognized outfitter (☞ Guided Tours *in* Northern Idaho A to Z *and* Idaho A to Z, *below*). Even then, you should be a good swimmer and in solid general health. Permits from the U.S. Forest Service are usually required to run these rivers, but they're often hard to get and may require waiting periods (another good reason to use an outfitter).

Skiing

There are three major downhill ski areas in the region. Brundage Mountain is 8 mi north of McCall. It catches some of the deepest powder in the Northwest and is known for its glade trails and vertical drop of 1,800 ft. Schweitzer Mountain Resort in Sandpoint is Idaho's northernmost major ski mountain in the Selkirk range. More than 300 inches of snow fall each season and the top-to-bottom descent is 2,400 ft. Silver Mountain is spread across north-facing slopes of the Bitterroot range near Kellogg in Idaho's silver mining district. The world's longest single-stage gondola shuttles to a lodge on top, overlooking a 2,200-ft vertical drop.

In addition to cross-country trails at the major downhill ski resort areas, there are several Nordic trails in and around Coeur d'Alene and Priest Lake, north of Sandpoint. Contact the Idaho Department of Parks and Recreation (☞ Camping *in* Idaho A to Z, *below*) for information and maps.

Water Sports

Boating is popular on the lakes of northern Idaho. Coeur d'Alene and Pend Oreille lakes have miles and miles of shoreline with small coves, bays, and stream inflow points. Though each has popular beaches, you can find your own secluded spot within minutes of leaving the boat dock.

McCall

⓭ *108 mi from Boise via Route 55 north.*

Although the town of McCall is close to Boise and falls within the capital's sphere of influence, it has the alpine feel of the northern half of the state. The 108-mi drive north from Boise on Route 55 is one of the most beautiful in Idaho, if not the country. The road, choked by recreational vehicles in summer, runs along the shore of the Payette River as it rollicks down the mountains, over boulders, and through alpine forests. The arid plains of the Snake River give way to higher and higher mountains covered by tremendous stands of pines.

McCall traces its beginnings to a wagon train and passengers Tom McCall and family, who after camping at what is now the town site decided to stay behind. Laid out in 1901, the town blossomed a few years later with the arrival of the Union Pacific Railroad. The area's first ski slope, Little Ski Hill, opened in 1937 with a T-bar carrying skiers up 405 vertical ft, and the film *Northwest Passage* was shot here in 1938. In 1948, a lodge was built on the shore of Payette Lake where the town sits today. Beginning in 1961 with plenty of powdery snow and the construction of Brundage Mountain Resort, McCall experienced a rebirth. Today, the Little Ski Hill is overshadowed by Brundage Mountain, which is still considered modest by ski-area standards, with 1,400 acres of skiable terrain.

During the 1980s, the area was discovered by Californians. Espresso shops and tourist-friendly stores line the streets. The 1948 lodge on Payette Lake was bought by a San Diego developer and has been remodeled and gone upscale. Locals are a little ambivalent about all this, but there's no doubt the changes have made McCall one of the most popular resort destinations in the state. The town hosts a popular Winter Carnival each January featuring massive, intricately detailed ice sculptures.

Dining and Lodging

$ ✕ **The Pancake House.** At the south edge of town, this breakfast spot has become a skiers' favorite, thanks to its massive pancakes. You may have a short wait, because everybody in McCall seems to eat here. ✉ *201 N. 3rd St.,* ☎ *208/634–5849. MC, V. No dinner.*

$–$$$ ✕🏨 **The Shore Lodge.** Inside there's lots of hunter green, dark wood, and plaid upholstery—an English hunting lodge moved to Idaho. Large, high-ceiling lakefront suites have excellent views; street-side units are like small motel rooms. At the Narrows restaurant, with antler chandeliers, burl-wood furniture, and a dramatic view of the lake, game selections include elk, venison, and duck. Try the creamy sharp-cheddar and beer soup with red pepper and potato. Summer brings outdoor lakefront dining. Service is friendly, but some diners may feel the restaurant overreaches its grasp. Lunch is not served. ✉ *501 W. Lake St., Box 1006, 83638,* ☎ *208/634–2244 or 800/657–6464,* FAX *208/634–7504. 116 rooms. Restaurant, bar, café, hot tub, sauna, exercise room. AE, D, MC, V.*

$$–$$$ 🏨 **Hotel McCall.** This hybrid between a hotel and a B&B is in the center of town. The building, constructed in 1939, is more attractive outside than in. Rooms and prices vary widely; six are small, dark, and share a bath, while others are almost grand and have lots of light and antique furnishings. Some have views of Payette Lake. A Continental breakfast is included. ✉ *3rd and Lake Sts., Box 1778, 83638,* ☎ *208/634–8105. 22 rooms, 16 with bath. Dining room. AE, MC, V.*

Outdoor Activities and Sports

GOLF

MeadowCreek Golf & Field Club (✉ 1 MeadowCreek Ct., New Meadows, ☎ 208/347–2555). **McCall Golf Course** (✉ Davis St., McCall, ☎ 208/634–7200).

SKIING

Brundage Mountain (✉ 8 mi north of McCall off Rte. 55, Box 1062, McCall, ☎ 208/634–4151) might be a small ski area as far as chairlifts and tows are concerned, but the area boasts an impressive vertical drop, ample treed terrain, and lots of powder. Although the runs are a little short and black diamond speed freaks may want to test their sanity elsewhere, Brundage does have enough to keep intermediates and beginners interested. Advanced skiers find solace in the powder glades. On top of the hill are spectacular views of the Seven Devils peaks and Payette Lake. With a vertical drop of 1,800 ft and 38 runs, Brundage has two triple chairs, two double chairs, a platter tow, and a handle tow.

Little Ski Hill (✉ Rte. 55, south of McCall, ☎ 208/634–5691) still serves downhill skiers, primarily those who want to make a few telemark turns (with free heel boots and bindings). It also has 30 mi of groomed Nordic skating and touring trails and is one of the five U.S. Olympic Committee–sanctioned biathlon courses in the nation.

En Route Route 55 reaches its peak a few miles outside McCall and then gradually snakes its way downhill. It joins U.S. 95 and the Little Salmon River at New Meadows and heads into mining territory, where gold and silver, and rumors of both, drew hundreds of mostly disappointed men.

Riggins

14 *45 mi from McCall via Rte. 55 and U.S. 95 north.*

About 33 mi north of the junction of Route 55 and U.S. 95, where the Little Salmon flows into the main Salmon River, the tiny town of Riggins is a wide spot in the road. It's also the last stop in the Mountain Time Zone; across the river, it's an hour earlier. Hunters and anglers flock here for chukar, elk, and steelhead.

Lodging

$$$ ★ **The Lodge at Riggins Hot Springs.** This lodge, named for hot springs that have been harnessed into pools on the bank of the Salmon River, is just over 10 mi upriver from Riggins along a narrow, winding road. Inside, Western antiques and Native American crafts abound, and a sitting room is dominated by a large rock fireplace. Rooms have pine paneling and wooden bed frames. Full country breakfasts, snack lunches, and fine dinners, such as lamb in raspberry sauce, are included. The lodge works with outfitters to create package excursions for hunters, anglers, and rafters. ✉ *Box 1247, 83549,* ☎ *208/628–3725,* FAX *208/628–3785. 10 rooms. Dining room, pool, hot tub, mineral baths, sauna, billiards, travel services. MC, V.*

$–$$ **Salmon River Motel.** The rooms are clean, comfortable, and spare; they also offer TVs and sounds of the river. One of Riggins's four restaurants is on site. ✉ *1203 U.S. 95, 83549,* ☎ *208/628–3231 or 888/628–3025. 16 rooms. Restaurant. MC, V.*

Nightlife

Locals hang out at the **Ruby Rapids** (✉ U.S. 95, ☎ 208/622–3914), that rare establishment that gives drinks on credit to folks it knows. Yes, it's a small-town dive, but a dive of the best kind.

En Route Immediately outside Riggins, U.S. 95 crosses the Salmon and begins the 40-mi climb toward **White Bird Summit,** which rises 4,245 ft above sea level. There were no roads from north to south Idaho until 1915, when the White Bird Grade was finished. It climbed nearly 3,000 ft in 14 mi of agonizing hairpins and switchbacks. The new road was finished in 1975. A little more than halfway up the new grade, a small scenic overlook sits above the valley where the Nez Perce War started. In 1877, Chief Joseph and his band of Nez Perce, who had not signed a treaty with the whites (as had other bands), were nevertheless on their way to resettle at the nearby reservation when trouble broke out. About 80 Native Americans decimated a much larger white force without losing a person. The army retreated, but the legendary pursuit of Joseph's band across 1,500 mi of Idaho and Montana began. An interpretive shelter tells the story of the battle. From White Bird Summit, U.S. 95 plunges rapidly into the Camas Prairie and into Grangeville, a farming town. Here, the Nez Perce dug the roots of the camas plant, a dietary staple.

Spalding

90 mi from Riggins via U.S. 95 north.

About 53 mi north of Riggins, U.S. 95 enters the modern Nez Perce Indian Reservation, home to treaty and nontreaty Nez Perce. (There
15 is still some minor antagonism between the groups.) **Nez Perce National Historical Park** is really a series of 24 sites spread across three states. Park headquarters is in Spalding (11 mi east of Lewiston), where a visitor center gives a detailed look at the Nez Perce, or Ne-Mee-Poo, as they called themselves, and their history. A 30-minute film details the tribe's contacts with Lewis and Clark and their lives today. A small museum exhibits artifacts from chiefs Joseph and White Bird, including textiles; pipes; and, poignantly, a ribbon and a coin given to the tribe by Meriwether Lewis as thanks for help. ⊠ *U.S. 95,* ☎ *208/843–2261.* 🎫 *Free.* ⏲ *Memorial Day–Labor Day, daily 8–5:30; Labor Day–Memorial Day, daily 8–4:30.*

Lewiston

16 *11 mi from Spalding via U.S. 95 north and U.S. 12 west.*

The hardworking mill town of Lewiston is tucked into the hills at the junction of the Snake and Clearwater rivers. It was once the capital of the Idaho Territory but is now known regionally for its relatively mild temperatures and early golf season. Its blue-collar economy is based on its inland port and the giant paper mill just on its eastern edge.

Lewiston and Clarkston (its twin city in Washington), named for you know whom, are also known as the gateways to **Hells Canyon,** a geologic wonder deeper than the Grand Canyon. Canyon tours have become big business in Lewiston (☞ Guided Tours *in* Northern Idaho A to Z, *below*). The hills in the canyon resemble ancient Mayan temples as they rise high above the waterway. Columnar basalt, rock formations that look like giant black pencils, frame the river. In some spots, ancient Native American pictographs can be seen on smooth rock faces. Bald eagles swoop down from cliffs to hunt for fish, and deer scatter along the hillsides.

Miners tried to exploit the area, but they gave up. Today a few hardy sheep and cattle ranchers are all that's left of the pioneers who first settled here. The **Kirkwood Historic Ranch** (☎ 208/628–3916), a long backpack past mining-camp sites and petroglyphs or a four-hour jetboat ride from Lewiston (☞ Guided Tours *in* Northern Idaho A to Z, *below*), has been preserved to show how the pioneers lived. Although they make their homes from cut lumber instead of logs, ranchers today live in nearly the same style.

Dining and Lodging

$$ ✕ **Bojack's.** Frankly, the pickings are slim for good dining spots in Lewiston, but this downtown eatery is renowned locally for good steaks, spaghetti, and salads. From the outside it doesn't look like much more than a dark lounge, but inside, it's, umm, a dark lounge with a restaurant added on. ⊠ *311 Main St.,* ☎ *208/746–9532. AE, MC, V. No lunch.*

$–$$ ✕🏨 **Sacajawea Motor Inn.** The basic motel-type rooms were recently remodeled and are clean, quiet, and a good bargain. Lots of locals eat at the attached restaurant, the Helm, because they know exactly what to expect: good, reliable, simple food for breakfast, lunch, or dinner.

It is much like a Denny's with its counter and vinyl booths. The menu carries steaks, burgers, chops, chicken, pancakes, and a variety of sandwiches. ✉ *1824 Main St., 83501,* ☎ *208/746–1393 or 800/333–1393,* FAX *208/743–3620. 90 rooms. Restaurant, pool, hot tub, exercise room, coin laundry. AE, D, DC, MC, V.*

$–$$$ **Grand Plaza Ramada Inn.** On the east side of town, this former Ramada Inn is often used for local meetings. The sports bar, with its own microbrewery serving up five specially brewed beers, stocks 100 brands, including local microbrews and imports. ✉ *621 21st St., 83501,* ☎ *208/799–1000 or 800/232–6730,* FAX *208/746–8321. 134 rooms. Restaurant, bar, pool, hot tub. AE, D, DC, MC, V.*

Outdoor Activities and Sports

Sitting high on a hill overlooking the Lewiston/Clarkston Valley and the Snake and Clearwater rivers, the 18-hole **Bryden Canyon Golf Course** (✉ 445 O'Connor Rd., ☎ 208/746–0863) is blessed with generally temperate conditions and is open almost year-round and offers views of the valley and the Snake and Clearwater rivers below.

En Route From Lewiston, U.S. 95 climbs 2,000 ft virtually straight up out of the valley and into rolling farmland. About 40 mi later, it cuts through the middle of **Moscow,** home of the University of Idaho. Students often joke that the university was placed in Moscow because there is absolutely nothing to do here except study. The city does feature a fine set of late-19th-century buildings, however, and one of the best jazz festivals in the country (☞ Festivals and Seasonal Events *in* Chapter 1).

Coeur d'Alene

17 *120 mi from Lewiston via U.S. 95 north.*

Idaho's second-most-famous resort town sits on the shores of lovely Coeur d'Alene Lake, surrounded by evergreen-covered hills. Originally a Native American settlement, then a U.S. Army fort, the town has always attracted visitors. Now it does so with a vengeance, but it retains a pleasant village atmosphere, especially along Sherman Avenue, the main drag. Although primarily known as a summer destination and as Spokane's playground, Coeur d'Alene has boosted its number of winter visitors by promoting Silver Mountain, a ski area about 50 mi to the east (☞ Outdoor Activities and Sports, *below*).

In between shopping, swimming, sailing, and fishing in Coeur d'Alene, visit **Tubbs Hill.** A 2-mi loop trail winds around the hill. Small wooden signs describe plant and rock types found in the area as well as the remnants of historical buildings. An interpretive guide is available from the city's parks department. ✉ *221 S. 5th St.,* ☎ *208/769–2250.* *Free.* ⏲ *Daily sunrise–sunset.*

Ten miles south on U.S. 95 is the **Coeur d'Alene Indian Reservation.** French-Canadian trappers mingled with the local Native Americans in the early 1800s and found them to be astute traders. Possibly because of their tough bargaining skills, the trappers called them *Coeurs d'Alenes* (Pointed Hearts).

Silverwood Amusement Park, 14 mi north of Coeur d'Alene, is Idaho's only amusement park and features a perfectly reconstructed turn-of-the-20th-century mining town, with rides on a narrow-gauge steam train or in a vintage biplane, and old-fashioned barnstorming performances. The eight-story, 55 mph, wooden roller coaster called "Tremors" is a prime attraction. ✉ *26225 N. U.S. 95, Athol,* ☎ *208/683–3400.* *$22.* ⏲ *Daily Memorial Day–Labor Day; hours vary.*

Dining and Lodging

$$–$$$ ✕ **Cedars Floating Restaurant.** This restaurant is actually *on* the lake, giving it wonderful views and drawing diners from miles away for seafood and beef and a supper-club atmosphere with a boat dock and outside deck dining. Beer-marinated, charbroiled steak is a specialty. ✉ *U.S. 95, ¼ mi south of I–90,* ☎ *208/664–2922. AE, DC, MC, V. No lunch.*

$–$$$ ✕ **Jimmy D's.** This comfortable downtown spot across from the lakefront is a favorite of locals, including several inn owners who have their food catered. Redbrick walls decorated with art, candlelit tables, and a small bar forge a bistrolike atmosphere. The menu is uncomplicated but well done: pastas, steaks, chicken, fish, and a seasonal weekend brunch. There is also a strong selection of wines, perhaps because the former owner runs a wine store and nightclub across the street. ✉ *320 Sherman Ave.,* ☎ *208/664–9774. AE, D, MC, V.*

$–$$ ✕ **T. W. Fisher's—A Brewpub.** Fisher's microbrewery offers daily tours of the brew works and some of the best beer made in Idaho, along with a solid menu of burgers, chicken, salads, and pizza, a specialty. The pub is a lively place, with sports on TV, a wood and brass U-shape bar, and a mostly young crowd. Brewery tours are given at 1:30 and 5:30 daily. ✉ *204 N. 2nd St.,* ☎ *208/664–2739. AE, D, MC, V.*

$ ✕ **Hudson's Hamburgers.** When they say hamburgers, they mean it. It's burgers, ham and cheese, or egg sandwiches, and that's it. These folks have been in business since 1907, and even local rivals have been forced to admit that Hudson's basic burgers are the town favorites. Sit at the counter and watch how burgers used to be made. ✉ *207 Sherman Ave.,* ☎ *208/664–5444. No credit cards. Closed Sun. No dinner.*

$$$ ✕🏨 **Coeur d'Alene Resort.** The modern tower was controversial in 1986, but its effect has been mitigated somewhat by the long floating boardwalk around the marina. Inside, the lobby boasts small eateries, shops, and sunny nooks from which to people-watch. Standard rooms, especially in the former motel, are small, with very basic amenities dating from the 1960s; more expensive tower rooms are more spacious. Many feature fireplaces or balconies with terrific views of the lake. Atop the tower, with expansive windows and contemporary decor, Beverly's ($$–$$$) creates an airy, relaxed setting for a Northwest-inspired menu including grilled salmon drizzled with huckleberry salsa. In winter, buses to Silver Mountain (☞ Silver Valley and Cataldo Mission, *below*) cost $15, and ski packages are available. ✉ *2nd and Front Sts., 83814,* ☎ *208/765–4000 or 800/688–5253;* FAX *208/667–2707. 336 rooms. 4 restaurants, 3 bars, lobby lounge, indoor pool, sauna, 18-hole golf course, bowling, exercise room, beach, shops, recreation room, children's programs (ages 4–14), travel services. AE, D, DC, MC, V.*

$$$ 🏨 **Berry Patch Inn Bed and Breakfast.** On 2 acres of landscaped grounds (complete with gardens and a waterfall) atop a hill just west of Coeur d'Alene Lake, this 4,500-square-ft cedar chalet has wonderful views of Mt. Spokane and the Cabinet Mountains to the north. Paths through an adjacent forest are perfect for summer strolls. Inside, the spacious living room has a large stone fireplace, and a TV, VCR, and stereo. Decor throughout is country elegant. Breakfasts include an abundance of fresh fruit with poppy-seed dressing and such entrées as griddle cakes stuffed with oats and green apple and topped with huckleberries in sour cream. ✉ *1150 N. Four Winds Rd., 83814,* ☎ *208/775–4994,* FAX *800/667–7336. 3 rooms, 1 with bath. Breakfast room. MC, V.*

$$–$$$ 🏨 **The Blackwell House.** This late-Victorian jewel sits among several impressive residences in the historic district two blocks from the city's center. Built in 1904, the three-story, whitewashed mansion with towering columns and a wraparound porch has been restored to its original luster. Inside, rich wood paneling and patterned wallpaper in subdued hues of rose and burgundy, Victorian steamer trunks, and white wicker create a handsomely furnished, warm setting. The morning room, where a full breakfast is served, overlooks the manicured lawn, gardens, and gazebo. The only drawback to the rooms at the front of the house is traffic noise, which is noticeable but not unbearable. ✉ *820 Sherman Ave., 83814,* ☎ *208/664–0656 or 800/899–0656. 8 rooms, 6 with bath. Dining room. AE, D, MC, V.*

$$–$$$ ★ **Clark House on Hayden Lake.** Half hidden in the trees across the street from Hayden Lake, this B&B on steroids was built in 1910 by an eccentric millionaire as a copy of a Kaiser Wilhelm palace. By the late 1980s, the local fire department was ready to torch it for practice, but a nearly $1 million restoration has resulted in a giant wedding cake of a place with wide-open rooms, an art deco feel, hardwood floors in public areas, luxurious guest rooms, and an expansive walled garden. A formal, four-course breakfast (included in the room rate) and dinner (reservations essential) are served. ✉ *E. 4550 S. Hayden Lake Rd., Hayden Lake 83835,* ☎ *208/772–3470 or 800/765–4593,* FAX *208/772–6899. 10 rooms. Dining room. AE, D, DC, MC, V.*

Outdoor Activities and Sports

CYCLING

The premier cycling route is the **Centennial Trail,** a new paved path leading from east of Coeur d'Alene all the way to Spokane. Silver and Schweitzer ski areas (☞ Skiing, *below*) are renowned for mountain biking. In Coeur d'Alene, rent bikes at the activities desk of the **Coeur d'Alene Resort** (☞ Dining and Lodging, *above*) or from **Coeur d'Alene Surrey Cycles** (✉ Box 14, Hayden Lake, ☎ 208/664–6324).

GOLF

Coeur d'Alene Resort (✉ 900 Floating Green Dr., ☎ 208/765–4000 or 800/688–5253) claims that its 18-hole course has the only floating green in the nation.

Other 18-hole courses in the area are **Avondale-on-Hayden Golf Club** (✉ 10745 Avondale Loop, Hayden Lake, ☎ 208/772–5963), **Coeur d'Alene Golf Course** (✉ 2201 Fairway Dr., ☎ 208/765–0218), and **Highlands Golf and Country Club** (✉ 701 N. Inverness Dr., Post Falls, ☎ 208/773–3673).

Shopping

Plaza Shops at the Coeur d'Alene (✉ 210 Sherman Ave., at 2nd St., ☎ 208/664–1111) is an enclosed minimall with 22 small shops, several selling merchandise with a Northwest emphasis. There are resortwear retailers, including United Colors of Benetton and Worn Out West, which specializes in shirts with wildlife designs; an espresso shop; and an Italian bistro-style restaurant, Tito Macaroni's.

Nearby, the **Original Penny Candy Store** (✉ 325 Sherman Ave., ☎ 208/667–0992), a re-created turn-of-the-20th-century dry-goods and candy store, carries exotic candies from around the world, from sour-green-apple balls to strawberry bonbons. **Wilson's Variety** (✉ 401 Sherman Ave., ☎ 208/664–8346) carries a wide selection of books about Idaho, including guides on geology and history, and topographical maps. Lodge decor reigns at **Partners** (✉ 404 Sherman Ave., ☎ 208/664–4438), where you can find everything from beds to love seats to tables, all made from peeled-pine tree trunks and limbs; decorative birdhouses and Navajo-print pillows are also for sale. Antique lodge furnishings are available at **Sherman Arms Antiques** (✉ 412 Sherman Ave., ☎ 208/667–0527).

Journeys American Indian Arts (✉ 117 S. 4th St., ☎ 208/664–5227) carries beads and other jewelry supplies, as well as a wealth of Native American drums, moccasins, baskets, and books.

Silver Valley and Cataldo Mission

24 mi from Coeur d'Alene via I–90 east.

18 One of the best historical attractions in the area is the **Cataldo Mission.** Influenced by trappers and visited by missionaries, a group of Coeur d'Alenes took up Roman Catholicism. In 1850, together with Father Anthony Ravalli, they began construction of the mission, now the oldest building in Idaho. The mission church is massive, considering that it was built almost totally by hand with an ax and a few other hand tools. Behind the altar you can see the mud-and-stick construction used on the walls. The giant beams overhead were dragged from the forest, and rock for the foundation was quarried from a hill ½ mi away. The adjacent mission house, home to generations of priests, is furnished the way it would have been at the turn of the 20th century. An interpretive center provides more details about the Coeur d'Alenes and the site, which is accessible to travelers with mobility impairments. ✉ *Old Mission State Park, Exit 39, I–90, Cataldo,* ☎ *208/682–3814.* *$2 per vehicle.* ⏲ *Memorial Day–Labor Day, daily 8–6; Labor Day–Memorial Day, daily 9–5.*

19 The historic mining town of **Wallace,** 37 mi east of Coeur d'Alene off I–90, is one of the few towns to be included in its entirety on the National Register of Historic Places. It was first settled in the 1880s mining rush, and today much of the town center looks exactly as it did at the turn of the 20th century.

Dining and Lodging

$$ ✕ **The Historic Jameson.** The redbrick, downtown Jameson Building (opened 1908, restored 1979) houses a saloon and restaurant on the first floor, second-floor conference space, and B&B accommodations on the third floor, reached by stairs. Small rooms have been carefully furnished with choice antiques. The softened Victorian decor features warm hues of brown and tan and is spiced up with dainty floral wallpaper. Complimentary Continental breakfast is served in guest rooms or the parlor. The Jameson Restaurant ($–$$) serves classic American cuisine, including steaks and pasta dishes. Ceiling fans, bentwood chairs, polished brass, chandeliers, and oriental carpets are reminiscent of a fancy Old West saloon and hotel. If you're lucky, the Jameson's three resident ghosts may visit! ✉ *314 6th St., Wallace 83873,* ☎ *208/556–1554 or 800/643–2386,* FAX *208/753–0981. 6 rooms, 1 with bath. Restaurant, meeting rooms. MC, V.*

Outdoor Activities and Sports

SKIING

Silver Mountain (✉ 610 Bunker Ave., Kellogg 83837, ☎ 208/783–1111) solved an accessibility problem by installing the world's longest single-stage gondola. Near Kellogg, the hill offers a complete family learning program. Locals think the advanced terrain at Schweitzer is better, but Silver offers some excellent wooded powder skiing and some steep runs. Fifty-two trails cover a vertical drop of 2,200 ft and are reached by a quad, two triple chairs, two double chairs, and a surface lift in addition to the gondola.

Sandpoint

20 *40 mi from Coeur d'Alene via U.S. 95 north.*

Sandpoint lies on the shore of Lake Pend Oreille, the second-deepest lake in the United States. Nestled between the lake and the Selkirk and Cabinet mountain ranges, Sandpoint has been a railroad depot and a mining town, but now it survives on tourism and lumber. The town is small—five blocks of shops and restaurants form its core—and the brick and stone buildings are almost unchanged since the early 1900s. Locals say the town is 20 years behind Coeur d'Alene. They mean it as a boast. Like Coeur d'Alene, this is a summer destination with fine lake beaches, extensive woodlands, and nearby mountains. However, the local ski hill, Schweitzer (☞ Outdoor Activities and Sports, *below*), is transforming itself into a first-class ski area. Sandpoint, it has been said, is what places such as Vail, Colorado, and Jackson, Wyoming, were like just before they expanded.

Dining and Lodging

$–$$$ ★ ✕ **The Garden Restaurant.** This restaurant overlooking Lake Pend Oreille has been the Sandpoint standard since 1971, thanks to its eclectic menu and greenhouse ambience. Fare ranges from sandwiches, pastas, and steaks to sophisticated items such as owner (and expert mushroom hunter) Richard Hollars's exotic mushroom soups. The wine list features West Coast and European varietals. Sunday brunch is very popular. ✉ *115 E. Lake St.,* ☎ *208/263–5187. AE, D, MC, V. Closed Tues. in winter.*

$$–$$$ ★ ✕🏨 **Best Western Connie's Motor Inn.** This may be the best-maintained motel in Idaho. Rooms are spotless and tastefully decorated for a motel, with special touches such as marbleized wallpaper. Most rooms come with a small refrigerator and two sinks. Family suites offer microwaves. A two-room suite with a whirlpool tub and a wet bar feels downright decadent. At Connie's Café, locals gather at the counter for breakfast, but the same basic, affordable fare—pancakes, eggs, cereal, sandwiches (often big enough for two), steaks, and chicken—is also served in the café, cocktail lounge, and dining room with fireplace. ✉ *323 Cedar St., 83864,* ☎ *208/263–9581 or 800/282–0660,* FAX *208/263–3395. 52 rooms, 1 suite. Restaurant, pool, hot tub, meeting rooms. AE, D, MC, V.*

$$–$$$ 🏨 **Green Gables Lodge.** At ski resorts you pay for location, and that's what this lodge 50 yards from the ski lift at Schweitzer's, 11 mi northwest of Sandpoint off U.S. 95, offers. There is a cozy, European-chalet feeling in the public areas. Standard rooms are basic, motel-type units, while more deluxe rooms, with whirlpool tubs, are bigger and offer microwave/wet-bar facilities. ✉ *Schweitzer Mountain Resort, Box 815, Sandpoint 83864,* ☎ *208/265–0257 or 800/831–8810,* FAX *208/263–7961. 82 rooms. 2 restaurants, pool, 2 hot tubs. AE, MC, V.*

$$ 🏨 **Sandpoint Quality Inn.** The rooms are clean and pleasant, and units on the second floor have water views. ✉ *807 N. 5th Ave., 83864,* ☎ *208/263–2111 or 800/635–2534,* FAX *208/263–3289. 57 rooms. Restaurant, bar, indoor pool, hot tub. AE, D, MC, V.*

Nightlife

The **Kamloops** (✉ 302 N. 1st St., ☎ 208/263–6715) often leaves its mike open for blues and R&B musicians during the week, so you never know what you'll hear. On weekends, it has live rock and blues acts.

Outdoor Activities and Sports

You can rent bicycles at **Sandpoint Recreational Rentals** (✉ 209 E. Superior St., ☎ 208/265–4557). **Hidden Lakes Country Club** (✉ 8838 Lower Pack River Rd., 8 mi east of Sandpoint, ☎ 208/263–1621) has 18 holes and an abundance of water hazards and sand traps on its golf course.

SKIING

For years, only people in Spokane and Sandpoint knew much about **Schweitzer** (✉ 11 mi northwest of Sandpoint off U.S. 95, Box 815, Sandpoint 83864, ☎ 800/831–8810), but it's on the way to becoming a top western ski destination. It offers on-hill accommodations, children's programs, and a full-service ski school, in addition to two mountain bowls with spine-tingling black diamond runs so steep your elbows scrape the snow on turns. Open-bowl skiing is available for the intermediate and advanced, and beginners can choose from among half a dozen tree-lined runs. There is a vertical drop of 2,400 ft. A quad and five double chairs access 55 runs.

Shopping

The next time you need a custom Mongolian yurt, try **Little Bear Trading Company** (✉ 324 1st St., ☎ 208/263–1116). The shop owner, Bear (yes, just Bear), makes tepees and yurts for clients around the country. The small store also carries Native American crafts, beads, and feathers, as well as materials from Africa and Central and South America.

Cabin Fever (✉ 113 Cedar St., ☎ 208/263–7179) has one of the best assortments of gifts, home-decor items, garden adornments, and curios for cabins in North Idaho. The second **Cabin Fever** store (✉ 309 1st St., ☎ 208/263–7178) sells casual, Northwestern-style clothing.

The only retail outlet for the mail-order **Coldwater Creek** (✉ 1st and Cedar Sts., ☎ 208/263–2265) took over the Cedar Street Bridge Public Market, which now comprises six stores and restaurants in a split-level arcade of native tamarack and fir timbers spanning a mountain creek. Merchandise includes wildlife-inspired jewelry, posters, and books; bird feeders; and other nature-oriented gifts.

Northern Idaho A to Z

Arriving and Departing

BY BUS

Greyhound Lines stops at the **Coeur d'Alene Bus Depot** (✉ 1923½ N. 4th St., Coeur d'Alene, ☎ 208/667–3343). **Northwestern Greyhound Bus Lines** (✉ 1002 Idaho St., ☎ 208/746–8108) serves Lewiston. Sandpoint's **Empire Bus Lines** (✉ 402 5th Ave., Sandpoint, ☎ 208/263–7721) offers service to other cities.

BY CAR

From Boise, Route 55 heads north to McCall. From Spokane take U.S. 2 north to Sandpoint. From western Montana, you can take I–90 to Coeur d'Alene and then U.S. 95 north to Sandpoint.

BY PLANE

Horizon serves Lewiston/Clarkston, the only commercial airport north of Boise. Spokane, Washington, a 35-minute drive from Coeur d'Alene, is a popular hub for those traveling to the Idaho Panhandle. The airport is served by Alaska, Delta, Northwest, Southwest, United, and Horizon.

BY TRAIN

The ***Empire Builder*** stops at the Sandpoint Amtrak Depot (✉ 409 Railroad Ave., ☎ 800/872–7245), bound for Seattle or Chicago.

Getting Around

BY CAR

The primary north–south highway is U.S. 95; I–90 and U.S. 2 run east–west. During the winter, storms can slow interstate travel, but major highways are usually cleared promptly and are rarely closed.

Contacts and Resources

DOCTORS AND DENTISTS

Kootenai Medical Center (✉ 2003 Lincoln Way, Coeur d'Alene, ☎ 208/667–6441). **St. Joseph Hospital** (✉ 5th Ave. and 6th St., Lewiston, ☎

208/743–2511). **Bonner General Hospital** (✉ 3rd and Fir Sts., Sandpoint, ☎ 208/263–1441 or, for the emergency room, 208/265–4733).

GUIDED TOURS

Hells Canyon and other river tours are a thriving business. Most tour operators give historical and geological information on one- or two-day trips on the Snake River in Hells Canyon. Some outfitters run jet boats upriver from Lewiston into the Hells Canyon National Recreation Area, while others put rafts in near Oxbow Dam and float downstream. Rafting tours range from mild floats to white-water adventures. Some offer lodging at cabins or lodges along the way or combine river activities with horseback riding and mountain biking. **Beamer's Landing Hells Canyon Tours** (✉ Box 1223, Lewiston 83501, ☎ 800/522–6966) has the contract to deliver the U.S. mail to remote ranches in the canyon and offers a two-day mail-run via water, a jet-boat trip that includes a stop at a sheep ranch. **Salmon River Challenge** (✉ Box 1299, Riggins 83549, ☎ 800/727–9977) offers half-day to week-long rafting tours of the River of No Return Wilderness, including lodging at a backcountry ranch. **ROW** (✉ River Odysseys West, Box 579–TO, Coeur d'Alene 83816, ☎ 800/451–6034) plies a number of waters throughout the state, including the Snake River in Hells Canyon, the Middle Fork of the Salmon River, and a Snake/Lochsa Rivers combination. Specialized tours cater to senior citizens or parents with teenagers.

VISITOR INFORMATION

North Idaho Travel Association (✉ Greater Sandpoint Chamber of Commerce, Box 928, Sandpoint 83864, ☎ 208/263–2161). **North Central Idaho Travel Association** (✉ Lewiston Chamber of Commerce, 2207 E. Main St., Lewiston 83501, ☎ 208/743–3531 or 800/473–3543). **Coeur d'Alene Convention and Visitors Bureau** (✉ Box 1088, Coeur d'Alene 83816, ☎ 208/664–0587). **McCall Area Chamber of Commerce** (✉ 116 N. 3rd St., Box D, McCall 83638, ☎ 208/634–7631).

IDAHO A TO Z

Getting Around

By Bus

Major Idaho towns are served by **Greyhound Lines** (☎ 800/231–2222) and by **Boise–Winnemucca Stages** (☎ 208/336–3300).

By Car

The best way to see the state is by car—this is the West, after all, and interesting sights are sometimes spread out. Remember that Westerners often have an expanded view of distance. So when an Idahoan says "right around the corner," translate that as under an hour's drive. Interstates and the much more interesting two-lane state and U.S. highways are uncrowded, with rare exceptions (such as Boise to McCall on Friday at 5:30). Best of all, a car allows you to travel the back roads, where some of Idaho's unique sights await. Be sure to keep an eye on your gas gauge; in some parts of the state, the next gas station may be no closer than "right around the corner."

As a rule of thumb, the state's network of improved and unimproved roads are open in the summer and early fall months. Winter travel can be unpredictable, with many state highways and particularly smaller unimproved roads rendered impassable for varying lengths of time. In winter, snowstorms in the mountainous regions can make tire chains mandatory. Many of Idaho's unimproved roads in the backcountry are accessible only by 4-wheel-drive vehicles, even in summer, and are shut down for the winter. Major newspapers carry road-condition reports on their weather pages. Or, call the state's **road report hot line** (☎ 208/336–6600) or **hot lines for specific regions:** Boise (☎ 208/334–3731), Coeur d'Alene (☎ 208/772–0531), Idaho Falls (☎ 208/522–5141), Lewiston (☎ 208/743–9546), Pocatello (☎ 208/232–1426), and Twin Falls (☎ 208/733–7210).

In Idaho you may make a **right turn** on a red light, after stopping, unless there is a sign posted forbidding it.

By Plane

Commuter airlines serve airports in Idaho Falls, Lewiston, Pocatello, Sun Valley, and Twin Falls. Major airlines serve Boise and Spokane, Washington, a gateway to the Panhandle. (☞ Arriving and Departing sections *in* individual regions, *above*). In addition, there are many airstrips scattered around Idaho, especially in wilderness areas. These strips, open only in summer and early fall, are used by private planes and those chartered by outfitters.

By Train

Amtrak's *Empire Builder* (☎ 800/872–7245) cuts across the Panhandle, stopping in Sandpoint on its way between Chicago and Seattle.

Contacts and Resources

Camping

Primitive campsites at Idaho state parks cost $5 per day, basic sites are $7, and developed sites cost $8. Electric and sewer hookups cost an additional $4. There is an entrance fee of $2 for motorized vehicles at most parks, but it is incorporated into camping fees. An annual passport for $25 provides unlimited entrance to all state parks for one calendar year. Group facilities are available at some parks. For a complete guide, contact the **Idaho Department of Parks and Recreation** (✉ Box 65, Boise 83720, ☎ 208/334–4199 or 800/635–7820).

Emergencies

Ambulance (☎ 911). **Police** (☎ 911).

For hospital emergency rooms, *see* Doctors and Dentists *in* individual A to Z sections, *above*.

Fishing

Idaho Department of Fish and Game (✉ 600 S. Walnut St., Box 25, Boise 83707, ☎ 208/334–3700 or 800/554–8685). **Idaho Outfitters and Guides Association** (✉ Box 95, Boise 83701, ☎ 208/342–1919).

Guided Tours

Most tourism in Idaho is related to the outdoors. Packagers can combine different sites, such as the Salmon and Snake rivers, or activities, such as fishing and rafting, on their trips. It is against the law for anyone who is not a member of the **Idaho Outfitters and Guides Association** (✉ Box 95, Boise 83701, ☎ 208/342–1919) to provide guiding or outfitting services; contact the association for a free directory of members.

Visitor Information

Idaho Travel Council (✉ 700 W. State St., Box 83720, Boise 83720, ☎ 208/334–2470 or 800/635–7820).

6 MONTANA

They call it Big Sky Country, but that's only part of the story; the land is big, too: The fourth-largest state, Montana stretches from North Dakota on the eastern side to Idaho on the west, 600 and some odd miles. From north to south, meanwhile, is a distance of about 400 mi. Not only is this a massive chunk of land, but it's also sparsely peopled. There are roughly 900,000 Montanans on all this ground, most of them in the major cities of Billings, Great Falls, Missoula, and Helena.

By Jim Robbins

Revised and updated by Kristin Rodine

MONTANA IS DIVIDED INTO TWO REGIONS: the Rocky Mountain cordillera, which enters Montana in the northwest corner, taking up most of the western half of the state with timbered mountains and broad, grassy river valleys; and the plains and rolling hills to the east. When night comes down, the skies are so dark and clear that the stars look like shiny glass beads suspended in a midnight sky. Northern lights shimmer like red and green curtains against velvet black skies and at other times scream across the full scope of the sky, ending only when the light of dawn erases them. If there is a factor that makes Montana so unusual, it is the light. Sometimes it shoots down from behind the clouds in long, radiant spotlight shafts, outlining the clouds in gold. A pink and orange light falls gently like dust on western slopes. A brilliant crimson takes over clouds at sunset. The fiery red and orange light of sunset in the Rockies illuminates the mountains so intensely, they appear to be lit from within like glowing coal.

The land here teems with wildlife. Bald eagles soar by the thousands and zero in on streams flush with fish: rainbow, brown, cutthroat, and brook trout among them. Cougars scream in the night, and grizzlies and wolves move through the darkness. With manes flapping, wild horses gallop over red hillsides. Thousands of elk move from the high country to the lowlands in the fall, and head back to the high country come summer.

Long gone, but not forgotten, are some of Montana's most famous wildlife, whose skeletons remain as evidence of their greatness. Some of the richest dinosaur fossil beds in the world are found in the Rocky Mountain Front Range, where the mountains meet the plains. Recently, discoveries of fossils and dinosaur eggs have challenged the notion that dinosaurs were cold-blooded; it's possible they were warm-blooded animals who cared for their young, closer to mammals than reptiles.

Evidence of early human occupation dates back 12,000 years. For generations before the Europeans arrived here, Native Americans inhabited what is now Montana. In 1805–06, the Lewis and Clark Expedition came through, seeking a transcontinental route to the Pacific, and expanded trade relations with the natives.

Montana remained a remote place, however, through much of the 19th century, and it was valued for its rich trade in buffalo hides and beaver pelts. It was the discovery of gold at Gold Creek (between Missoula and Helena) in 1858 that began to change the region dramatically. After large gold strikes at Grasshopper Creek and Alder Gulch, miners came to the southwest mountains of Montana by the thousands. In 1862, the Territory of Montana was created. Pressure by miners and settlers for Native lands in the area was unrelenting; inhabitants were forced from their homelands and restricted to reservations. Major events in the West's Indian wars—the Battle of the Little Bighorn and the Flight of the Nez Perce—were played out in Montana, indelibly shaping the history of this region and the nation.

The state of Montana entered the Union in 1889, and its motto "Oro y Plata" (gold and silver) stands. With the landscape relatively untouched, history remains alive here. Ranching and farming, mining and logging are still the ways of life, and a small-town atmosphere and friendly outlook greet travelers even in the state's larger cities. The natural splendor, free-running rivers, vast mountain ranges, and large populations of wildlife make this what Montanans call the "Last Best Place."

Pleasures and Pastimes

Dining

No matter where you eat in Montana, dress is casual. Leave your ties at home. Fine steaks and home-style cooking can be found throughout the state, along with a surprising number of upscale eateries with casually chic atmosphere and fine Continental food. Good ethnic cuisine is a rarity.

CATEGORY	COST*
$$$$	over $35
$$$	$25–$35
$$	$15–$25
$	under $15

**per person for a three-course dinner, not including drinks and tip; there is no tax on meals*

Lodging

Montana's lodging falls generally into three categories: historic hotels and bed-and-breakfasts; newer motels along commercial strips; and resort communities offering a wide range of accommodations and a dizzying array of seasonal recreational pursuits.

CATEGORY	COST*
$$$$	over $225
$$$	$150–$225
$$	$75–$150
$	under $75

**Prices are for a standard double room in high season, not including the 4% tax and service.*

Outdoor Activities and Sports

Cycling, hiking, fishing, and skiing opportunities abound in fitness-oriented Montana, and outfitters are available for almost every sport. Many of the cycling and hiking trails involve arduous climbing, changeable weather, and wild animals: It's best to know what you are getting into before you go. *Hiking Montana,* by Bill Schneider, offers a lot of useful, basic information and is available at most bookstores.

Montana has the best rainbow, brown, and brook trout fishing in the country. The Yellowstone, Missouri, Madison, Beaverhead, Gallatin, and Bighorn rivers are the cream of the crop, and there are numerous lakes and small streams. State law says that all land along rivers to the high-water mark is publicly owned, and access is guaranteed.

Wildlife

This state is home to almost 1,000 species of animals, from deer to dippers, mountain lions to moose. The Montana Department of Fish, Wildlife, and Parks operates a Watchable Wildlife program. Signs along the highways, marked with an icon that represents a pair of binoculars, indicate 100 of the best places to see some of the state's wildlife.

Exploring Montana

To really explore Montana, you must spend a lot of time on the road. Towns and attractions are widely spaced, especially in the east. Most of the state's tourist magnets and awe-inspiring scenery lie along the Rocky Mountains between two of the west's great national parks—Glacier in the north and Yellowstone on the state's southern border. But to get a real feel for Montana, venture through the rolling agricultural plains to Billings and points east.

Numbers in text correspond to numbers in the margin and on the Montana map.

Great Itineraries

IF YOU HAVE 4 DAYS

The mountains and wildlife of western Montana are its most prized attractions, and this tour offers plenty of both. Begin your day in **Missoula** ① with a visit to the **Rocky Mountain Elk Foundation Wildlife Visitor Center,** then head north to the **National Bison Range** ② near Moiese. The self-guided auto tour takes at least two hours, allowing for frequent stops to gaze at bighorn sheep, deer, elk, and the massive mammals that give the range its name. Enjoy a picnic lunch on the grounds or at your next stop, the historic mission in **St. Ignatius** ③. After admiring the mission's 58 frescoes, continue north along the east shore of **Flathead Lake,** the largest freshwater lake west of the Mississippi. Take in the shops and scenery of small, vibrant **Bigfork** ⑤, then visit one of the village's fine restaurants and enjoy a production of the Bigfork Summer Playhouse.

Day two takes you to the "Crown of the Continent," **Glacier National Park** ⑦. Take a leisurely stroll along the fragrant, wheelchair-accessible Trail of the Cedars before continuing up steep, scenic Going-to-the-Sun Road, with views of waterfalls and wildlife to the left and an awe-inspiring, precipitous drop to the right. At the summit, **Logan Pass,** stop in at the visitor center. As your eyes strain to focus on mountain goats on the distant cliffs, don't be surprised if one walks past you on the side of the road. A boardwalk protects the abundant wildflowers and spongy tundra on the hike up to prime wildlife-viewing spots, where it is not uncommon to glimpse a grizzly. Note the changing landscape as you drop over the mountains to the east side of the park, where the forest thins, the vistas grow broader, and a gradual transition to the plains begins. Spend the night in **Many Glacier.**

The next day, head for **Browning** ⑧ to enhance your appreciation for the first residents of this landscape at the **Museum of the Plains Indian.** Then it's on to **Helena** ⑩, where you can explore the **Montana Historical Society Museum,** then hop aboard the *Last Chancer* automotive train for an hour-long tour through Helena's historic neighborhoods. After the tour, amble down to **Last Chance Gulch** for dinner and window-shopping.

On day four, stop in at the **Holter Museum of Art** before heading back across the Continental Divide. For a kitschy approximation of frontier life, stop in at **Frontier Town,** then continue west back to **Missoula** ①, where you can stroll along the downtown river paths and take a ride on the old-fashioned **carousel** before selecting a restaurant and settling in for the night. If you'd prefer, you can skip Frontier Town to give you more time to explore Missoula, including the **Historical Museum at Fort Missoula.**

IF YOU HAVE 7 DAYS

Start as for the four-day itinerary, from Missoula through Glacier, possibly spending the second night in **East Glacier** or St. Mary. On day three, enjoy a last wander in Glacier before heading southeast to **Great Falls** ⑨ and the **C. M. Russell Museum.**

Get an early start the next day for the trek east through Montana's wide-open ranch land to Lewistown, then south to **Billings** ⑪. The journey through rolling plains and tiny communities takes about four hours, bringing you to the "Magic City" in time for lunch. Shop for a custom-fitted hat or other Western accessory in downtown Billings, then learn about the culture and history of the area at the **Western Her-**

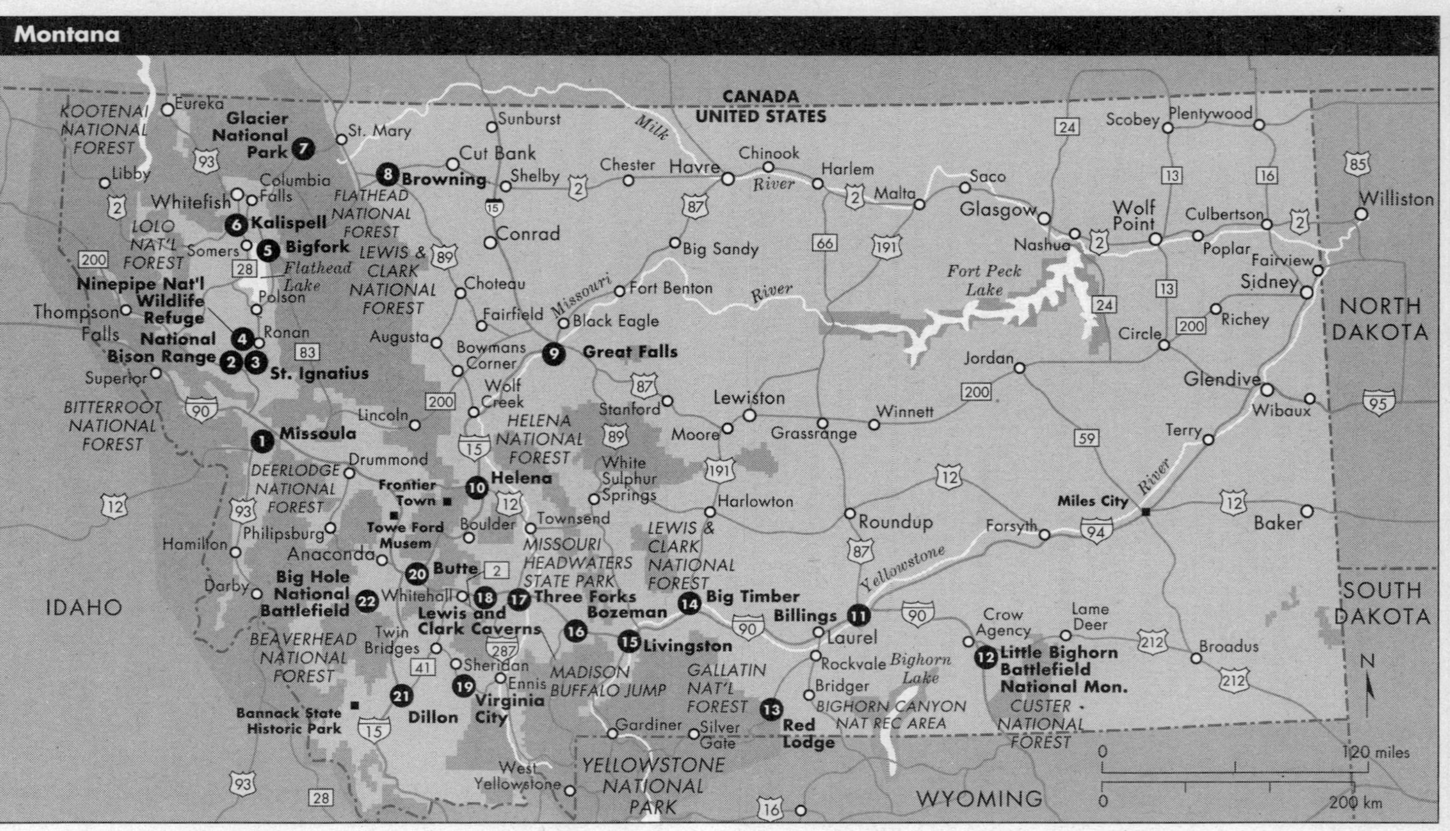
Montana
CANADA
UNITED STATES
NORTH DAKOTA
SOUTH DAKOTA
WYOMING
IDAHO
N
120 miles
200 km
0
1 Missoula
2 3 St. Ignatius
2 National Bison Range
4 Ninepipe Nat'l Wildlife Refuge
5 Bigfork
6 Kalispell
7 Glacier National Park
8 Browning
9 Great Falls
10 Helena
11 Billings
12 Little Bighorn Battlefield National Mon.
13 Red Lodge
14 Big Timber
15 Livingston
16 Bozeman
17 Three Forks
18 Lewis and Clark Caverns
19 Virginia City
20 Butte
21 Dillon
22 Big Hole National Battlefield
Frontier Town
Towe Ford Musem
Bannack State Historic Park
Miles City
KOOTENAI NATIONAL FOREST
LOLO NAT'L FOREST
FLATHEAD NATIONAL FOREST
LEWIS & CLARK NATIONAL FOREST
BITTERROOT NATIONAL FOREST
DEERLODGE NATIONAL FOREST
HELENA NATIONAL FOREST
BEAVERHEAD NATIONAL FOREST
GALLATIN NAT'L FOREST
CUSTER NATIONAL FOREST
MISSOURI HEADWATERS STATE PARK
MADISON BUFFALO JUMP
BIGHORN CANYON NAT REC AREA
YELLOWSTONE NATIONAL PARK
Fort Peck Lake
Flathead Lake
Bighorn Lake
Milk River
Missouri River
Yellowstone River
Eureka
Libby
Whitefish
Columbia Falls
Somers
Polson
Ronan
Thompson Falls
Superior
St. Mary
Cut Bank
Sunburst
Shelby
Conrad
Chester
Havre
Chinook
Harlem
Malta
Saco
Glasgow
Nashua
Wolf Point
Scobey
Plentywood
Poplar
Culbertson
Fairview
Sidney
Williston
Richey
Circle
Glendive
Wibaux
Terry
Baker
Jordan
Big Sandy
Fort Benton
Black Eagle
Choteau
Fairfield
Augusta
Bowmans Corner
Wolf Creek
Lincoln
Drummond
Philipsburg
Anaconda
Hamilton
Darby
Stanford
Lewiston
Moore
Grassrange
Winnett
Roundup
Harlowton
White Sulphur Springs
Townsend
Boulder
Whitehall
Twin Bridges
Sheridan
Ennis
West Yellowstone
Gardiner
Silver Gate
Laurel
Rockvale
Bridger
Forsyth
Crow Agency
Lame Deer
Broadus
85
95
2
16
13
200
24
59
12
94
212
191
66
87
90
89
15
93
83
28
41
287
16

itage Center. Next, journey southeast to the famed **Little Bighorn Battlefield National Monument** ⑫, exploring the site and interpretive displays that examine both sides of the conflict. Return to Billings for a sunset drive along the buckskin-color rimrocks.

The fifth day sends you southwest to charming **Red Lodge** ⑬ and one of the West's most scenic drives, the Beartooth Scenic Highway, which leads over **Beartooth Pass** to the Silver Gate entrance to **Yellowstone National Park.** This route brings you briefly into Yellowstone as you traverse the northern reaches of the park before heading out of its north gate at Gardiner, Montana. Head north through the beautiful Paradise Valley and along the **Yellowstone River,** a route dotted with tempting spots to fish, picnic, or just relax and enjoy the spectacular views. When you reach lovely **Livingston** ⑮, check out the art and architecture of the old **Northern Pacific Depot.** Spend the night here or in nearby **Bozeman** ⑯.

The next morning, visit Bozeman's outstanding **Museum of the Rockies** for impressive displays on dinosaurs and more recent residents of this region. Head west through **Three Forks** ⑰, perhaps retracing Lewis and Clark's steps at **Missouri Headwaters State Park,** where three rivers join to form the Missouri River. Following a picnic lunch, your next stop should be the extensive subterranean passages of **Lewis and Clark Caverns** ⑱. A scenic drive south of the caverns will bring you to **Virginia City** ⑲ and Nevada City, lovingly restored remnants of Montana's frontier days. Tour the sites where gold was struck and vigilantes took the law—and suspects' necks—in their hands. Next, head back to I–90 and **Butte** ⑳. Peer into the gigantic **Berkeley Open Pit Mine** and wander the historic downtown area before settling in for a meal and a night's rest.

On the final day of the tour, journey southwest from Butte to the **Big Hole National Battlefield** ㉒ for a vivid glimpse at a decisive battle between Chief Joseph's Nez Perce and the U.S. Army. From Big Hole, travel briefly west, then north on U.S. 93 through the beautiful Bitterroot Valley back to **Missoula** ①. Enjoy the Garden City's charms with a walk along the Clark Fork River, a ride on a hand-carved steed on **A Carousel for Missoula,** and, if there's time, a trek through the city's past in the **Historical Museum at Fort Missoula.**

When to Tour Montana

Summer is the most popular time to visit Montana, when all of the state's attractions are open, mountain roads are passable, and high-country wildflowers put on gorgeous displays. In Glacier National Park, the spectacular Going-to-the-Sun Road across the Continental Divide is generally closed by snow from October until June, but off-season visitors to the park are rewarded by smaller crowds and greater opportunities for wildlife viewing. Winter offers fine skiing, inspiring snow-flocked vistas, and the longest dogsled race in the lower 48 states, the Race to the Sky. Festivals and celebrations are scattered throughout the year, from Butte's rollicking St. Patrick's Day celebration in March to the Pamplona-style Running of the Sheep in Reedpoint (off I–90, 21 mi east of Big Timber and 61 mi west of Billings) each August. Rodeos and Native American powwows abound in the summer, while Christmas strolls and winter carnivals brighten up the cold months.

MISSOULA TO HELENA

This trip starts in Missoula and makes its way through the heart of Montana's mountainous western third, highlighted by Glacier National Park. Its long, finger-shape lakes and towering pines frame the snow-mottled peaks of mountain range after mountain range as you continue toward Great Falls and Helena, the state capital. Thirty percent of Montana is publicly owned land, and the national park, national forests, and state parks on this drive have plenty of campgrounds and hiking and biking trails.

Missoula

❶ *115 mi west of Helena, via U.S 12 to I–90.*

The aptly nicknamed "Garden City" is one of the most beautiful in Big Sky Country, and its population of 50,000 makes it the largest city in western Montana. Maple trees line the residential streets, the **Clark Fork River** slices through the center of town, and the University of Montana cozies up against the slopes of Mt. Sentinel. A gravel trail along the river passes the university's campus en route to Hellgate Canyon; it is ideal for walking and cycling.

The **Smokejumper Visitor Center** has exhibits, motion pictures, and murals that detail and explain various fire-fighting techniques. From Memorial Day through Labor Day, the center offers tours by firefighter-guides who can provide first-hand accounts of jumping into blazing forests. ✉ *5765 Old Hwy. 10 W (west of town, off U.S. 93),* ☎ *406/329–4934.* 🎫 *Donations accepted.* ⏲ *Memorial Day–Labor Day, daily 8:30–5, tours on the hr from 10–11 and 2–4; by appt. the rest of the yr.*

The **Rocky Mountain Elk Foundation Wildlife Visitor Center** features natural-history displays, films, art, and wildlife information. ✉ *2291 W. Broadway,* ☎ *406/523–4545 or 800/225–5355.* 🎫 *Donations accepted.* ⏲ *Memorial Day–Labor Day, daily 8–6; Labor Day–Memorial Day, weekdays 8:30–5, weekends 11–4.*

The **Historical Museum at Fort Missoula,** at the western edge of town, sits at the center of the old fort that was established in 1877 at the height of the U.S. Army's conflict with the Nez Perce, led by Chief Joseph. Indoor and outdoor exhibits, including 13 historic structures relocated from nearby sites, recount the early settlement and industry of Missoula County. Guided tours are available by appointment. ✉ *Bldg. 32, Fort Missoula,* ☎ *406/728–3476.* 🎫 *Donations accepted.* ⏲ *Memorial Day–Labor Day, Mon.–Sat. 10–5, Sun. noon–5; Labor Day–Memorial Day, Tues.–Sun. noon–5.*

The **Missoula Museum of the Arts** has changing exhibits of contemporary work and a small permanent collection. ✉ *335 N. Pattee St., 1 block from the intersection with W. Broadway,* ☎ *406/728–0447.* 🎫 *$2; free on Tues.* ⏲ *Mon.–Sat. noon–5.*

A Carousel for Missoula offers old-fashioned charm and hand-carved steeds. The traditional carousel, built and run by community volunteers, is in downtown Caras Park along the Clark Fork River. The horses and chariots ride on a lovingly restored 1918 carousel frame, accompanied by tunes from the largest band organ in continuous use in the United States. ✉ *Ryman St. south of Broadway,* ☎ *406/549–8382.* 🎫 *$1 per ride.* ⏲ *Memorial Day–Labor Day, daily noon–7; Labor Day–Memorial Day, daily noon–5:30.*

Take a break while touring downtown Missoula and have a cappuccino or a glass of fresh-squeezed juice at **Butterfly Herbs** (✉ 232 N. Higgins Ave., ☎ 406/728–8780). If you can't decide what you fancy, try the "Over the Rainbow"—a drink with flavors including strawberry, hot pepper, orange, ginger, and mint. The shop also sells baked goods, candies, soaps, candles, china, and other odds and ends.

Dining and Lodging

$–$$$ ✕ **Shadows Keep.** This grand, turreted structure overlooking Missoula and the valley is the reincarnation of a local landmark mansion that burned down in 1992. The restaurant serves fine food with imaginative sauces in a casually elegant atmosphere. Popular dishes include the rack of lamb with plum sauce and melt-in-your-mouth grilled salmon. Views are outstanding, as is the wine list. Linger in the fireside lounge in the winter or watch golfers on the neighboring Highlands course from a terrace table in summer. ✉ *102 Ben Hogan Dr.,* ☎ *406/728–5132. AE, D, MC, V. No lunch.*

$–$$ ★ ✕ **Guy's Lolo Creek Steakhouse.** For a real taste of Montana, head for this steak house in a massive log structure 8 mi south of Missoula, in Lolo. The dining room has a hunting-lodge atmosphere, replete with stuffed wildlife on the walls. Although most diners opt for one of Guy's signature sirloins—cooked over a crackling open-pit barbecue and available in three sizes—there are other well-prepared meat, chicken, and seafood dishes to choose from. ✉ *6600 U.S. 12 W, Lolo,* ☎ *406/273–2622. AE, D, MC, V. Closed Mon. No lunch.*

$ ✕ **The Shack.** Innovative omelets and hash browns with herb-scented gravy draw a crowd of locals to this attractive eatery for breakfast. Creative lunch and dinner specials, often with a Southwestern flair, are served the rest of the day. ✉ *222 W. Main St.,* ☎ *406/549–9903. MC, V.*

$ ✕ **Zimorino's Red Pies over Montana.** Some of the best pizza that has ever been tossed anywhere is served here. The pasta and bruschetta are top notch, too. Eat in, take out, or call for a delivery. Beer and wine are served. ✉ *424 N. Higgins Ave.,* ☎ *406/549–7434. MC, V. No lunch.*

$$$$ 🏨 **Triple Creek Ranch.** This ranch is definitely off the beaten path—about a 90-minute drive from Missoula—but it's well worth the effort for those seeking utter seclusion and indulgence. Luxurious log cabins tucked into ponderosa forest offer the kind of privacy and pampering that attracts celebrities to this year-round, adults-only resort. The humblest accommodations here share a hot tub amid the trees, while the others (mostly one-bedroom suites) have roomy indoor Jacuzzis or hot tubs on decks overlooking the Bitterroot Range. Massive log beds, fireplaces, and his-and-her bathroom suites with steam showers grace cabins decorated in rich greens and reds. All meals and drinks, whether taken in the main lodge or in your cabin, are included, as are on-ranch trail rides and fly-casting instruction. The staff has that rare blend of friendliness and discretion. ✉ *5551 West Fork Stage Rte., Darby 59829,* ☎ *406/821–4600,* FAX *406/821–4666. 5 rooms, 15 suites. Restaurant, bar, in-room data ports, kitchenettes, minibars, in-room VCRs, pool, hot tub, massage, putting green, tennis court, hiking, horseback riding, fishing, cross-country skiing, snowmobiling, library, laundry service, business services, meeting rooms, airport shuttle. AE, D, DC, MC, V. FAP.*

$$ 🏨 **Doubletree Hotel Missoula/Edgewater.** Stretching along the Clark Fork River, this reliable chain offers inviting rooms, some of which face the mountains; others overlook the pool. Also on the grounds, which are close to the campus, is a lovely garden. ✉ *100 Madison Ave., 59802,* ☎ *406/728–3100,* FAX *406/728–2530. 172 rooms. Restaurant, bar, coffee shop, pool, hot tub. AE, D, DC, MC, V.*

$$ ★ 🏨 **Goldsmith's Bed and Breakfast.** Built in 1911 for the first president of the University of Montana, this lodging is on the shore of the Clark Fork River, at the end of a footbridge that leads to the campus. Within the prairie-style building, with big white eaves and a huge porch, are period furnishings, wool carpets, and fresh flowers. Each private room is unique, and public rooms include a library and TV sitting area. A bonus to staying at this B&B is that it's right next to Goldsmith's Premium Ice Cream, a café that features homemade ice cream and gourmet coffee. ✉ *809 E. Front St., 59801,* ☎ *406/721–6732. 3 rooms, 4 suites. AE, D, MC, V.*

$$ ☐ **Holiday Inn Missoula–Parkside.** The Missoula member of this chain is a large, comfortable hotel with a lush atrium in the center, and comfortable, modern rooms. The property's most valued asset is its location in Missoula's riverfront park, a stone's throw from the Clark Fork. ✉ *200 S. Pattee St., 59802,* ☎ *406/721–8550 or 800/465–4329,* FAX *406/721–7427. 200 rooms. Restaurant, bar, pool. AE, D, DC, MC, V.*

Outdoor Activities and Sports

CYCLING

The folks at **Adventure Cycling** (✉ 150 E. Pine St., ☎ 406/721–1776 or 406/721–8719) in downtown Missoula have good suggestions for nearby bike routes.

GOLF

Highlands Golf Club (✉ 102 Ben Hogan Dr., ☎ 406/728–7360) has nine holes. **Larchmont Golf Course** (✉ 3200 Old Fort Rd., ☎ 406/721–4416) has 18 holes.

Shopping

Rockin' Rudy's (✉ 237 Blaine St., ☎ 406/542–0077) could be called the store that has everything, including new and used records, CDs, and tapes; T-shirts; imported dresses, hats, and accessories; incense; greeting cards; and other gifts.

Want to bring an unusual gift home? How about an indoor trout stream? Steve Fisher of **Indoor Trout Streams** (✉ 6640 Old Hwy. 10 E, ☎ 406/258–6800) builds custom-made streams from 5 to 30 ft long, complete with insects and trout to match the new drapes. You can make an appointment to see his creations.

National Bison Range

❷ *49 mi north of Missoula, via U.S. 93 north to Ravalli, Rte. 200 west, and Rte. 212 north.*

A self-guided auto tour at the **National Bison Range** allows close-up views of bison, elk, antelope, deer, and mountain sheep. The 20,000-acre refuge at the foot of the Mission Mountains was established in 1908 by President Theodore Roosevelt. Today the U.S. Fish and Wildlife Service ranches a herd of several hundred bison. A visitor center explains the history, habits, and habitat of the bison. To reach the bison range, follow the signs west, then north from the junction of U.S. 93 and Route 200 in Ravalli. ✉ *Rte. 212, Moiese,* ☎ *406/644–2211.* 🎫 *$4 per vehicle.* ⏲ *Mid-May–Sept., daily 8–7; Oct.–mid-May, weekdays 8–4:30.*

St. Ignatius

❸ *40 mi north of Missoula, via U.S. 93 north.*

The **St. Ignatius Mission**—a church, cabin, and collection of other buildings—was built in the 1890s with bricks made of local clay by missionaries and Native Americans. The 58 murals on the walls and ceilings of the church were used to teach Bible stories to the natives. In the St. Ignatius Mission Museum, an old log cabin, is an exhibit of early artifacts and arts and crafts. In St. Ignatius, take Main Street south to Mission Drive. ✉ *1 Catholic Mission Dr.,* ☎ *406/745–2768.* 🎫 *Donations accepted.* ⏲ *June–Aug., daily 9–7; Sept.–May, daily 9–dusk.*

Ninepipe National Wildlife Refuge

❹ *9 mi north of St. Ignatius; 49 mi north of Missoula, via U.S. 93.*

Sprawling Ninepipe is *the* place for bird-watchers. This wetland complex in the shadow of the Mission Mountains is home to everything from marsh hawks to kestrels to red-winged blackbirds. It features rookeries for double-crested cormorants and great blue herons; bald eagles fish here in the winter. Roads through the center of the refuge are closed March through mid-July during nesting season, but visitors can drive along the periphery throughout the year. Maps are available from the nearby National Bison Range, which manages Ninepipe. ✉ *U.S. 93,* ☎ *406/644–2211.*

Bigfork

❺ *44 mi north of Ninepipe National Wildlife Refuge; 96 mi north of Missoula via U.S. 93 to Rte. 35.*

The Swan River empties into Flathead Lake at the small, idyllic resort community of Bigfork. The town is filled with shops and restaurants, and there is a host of activities in the area: boating, hiking, horseback riding, golf, and cross-country skiing. **Flathead Lake,** the largest natural freshwater lake in the western United States, is a wonderful place for sailing, fishing, or swimming. Toward the end of July, on the east side of the lake, farmers harvest cherries and sell them at roadside stands.

Dining and Lodging

$–$$ ✕ **Swan River Café and Dinner House.** This relaxed yet elegant eatery serves prime rib, seafood, and other fare inside or on the terrace overlooking Bigfork Bay. The Sunday brunch and dinner buffets attract throngs of hungry locals. ✉ *360 Grand Ave.,* ☎ *406/837–2220. AE, D, MC, V.*

$$ ★ **Best Western Kwa-Taq-Nuk.** Thirty miles south of Bigfork on the shore of crystalline Flathead Lake is this resort owned by the Confederated Salish and Kootenai tribes. In addition to the deluxe accommodations, guests enjoy sweeping views of the lake and the majestic Mission Mountains from their rooms. The hotel is well situated to provide visitors with golfing, rafting, and lake-cruise adventures. ✉ *303 U.S. 93 E, Polson 59860,* ☎ *406/883–3636 or 800/882–6363,* FAX *406/883–5392. 112 rooms. Restaurant, bar, lobby lounge, indoor and outdoor pools, hot tub, boating. AE, D, DC, MC, V.*

$$ **O'Duach'ain Country Inn Bed and Breakfast.** In a quiet lodgepole-pine forest near Flathead Lake and the Swan River, this lovely property consists of two log-cabin structures: a main house with three guest rooms and a smaller building with two suites. Rooms and common spaces are furnished with Old West antiques and Navajo rugs on the walls; two stone fireplaces warm the main house. A full breakfast, featuring stuffed Irish toast and other house specialties, is included in the room rate. ✉ *675 Ferndale Dr., 59911,* ☎ *406/837–6851,* FAX *406/837–4390. 5 rooms, 4 with bath. Dining room, hot tub, hiking. AE, MC, V.*

Nightlife and the Arts

From late June through Labor Day, the **Bigfork Summer Playhouse** (☎ 406/837–4886) presents repertory Broadway musicals each night except Sunday.

Shopping

Bigfork's Electric Avenue is lined with galleries and eclectic gift shops. A few spots to try are **Bigfork Bay Gift & Gallery** (✉ No. 491, ☎ 406/837–5850), **Beartree Gifts & Collectibles** (✉ No. 470, ☎ 406/837–2327), and **North American Wildlife Gifts** (✉ No. 459, ☎ 406/837–2311).

Kalispell

❻ *15 mi from Bigfork, via Rte. 82 west and U.S. 93 north; or 105 mi north of Missoula via U.S. 93 north.*

Local farmers harvest such produce as Christmas trees, peppermint, and sweet cherries in Kalispell, a lumber town and burgeoning tourist destination with a population of about 12,000. The mild climate of the Flathead Valley makes this area the recreation capital of northwest Montana, with opportunities for rafting, hiking, mountain biking, downhill skiing, and fishing, among other sports.

One of Kalispell's highlights is the **Conrad Mansion National Historic Site Museum,** a 26-room Norman-style mansion that was the home of C. E. Conrad, the manager of a freighter on the Missouri River and the founder of the town of Kalispell. Come Christmas, the mansion is lavishly decorated and filled with the wares of local artisans. ✉ *4th St. (6 blocks east of Main St.),* ☎ *406/755–2166.* 🎫 *$7.* ⏲ *Mid-May–mid-June, daily 10–5:30; mid-June–mid-Sept., daily 9–8; mid-Sept.–mid-Oct., daily 10–5:30.*

The **Hockaday Center for the Arts,** housed in the renovated Carnegie Library, presents national and international contemporary art exhibits. ✉ *2nd Ave. E and 3rd St.,* ☎ *406/755–5268.* 🎫 *Free.* ⏲ *Tues.–Fri. 10–5, Sat. 10–3.*

Dining and Lodging

$–$$ ✕ **Rocco's.** This bustling family eatery serves tasty Italian dishes, steak, and seafood in a casual atmosphere. ✉ *3796 Hwy. 2 E,* ☎ *406/756–5834. AE, D, MC, V. No lunch.*

$–$$ 🏨 **Stillwater Inn.** This lovely turn-of-the-20th-century home offers cozy rooms, gourmet breakfasts, and a convenient location. ✉ *206 4th Ave. E, 59901,* ☎ *406/755–7080 or 800/398–7024,* FAX *406/756–0020. 4 rooms, 2 with private bath. MC, V.*

$ 🏨 **Aero Inn.** Located 1 mi south of town near the airport, this motel boasts comfortable, modern rooms and free Continental breakfast. ✉ *1830 U.S. 93 S, 59901,* ☎ *406/755–3798,* FAX *406/752–1304. 62 rooms. AE, D, MC, V.*

Glacier National Park

❼ *30 mi from Kalispell (to town of Apgar), east on U.S. 2.*

The view into **Glacier National Park**'s interior from Apgar, at the foot of Lake McDonald, has few equals: Its majestic, snowcapped peaks look like an illusion rising out of the lake. Motorized access to the park is limited, but the few roads can take the traveler through a range of settings—from densely forested lowlands to craggy heights. Going-to-the-Sun Road, which snakes through the precipitous center of Glacier National Park, is one of the most dizzying rides on the North American continent. Navigating the narrow, curving highway, built from 1922 to 1932, you will understand why access is restricted. Vehicles more than 21 ft long and 8 ft wide (including mirrors) are not allowed to drive over Logan Pass—a restriction that is enforced at checkpoints at the east and west entrances. Most development and services are concentrated around St. Mary Lake, on the east side of the park; and Lake McDonald, on the west side. Other islands of development occur in Many Glacier, in the northeastern part of Glacier; Logan Pass Visitor Center; and Apgar village. The northern boundary of Glacier National Park coincides with the international border and the southern boundary of Canada's Waterton Lakes National Park. Together, the two parks are called Waterton/Glacier International Peace Park. ✉ *Glacier National Park Headquarters, West Glacier 59936,* ☎ *406/888–7800.* 🎫 *$10 for a 7-day permit.* ⏲ *Park: Open all year, but Going-to-the-Sun Rd. closed over Logan Pass Oct.–June. Limited services in winter. Visitor centers: Open all year, 8–4:30.*

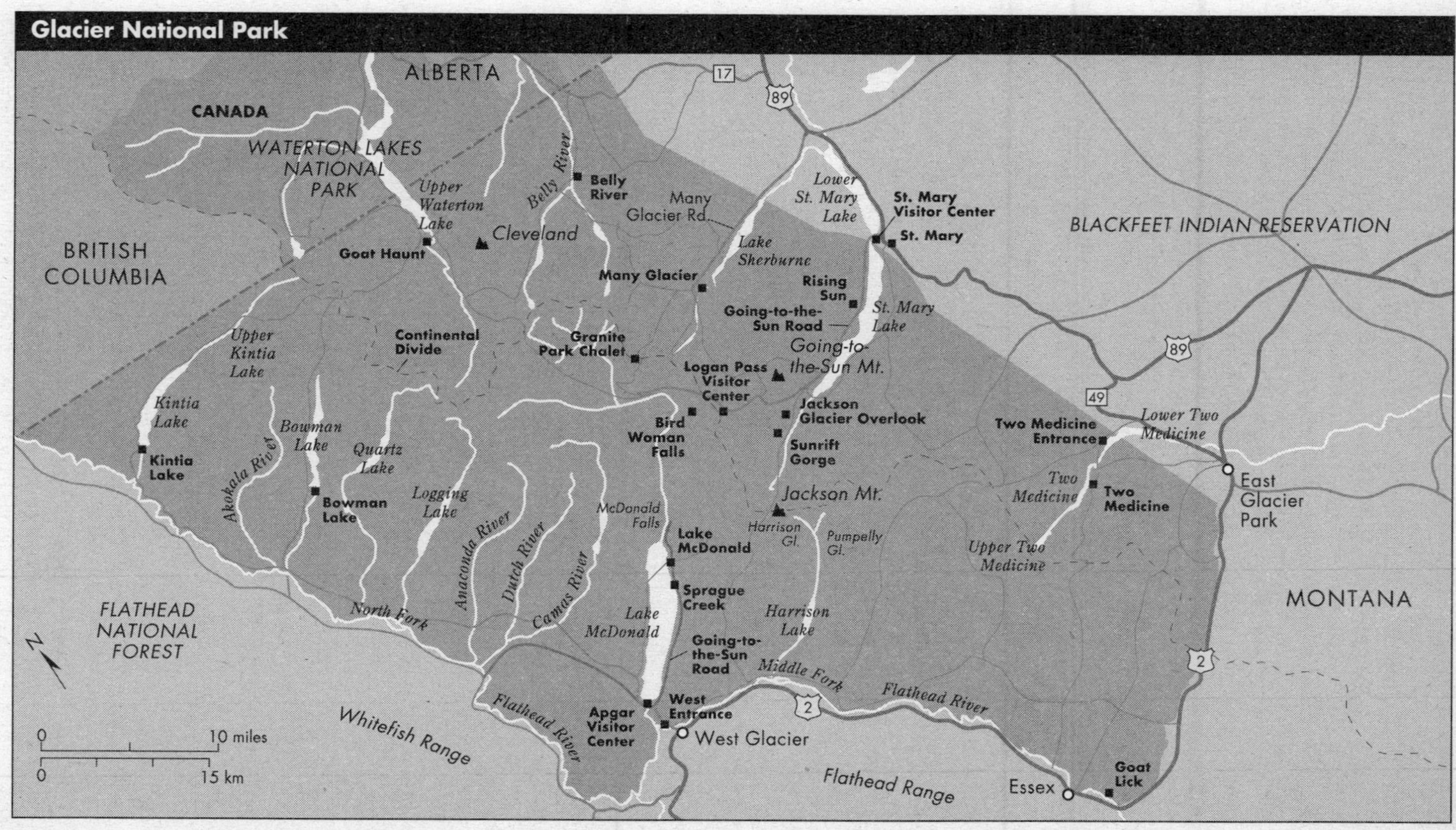
Glacier National Park
ALBERTA
CANADA
WATERTON LAKES NATIONAL PARK
BRITISH COLUMBIA
BLACKFEET INDIAN RESERVATION
MONTANA
FLATHEAD NATIONAL FOREST
Upper Waterton Lake
Goat Haunt
Cleveland
Belly River
Belly River
Many Glacier Rd.
Many Glacier
Lake Sherburne
Lower St. Mary Lake
St. Mary Visitor Center
St. Mary
Rising Sun
Going-to-the-Sun Road
St. Mary Lake
Going-to-the-Sun Mt.
Continental Divide
Granite Park Chalet
Logan Pass Visitor Center
Jackson Glacier Overlook
Bird Woman Falls
Sunrift Gorge
Jackson Mt.
Harrison Gl.
Pumpelly Gl.
Upper Kintia Lake
Kintia Lake
Kintia Lake
Akokala River
Bowman Lake
Bowman Lake
Quartz Lake
Logging Lake
Anaconda River
Dutch River
Camas River
North Fork
McDonald Falls
Lake McDonald
Sprague Creek
Lake McDonald
Harrison Lake
Going-to-the-Sun Road
Middle Fork
Flathead River
West Entrance
Apgar Visitor Center
West Glacier
Flathead River
Whitefish Range
Flathead Range
Two Medicine Entrance
Lower Two Medicine
Two Medicine
Two Medicine
Upper Two Medicine
East Glacier Park
Essex
Goat Lick
17
89
89
49
2
2
0
10 miles
0
15 km
N

Glacier is known as the "Crown of the Continent," for good reason. About 100 million years ago, continents collided and this part of the world was thrust skyward. The last of the massive Ice Age glaciers swept through here 10,000 years ago, acting like a giant rasp on the landscape, moving huge amounts of soil and rock and etching details such as waterfalls, some 200 lakes, knife-edge ridges, and spires into the mountains. Rivers, gravity, and the yearly cycle of freezing and thawing put the finishing touches on the landscape. The 50 glaciers that remain here now are relatively tiny year-round patches of ice and snow, hidden, like refugees, in the dark, cool, high-altitude recesses of the northern mountains. Triple Divide Peak in the backcountry north of the park is a real curiosity. When the snow from most mountains melts, the water drains to either the Pacific or Atlantic. This peak provides water to the Atlantic, Pacific, and Arctic oceans.

In spring and summer, the alpine wildflowers make up for their short season with an unmatched intensity of color. As the sun warms Glacier in the spring, lilies grow up next to the lip of receding snowbanks. Then the mountain meadows explode in pink and red devil's paintbrush, white phlox, lavender shooting stars, pale blue wild irises, moss campion, and mountain heather—all blooming together in a high-mountain Impressionist painting. Later in the summer, the fragrant white balls of bear grass bloom, each looking like a lightbulb on the end of a stick.

Glacier is one of the last enclaves of the grizzly bear, and the wild country in and around the park is home to the largest population of grizzlies in the lower 48 states. Snow-white mountain goats, with their wispy white beards and curious stares, are often seen in alpine areas, and surefooted bighorn sheep graze the high meadows during the short summers.

A haven for outdoor enthusiasts, Glacier National Park offers white-water river rafting, horseback riding, bird-watching, and scenery gazing, to name a few activities. Glacier is also a backpacker's heaven, and more than 700 mi of maintained trails twist and switchback through towering pines, steel gray mountains, and valleys; past turquoise high-alpine lakes; and over wind-whipped ridges that command vast expanses of wilderness.

Head east along the shore of finger-shape Lake McDonald on the serpentine, 52-mi, Going-to-the-Sun Road, one of the most scenic drives in the world. If you want a little exercise, stop near **Avalanche Creek,** where you can pick up a 3-mi trail leading to **Avalanche Lake,** one of many mountain-ringed lakes in the park. The walk is relatively easy, making this one of the most accessible backcountry lakes in the park.

At **Logan Pass**, at the summit of Going-to-the-Sun Road, there's a **visitor center** with crystalline Hidden Lake a short hike from its parking lot. Mountain goats climb rocky cliffs at the lake, wildflowers bloom, and ribbons of water pour off the rocks. Before you set out on any hike in the park, however, remember to grab a jacket: Locals say there are only two seasons here, winter and the Fourth of July—and the only one you can really count on is winter. There's another visitor center at the park's east entrance.

Dining and Lodging

Dining generally takes a back seat to other attractions in and around Glacier. The hotels listed below have dining rooms, and there are less formal cafés in Apgar Village and at Lake McDonald.

$$ **Izaak Walton Inn.** This small, out-of-the-way inn is off U.S. 2, which crosses the Marias Pass along the southern boundary of the park, between East and West Glacier. Originally built as a dormitory for railroad workers, the inn has a historic presence and is a convenient lodging for cross-country skiers, mountain bikers, and hikers. Just outside the front door are more than 18 mi of groomed trails for such activities. Also, for those who don't have a car, Amtrak trains stop right outside the inn, whose front overlooks the train yard. Ask for a room in the back where it's quieter. For train buffs, four cabooses have been renovated and are available for cabin-style lodging. ✉ *123 Izaak Walton Rd., Essex 59916,* ☎ *406/888–5700,* FAX *406/888–5200. 31 rooms, 11 with bath. Restaurant, sauna, recreation room, coin laundry. MC, V.*

GLACIER NATIONAL PARK PROPERTIES

The three massive stone and timber structures described below were built in the early part of this century by the Great Northern Railroad, and today are owned by **Glacier Park, Inc.** They are available June–September and should be reserved three–six months in advance because they book up early. ✉ *For all hotels contact: Glacier Park, Inc., Dial Corporate Center, Phoenix, AZ 85077,* ☎ *602/207–6000. D, MC, V.*

$$–$$$ **Glacier Park Lodge.** On the east side of the park and across from the Amtrak station is this beautiful hotel originally built in 1913. This full-service lodge is supported by 500- to 800-year-old fir and 3-ft-thick cedar logs. ✉ *Off U.S. 2, East Glacier,* ☎ *406/226–9311. 154 rooms. Restaurant, bar, snack bar, pool, 9-hole golf course, playground.*

$$–$$$ **Many Glacier Hotel.** The most isolated of the grand hotels—it's near Swiftcurrent Lake on the northeast side of the park—this is also one of the most scenic, especially if you nab one of the balcony rooms. There are several hiking trails nearby, and a large wrought-iron fireplace in the lobby where guests gather on chilly mornings. ✉ *Many Glacier Rd., 12 mi west of Babb,* ☎ *406/732–4411. 211 rooms. Restaurant, bar, ice cream parlor, hiking.*

$$ **Lake McDonald Lodge.** This former hunting lodge on the shore of lovely Lake McDonald offers cabins, which sleep up to four and don't have kitchens; motel rooms, which are the largest; and units in the lodge itself. The lobby is decorated with mounts of wild animals. ✉ *Going-to-the-Sun Rd.,* ☎ *406/888–5431. 100 rooms. Restaurant, bar, coffee shop, hiking, boating, fishing.*

Outdoor Activities and Sports

FISHING

Within Glacier National Park is an unlimited range of fishing possibilities, with a catch-and-release policy encouraged. The sport-fishing species include burbot (ling); northern pike; whitefish; kokanee salmon; grayling; and cutthroat, rainbow, lake (Mackinaw), and brook trout. You can fish in most waters of the park, but the best fishing is generally in the least accessible spots. A fishing license is free, but it is expected that you familiarize yourself with all park fishing regulations before you use any facilities. Stop by a park office to pick up a copy of the regulations and speak with a ranger. If you want a guide for fly-fishing, contact Glacier Raft Company (☞ Rafting, *below*).

GOLF

Glacier Park Lodge (☎ 406/226–9311), in East Glacier, has a nine-hole, par-36 course, as well as a nine-hole pitch-and-putt course. **Glacier View Golf Course** (☎ 406/888–5471), in West Glacier, is an 18-hole course. If you go on into the Canada park, you could play nine holes at the **Waterton golf course** (☎ 403/859–2114), just outside town. Don't be surprised if you see moose, elk, deer, bighorn sheep, and other wildlife on the greens while playing.

HIKING AND BACKPACKING

Maps for hiking are available at the Apgar Visitor Center (406/888–5441) near the western entrance of Glacier. If you want to backpack, you must pick up a backcountry permit at the same location. Trails of various lengths and levels are well marked within the park. Novices and those who want the help of an experienced guide can sign up with **Glacier Wilderness Guides** (☞ Rafting, *below*), which runs daylong to weeklong trips and also combines hiking and rafting expeditions.

HORSEBACK RIDING

Mule Shoe Outfitters (☎ 406/732–4203) runs the horseback riding concession in Glacier from early June on, as the weather allows. Stables are at Apgar, Lake McDonald, and Many Glacier. Different trips, all led by a guide who provides information on the national park, are for beginning to advanced riders and cover country both flat and mountainous. Rates run from $20 for an hour to $100 for a full day.

RAFTING

Glacier Wilderness Guides and Montana Raft Company (✉ U.S. 2, across from the Amtrak station, Box 535, West Glacier 59936, ☎ 406/387–5555 or 800/521–7238) and **Wild River Adventures** (✉ Box 272B, West Glacier 59936, ☎ 406/387–9453 or 800/826–2724) will take you on **raft trips** through the stomach-churning white water of the Middle Fork of the Flathead and combine it with a hike or horseback ride. Two outfitters working out of **resorts** that also rent cabins with kitchens are: **Glacier Raft Company** (✉ Box 218, West Glacier 59936, ☎ 406/888–5454 or 800/332–9995) and **Great Northern Whitewater** (✉ Box 278, West Glacier 59936, ☎ 406/387–5340 or 800/735–7897). Glacier Raft Company also can provide guides for fly-fishing and organize trips that combine rafting and horseback riding.

SKIING

Big Mountain (✉ Box 1400, Whitefish 59937, ☎ 406/862–3511 or 800/858–4439), 28 mi from Glacier National Park, has 63 marked runs; a 2,300-ft vertical drop; 3,000 skiable acres—plus out-of-bounds for Sno-Cat skiing—and nine lifts, including two high-speed quads. During summer, the gondola continues to operate high above the mountains, exposing the resort's beauty.

Cross-country skiing is increasingly popular in the park itself. It's a good way to observe wildlife, but be careful not to chase the animals; it causes unnecessary stress that could hamper their ability to survive the winter. Glacier National Park distributes a free pamphlet entitled "Ski Trails of Glacier National Park," which describes 16 ski trails that have been identified by the park.

En Route The fastest route east from West Glacier and Apgar to Browning (and the only route in winter, when Going-to-the-Sun Road is closed) is U.S. 2. Near Essex is a goat lick—a natural salt formation along the highway that attracts mountain goats. It's a good place to watch these animals. The highway travels over Marias Pass. At 5,216 ft, this is the lowest major pass over the Rocky Mountains, and the spot where the Great Northern Railroad crossed the Great Divide in 1891.

Browning

8 *13 mi east of Glacier National Park via U.S. 2.*

Browning, just east of the Continental Divide, is the center of the Blackfeet Nation. Until the late 19th century, the Blackfeet hunted the great northern buffalo, moving with them across the vast northern plains. At one time, the Blackfeet homeland stretched all the way from the Missouri River north to the Bow and Red Deer rivers in Canada, and from the Rocky Mountains 300 mi east. Rugged terrain and remoteness left Blackfeet territory some of the last Native American country in the contiguous United States to be opened to whites.

The **Museum of the Plains Indian,** on the north end of town, has been in operation since the 1930s. Now run by the Blackfeet, the museum houses a stunning collection of ancient artifacts from the Blackfeet and other Plains peoples. ✉ *Junction of U.S. 2 and U.S. 89,* ☎ *406/338–2230.* 🎟 *$4.* ⏲ *June–Sept., daily 9–5; Oct.–May, weekdays 10–4:30.*

During the second week of July, the Blackfeet host **North American Indian Days** (☎ 406/338–7276) in Browning. This gathering of tribes is a pageant of drumming, chanting, and tepees as far as the eye can see.

Great Falls

❾ *140 mi southeast of Glacier National Park and 127 mi southeast of Browning via U.S. 89.*

Montana's second-largest city, Great Falls was named for mighty Missouri River waterfalls that were both an inspiring spectacle and a formidable barrier to early navigation. Lewis and Clark were forced to spend nearly a month portaging around the falls in 1805. The mighty falls have been dammed, but much of the surrounding Missouri River country is much as it was in the early explorers' time. Great Falls was the home of famed cowboy artist Charles M. Russell, and the town celebrates his work the third weekend of March with the three-day C. M. Russell Art Auction. In late July and early August, the Montana State Fair is held here.

Russell's original home and log studio are now part of the **C. M. Russell Museum** complex, in the northeast section of town. The museum displays watercolors, sculptures, oil paintings, and illustrated notes and letters from the prolific artist. ✉ *400 13th St. N,* ☎ *406/727–8787.* 🎟 *$4.* ⏲ *May–Sept., Mon.–Sat. 9–6, Sun. 1–5; Oct.–Apr., Tues.–Sat. 10–5, Sun. noon–5.*

Dining and Lodging

$–$$ ✕ **Jaker's.** Ample portions of well-prepared ribs, steaks, and seafood are served in a cozy, inviting atmosphere. ✉ *1500 10th Ave. S,* ☎ *406/727–1033. AE, D, MC, V.*

$–$$ 🏨 **Old Oak Inn.** This lovingly restored Victorian B&B features antique furnishings in the rooms and public areas. The complimentary breakfast is Continental style. ✉ *709 4th Ave. N, 59405,* ☎ *406/727–5782. 6 rooms, 1 with bath. MC, V.*

$ 🏨 **Great Falls Inn.** This attractive, modern motel offers stylishly decorated rooms near the local hospital. Free Continental breakfast is served. ✉ *1400 28th St. S, 59405,* ☎ *406/453–6000,* FAX *406/453–6078. 45 rooms. AE, D, MC, V.*

Helena

❿ *89 mi south of Great Falls via I–15.*

This jewel of a town, where the prairie meets the mountains, started as a rowdy mining camp in 1864 and became a banking and commerce center in the Montana Territory. With statehood came a fight between the towns of Anaconda and Helena over which would be the capital. In a notoriously corrupt campaign in which both sides bought votes, Helena won. The iron ball of urban renewal robbed the town of much of its history, but Helena still has ornate brick and granite historic buildings along the Last Chance Gulch, of early mining fame.

The turn-of-the-20th-century **state capitol** boasts a dome of Montana copper and the largest work Charlie Russell painted, a 12- by 25-ft depiction of Lewis and Clark. Guided tours are offered on the hour in summer. ✉ *6th and Montana Sts.,* ☎ *406/444–4789.* 🎫 *Free.* ⏲ *Daily 8–5.*

The **Montana Historical Society Museum** displays one of the most important collections of Russell's work in its MacKay Gallery. Early black-and-white photos of Yellowstone National Park taken by F. Jay Haynes are on display in the Haynes Gallery. The expansive Montana Homeland exhibit, which features nearly 2,000 historical artifacts, documents, and photographs, gives visitors a thorough look at Montana from the time of the first native settlers to the present. The venue also hosts special events and "family days" during the summer, including programs on folk music, Native American culture, and cowboys. Call ahead for information on upcoming events. ✉ *225 N. Roberts St. (across from the State Capitol),* ☎ *406/444–2694.* 🎫 *Donations accepted.* ⏲ *Memorial Day–Labor Day, weekdays 8–6, weekends and holidays 9–5; Labor Day–Memorial Day, weekdays 8–5, Sat. 9–5.*

Out in front of the Historical Society Museum, catch the ***Last Chancer*** (☎ 406/442–1023), an hour-long, $5 train tour that threads through Helena's historic neighborhoods, from the stately miners' mansions on the west side to the site where four miners made their first discovery on the gulch. It runs from May until September, from 9 to 6, on the hour. Walk a few blocks down 6th Avenue to the center of historic downtown Helena, and ask at the Downtown Helena Office (✉ 121 N. Last Chance Gulch, ☎ 406/442–9869) for **"The Heart of Helena,"** a self-guided walking tour of historic downtown.

On the corner of Last Chance Gulch and Lawrence Street, the lobby of the **Norwest Bank** displays a collection of gold nuggets taken from area diggings. ✉ *350 N. Last Chance Gulch,* ☎ *406/447–2000.* 🎫 *Free.* ⏲ *Weekdays 9:30–4.*

The **Holter Museum of Art,** a block off Last Chance Gulch, houses both permanent and changing exhibits of visual arts. The emphasis is on Montana artists, folk art, crafts, photography, painting, and sculpture. ✉ *12 E. Lawrence Ave.,* ☎ *406/442–6400.* 🎫 *Free.* ⏲ *Memorial Day–Labor Day, Tues.–Sat. 10–5, Sun. noon–5; Labor Day–Memorial Day, Tues.–Sun. noon–5.*

If you're tired of looking at attractions and want to stretch your legs, consider taking an hour-long hike to the top of Mt. Helena, which towers over the Last Chance Gulch Mall on the west edge of town. From the summit, you'll have panoramic views of Helena, the Helena Valley, and the Rocky Mountains to the west.

For an old-fashioned sweet treat, pull up a stool at the **Parrot** (✉ 42 N. Last Chance Gulch, ☎ 406/442–1470), a soda fountain and candy store built in the 1920s that sells everything from chocolate malts with homemade ice cream to hand-dipped chocolates.

OFF THE BEATEN PATH

FRONTIER TOWN – Frontier-style buildings handmade from huge trees and mammoth boulders are filled with reproduction and antique furnishings at this kitschy, eccentric tourist attraction built in the 1950s. Swagger into the saloon and order a beer at the long bar cut from a single huge tree. There is also a good restaurant. ✉ *U.S. 12, 15 mi west of Helena,* ☎ *406/442–4560.* 🎫 *Free.* ⏲ *Apr.–Oct., daily 9 AM–10 PM.*

Dining and Lodging

$ ✕ **On Broadway.** Wooden booths, discreet lighting, and brick walls contribute to the comfortable ambience at this Italian restaurant. Popular dishes include New York strip steak and scampi *fra diavolo* (shrimp with mushrooms, peppers, spices, wine, and tomato sauce). On Broadway is a nice place to chat and has a leisurely dining pace. ✉ *106 Broadway,* ☎ *406/443–1929. Reservations not accepted. AE, DC, MC, V. Closed Sun.*

$ ★ ✕ **Windbag Saloon & Grill.** This historic restaurant in the heart of downtown was a sporting house called Big Dorothy's until 1973, when a crusading county attorney forced Dorothy to close up shop. Now it's a family restaurant, named for the political debates you're likely to hear while dining on burgers, quiche, salads, and sandwiches. Inside the historic building is a bounty of cherry wood that gives this place a warm, comfortable feel. It also has a large selection of imported beer, on tap and in bottles. ✉ *19 S. Last Chance Gulch,* ☎ *406/443–9669. AE, DC, MC, V. No lunch Sun.*

$$ ★ **Sanders Bed and Breakfast.** This three-story Victorian mansion was built in 1875 by Colonel Wilbur Sanders, the prosecuting attorney at some of the summary trials hosted by the Montana vigilantes. The colonel's rock collection is still in the front hall, and the B&B has retained his furnishings. Most of the rooms have beautiful views overlooking mountain-ringed downtown Helena, and the breakfasts are something to behold. ✉ *328 N. Ewing St., 59601,* ☎ *406/442–3309,* FAX *406/443–2361. 7 rooms, 6 with bath. AE, MC, V.*

$–$$ ★ **Jorgenson's Holiday Motel, Restaurant, and Lounge.** This pleasant, modern motel is conveniently located next to a shopping mall and near the capitol. Its friendly, family-style restaurant is popular with locals from breakfast through dinner. ✉ *1714 11th Ave., 59624,* ☎ *406/442–1770,* FAX *406/449–0115. 17 rooms. Restaurant, bar, pool. AE, MC, V.*

Nightlife and the Arts

In Helena, an oasis for the arts is the **Myrna Loy Center for the Performing Arts** (✉ 15 N. Ewing, ☎ 406/443–0287). In a remodeled historic jail, the center—named after the Montana-born actress—offers live performances by nationally and internationally recognized musicians and dancers. There are also two theaters here that show foreign and independent films.

Outdoor Activities and Sports

CYCLING

Old logging roads running through the mountains of western Montana and in national forest land offer some of the best mountain biking in the state. Trail biking is not allowed in the national parks. For route information, call the **Helena National Forest** (☎ 406/449–5201).

FISHING

High Plains Outfitters of Helena (✉ 31 Division St., ☎ 406/442–9671) offers guided trips on various rivers in Montana, including the Missouri, the Big Hole, and the Blackfoot, and wading on smaller rivers and streams.

Shopping

Many of the nation's best ceramic artists come to work in residency at the **Archie Bray Foundation** (✉ 2915 Country Club Ave., ☎ 406/443–3502). Wander near the five antiquated, 8-ft-high, dome-shape brick kilns on a self-guided walking tour, and visit the gift shop, which sells work produced by foundation artists. It's open Monday through Saturday 10–5 and Sunday 1–5.

Missoula to Helena A to Z

Arriving and Departing

BY BUS

Greyhound Lines (☎ 800/231–2222) serves Missoula. **Intermountain Bus Company** stops in Kalispell (☎ 406/755–4011) and Helena (☎ 406/442–5860).

BY CAR

I–90 and U.S. 93 pass through Missoula. U.S. 93 and Route 35 lead off I–90 to Kalispell in the Flathead Valley; from there, U.S. 2 heads to Glacier National Park. If you're traveling to Glacier from the east, take I–15 to Great Falls and U.S. 89 to the east entrance to the park.

BY PLANE

Missoula International Airport (☎ 406/728–4381), on U.S. 93 just north of Missoula, is served by Delta, Northwest, Horizon, Big Sky, and Sky West. **Glacier Park International Airport** (☎ 406/257–5994), 8 mi northeast of Kalispell on U.S. 2, is serviced by Delta, Northwest, Horizon, and Big Sky. **Helena Regional Airport** (☎ 406/442–2821) offers flights on Delta, Horizon, and Big Sky. **Great Falls Airport** (☎ 406/727–3404) is served by Delta, Northwest, Horizon, and Big Sky.

BY TRAIN

Amtrak (☎ 800/872–7245) stops in Whitefish, Essex, East Glacier Park, and Browning.

Contacts and Resources

DOCTORS AND DENTISTS

Missoula: St. Patrick Hospital (✉ 500 W. Broadway, ☎ 406/543–7271).

Kalispell: Kalispell Regional Hospital (✉ 310 Sunnyview La., ☎ 406/752–5111).

GUIDED TOURS

Glacier Park, Inc. (☎ 406/226–5551 or 800/332–9351) operates a fleet of vintage-1930s red-and-black buses that navigate along Going-to-the-Sun Road. **Sun Tours** (☎ 406/226–9220) offers tours of Glacier from a Native American perspective.

VISITOR INFORMATION

Blackfeet Nation (✉ Box 850, Browning 59417, ☎ 406/338–7276). **Glacier National Park** (✉ West Glacier 59936, ☎ 406/888–5441). **Great Falls Chamber of Commerce** (✉ 815 2nd St. S, 59403, ☎ 406/761–4434). **Helena Chamber of Commerce** (✉ 201 E. Lyndale, 59601, ☎ 406/442–4120 or 800/743–5362). **Missoula Chamber of Commerce** (✉ Box 7577, 59807), ☎ 406/543–6623 or 800/526–3465).

BILLINGS TO BIG HOLE

This tour captures some of the diversity of Montana, moving from the rolling, grassy plains and rimrocks of eastern Montana to the Rocky Mountain Front and across the Continental Divide to southwestern Montana. The route follows I–90 along the meandering Yellowstone River before heading up U.S. 287 toward the timber-draped mountains of the west. Along the way it reveals much of Montana's history, from gold strikes to Indian wars. Mining towns and resort communities, cowboys and capitalists blend effortlessly in the heart of Big Sky Country.

Billings

11 *224 mi from Helena, south via U.S. 12/287 and east via I–90.*

Billings, the regional capital of the coal and oil industry, is, with nearly 100,000 residents, not only the largest city in Montana but also the largest city for 500 mi in any direction. The "Magic City" was developed in 1882 with the coming of the railroad and was named after a member of its board of directors, Frederick Billings. Billings is in the middle of the rolling plains of eastern Montana, at the foot of buckskin-color cliffs dubbed the rimrocks. The Bighorn Mountains are about an hour's drive south and offer hiking, fishing, camping, and all kinds of recreation.

Moss Mansion, at 3rd and Division streets, was built in 1903 for businessman P. B. Moss by Dutch architect Henry Hardenbergh (designer of the original Waldorf-Astoria Hotel in New York City). It still contains many of the elaborate original furnishings, ranging in style from Moorish to Art Nouveau Empire. Guided tours are offered on the hour. ✉ *914 Division St.,* ☎ *406/256–5100.* *$6.* ⏲ *June–Labor Day, Mon.–Sat. 10–4, Sun. 1–3; Labor Day–May, daily 1–3.*

A worthwhile attraction that offers insight into the history and culture of the Yellowstone River region is the **Western Heritage Center,** on the corner of 29th and Montana avenues. Its permanent exhibit includes oral histories, artifacts, and interactive displays tracing the lives of Native Americans, ranchers, homesteaders, immigrants, and railroad workers during the period 1880–1940. ✉ *2822 Montana Ave.,* ☎ *406/256–6809.* *Donations accepted.* ⏲ *June–Aug., Tues.–Sat. 10–6, Sun. 1–5; Sept.–May, Tues.–Sat. 10–6.*

The **Yellowstone Art Center,** in the original county jail, reopened in fall 1997 after an extensive renovation and expansion project. It features a permanent collection of western art along with changing exhibitions of regional artists' works. ✉ *401 N. 27th Ave.,* ☎ *406/256–6804.* *$3.* ⏲ *Tues.–Sat. 10–5, Sun. noon–5.*

OFF THE BEATEN PATH

PICTOGRAPH CAVE STATE PARK – Just 7 mi east of town, off I–90 (follow the signs from the Lockwood exit), is this state monument with ocher and black-and-white early drawings of figures, tepees, and wildlife. The complex of three caves was home to generations of prehistoric hunters. More than 30,000 artifacts have been identified from the park. Rock paintings in Pictograph Cave, the largest of the three, can be viewed from a short paved trail. ☎ *406/245–0227.* *$3 per car.* ⏲ *Mid-Apr.–mid-Oct., daily 8–8.*

Dining and Lodging

$–$$$ ✕ **Jake's.** This pleasant downtown eatery features steaks, seafood, and an inspired salad bar. The dimly lit restaurant, decorated with brass and wood, can seat 130 guests. ✉ *2701 1st Ave. N,* ☎ *406/259–9375. AE, MC, V. Closed Sun.*

$–$$ ✕ **CJ's Restaurant.** The kitchen at this popular spot turns out juicy mesquite-grilled ribs, steaks, chicken, and seafood, with a choice of three barbecue sauces—from mild to three-alarm. The wine list is well chosen. High-back chairs and intimate dining areas create a comfortable, casual atmosphere. ✉ *2456 Central Ave.,* ☎ *406/656–1400. AE, D, DC, MC, V.*

$–$$ ✕ **George Henry's Restaurant.** This popular spot is a remodeled 1882 home with stained-glass windows and delicious seafood specialities. ✉ *404 N. 30th St.,* ☎ *406/245–4570. AE, D, MC, V. Closed Sun.*

$ ✕ **Café Jones.** Have a slice of homemade quiche at this small downtown bistro. The chrome tables and unusual lamps give the place a 1950s flair, but a 1990s appreciation for java is demonstrated by a tasty selection of coffee drinks. ✉ *2712 2nd Ave. N,* ☎ *406/259–7676. No credit cards.*

$–$$ 🏨 **Radisson Northern Hotel.** This historic 1905 building in downtown Billings was destroyed by fire in 1940, then rebuilt. Although remodeled in 1990, it still provides a sense of the city's past. Rooms follow an American West theme, with woven rugs, bedspreads, and a gaming table. Views are glorious. The massive fireplace is the centerpiece of a comfortable lobby—a common gathering place for guests and locals. The Golden Belle serves fine Continental cuisine in an atmosphere that's fancier than usual for Montana. ✉ *Broadway at 1st Ave. N, Box 1296, 59101,* ☎ *406/245–5121 or 800/333–3333,* FAX *406/259–9862. 160 rooms. Restaurant, bar. AE, D, DC, MC, V.*

$ 🏨 **Hilltop Inn.** This quiet, well cared-for motel offers comfortable rooms and attractive public spaces. Amenities include a Continental breakfast and a coin laundry. ✉ *1116 N. 28th St., 59101,* ☎ *406/245–5000 or 800/878–9282,* FAX *406/245–7851. 45 rooms. Coin laundry. AE, D, DC, MC, V.*

$ 🏨 **Ponderosa Inn Best Western.** Rooms in this comfortable, modern motel are painted in pastel colors. There's a heated pool in the courtyard, surrounded by plenty of greenery. ✉ *2511 1st Ave. N, 59101,* ☎ *406/259–5511 or 800/628–9081,* FAX *406/245–8004. 130 rooms. Bar, café, pool, hot tub, sauna, exercise room. AE, D, DC, MC, V.*

$ 🏨 **Rimview Inn.** This clean, convenient motel boasts Montana's largest saltwater aquarium—a 1,000 gallon tank in the lobby. Free Continental breakfast is provided, and some suites have hot tubs and kitchens. ✉ *1025 N. 27th St., 59301,* ☎ *406/248–2622,* FAX *406/248–2622. 34 rooms, 20 suites. AE, D, DC, MC, V.*

Nightlife and the Arts

The **Alberta Bair Theater for the Performing Arts** (✉ 2801 3rd Ave. N, ☎ 406/256–6052 tickets, 406/256–8915 office) presents music, theater, dance, and other cultural events.

Outdoor Activities and Sports

Lake Hills (✉ 1930 Clubhouse Way, ☎ 406/252–9244) has 18 holes of golf.

Shopping

WESTERN PARAPHERNALIA

Rand's Custom Hats (✉ 2205 1st Ave. N, ☎ 406/259–4886 or 800/346–9815) creates cowboy hats for working cowboys as well as the celluloid variety and will make a felt fur hat exactly the size and shape of your head. Prices range from $200 to $2,000. They also produce custom leather carrying cases.

Stillwater Traders (✉ 2821 2nd Ave. N, ☎ 406/252–6211) corrals unique items such as night-lights shaped like trout, cowboy dishes, western-style clothing, and toys and T-shirts with a Western theme.

OFF THE BEATEN PATH

MILES CITY – History buffs may want to travel east from Billings (145 mi via I–94) to the ranch town of Miles City (population 10,000), at the confluence of the cottonwood-lined Tongue and Yellowstone rivers. The federal Treaty of 1868 said this would be "Indian country as long as the grass is green and the sky is blue." That promise changed, however, when gold was found in the Black Hills of South Dakota to the east, and white settlers streamed into this part of the world. Ranchers eventually took over, and in 1884, the last of the great herds of buffalo was slaughtered near here to make room for cattle. Ranching has been a way of life ever since. In May, Miles City holds the **Bucking Horse Sale** (☏ 406/232–2890) a three-day event with a rodeo and a giant block party. The **Range Riders Museum** (✉ Old Hwy. 10, 1 mi from Miles City, Exit 135 off I–94, ☏ 406/232–4483) is open daily from April to October, from 8 to 8, and costs $3.50. It's jammed to the rafters with saddles, chaps, spurs, guns, and other cowboy paraphernalia.

Little Bighorn Battlefield National Monument

⓬ *60 mi southeast of Billings via I–90 to U.S. 212.*

When the smoke cleared on June 25, 1876, neither Lieutenant Colonel George Armstrong Custer nor his 200 or so blue-shirted troopers were alive to tell the story of their battle against several thousand Northern Plains natives on this rolling, windswept prairie along the Little Bighorn River. It was a Pyrrhic victory for the tribes; the loss would force the U.S. government to redouble its efforts to clear them off the plains. Now a national monument, the site, on the Crow Indian Reservation, has a new interpretive display that includes material from recent archaeological excavations. The display explains what led to the momentous clash of two cultures and speculates on what might have happened during the battle. ✉ *U.S. 212, 15 mi from I–90, Exit 510,* ☏ *406/638–2621.* *$6 per vehicle.* ⏲ *Memorial Day–Labor Day, daily 8–8; Sept., Apr., and May, daily 8–6; rest of yr, daily 8–4:30.*

Red Lodge

⓭ *60 mi southwest of Billings via U.S. 212.*

Nestled against the foot of the pine-draped Pryor Mountains, Red Lodge was named for a band of Cheyenne who marked their settlement with paintings of red earth. It became a town in the late 1880s when the Northern Pacific Railroad laid tracks here to take coal back to Billings. At one time, "Liver Eatin' " Jeremiah Johnson, subject of much Western lore and a Robert Redford movie, was sheriff here. Now the historic little burg is listed on the National Register of Historic Places and is in the process of becoming a full-blown resort town, complete with a ski area, trout fishing, horseback riding, and a golf course.

Each August, Red Lodge holds a nine-day **Festival of Nations** (☏ 406/446–1718) to celebrate the numerous ethnic heritages of people who worked in the mines nearby.

From Red Lodge, you can continue south on U.S. 212 over the precipitous **Beartooth Pass,** which winds its way through lush alpine country to the "back door" of Yellowstone National Park in Wyoming (☞ Off the Beaten Path *in* Yellowstone National Park *in* Chapter 8). The highway is usually open from May to September, but bad weather can close it at any time.

Dining and Lodging

$–$$ ✕ **Bogart's.** Humphrey Bogart memorabilia abounds in this popular spot, which offers an eclectic mix of pizza, Mexican food, and standard American dishes. ✉ *11 S. Broadway,* ☏ *406/446–1784. MC, V.*

$$–$$$$ ★ **Pollard Hotel.** This 1893 landmark in the heart of Red Lodge's historic district has been lovingly restored to the charms of an earlier era. Public rooms have handsome oak paneling and green, brown, and gold flocked wallpapers. Enjoy a drink in the History Room surrounded by photos recalling the hotel's past. Reproduction Victorian furniture throughout vivifies a fin-de-siècle feeling. Greenlee's Dining Room is also a public restaurant specializing in steaks, chops, and exotic game such as ostrich. ✉ *2 N. Broadway, Box 1217, 59068,* ☏ *406/446–*

0001 or 800/765–5273, FAX 406/446–3733. 38 rooms. Bar, dining room, no-smoking rooms, hot tub, sauna, racquetball, exercise room. AE, DC, MC, V.

$$ **Rock Creek Resort.** This resort, which added a handsome rustic lodge facility in 1995, is just 4½ mi south of town. It's built along a babbling, rock-strewn creek and decorated in a Southwestern motif. It has a wonderful restaurant—the Old Piney Dell—in a historic old cabin. The menu features simple American, Mexican, and regional food. ✉ *U.S. 212, HC 49, Box 3500, 59068,* ☎ *406/446–1111,* FAX *406/446–3688. 90 rooms. 2 restaurants, 2 bars, indoor pool, sauna, 4 tennis courts, basketball, soccer, volleyball, fishing, cross-country skiing, playground. AE, D, DC, MC, V.*

Outdoor Activities and Sports

The 18-hole **Red Lodge Mountain Golf Course** (✉ 828 Upper Continental St., ☎ 406/446–3344) offers a beautiful view of the mountains.

In winter, there are 25 mi of skiing trails and a 2,350-ft vertical drop at **Red Lodge Mountain** (✉ 101 Ski Run Rd., ☎ 406/446–2610).

Shopping

Kibler and Kirch (✉ 22 N. Broadway, ☎ 406/446–2802) sells lodgepole pine beds, cowboy pillows, antiques, and original art.

Big Timber

⓮ *81 mi from Billings via I–90 west; 88 mi from Red Lodge via Rte. 78 north and I–90 west.*

Nestled at the foot of the Crazy Mountains, Big Timber offers galleries, antiques shops, and blue-ribbon trout streams. Explore the Boulder Valley and drop by the **Yellowstone River Trout Hatchery** (☎ 406/932–4434) to gaze at cutthroat trout. The Chamber of Commerce (☎ 406/932–5131) can provide information about sightseeing (a prairie-dog town and a natural bridge) in the region.

Lodging

$–$$ ★ **Grand Hotel.** This is a renovated classic Western hotel in the middle of downtown Big Timber—on I–90 between Billings and Livingston. The rooms are small, clean, and comfortable, and furnished with antiques—the kind of accommodations you might find over the Longbranch Saloon in *Gunsmoke.* A full breakfast is included in the daily room rate. The romantic restaurant serves decadent desserts. ✉ *139 McLeod St., 59011,* ☎ *406/932–4459. 10 rooms, 2 with bath. Bar, dining room, meeting room. D, DC, MC, V.*

Livingston

⓯ *35 mi west of Big Timber, 116 mi west of Billings via I–90.*

The stunning mountain backdrop to this town was once Crow territory, and a chief called Arapooish said about it: "The Crow country is good country. The Great Spirit has put it in exactly the right place. When you are in it, you fare well; when you go out of it, you fare worse."

The railroads brought white settlers, and Livingston, along the banks of the beautiful Yellowstone River, was built to serve the railroad. The railroad has been replaced by small businesses that cater to tourists, but the town of 12,000 has retained much of its turn-of-the-20th-century flavor. Perhaps you'll recognize it from Robert Redford's movie *A River Runs Through It* (adapted from the book of the same title by Norman Maclean), which was filmed here.

The old **Northern Pacific Depot** (take Exit 333 off I–90 and turn right onto Park Street) is now a museum with displays on Western and railroad history and works by artists from the region and around the country. The 1902 depot, an Italian villa–style structure, has mosaic trim, a terrazzo floor, and wrought-iron ticket windows. ✉ *200 W. Park St.,* ☎ *406/222–2300.* *$3.* ⊙ *Mid-May–Sept., Mon.–Sat. 9–5, Sun. 1–5.*

The **Park County Museum,** on the north side of town in an old schoolhouse, holds an old caboose, a sheep wagon, a stagecoach, and other pioneer memorabilia. ✉ *118 W. Chinook St.,* ☎ *406/222–3506.* *$3.* ⊙ *June–Labor Day, daily 9–5.*

OFF THE BEATEN PATH

YELLOWSTONE RIVER – Just south of Livingston and north of Yellowstone National Park, the Yellowstone River comes roaring down the Yellowstone Plateau and flows through Paradise Valley. Primitive public campsites (available on a first-come, first-served basis) and fishing access sites can be found at various places along the river, which is especially popular for trout fishing, rafting, and canoeing. U.S. 89 follows the west bank of the river, while East River Road runs along the east side.

Dining and Lodging

$–$$ ✕ **Uncle Louie's.** The food's Italian and the decor has a Mediterranean flavor in this popular restaurant and bar across the street from the train station. ✉ *119 W. Park Rd.,* ☎ *406/222–7177. AE, D, DC, MC, V.*

$$$$ **Mountain Sky Guest Ranch.** This full-service guest ranch in the middle of scenic Paradise Valley has riding, tennis, fishing, a heated pool, and a sauna. To get to the ranch, take U.S. 89 27 mi south of I–90 and then go 4½ mi west at the Emigrant turnoff. This leaves you only 30 mi north of Yellowstone National Park for some fine sightseeing if you want to leave the ranch. There's a seven-night minimum stay mid-June–Labor Day and a three-night minimum the rest of the year. ✉ *Big Creek Rd., Emigrant; mailing address: Box 1128, Bozeman 59715;* ☎ *406/587–1244 or 800/548–3392,* FAX *406/333–4911. 27 rooms. Dining room, pool, sauna, 2 tennis courts, horseback riding, fishing. MC, V. FAP.*

$$ **63 Ranch.** This dude ranch, 12 mi southeast of Livingston, is one of Montana's oldest, and it rests on 2,000 acres of land. It has been owned by the same family since 1929. A full range of activities is offered, from horseback riding to fishing to pack trips, but only seven-night (Sunday–Sunday) packages are offered for stays in their eight commodious, rustic cabins. ✉ *Box 979A, 59047,* ☎ *406/222–0570,* FAX *406/222–9446. 18 rooms. Dining room, horseback riding, fishing, coin laundry. No credit cards.*

$–$$ ★ **Murray Hotel.** In the old days, this hotel in downtown Livingston catered to early visitors to Yellowstone who came by train. Visitors ranged from Will Rogers to the Queen of Denmark. It has been remodeled, and the simple, elegant dining room, now called the Winchester Café, is excellent. Public spaces re-create the hotel's 1904 beginnings, and renovated guest rooms retain the charm of an earlier era. Each antiques-filled room reflects a different theme, and the staff tries to match guests with a room to fit their needs and interests. One room boasts furnishings used in the film *A River Runs Through It.* Another commemorates the five years director Sam Peckinpah lived at the Murray; it's decorated with movie posters and memorabilia along with furnishings from the director's room. ✉ *201 W. Park St., 59047,* ☎ *406/222–1350.* FAX *406/222–6745. 32 rooms, 30 with bath. Restaurant, bar. AE, MC, V.*

Shopping

ART GALLERIES

Livingston's beauty has inspired artists, as evidenced by the many fine art galleries in town. Paintings, sculptures, and works in other media can be found at the **Wishing Tree Gallery** (✉ 113 W. Callender St., ☎ 406/222–7528). The **Danforth Gallery** (✉ 106 N. Main St., ☎ 406/222–6510) is a community art center that displays and sells contemporary works by local and regional artists. **Visions West Gallery** (✉ 108 S. Main St., ☎ 406/222–0337) specializes in Western and wildlife art, including a wide range of works on the fly-fishing theme, from paintings and bronzes to hand-carved flies.

BOOKS

The floorboards creak as you walk through **Sax and Fryer's** (✉ 109 W. Callender St., ☎ 406/222–1421), an old-time bookstore specializing in Western literature. It also sells gifts.

Bozeman

16 *25 mi west of Livingston via I–90.*

In 1864, a trader named John Bozeman led his wagon train through this valley en route to the booming goldfields at Virginia City and southwest Montana. For several years it was the site of Ft. Ellis, established to protect settlers making their way west along the Bozeman Trail, which extended into Montana Territory. Recently the city, with a population of 25,000, has become a recreation capital for everything from trout fishing to white-water river rafting to backcountry mountain biking. The arts have also flowered here, in the home of the state's second-largest university (Montana State University). Each April, for example, members of New York's Metropolitan Opera stage a performance in Bozeman.

The town has a strong Western heritage, and each June the **College National Rodeo Finals** (☎ 406/587–2637) are held at the Montana State University (MSU) field house.

At the southern edge of the Montana State University campus, the **Museum of the Rockies** celebrates the history of the Rockies region. Eclectic exhibits include everything from prehistory to pioneers and a planetarium. There are dinosaur displays, complete with bones and eggs dug up in Montana, and a room where visitors can watch workers clean dinosaur fossils. Children love the hands-on science activities in the Martin Discovery Room and the Tensley Homestead, with home-crafts demonstrations including butter churning, weaving, and blacksmithing. ✉ *600 W. Kagy Blvd.,* ☎ *406/994–3466.* *$5.* *Memorial Day–Labor Day, daily 9–9; Labor Day–Memorial Day, Mon.–Sat. 9–5, Sun. 12:30–5.*

Dining and Lodging

$–$$ ★ ✕ **John Bozeman's Bistro.** It may be small, but the menu—from hot seafood stir-fry and Cajun cookery to creative sandwiches and soups—is one of the best in the state. Bozeman's Bistro is also known for its setting in a National Historic Register building, with a brick interior and well-preserved wood floors. In bustling downtown Bozeman, the bistro isn't far from some good antiques and furniture shops. ✉ *242 E. Main St.,* ☎ *406/587–4100. AE, D, MC, V. Closed Mon.*

$–$$ ✕ **Mackenzie River Pizza.** Zesty gourmet pizzas featuring tomato or pesto sauces, sun-dried tomatoes, artichoke hearts, and more are baked in a brick oven before your eyes. Eat here in this bustling joint, or take it to go. ✉ *232 E. Main St.,* ☎ *406/587–0055. Reservations not accepted. AE, MC, V.*

$$ **Gallatin Gateway Inn.** Built by the Milwaukee Railroad as a stopping-off point for visitors to Yellowstone National Park, this sumptuous inn is conveniently situated just 10 mi from town on U.S. 191 and 30 minutes from Big Sky Ski Resort. It did have its dog days, however, when it fell into disrepair and became a seedy bar that featured female

Jell-O wrestling (honest). After a renovation in 1987, the inn recaptured its reputation, with a wonderful restaurant and an outdoor swimming pool. The uniquely furnished rooms have contemporary, modern western decor and are painted in soothing pastels. The bathrooms, with original tile work and brass fixtures, exude simple elegance. ✉ *U.S. 191, Box 376, Gallatin Gateway 59730,* ☎ FAX *406/763–4672. 32 rooms, 29 with bath. Restaurant, pool, tennis court. AE, DC, MC, V.*

$$ ★ **Voss Inn.** This B&B occupies an elegant 1883 Victorian house and is lavishly furnished with antiques. Stop by the parlor for afternoon tea or to catch up on the news with other guests who drop in to watch TV or to chat. The lovely English garden makes a great spot for a quiet conversation. ✉ *319 S. Willson Ave., 59715,* ☎ *406/587–0982,* FAX *406/585–2964. 6 rooms with bath. MC, V.*

Outdoor Activities and Sports

Backcountry Bicycle Tours of Bozeman (✉ Box 4209, 59772, ☎ 406/586–3556) offers touring in the Gallatin Valley and all over the state.

Montana Whitewater (✉ Box 1552, 59771, ☎ 406/763–4465 or 800/799–4465) provides guided raft trips and horseback/raft packages.

Wildlife Safari (✉ Box 42, 59771, ☎ 406/586–1155) offers expeditions throughout Montana and Yellowstone guided by a wildlife biologist. Hikes, raft trips, and auto tours are available.

SKIING

Bridger Bowl (✉ 15795 Bridger Canyon Rd., ☎ 406/587–2111) is a top-ranked ski area. There's a variety of terrain, from steep, rocky chutes to gentle slopes and meadows. **Big Sky Resort** (✉ 1 Lone Mountain Trail, Big Sky, ☎ 406/995–5000 or 800/548–4486), 43 mi from Bozeman, is a beautiful, family resort with 75 mi of groomed downhill trails and cross-country skiing at Big Sky's Lone Mountain Guest Ranch (✉ U.S. 191, between Bozeman and West Yellowstone, ☎ 406/995–4644 or 800/514–4644). For more information about Big Sky, *see* Chapter 2.

Three Forks

17 *29 mi west of Bozeman via I–90.*

Sacajawea, famed for helping Lewis and Clark, lived in the Three Forks area with the Shoshone before she was kidnapped as a child by a rival tribe. A plaque in the city park commemorates her contribution to the expedition's success.

The Madison, Jefferson, and Gallatin rivers come together to form the mighty Missouri River within **Missouri Headwaters State Park,** a National Historic Landmark. Lewis and Clark named the three forks after Secretary of the Treasury Albert Gallatin, Secretary of State James Madison, and President Thomas Jefferson. The park has historical exhibits, interpretive signs, picnic sites, hiking trails, and camping. ✉ *Trident Rd., 3 mi northeast of Three Forks,* ☎ *406/285–3198.* *$3 per vehicle (includes admission to Madison Buffalo Jump* ☞ *below).* ⏲ *Daily dawn–dusk.*

Within **Madison Buffalo Jump** historic site is the cliff where Plains natives stampeded bison to their deaths more than 2,000 years ago. An interpretive center explains how the technique enabled Native Americans to gather food and hides. Picnic areas provide a restful break from touring. From Bozeman head west 23 mi on I–90 to the Logan exit and then follow the signs south along Buffalo Jump Road for 7 mi. ✉ *Buffalo Jump Rd., 30 mi west of Bozeman,* ☎ *406/285–3198.* *$3 per vehicle (includes admission to Missouri Headwaters State Park,* ☞ *above).* ⏲ *Daily dawn–dusk.*

18 **Lewis and Clark Caverns,** Montana's oldest state park, offers some of the most beautiful underground landscape in the nation. Two-hour tours lead through narrow passages and vaulted chambers past colorful, intriguingly varied limestone formations. The temperature stays in the 50s year-round; jackets and rubber-sole shoes are recommended. The hike to the cavern entrance is mildly strenuous. ✉ *Rte. 2, 19 mi west of Three Forks,* ☎ *406/287–3541.* *$7.* ⏲ *June–Labor Day, 9–6:30; May and Sept., 9–4:30.*

Dining and Lodging

$–$$ ✕▣ **Sacajawea Inn.** This carefully restored historic hotel—built in 1910—has 33 rooms decorated with arts and crafts reminiscent of the early 1900s. On summer evenings, the owners serve iced tea to guests, who sit in a line of wooden rockers on the expansive front porch. The restaurant serves a sumptuous Sunday brunch. Dinners feature Montana beef, seafood, and pasta dishes. ✉ *5 N. Main St., Box 648, 59752,* ☎ *406/285–6515 or 800/821–7326,* FAX *406/285–6515. 33 rooms. Restaurant, no-smoking rooms, meeting room. AE, D, MC, V.*

Virginia City

19 *66 mi from Three Forks, via I–90 west, U.S. 287 south, and (at Ennis) Rte. 287 west.*

Remnants of Montana's frontier days, Virginia City and its smaller neighbor Nevada City are two of the most unusual attractions the state has to offer, with lovingly restored historic buildings. When miners stampeded into the state in the 1860s, one of the places where the diggings were rich was in Virginia City's Alder Gulch; the city prospered and eventually became the capital of Montana Territory. The success of the city enticed criminals, who held up miners; in turn, vigilance committees—eager to maintain order—grew, held lightning-fast trials, and strung up the bad guys. Some of the graves of those hung by vigilantes remain atop a hill overlooking town. You can tour Virginia City on an old-time fire truck, walk along a boardwalk, wander through stores stocked with 19th-century goods, and ride a narrow-gauge railroad. Nevada City has a smaller collection of historic buildings, a music hall with fascinating coin-operated instruments, and all sorts of restaurants and shops.

Butte

20 *53 mi west of Three Forks via I–90; 79 mi northwest of Virginia City via Rte. 287 and Rte. 55.*

Dubbed the "Richest Hill on Earth," Butte was once a wealthy and rollicking copper-, gold-, and silver-mining town. The underground copper mines were dug up in the 1950s, creating the **Berkeley Open Pit Mine,** which is more than 1 mi across and reaches 1,800 ft deep. A viewing platform allows you to look into the now-abandoned, mammoth pit. ✉ *Continental Dr.,* ☎ *406/494–5595.* *Free.* ⏲ *Daily 8–dusk, weather permitting.*

Downtown Butte, a National Historic Landmark area, has numerous ornate buildings reminiscent of the Old West days. While meandering through the streets, consider this: Butte has the dubious distinction of containing the largest toxic waste site in the country—thanks to the old mining wastes. The city maintains a strong Irish flavor, and its St. Patrick's Day celebration is one of the region's finest.

Keeping watch over Butte—as seen from the east ridge of the Rocky Mountains—is **Our Lady of the Rockies,** a 90-ft-tall, 80-ton statue of the Virgin Mary on the Continental Divide; it's lit at night. For a two-hour bus tour, stop by the visitor center. ✉ *434 N. Main St.,* ☎ *406/782–1221 or 800/800–5239.* 🎫 *$10.* ⊙ *June–Sept., Mon.–Sat. 10–2, Sun. 11–2.*

Dining and Lodging

$–$$ ✕ **Uptown Café.** Fresh seafood, steaks, poultry, and pasta are served in this informal, smoke-free café. ✉ *47 E. Broadway,* ☎ *406/723–4735. AE, D, MC, V.*

$ ✕ **Pork Chop John's Sandwich Shop.** This small eatery serves up Butte's signature sandwich, a breaded pork sirloin that's been savored by residents since 1920. ✉ *2400 Harrison Ave.,* ☎ *406/782–1783. No credit cards.*

$$ ★ **Fairmont Hot Springs.** If you have children, you should bring them to this resort near Anaconda and 20 mi west of Butte. Although not much as far as architecture goes, it has naturally heated indoor and outdoor swimming pools, a water slide, and a petting zoo in a beautiful setting. There's an 18-hole golf course on the grounds. ✉ *1500 Fairmont Rd., Gregson 59711,* ☎ *406/797–3241 or 800/332–3272,* FAX *406/797–3337. 130 rooms, 28 suites. Restaurant, bar, coffee shop, indoor and outdoor pools, massage, 18-hole golf course, 2 tennis courts, volleyball. AE, D, DC, MC, V.*

$$ **War Bonnet Inn.** This attractive motel is next to a park with a running track and tennis courts. ✉ *2100 Cornell Ave., 59701,* ☎ *406/494–7800 or 800/443–1806,* FAX *406/494–2875. 134 rooms. Restaurant, bar, pool, whirlpool, sauna, exercise room. AE, D, MC, V.*

OFF THE BEATEN PATH

MONTANA AUTO MUSEUM – Part of a complex of museums based around the old state penitentiary, this one is a car buff's delight. Displays include more than 100 vintage Fords and Lincolns dating from 1903 to the 1970s, including such rarities as a Fordson tractor and a Model A snowmobile. Admission here also grants you passage to the Old Montana Prison, Frontier Montana Museum, and Yesterday's Playthings Doll and Toy Museum. ✉ *1106 Main St., Deer Lodge, 41 mi west of Butte via I–90,* ☎ *406/846–3111.* 🎫 *$8.* ⊙ *June–Aug., daily 8 AM–8 PM; Sept.–Oct. and Apr.–May, daily 8:30–5:30. Hrs vary at other times of the year.*

Dillon

㉑ *65 mi south of Butte, via I–90 west and I–15 south.*

Dillon is a capital of southwestern Montana's ranch country and was a shipping point for cattle and sheep on the Union Pacific Railroad. There is hiking and mountain biking in the nearby Ruby and Tendoy mountains, and the fishing on the Beaverhead River is very good. The **Beaverhead County Museum** exhibits Native American artifacts; ranching and mining memorabilia; a homesteader's cabin; mining equipment and agricultural artifacts; and a boardwalk imprinted with the area's ranch brands. ✉ *15 S. Montana St.,* ☎ *406/683–5027.* 🎫 *Donations accepted.* ⊙ *Memorial Day–Labor Day, weekdays 10–8, weekends 1–5; Labor Day–Memorial Day, weekdays 10–noon, weekends 1–5.*

OFF THE BEATEN PATH

BANNACK STATE HISTORIC PARK – Bannack was Montana's first territorial capital. Today, protected as a state park, it is a good example of a frontier boomtown. Montana's vigilantes were active here, and one of the most notorious was Henry Plummer, the sheriff himself. The gallows on which he was hanged still stands in Bannack. Rumors persist that Plummer's stash of stolen gold was hidden somewhere in the mountains near here and never found. To get to Bannack, follow Route 278 21 mi west out of Dillon and watch for a sign just before Badger Pass; take the well-maintained gravel road for 3 mi. ☎ *406/834–3413.* 🎫 *$4 per vehi-*

cle. ⏲ Park: daily dawn–dusk; visitor center: Memorial Day–Labor Day, daily 10–6.

Big Hole National Battlefield

㉒ *87 mi southwest of Butte, via I–90 west, I–15 south, and Rte. 43 west.*

One of the West's greatest and most tragic stories played out on this battlefield. In 1877, Nez Perce warriors in central Idaho killed some white settlers as retribution for earlier killings by whites. The Nez Perce, knowing the army would make no distinction between the guilty and innocent, fled—the beginning of a 1,500-mi odyssey. They engaged 10 separate U.S. commands in 13 battles and skirmishes. One of the fiercest of these was here at Big Hole Battlefield, where both sides suffered serious losses. From here, the Nez Perce headed toward Yellowstone. A visitor center overlooks the meadows of the Big Hole, which remain as they were at the time of the battle. Tepee poles erected by the park service mark the site of the Nez Perce village and serve as haunting reminders of what transpired here. ☎ *406/689–3155,* 🎫 *$4 per vehicle Memorial Day–Labor Day, free rest of year.* ⏲ *May–Labor Day, daily 8–8; rest of year, daily 8–5.*

En Route If you're heading back to Missoula from Big Hole, take Route 43 west to U.S. 93 for an 80-mi drive through the beautiful **Bitterroot Valley.** The route is flanked by scenic peaks—the Bitterroot Range to your left, the Sapphire Range to your right—and signs along the road mark abundant hiking trails. If you're in need of refreshment, stop in the small town of Victor at the **Hamilton** (✉ 104 Main St., ☎ 406/642–6644), an authentic Scottish pub replete with great fish-and-chips and a kilt-wearing owner.

Billings to Big Hole A to Z

Arriving and Departing

BY BUS

Intermountain Transportation Company buses stop in Butte (☎ 406/723–3287). **Greyhound Lines** (☎ 800/231–2222) and **Rimrock Stages** (☎ 406/442–5860) serve Billings and Bozeman. In summer, **Karst Stage** (☎ 406/586–8567 or 800/332–0504) runs between Bozeman, Livingston, Billings, and Yellowstone.

BY CAR

Use I–90 for Billings, Livingston, Bozeman, and Butte. U.S. 89 and U.S. 212 link this region with Yellowstone National Park.

BY PLANE

Logan Field International Airport (☎ 406/657–8495) in Billings is the largest in the state and is served by Big Sky, Delta, Horizon, Northwest, Sky West, and United. Farther west, in Bozeman, **Gallatin Field Airport** (☎ 406/388–6632) is served by Delta, Horizon, Northwest, and Sky West. Butte's **Bert Mooney Airport** (☎ 406/494–3771) is served by Horizon and Sky West.

Contacts and Resources

DOCTORS AND DENTISTS

Billings Deaconess Medical Center (✉ 2800 10th Ave. N, Billings, ☎ 406/657–4000). **Bozeman Deaconess Medical Center** (✉ 915 Highland Blvd., Bozeman, ☎ 406/585–5000). **St. Peter's Community Hospital** (✉ 2475 Broadway, Helena, ☎ 406/442–2480).

GUIDED TOURS

Karst Stage (☎ 406/586–8567 or 800/332–0504) in Bozeman conducts group tours of the state and one-day tours of Yellowstone National Park for individuals.

VISITOR INFORMATION

Butte Chamber Visitor and Transportation Center (✉ 1000 George St., 59701, ☎ 406/723–3177 or 800/735–6814). **Billings Chamber of Commerce** (✉ Box 31177, 59107, ☎ 406/245–4111). **Bozeman Convention and Visitors Bureau** (✉ Box B, 59715, ☎ 406/587–2111 or 800/228–4224). **Livingston Chamber of Commerce** (✉ 212 W. Park St., 59047, ☎ 406/222–0850). **Miles City Chamber of Commerce** (✉ 901 Main St., 59301, ☎ 406/232–2890). **Red Lodge Chamber of Commerce** (✉ Box 998, 59068, ☎ 406/446–1718). **Virginia City Chamber of Commerce** (✉ Box 218, 59755, ☎ 406/843–5345).

MONTANA A TO Z

Getting There

By Bus

Greyhound (☎ 800/231–2222) carries passengers into Montana from all neighboring states.

By Car

Primary routes into Montana from Idaho include I–90, I–15, and scenic U.S. 12. I–90 enters the state from Wyoming. I–95 and U.S. 12 are popular access routes from North Dakota, and U.S. 212 is the route from the Black Hills of South Dakota.

By Plane

Billings's **Logan Field International Airport** (☎ 406/657–8495) is the largest in the state. **Gallatin Field Airport** (☎ 406/388–6632) is just outside Bozeman. **Glacier International Airport** (☎ 406/257–5994) is in Kalispell. **Missoula International Airport** (☎ 406/728–4381) is the fourth major facility in the state.

By Train

Amtrak's (☎ 800/872–7245) *Empire Builder* runs east–west across Montana's Highline, the most northern part of the state, on its way from Chicago to Portland and Seattle. Major stops along the route, which parallels U.S. 2, include Havre, Shelby, Glacier National Park, and Whitefish.

Getting Around

By Bus

Greyhound Lines (☞ above) services the southern part of the state. **Rimrock Stages** (☎ 406/549–2339) runs regular bus service between Missoula, Bozeman, and Billings.

By Car

Drivers on the interstate now face a daytime speed limit after several years of a "reasonable and prudent" rule that transformed some stretches into an American autobahn. But a speed limit was reinstated in May 1999, limiting drivers to 65 mph in urban areas and 75 in the wide open spaces. At night, the speed limit is 65. Going east to west, I–94 runs from the North Dakota border and into I–90 near Billings, where it becomes I–90 all the way to the Idaho border. Interstate 90, meanwhile, comes up from Wyoming to join I–94. From north to south, I–15 comes into southern Montana from Idaho, and it runs through Dillon, Butte, Helena, and Great Falls on its way to the Canadian border.

In Montana you may make a right turn at a red light, after stopping, unless there is a sign posted forbidding it.

Contacts and Resources

Camping

The Montana state highway map, which is free from gas stations, hotels, and Travel Montana (☞ Visitor Information, *below*), lists many of the campgrounds. The U.S. Forest Service, Northern Region Office (✉ Missoula 59801, ☎ 406/329–3511) and any of the national forest offices around the state can provide information on camping in Montana's forests.

Cycling

For information on cycling in the state, contact **Adventure Cycling** (☎ 406/721–1776 or 406/721–8719).

Emergencies

Ambulance (☎ 911). **Police** (☎ 911). The **Montana Highway Patrol** can be reached at ☎ 800/525–5555.

Fishing

Licenses are required for fishing. An annual, nonresident season license costs $45 and is good through February of the season it was purchased. A two-day license is $15 for the first two days and $10 for every two days after that. For more information, contact the **Montana Department of Fish, Wildlife, and Parks** (✉ 1420 E. 6th Ave., Helena 59601, ☎ 406/444–2535).

Guided Tours

Glacier Wilderness Guides and its affiliate Montana Raft Company (✉ Box 535, West Glacier 59936, ☎ 800/521–7238) lead trips through stomach-churning white water, and they often combine the adventure with horseback riding or hiking.

Wild Horizon Expeditions (✉ West Fork Rd., Darby 59829, ☎ 406/821–3747) is a wilderness guide service that specializes in six- to eight-day backpack trips into some of Montana's remotest wild places, where you're not likely to see other people. Expert guides discuss the plants, wildlife, and geology.

Visitor Information

Travel Montana (✉ Dept. of Commerce, 1424 9th Ave., Helena 59620, ☎ 406/444–2654 or 800/847–4868) provides information and free publications, including a comprehensive directory of lodgings, guest ranches, campgrounds, outfitters, and special events.

By Scott Warren

Updated by Kurt Repanshek

GIVEN THAT SPECTACULAR SCENERY pervades virtually every corner of Utah, visitors can be thankful that much of the state falls under public domain. Federally owned lands include five national parks, seven national monuments, a national historic site, two national recreation areas, seven national forests, and more than 22 million acres held by the Bureau of Land Management (BLM). Add to this nearly four dozen state parks, and it's easy to see why there are unlimited opportunities to enjoy the great outdoors. Whether your interest is hiking a trail, touring a scenic byway, skiing a powdery slope, fishing a lake, setting sails to the wind, watching wildlife, shooting the rapids, or capturing a scenic panorama on film, you can find it in Utah.

Its natural beauty notwithstanding, Utah is unique in other respects. Prior to 1847, Utah was like many other western areas. It was home to the Ute, Navajo, Paiute, Gosiute, and Shoshone Indians. It had witnessed the birth and eventual disappearance of the Fremont and Anasazi peoples. Spanish expeditions had come and gone, and streams and river valleys were stalked by rough-and-ready mountain men.

But on July 24, 1847, an event took place that would set Utah on a unique course. On that day, a small band of Mormons led by Brigham Young got its first look at the Great Salt Lake Valley. Casting his gaze over the arid land, Young declared to his followers: "This is the place." Within hours the pioneers began planting crops and diverting water for irrigation, and within days Brigham Young drew up plans for what would become one of the most successful social experiments ever.

As members of the relatively new Church of Jesus Christ of Latter-day Saints (LDS), these pioneers had migrated west to escape religious intolerance. Establishing a new promised land adjacent to the Great Salt Lake, they were joined by tens of thousands of other Mormons in the two decades that followed. Many settled in Salt Lake City, while others were directed by Young to establish smaller towns in distant corners of the territory. To populate this particularly harsh land took an effort that was no less than heroic, but the reward was to be a society free from outside influence and control. Or so the pioneers had hoped.

Although the Mormons were determined to keep to themselves, their land of Zion was not to be. In 1862, U.S. troops were dispatched to Salt Lake City to keep an eye on them. In 1868, the discovery of silver in the nearby Wasatch mountains led to a flood of prospectors and miners and, as a result, to the growth of riotous mining camps. In the year following, the completion of the first transcontinental railroad ushered in additional waves of non-Mormon ("gentile" in LDS terminology) settlers. By the turn of the 20th century, Utah's religious and social homogeneity had been effectively destroyed.

Today, because about 75% of all Utahns count themselves as members of the Mormon church, Utah is decidedly conservative. Utah was, for instance, the only state in the nation that placed Bill Clinton third behind George Bush and Ross Perot in the 1992 presidential election. Politics aside, Utah is not nearly as provincial as many nonresidents have come to believe. When it comes to hotels, restaurants, the arts, and other worldly pleasures, places such as Salt Lake City, Park City, and Ogden have no shortage of acceptable, and sometimes excellent, options. A legislative overhaul of Utah's infamous drinking laws has rendered those beasts essentially harmless. However, many nightspots require that you purchase temporary "membership" for about $5 (which entitles you to order liquor). Combine the state's burgeoning

7 UTAH

Although 10 other states exceed Utah's 84,990-square-mi area, few, if any, can match the breadth and diversity of its topography. Around virtually every bend, mountains pierce the skyline. Oceans of sagebrush roll out to the horizon. Improbable canyons score the earth. Snow-white salt flats shimmer, lush evergreen forests rim alpine meadows, and azure lakes glisten in the sun.

sophistication with its natural splendor, wealth of recreational opportunities, and a growing list of guest services and facilities, and it can safely be said that having fun is not prohibited in Utah.

Pleasures and Pastimes

Dining

There are a growing number of fine restaurants in Salt Lake and Park City, and culinary jewels are cropping up in various other areas. But generally, options lean toward more traditional, family-style eateries serving up meat and potatoes (and a little fresh fish). Having a drink with dinner is not a problem, nor, at most places, is getting a table. Men might want to wear a jacket at the more expensive restaurants in Salt Lake City; otherwise, dress is casual.

CATEGORY	COST*
$$$$	over $35
$$$	$25–$35
$$	$15–$25
$	under $15

**per person, excluding drinks, service, and approximately 61/4% sales tax (rates vary depending on location)*

Lodging

Chains are everywhere. Other than that, accommodations are varied—from entire ski villages under one roof at some of the resorts; the tall, modern business hotels in downtown Salt Lake City; and historic bed-and-breakfast inns and modest motels that simply provide a good place to rest after a day of sightseeing. No-smoking rooms are available; ask when making reservations. Rooms have private baths unless otherwise noted in the reviews.

CATEGORY	COST*
$$$$	over $125
$$$	$100–$125
$$	$75–$100
$	under $75

**All prices are for a standard double room, excluding approximately 61/4% sales tax and 3%–11% room tax (rates vary depending on location).*

Outdoor Activities and Sports

During winter, skiing is king, and a number of first-class resorts bring skiers from all over the country and the world. In the summer, Utah is filled with hikers, campers, and, increasingly, mountain bikers. Perhaps most surprising in this second-driest state, boating on the many lakes, rafting on the rivers in the south and east, and fishing (for bass, pike, kokanee salmon, and cutthroat trout), are extremely popular activities. Golf courses are throughout the state, and reservations are generally necessary.

Parks

With five, Utah has more national parks than any other state except Alaska and California. Though Bryce and Zion are the best known, fascinating landscape can be seen at Arches, Canyonlands, and Capitol Reef national parks. Utah's 45 state parks range from historic monuments to recreation areas, many of which have public lakes, often reservoirs, that are popular spots for camping as well as boating and other water sports. Officially, national and state parks are open 24 hours a day, but visitor centers are usually open 8–sunset.

Exploring Utah

Utah's landscape is remarkably diverse. Salt Lake City sprawls at the western base of the Wasatch Range. It's the largest in a string of cities known locally as the Wasatch Front. The Wasatch mountains themselves form a rugged divider spanning the center of the state for 300 mi from north to south. East of the Wasatch Range, northeastern Utah is dominated by the east/west-oriented Uinta Mountains and their foothills, which give way to the rural and ranching country of the Uinta Basin. Millions of years ago, dinosaurs rumbled through this part of the state. Today, their remnants have earned this region the moniker, "Dinosaurland." To the south, the geologic division known as the Colorado Plateau dominates the red-rock country of southeastern Utah, where the ancient Fremont and Anasazi cultures once made their homes. In the southwestern portion of the state, colorful deserts mingle with forested mountains and stretch north to meet the Great Basin. All of Utah's national parks are in the southern reaches of the state, which typically offer a climate much more mild and dry year-round than northern Utah's.

Numbers in the text correspond to numbers in the margin and on the Utah, Salt Lake City, and Salt Lake City Vicinity maps.

Great Itineraries

IF YOU HAVE 3 DAYS

You'll have little trouble filling a day in and around **Salt Lake City.** Begin at the **Great Salt Lake**'s south shore. During spring and fall migrations there will be hundreds of shore and wading birds. Back in the city, enjoy an early lunch and some shopping at the **ZCMI Center** or **Crossroads Plaza,** then walk across the street to tour **Temple Square** ① or just enjoy the beautiful grounds. Dinner at **Trolley Square** ⑳ could be followed by a movie, unless you'd rather take in a **Utah Jazz basketball game** at the Delta Center or a **Salt Lake Buzz baseball game** at Franklin Covey Field. In the morning drive to **Park City** ㉚ and spend the day skiing, golfing, or browsing the shops on historic Main Street. Do visit the **Winter Sports Park** to watch would-be Olympians train, or maybe try a ski jump or bobsled run yourself. This evening, enjoy one of Park City's fine restaurants or clubs. If day three dawns on a weekend, drive to Midway for brunch at the **Homestead.** Swing down Provo Canyon to experience "rustic chic" at **Sundance Resort** ㊴, or continue on to Provo and visit the fine museums on the Brigham Young University campus before returning to Salt Lake City.

IF YOU HAVE 7 DAYS

It's difficult to experience all of Utah's best in only one week—better to choose specific parts of the state and give them your full attention. The two itineraries that follow do just that. The first begins in Salt Lake City and explores southeastern Utah. The second begins in Las Vegas and highlights the attractions of southwestern Utah.

Begin your week in Salt Lake City. After a morning of sightseeing and a light lunch, head toward **Park City** ㉚, stopping at the **Factory Stores** just outside town, before checking into one of Park City's hotels or inns. Splurge on an elegant dinner at Deer Valley Resort's **Glitretind** restaurant or Park City's **Grappa.** Spend the next morning skiing, golfing, or just relaxing. In the afternoon, try the **Silver Mine Adventure,** then drive to **Sundance Resort** ㊴ for dinner and evening entertainment. Spend the night in one of the resort's elegant mountain cabins. After breakfast, drive south to **Capitol Reef National Park** ㊻. You should have an entire afternoon to hike and explore the park. During late summer and early fall you can pick fruit in the pioneer orchards along the Fremont River. Overnight in nearby **Torrey,** dining at one of the tiny town's surprisingly good restaurants. In the morning, pick up some freshly baked bread and other picnic staples at the small store on Route 24, and drive east and north from Torrey to I–70 eastbound, then south on U.S. 191 to **Moab** 51. Choose a spot along the Colorado River to enjoy your picnic lunch beneath soaring sandstone cliffs. After lunch, head north on U.S. 191 and west on Route 313 to enjoy the view from **Dead Horse Point State Park** and the **Island in the Sky District** of **Canyonlands National Park,** of the Colorado and Green rivers, thousands of feet below, flowing through the incredible landscape they have carved. Toward evening, head back to Moab for dinner and a good night's sleep. On day five, join a day trip on the Colorado River, rent a bicycle, or head into the surrounding red-rock landscapes on foot, or with a guide in a four-wheel-drive vehicle. End your day with the guided **Canyonlands by Night,** a relaxing after-dark float on the Colorado, and overnight again in Moab. After breakfast and a stop at one of Moab's well-stocked grocery stores for lunch fixings, head north to **Arches National Park.** Between the stunning scenic drive, and the myriad hiking opportunities, there is plenty here to fill your day. Enjoy dinner, and a night in the cabins at **Pack Creek Ranch** south of Moab. On your final day, pick up a few souvenirs in Moab's various gift shops, or browse for Southwestern art in any of several galleries. Then head north east from Moab along the **Colorado River Scenic Byway** (Route 128) to I–70, then west to the town of Green River. Grab a burger at **Ray's Tavern,** guaranteed to satisfy your appetite all the way back to Salt Lake City.

If you choose to explore southwestern Utah, embarking from Las Vegas via I–15, it is a three hour drive to **St. George** 66, leaving plenty of time for golf, shopping, or a tour of the city's historic district. In the late afternoon, drive through Snow Canyon State Park to enjoy the evening views. Return to St. George for dinner and a night at one of the city's historic B&Bs. In the morning, head for **Zion National Park** 67. Try the open-air car tour of Zion Canyon to fully appreciate its grandeur. Have dinner and a restful night in one of the small communities near the southern entrance to the park. On your third day, skirt through Zion's east side on Route 9, then follow U.S. 89 north to Route 14 and west to **Cedar City** 65. During the summer, don't miss the **Utah Shakespearean Festival,** including a Royal Feaste for dinner. If the festival is not going on during your visit, drive Route 14 through Cedar Canyon to visit **Cedar Breaks National Monument** 64, and have a meal at Milt's Stage Stop on your way back to Cedar City for the night. In the morning, take Route 14 and Route 143 to Panguitch, then continue east on Route 12 to **Bryce Canyon National Park** 69. You should arrive in plenty of time to explore the amphitheaters of Bryce on foot or horseback. Don't miss the spectacle of sunset on the colorful formations. From April to October, you can sign up for a chuck-wagon dinner at **Best Western Ruby's Inn,** then take in the **nightly rodeo.** Spend the night in the historic Bryce Canyon Lodge. From Bryce on day five, follow Route 12 east to **Escalante** 70 and across the **Grand Staircase–Escalante National Monument** to **Calf Creek Falls,** a perfect place to enjoy a picnic lunch. Continue north on Route 12, over Boulder Mountain. Take time to stop and savor the incredible views along the way. The town of **Torrey** sits at the junction of Route 12 and Route 24; overnight here, and try the funky Southwestern cuisine at Café Diablo. In the morning, take Route 24 east to **Capitol Reef National Park** 72. Spend the day hiking and discovering the history of the Fremont Culture and the 19th-century pioneers, who both settled along the banks of the Fremont River, which runs through the park. Overnight again in Torrey, or nearby Loa.

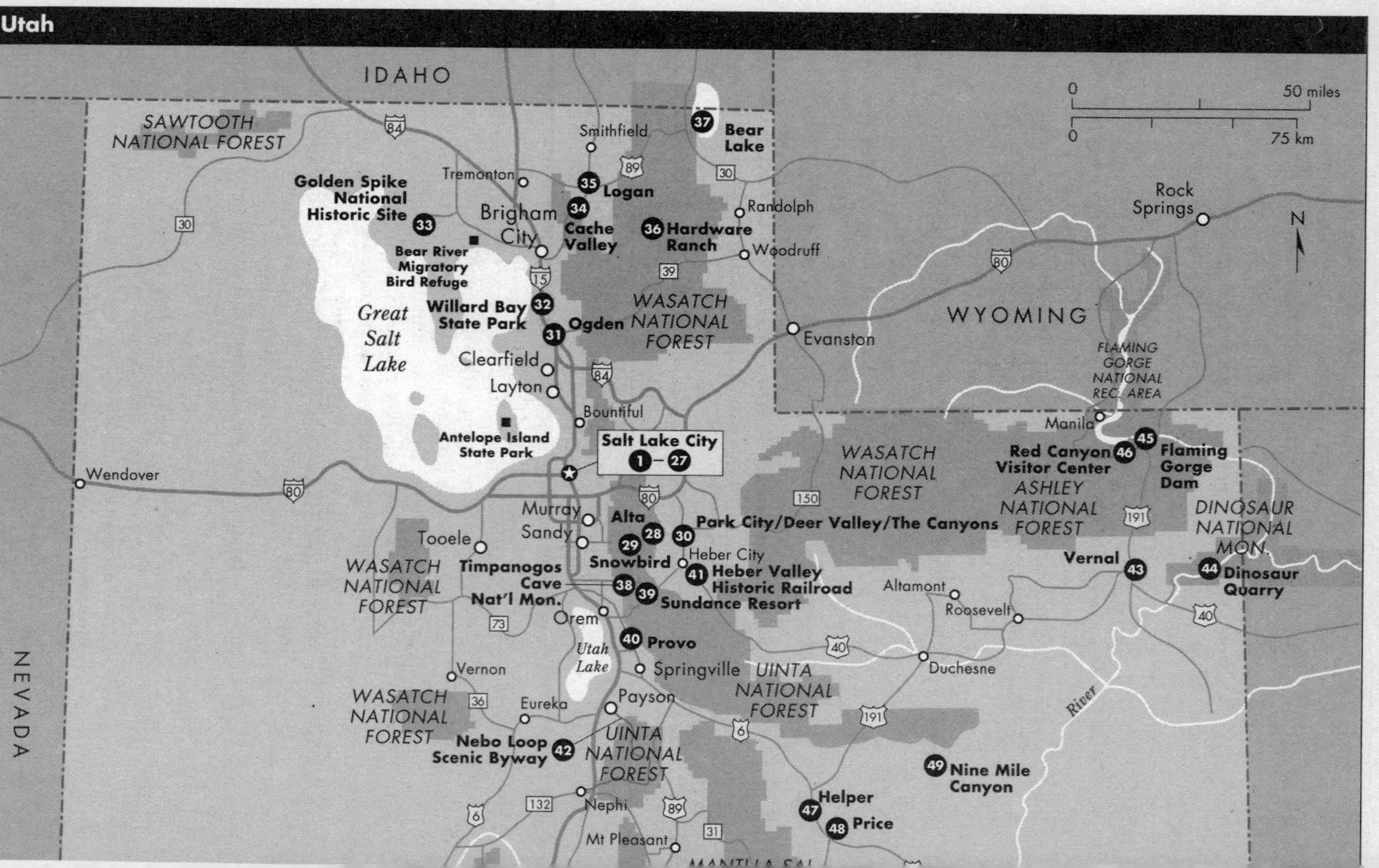
IDAHO
WYOMING
NEVADA
0 50 miles
0 75 km
N
SAWTOOTH NATIONAL FOREST
Smithfield
37 Bear Lake
Tremonton
35 Logan
34 Cache Valley
Golden Spike National Historic Site
33
Brigham City
36 Hardware Ranch
Randolph
Woodruff
Bear River Migratory Bird Refuge
Great Salt Lake
Willard Bay State Park
32
31 Ogden
WASATCH NATIONAL FOREST
Clearfield
Layton
Bountiful
Antelope Island State Park
Salt Lake City
1 – 27
Wendover
Evanston
Rock Springs
FLAMING GORGE NATIONAL REC. AREA
Manila
45 Flaming Gorge Dam
Red Canyon Visitor Center 46
ASHLEY NATIONAL FOREST
DINOSAUR NATIONAL MON.
44 Dinosaur Quarry
Vernal 43
Murray
Sandy
Alta
28
29
30 Park City/Deer Valley/The Canyons
Snowbird
Heber City
41 Heber Valley Historic Railroad
38
39 Sundance Resort
Tooele
Timpanogos Cave Nat'l Mon.
Orem
40 Provo
Utah Lake
Springville
UINTA NATIONAL FOREST
Altamont
Roosevelt
Duchesne
River
Vernon
Eureka
Payson
Nebo Loop Scenic Byway 42
Nephi
Mt Pleasant
49 Nine Mile Canyon
47 Helper
48 Price
84
89
30
39
15
80
150
191
40
73
36
6
132
31

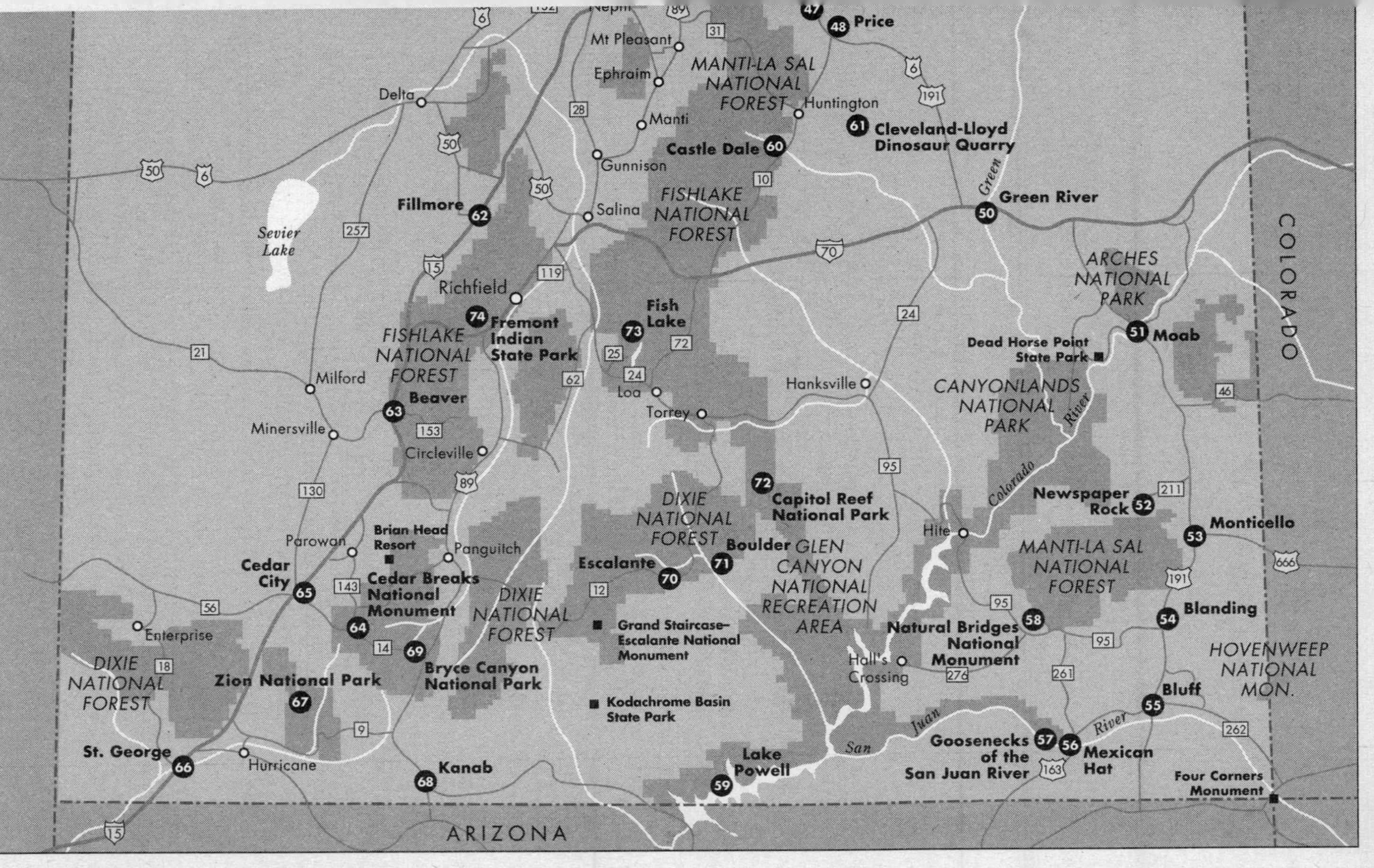
Price
Mt Pleasant
Ephraim
MANTI-LA SAL NATIONAL FOREST
Huntington
Manti
Cleveland-Lloyd Dinosaur Quarry
Delta
Castle Dale
Gunnison
FISHLAKE NATIONAL FOREST
Fillmore
Salina
Green River
Green
Sevier Lake
COLORADO
ARCHES NATIONAL PARK
Richfield
Fremont Indian State Park
Fish Lake
Moab
Dead Horse Point State Park
FISHLAKE NATIONAL FOREST
Milford
Beaver
Hanksville
Loa
Torrey
CANYONLANDS NATIONAL PARK
River
Minersville
Circleville
DIXIE NATIONAL FOREST
Capitol Reef National Park
Colorado
Newspaper Rock
Monticello
Brian Head Resort
Parowan
Panguitch
Boulder
GLEN CANYON NATIONAL RECREATION AREA
Hite
MANTI-LA SAL NATIONAL FOREST
Cedar City
Cedar Breaks National Monument
Escalante
DIXIE NATIONAL FOREST
Blanding
Enterprise
Grand Staircase–Escalante National Monument
Natural Bridges National Monument
Hall's Crossing
HOVENWEEP NATIONAL MON.
DIXIE NATIONAL FOREST
Zion National Park
Bryce Canyon National Park
Kodachrome Basin State Park
Bluff
San Juan
River
Goosenecks of the San Juan River
Mexican Hat
St. George
Hurricane
Kanab
Lake Powell
Four Corners Monument
ARIZONA

On day seven, travel back to Salt Lake City via Route 24, U.S. 50 and I–15, detouring across the **Nebo Loop Scenic Byway** ⓸⓶ for an alpine diversion before rejoining the interstate.

SALT LAKE CITY

Nestled at the foot of the rugged Wasatch mountains and extending to the south shore of the body of water for which it's named, Salt Lake City features one of the most scenic backdrops in the country. As the capital of progress-minded Utah, it is emerging as a prominent population and economic center of the Rocky Mountains. Within the last decade, the number of people living in the Salt Lake Valley has climbed to more than 800,000. As a reflection of this growth, a small but dynamic skyline has sprouted, along with ever-widening rings of suburbia. Smog occasionally bedevils the town, and crime is present, but for all intents and purposes Salt Lake maintains the charm of a small, personable city. It is still an easy place to get around, and its residents are as down-to-earth as you will find anywhere.

Just as Salt Lake has grown considerably in recent years, so too has it come of age. The downtown now features several high-rise hotels, Salt Lake restaurants serve up a whole world of tastes, and there is nightlife worthy of discussion. The Salt Lake arts scene is as prodigious as you'd expect to find in a city twice its size. All over town, fashionable retail enclaves are springing up. The community takes great pride in its NBA team, the Utah Jazz, and it is eagerly planning for its role as host of the 2002 Olympic Winter Games.

As with most Utah municipalities, Salt Lake City is based on a grid plan that was devised by Brigham Young in the 19th century. Most street names have a directional and a numerical designation, which describes their location in relation to one of two axes. Streets with "East" or "West" in their names are east or west of (and parallel to) Main Street, which runs north–south, while "North" and "South" streets run parallel to South Temple Street. The numbers tell how far the streets are from the axes. (For example, 200 East Street is two blocks east of Main Street.) To confuse the matter further, addresses typically include two directional references and two numerical references; 320 East 200 South Street, for instance, is in the east 300 block of 200 South Street. As an added complication, three of Salt Lake's most prominent streets are named after the Mormon Temple: North Temple, South Temple, and West Temple. However, this simply indicates that the streets' locations run parallel to the north, south, and west borders of Temple Square. Main Street borders the square's east side.

The pervasiveness of the Mormon religion notwithstanding, Salt Lake City is not and was not devoid of representation by other faiths, especially in its early years. In the blocks east of downtown are three impressive houses of worship. Dating back to 1871, the Episcopal **Cathedral Church of St. Mark** (⊠ 231 E. 100 South St.) is Salt Lake's oldest non-Mormon church. The Gothic-inspired **Catholic Cathedral of the Madeleine** (⊠ 331 E. South Temple St.) features twin spires, gargoyles, and plenty of stained-glass windows. Nearby, the **First Presbyterian Church** (⊠ 371 E. South Temple St.) features beautifully crafted red sandstone construction. In addition to being home to the Mormon church's competition, the eastern portion of South Temple Street was also a favored neighborhood for early Salt Lake's well-to-do. Many fine mansions remain.

eehive House, **7**
righam Young Memorial Park, **6**
City and County Building, **12**
Delta Center, **15**
Exchange Place Historic District, **11**
Family History Library, **3**
Gallivan Utah Center, **10**
Hansen Planetarium, **9**
Joseph Smith Memorial Building, **4**
Kearns Mansion, **8**
LDS Church Office Building, **5**
Marmalade Historic District, **19**
Museum of Church History and Art, **2**
Pioneer Memorial Museum, **18**
Rio Grande Depot, **13**
Salt Palace, **16**
Temple Sq., **1**
Union Pacific Railroad Depot, **14**
Utah State Capitol, **17**

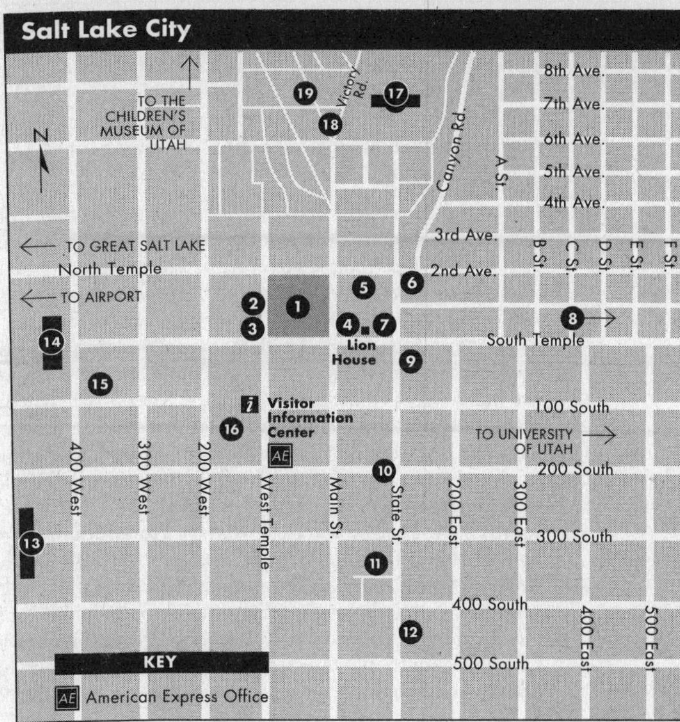

for mammoth bones as part of the many interactive exhibits. ✉ *840 N. 300 West St.,* ☎ *801/328–3383.* 🎟 *$3.* ⏲ *Mon.–Thurs. and Sat. 10–6, Fri. 10–8.*

12 **City and County Building.** This seat of city government is situated on Washington Square, the site where the original Mormon settlers circled their wagons on their first night in the Salt Lake Valley. Said to be modeled after the London City Hall, the massive building has ornate details common to the Romanesque Revival style. Construction began in 1892 and took two years to complete, at a cost of $900,000. When Utah achieved statehood in 1896, this building served as the state capitol for 19 years until the current capitol was constructed. In 1989, this building was renovated at a cost of nearly $35 million. ✉ *State St., between 400 and 500 South Sts.*

15 **Delta Center.** From the outside, this structure, built in the early 1990s, resembles an enormous block of ice. But from the inside, the views of the surrounding city and the Wasatch mountains are stunning. The Delta Center arena seats 20,000 and is home court for the Utah Jazz (☞ Spectator Sports, *below*). Concerts, rodeos, ice shows, and other touring entertainments are also held here. An information desk and a gift shop are open daily. The gift shop stocks the city's best assortment of Utah Jazz basketball paraphernalia. ✉ *300 W. South Temple St.,* ☎ *801/325–7328.*

11 **Exchange Place Historic District.** Reminiscent of early Chicago, this cluster of buildings reaching 11 stories includes the Boston and Newhouse buildings, Salt Lake's first skyscrapers. As the city's center for non-Mormon commerce, this was one of the West's leading business centers early in the 1900s. Today, the quiet street has restaurants, small shops, and an art gallery. These "skyscrapers" of the past are easily dwarfed by

Downtown Salt Lake

Although businesses and homes stretch in all directions, the core of d town Salt Lake City is a compact, four-block-by-four-block area includes several buildings central to Mormonism, two large shopp malls, historic buildings, and entertainment venues.

A Good Walk

If for no other reason than to orient yourself to Salt Lake's street system, **Temple Square** ① is a good place to begin a walking tour of the city. Across West Temple Street from Temple Square are two Mormon-owned and -operated institutions: the **Museum of Church History and Art** ② and the **Family History Library** ③. East of Temple Square across Main Street is the **Joseph Smith Memorial Building** ④, a community center. Dominating the block east of Temple Square is the **LDS Church Office Building** ⑤. To the east, just across State Street, are **Brigham Young Memorial Park and City Creek Park** ⑥. Around the corner, south of the Church Office Building, is the **Beehive House** ⑦, Brigham Young's official residence. It's a bit of a walk east on South Temple Street to get to **Kearns Mansion** ⑧, now the Utah governor's residence. A half-block south of the Beehive House is **Hansen Planetarium** ⑨. A block and a half south, on the west side of State Street at 200 South Street, is the **Gallivan Utah Center** ⑩, an outdoor gathering place with year-round activities. Continue south on State Street to the middle of the 300 South block, and turn right to see the **Exchange Place Historic District** ⑪. One-half-block south on State Street, the beautiful grounds of the **City and County Building** ⑫ are a fine spot for a rest or even a picnic.

Salt Lake City's two enormous train stations underscore the two railways' fierce competition for dominance in the region at the time they were built. The **Rio Grande Depot** ⑬ is at the west end of 300 South Street. Head up 400 West Street for three blocks to get to the **Union Pacific Railroad Depot** ⑭. Heading back toward Temple Square, you'll see the modern **Delta Center** ⑮ at 300 West and South Temple Street and the **Salt Palace** ⑯ just south of South Temple Street on West Temple Street. These are the current and former homes, respectively, of the Utah Jazz. Each offers visitor information and brochures, as well as an opportunity to purchase good-quality Utah souvenirs.

TIMING

Allot half a day to enjoy this part of the city, not because it's a big area, (it's not) but because it's historic, interesting, entertaining, and pretty in any season. You will find that with this many attractions this close together, once you start touring, you may not want to stop.

Sights to See

7 **Beehive House.** Brigham Young's home, a national historic landmark, was constructed in 1854 and is topped with a replica of a beehive, symbolizing industry. Young built the Lion House next door to house his 27 wives and 56 children; now a social center and restaurant, it isn't open for tours. ✉ *67 E. South Temple St.,* ☎ *801/240–2672.* 💌 *Free.* ⏲ *Mon.–Sat. 9:30–4:30, Sun. 10–1.*

6 **Brigham Young Memorial Park and City Creek Park.** These tiny, twin parks divided by Second Avenue are a pretty diversion from the cityscape. Paths are inlaid with the footprints and names of native animals and birds, and a stone-lined stream drives a lazy mill wheel. ✉ *East side of State St. at North Temple St.*

OFF THE BEATEN PATH

CHILDREN'S MUSEUM OF UTAH – The goal of this museum is to "create the love of learning through hands-on experience," and that's exactly what it does. Children can pilot a jetliner, draw with computers, or dig

Close-Up

THE MORMON INFLUENCE

FROM ITS BEGINNINGS IN 1830 with just six members, the Church of Jesus Christ of Latter-day Saints has evolved into one of the fastest growing religions in the world. There are more than 10 million members in more than 160 countries and territories. The church was conceived and founded in New York by Joseph Smith, who said God the Father and his son, Jesus Christ, came to him in a vision when he was a young boy. Smith said he also saw a resurrected entity named Moroni, who led him to two metal plates that were engraved with the religious history of an ancient American civilization. In 1827, Smith translated this record into the Book of Mormon, which was named for a prophet.

Not long after the Church's creation, religious persecution forced Smith and his followers to flee New York, and they traveled first to Ohio, and then Missouri, before settling in Nauvoo, Illinois, in 1839. But even here the fledgling church was ostracized, and Smith was killed by a mob in June 1844 in Carthage, Illinois. To escape the mounting oppression, Brigham Young, who ascended to the Church's leadership following Smith's death, led a pilgrimage to Utah, then a territory, with the first group arriving in the Salt Lake Valley on July 24, 1847. Here, under Young's guidance, the Church quickly grew and flourished.

In keeping with the Church's emphasis on proselytizing, Young laid plans to both colonize Utah and spread the Church's word. This work led to the founding of small towns not only throughout the territory but from southern Canada to Mexico. Today the Church continues that work through its young people, with most taking time out from college or careers to spend two years abroad on a mission.

Latter-day Saints believe that they are guided by divine revelations received from God by the Church president, who is viewed as a modern-day prophet in the same sense as other biblical leaders. The Book of Mormon is viewed as divinely inspired scripture and is used side-by-side with the Holy Bible. Families are highly valued in the Church, and marriages performed in the Church's temples are thought to continue through eternity.

Under the Church's guidance, Utah has evolved into a somewhat progressive, albeit conservative, state where the good of the Church is placed above most other concerns. Despite most states' belief that church and government should be separate, in Utah legislative leaders regularly consult with Church officials on key legislation. And the Church's opposition to alcoholic products has led to the state's peculiar liquor laws. To enter a bar that sells liquor, you first must purchase a "membership," usually for $5. Beer bars, however, do not require such memberships, nor do restaurants that serve food with liquor.

While only about 50% of Salt Lake City residents belong to the Church, statewide the number is closer to 75% of Utah's two million population. The Church's influence has created a largely tight-knit state, where people generally are willing to help friends and strangers alike without hesitation.

The state's political leaders and business community tend to reflect the visionary nature that Brigham Young brought to Utah. Salt Lake City is a clean, burgeoning metropolis with vibrant financial, high-tech, and medical communities. Utah also is one of the West's preeminent playgrounds, as evidenced by the many winter resorts in the Wasatch Range that attracted the 2002 Winter Games as well as the five red-rock national parks in the southern half of the state that entice millions of tourists each year.

–Kurt Repanshek

surrounding structures. ✉ *Between State and Main Sts. at 350 South St. Access is from State St. only.*

3 **Family History Library.** Genealogy is important to Mormons because they believe in baptizing their ancestors, even after death. This library houses the largest collection of genealogical data in the world. Mormons and non-Mormons are allowed to visit the facility and make use of the records for research. ✉ *35 N. West Temple St.,* ☎ *801/240–2331.* 🎟 *Free.* ⏲ *Mon. 7:30–5, Tues.–Sat. 7:30–10.*

10 **Gallivan Utah Center.** This outdoor plaza hosts daily entertainments including an ice rink, a giant outdoor chessboard, farmers' markets, lunchtime and evening concerts, and unique art projects for all ages. ✉ *36 E. 200 South St.,* ☎ *801/532–0459.* 🎟 *Free.* ⏲ *Daily 7 AM–10 PM.*

9 **Hansen Planetarium.** This stargazer's delight features various exhibits, including a moon rock display. There is a great book and gift shop and, of course, a domed theater. Special events include laser shows set to music and live stage performances. ✉ *15 S. State St.,* ☎ *801/538–2098.* 🎟 *Free; shows cost $2–$5.* ⏲ *Weekdays 9–8, Sat. 10 AM–midnight, Sun. 1–5.*

4 **Joseph Smith Memorial Building.** Once the Hotel Utah, this building on the National Historic Register is now a community center owned and operated by the Mormon church. Visitors can use a computer program to learn how to do genealogical research or watch an hour-long film on early Mormon history and the emigration of Mormons to the Salt Lake Valley in the mid-19th century. The center also has two restaurants and an elegantly restored lobby. ✉ *South Temple and Main Sts.,* ☎ *801/240–1266 or 800/537–9703.* 🎟 *Free.* ⏲ *Mon.–Sat. 9–9.*

8 **Kearns Mansion.** Built by silver-mining tycoon Thomas Kearns in 1902, this impressive structure is now the official residence of Utah's governor. A devastating Christmas fire in 1993 destroyed and damaged much of the mansion's interior. Restoration took three years and included faithful recreation of the colors and patterns used in the original decor. ✉ *603 E. South Temple St.,* ☎ *801/538–1005.* 🎟 *Free.* ⏲ *Tours: Apr.–Nov., Tues. and Thurs. 2–4.*

5 **LDS Church Office Building.** Standing 28 stories high, this is Salt Lake's tallest structure. Although there is not a lot to see here, tours do include a visit to an observation deck on the 26th floor. Separate tours of the lovely gardens on the building's plaza are offered spring through fall. Indicative of the breadth of the church's business dealings, this building has its own zip code just to deal with the volume of mail it receives. ✉ *50 E. North Temple St.,* ☎ *801/240–2190.* 🎟 *Free.* ⏲ *Mon.–Sat. 9–4:30.*

2 **Museum of Church History and Art.** The museum houses a variety of artifacts and works of art related to the history and doctrine of the Mormon faith, including belongings of church leaders Joseph Smith, Brigham Young, and others. There are also samples of Mormon coins and scrip used as standard commerce in Utah during the 1800s, and beautiful examples of quilting, embroidery, and other handwork. Upstairs galleries exhibit the works of Mormon artists from all over the world, on both religious and secular themes. ✉ *45 N. West Temple St.,* ☎ *801/240–3310.* 🎟 *Free.* ⏲ *Weekdays 9–9, weekends 10–7.*

13 **Rio Grande Depot.** This 1910 depot was built to compete with the showy Union Pacific Railroad Depot (☞ *below*) three blocks north. It is still in operation, handling Salt Lake's Amtrak service. It also houses the Utah State Historical Society Museum, which has rotating exhibits on various aspects of the history of Utah and of the West. An eclectic gift

shop is packed with tidbits of history, from Victorian paper doll reproductions to scholarly tomes and sepia-tone photographs printed from the Historical Society's extensive collection. ✉ *320 S. Rio Grande St.,* ☎ *801/533–3500.* 🎫 *Free.* ⏲ *Weekdays 8–5, Sat. 10–3.*

16 **Salt Palace.** The former home of the National Basketball Association's Utah Jazz has received a massive face-lift, and it is now an elegant convention center. Frequently the site of large consumer shows, community events, and factory-outlet sales, it also has a conveniently located visitor information outlet and a gift shop offering Utah-theme books and gifts of better than average quality. ✉ *100 S. West Temple St.,* ☎ *801/534–4777.*

1 **Temple Square.** Brigham Young chose this spot for a temple upon arriving in the Salt Lake Valley, but work on the building did not begin for another six years. Constructed with blocks of granite hauled by oxen and then by train from Little Cottonwood Canyon, the Mormon Temple took 40 years to the day to complete. Its walls measure 16 ft thick at the base. Perched 210 ft above ground level is a golden statue of the trumpeting angel Moroni. Off-limits to all but faithful followers of the Mormon religion, the temple is used for marriages, baptisms, and other religious functions. Non-Mormons can learn more about the activities within the temple at the North and South visitor centers. Dioramas, photos of the temple interior, a baptismal font, and other displays offer considerable insight into the Mormon religion.

Other buildings of interest at Temple Square include the **Assembly Hall,** which was completed in 1882 with leftover granite from the temple, and the **Tabernacle,** home of the world-renowned Mormon Tabernacle Choir (☞ Nightlife and the Arts, *below*). This unusual dome-shape structure was built in the 1860s as a meeting place. Void of interior supports, the 8,000-seat building is known for its exquisite acoustics.

As impressive as the architectural trappings of Temple Square are, don't forget to enjoy the quiet environs of the 10-acre grounds themselves. But don't be surprised if a member of the church politely inquires about any interest you might have in learning more about Mormonism. ✉ *50 W. North Temple St.,* ☎ *801/240–2534.* 🎫 *Free.* ⏲ *Memorial Day–Labor Day, daily 9 AM–9:15 PM; Labor Day–Memorial Day, daily 9 AM–9 PM.*

14 **Union Pacific Railroad Depot.** This now-vacant depot, built in 1909 at a cost of $300,000, is a vivid monument to the importance that the railroad played in the settling of Utah and the West. The black, slate-shingle mansard roof sets a distinctive French Second Empire tone for the exterior. Inside, Western-theme murals and stained-glass windows create a setting rich with color and texture. ✉ *South Temple and 400 West Sts.*

Capitol Hill and the University of Utah

A Good Tour

North of downtown but still within walking distance is the **Utah State Capitol** ⑰, one of the nation's finest examples of Renaissance Revival architecture. Also on Capitol Hill is the **Pioneer Memorial Museum** ⑱. Northwest of Capitol Hill are the small Victorian homes of the **Marmalade Historic District** ⑲. At this point, you'll probably want to switch to a car to visit the sights outside central Salt Lake City. About 10 blocks south of Capitol Hill at 600 South, then six blocks east on 700 East Street, is another of the town's historical treasures, **Trolley Square** ⑳, now a shopping, restaurant, and entertainment complex. From here, head south on 700 East to 900 South Street to get to expansive Liberty Park and the **Tracy Aviary** ㉑. Continue east on 900 South Street and then turn north on 1300 East to reach the campus of the **University of Utah** and its **Utah Museum of Natural History** ㉒ and **Utah Museum of Fine Art** ㉓.

Just east of the University of Utah campus is **Ft. Douglas** ㉔, set up by Union-loyal Westerners to keep an eye on the Mormon settlers during the Civil War. Drive three blocks east and curve south, via 400 South Street and Foothill Drive, then east three blocks on Wakara Way, to **Red Butte Garden and Arboretum** ㉕; this is a great respite from the bustle of the city. Farther east, at the mouth of Emigration Canyon (take Wakara Way west, Foothill Drive south ½ mi, then Sunnyside Avenue east six blocks to the park entrance) is **This Is The Place Heritage Park** ㉖, which commemorates the Mormons' arrival in Salt Lake. Directly south across Sunnyside Avenue, just east of the state park entrance, is **Utah's Hogle Zoo** ㉗.

TIMING

This tour is a wonderful way to spend a day. Though it is somewhat spread out, the points of interest are in clusters, so even if the weather is inclement, you'll be able to enjoy yourself. Try exploring the Capitol Hill attractions in the morning and save Trolley Square, the aviary, or the zoo for the lunch hour, as they are the most likely spots to find a meal or snack. Visit the museums at the University of Utah in the afternoon because fewer students attend in the afternoon than in the morning, so parking is more plentiful. Because of its location in the eastern foothills of the city, early evening is a good time to visit Red Butte Gardens and Arboretum and see the alpenglow on the Wasatch mountains. In the evenings at This Is The Place Heritage Park, there are special activities, such as Dutch-oven cookouts, hay rides, or candlelight tours during the holiday season.

Sights to See

24 **Ft. Douglas.** Established in 1862, this former military post resulted from strained relations between the U.S. government and the Mormon settlers. Acting on the assumption that Brigham Young might side with the Confederates during the Civil War, a brigade of California and Nevada volunteers set up shop on this site to keep an eye on things. During their free time, the soldiers took to prospecting in the nearby mountains, which in turn led to the establishment of such mining camps as Park City (☞ The Wasatch Range, *below*). Today Ft. Douglas showcases several examples of military architecture spread out across manicured grounds. There's also a small museum highlighting the fort's military history. ✉ *East side of Wasatch Blvd. at 300 South St.,* ☎ *801/581–1710.* ⏲ *Grounds: daily till dusk; museum: Tues.–Sat. 10–noon and 1–4.*

19 **Marmalade Historic District.** So called because its streets were named after fruit trees, this small but interesting neighborhood between 300 and 500 North streets, with Quince Street as the western boundary and Center Street as the eastern, has been restored thanks to the efforts of the Utah Heritage Foundation. In contrast to most of Salt Lake City's streets, these avenues are steep and narrow. The foundation (☞ Guided Tours *in* Salt Lake City A to Z, *below*) sells a brochure about the district, including a self-guided tour, for $3.

18 **Pioneer Memorial Museum.** Featuring four floors of exhibits, many of which relate to the area's settlement by Mormon pioneers, the museum has one of the most extensive collections of settlement-era relics in the West. ✉ *300 N. Main St.,* ☎ *801/538–1050.* 🎫 *Free, but donations accepted.* ⏲ *Mon.–Sat. 9–5.*

25 **Red Butte Garden and Arboretum.** With 25 acres of gardens and 150 acres of natural areas, the grounds provide many pleasurable hours of strolling through flora from various corners of the earth. Trails access the nearby mountain terrain. ✉ *Enter on Wakara Way, east of Foothill Dr.,* ☎ *801/581–5322.* 🎫 *$5.* ⏲ *Oct.–Apr., daily 9–sunset.*

Fort Douglas, **24**
Red Butte Garden and Arboretum, **25**
This Is the Place Heritage Park, **26**
Tracy Aviary, **21**
Trolley Square, **20**
Utah Museum of Fine Art, **23**
Utah Museum of Natural History, **22**
Utah's Hogle Zoo, **27**

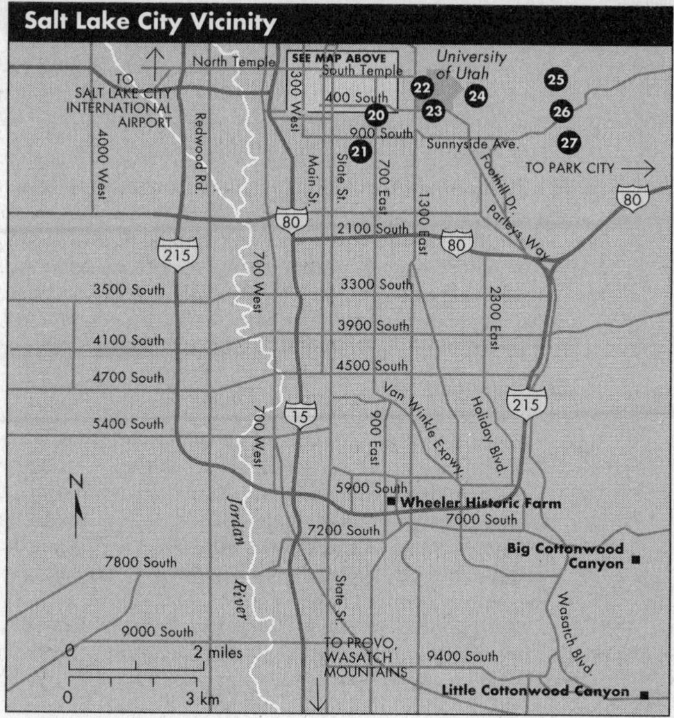

26 **This Is The Place Heritage Park.** Certainly Utah's premier historic park, this compound includes Old Deseret Village, a re-created community typical of Utah in the mid- to late 1800s; and an impressive monument adorned with larger than life statues of explorers and settlers from Utah's past. Volunteers staff seasonal activities and events. ✉ *2601 Sunnyside Ave.,* ☎ *801/584–8391.* 🎫 *$6 per vehicle.* ⏲ *Daily 7:30–dusk; some special evening activities offered.*

21 **Tracy Aviary.** Set on 11 acres, this facility features some 250 species of birds from around the globe: ostriches, bald eagles, flamingos, parrots, several types of waterfowl, and many more. There are two free-flight bird shows daily during the summer. ✉ *700 E. 900 South St.,* ☎ *801/596–8500.* 🎫 *$3.* ⏲ *Nov.–Mar., 9–4:30; Apr.–Oct., 9–6.*

20 **Trolley Square.** From 1908 to 1945, this sprawling redbrick structure housed nearly 150 trolleys and electric trains for the Utah Light and Railway Company. In the face of more contemporary modes of transport, however, the facility was closed. After a complete overhaul, the mission-style edifice reopened in 1972 and today is home to a collection of more than 100 boutiques, shops, movie theaters, and restaurants, making it one of the more intriguing retail centers in the West. ✉ *600 S. 700 East St.,* ☎ *801/521–9877.*

23 **Utah Museum of Fine Art.** Included in the permanent collection here are ancient Egyptian relics, Italian Renaissance paintings, Chinese ceramics, traditional Japanese screens, Navajo rugs, and American art from the 17th century to the present. Special exhibits are regularly mounted. ✉ *1530 E. South Campus Dr. (a continuation of 400 South St.), just south of Marriott Library,* ☎ *801/581–7332.* 🎫 *Free.* ⏲ *Weekdays 10–5, weekends noon–5.*

22 **Utah Museum of Natural History.** In addition to collections of rocks, minerals, dinosaurs, and other fossils, there are displays about the prehistoric human inhabitants of the West. Utah wildlife is well represented, and you can even learn why Utah is so enamored of seagulls. ✉ *1340 E. 200 South St., on President's Circle,* ☎ *801/581–4303.* *$3.* *Mon.–Sat. 9:30–5:30, Sun. and holidays noon–5.*

27 **Utah's Hogle Zoo.** The zoo houses more than 1,400 animals, big and small, from all over the world. There is a children's zoo and an outdoor Discovery Area with interactive exhibits. During the summer, a miniature train conducts young visitors on make-believe journeys. One of the zoo's newest exhibits is a primate forest featuring spider, colobus, and capuchin monkeys. ✉ *2600 Sunnyside Ave.,* ☎ *801/582–1631.* *$6.* *Daily 9–5.*

17 **Utah State Capitol.** In 1912, after the state happened upon $800,000 in inheritance taxes from the estate of Union Pacific Railroad president Edward Harriman, work was begun on the marvelous Renaissance Revival structure that tops Capitol Hill. Beneath the 165-ft-high rotunda is a series of murals, commissioned during the Depression, that depict the state's history. From the steps outside, you get a marvelous view of the entire Salt Lake Valley. ✉ *Capitol Hill, 400 N. State St.,* ☎ *801/538–3000.* *Free.* *Guided tours of interior: weekdays, every ½ hr, 9–4.*

OFF THE BEATEN PATH

WHEELER HISTORIC FARM – Come here to experience 1890s-era farm life by taking an "afternoon chores tour," trying your hand at milking a cow, or riding a draft horse–drawn wagon. ✉ *6351 S. 900 East St.,* ☎ *801/264–2212.* *$1.* *Daily 10–5.*

Side Trips from Salt Lake City

Depending on your point of view, the **Bingham Canyon Copper Mine** is either a marvel of human engineering or simply a great big eyesore. At any rate, this enormous open-pit mine is touted as the world's largest excavation. Measuring nearly 2½ mi across and ½ mi deep, it is the result of the removal of 5 billion tons of rock. Since operations began nearly 90 years ago by the Kennecott Utah Copper company, more than 12 million tons of copper have been produced. Visitors may view the mine from an overlook, but be sure to check on hours before making the 22-mi trip out there (take I–15 to the 7200 South exit; drive south to 7800 South, then west to Route 48, which leads to the mine). The site also has a visitor center. ✉ *Rte. 48, Copperton,* ☎ *801/252–3234.* *$2 per vehicle.* *Apr.–Oct., daily 8–dusk.*

As one of the West's most unusual natural features, the Great Salt Lake is second only to the Dead Sea in saltiness. (It is up to eight times saltier than the ocean.) Ready access to this natural wonder is possible at the **Great Salt Lake State Park,** 16 mi west of Salt Lake City, on the lake's south shore. Here a marina allows you to set sail across the buoyant water. What makes the lake so salty? Because there is no outlet to the ocean, salts and other minerals carried down by rivers and streams become concentrated in this enormous evaporation pond (☞ Antelope Island State Park, *below*). ✉ *Frontage Rd., 2 mi east of I–80, Exit 104,* ☎ *801/250–1898.* *Free.* *Daily 7 AM–10 PM.*

The **Bonneville Salt Flats,** west of Salt Lake City on I–80, past the Great Salt Lake, are nearly as devoid of life as the surface of the moon. Left behind by the receding waters of ancient Lake Bonneville, these extremely level salt flats support precious little in the way of plants and animals. One thing you will find here, however, is the Bonneville Speedway. Vehicles of varying designs have topped 600 mph on the 80-ft-wide, 9-

mi-long track, first used in 1896. The BLM's Salt Lake District (☎ 801/977–4300), managing agency of the salt flats, has seen an alarming 30% reduction in salt volume in the last 30 years.

Jordan River State Park, a 5-mi riverside complex accessed from North Temple Street at Redwood Road (1700 West), runs from North Temple Street to 2200 North Street. It has jogging paths, canoeing, picnic facilities, a golf course, and bicycling areas. Like the river for which it's named, Utah's Jordan River runs from fresh water (Utah Lake) to salt (Great Salt Lake). ✉ *1084 N. Redwood Rd., Salt Lake City,* ☎ *801/533–4496.* *Free.* *Daily 8 AM–sunset.*

Calling itself the largest amusement park between Kansas City and the West Coast, **Lagoon** includes all the rides and attractions you'd expect, plus the adjacent Lagoon-A-Beach water park. In operation for more than a century, Lagoon is a Utah landmark. ✉ *375 N. Lagoon Dr., Farmington, 14 mi north of Salt Lake City, Exit 326 off I–15,* ☎ *801/451–8000.* *$28.* *Memorial Day–Labor Day, 10 AM–midnight.*

From I–15, 30 mi north of Salt Lake City, **Antelope Island State Park** appears to be a desolate and deserted, water-bound mountain. In reality, this, the largest island in the Great Salt Lake, is home to a variety of wildlife, including a herd of 600 bison, descendant from a group of 12 placed on the island in 1893. In 1983, the Great Salt Lake's level rose dramatically and flooded the 7-mi causeway that leads to the island. The water has since receded, and the 28,000-acre island's beaches, campground, and hiking areas are again accessible. A concessionaire, **R&G Horseback** (☎ 801-782–4946), rents horses for island explorations. ✉ *Rte. 127, Syracuse, 7 mi west of I–15, Exit 335,* ☎ *801/773–2941.* *$7 per vehicle, including fee for causeway; $9 camping per night.* *Daily 7 AM–10 PM.*

Dining

American

$$–$$$ ✕ **Lamb's Restaurant.** Having opened its doors in 1919, Lamb's claims to be Utah's oldest restaurant. The decor is reminiscent of a classy 1930s diner, and this is where most of Salt Lake City's "movers and shakers" convene for breakfast. The lunch and dinner menus have beef, chicken, and seafood dishes, plus a selection of sandwiches. ✉ *169 S. Main St.,* ☎ *801/364–7166. AE, D, DC, MC, V. Closed Sun.*

$$–$$$ ✕ **Squatter's Pub Brewery.** It might seem delightfully sinister to enjoy home-brewed beer in such a conservative state as Utah, but that's exactly what you'll find in this pub on the first floor of the old Boston Hotel. Combining a lively atmosphere with great food and drink, Squatter's comes highly recommended by locals and visitors alike. In addition to the popular Squatterburger, the Margherita pizza, and the generous plate of fish-and-chips, it also serves killer bread pudding, plus eight different ales. Because it bases production on demand, the pub promises the freshest brew in town. From pale ale to cream stout, no preservatives are used. ✉ *147 W. Broadway,* ☎ *801/363–2739. Reservations not accepted. AE, D, DC, MC, V.*

Contemporary

$$$–$$$$ ★ ✕ **Log Haven.** Nestled near the head of Millcreek Canyon, just south of Salt Lake City, this 80-year-old rustic retreat in the pines has lured the likes of Margaret Thatcher and pampered members of the International Olympics Committee for dinner. Chef David Jones has fused the world's finest cuisines into his own unique creation, with dishes influenced by the Pacific Rim, California, the Southwest, and France. Appetizers range from lemon-pepper smoked salmon to Mandarin duck tacos. House spe-

cialties include coriander-rubbed ahi tuna, pepper-seared filet mignon, and Cajun-spiced duck confit. ✉ *4 mi up Millcreek Canyon, From I–15, take I–80 East to I–215 South. Take exit for 39th South, turn left at the end of the ramp, left onto Wasatch Blvd., then turn right at 3800 South traffic light,* ☎ *801/272–8255. AE, D, DC, MC, V.*

French

$$$$ ★ ✕ **La Caille.** It's hard to imagine a dining experience as interesting and tasty as the one here. Start with the escargots à la Bourguignonne, followed by the best wilted-spinach salad anywhere. Then choose from such treats as fresh Norwegian silver salmon baked in parchment or Chateaubriand served with bearnaise sauce and brittle pommes frites. Add personable servers dressed in period costume, the stately surroundings of an 18th-century French château replica, and a 22-acre nature preserve. The result is a dinner worth every penny. ✉ *9565 Wasatch Blvd.,* ☎ *801/942–1751. Reservations required. AE, D, DC, MC, V.*

Italian

$$$–$$$$ ★ ✕ **Tuscany.** Nestled among mature trees in a quiet part of the city, Tuscany has six candlelit dining areas, including a cellar and two wrought-iron balconies. Even the written description of the appetizers (such as "herb crusted beef carpaccio with caper vinaigrette and shaved Parmesan") is enough to awaken the taste buds. Entrées are creative: Italian sausage, vegetables, and sun-dried tomatoes over fusilli pasta in a Madeira herb reduction, or pesto salmon with toasted vegetable couscous, for example. The dessert tray includes slabs of a 7-ft chocolate layer cake served in honor of retired Utah Jazz center, Mark Eaton, one of the restaurant's owners. Tuscany boasts one of the best wine cellars in the city. ✉ *2832 E. 6200 South St.,* ☎ *801/277–9919. AE, DC, MC, V.*

$ ✕ **Spaghetti Factory.** In historic Trolley Square, this animated restaurant serves a lot of spaghetti for very little money. It's a good place to take a hungry family. ✉ *600 S. 700 East St., Trolley Sq.,* ☎ *801/521–0424. D, DC, MC, V.*

Seafood

$$–$$$$ ★ ✕ **Market Street Grill.** Known for its fresh and well-prepared seafood, this restaurant has a lively atmosphere. It is owned by Gastronomy, Inc., a Salt Lake chain that transforms historic buildings into tasteful dining spots. Although you can count on every entrée being a winner, be sure to check the daily fish specials before ordering. ✉ *48 Market St.,* ☎ *801/322–4668. Reservations not accepted. AE, D, DC, MC, V.*

Southwestern

$$–$$$ ★ ✕ **Café Pierpont.** Tasty Southwestern cuisine is served in a family-oriented setting. Children small enough to walk through the wrought-iron cactus at the door eat for free. The menu includes four fajita, nine combination, and several enchilada plates, plus beef, chicken, and seafood. ✉ *122 W. Pierpont Ave.,* ☎ *801/364–1222. Reservations not accepted. AE, D, DC, MC, V. No lunch weekends.*

$–$$ ✕ **Santa Fe Restaurant.** This restaurant, in scenic Emigration Canyon, has earned acclaim for its cuisine. The extensive menu offers a variety of appetizers; salads; and regional selections, such as chicken roulade stuffed with vegetables and rainbow trout, all served with unusual sauces. Brunch is served on Sunday. ✉ *2100 Emigration Canyon,* ☎ *801/582–5888. MC, V. No lunch Sat. No dinner Sun.*

Thai

$$–$$$ ✕ **Bangkok Thai.** With a wide selection of authentic Thai dishes, this is a good place to find something different. Categories include curry, wok-fried, seafood, rice and noodle, and vegetarian dishes. ✉ *1400 S. Foothill Dr.,* ☎ *801/582–8424. AE, D, DC, MC, V. No lunch weekends.*

Lodging

Downtown

$$$$ **Doubletree Hotel.** This hotel is one of the city's largest, and it's certainly one of the best-appointed. Within walking distance of many downtown attractions, it is also within a block of several great restaurants, though a complimentary Continental breakfast is offered. The hotel caters to skiers, making available such things as lift tickets and complimentary ski storage. ✉ *255 S. West Temple St., 84101,* ☎ *801/328–2000 or 800/547–8010,* FAX *801/532–1953. 496 rooms. 2 restaurants, 2 bars, pool, hot tub, sauna, exercise room, coin laundry, airport shuttle. AE, D, DC, MC, V.*

$$$$ **Hotel Monaco Salt Lake City.** This boutique hotel's 1999 arrival in the heart of downtown added a needed dose of lodging pizazz to the city. Ensconced in the former Continental Bank Building on the southwest corner of Main and 200 South streets, the 225-room hotel caters to business travelers, skiers, and tourists. The 14-story building retains its classical cornice, cartouches, and carved stone faces of Norse gods, and the interior still features its bronze and glass walls. The revived lobby's high ceiling, plush furnishings, and grand fireplace try to evoke the swagger of 1940s Hollywood. Guest rooms have cool green and cream tones with bronze accents, and granite-floor bathrooms. Amenities include ski storage and transportation to the slopes. There's also an unusual program that allows you to adopt a goldfish during your stay. Suites have whirlpool tubs, stereo systems, and VCRs. ✉ *15 W. 200 South St., 84101,* ☎ *801/595–0000 or 877/294–9710,* FAX *801/532–8500. 187 rooms, 38 suites. Room service, in-room data ports, health club, laundry service, business services, meeting rooms. AE, D, DC, MC, V.*

$$$–$$$$ **Shilo Inn.** A couple of blocks from Temple Square, this hotel combines the convenience of being right downtown with good rates. Service is reasonable, and the amenities, such as the complimentary breakfast buffet, are better than what you'd expect for the price. ✉ *206 S. West Temple St., 84101,* ☎ *801/521–9500 or 800/222–2244,* FAX *801/359–6527. 200 rooms. 2 restaurants, bar, pool, hot tub, saunas, coin laundry, airport shuttle. AE, D, DC, MC, V.*

$$–$$$$ **Anton Boxrud Bed and Breakfast.** Antiques and unusual furnishings from all over the world fill the rooms of this elegant, yet casual, Victorian manor just down the street from the Governor's mansion and a 15-minute stroll from the city center. The complimentary evening snacks and beverages offered near the parlor's bay window are as delicious as the bountiful breakfasts. ✉ *57 S. 600 East St., 84102,* ☎ *801/363–8035 or 800/524–5511,* FAX *801/596–1316. 7 rooms. Hot tub. AE, D, DC, MC, V.*

$$–$$$$ **Brigham Street Inn.** If you love historic B&Bs, this is the place to stay. On East South Temple (formerly Brigham Street), this turn-of-the-century mansion was carefully restored by Salt Lake architect John Pace. Each of the nine guest rooms was decorated by a different interior designer. The result: a collection of superbly appointed rooms, each with its own personality. Some are decorated in pastels, with the visual focus being the inn's large tree-shaded windows; others are dramatic with jewel-tone furniture and recessed lighting. The original woodwork has been preserved throughout, one example of the special attention paid to preserving the home's character. The breakfast is Continental. ✉ *1135 E. South Temple St., 84102,* ☎ *801/364–4461,* FAX *801/521–3201. 9 rooms. Breakfast room. AE, D, DC, MC, V.*

$$–$$$$ ★ **Little America Hotel & Towers.** Inside Salt Lake's largest hotel are such niceties as brass railings, chandeliers, and marble tubs. Perhaps because Little America is a small regional chain (six properties in all), it can afford to pay close attention to details in service and in the decor of guest rooms, which are not standard hotel issue, but lean to elegance *with textured fabrics, plush seating, and variable lighting. A sister 900-room hotel is scheduled to open across the street in 2000. ✉ 500 S. Main St., 84101, ☎ 801/363–6781 or 800/453–9450, FAX 801/596–5911. 850 rooms. 2 restaurants, bar, indoor pool, hot tub, exercise room, coin laundry, airport shuttle. AE, D, DC, MC, V.*

$$–$$$$ **Saltair Bed and Breakfast.** The history of this 1903 Victorian home landed it on the state and national registers of historic places. Fine oak woodwork and period antiques lend elegance to the setting. Sitting in the formal parlor with a book before a roaring fire is the perfect way to end the day. ✉ *164 S. 900 East, 84102,* ☎ *801/533–8184 or 800/733–8184,* FAX *801/595–0332. 7 rooms, 9 suites. Full breakfast. AE, D, DC, MC, V.*

$$ **Holiday Inn Express.** Located between the airport and downtown, this chain property offers no frills or surprises. There is a complimentary Continental breakfast. ✉ *2080 W. North Temple St., 84116,* ☎ *801/355–0088 or 800/465–4329,* FAX *801/355–0099. 93 rooms. Restaurant, pool, airport shuttle. AE, D, DC, MC, V.*

Airport and Greater Salt Lake Valley

$$$$ ★ **La Europa Royale.** Set on a large, wooded lot in south Salt Lake, this small, elegant hotel pampers guests. For skiers, there's easy access to the resorts in Big and Little Cottonwood Canyons as well as individual ski lockers and gas fireplaces in each room. For business travelers, rooms come with data-grade phone systems, data ports, and desks. The comfortable guest rooms are individually decorated, but not fussy, and the common areas are elegant. Outside, two landscaped acres invite after-meal walks. Complimentary sit-down breakfasts are creative and well prepared. ✉ *1135 E. Vine St., 84107,* ☎ *801/263–7999 or 800/523–8767,* FAX *801/263–8090. 9 rooms. Dining room, in-room data ports, hot tub, exercise room, laundry service and dry cleaning, airport shuttle. AE, D, DC, MC, V.*

$$$$ **Radisson Hotel Airport.** This hotel is elegant and very comfortable. Rooms include a wet bar and refrigerator. Try the free Continental breakfast and the Club Room for fun dining possibilities. This is the best bet near the airport. ✉ *2177 W. North Temple St., 84116,* ☎ *801/364–5800 or 800/333–3333,* FAX *801/364–5823. 127 rooms. Restaurant, pool, hot tub, exercise room, airport shuttle. AE, D, DC, MC, V.*

$$–$$$$ **Reston Hotel.** This property is just 10 minutes from downtown and 15 minutes from the airport. Renovated in 1998, the three-story hotel offers meeting rooms, an indoor pool and hot tub, and a restaurant. ✉ *5335 College Dr., 84123,* ☎ *801/264–1054 or 800/231–9710,* FAX *801/264–1054. 98 rooms. Restaurant, room service, indoor pool, indoor hot tub, meeting rooms, airport shuttle. AE, D, DC, MC, V.*

$–$$ **Hampton Inn–Sandy.** Because Hampton Inns generally offer pleasant rooms with nice furnishings for a moderate price, this is a worthwhile place to stay if you're just passing through. It's close to I–15, and there are a large shopping mall, movie theaters, and several restaurants within 1 mi. ✉ *10690 S. Holiday Park Dr., Sandy 84070,* ☎ *801/571–0800,* FAX *801/572–0708. 131 rooms. Indoor pool, hot tub, coin laundry. AE, D, DC, MC, V.*

Nightlife and the Arts

BARS AND LOUNGES

The **Bay** (✉ 404 S. West Temple St., ☎ 801/363–2623) is a smoke- and alcohol-free club with three dance floors. The **Hard Rock Café** (✉ 505 South, 600 East, ☎ 801/532–7625) features burgers and rock 'n roll memories. A good place for spotting Utah Jazz basketball players and their visiting competitors is **Port O' Call** (✉ 78 W. 400 South St., ☎ 801/521–0589), a sports bar with 14 satellite dishes and 26 TVs.

COMEDY CLUBS

A short drive south of town, **The Comedy Circuit** (✉ 10 N. Main St., Midvale, ☎ 801/561–7777) offers a variety of shows.

DANCE

Salt Lake's three main dance companies perform at the historic **Capitol Theatre** (✉ 50 W. 200 South St., ☎ 801/355–2787). **Ballet West** (☎ 801/355–2787) is considered one of the nation's top ballet companies, performing both classical and original works. **Repertory Dance Theatre** (☎ 801/534–1000) presents modern-dance performances. **Ririe-Woodbury Dance Company** (☎ 801/328–1062) is Salt Lake's premier modern-dance troupe. It's recognized for its innovation and commitment to community education.

MUSIC

The **Mormon Tabernacle Choir** (✉ Temple Sq., ☎ 801/240–2534) may be heard in performance in the Tabernacle on Sunday morning at 9:30 (be seated by 9:15) or during rehearsals on Thursday at 8 PM. The **Utah Symphony** (✉ 123 W. South Temple St., ☎ 801/533–6683) performs 260 concerts annually, both at home in the acoustically acclaimed Maurice Abravanel Concert Hall (part of the Salt Palace Convention Center) and in cities across the nation and abroad.

NIGHTCLUBS

Club Max (✉ 255 S. West Temple St., ☎ 801/328–2000) is a high-energy dance club in the Red Lion Hotel. The **Dead Goat Saloon** (✉ 165 S. West Temple St., ☎ 801/328–4628) features live music nightly. The tempo is upbeat, and the grill is fired up every day for lunch and dinner. **Green Street Social Club** (✉ 602 E. 500 South 500 St., ☎ 801/532–4200) is a fine spot to meet or make friends while enjoying light food and live acoustic music or jazz. **The Zephyr Club** (✉ 301 S. West Temple St., ☎ 801/355–2582) showcases both local and nationally recognized bands in a lively atmosphere. The decor is art deco.

OPERA

Utah Opera Company (✉ Capitol Theatre, 50 W. 200 South St., ☎ 801/355–2787) produces four operas a year, which often feature nationally recognized stars. Even if you don't care for opera, check out the ornate facade of the Capitol Theatre.

THEATER

Desert Star Playhouse (✉ 4861 S. State St., ☎ 801/266–7600) specializes in musical-comedy melodrama. You are encouraged to hiss at the bad guy and cheer for the hero. **Pioneer Theatre Company** (✉ 300 S. 1340 East St., ☎ 801/581–6961) features several different classic and contemporary musicals during its season, which runs from September through May. **Salt Lake Acting Company** (✉ 168 W. 500 North St., ☎ 801/363–7522) is nationally recognized for its development of new plays. Performances run year-round.

Outdoor Activities and Sports

Participant Sports

CYCLING

Salt Lake City is a comparatively easy city to tour by bicycle, thanks to its extra-wide streets and not-so-frenetic traffic. An especially good route is **City Creek Canyon,** east of the state capitol. On odd-number days from mid-May through September the road is closed to motor vehicles. City Creek Canyon is also a popular jogging spot, as are Liberty Park, Sugarhouse Park, and Jordan River State Park.

GOLF

Some good 18-hole golf courses include **Bonneville** (✉ 954 Connor Rd., ☎ 801/583–9513), **Meadow Brook** (✉ 4197 S. 1300 West St., Murray, ☎ 801/266–0971), **Rose Park** (✉ 1386 N. Redwood Rd., ☎ 801/596–5030), **University** (✉ 100 S. 1900 East St., ☎ 801/581–6511), and **Wingpointe** (✉ Salt Lake International Airport, ☎ 801/575–2345).

SKIING

Salt Lake City is a gateway to the excellent ski resorts strung along the Wasatch Range. Seven of these are accessible in less than ½ hour from Salt Lake (☞ The Wasatch Range, *below*).

Spectator Sports

BASEBALL

The Pacific Coast League, Triple A **Salt Lake Buzz** (✉ 77 W. 1300 South St., ☎ 801/485–3800) play at Franklin Covey Field, which has the Wasatch Range for a backdrop.

BASKETBALL

The **Utah Jazz** (✉ 301 W. South Temple St., ☎ 801/355–3865) is Salt Lake City's NBA team and a real crowd-pleaser. Home games are played at the Delta Center.

HOCKEY

Turner Cup Champions for 1995 and 1996, the **Utah Grizzlies** (✉ 3200 S. Decker La., West Valley City, ☎ 801/988–8000) play IHL hockey on the E Center ice.

Shopping

Crossroads Plaza (✉ 50 S. Main St., ☎ 801/531–1799) is an all-inclusive downtown shopping experience. Among its 140 stores and restaurants are Nordstrom and Mervyn's.

East of I–15 in the south end of the city, **The Factory Stores of America Mall** (✉ 12101 S. Factory Outlet Dr., ☎ 801/572–6440) offers outlet discounts on everything from cookware and coats to luggage, books, and Doc Martens.

Under the commission of Brigham Young, Archibald Gardner built a flour mill in 1877. Today you can visit the mill and stroll among a number of stores in the adjacent **Gardner Historic Village** (✉ 1100 W. 7800 South St., ☎ 801/566–8903). Items for sale include furniture, collectibles, and knickknacks.

The wares at **Trolley Square** (☞ Capitol Hill and the University of Utah, *above*) run the gamut from estate jewelry and designer clothes to bath products, baskets, and saltwater taffy. Stores include Laura Ashley, the Gap, Williams-Sonoma, and Banana Republic.

Founded by Brigham Young in 1868, the Zion's Cooperative Mercantile Institution was America's first department store. The cast-iron facade on the Main Street entrance of the **ZCMI Center** (✉ 36 S. State St., ☎ 801/321–8745) dates to 1902. History notwithstanding, this thoroughly modern shopping center features not only a ZCMI store but also Eddie Bauer and Gart Brothers outlets. The center is closed Sunday.

ANTIQUES

Honest Jon's Hills House Antiques (✉ 126 S. 200 West St., ☎ 801/359–4852) carries a nice collection of American furniture. **Salt Lake Antiques** (✉ 279 E. 300 South St., ☎ 801/322–1273) is a 17,000-square-ft jumble of art, furniture, jewelry, and knickknacks. The vicinity of **300 South and 300 East Streets** has several small shops specializing in antique jewelry, furnishings, art, and collectibles. **Circa** (✉ 635 S. State St., ☎ 801/

532–2542) has furniture and "kitsch" that's not necessarily antique, but definitely out-of-the-ordinary. The accent at **Elementé** (✉ 353 W. Pierpont Ave., ☎ 801/355–7400) is on unique and unusual period pieces. Don't miss the Bargain Basementé. Neighboring **Ec-lec-tic** (✉ 380 W. Pierpont Ave., ☎ 801/322–4804) has a nice selection of furniture, antique linens, and clothing.

BOOKS

Deseret Book, purveyor of books and materials related to the Mormon church and its doctrine, has several Salt Lake locations, the largest of which is in the ZCMI Center (☞ *above*). In a rambling house, with room after room filled with books, **The King's English** (✉ 1511 S. 1500 East St., ☎ 801/484–9100) is a fun place to browse. **Sam Weller's Zion Book Store** (✉ 254 S. Main St., ☎ 801/328–2586) stocks more than half a million new and used books.

CRAFTS

Mormon Handicraft (✉ 36 S. State St., ☎ 801/355–2141) sells exquisite quilts, crafts, and children's clothing made by valley residents. **The Quilted Bear** (✉ 145 W. 7200 South St., ☎ 801/566–5454) is a co-op with gifts, decor, and collectibles created by more than 600 different craftspeople.

Salt Lake City A to Z

Arriving and Departing

BY BUS

Greyhound Lines (☎ 801/355–9579) runs several buses each day to the terminal at 160 West South Temple Street.

BY CAR

From I–80, take I–15 north to 600 South Street to reach the city center. I–15 will be under major construction until 2001. Count on just two lanes in either direction along the entire urban corridor from Ogden on the north to Provo on the south. Once off the Interstate, Salt Lake City's streets are extra wide and typically not congested. Most are two-way.

BY PLANE

Salt Lake City International Airport (☎ 801/575–2400) is 7 mi northwest of downtown Salt Lake City. It is served by American, America West, Continental, Delta, Northwest, Southwest, TWA, and United.

Between the Airport and Center City. All major car-rental agencies have desks at Salt Lake International. From the airport, drive 7 mi east on I–80 to 600 South Street and follow the signs for city center. The **Utah Transit Authority** (☎ 801/287–4636) runs bus service between the airport and downtown. Buses run regularly and are less expensive than cabs. In addition, most downtown hotels offer free airport pickup for guests. **Yellow Cab** (☎ 801/521–2100) provides 24-hour service to all of the Salt Lake Valley. The cost of a ride into town is about $15.

BY TRAIN

Amtrak serves the area daily out of **Rio Grande Depot** (✉ 300 S. Rio Grande St., ☎ 801/531–0188).

Getting Around

BY BUS

Salt Lake has a very workable public transportation system in the **Utah Transit Authority** (☎ 801/287–4636). A Free Fare Zone covers a 15-block area downtown and on Capitol Hill. Round-trip service to the ski resorts costs $9; most other routes cost $1 per ride.

Contacts and Resources

DOCTORS AND DENTISTS

Columbia St. Mark's Hospital (✉ 1200 E. 3900 South St., ☎ 801/268–7111). **Salt Lake Regional Medical Center** (✉ 1050 E. South Temple St., ☎ 801/350–4111). **LDS Hospital** (✉ 8th Ave. and C St., ☎ 801/321–1100). **Primary Children's Medical Center** (✉ 100 N. Medical Dr., ☎ 801/588–2000). **University Hospital and Clinics** (✉ 50 N. Medical Dr., ☎ 801/581–2121).

GUIDED TOURS

Lewis Brothers Tours (✉ Box 510247, 84151, ☎ 801/359–8677 or 800/826–5844) conducts tours of Salt Lake City sights in *Old Salty,* an open-air, rubber-tire train. Tours depart from Temple and Trolley squares. **Utah Heritage Foundation** (✉ 485 Canyon Rd., ☎ 801/533–0858) offers the most authoritative tours of Salt Lake's historic sights. Two-week advance notice is required for groups of 20 or more.

LATE-NIGHT PHARMACIES

Broadway Pharmacy (✉ 243 E. 300 South St., ☎ 801/363–3939) is open 365 days a year, 9–9 on weekdays and 9–7 on weekends. The pharmacy at **Harmon's Supermarket** (✉ 3200 S. 1300 East St., ☎ 801/487–5461) is open until midnight.

VISITOR INFORMATION

The **Salt Lake Convention and Visitors Bureau** (✉ 90 S. West Temple St., 84101, ☎ 801/521–2822) is open weekdays 8–5 and weekends 9–4.

THE WASATCH RANGE

Rising to elevations of more than 11,000 ft and stretching some 160 mi from the Idaho border to central Utah, the Wasatch Range is an imposing and important geographic feature in the western United States. From a geologic perspective, the mountains are a complex assemblage of igneous, sedimentary, and metamorphic formations. From a demographic one, these mountains or, more precisely, their western base—a corridor known as the Wasatch Front—is home to three-quarters of all Utahns. Not only Salt Lake City residents but also those in Ogden, Logan, and Provo are greeted each morning with a spectacular view of the Wasatch.

Scientific and social implications aside, the Wasatch Range is one of the nation's premier mountain playgrounds. Uppermost in many visitors' minds is the legendary skiing found at resorts such as Snowbird, Alta, and Park City. What many don't realize, however, is that these same ski towns double as wonderful summer destinations. Picturesque mountain communities, miles of hiking and bicycling trails, bright blue lakes, and truly spectacular alpine scenery add up to a vacation that's hard to beat.

Note: Although not far from Alta and Snowbird as the crow flies, Park City, and its three ski resorts, is best accessed by following I–80 east from Salt Lake City through Parley's Canyon. On the back side of the Wasatch Range, it is Utah's only real ski town, and because it is a mere 40-minute drive from Salt Lake International Airport, it is the most accessible ski town in the country.

Camping

Across the Wasatch–Cache and Uinta national forests are a number of wonderful campgrounds. Between Big and Little Cottonwood canyons there are four higher-elevation camping facilities. Of the nine facilities in Logan Canyon, Guinavah-Malibu and Tony Grove campgrounds are the nicest. Near Nephi a pair of campgrounds are found along the

Nebo Loop Scenic Byway. All 11 campgrounds in the Huntsville area up Ogden Canyon offer swimming and fishing. In the Provo area, American Fork, Provo Canyon, and the Hobble Creek drainage hold dozens of possibilities. In Sanpete County, most campground facilities are found to the east in the Manti–La Sal National Forest (☎ 435/637–2817 for information). Additional campgrounds await visitors at the region's state parks (☞ State Parks *in* The Wasatch Range A to Z, *below*) and national monuments and at the Little Sahara Recreation Area (☞ Off the Beaten Path, *below*).

Fishing

Good fishing can be found at the following locations: Bear Lake; the Logan and Blacksmith Fork rivers, outside Logan; Willard Bay and Pineview Reservoir, near Ogden; the Provo River and Deer Creek Reservoir, northeast of Provo; and Jordanelle Reservoir in the Heber Valley.

Water Sports

Water-sports enthusiasts will find a surprising number of places to boat, windsurf, water ski, and sail. The most popular of these spots are state park facilities (☞ State Parks *in* The Wasatch Range A to Z, *below*). They include Bear Lake, Willard Bay, Pineview Reservoir, Rockport Reservoir, Deer Creek Reservoir, Hyrum Reservoir, Jordanelle Reservoir, and Utah Lake.

Alta

28 *28 mi from Salt Lake city via I–15 south, I–215 east, and Rte. 210 south.*

The nation's second-oldest ski area began as a silver-mining camp in the 1800s. So frenzied was the pace back then that the year-round population topped 8,000. The eventual crash of the silver market, however, left the canyon virtually empty until it was recognized for its potential as a winter sports area. A lift was pieced together from an old mine tram, and in January of 1939 the Alta Lifts Company was in business. Today Alta is widely acclaimed for both what it has and what it doesn't have. The ski area (☞ Outdoor Activities and Sports, *below*) promises a generous helping of Wasatch powder—up to 500 inches a year. What you won't find is the glitz and pomp that other resorts exude.

Dining and Lodging

$$–$$$$ ✕ **The Shallow Shaft.** For fine beef, seafood, poultry, and pasta dishes, Alta's only base-area sit-down restaurant that is not part of a lodging property is the place to go. The small interior is cozy and decorated in funky Southwestern style with a sandy color scheme and walls adorned with 19th-century mining tools found on the mountain. The menu is also Southwestern, with adventurous specials including lamb chops grilled and served in ancho-chili sauce and pork medallions braised in apple cider. The restaurant makes its own ice cream daily. Homemade pizza is also served, as is liquor. ✉ *Across from the Alta Peruvian,* ☎ *801/742–2177. AE, D, MC, V.*

$$$$ ★ **Alta Peruvian Lodge.** Comfortably rustic is the best way to describe the Alta Peruvian. You'll first enter the plant-filled lobby, where a large stone fireplace dominates a room with handcrafted blond-wood furniture, books, and hotel guests relaxing after an intense day on the slopes. A picture window overlooks the outdoor swimming pool and hot tub, with the mountain in the background. This is the quintessential unpretentious classic ski lodge where après-ski means hot chocolate, apple cider, and brownies set out on tables around the room. The family-style dining room and the bar upstairs are equally cozy, but the rooms can be tiny, and more than half have shared bathrooms down the hall. Guest

rooms range from simple dormitory style to cozy, simply furnished two-bedroom suites. Breakfast, lunch, and dinner at the in-house restaurant are included in all lodging packages. Combine this American meal plan with complimentary lift tickets, and you have one-stop shopping—Alta style. ✉ *Box 8017, 84092,* ☎ *801/742–3000 or 800/453–8488,* FAX *801/742–3007. 80 rooms, 4 dorms. Restaurant, bar, outdoor pool, outdoor hot tub, sauna, coin laundry, ski shop. AE, D, MC, V.*

$$$–$$$$ **Rustler Lodge.** The fanciest lodge in Alta most resembles a traditional full-service hotel. The interior is decidedly upscale, with dark wood paneling, burgundy chairs and couches, handsome wooden backgammon tables, and a grand piano dominating a small sitting room off the main lobby. Guest quarters are handsomely decorated with dark woods, white brick walls, and richly colorful coverings and drapes. All but three units have a private bathroom. Offering some of Alta's most elegant rooms, this property has comfortable furnishings such as sofas and seating areas in deluxe rooms and a pleasant atmosphere. As at all of Alta's lodges, breakfast and dinner are included in the price. ✉ *Box 8030, 84092,* ☎ *801/742–2200 or 888/532–2582,* FAX *801/742–3832. 85 rooms, 4 dorms. Restaurant, bar, outdoor pool, indoor hot tub, 2 saunas, ski shop, coin laundry. No credit cards.*

Outdoor Activities and Sports

CYCLING AND HIKING

Many cycling and hiking trails access the higher reaches of the Wasatch–Cache National Forest from Alta. The trails over Catherine Pass will put you at the head of Big Cottonwood Canyon at the Brighton Ski Area. The hike to Catherine Pass is relatively easy and quite scenic.

SKIING

Alta (✉ Box 8007, 84092, ☎ 801/359–1078) is noted for both steep runs and ski-where-you-please openness. From the lifts to lodging, everything here is unpretentious. Fortunately, so is the price. Where other major ski resorts will charge upward of $60 for a lift ticket, Alta comes in at nearly half that rate (☞ Chapter 2).

Snowbird

 *1 mi from Alta via Rte. 210 west.*

Since the early '70s, "the Bird," has taken skiing to new heights. The Snowbird Ski and Summer Resort (☞ Outdoor Activities and Sports, *below*), in **Little Cottonwood Canyon,** is one of the nation's most modern ski facilities, and at the base area a cluster of modern structures house elegant guest rooms, exquisite restaurants, and pleasurable nightclubs. The largest of these buildings, the Cliff Lodge (☞ Dining and Lodging, *below*), is like an entire ski town under one roof. During the summer, Little Cottonwood Canyon is still the place to be for outdoor fun. From Memorial Day weekend to October, Snowbird fires up its tram to ferry sightseers and hikers to the top. From here you get one of the most spectacular views in the West.

Up range (north) from Little Cottonwood Canyon is **Big Cottonwood Canyon**—home to two smaller ski areas, Brighton and Solitude (☞ Outdoor Activities and Sports, *below*).

Dining and Lodging

$$$ ★ ✕ **Aerie.** In what may just be Utah's most scenic dining spot, this restaurant serves sumptuous seafood, beef, and poultry dishes. Try the grilled free range chicken with winter vegetable pastina or the aged New York strip steak with cognac peppercorn sauce. In keeping with the elegance of its 10th-floor setting, much attention is paid to preparation and presentation. There is a sushi bar, and even if you are stay-

ing for only one night, it's worth dining here simply to be able to select from the impressive wine list. ✉ *Top floor of Cliff Lodge (☞ below), ☎ 801/742–2222, ext. 5500. AE, D, DC, MC, V.*

$$$$ ★ **Cliff Lodge.** To some, this 10-story structure with bare concrete walls initially looks a bit bland, but it doesn't take long to realize that the real beauty of its design is that it blends nicely with the surrounding scenery. The rooms in this large hotel are decorated mainly in mountain colors and desert pastels. Wonderful views are to be found from every window, and service is friendly and helpful. Even in summer, guests may use the Cliff Spa, on the top two floors, with its rooftop pool, massage rooms, hot tubs, and steam rooms. In addition, you have your choice of several fine restaurants in the Snowbird base area. This is one of the finest ski-resort accommodations in the Rocky Mountains. ✉ *Snowbird Ski and Summer Resort (☞ Outdoor Activities and Sports, below), 84092, ☎ 801/742–2222 or 800/453–3000, FAX 801/947–8227. 460 rooms, 47 suites. 3 restaurants, 6 bars, 2 pools, beauty salon, 4 hot tubs, sauna, spa, 3 tennis courts, exercise room, baby-sitting, children's programs (ages 3–12), coin laundry, laundry service and dry cleaning, convention center, meeting rooms. AE, D, DC, MC, V.*

Nightlife and the Arts

Snowbird Special Events Department (☎ 801/933–2110) mounts a variety of events throughout the year. Included are performances by the Utah Symphony, outdoor concerts, a jazz and blues festival, and murder mystery weekends.

As a guest at Snowbird, you receive a complimentary membership to the **"Club at Snowbird"** and can enjoy a drink at any of several lounges spread about the base area.

Outdoor Activities and Sports

CYCLING AND HIKING

Off-road cyclists are discovering that Snowbird's ski slopes make for some excellent, if strenuous, riding. Down the canyon from Snowbird is the trailhead for the Red Pine Lake and White Pine Lake trails. Located 3½ mi and 5 mi in, respectively, these mountain lakes make for great day hikes.

SKIING

Snowbird Ski and Summer Resort (☎ 801/742–2222 or 800/453–3000) has plenty of powder-filled chutes, bowls, and meadow areas. Like its neighbor, Alta, it's known for its expert runs; 40% of Snowbird is black diamond terrain. In contrast, however, an extra $15 for a lift ticket will get you the speed, convenience, and impressive vertical drop (3,240 ft in one fell swoop) that only Snowbird's 125-passenger aerial tram can provide (☞ Chapter 2). Camp Snowbird provides summer activities for children to enjoy without their parents.

With 850 and 1,200 skiable acres, respectively, **Brighton Ski Resort** (☎ 801/532–4731 or 800/873–5512) and **Solitude** (✉ 1200 Big Cottonwood Canyon, Solitude, ☎ 801/534–1400 or 800/748–4754) are roughly half the size of Alta and Snowbird, but they still offer the same fluffy powder that has made Utah skiing so exemplary. Because these **ski resorts** are less crowded, locals often purchase their season passes here and save the bigger resorts for special occasions.

Park City/Deer Valley/The Canyons

30 *33 mi from Salt Lake City via I–80 east (to Exit 145) and Rte. 224 south.*

Park City was a rip-roaring mining town like no other. Silver was discovered here in 1868, and in the years immediately following, the town's population grew by leaps and bounds. In the process it earned the nickname "Sin City." Certainly, it was uncommon for any municipality within spitting distance of Salt Lake to have more than two dozen saloons and a thriving red-light district. Despite the generosity of the mountains, Park City eventually fell victim to depressed silver prices. It was not until 1946 that its current livelihood began to take shape in the form of the small Snow Park ski hill, which opened a few miles south. In 1963, Treasure Mountain Resort began operations with its skier's subway—an underground train and hoist system that ferried skiers to the mountain's top via old mining tunnels. In the years since, facilities were upgraded, and Treasure Mountain became the Park City Mountain Resort (☞ Outdoor Activities and Sports, *below*).

Today, because Park City includes a mind-numbing collection of condominiums, it could be considered just another ill-conceived resort town. At its heart, however, is a historic downtown district that rings with authenticity. "Charming" is a word that comes to mind when describing the buildings that line Main Street, but, what's more important, this collection of turn-of-the-century edifices reminds visitors that Park City is a real town with real roots.

Although it's the skiing that attracts most visitors to Park City, the town also serves as an excellent base camp for summer activities. Hiking trails are plentiful. A scenic drive over Guardsman Pass (via a gravel road that is passable for most vehicles) reveals incredible mountain vistas and a plethora of alpine wildflowers. There are some acclaimed golf greens, hot-air ballooning is available, and an increasing number of mountain bikers are finding that the ski slopes make for truly exceptional pedaling. The Canyons (☞ Outdoor Activities and Sports, *below*) is a growing destination resort just north of town.

The **Alpine Slide** (✉ 1345 Lowell Ave., Park City, ☎ 435/649–8111) is a big attraction during the summer at the Park City Mountain Resort. Children of all ages can fly down the curving track on a sled that is easy to control. The **Park City Silver Mine Adventure** (✉ Ontario Canyon, 1½ mi south of Park City via Rte. 224, ☎ 435/655–7444 or 800/467–3828) provides a look at the town's mining heritage with interactive displays, and a tour 1,500 ft below the ground of an actual mine shaft. The **Utah Winter Sports Park** (✉ 3000 Bear Hollow Dr., Park City, ☎ 435/658–4200) is the official site of the 2002 Olympic bobsled, luge, and ski-jumping events. But anyone who dreams of Olympic glory can enjoy the recreational ski-jumping lessons and bobsled instruction offered to the public each winter on actual Olympic courses. The Winter Sports Park also serves as a year-round training site for members of the U.S. Ski Team and other athletes training for amateur competition. In summer, check out the freestyle ski jumpers who practice their form on a special jump with a splash pool at the bottom.

Dining and Lodging

$$$–$$$$ ★ ✕ **Gamekeeper's Grill.** Housed in a historic, two-story brick building with copper highlights, this restaurant's menu reflects its name. You'll find pan-seared elk medallions, smoked buffalo ravioli, and wild game chili competing against grilled salmon, Utah red trout, and herb-crusted rack of lamb for your attention. The large portions leave little room for dessert. ✉ *508 Main St., Park City,* ☎ *435/647–0327. AE, MC, V.*

$$$–$$$$ ★ ✕ **Glitretind.** It's worth breaking open the piggy bank for this fabulous restaurant, a source of Deer Valley's unsurpassed reputation in ski-resort dining. The Glitretind is posh without being ostentatious, gracious without being overbearing, exemplary in service, and impeccable in decor, with softly colored textured walls, handsome wood trim, cranberry tablecloths, crystal glasses, hand-painted china, and fresh-cut flowers. It is, in a word, exquisite. Selections include various seafood, beef, and poultry dishes, which are prepared with a creative selection of ingredients. How does pepper-crusted beef tenderloin with cabernet wine sauce and basil mashed potatoes sound? This is the stuff that travel, food, and ski magazines rave about when Deer Valley is the topic of discussion. ✉ *Stein Eriksen Lodge, Deer Valley,* ☎ *435/649–3700. Reservations essential. AE, DC, MC, V.*

$$$–$$$$ ✕ **The Riverhorse Café.** The two large upper-level warehouse rooms that make up this café resemble an ultramodern big-city supper club, with exposed beams, polished hardwood floors, black and white furnishings, and walls adorned with huge portraits of such well-known Native Americans as Sitting Bull and Geronimo. House specialties include ahi tuna in a puff pastry tart with eggplant and citrus sauce; charred rack of Utah lamb in a cabernet demiglace; and goat cheese ravioli with roasted garlic and fresh herbs. Don't miss the restaurant's signature mashed potatoes. ✉ *540 Main St., Park City,* ☎ *435/649–3536. Reservations essential. AE, MC, V.*

$$–$$$$ ✕ **Café Terigo.** This airy café serves several well-prepared pasta and seafood dishes using only fresh ingredients. Good picks include almond-encrusted salmon or smoked chicken with sun-dried tomatoes over fettuccine. Be sure to top your meal off with a helping of bread pudding or mud pie. ✉ *424 Main St., Park City,* ☎ *435/645–9555. AE, MC, V.*

$$–$$$$ ✕ **Zoom.** Owned by Robert Redford, this "western chic" eatery's specialty is . . . drum roll, please . . . macaroni and cheese! Suffice it to say it's nothing like the stuff in the box. The rest of the menu offers other comfort foods, but always with a twist. Locals favor the tri-tip steak served with grits disguised by garlic and Asiago cheese, or the beefed-up, but totally meatless, Portobello mushroom burger. Don't forget to save room for the chocolate mousse cake with raspberry sauce. ✉ *660 Main St., Park City,* ☎ *435/649–9108. AE, MC, V.*

$$$ ★ ✕ **Grappa.** In Park City's historic old town district, this restaurant specializes in ambience and northern Italian dishes. Heavy floor tiles, bricks, and timbers lend a rustic, warm, farmhouse feel. Tables on the wrap-around balcony overlook those on the first floor. The menus, which change seasonally, offer appetizers such as homemade duck prosciutto with a summer pear and balsamic vinegar salad, and fried calamari served with basil aioli and fresh marinara. Innovative entrées include crisp, panfried game hen with spinach tortellini and roasted garlic velouté, as well as pancetta-wrapped chicken fricassee filled with spinach and mushroom risotto, served with summer squash and greens. ✉ *151 Main St., Park City,* ☎ *435/645–0636. AE, D, MC, V.*

$–$$ ✕ **Nacho Mamma's.** Located in Prospector Square just a few minutes from Main Street, this local favorite features Southwestern dishes that will test the strength of your taste buds. The chili *rellenos,* which come with chicken, beef, or shrimp, push the upper limits of spicy, while the beef *chipotle,* with its thinly sliced beef and tangy sauce, will sate any meat-lover's appetite. ✉ *1821 Sidewinder Dr., Park City,* ☎ *435/645–8226. Reservations accepted. AE, D, MC, V.*

$$$$ 🏨 **Olympia Park Resort Hotel.** As one of Park City's largest, this hotel includes a full array of amenities. On the premises is a restaurant plus a nice atrium area with a pool. ✉ *1895 Sidewinder Dr., Box 4439, Park City 84060,* ☎ *435/649–2900 or 800/234–9003,* FAX *435/649–4852. 226 rooms. Restaurant, bar, indoor pool, hot tub, sauna, exercise room. AE, D, DC, MC, V.*

$$$$ 🏨 **Shadow Ridge Resort.** Few other hotels in town can match the Shadow Ridge for convenience and comfort. Just a few feet from the Park City Mountain Resort, you can amble to the slopes in less time than it takes to warm up your car. Accommodations range from a single hotel room to a two-bedroom condominium suite. With full kitchens,

these suites are a sweet deal for families. All rooms have sturdy furnishings in the colors of a mountain summer. The staff here is friendly and experienced. ✉ *50 Shadow Ridge St., Box 1820, Park City 84060,* ☎ *435/655–3315 or 800/451–3031,* FAX *435/649–5951. 150 units. Restaurant, bar, pool, hot tub, sauna, coin laundry. AE, D, DC, MC, V.*

$$$$ ★ **Washington School Inn.** Although it is hard to imagine an old schoolhouse making a great B&B, this inn (circa 1890) proves that it can be done. It was home to thousands of students during its heyday, but in the mid-1930s it closed and then fell into disrepair. It was reincarnated as an elegant country inn in the 1980s. The exterior of the three-story stone structure was carefully restored and the inside completely gutted to make way for the guest rooms, kitchen, and common areas. The interior is spacious and designer-perfect, with high, vaulted ceilings, cherry-wood wainscoting, and a stunning center staircase leading to the bell tower. The large rooms and suites are elegant, with country-style wall coverings, handwoven area rugs, tile-and-stone flooring, and four-poster canopy beds. Each room is appointed with Victorian-era furnishings and down pillows and comforters. Of course, breakfast is included. ✉ *543 Park Ave., Box 536, Park City 84060,* ☎ *435/649–3800 or 800/824–1672,* FAX *435/649–3802. 12 rooms, 3 suites. Hot tub, sauna, exercise room, laundry room. AE, D, DC, MC, V.*

$$$–$$$$ **Best Western Landmark Inn.** Out by the interstate, this property makes a great stopover for travelers. The rooms are nicely furnished, and the location is convenient for those visitors splitting their time between Park City and Salt Lake. ✉ *6560 N. Landmark Dr., 84098,* ☎ *435/649–7300 or 800/548–8824,* FAX *435/649–1760. 106 rooms. Restaurant, indoor pool, hot tub, exercise room, coin laundry. AE, D, DC, MC, V.*

Nightlife and the Arts

Park City hosts a variety of performing-arts events throughout the summer. The **Park City International Chamber Music Festival** (☎ 435/649–5309) runs from early July through mid-August. The historic **Egyptian Theatre** (✉ 328 Main St., ☎ 435/649–9371), in downtown Park City, stages many different plays. Deer Valley Resort's outdoor **Summer Concert Series** (☎ 435/649–1000) includes everything from classical to country music. The **Summit Institute** (☎ 435/649–2315) at Deer Valley puts on a variety of musical and dance events throughout the summer. Included are performances by the Ririe-Woodbury Dance Company, a String Chamber Music Festival, and several artist-in-residence programs.

Among Park City's lively **bars** are Cicero's (✉ 306 Main St., ☎ 435/649–6800) and The Alamo (✉ 447 Main St., ☎ 435/649–2380).

Outdoor Activities and Sports

CYCLING

Several mountain bike trails are accessible from the **Guardsman Pass Road** in Park City. Both **Deer Valley Ski Resort** and the **Park City Mountain Resort** (☞ *below*) run lifts in the summer to facilitate fun descents by bike. **The Canyons** (☞ *below*) also has cycling trails on the resort property. The **Historic Union Pacific Rail Trail** (☎ 435/649–3602) is a 28-mi trail popular with cyclists. It begins at Park City and follows I–80 to Echo Reservoir.

GOLF

The **Park City Municipal Golf Course** (✉ 1541 Thaynes Canyon Dr., ☎ 435/649–8701) offers 18 holes.

SKIING AND SNOWBOARDING

With 97 trails and 3,000 acres of skiable terrain, including 650 acres of open bowls, the **Park City Mountain Resort** (✉ Box 39, 84060, ☎ 435/649–8111 or 800/222–7275) is one of Utah's largest ski complexes.

The mountain is accessed by 14 chairlifts, four of which are six-person chairs. Roughly half of Park City's terrain is rated as intermediate, but the slopes that line Jupiter Mountain are revered by experts as well. Snowmaking covers 475 acres, and night skiers will delight in Pay Day, the longest artificially lighted run in the Rockies. If you want to ski Park City but your youngsters do not, the city has several licensed child care agencies. Call 801/649–6100 for suggestions, or inquire at the resort where you are planning to ski.

The Canyons (✉ 4000 The Canyons Dr., Park City 84098, ☎ 435/649–5400 or 888/226–9667) is a fast-growing player in Utah's ski industry. Formerly known as Wolf Mountain, the resort is nearing 3,000 acres in skiable terrain and is building a year-round base resort. There are 11 lifts, including an eight-passenger gondola, and several on-mountain restaurants. As the first Park City mountain to allow snowboarding (only Deer Valley prohibits it now) this resort has enjoyed popularity with younger crowds. The resort area boasts a vertical drop of 3,190 ft.

Deer Valley (✉ Box 1525, Park City 84060, ☎ 435/649–1000 or 800/424–3337), just south of Park City, broke new ground in the ski industry by providing such amenities as ski valets, on-slope telephones, grooming fit for a king, and slope-side dining of the highest caliber. For such pampering, the resort has won rave reviews from virtually every ski and travel magazine. While Deer Valley has elevated grooming to an art, it also offers extreme terrain in Empire Canyon. For more about Deer Valley, *see* Chapter 2.

Shopping

Within the colorful structures that line **Main Street** in Park City are a number of clothing boutiques, sporting-goods stores, and gift shops. Check out **Wyoming Wear** (✉ 518 Main St., ☎ 435/645–9427) for regional favorites in stylish outdoor clothing. **Christmas on Main Street** (✉ 442 Main St., ☎ 435/645–8115) carries ornaments year-round. Visit **Jan's Mountain Outfitters** (✉ 1600 Park Ave., ☎ 435/649–4949) to pick up skiing, bicycling, camping, and fly-fishing gear. A few miles north of Park City, next to I–80, are the **Factory Stores at Park City** (✉ 6699 N. Landmark Dr., ☎ 435/645–7078). Represented in this collection of 47 outlets are Nike, Brooks Brothers, Eddie Bauer, Guess, and Corning, among others.

Ogden

31 *35 mi from Salt Lake City via I–15 north.*

With a population of more than 65,000, Ogden combines a small-town feel with the infrastructure of a larger city. Upon the site of a stockade and trading post built by mountain man Miles Goodyear, Brigham Young directed the settlement of Ogden in 1850. Despite its Mormon roots, however, Ogden was to change radically with the arrival of the transcontinental railroad in the area in 1869. The town quickly became a major western crossroads, and it received a great influx of non-Mormons. With the advent of World War II, the military began to have a considerable presence in town, which, with Hill Air Force Base nearby, it still has today. Ogden is also a college town; Weber State University is within the city limits.

On your way into town from the south, at Exit 341 off I–15, are Hill Air Force Base and the **Hill Aerospace Museum.** Among the many interesting planes housed in this large hangar are the SR-71 Blackbird (a reconnaissance aircraft that made a transatlantic flight in less than two hours) and a B-17 Flying Fortress. ✉ *Hill Air Force Base,* ☎ *801/777–6868.* 🎫 *Free.* ⏲ *Daily 9–4:30.*

Given Ogden's history, it's safe to assume that it has a number of vintage buildings and museums. The best of the latter are found in the **Ogden Union Station.** Built in 1924, this impressive Spanish Revival structure demonstrates the considerable esteem railroad travel once enjoyed and houses some interesting museums: the Utah State Railroad Museum, the Browning-Kimball Car Museum, and the Browning Firearms Museum. (Browning is a renowned gun manufacturer.) ✉ *25th St. and Wall Ave.,* ☎ *801/629–8444.* 🎫 *$3.* ⏲ *Mon.–Sat. 10–5, Sun. 11–3.*

Highlighting a chapter in history that unfolded decades prior to the railroad era, **Ft. Buenaventura State Park** is a 32-acre tract with exact replicas of the stockade and cabins that Miles Goodyear built in 1846. Guides in period costume interpret the ways of the early trappers, and hundreds of mountain-man enthusiasts rendezvous at the fort in September, at Thanksgiving, and over Easter weekend. Camping and picnicking facilities are available. ✉ *2450 A Ave.,* ☎ *801/621–4808.* 🎫 *$3 per vehicle.* ⏲ *Daily 8–sunset.*

Back in downtown Ogden, the **Ogden River Parkway** follows the banks of the Ogden River for 3 mi to the mouth of Ogden Canyon. A real people place, this urban greenway hosts a number of outdoor activities, including bicycling, walking, jogging, tennis, baseball, and fishing. What really distinguishes the Ogden River Parkway, however, are the two parks found along the way: the MTC Learning Park, which has botanical gardens and pavilion facilities, and the **George S. Eccles Dinosaur Park,** which features dozens of life-size dinosaur replicas, one of the largest collections of its kind in the nation. ✉ *1544 E. Park Blvd.,* ☎ *801/393–3466.* 🎫 *$3.* ⏲ *Apr.–Nov., daily 10–dusk.*

With the Ogden River Parkway pointing the way, follow Route 39 (a designated scenic byway) into **Ogden Canyon.** A few miles beyond the canyon mouth, the mountains open up to make room for **Pineview Reservoir.** During the summer, this 2,000-acre lake is festooned with colorful sailboards and the graceful arcs of water-skiers. The fishing is good, and some nice beaches, campgrounds, and marinas dot the shore. **Anderson Cove,** along the southern end of the lake, is quite popular, as is **Middle Inlet,** along the eastern shore. During the winter, Ogden Canyon reveals some great (and inexpensive) alternatives to the Salt Lake City ski scene, including Snowbasin and Powder Mountain (☞ Outdoor Activities and Sports, *below*).

32 After you return to I–15 north, the next point of interest is **Willard Bay State Park.** About 10,000 acres in size, the bay is actually a freshwater arm of the Great Salt Lake. Fed by canals in the spring, it is effectively protected from saltwater intrusion by dikes, and because it is freshwater, Willard Bay is a popular fishing, boating, and bird-watching area. ✉ *15 mi north of Ogden off I–15,* ☎ *435/734–9494.* 🎫 *$4 per vehicle.* ⏲ *Daily 6 AM–10 PM.*

If you happen to be passing through in the late summer or early fall, drive up U.S. 89/91 from Ogden to Brigham City to enjoy Utah's **Fruitway.** You'll find many produce stands and the peach, apple, cherry, plum, pear, and apricot orchards from which the fruit came.

Dining and Lodging

$$–$$$$ ✕ **Prairie Schooner.** The atmosphere might be overkill for some, but it's fun nevertheless. Steaks, prime rib, and seafood are served in a recreated Western setting; each table is enclosed in a covered wagon. Underneath it all, however, the food is good. ✉ *445 Park Blvd.,* ☎ *801/392–2712. AE, D, DC, MC, V.*

$$–$$$ ✕ **Gray Cliff Lodge Restaurant.** Set in scenic Ogden Canyon, this local favorite features Utah trout, prime rib, lamb, and seafood as well as

great atmosphere. ✉ *508 Ogden Canyon,* ☎ *801/392–6775. AE, D, DC, MC, V.*

$–$$$ ★ ✕ **Rooster's.** Located on historic 25th Street, this brew pub offers excellent food, and libations brewed on site. Pizzas, prime rib, and daily seafood specials are popular, as is the spicy seafood jambalaya. Wash down your meal with a tall Golden Spike Ale, or any of the Brewmaster's Specials, which vary by season. Sunday brunch at Rooster's is a lazy pleasure. ✉ *253 25th St.,* ☎ *801/627–6171. AE, D, DC, MC, V.*

$ ✕ **Lee's Mongolian Barbecue.** In a simple setting, the tasty (and occasionally spicy) food reflects its Mongolian roots. The food is as exotic as the way in which it is prepared. After selecting your ingredients, you hand over your dish to the chef, who stir-fries the meal before your eyes on a large hot plate. ✉ *2866 Washington Blvd.,* ☎ *801/621–9120. MC, V.*

$ ✕ **Shooting Star Saloon.** For what some consider to be the best burger in the country, as well as the most down-home barroom atmosphere in Utah, visit this Huntsville tavern. From the dollar bills pinned to the ceiling to the stuffed head of a 300-pound St. Bernard on the wall to the graffiti in the bathrooms, there is something to look at in every corner. ✉ *7350 E. 200 South St., Huntsville, 17 mi. from Ogden via Rte. 39,* ☎ *801/745–2002. No credit cards.*

$$–$$$ ★ **Radisson Suite Hotel Ogden.** Combining the luxurious suites for which Radisson is known with the allure of a historic downtown building, this hotel is one of Ogden's most visually important structures and is listed on the National Register of Historic Places. In addition to its elegant rooms, furnished with quality antique reproductions, the hand-painted ceiling tiles and chandeliers in the lobby area are worth a look. A full breakfast is included. ✉ *2510 Washington Blvd., 84401,* ☎ *801/627–1900 or 800/333–3333,* FAX *801/393–1258. 144 rooms. Restaurant, bar, exercise room. AE, D, DC, MC, V.*

$$ **Snowberry Inn.** Overlooking Pineview Reservoir in the Wasatch mountains above Ogden, this cozy inn is everything a rural B&B should be. Many will find the quiet environment and views are a welcome replacement for luxurious amenities. The rooms are rustic yet comfortable, and the vegetarian breakfast is complete and country good. The inn is near three ski areas. ✉ *1315 N. Rte. 158, Box 795, Eden 84310,* ☎ *801/745–2634. 5 rooms. Hot tub, coin laundry. AE, D, MC, V.*

$ **Best Western High Country Inn.** Conveniently located near I–15, this motel is spacious and comfortable. An upgrade in 1995 spruced up the facilities with a decor done in maroons and greens. ✉ *1335 W. 12th St., 84404,* ☎ *801/394–9474 or 800/594–8979,* FAX *801/392–6589. 111 rooms. Restaurant, pool, hot tub, exercise room, coin laundry. AE, D, DC, MC, V.*

Nightlife and the Arts

The **Eccles Community Art Center** (✉ 2580 Jefferson Ave., ☎ 801/392–6935) displays a permanent art collection plus special showings in an impressive Victorian mansion. **Weber State University** (✉ 3750 Harrison Blvd., ☎ 801/626–6000) regularly offers theater, music, and dance performances by students and visiting artists at the **Val A. Browning Center for the Performing Arts.** The **Perry Egyptian Theater** (✉ 2415 Washington Blvd., ☎ 801/395–3200), renovated in 1996, is an Art Deco jewel where live theater is staged. Occasionally, films, such as those of the Sundance Film Festival, are shown.

Outdoor Activities and Sports

GOLF

There are three 18-hole courses in the area: **Ben Lomond Golf Course** (✉ 1800 N. Hwy. 89, Harrisville, ☎ 801/782–7754). **Mount Ogden Golf Course** (✉ 3000 Taylor Ave., Ogden, ☎ 801/629–8700). **Riverside Golf Course** (✉ 460 S. Weber Dr., ☎ 801/399–4636).

SKIING

Rising north of Ogden Canyon's Pineview Reservoir is **Powder Mountain** (✉ Box 450, Eden 84310, ☎ 801/745–3772). As the name suggests, Powder Mountain receives a generous helping of the white stuff for which Utah is known. It offers just under 2,000 vertical ft, three chairlifts, and three surface tows. Skiable acreage totals 1,800, and two slope-side eateries provide après-ski diversions.

With a vertical drop of 2,950 ft, **Snowbasin** (✉ Box 460, Huntsville 84317, ☎ 801/399–1135) is ready to host the downhill ski races during the 2002 Olympic Winter Games. With nine chairlifts accessing more than 3,000 acres of skiable terrain, this is one of Utah's largest ski resorts. Only 17 mi from Ogden, Snowbasin has no base-area accommodations.

Shopping

East of the train depot in Ogden, **25th Street** first served as a center for immigrants before becoming the town's shadiest avenue in the 1870s. Today the historic street is a shopping district. Behind the old brick fronts that once housed gambling halls, saloons, opium dens, and the like is a variety of antiques shops, gift boutiques, and restaurants.

OFF THE BEATEN PATH

BEAR RIVER MIGRATORY BIRD REFUGE – Thirty-seven miles from Ogden via I–15 north (to Exit 366 at Brigham City) and Forest Street (which becomes Bird Refuge Road) west, this was originally a series of freshwater lagoons ideally suited for waterfowl; however, in 1983 the 73,000-acre preserve was inundated by the rising Great Salt Lake. Ice floes destroyed all facilities at the refuge, but a considerable amount of work by the U.S. Fish and Wildlife Service has resurrected a driving-tour route that follows various dikes. The habitat has been reclaimed, and the refuge once again hosts seasonal influxes of ducks, geese, and shorebirds. A new visitor center and a 17,000-acre expansion are being constructed. ✉ *Bird Refuge Rd., 16 mi west of Brigham City,* ☎ *435/723–5887.* *Free.* *Daily 9–sunset.*

Golden Spike National Historic Site

33 *54 mi from Ogden via I–15 north (to Exit 368 at Brigham City), Rte. 83 west, and Rte. 13 south.*

The Union Pacific and Central Pacific railroads met here at Promontory Summit on May 10, 1869, completing the first transcontinental route. Under the auspices of the National Park Service, Golden Spike features a visitor center, an auto tour, and some vintage locomotives on display. Every May 10, a reenactment of the driving of the golden spike is held. ✉ *Rte. 13, 29 mi west of Brigham City,* ☎ *435/471–2209.* *$5 per vehicle.* *Daily 8–4:30.*

Cache Valley

34 *18 mi from Brigham City via U.S. 89/91 north.*

East of Brigham City, U.S. 89/91 tops Sardine Summit in Wellsville Canyon before dropping into the highly scenic Cache Valley. Walled in to the west by the imposing Wellsville Mountains (often touted as the steepest incline of any range in the country) and by the Bear River Range (a sub-range of the Wasatch) to the east, Cache Valley is 15 mi wide and 60 mi long. Although first successfully settled in 1856 by Mormon pioneer Peter Maughan, during the 1820s Cache Valley was a favorite haunt for mountain men, who held many rendezvous here. These early trappers often stashed their furs in the valley, hence the name. Today Cache Valley is one of the most important agricultural regions in Utah. Topping the list of foods produced here is cheese. One of three cheese factories in the valley, Cache Valley Cheese is the nation's largest producer of Swiss cheese.

To learn about agriculture's early days in the valley, visit the **American West Heritage Center and Ronald V. Jensen Living Historical Farm,** a 1917 dairy farm. Numerous antique farm implements are on display. Draft horses still pull their weight. Workers dressed in period clothing demonstrate such tasks as sheepshearing and quilting, and a variety of special events takes place throughout the year. ✉ *4025 S. U.S. 89/91, Wellsville,* ☎ *435/245–4064.* 🎫 *$3.* ⏲ *May–Oct., Tues.–Sat. 10–4, and on special occasions year-round.*

Logan

35 *25 mi from Brigham City via U.S. 89/91 north.*

Logan is home to **Utah State University,** a land-grant college that began in 1888. Today, USU has an enrollment of about 19,800 and is a leader in such diverse fields as agriculture, natural resources, and space technology. On a benchland just east of downtown Logan, the USU campus is best toured by starting at the historic **Old Main** administration building. Across campus, the Chase Fine Arts Center includes the **Nora Eccles Art Museum** (☎ 435/797–1412), which features exhibits by local and nationally recognized artists. For further information about USU, contact the University Public Relations Department (☎ 435/797–1000). No visit to USU would be complete without a stop at the **Food Science Building** (✉ 1200 East and 750 North Sts.), open 9–9, for a scoop of the university's famous ice cream. You can also get soup and sandwiches here.

Just as Old Main's bell tower signifies that Logan is a college town, the twin towers of Logan's **Mormon Temple** (✉ 100 North and 200 East Sts.) remind all that it's also a somewhat conservative community with Mormon roots. Rising from a grassy knoll, this impressive limestone edifice took settlers seven years to complete. The site was chosen by Brigham Young in 1877, and the work was directed by architect Truman O. Angell, designer of the Salt Lake temple. As with all Mormon temples, this structure is open only to followers of the faith.

A Mormon landmark that can be visited by all is the **LDS Tabernacle and Genealogical Library** (✉ Center and Main Sts.). Holding court over downtown Logan, the Tabernacle is one of several structures featured on a walking tour of historic Main Street. An illustrated brochure, available from the Chamber of Commerce (✉ 160 N. Main St.), guides you along both sides of Main Street and up a few cross streets. The more interesting buildings along the walk include St. John's Episcopal Church, representing Cache Valley's first non-Mormon denomination; the Ellen Eccles (formerly Capitol) and Lyric theaters; and the Cache County Courthouse, with its restored cupola.

If you pass through in the winter, be sure to drive up Blacksmith Fork
36 Canyon to **Hardware Ranch.** Here the state Division of Wildlife Resources feeds several hundred head of elk throughout the snowy months. A 20-minute sleigh ride takes you up close to the majestic creatures for some great pictures. There is also a visitor center and café. ✉ *Rte. 101, 24 mi southwest of Logan via U.S. 89/91 and Rte. 101, Hyrum,* ☎ *435/753–6168.* 🎫 *Sleigh rides: $4 (over age 3);* ⏲ *Mid-Dec.–mid-Mar., daily 10–5, snow conditions permitting.*

Dining and Lodging

$$$–$$$$ ✕ **The Grapevine Restaurant.** Located in a converted Victorian house on a quiet side street, this is one of Logan's most upscale dining options. Fish, lamb, poultry, beef, or wild game are all prepared with a Continental flair. Locally grown fruit, and chocolate treats such as cheesecake or torte, make frequent appearances on the dessert menu. In summer, you can dine with white linens and silver on a patio shaded by tall sycamores. ✉ *129 N. 100 East St.,* ☎ *435/752–1977. AE, D, MC, V.*

$–$$$$ ✕ **Café Habanero.** You may catch yourself staring as much at the woodwork and high ceilings in this restaurant in a restored train depot as at the menu, which includes steak, lobster, and salmon, as well as more traditional Mexican dishes. Try the *carnita,* a house favorite of slowly simmered pork served on a corn tortilla. ✉ *600 W. Center St.,* ☎ *435/753–8880. AE, DC, MC, V.*

$–$$$ ✕ **Gia's Italian Restaurant.** Upstairs you will find sit-down service and carefully prepared Italian dishes. Downstairs, in the Factory, the service is strictly cafeteria style, the food includes pizza and sandwiches, and the atmosphere is lively. As any college student will tell you, the basement is where you go to meet friends for a beer, while upstairs is reserved for entertaining a date or parents. ✉ *119 S. Main St.,* ☎ *435/752–8384. AE, MC, V.*

$$$–$$$$ ★ **Center Street Inn.** This wonderful B&B on Logan's most prestigious historic boulevard is actually three separate buildings on one city lot: the 22-room mansion that dates to the late 1800s; the Carriage House; and the White House. Guest rooms, called fantasy suites, range from smaller models to full suites, each with a different decor. Honeymooners enjoy the Garden Suite, but travelers may find the Arabian Nights Suite, the Jungle Bungalow, or Aphrodite's Court more inviting. A Continental breakfast is delivered to your room, and there is no smoking in the rooms. ✉ *169 E. Center St., 84321,* ☎ *435/752–3443. 18 rooms. Hot tub. AE, MC, V.*

$ **Baugh Best Western Motel.** These basic, yet comfortable, accommodations are one of the best deals in town. Because it is locally owned, the service is personable enough to make up for the standard motel-style furnishings. ✉ *153 S. Main St., 84321,* ☎ *435/752–5220 or 800/462–4145,* FAX *435/752–3251. 78 rooms. Restaurant, pool. AE, D, DC, MC, V.*

Nightlife and the Arts

Thanks to both the presence of Utah State University and the community's keen interest in the arts, Logan is home to many fine productions. USU's theater and music departments host a variety of exciting performances. The **Ellen Eccles Theatre** (✉ 43 S. Main St., ☎ 435/752–0026) is home to the Utah Festival Opera Company. The **Lyric Theatre** (✉ 28 W. Center St., ☎ 435/797–0305) features performances by the university's repertory company.

Outdoor Activities and Sports

CANOEING

Although you can canoe on virtually any body of water in the region, the best places include Tony Grove Lake in Logan Canyon (☞ Off the Beaten Path, *below*) and the Bear River, northwest of Logan. Winding in serpentine fashion through Cache Valley, the Bear River features several nice stretches, including a particularly satisfying one that runs 11 mi from Amalga to Tremonton. Canoeists pass a blue heron rookery along the way, so this is a good float for bird-watchers.

CYCLING AND HIKING

Road cyclists will enjoy heading out into scenic Cache Valley on country roads or up Logan and Blacksmith Fork canyons. Mountain bikers can enjoy the 7-mi ride to White Pine Lake near the Mt. Naomi Wilderness Area or the strenuous climb to the top of Logan Peak. Of the hiking trails that give access to the wilderness area, a good pick is the 3-mi route from Tony Grove Lake to the summit of Naomi Peak. The Limber Pine Trail is a popular and easy hike (1-mi round-trip) at the summit between Logan Canyon and Bear Lake. In the Wellsville Mountains, a 2-mi trail climbs steeply from Maple Bench to Stewart Pass, a lofty ridge top with a spectacular view.

GOLF

Logan River Municipal Golf Course (✉ 1000 S. U.S. 89/91, Logan, ☎ 435/750–0123) has 18 holes.

OFF THE BEATEN PATH

LOGAN CANYON – From Logan, U.S. 89 continues for 30 mi up the scenic Logan Canyon before topping out at the crest of the Bear River Range. Within the canyon are a number of campgrounds and picnic areas administered by the Wasatch–Cache National Forest. For a particularly satisfying excursion, climb the 7 mi to Tony Grove Lake. At more than 8,000 ft, this subalpine jewel is surrounded by beautiful scenery. A short trail circles the lake, and other backcountry routes enter the Mt. Naomi Wilderness Area to the west.

Bear Lake

37 *41 mi from Logan (to Garden City) via U.S. 89 north.*

Eight miles wide and 20 mi long, the lake is an unusual shade of blue, thanks to calcium carbonate in the water. It is home to four species of fish found nowhere else, including the Bonneville cisco, which draws fishermen during spawning in January. Among the lake's more discreet inhabitants is the Bear Lake Monster, which for more than a century has lurked in local lore, like its Loch Ness counterpart.

There are three state park facilities on the lake. **Bear Lake State Park–Marina** (✉ U.S. 89, 2 mi north of Garden City) contains a marina, beach, picnic area, campground, and visitor center. At **Eastside State Park** (✉ 10 mi north of Laketown), the lake bottom drops off quickly, making this site a favorite among anglers and scuba divers. Facilities include a primitive campground and boat ramp. **Rendezvous Beach State Park** (✉ Rte. 30, near Laketown) is on the south shore of Bear Lake and has more than a mile of sandy beaches, three campgrounds, and picnic areas. Getting its name from the mountain-man gatherings that took place here in 1827 and 1828, Rendezvous Beach hosts a reenactment of the events each September. For information on any of these parks, call ☎ 435/946–3343 or 800/322–3770.

Dining and Lodging

The Bear Lake area's most famous cuisine centers around raspberries, which grow wonderfully well in this mountain valley. Several fast-food joints, open May–September, offer huge fresh raspberry shakes along with typical fast-food fare. Year-round restaurants are few and far between in this area, and though the food is plentiful at the few there are, it is also pretty standard. Several small resorts provide condominium-style lodging with beachfront access to Bear Lake and nightly or weekly rates.

$$–$$$$ ✕🏨 **Harbor Village Resort.** This resort has direct access to 300 mi of snowmobile trails. Condo sizes vary and they are pleasantly furnished. Resort guests mingle with locals and campers at Harbor Village's restaurant ($–$$$). ✉ *900 N. Bear Lake Blvd., Box 201, Garden City 84028,* ☎ *435/946–3448,* FAX *435/946–2819. 40 condos. Restaurant, pool, hot tub, sauna, exercise room. AE, D, DC, MC, V.*

Outdoor Activities and Sports

CYCLING

In addition to the mountain bike trails minutes away in Logan Canyon, a 48-mi loop trail circles Bear Lake. Cyclists of all abilities can enjoy all, or any portion, of this fairly level ride. The paved **Lakeside Bicycle Path** curves from Bear Lake Marina south and east along the shore, with several rest stops. Interpretive signs contain stories about Bear Lake's history, as well as tales from local lore.

GOLF

Bear Lake Golf Course (✉ Garden City, ☎ 435/946–8742) has nine holes.

Timpanogos Cave National Monument

38 *36 mi from Salt Lake City via I–15 south and Rte. 92 east.*

The soaring, 11,750-ft **Mt. Timpanogos** is the centerpiece of a wilderness area of the same name and towers over **Timpanogos Cave National Monument,** along Route 92 within American Fork Canyon. After hiking a steep 1½-mi trail to the cave entrance, visitors may explore three separate caves connected by tunnels. A variety of well-preserved stalactites and stalagmites, plus other formations, make the three-hour tour well worth the effort. ✉ *Rte. 92, 3 mi from American Fork,* ☎ *801/756–5239. Tours:* *$6* *Mid-May–mid-Oct., daily 9–sunset.*

OFF THE BEATEN PATH

ALPINE LOOP SCENIC BYWAY – Beyond Timpanogos Cave, Route 92 continues up American Fork Canyon before branching off to climb behind Mt. Timpanogos itself. Designated the Alpine Loop Scenic Byway, this twisting mountain road reveals some stunning mountain scenery before dropping into Provo Canyon to the south. Closed in winter, the Alpine Loop is not recommended for recreational vehicles. While the Alpine Loop Scenic Byway provides a roundabout way to get to scenic Provo Canyon from I–15, a more direct route follows U.S. 189 east from Orem.

Sundance Resort

39 *51 mi from Salt Lake City via I–15 south and Rte. 52 east.*

The small but distinctive Sundance Resort (☞ Outdoor Activities and Sports, *below*), best accessed from Provo Canyon, came into being when Robert Redford purchased a ski hill in 1969. Reflecting the actor's interests in the environment, the arts, and outdoor recreation, the resort was designed to blend in with the natural surroundings. In the summer, a number of hiking and biking trails, as well as theater productions, entice visitors. In winter, the yearly Sundance Film Festival draws a wide audience. It has become an internationally recognized venue for showing important low-budget films produced outside the mainstream studio system.

Dining and Lodging

$$$–$$$$ ★ ✕ **The Tree Room.** In addition to serving up great Continental cuisine, such as the black bass with pureed morels in a truffle sauce, this restaurant has a special ambience. The place is filled with exquisite Native American art and western memorabilia collected by Robert Redford. The man does have good taste. ✉ *Sundance Resort,* ☎ *801/225–4107. AE, MC, V.*

$$–$$$$ ★ **The Foundry Grill.** Wood-oven cooked pizzas, double-cut pork chops with mashed potatoes, and spit-roasted chickens are among the hearty staples served up at the resort's other full-service restaurant. The view

of alplike Mount Timpanogos isn't bad, either. ✉ *Sundance Resort,* ☎ *801/225–4107. AE, MC, V.*

$$$$ ★ **The Sundance Cottages.** Ranging in size from one to three bedrooms, these self-sufficient cottages lie in an appealing forest setting. Units feature natural wood trim, rock fireplaces, decks, and handmade furniture. This is a great getaway place, especially in summer. ✉ *R.R. 3, Box A-1, 84604,* ☎ *801/225–4107 or 800/892–1600,* FAX *801/226–1937. 93 suites. Restaurant, bar. AE, D, DC, MC, V.*

Nightlife and the Arts

The Sundance Institute (☎ 801/225–4107 or 800/892–1600) presents the **Sundance Film Festival,** a renowned showcase for independent filmmakers with screenings and workshops at Sundance, and in Salt Lake City, Ogden, and Park City each January. Sundance Resort also hosts the **Sundance Summer Theatre** from mid-June through August. Broadway musicals are staged under the stars in a spectacular outdoor theater. The summer **Children's Theatre** (✉ Sundance Resort, ☎ 801/225–4107 or 800/892–1600) features outdoor musicals for the little ones.

Like the mind-set labeled the "Sundance ethic," nightlife at the resort is low-key. Many guests opt to spend the evenings relaxing in their cottages. The General Store (☞ Shopping, *below*) carries a good selection of beer, wine, and other spirits. For a little more action, Sundance's **Owl Bar** (☎ 801/225–4107) has an ornate Western bar (bullet holes and all) that was originally in a Thermopolis, Wyoming, establishment frequented by the "Hole in the Wall" outlaws. There is live music nightly.

Outdoor Activities and Sports

Winter visitors to the **Sundance Resort** (✉ R.R. 3, Box A-1, Sundance 84604, ☎ 801/225–4107 or 800/892–1600) will find 42 runs across 450 acres of terrain and four lifts that access the mountain's 2,150 vertical ft. In summer, Sundance lets guests explore the mountain and its series of trails on foot or bicycle.

Shopping

The General Store (✉ Sundance Resort, ☎ 801/225–4107) features distinctive home furnishings, clothing, and jewelry reflecting the Sundance ethic and taste. The shop is home base for the award-winning Sundance catalog.

Provo

40 *15 mi from Sundance via Rte. 52 west; 45 mi from Salt Lake City via I–15 south.*

South of Salt Lake City, around Point of the Mountain (a popular hang-gliding haven and site of the Utah State Prison), I–15 drops into Utah Valley, much of which is covered by **Utah Lake.** Although this, Utah's largest freshwater lake, is 11 mi wide and 24 mi long, it averages a scant 9 ft deep. Boating and fishing are popular, but the cloudy (some would say polluted) water makes swimming questionable. On the east shore, Utah Lake State Park (✉ 4400 W. Center St., ☎ 801/375–0731) is the lake's best access point. In addition to a boat ramp, campgrounds, picnic areas, and a marina, the park has an ice-skating rink in the winter and a wheelchair-accessible fishing area.

Although the scenic resources in and around Utah Valley are considerable, Provo and the entire region are probably best known as the home of **Brigham Young University.** As one of the largest religiously affiliated universities in the world, BYU reflects the conservative nature of the Mormon church. Students must adhere to a strict dress code, and they are supposed to refrain from alcohol, tobacco, and caffeine. The university is known for a variety of undergraduate and graduate programs, is a considerable force in regional athletics, and serves as a cultural center for the southern Wasatch area. Heading up BYU attractions is a quartet of museums.

The **Museum of Art at Brigham Young University** opened in 1994. Its collection of more than 14,000 objects is anchored by its large number of works by American artists. Utah artists are represented by work from the Mormon pioneer era to the present. Rembrandt, Monet, and Rubens are also in the collection, along with some fine Far Eastern selections. ✉ *N. Campus Dr., southeast of Cougar Stadium,* ☎ *801/378–2787.* 🎫 *Free.* ⏲ *Mon., Thurs., 10–9; Tues., Wed., Fri. 10–6, Sat. noon–5.*

The **Monte L. Bean Life Science Museum** includes exhibits on wildlife from around the world plus live reptile displays. ✉ *On 1430 North, east of the Marriott Center and north of the bell tower,* ☎ *801/378–5051.* 🎫 *Free.* ⏲ *Weekdays 10–9, Sat. noon–5.*

The **Earth Sciences Museum** features dinosaur bones, fossils, and various hands-on activities. ✉ *1683 N. Canyon Rd., across from Cougar Stadium,* ☎ *801/378–3680.* 🎫 *Free.* ⏲ *Mon. 9–9, Tues.–Fri. 9–5, Sat. noon–4.*

The **Museum of Peoples and Cultures** is an interesting collection of artifacts relating to cultures from all over the earth. ✉ *700 N. 100 East St.,* ☎ *801/378–6112.* 🎫 *Free.* ⏲ *Weekdays 9–5.*

One other museum of interest in Provo is the **McCurdy Historical Doll Museum.** Covering global themes, this collection of more than 3,000 dolls was started by Laura McCurdy Clark. The facility includes a doll hospital (for repairs) and a gift shop. ✉ *246 N. 100 East St.,* ☎ *801/377–9935.* 🎫 *$2.* ⏲ *Jan.–Apr., Tues.–Sat. 1–5; May–Dec., Tues.–Sat. noon–6.*

Seven Peaks Resort Water Park and the Peaks Ice Arena includes 26 acres of waterborne fun, and year-round ice-skating on two rinks that will be used for the 2002 Winter Games. ✉ *1334 E. 300 North St.,* ☎ *801/373–8777.* 🎫 *$15 water park, $4.50 ice skating.* ⏲ *Water park, Mid-May–Labor Day, 10–7 and 7:30–9:30; call for skating hrs.*

Dining and Lodging

$$–$$$$ ✕ **Magelby's.** Steaks, seafood, and chicken are served in a European ambience. The nearly three dozen homemade desserts here are famous. ✉ *1675 N. 200 West St.,* ☎ *801/374–6249. AE, D, MC, V. Closed Sun.*

$$–$$$$ ✕ **The Restaurant Roy.** Freshly made pastas, meat dishes, and seafood can be found in this European-flavored restaurant. Both the pepper steak and Macadamia-encrusted halibut are popular. The view of the Wasatch Front is enticing, too. ✉ *2005 S. State St., Orem,* ☎ *801/235–9111. AE, D, MC, V.*

$$$–$$$$ **Provo Marriott Hotel.** A large facility, this hotel close to the downtown area offers good service. The guest rooms and common areas have more sophisticated colors and furniture styles than many properties in this price range. ✉ *101 W. 100 North St., 84601,* ☎ *801/377–4700 or 800/777–7144,* FAX *801/377–4708. 331 rooms. Restaurant, pool, hot tub, sauna, exercise room. AE, D, DC, MC, V.*

$–$$ **Best Western Cottontree Inn.** Close to Brigham Young University as well as downtown, this is a good choice for moderately priced lodging. There are indoor and outdoor pools on site, and you can get a pass to a nearby gym to work out. A Continental breakfast is included in the rates. ✉ *2230 N. University Pkwy., 84604,* ☎ *801/373–7044 or 800/662–6886,* FAX *801/375–5240. 80 rooms. In-room data ports, 2 pools, laundry facilities. AE, D, DC, MC, V.*

Nightlife and the Arts

Although Provo is not "dry," the standards of Brigham Young University are very evident in the city's entertainment options. Check with hotel staff for nightlife suggestions.

Because **Brigham Young University** (☎ 801/378–4636) has a considerable interest in the arts, Provo is a great place to catch a play, dance performance, or musical production. There are a dozen performing groups in all. Of special note are the BYU International Folk Dancers and Ballroom Dancers.

Outdoor Activities and Sports

In the Provo area, road **cyclists** may make a 100-mi circumnavigation of Utah Lake or tackle U.S. 189 through Provo Canyon or the Alpine Loop Scenic Byway.

The best **hiking** trails take off from the Alpine Loop Scenic Byway. The 9-mi Timpooneke Trail and the 8-mi Aspen Trail both reach the summit of Mt. Timpanogos.

At **Thanksgiving Point** (✉ 2095 N. West Frontage Rd., Lehi, ☎ 801/768–2300) you can find something for just about everyone. There's an 18-hole championship golf course designed by Johnny Miller, greenhouses, gardens, and a barnyard animal park.

There are 27 holes at **East Bay Golf Course** (✉ 1860 S. East Bay Blvd., ☎ 801/373–6262).

OFF THE BEATEN PATH

SPRINGVILLE MUSEUM OF ART – Springville, 10 mi south of Provo on I–15 or U.S. 89, is known for its support of the arts, and the Springville Museum of Art is a must stop for fine-arts fans. Beginning as a warehouse for works produced at the local high school, the museum later began to accept gifts from major artists. The present facility was built in 1937 and features mostly works by Utahns, but it also has a collection of Soviet working class impressionism. ✉ *126 E. 400 South St.*, ☎ *801/489–2727.* 🎫 *Free.* ⏲ *Tues.–Sat. 10–5, Sun. 3–6.*

The Heber Valley

30 mi from Provo (to Heber City) via U.S. 189 north; 20 mi from Park City via U.S. 40.

In April of 1859, 11 men fought their way through a snowslide in Provo Canyon to settle the verdant Heber Valley. Today this area, with several small towns, including Heber City and Midway, still bears a resemblance to the farm valley of those settlers' dreams. It truly seems a world away from the sophisticated sprawl of Park City to the north. But how long Heber Valley will be able to maintain its easy charm is anybody's guess. The area has a growing reputation as a gateway to recreation on the east side of the Wasatch Range, a status that is certainly responsible for the dozen or more fast-food purveyors along Heber's Main Street. U.S. 189 passes **Deer Creek Reservoir** (☎ 801/654–0171 for information on boating, swimming, and camping) in the south end of the Heber Valley.

The railroad tracks running along U.S. 189 are part of the scenic
41 **Heber Valley Historic Railroad.** Following a line that first ran in 1899, trains take passengers on a nostalgic trip through beautiful Provo Canyon. Each car has been carefully restored, and two of the engines—Number 618 and Number 1907—are fully operational, steam-powered locomotives. ✉ *450 S. 600 West St., Heber City,* ☎ *435/654–5601.* 🎫 *$10 and up.* ⏲ *Daily 9–5.*

Jordanelle State Park has two recreation areas on a large mountain reservoir. The **Hailstone Area** is 10 mi north of Heber City via U.S. 40, with tent and RV camping, and day use areas. There are also boat ramps, a children's playground, a visitor center, and a marina store where water toys (wave runners, and the like) can be rented. To the east, across the reservoir on Route 32, the **Rock Cliff** facilities are near the Provo River. This is a quiet area known for excellent wildlife watching, particularly along a series of elevated boardwalks winding through aspen forest. The 50 campsites here are all "walk-ins." The Rock Cliff Nature Center provides interpretation of the area's natural history. ☎ *435/649–9540, Hailstone; 435/783–3030, Rock Cliff.* *$5 per vehicle.* *May–Sept., daily 6–10; Oct.–Apr., daily 8–5.*

Dining and Lodging

$$$–$$$$ ★ **The Homestead.** The Homestead, in Midway, 4 mi west of Heber City via Midway Lane, combines the facilities of a complete resort with the charm of a country inn. The centerpiece is a natural hot spring once popular with the silver miners of Park City. The site was first developed in 1886 as an inn and restaurant. An expansion in 1952 turned the property into a rustic yet elegant year-round resort. In addition to a soak in the hot spring, you can enjoy a championship golf course, cross-country ski touring, hot-air ballooning, snowmobiling, and exceptionally fine dining. At Simon's, an upscale restaurant on the premises (reservations essential, $$$$), the menu includes such dishes as Mountain Meadow strudel, a vegetarian strudel, pan-roasted Alaskan halibut, and rack of lamb, all meticulously prepared and served. ✉ *700 N. Homestead Dr., Box 99, Midway 84049,* ☎ *435/654–1102 or 800/327–7220,* FAX *435/654–5087. 154 rooms. 2 restaurants, bar, pool, hot spring, hot tub, sauna, 18-hole golf course, 2 tennis courts, exercise room, horseback riding, cross-country skiing, convention center. AE, D, DC, MC, V.*

Nephi

30 mi from Springville via I–15 south; 50 mi from Springville via Nebo Loop Scenic Byway (Forest Service Rd. 15).

South of Springville on I–15, you will soon leave behind the more populated area of the state for more rural surroundings. Towering over this area is Mt. Nebo, which at 11,877 ft is the tallest peak in the Wasatch Range. From the town of Payson, the 43-mi **Nebo Loop Scenic Byway** (42) circles east of Mt. Nebo's summit to access impressive panoramas and some alluring hiking trails. A ¼-mi walk leads to the Devil's Kitchen Geologic Area, a collection of strangely eroded spires and ridges. The Nebo Loop Scenic Byway returns to I–15 at Nephi, a small town that provides basic services.

Lodging

$–$$$$ **Whitmore Mansion Bed & Breakfast.** Built at the turn of the 20th century, this opulent Queen Anne–style home is now listed on the National Register of Historic Places. Antiques and fine woodwork add to its Victorian charm. Guest rooms have a formal tone apparent in the liberal use of rich velvets and creamy lace. Breakfast is complimentary, and there is no smoking in the rooms. ✉ *110 S. Main St., 84648,* ☎ *435/623–2047. 8 rooms. Breakfast room. MC, V.*

Outdoor Activities and Sports

The laborious grades of the Nebo Loop Scenic Byway provide a test of endurance for **cyclists.** A challenging 6-mi **hiking** route climbs Mt. Nebo from a trailhead along the Nebo Loop Scenic Byway. It is administered by the Uinta National Forest (☎ 801/377–5780).

OFF THE BEATEN PATH

LITTLE SAHARA RECREATION AREA – These expansive sand dunes originated as sandbars in Lake Bonneville, but they have moved 150 mi in the 10,000 years since the lake receded. Although much of this 60,000-acre sandbox is popular with off-road vehicle enthusiasts, the BLM has established three campgrounds and an area especially for children. Nine thousand acres in the western portion of the recreation area have been set aside as a nature preserve. ✉ *From Nephi, follow Rte. 132 west for 13 mi; then turn north and follow a paved BLM road 8 mi to Jericho Junction,* ☎ *435/743–4116.* *$6 per vehicle.*

Sanpete County

43 mi from Nephi (to Manti) via Rte. 132 and U.S. 89 south.

Colorful towns dot Sanpete County. The area, nicknamed "Little Denmark," was settled mainly by Mormon pioneers of Scandinavian extraction. The county seat, **Manti,** is Sanpete's largest community and one of Utah's oldest, established in 1849. Several buildings date back more than a century, including the Manti Temple, completed in 1888. The town of **Ephraim** is home to Snow College, a two-year institution that also dates to 1888; several historic buildings; and turkey farms. Nearly all of nearby **Spring City** is listed on the National Register of Historic Places, and the town has become an arts colony of sorts, with dozens of potters, painters, and sculptors among its residents.

To return to Salt Lake City, either backtrack on I–15 or follow U.S. 89 north to Spanish Fork, just south of Provo. On U.S. 89 near Thistle, now a ghost town, watch for evidence of the **landslide and flood** that inundated the town in 1983. A new stretch of highway was subsequently built around the area, and an interpretive sign describes the disaster, and its aftermath, in some detail.

Lodging

$–$$$ **Manti House Inn Bed & Breakfast.** This 1880 home was built by the same workers who built the Manti Temple. Known locally as the McAllister House, the inn is now a state historic site, and it is one of several fine B&Bs in Manti. Breakfast is, of course, included, and, for snacks, there is an ice-cream parlor on the premises. Rooms are no-smoking. ✉ *401 N. Main St., 84642,* ☎ *435/835–0161,* FAX *435/835–0161. 7 rooms. Ice-cream parlor, hot tub. AE, D, MC, V.*

The Wasatch Range A to Z

Arriving and Departing

BY BUS

Greyhound Lines (☎ 800/231–2222) serves many towns along the Wasatch Front: Tremonton, Logan, Brigham City, Ogden, and Provo. The **Utah Transit Authority** (☞ By Bus *in* Getting Around, *below*) connects Salt Lake City to many spots in the area.

BY CAR

If you're driving into the area, chances are you'll be coming on either I–15 or I–80. Even if you fly into Salt Lake City, it's a good idea to rent a car at the airport and drive to the section of the Wasatch you want to visit. Until the summer of 2001, I–15 will be in the midst of a major reconstruction effort between Ogden and Provo. However, two lanes should be open at all times, both north and south.

BY TRAIN

Amtrak (☎ 800/872–7245) has service to Ogden and Provo.

Getting Around

BY BUS

The **Utah Transit Authority** (☎ 801/287–4636) has frequent service to all of Salt Lake Valley, Davis and Weber counties, and Utah Valley. Buses, with ski racks, also make several runs a day to the ski areas in Little and Big Cottonwood canyons.

BY CAR

The main thoroughfare along the Wasatch mountains is I–15. From this trunk, I–80 heads east toward Park City, U.S. 89 branches to the far north, U.S. 189 runs up Provo Canyon, and Route 132 winds into Sanpete County. All these routes feature spectacular mountain views. Winter visitors should be versed in driving on snowy roads; cars should be equipped with snow tires or chains.

Contacts and Resources

DOCTORS AND DENTISTS

Logan: Logan Regional Hospital (✉ 1400 N. 500 East St., ☎ 435/752–2050).

Ogden: Columbia-Ogden Regional Medical Center (✉ 5575 S. 500 East St., ☎ 801/479–2111).

Park City: Family Health and Emergency Center (✉ 1665 Bonanza Dr., ☎ 435/649–7640).

Provo: Utah Valley Regional Medical Center (✉ 1034 N. 500 West St., ☎ 801/373–7850).

STATE PARKS

The following is not a complete list of Wasatch Range state parks, but all of these do have excellent camping facilities with modern rest rooms and showers:

Deer Creek State Park (✉ 11 mi northeast of Provo on U.S. 189, ☎ 435/654–0171) is popular with anglers and boaters. **East Canyon State Park** (✉ 5535 S. Rte. 66, Morgan, ☎ 435/829–6866) is on a 680-acre reservoir in the mountains northeast of Salt Lake City. **Hyrum State Park** (✉ 405 W. 300 South St., in the northwest corner of Hyrum, ☎ 435/245–6866) features boating on a 450-acre reservoir. **Palisade State Park** (✉ southeast of Manti off U.S. 89, ☎ 801/835–7275) has a small reservoir and nine-hole golf course. **Rockport State Park** (✉ 9040 N. Rte. 302, Peoa, 7 mi south of Wanship on Rte. 32, ☎ 435/336–2241) is northeast of Park City and is quite nice for boating and fishing. There are eight camping areas, offering both developed and primitive camping. **Wasatch Mountain State Park** (✉ 1281 Warmsprings Dr., off Rte. 224, Midway, ☎ 435/654–1791) is known for its 27-hole golf course but also offers hiking and riding trails in the summer and Nordic skiing in the winter. It is Utah's largest state park and will be the site of the cross-country ski events for the 2002 Winter Games.

VISITOR INFORMATION

Bridgerland (✉ 160 N. Main St., Logan 84321, ☎ 435/752–2161 or 800/882–4433). **Brigham City Chamber of Commerce** (✉ 6 N. Main St., Brigham City 84302, ☎ 435/723–3931). **Golden Spike Empire** (✉ 2501 Wall Ave., Ogden 84401, ☎ 801/627–8288 or 800/255–8824). **Great Salt Lake Country** (✉ 90 S. West Temple St., Salt Lake City 84101, ☎ 801/521–2822 or 800/541–495). **Heber Valley County Chamber of Commerce** (✉ 475 N. Main St., Heber 84032, ☎ 435/654–3666). **Mountainland** (✉ 586 E. 800 North St., Orem 84097, ☎ 801/229–3800). **Utah County Convention and Visitors Bureau** (✉ 105 E. Center St., Suite 3200, Provo 84606, ☎ 801/370–8393 or 800/222–8824). **Panoramaland** (✉ 4 S. Main St., Box 71, Nephi 84648, ☎ 435/623–5203 or

800/748–4361). **Park City Chamber of Commerce/Convention and Visitors Bureau** (✉ Box 1630, Park City 84060, ☎ 435/649–6100 or 800/453–1360). **Springville Chamber of Commerce** (✉ 50 S. Main St., Springville 84663, ☎ 801/489–4681).

NORTHEASTERN UTAH

With the western portion of Dinosaur National Monument within its borders, northeastern Utah counts the remains of Jurassic giants as its primary attraction. While the monument and related sites explore the lives of long-extinct creatures, the region also showcases some beautiful landscape: colorful slickrock canyons and deserts, a scenic stretch of the Green River, and the Uinta Mountains—Utah's highest mountain range. Boating, waterskiing, and windsurfing are popular at Flaming Gorge Reservoir, Red Fleet Reservoir, Starvation Reservoir, Steinaker Lake, and Strawberry Reservoir, all of which have boat-ramp facilities. Add to these natural wonders some Fremont rock art and relics of 19th-century pioneers and outlaws, and you have a worthwhile tour to a remote corner of the West.

The Uinta Basin

116 mi (to Duchesne) from Salt Lake City via I–80 and U.S. 40 east.

Sprawling across northeastern Utah at the southern base of the Uinta Mountains, the small towns of the Uinta Basin provide access to the recreational and historic destinations unique to this isolated portion of the state

Duchesne serves as the seat of government for the county of the same name. The town was settled in the early 1900s when portions of the Ute Indians' Uintah and Ouray Reservation were opened to Anglo settlement. Anglers cast for walleye, German brown trout, and bass at 3,500-acre **Starvation Reservoir** (✉ 4 mi northwest of Duchesne on U.S. 40, ☎ 435/738–2326).

Situated on the south slope of the Uinta Mountains (✉ 17 mi north and east of Duchesne on Rte. 87), **Altamont** is not really much of a town, as towns go. Mostly, it's a place for the far-flung ranchers of the Uinta Basin to come for church services, pick up mail, or have a look at the people who've stopped to get directions on their way to the several guest ranches in the area.

Roosevelt (✉ 28 mi northeast of Duchesne via U.S. 40 or 18 mi southeast of Altamont via Rte. 87 and U.S. 40) has a population hovering around 4,000, and was named for President Theodore Roosevelt, who signed a declaration in 1902 allowing whites to settle on Ute lands. The nearby town of Duchesne was originally called Theodore, but the community eventually adopted the name of a French nun instead.

Travel north from Roosevelt or Duchesne, and you'll soon cross portions of the **Uinta and Ouray Indian Reservation.** Nearly 1 million acres in size, this sovereign land is spread out across northeastern Utah in several units. Visitors are asked to stay on the main roads, although camping and hiking are allowed with a permit. The tribe hosts the Northern Ute Indian Pow Wow in early July at tribal headquarters in Fort Duchesne (☎ 435/722–5141).

Dining and Lodging

$–$$$ ★ ✕ **Frontier Grill.** Affiliated with a locally owned motel, this family restaurant is known for its great sandwiches and salads during the noon hour, its prime rib and seafood at night, and its homemade pies any time of the day. ✉ *65 S. 200 East St., Roosevelt,* ☎ *435/722–3669. AE, DC, MC, V.*

$$$$ ✕🏨 **Falcon's Ledge Lodge.** This modern stucco lodge in pristine Stillwater Canyon offers multi-day packages, including meals, that involve falconry, fly-fishing, and horseback or llama pack-trips into the High Uintas Wilderness. Guest rooms are luxurious; some have vault ceilings and Jacuzzis. The spacious lobby has sweeping views of the high desert scenery. The restaurant's meals are the best in the area; specialties include fresh trout and "olive lover's" steak. Fresh home-baked bread is served at every meal. ✉ *Stillwater Canyon, Box 67, Altamont 84001,* ☎ *435/454–3737,* FAX *435/454–3392. 9 rooms. Restaurant, fishing, horseback riding. AE, MC, V.*

$ 🏨 **Best Western Inn.** Clean and comfortable rooms, plus a pool and a coffee shop make this the place to stay in Roosevelt. There's also a restaurant nearby. ✉ *Rte. 1, Box 2860, E. Hwy. 40, Roosevelt 84066,* ☎ *435/722–4644,* FAX *435/772–0179. 40 rooms. Coffee shop, pool, hot tub. AE, D, DC, MC, V.*

Outdoor Activities and Sports

Campgrounds abound in the **Ashley National Forest** (☞ Other Recreation Areas, *below*) north of Duchesne and Roosevelt and west of Flaming Gorge. **Flaming Gorge National Recreation Area** (administered by the Ashley National Forest) contains more than a dozen campgrounds within the Utah portion, including those in the Dutch John and Antelope Flat areas. Several commercial campgrounds are also in the area.

Vernal

43 *30 mi from Roosevelt via U.S. 40 east.*

The largest town (population 6,800) in the northeast corner of the state, Vernal serves as a hub for visiting the area, which was frequented by mountain man William Ashley in the 1820s and first settled during the 1870s.

Because Vernal was so isolated in its early days, shipping was expensive. To avoid high freight costs, one businessman had a bank facade shipped in brick by brick by U.S. mail. Nicknamed the **Parcel Post Bank,** the 1916 structure still stands and is part of the Zions First National Bank building in downtown Vernal.

Other historic sites in and about Vernal include an 1877 log post office and store (✉ 1255 W. 2000 North St.) and the old Oscar Swett Ranch (☞ Flaming Gorge, *below*). Additionally, two museums feature relics and memorabilia from Vernal's yesteryear. **The Daughters of Utah Pioneers Museum** (✉ 158 S. 500 West St.), open during the summer months, offers some perspective on what pioneer life was like. The **Western Heritage Museum** (✉ 302 E. 200 South St., ☎ 435/789–7399) highlights, among other Old West themes, 19th-century outlaws of the Vernal area.

One hundred and fifty million years ago, this land was the stomping ground of dinosaurs, both large and small. A good place to initiate an investigation is the **Utah Field House of Natural History State Park.** In its museum, numerous rock samples and fossils (including dinosaur bones) are housed. A large mural depicts the last 2.7 billion years of the Uinta Basin's geologic history, and Fremont and Ute artifacts offer insight into the early presence of humans in the area. Outside, the Dinosaur Garden features 17 life-size dinosaur models in a primordial setting. ✉ *235 E. Main St.,* ☎ *435/789–3799.* 🎫 *$5.* ⏲ *June–Sept., daily 8 AM–9 PM; Oct.–May, daily 9–5.*

Dinomania rules at **Dinosaur National Monument** (☞ Chapter 4), which straddles the Utah-Colorado border. Located 20 mi east of Vernal are
44 the monument's visitor center and astounding **Dinosaur Quarry,** where, inside a large enclosure, there are some 2,000 dinosaur bones encased in a 200-ft-long sandstone face. This collection of fossils resulted when floods brought the bodies of several dinosaurs to rest on a sandbar; subsequent deposits covered the carcasses where they lay, becoming part of the Morrison Formation. The cache of paleontological treasures was discovered by Earl Douglass in 1909. Today visitors must ride a shuttle bus from the visitor center to the quarry during busy times of the year. ✉ *20 mi east of Vernal on Rte. 149,* ☎ *435/789–2115 quarry.* *$10 per vehicle.* ⏲ *June–Sept., 8–7; Oct.–May, 8–4:30.*

Although most people visit Dinosaur National Monument to see dinosaur bones, this 200,000-acre park also offers a generous supply of alluring backcountry to explore, either on foot or by vehicle. An especially scenic drive runs 6 mi east from the quarry to the **Josie Morris Cabin.** A rugged individualist, Ms. Morris kept company with the likes of Butch Cassidy. For wonderful vistas along the Utah-Colorado border, take the Harpers Corner Road. The drive into Rainbow Park not only passes some impressive Fremont petroglyph panels but also reaches a put-in point for rafters, who will find a variety of white-water thrills on the Green and Yampa rivers (☞ Outdoor Activities and Sports, *below*).

Boating and waterskiing enthusiasts will love **Steinaker Lake State Park** (✉ 7 mi north of Vernal on U.S. 191, ☎ 435/789–4432). More than 2 mi long, Steinaker Reservoir also relinquishes a fair number of large-mouth bass and rainbow trout.

Red Fleet State Park (✉ 10 mi north of Vernal off U.S. 191, ☎ 435/789–4432), like the other reservoirs in the region, is great for boat and bait. The real attraction here, though, is the colorful sandstone formations in which the lake is nestled. In addition, a section of 200-million-year-old dinosaur tracks can be reached by a short hike or by boat.

Dining and Lodging

$$–$$$$ ✕ **The Curry Manor.** The diverse menu includes entrées such as Parmesan-pesto chicken, baked salmon stuffed with crab, and pork tenderloin with wild-berry sauce. This restaurant serves old-fashioned breakfasts and burgers at lunch. ✉ *189 S. Vernal Ave.,* ☎ *435/789–2289. AE, D, MC, V.*

$ ✕ **Casa Rios.** If you're in search of south-of-the-border flavors, this is a good bet. Try the special beef burrito or the chimichangas. ✉ *2015 W. Rte. 40,* ☎ *435/789–0103. MC, V. Closed Sun. and Mon.*

$–$$ **Best Western Antlers Motel.** Locals rate this as Vernal's best accommodations. The motel offers good-size rooms decorated in quiet colors, and the staff is friendly and helpful. A wading pool and playground delight young guests. ✉ *423 W. Main St., 84078,* ☎ *435/789–1202 or 800/524–1234,* FAX *435/789–4979. 44 rooms. Restaurant, pool, hot tub. AE, D, DC, MC, V.*

$ **Weston Lamplighter Inn.** Close to shopping, theaters, and restaurants, this motel has rooms that are simply furnished, and a more than adequate restaurant. ✉ *120 E. Main St., 84078,* ☎ *435/789–0312,* FAX *435/781–1480. 94 rooms. Restaurant, pool. AE, D, DC, MC, V.*

Outdoor Activities and Sports

CAMPING

Dinosaur National Monument (✉ Box 4545, Dinosaur, CO 81610, ☎ 303/374–2216 or 435/789–2115) has two campgrounds, one near the quarry and the other in a more remote section of the monument.

RAFTING

White-water enthusiasts find challenging stretches on the Green and Yampa rivers in Dinosaur National Monument. Joining forces near Echo Park in Colorado, the two waterways have each carved spectacular canyons through several aeons' worth of rock, and they are still at it in rapids such as Whirlpool Canyon, SOB, Disaster Falls, and Hell's Half Mile. Day-trippers will enjoy a float down the Green River below the Flaming Gorge Dam. The **Utah Travel Council** (☎ 800/200–1160) can provide a directory detailing river routes and which outfitters run them.

OFF THE BEATEN PATH

BROWNS PARK AND THE JOHN JARVIE RANCH – If visiting the back of beyond is your interest, then drive 65 mi northeast from Vernal on U.S. 191 to Browns Park. Lying along a quieter stretch of the Green River and extending into Colorado, this area features plenty of high desert scenery and a fascinating historic site, the John Jarvie Ranch (follow signs off Rte. 191). Operated by the BLM, the ranch includes four original buildings constructed by Scotsman John Jarvie more than a century ago. Jarvie was a colorful addition to Browns Park settlement. He was a storekeeper, an accomplished musician, and a prospector. His even-handed treatment of his customers earned respect from the area's ranchers and from the many outlaws who frequented the area en route to more remote hideouts. Because the road into Browns Park can be rough at times, be sure to check with the BLM's Vernal office (☎ 435/789–1362) about road conditions, or call the Jarvie Ranch directly (☎ 435/885–3307).

En Route

For more recreational opportunities, return to Vernal and head north on U.S. 191. Steinaker Lake and Red Fleet state parks (☞ *above*) both have reservoirs ideally suited to water sports and fishing. Past Red Fleet Reservoir, U.S. 191 begins to ascend the eastern flank of the Uinta uplift. This section of the tour follows what is known as the **Drive Through the Ages.** Within a distance of 30 mi, the road passes 19 geologic formations, including the billion-year-old exposed core of the Uinta Mountains, with signs identifying and describing them. This route also provides plenty of opportunity for wildlife watching. A road guide is available at the Vernal Welcome Center.

Flaming Gorge National Recreation Area

40 mi from Vernal (to Flaming Gorge Dam) via U.S. 191 north.

In May of 1869, during his mapping expedition on the Green and Colorado rivers, explorer John Wesley Powell named this canyon Flaming Gorge for its "flaming, brilliant red" color. Powell was not the first traveler to be in awe of the landscape. The first recorded visitors were fur trappers who set up a long-term camp in 1825. By the late 1800s, scores of cattlemen and farmers, followed by rustlers and outlaws, had come to live in the area. The people came, but not the conveniences that generally follow. Flaming Gorge remained one of Utah's most remote and least developed inhabited areas well into the 1950s. In 1964, Flaming Gorge Canyon and the Green River running through it were plugged with a 500-ft-high wall of concrete. The result is a 90-mi-long reservoir that twists and turns among canyon walls. Although much of the lake stretches north into Wyoming, most facilities lie south of the state line in Utah.

Upon reaching Greendale Junction, 36 mi north of Vernal, stay right on
45 U.S. 191 if you wish to visit the **Flaming Gorge Dam** itself. Displays at the nearby visitor center explain aspects of this engineering marvel, and the dam is open for self-guided tours Memorial Day–Labor Day, daily 9–5.

46 Inside the **Red Canyon Visitor Center** are displays covering the geology, flora and fauna, and human history of the Flaming Gorge area,

but the most magnificent thing about the center is its location atop a cliff that towers 1,300 ft above the lake. The views here are outstanding. ✉ *Turn left onto Rte. 44 at Greendale Junction and follow signs to visitor center turnoff,* ☎ *435/889–3713.* ⊙ *Memorial Day weekend–Sept., daily 9:30–5.*

Numerous hiking trails and a scenic drive traverse the **Sheep Creek Canyon Geological Area** (✉ Sheep Creek Canyon Loop Rd., 28 mi west of U.S. 191 and Rte. 44 junction, ☎ 435/784–3445), which is full of upturned layers of rock.

The quickest route from Flaming Gorge to Salt Lake City cuts northwest across Wyoming to I–80, or, of course, you can return the way you came and enjoy the attractions of Northeastern Utah once again.

Lodging

$–$$$ **Flaming Gorge Lodge.** Probably the best accommodations in the vicinity of Flaming Gorge, the lodge has a great restaurant, plus a store, raft rentals, and fishing guide service. The rooms, although simple, are not spartan. The emphasis here is on comfort, not frills. ✉ *Greendale, U.S. 191, Dutch John 84023,* ☎ *435/889–3773,* FAX *435/889–3788. 21 rooms, 24 condos. Restaurant. AE, D, MC, V.*

$–$$$ **Red Canyon Lodge.** Cabins, termed "rustic," "deluxe," and "luxury," compose this property. The basic difference between them is bathroom facilities. "Rustic" means a shared shower house and rest room. Deluxe cabins have their own rest rooms and shower facilities. Luxury means a bigger cabin with living room, vault ceilings, kitchenette, and full bathrooms. Although none of the options are truly luxurious, the plain but functional accommodations feel just fine in this wild setting. ✉ *790 Red Canyon Rd., off Rte. 44, Dutch John 84023,* ☎ *435/889–3759,* FAX *435/889–5106. 24 cabins. Restaurant. AE, D, MC, V.*

Outdoor Activities and Sports

CYCLING

Because it mixes high desert vegetation—blooming sage, rabbit brush, cactus, and wild flowers—and red-rock terrain with a cool climate, Flaming Gorge National Recreation Area is an ideal destination for road and trail biking. The 3-mi-round-trip **Bear Canyon–Bootleg ride** begins south of the dam off U.S. 191 at the Firefighters' Memorial Campground and runs west to an overview of the reservoir. A 6-mi-round-trip spur shared by cyclists and cars begins at the Greendale rest area on Route 44. It leads to the historic **Swett Ranch,** where Oscar Swett began homesteading in 1909 and continued to work the land with his wife—and, later, nine children—until he died in 1968. Equipment powered by horses, rather than gasoline, was used for daily chores until 1970. Many of these implements are displayed on the ranch, which is now administered by the Ashley National Forest (☎ 435/784–3445). A free brochure, **Flaming Gorge Trails,** describes these and other cycling routes. It is distributed at area visitor centers.

FISHING

Strawberry Reservoir (✉ 25 mi south of Heber City on U.S. 40, ☎ 435/548–2321) covers 17,000 acres. Construction on the original reservoir, part of a federal project designed to bring water from the Colorado River basin to the Wasatch Front, began in 1906. In 1973, the Soldier Creek Dam was built downstream, and the original Strawberry Reservoir dam was eventually removed. The result was a much larger storage facility, which boaters and anglers alike now relish. Ice fishing is also popular. Four U.S. Forest Service campgrounds and three marinas dot the lakeshore.

Fishing fans can try their luck at all of this region's reservoirs, but "old-timers" maintain that Flaming Gorge and Starvation reservoirs provide the best lake fishing. For the best river fishing, experts suggest the Green River below the Flaming Gorge Dam. Fed by cold water from the bottom of the lake, this stretch has been identified as one of the best trout fisheries in the world.

WATER SPORTS

At Flaming Gorge, three marinas offer boat rentals and supplies: **Cedar Springs Marina** (✉ Box 337, Dutch John, ☎ 435/889–3795), near the dam; **Lucerne Valley Marina** (✉ Box 356, Manila, ☎ 435/784–3483), east of Manila; and the **Buckboard Marina** (✉ Star Rte. 1, Green River, ☎ 307/875–6927) in Wyoming.

Other Recreation Areas

Although the Wasatch may be Utah's best-known mountain range, the **Uinta Mountains,** the only major east–west mountain range in the Rockies, are its tallest, topped by 13,528-ft Kings Peak. Though the mountains lie north of the Uinta and Ouray Indian Reservation, the quickest, easiest (read: paved) route to Uinta country is the Mirror Lake Scenic Byway, which begins in Kamas. The 65-mi drive follows Route 150 into the heavily wooded canyons of the **Wasatch–Cache National Forest** (✉ 50 E. Center St., Box 68, Kamas, ☎ 435/783–4338), cresting at 10,687-ft Bald Mountain Pass. At nearby Mirror Lake, campgrounds provide a base for hikes into the surrounding mountains, and Highline Trail accesses the 460,000-acre High Uintas Wilderness Area to the east. Still farther east, accessible by dirt roads from the reservation, are several recreation areas in the **Ashley National Forest** (✉ 244 W. U.S. 40, Roosevelt, ☎ 435/722–5018). One of these, Moon Lake, features a U.S. Forest Service campground and private resort. Another, along the Yellowstone River, has five campgrounds. These areas also have trails that lead to the High Uintas Wilderness Area.

Northeastern Utah A to Z

Arriving and Departing

BY BUS

Greyhound Lines (☎ 800/231–2222) serves Vernal.

BY CAR

The best way to reach the area is by car, whether you're coming from Salt Lake or Colorado on U.S. 40, or Wyoming on U.S. 191.

Getting Around

BY CAR

Both U.S. 40 and U.S. 191, the tour's main routes, are well maintained; however, there are some curvy, mountainous stretches. If you're headed for the wilderness, be prepared for dirt roads.

Contacts and Resources

DOCTORS AND DENTISTS

Vernal: Ashley Valley Medical Center (✉ 151 West 200 N, ☎ 435/789–3342).

Roosevelt: Uinta Basin Medical Center (✉ 250 West 300 N, ☎ 435/722–4691).

GUIDED TOURS

Dinaland Aviation (✉ 830 E. 500 South St., Vernal, ☎ 435/789–4612) offers flights over Dinosaur National Monument, Flaming Gorge, and the canyons of the Green River. Prices start at $29 per person.

Guided river trips are available from **Adrift Adventures–Dinosaur** (✉ Box 192, Jensen 84035, ☎ 435/789–3600 or 800/824–0150), **Hatch River Expeditions** (✉ 55 E. Main St., Box 1150, Vernal 84078, ☎ 435/789–4316 or 800/342–8243, FAX 435/789–8513), and **Holiday Expeditions** ✉ 793 S. 1500 East, Vernal 84078, ☎ 435/789–4586 or 800/624–6323. Trips run one to six days and cost $63 and up.

VISITOR INFORMATION

Dinosaurland Welcome Center (✉ off U.S. 40 at the Jensen exit, ☎ 435/789–4002). **Vernal Information Centers** (✉ Utah Fieldhouse of Natural History, 235 E. Main St., Vernal 84078, and ✉ 25 E. Main St., ☎ 435/789–6932 or 800/477–5558 for both centers). **Vernal Chamber of Commerce** (✉ 134 W. Main St., Vernal 84078, ☎ 435/789–1352). **Duchesne County Chamber of Commerce** (✉ 48 South 200 E, Roosevelt 84066, ☎ 435/722–4598).

SOUTHEASTERN UTAH

Characterized by multihue buttes, bizarre rock formations, deep canyons, and lonesome plateaus, southeastern Utah stirs the imagination as few other places can. The broad and open desert topography provides grand vistas, where scale is often an intangible element. Storm clouds billow high into the sky, and spectacular sunsets routinely light up an already colorful landscape. Add to this incredible natural beauty a wealth of paleontological, archaeological, and historical treasures, plus a broad range of outdoor recreational opportunities, and you have one of the most alluring travel destinations to be found anywhere.

If you do set out for this distant corner of the state, be prepared for some of the most desolate stretches of highway in the country. In addition to stocking up on extra supplies and making sure that your vehicle is in good mechanical condition, you should also prepare yourself mentally for the vast stretches of nothingness that lie ahead. Although some travelers thrive on the extra elbow room, others may become a bit unnerved when they learn just how spacious this corner of the West really is.

Because of vast distances, it is a good idea to plan southeastern Utah explorations in advance. This loop tour, in its entirety or just a portion, gives a good taste of the area. However, don't be afraid to strike out on your own. Excellent information is available throughout the region to help you do so in safety.

Helper

47 *63 mi from Provo via U.S. 6 south.*

If you're headed into the area from the north, making a brief stop in Helper yields a worthwhile tribute to the local area's history. The **Western Mining and Railroad Museum,** housed in a former hotel that is part of a national historic district, features displays on the development of mining in Castle Country, Depression-era paintings, an archive room for researchers, and an outdoor display of trains and mining equipment. ✉ *296 S. Main St.,* ☎ *435/472–3009.* *$1 suggested donation.* *May–Sept., Mon.–Sat. 9–5; Oct.–May, Tues.–Sat. 11–4.*

Price

48 *11 mi from Helper via U.S. 6 south.*

Price is the hub of Utah's Castle Country (so called because many rock formations resemble castles). As with virtually every other community in southern Utah, Price began as a Mormon farming enclave in the late

19th century. Shortly after it was established, however, the town took on a noticeably different character. In 1883 the railroad arrived, bringing with it immigrants from around the world. Nearby coal reserves were tapped, and the town has counted mining, not agriculture, as its primary industry ever since. Today, because many of Price's nearly 10,000 residents are still employed in the coalfields, there are strong labor union ties in the community, a fact that makes Price and nearby Helper bastions of liberalism and the Democratic party in an otherwise conservative state.

Although in many ways a modern town, Price has not forgotten its heritage and celebrates its ethnic diversity with two summer festivals. Song, dance, and food reminiscent of old Greece are the highlights of Greek Days in mid-July. International Days, which takes place during the first or second week in August in conjunction with the county fair, is a real local's event. If you should miss these colorful festivals, then be sure to visit the **Price Mural** in the Municipal Building (✉ 185 E. Main St.). A Works Progress Administration project, this 200-ft-long mural was painted between 1938 and 1941 by Lynn Fausett. It narrates the modern history of Price and surrounding Carbon County, beginning with the first white settlers.

As in other parts of Utah, the past in Castle Country extends at least a few years prior to the arrival of Mormon farmers in the 19th century—to about 150 million years ago. Housing one of the best collections of dinosaur memorabilia in the region is the **College of Eastern Utah Prehistoric Museum,** next to the Price Municipal Building. Front and center in the museum's Hall of Dinosaurs are several complete dinosaur skeletons, and that of an 11,000-year-old mammoth excavated locally. A rare dinosaur egg is on display, as are dinosaur tracks unearthed by miners in nearby coal beds. ✉ *155 E. Main St.,* ☎ *435/637–5060.* *$1 suggested donation.* ⊙ *Apr.–Sept., daily 9–6; Oct.–March, Mon.–Sat. 9–5.*

Dining and Lodging

$–$$ ✕ **Greek Streak.** For genuine and delicious Greek food, this is the place in Price. Family owned, the restaurant serves up gyros, lamb stew, and roast lamb, among other authentic dishes. The Greek pastries served here are considered the best in the state. ✉ *84 S. Carbon Ave.,* ☎ *435/637–1930. MC, V. Closed Sun. and Mon. in summer.*

$ **Best Western Carriage House Inn.** Unlike some locally owned motor inns, which can disappoint, this one in downtown Price outpaces the big national chains in all respects. For a good price, you get a clean and comfortable room, plus personal service. ✉ *590 E. Main St., 84501,* ☎ *435/637–5660,* FAX *435/637–5660. 41 rooms. Indoor pool, hot tub. AE, D, DC, MC, V.*

Outdoor Activities and Sports

CAMPING

Price Canyon Recreation Area (✉ 18 mi northwest of Price along U.S. 6) is operated by the BLM, and with RV and tent camping sites, picnic tables, and flush toilets, is more accommodating than most BLM facilities (☎ 435/636–3600).

GOLF

The **Carbon Country Club Golf Course** is the oldest in the eastern half of the state, and it's one of the most unusual. The original nine holes, built just after World War II, are tree-lined and require disciplined play. By contrast, the back nine holes, created in 1994, have spacious, open fairways. ✉ *Between Helper and Price on U.S. 6,* ☎ *435/637–2388.*

Nine Mile Canyon

49 *7½ mi from Price via U.S. 6/191 south.*

Nine Mile Canyon, an enormous gallery of hundreds of petroglyphs etched into its boulders and cliffs, is the handiwork of the Fremont Indians, who lived in much of what is now Utah from AD 300 to 1250. Indeed, the meaning of these images is one of the most mystifying puzzles of the area, but almost as confounding is how a canyon 40 mi long came to be named "Nine Mile." One explanation points to John Wesley Powell's epic float down the nearby Green River in 1869. It seems the expedition's mapmaker drew up a 9-mi triangulation, which he titled Nine Mile Creek. The canyon has the remnants of many homesteads, stage stops, and ranches. However, the petroglyphs and pictographs are the main draw. It's important not to disturb the fragile rock art in any way. Because most of this 80-mi round-trip is on a gravel road, plan to take most of a day to complete it. A brochure detailing significant sites is available at visitor centers in Price. Without it, many panels will go unnoticed. Of course, the best way to experience Nine Mile Canyon is to go with a guide. **Reflections on the Ancients** (✉ Box 444, Wellington, UT 84542, ☎ 435/637–5801 or 800/468–4060) offers archaeologist-led tours. General information is available from the BLM (☞ Cycling *in* Green River, *below*).

En Route Southeast of the turnoff for Nine Mile Canyon, U.S. 6/191 continues into some of the most desolate terrain anywhere. Known as the **San Rafael Desert,** this barren landscape can be a bit overwhelming, but views of the Book Cliffs to the east do lessen the monotony somewhat. Because this drive includes some lengthy straightaways, you may find yourself developing a heavy foot, but beware: The Utah Highway Patrol watches this stretch closely.

Green River

50 *65 mi from Price via U.S. 6/191 south and I–70 east.*

Today travelers can avoid Green River completely, but not so long ago the highway traffic cruised right through town, and the town fathers fought a bypass in the name of commerce. Although no longer compulsory, a visit to Green River can be a pleasant experience. Thanks to irrigation water siphoned from the river of the same name, the town is known for its watermelons and its annual **Melon Days** celebration. Held the third weekend in September, this small-town event features a parade and fair, plenty of music, and a canoe race.

Green River's claim to agricultural fame notwithstanding, the town is known as a base for several river-running outfits—and for good reason. To the north, the Green River has carved two spectacular canyons, Desolation and Gray, whose rapids make them a favorite haunt of rafters. South of town, it drifts at a lazier pace through Labyrinth and Stillwater canyons, and the 68-mi stretch of river that runs south to Mineral Bottom in Canyonlands National Park is best suited to canoes and motorized boats.

Exploration of Utah's wild waterways enjoys a rich history—more than a century's worth. The largest tributary of the Colorado River, the Green was the last major river in the continental United States to be explored. John Wesley Powell and a party of nine men rectified the situation with an epic voyage in 1869. Commemorating this feat is the **John Wesley Powell River History Museum.** In addition to various exhibits, artifacts, and works of art concerning 19th-century western exploration, it also houses the River Runner's Hall of Fame, a tribute to those who have followed in Powell's wake. ✉ *885 E. Main St., on the Green River,* ☎ *435/564–3427.* *$2 per person, $5 per family.* ⏲ *June–Sept., daily 8–8; Oct.–May, daily 9–5.*

For a bit of exploring on "dry" land, drive out to **Crystal Geyser,** 10 mi south of town on good, graded road. Reaching up to 60 ft high, this cold-water eruption blows two or three times a day and usually lasts for seven minutes. The staff at the Green River Information Center, which is in the John Wesley Powell River History Museum, can provide approximate eruption times, detailed directions, and updated road conditions.

Another worthwhile excursion is the **Green River Scenic Drive,** which descends into the lower portion of Gray Canyon. Following the west bank of the river, this 10-mi route provides spectacular views of the Beckwith Plateau. After passing some sandy beachfront and a set of rapids, you'll know you're nearing the end as the Nefertiti rock formation, an aptly named local landmark, comes into view. A primitive campground is here, and it is possible to hike upstream for several miles along old cattle trails. Because all but 1½ mi of this drive is on dirt road, be sure to check with the Green River State Park office (☎ 435/564–3633) about conditions beforehand. Wet weather renders the drive impassable, but when dry it's suitable for cars with good clearance. From Main Street, follow 1200 East Street, known locally as the Hastings Road.

Dining and Lodging

$–$$ ★ ✕ **Ray's Tavern.** Stop here for one of the best burgers in the state. Topped with a thick slice of onion, tomato, and lettuce, this all-beef monstrosity is nestled in a large helping of steak fries. Although a draw of cold beer is optional, interesting conversation is not. Ray's is a favorite hangout for river runners. Although at times a surly bunch, they're always ready with some great tale about working on the river. If you have time, be sure to rack up a game of pool. ✉ *25 S. Broadway,* ☎ *435/564–3511. AE, D, MC, V.*

$–$$ ✕ **Tamarisk Restaurant.** This sit-down eatery features homemade pies and fudge in addition to dinner specials. The riverside setting makes dining here a treat. ✉ *870 E. Main St.,* ☎ *435/564–8109. AE, D, DC, MC, V.*

$–$$ **Best Western River Terrace Hotel.** The setting, on the bank of the Green River, is conducive to a good night's rest. Comfortable rooms are furnished with large beds, and the premises are clean. The lovely river views are more memorable than the decor. ✉ *880 E. Main St.,* ☎ *435/564–3401 or 800/528–1234,* FAX *435/564–3403. 51 rooms. Pool, hot tub. AE, D, DC, MC, V.*

Outdoor Activities and Sports

CYCLING

West of Green River, the San Rafael Swell, north and south of I–70, presents a wild landscape where outlaws once camped in twisting canyons, and cowboys galloped across vast tracts of desert grazing land. In modern times, off-road vehicle trails carved the area, providing easy access for cyclists. A free bike-trail guide is available from the **Castle Country Travel Region** (☎ 435/637–3009 or 800/842–0789). There are no reliable water sources in the desert of the San Rafael, so carry plenty of water on any ride or hike. Another great place to explore on a bicycle is **Nine Mile Canyon** (☞ *above*). For information on both areas, check with the BLM (✉ 900 N. 700 East St., Price 84501, ☎ 435/636–3600).

RAFTING AND CANOEING

Raft trips on the **Green River,** both above and below the town of the same name, are generally arranged by companies headquartered in Vernal or Moab. The annual Raft Utah directory available from the Utah

Travel Council (☎ 800/200–1160) has descriptions of the river canyons and information on guides and outfitters.

Green River City serves as a put-in point for those headed into **Labyrinth Canyon.** Here canoeists are king, for there is barely a ripple along the entire route. For information, contact the BLM in Price (☞ Cycling, *above*).

FOUR-WHEELING

The **San Rafael Swell,** west of Green River, is sort of a cult classic among four-wheelers. Routes such as Buckhorn Draw, Hidden Splendor, and the Copper Globe Loop are favored destinations. Contact the BLM in Price (☞ Cycling, *above*) for maps of the area and trip suggestions.

GOLF

The nine-hole **Green River State Park Golf Course** (☎ 435/564–8882) meanders along the scenic bank of the river for which it was named.

Moab and Environs

51 *52 mi from Green River via I–70 east and U.S. 191 south.*

Established in the 1870s adjacent to the Colorado River, Moab was supposed to be a Mormon farming community. The discovery of uranium in the early 1950s, however, changed the town's character. Within a few years the town's population tripled, as prospectors armed with Geiger counters flooded in. One of these was Charlie Steen, a penniless young man from Texas. Striking it very rich with his Mi Vida mine, Steen built a mansion overlooking town in which he threw lavish parties. Although he may have been a bit more eccentric than most of his neighbors, Steen and his lifestyle were characteristic of the town's freewheeling ways.

Moab is still quite lively and enjoys a greater-than-average influx of outsiders, but it is no longer mineral wealth that draws visitors. Rather, it is the beauty of the surrounding canyons, mesas, and mountains. First lured to Moab by the establishment of Canyonlands National Park in 1964, a small but dedicated corps of outdoor enthusiasts has long known of the area's outstanding rafting and hiking opportunities (☞ Outdoor Activities and Sports, *below*). Similarly, four-wheelers have rallied in Moab every Easter since 1966 to participate in the Moab Jeep Safari. Within the last decade, however, Moab's tourism industry has grown by leaps and bounds. Strings of new motels, T-shirt shops, and restaurants have sprung up. A McDonald's was built on south Main Street, paving the way for several other national chains. A brew pub now serves homemade beer, and Utah's only commercial winery has opened just south of town. The banks have even installed automatic teller machines. What could bring such unprecedented change to this distant corner of the state? Move over, boaters, hikers, and Jeep drivers: Meet the mountain bike.

All-terrain bicycles are well suited to the many miles of rugged back roads left behind by uranium prospectors. What has really put Moab on every mountain biker's map, though, is a simple matter of geology; the asphalt-smooth sandstone, or slickrock, that characterizes much of canyon country is to mountain biking what powder snow is to skiing (☞ Outdoor Activities and Sports, *below*).

If you happen to visit Moab sans raft, backpack, four-wheel-drive vehicle, or mountain bike, don't despair. The area still offers plenty of places that require nothing more than a car and your own two feet to explore. Perhaps the handiest of these is **Arches National Park,** a few miles north. Boasting the largest collection of natural arches in the world, the park is a geologic wonderland unlike any other. Although the process by which these spans of red rock were formed is complex, geologists do point to an underlying bed of salt as the main impetus. As this material shifted, fissures formed in the overlying layer of sandstone. Wind and water then eroded this rock into freestanding fins, which were in turn sculpted into the arches and formations seen today. Many of the park's premier sights, including the Courthouse Towers, Balanced Rock, the Windows, and Skyline Arch, are found along the park's 21-mi paved road. Others, such as Delicate Arch, the Fiery Furnace, and Devil's Garden, are accessible only by foot. Other than the visitor center at the park entrance and the 50-site Devil's Garden Campground, which lies at road's end, there are no services in Arches. *5 mi north of Moab on U.S. 191, 435/259–8161. $10 per vehicle. Visitor center: daily 8–sunset.*

For a taste of history in the Moab area, stop by the **Dan O'Laurie Museum.** The Fremont and Anasazi Indians are remembered in exhibits of sandals, baskets, pottery, and other artifacts. The Ute, a Native American group that has lived in the region during more recent times, command some attention here. A display on the 1776 Dominguez–Escalante Expedition reveals the role that the Spanish played in exploring this part of the West, and the variety of rocks, fossils, and dinosaur bones speaks of the influence that geology has had in shaping life in southeastern Utah. *118 E. Center St., 435/259–7985. Free. Apr.–Oct., Mon.–Sat. 1–5 and 7–9; Nov.–Mar., Mon.–Thurs. 3–5, Fri. and Sat. 1–7.*

Hole 'n the Rock is a 14-room, 5,000-square-ft home carved into a solid rock wall. It would be just another funky roadside attraction if it didn't represent 20 years of toil for Albert and Gladys Christensen. Children can run around all over it. *15 mi south of Moab on U.S. 191, 435/686–2250. $2.50. June–Sept., daily 8–8; Oct.–May, daily 9–5.*

Encompassing some 500 square mi of rugged desert terrain, **Canyonlands National Park** is naturally divided by the Colorado and Green rivers into three districts. Although the Needles and Maze districts are accessible from points farther on in this tour, the **Island in the Sky District** is reached from Moab. As the name suggests, this portion of the park features a high plateau ringed by thousand-foot cliffs. A favorite among photographers is Mesa Arch, which is reached by hiking a ¼-mi trail. A number of scenic overlooks, each of which is precariously perched at land's end, are accessed by 20 mi of paved road. From the Shafer Canyon Overlook, you gaze down upon the twisted Shafer Trail—an early 1900s cattle route that was later upgraded for high-clearance vehicles. From Grand View Point, you can take in spectacular views of the meandering Colorado and Green rivers, the sandstone pinnacles of the Needles District far to the south, and the labyrinths of the Maze District to the southwest. *33 mi from Moab via U.S. 191 north and Rte. 313 west, 435/259–7164. $10 per vehicle. Visitor center: daily 8–sunset.*

Dead Horse Point State Park, one of the finest of Utah's state parks, overlooks a sweeping oxbow of the Colorado River, some 2,000 ft below, and the upside-down landscapes of Canyonlands National Park. Dead Horse Point itself is a small peninsula connected to the main mesa by a narrow neck of land. As the story goes, cowboys used to drive wild horses onto the point and pen them there with a brush fence. Some were accidentally forgotten and left to perish. Facilities at the park include a modern visitor center and museum, a campground with drinking water, and an overlook. *34 mi from Moab at the end of Rte. 313, 435/259–2614. $5 per vehicle. Daily 8–sunset.*

Although the stretches of the Colorado River visible from the Island in the Sky and Dead Horse Point can be accessed only by boat, other portions can be enjoyed up close along two scenic drives. Branching off from U.S. 191 2 mi north of Moab is the **Colorado River Scenic Byway.**

Also known as Route 128, this paved road follows the Colorado River northeast to I–70. First passing through a high-walled corridor, the drive eventually breaks out into Professor Valley, home of the monoliths of Fisher Towers and Castle Rock, which you may recognize from various car commercials. The byway also passes the single-lane Dewey Bridge, in use from 1916 to 1986. Near the end of the 44-mi drive is the tiny town of Cisco. Although a thriving community during the uranium boom, Cisco is today all but abandoned. It is worth a visit just to see what has to be one of the smallest post offices in the nation.

A second interesting drive follows the Potash Road, or Route 279, west from U.S. 191 for 15 mi. After entering the Portal (a break in the high cliffs northwest of town), the **Potash Scenic Byway** continues through a gorge with a number of petroglyph panels. The canyon's walls are also a favorite of rock climbers. Several hiking trails lead to rock formations in side canyons. At the end of the pavement is the Moab Salt Plant, formerly known as the Potash Plant. This facility extracts salt and potash from deposits hundreds of feet below by injecting a solution into drill holes and then pumping it out to large evaporation ponds. Beyond the plant, a rough dirt road continues on to the Shafer Trail, which can be observed from the Shafer Canyon Overlook in Canyonlands National Park.

Although Moab is best known for its slickrock desert, it is also the gateway to the second-highest mountain range in the state—the 12,000-ft La Sal Mountains. Because these peaks remain snowcapped a good part of the year, they provide a striking contrast to the red-rock desert of lower elevations. Exploring them is easy, thanks to the paved **La Sal Mountain Loop.** Beginning 8 mi south of Moab, this 62-mi drive climbs up and over the western flank of the range before dropping into Castle Valley and Route 128 to the north. Along the way a number of scenic turnouts and hiking trails are accessible. Long a favorite haunt of locals, the La Sal Mountain Loop is now being discovered by out-of-towners as a welcome retreat from the summer heat. Once snow flies, portions of this road are impassable. But a well-maintained hut-to-hut system, and both groomed trails and backcountry terrain make this a wonderful place to cross-country ski.

Dining and Lodging

$$–$$$$ ★ ✕ **Center Café.** This is Moab's version of nouvelle cuisine, and a successful one at that. It features the likes of grilled prawns with basil-crab flan and spicy gazpacho sauce, lamb with chanterelle mushrooms, and sautéed free-range chicken breast, among other culinary delights. ✉ *92 E. Center St.,* ☎ *435/259–4295. D, MC, V. No lunch.*

$$–$$$ ✕ **Eddie McStiff's.** This casual restaurant and microbrewery serves up pizzas and zesty Italian specialties to go with 13 freshly brewed concoctions such as raspberry and blueberry wheat beer and a smooth cream ale. ✉ *57 S. Main St.,* ☎ *435/259–2337. MC, V.*

$–$$ ✕ **La Hacienda.** This restaurant has a reputation for serving good south-of-the-border meals at an equally good price. The helpings are generous and the service is friendly. And yes, you can order a margarita, too. ✉ *574 N. Main St.,* ☎ *435/259–6319. AE, D, MC, V.*

$–$$ ✕ **Poplar Place.** This local landmark for fun and lively dining is known for its appetizers, pizzas, and sandwiches. If you're not too hungry, just stop in for a drink and some Poplar Hot Wings. ✉ *11 E. 100 N. Main St.,* ☎ *435/259–6018. MC, V.*

$ ✕ **Jail House Café.** Breakfast here will keep you going long into the afternoon. From eggs Benedict to Grand Marnier-flavored French toast, the menu is guaranteed to fill you up. Housed in what once was the county courthouse, the building held prisoners in the past. ✉ *101 N. Main St,* ☎ *435/259–3900. MC, V. Closed Nov.–Mar.*

$$$$ ★ 🏨 **Sunflower Hill Bed and Breakfast.** There are more than two dozen properties in Moab and vicinity billing themselves as B&Bs. This is the best of the bunch. Country touches and elaborate gardens mark the decor of this stucco-and-weathered-wood dwelling built at the turn of the 20th century and enlarged and renovated in the early 1990s. The breakfast spread might include yogurt, homemade bread, or huge fruit muffins. There is a kitchenette in the common area. ✉ *185 N. 3rd East St., 84532,* ☎ *435/259–2974. 11 rooms and suites, 9 with bath. AE, D, MC, V.*

$$$–$$$$ 🏨 **Pack Creek Ranch.** A real treat, this out-of-the-way (and glad of it) guest ranch sits beneath the snowcapped summits of the La Sal Mountains. Wildlife abounds in this natural setting off the southern end of the La Sal Mountain Loop. Cabins, with one to four bedrooms, are spacious and luxurious, including woven rugs, bent-willow furnishings, and full kitchens; most have stone fireplaces. This is one of those places that can get away with no TVs or phones in the cabins. The main feature here is peace and solitude in a spectacular setting. A full breakfast is included in the price of the room. The ranch's lodge is open for groups and dinners with advance arrangements. The pool, hot tub, and sauna are within earshot of the creek. ✉ *La Sal Mountain Loop, 20 mi from Moab; Box 1270, Moab 84532,* ☎ *435/259–5505,* FAX *435/259–8879. 11 cabins, 1 ranch house that sleeps 12. Pool, hot tub, sauna, horseback riding. AE, D, MC, V.*

$–$$$$ 🏨 **Aarchway Inn.** On the north end of Moab, this 97-room inn is designed for multi-day stays with suites and apartments as well as outdoor grills. If you have any energy left after visiting nearby Arches or Canyonlands national parks you can work it off in the heated outdoor pool or exercise room. ✉ *1551 N. Hwy. 191, Box 358, 84532,* ☎ *435/259–2599 or 800/341–9359,* FAX *435/259–2270. 97 rooms. Refrigerators, pool, indoor hot tub, exercise room, meeting rooms. AE, D, DC, MC, V.*

$–$$ 🏨 **Comfort Suites.** When it was built in 1993, as the first major chain accommodation in town, this property represented a sure sign of things to come. It has comfortable, roomy suites done in colors that echo the surrounding desert, a handsome lobby, and an impressive fitness facility. A complimentary Continental breakfast is served daily. ✉ *800 S. Main St., 84532,* ☎ *435/259–5252 or 800/228–5150,* FAX *435/259–7110. 75 rooms. Indoor pool, hot tub, exercise room. AE, D, DC, MC, V.*

$–$$ 🏨 **Landmark Motel.** Since it's been here for decades, this truly is a Moab landmark. It offers deluxe rooms in a convenient location near many downtown restaurants and shops. ✉ *168 N. Main St., 84532,* ☎ *435/259–6147 or 800/441–6147,* FAX *435/259–5556. 36 rooms. Pool, hot tub, coin laundry. AE, D, DC, MC, V.*

Nightlife

Most nightlife is concentrated in Moab. **Poplar Place** (☞ Dining and Lodging, *above*) offers live music, usually folk or soft rock. On weekends, there's live country music at **Rio Colorado Restaurant** (✉ 2 S. 100 West St., ☎ 435/259–6666) and the **Sportsman's Lounge** (✉ 1991 S. U.S. 191, ☎ 435/259–9972). At **Eddie McStiff's** (☞ Dining and Lodging, *above*), when there is something worth watching, several televisions draw a crowd to the separate barroom. The house brews on tap may help, too.

Operating from May to November, **Canyonlands by Night** (✉ on U.S. 191, just south of the bridge over the Colorado River north of Moab, ☎ 435/259–5261) is a two-hour boat trip on the Colorado River after dark. Virtually unchanged since it was developed in 1966, the experience includes spotlight viewing of the towering canyon walls, and narration interspersed with mood music. The focus is on natural history, local lore, and Native American stories of the Colorado River.

Outdoor Activities and Sports

CAMPING

Of the many appealing **public campgrounds** found in the Moab area, Devil's Garden in Arches National Park, Squaw Flat in the Needles District of Canyonlands National Park, and Dead Horse Point State Park are the best bets for finding good facilities along with interesting vistas or hiking trails. Another nice spot is the Wind Whistle Campground in the BLM's Canyon Rims Recreation Area (☞ Off the Beaten Path, *below*), south of Moab, on the west side of U.S. 191. There are a number of excellent commercial campgrounds in and around Moab. Some are open year-round, others close from November to March. The **Moab Information Center** (✉ Main and Center Sts., ☎ 435/259–8825) and the **Grand County Travel Council** (☎ 800/635–6622) carry a complete listing.

CYCLING

Mountain bikes are the bicycle of choice in southeastern Utah and are at home on most any back road or trail (provided they are allowed). In the slickrock desert that surrounds Moab, the possibilities are inexhaustible. The most popular off-road cycling route is the **Slickrock Trail**, a few miles east of Moab. Beginners should master the 2½-mi practice loop before tackling the longer and more difficult 10⅓-mi main loop. Another popular ride is the one to **Gemini Natural Bridges,** which begins a few miles north of town along U.S. 191. **The Monitor and Merrimac Buttes Trail** also starts from U.S. 191 north of Moab, and it's a good introduction to mountain biking, with a variety of terrain to conquer. For expedition-length rides, try either the 100-mi **White Rim Trail** (backcountry permit required) in Canyonlands National Park or the 140-mi **Kokopelli Trail,** which runs from Grand Junction, Colorado, to Moab. The Moab Information Center (☞ Visitor Information, *below*) carries a free biking trail guide. For bike and helmet **rentals,** solid advice on trails, and guided tours, try **Rim Cyclery** (✉ 1233 S. Hwy. 191, ☎ 435/259–5223 or 800/626–7335) or **Western Spirit Cycling** (✉ 478 Mill Creek Dr., ☎ 435/259–8732 or 800/845–2453).

FOUR-WHEELING

With routes such as the White Rim Trail, Elephant Hill, and the Moab Rim, Moab has been a mecca for off-road lovers for decades. *See* Guided Tours *in* Southeastern Utah A to Z, *below* for tour operators, or contact the Moab Information Center (☞ Visitor Information, *below*) for a complete listing.

GOLF

Moab Golf Course (✉ 2705 S. East Bench Rd., ☎ 435/259–6488) has 18 holes. The course has lush greens against a ruddy sandstone backdrop, a lovely visual combination that's been known to distract even the most focused golfer.

HIKING

There are countless hiking trails around Moab. In **Arches National Park,** there are several short roadside trails, such as the one to **Sand Dune Arch,** perfect for children to hike. Longer routes access the **Courthouse Towers, Windows,** and **Devil's Garden** areas. Among the many trails in the Needles District of **Canyonlands National Park,** the **Joint Trail,** and the **Chesler Park Trail** are very interesting. In a BLM-administered side canyon northeast of Moab, the hike to **Corona and Bow Tie arches** makes for a pleasant morning jaunt. South of town, the hike to **Mill Creek Canyon** is popular. Also south of town is the popular **Hidden Valley Trail.** Heading south toward Monticello on U.S. 191, you might stop about 20 mi south of Moab for a quick, roadside scramble to the base of **Wilson Arch.**

RAFTING

As it flows through Moab, the **Colorado River** is misleadingly calm; white-water adventures await rafters both upstream and down. Upriver, near the Colorado state line, is **Westwater Canyon,** an exciting one- or two-day float that includes legendary rapids. Moab's **Daily** river run, which begins along Route 128, offers somewhat tamer waters just out of town. Downstream from Moab, in the heart of Canyonlands National Park, is **Cataract Canyon,** which features more than two dozen rapids in a 14-mi stretch. A permit is required from the BLM (✉ Grand Resource Area, Box M, Moab 84532, ☎ 435/259–8193) to run Westwater, and a trip down Cataract Canyon requires one from Canyonlands National Park (☞ State Parks *in* Utah A to Z, *below*).

If you want to hook up with an experienced raft-outfitting company, try **Adrift Adventures** (✉ 378 N. Main St., Box 577, ☎ 435/259–8594 or 800/874–4483, FAX 435/259–7628) or **Holiday Expeditions** (✉ 1055 E. Main St., Green River, ☎ 435/564–3272 or 800/624–6323). **Tag-A-Long Expeditions** (✉ 452 N. Main St., Box 1206, ☎ 435/259–8946 or 800/453–3292) has been in Moab for many years and has a good reputation.

Shopping

In Moab, shopping opportunities are plentiful from March until the end of October, with art galleries, jewelry stores, and shops carrying T-shirts and souvenirs on every block. Many of these stores close from November to February. During this off-season, shoppers can pick up real bargains at stores that are open. Be sure to check out the **Moab Rock Shop** (✉ 600 N. Main St., ☎ 435/259–7312) for one of the most interesting rock collections in the state. The shop is owned by Lin Ottinger, a longtime resident of Moab and a backcountry tour guide. **Rim Cyclery** (☞ Cycling, *above*) offers a wide array of bicycles, plus a full line of accessories, parts, rock-climbing equipment, and outdoor clothing. Here, unlike at some bike shops in town, you'll never get laughed at for asking questions.

OFF THE BEATEN PATH

CANYON RIMS RECREATION AREA – With a few hours to spare, you can enjoy two remarkable canyon-country vistas. Turn off U.S. 191 at a point centered between Moab and Monticello (about 27 mi south of Moab, and 26 mi north of Monticello), and the paved Needles Overlook Road runs 22 mi west to Needles Overlook, which takes in the southern end of Canyonlands National Park. Less than 20 mi farther on a good, graded road is the Anticline Overlook, which encompasses the Colorado River, Dead Horse Point, and other locales to the north. For more information, contact the Moab district office of the BLM (✉ 82 E. Dogwood St., Moab 84532, ☎ 435/259–6111).

Newspaper Rock

52 *51 mi from Moab via U.S. 191 south and Rte. 211 west.*

Beginning 2,000 years ago, prehistoric inhabitants of this region began etching cryptic images on a large rock face. In the centuries following, subsequent chapters of an undecipherable history were added, resulting in an impressive collection of petroglyphs that archaeologists cite as one of the most comprehensive in the Southwest. An interpretive trail and small campground are provided. ✉ *12 mi west of U.S. 191 on Rte. 211,* ☎ *435/587–2141.* *Free.* *Always open.*

Monticello

53 *53 mi from Moab via U.S. 191 south; 26 mi from Newspaper Rock via Rte. 211 east and U.S. 191 south.*

Monticello, the seat of San Juan County, is a mostly Mormon community. This quiet town has seen some growth in recent years, mostly in the form of new motels made necessary by a steady stream of tourists venturing south of Moab. At 7,000 ft, Monticello provides a cool respite from the summer heat of the desert, and it's at the doorstep of the Abajo Mountains. The highest point in the range, 11,360-ft Abajo Peak, is accessed by a road that branches off the graded, 22-mi Blue Mountain Loop (Forest Service Road 105, which begins in Monticello). Although the **Manti–La Sal National Forest** (☎ 435/587–3235) is suited to most four-wheel-drive, high-clearance vehicles, be sure to inquire about road conditions ahead of time.

Dining and Lodging

Monticello's restaurant options are a bit sparse. Family-style dining and fast food are the norm, but there are some options with a touch of variety, and more restaurants are being built each year.

$–$$ ✕ **Lamplight Restaurant.** This quiet eatery has one of the only liquor licenses in town, and it serves passable steaks, chicken, and seafood in a Victorian atmosphere. ✉ *Hwy. 666,* ☎ *435/587–2170. MC, V.*

$–$$ ★ **Grist Mill Inn.** A B&B like this deserves more than the usual accolades. Housed in a 1933 flour mill—yes, a flour mill—are beautiful suites filled with antiques and unique accessories such as treadle sewing machines, a turn-of-the-century medical scale, and a collection of vintage telephones. There is a library on the third floor, a sitting room with a fireplace, and plenty of charm to spare. Additional guest rooms are next door. Smoking is not permitted in the rooms. A full breakfast is included in the rate, and dinner is also served. ✉ *64 S. 300 East St., Box 156, 84535,* ☎ *435/587–2597 or 800/645–3762,* FAX *435/587–2580. 11 rooms. Dining room, hot tub, library. AE, D, DC, MC, V.*

$ **Days Inn.** This is one of the largest properties in town. With a heated indoor pool and a hot tub for soaking adventure-weary bodies, it's also one of the nicest. ✉ *549 N. Main St., Box 759,* ☎ *435/587–2458 or 800/329–7466,* FAX *435/587–2191. 43 rooms. Indoor pool, hot tub. AE, D, DC, MC, V.*

Blanding

54 *25 mi from Monticello via U.S. 191 south.*

Conservative Blanding is dry: That is, there is no state liquor store, and no beer is sold in grocery or convenience stores. What Blanding does offer, however, is the **Edge of the Cedars State Park.** Here, one of the nation's foremost museums dedicated to the Anasazi Indians displays a variety of pots, baskets, spear points, and such. Interestingly, many of these artifacts were donated by guilt-ridden pot hunters, or archaeological looters. Behind the museum, you can visit an actual Anasazi ruin. ✉ *660 W. 400 North St.,* ☎ *435/678–2238.* *$5 per vehicle.* ⏲ *May–Oct., daily 8–8; Nov.–Apr., daily 9–5.*

Lodging

$ **Comfort Inn.** A national chain in remote Blanding suggests that southeastern Utah is gaining prominence as a travel destination. Because this is a fairly new property, it includes a variety of amenities. A complimentary Continental breakfast is included. ✉ *711 S. Main St., 84511,* ☎ *435/678–3271 or 800/622–3250,* FAX *435/678–3217. 52 rooms. Restaurant, indoor pool, hot tub, exercise room, coin laundry. AE, D, DC, MC, V.*

OFF THE BEATEN PATH **HOVENWEEP NATIONAL MONUMENT** – For anyone with an abiding interest in the Anasazi Indians, a visit to this monument is a must. Along a remote stretch of the Utah-Colorado border southeast of Blanding,

Hovenweep features several unusual tower structures that may have been used for making astronomical observations. By marking the summer solstice, these early farmers knew the best times of the year to plant their crops. If you travel to Hovenweep with bicycles in tow, take them down off the rack to explore the monument's six clusters of ruins linked by paths. Because Hovenweep is accessible only by a lonely paved, then gravel, road, it is not uncommon to have the monument pretty much to yourself. ✉ *21 mi east of U.S. 191 on Rte. 262,* ☎ *970/749–0510.* *$6.* ⊙ *Daily 8 AM–sunset.*

Bluff

55 *25 mi from Blanding via U.S. 191 south.*

Bluff, one of southeastern Utah's oldest towns, began as a farming community in the 1880s. Helped by Navajo neighbors skilled at raising crops and livestock in the desert, Bluff's settlers built a ranching empire that made the town the richest per capita in the state at one time. Reminders of this affluent past include several historic Victorian-style homes that were skillfully fashioned from blocks of local sandstone. The area, astride the San Juan River, also includes small kivas and cliff dwellings that attest to the presence of the Anasazi centuries ago. Today residents of the Navajo Indian Nation, the largest Native American reservation, visit Bluff to shop, gas up, or eat out. Today Bluff witnesses a steady stream of boaters setting out for a float down the San Juan from the **Sand Island Recreation Site** (✉ 3 mi west of Bluff). In addition to a developed launch site, this BLM facility includes a primitive campground and one of the largest panels of rock art in the Four Corners area. The panel includes several large images of Kokopelli, the mischief maker for Pueblo Indian lore.

OFF THE BEATEN PATH

FOUR CORNERS MONUMENT – Head south from Bluff on U.S. 191 for about 35 mi, to its junction with U.S. 160. (The U.S. 191/U.S. 160 junction is south of the Utah/Arizona border in the Navajo Nation.) Drive east on U.S. 160 for about 30 mi. At this point, U.S. 160 curves north to the only place in the country where four states, Utah, Arizona, New Mexico, and Colorado (☞ Cortez *in* Chapter 4), meet. Administered by the Navajo Nation, Four Corners offers not only a geography lesson but also a great opportunity to buy Native American jewelry or mud toys and other traditional crafts directly from the Navajo themselves. Bring cash, as credit cards and checks may not be accepted, particularly when buying from roadside displays or other impromptu marketplaces.

Dining and Lodging

$–$$ ✕ **Cow Canyon Trading Post.** This small restaurant next to a funky trading post serves three dinner entrées daily—perhaps chicken-and-vegetable shish kebabs on a bed of wild rice, lamb-stuffed onions, or a phyllo pie stuffed with spinach and ham. Many of the meals have some Navajo influence. ✉ *Intersection of Hwy. 191 and Hwy. 163,* ☎ *435/672–2208. MC, V.*

$ **Recapture Lodge.** In addition to providing plain but comfortable rooms, this locally owned motel offers guided tours into the surrounding canyon country. Slide shows examining local geology, art, and history are presented at night. ✉ *U.S. 191, Box 309, 84512,* ☎ *435/672–2281,* FAX *435/672–2284. 28 rooms. Pool, hot tub. AE, D, MC, V.*

Outdoor Activities and Sports

While somewhat calmer than the Colorado, the **San Juan River** offers some truly exceptional scenery. It can be run in two sections: from Bluff to Mexican Hat and from Mexican Hat to Lake Powell. For permits, contact the BLM (✉ San Juan Resource Area, Box 7, Monticello 84535, ☎ 435/587–1544).

Mexican Hat

56 *20 mi from Bluff via U.S. 163 south.*

Small Mexican Hat lies on the north bank of the San Juan River. Named for a nearby rock formation, which you can't miss on the way into town, Mexican Hat is a jumping-off point for visiting two geological wonders.

By crossing the San Juan River and driving 21 mi south on U.S. 163 across Navajo land, you will reach the **Monument Valley Tribal Park.** Thanks to its striking red-rock spires, buttes, and mesas, Monument Valley has earned international recognition as the setting for dozens of movies and television commercials. Just as memorable as the scenery, though, is the taste of Navajo culture you can get here. In addition to visiting the historic Gouldings Trading Post (☞ Shopping, *below*) and shopping at its rows of arts and crafts booths, plan to take a Navajo-guided tour of the valley. These informative excursions invariably include a stop at a hogan, the traditional Navajo home. Guide services can be acquired at the **Tribal Park headquarters** (✉ Box 360289, Monument Valley, ☎ 435/727–3287), which is on a paved spur off U.S. 163 at the Utah-Arizona border. The costs for guided tours in Monument Valley vary based on the length of the tour and the season of the year. The headquarters office is open daily, 10 AM–sunset.

57 From the overlook at **Goosenecks of the San Juan River** (✉ 10 mi northwest of Mexican Hat off Rte. 261) you can peer down upon what geologists claim is the best example of an "entrenched meander" in the world. The river's serpentine course resembles the necks of geese in spectacular 1,000-ft-deep chasms. Although the Goosenecks of the San Juan River is actually a state park, no facilities other than pit toilets are found here, and no fee is charged.

Lodging

$–$$$$ **Gouldings Lodge.** This is the best place from which to tour Monument Valley and the surrounding Navajo Nation. Rooms are better than those at most motels this far out of the way. Most rooms have stunning views, and the service here is quite friendly. Part of the 1923 Gouldings Trading Post, the lodge gives guests a good feel for the history of the area. Be sure to peruse the shop for Native American arts and crafts. ✉ *Box 360001, 84536,* ☎ *435/727–3231,* FAX *435/727–3344. 64 rooms. Restaurant, pool. AE, D, DC, MC, V.*

Shopping

When in Monument Valley, be sure to stop at **Gouldings Trading Post** (☞ Lodging, *above*) for a wide selection of fine handcrafted jewelry, Navajo rugs, pottery, and such. You can be sure that everything sold here is authentic, as the store has a reputation that extends back to 1923 to protect. Another trading post is about 5 mi east at **Oljato** (☎ 435/727–3210).

En Route From the turnoff for the Goosenecks, Route 261 heads north toward what looks to be an impregnable 1,200-ft wall of rock. In actuality, the road climbs this obstacle in a steep, 3-mi ascent known as the Moki Dugway. Unpaved but well graded, the series of tight curves is manageable by passenger car. Be sure to stop at an overlook near the top to take in the superb view of the **Valley of the Gods.** Featuring scattered buttes and spires, this lonesome valley is accessed by a 17-mi dirt road that begins just south of the dugway. At the top of the Moki Dugway, the drive returns to pavement as Route 261 tracks north across Cedar Mesa—relatively flat terrain that is thick with piñon and juniper, but not cedar. On occasion, you might spy a canyon break in the distance. Actually, several canyons divide this plateau land. Once home to the Anasazi, these drainages feature hundreds, if not thousands, of their cliff dwellings. Grand Gulch, the largest of these drainages, is today protected as a primitive area and is quite popular among backpackers.

Natural Bridges National Monument

58 *33 mi from Mexican Hat via Rtes. 261 and 275 north; 38 mi from Blanding via Rtes. 95 and 275 east.*

The three stone bridges showcased here are unique because they are very close to one another. Different from an arch, a natural bridge, which spans a drainage or streambed, is created by the erosive powers of running water. Each of the three bridges of Natural Bridges National Monument—Sipapu, Kachina, and Owachomo—is visible from a 9-mi scenic drive that loops through the small monument. The desert setting is quiet, colorful, and often fragrant with a mix of sage, juniper, and wildflowers. Also of interest is the monument's impressive bank of solar panels. Upon completion in 1980, it was the largest solar-energy system in the world. There is also a visitor center and a primitive campground. ✉ *Rte. 275 off Rte. 95,* ☎ *435/692–1234.* 🎫 *$6 per vehicle.* ⏲ *Daily 8–sunset.*

Lake Powell

59 *50 mi from Natural Bridges Monument (to Hall's Crossing) via Rtes. 275, 95, and 276.*

Lake Powell, the recreational focus of Glen Canyon National Recreation Area, is the second-largest man-made lake in the United States. To explore it fully would take years. Certainly, the most pleasurable way to see the lake is to rent a houseboat at any of the lake's marinas and set out across the intriguing blue waters. However, guided day tours are also available. A popular excursion sets out from the Bullfrog, Hall's Crossing, or Wahweap (in Arizona) marinas to **Rainbow Bridge**. The largest natural bridge in the world, this 290-ft-high, 275-ft-wide span is breathtaking. Lake Powell is also known for its bass fishing. A Utah fishing license and further information may be obtained at any of the marinas. For rentals and tours, contact **Lake Powell Reservations** (✉ Box 56909, Phoenix, AZ 85079, ☎ 800/528–6154). Houseboat rentals begin at $539 for 3 days in off-season; a day trip to Rainbow Bridge starts at $91.

If you're traveling west on Route 95, Lake Powell can be crossed by bridge at Hite Crossing, or by ferry from Hall's Crossing. If you choose to cross by ferry, a most scenic journey, and the best way to get a sense of the vastness of this water and sandstone mingling, turn south at the junction of Routes 95 and 276. Follow Route 276 west for 40 mi to the **Hall's Crossing Marina,** the eastern terminus of the **Lake Powell Ferry**. From here the 100-ft *John Atlantic Burr* will float you and your car across a 3-mi stretch of the lake to the Bullfrog Basin Marina, from which it's an hour's drive north to rejoin Route 95. ✉ *Hall's Crossing Marina, Rte. 276,* ☎ *435/684–7000. Reservations not accepted.* 🎫 *$2 per foot passenger; $10 per car, including all passengers.* ⏲ *Crossings: mid-May–Sept., 6 per day; Oct.–mid-May, 4 per day.*

Dining and Lodging

All of Lake Powell's major **marinas** have a gas station, campground, lodging, a general store, and boat docks. Surprisingly, in this wilderness of water and stone, there are also a couple of upscale dining and lodging options. Wahweap Lodge (in Arizona) and **Defiance House Lodge** at Bullfrog (☎ 435/684–2233) have amenities ranging from premium movie service to private decks, heated pools, and exercise rooms. These two lodges also have excellent restaurants serving three sit-down meals a day.

Hanksville

95 mi from Natural Bridges National Monument via Rte. 275 south and Rte. 95 north.

If you don't have the time or inclination to cross Lake Powell by ferry, simply follow Route 95 to Hite Crossing. (Just before the bridge, a left turn leads to Hite Marina—the only services for miles around.) Upon crossing the bridge, continue north past the 11,000-ft Henry Mountains to Hanksville, a good place to gas up. Here, pick up Route 24, and head northeast toward I–70. About a dozen miles out of Hanksville, signs point the way to **Goblin Valley State Park.** As the name implies, the area is filled with hundreds of gnomelike rock formations, and there's a small campground with modern rest rooms and showers. ✉ *12 mi north of Hanksville via Rte. 24,* ☎ *435/564–3633.* *$4 per vehicle.* ⏲ *Daily 8–sunset.*

OFF THE BEATEN PATH

THE MAZE – Of the three districts within Canyonlands National Park, the Maze is by far the most remote. Requiring a four-wheel-drive vehicle and a steady hand at the wheel, the signed, but unimproved, route into the Maze begins 50 mi north of Hanksville, almost exactly east of the paved route leading west from Highway 24 to Goblin Valley State Park. It crosses nearly 50 mi of high-clearance dirt road before reaching its second stage, the incredibly rugged Flint Trail. At the journey's end, intrepid travelers will find not only a wonderful view of the Maze but also a trail of sorts that runs to the bottom. A scrambled collection of sandstone canyons, the Maze is one of the most appropriately named features in southern Utah. If you do make the drive into the Maze, consider a visit to nearby Horseshoe Canyon. Featuring larger-than-life-size pictographs that may date back several thousand years, this isolated annex of Canyonlands National Park is well worth the bumpy ride and the 4-mi hike to the canyon. ☎ *435/259–7164.* *$10 per vehicle or $5 for individuals.*

En Route Heading north on Route 24, a bit north of Goblin Valley you may notice a long line of flatiron-shape cliffs jutting from the desert floor to the west. This is the San Rafael Reef—the front of the 80-mi-long **San Rafael Swell.** Rugged and quite expansive, the San Rafael Swell is a popular destination for outdoors lovers. After turning west on I–70, you can get an up-close look at this impressive landform from a turnoff where the interstate passes through the sawtooth ridge. A little more than 50 mi west of the Route 24 interchange, turn north on Route 10 to complete the last leg of this tour. After passing through the small towns of Emery (the first outpost of civilization since Hanksville) and Ferron, you'll reach Castle Dale.

Castle Dale

60 *135 mi from Hanksville via Rte. 24 north, I–70 west, and Rte. 10 north.*

At Castle Dale you may notice that the surrounding countryside is beginning to look familiar. That's because you have re-entered Castle Country, the northern half of which includes Price. In Castle Dale, the **Museum of the San Rafael** provides an overview of the ancient Anasazi and Fremont Indian cultures. As further proof that you are indeed closing in on Price, there are a number of dinosaur bones on display. ✉ *64 N. 100 East St.,* ☎ *435/381–5252.* *Free.* ⏲ *Mon.–Sat. 10–4.*

OFF THE BEATEN PATH

THE MANTI MOUNTAINS – Two scenic byways climb west from Castle Country into the nearby Manti Mountains. The first travels for a little over 20 mi on Route 29 from Castle Dale to the subalpine setting of Joe's Valley. The second begins in Huntington, to the north, and follows Route 31 for 50 mi to Electric Lake. Both drives offer stunning fall colors in late September and early October.

Huntington

9 mi from Castle Dale via Rte. 10 north.

As a nearby power plant suggests, the town of Huntington counts its coal reserves as its most valuable resource. It is also home to Huntington State Park, with a 237-acre reservoir, and it's the nearest sizable community to the **Cleveland-Lloyd Dinosaur Quarry.** Reached by Route 155 and a series of graded roads, the enclosed quarry has a visitor center and an outdoor nature trail. Having produced more complete skeletons than any other site in the world, the Cleveland-Lloyd Quarry is one of the state's premier destinations for dinosaur aficionados. ⊠ *20 mi east of Huntington via Rte. 155,* ☎ *435/636–3600.* *$2.* *Easter–Memorial Day, weekends 10–5; Memorial Day–Labor Day, daily 10–5.*

61

Southeastern Utah A to Z

Arriving and Departing

BY BUS

Price is served by **Greyhound Lines** (☎ 800/231–2222).

BY CAR

To reach southeastern Utah, take I–15 to U.S. 6 from Salt Lake City and the northwest, I–70 or U.S. 666 from Colorado and the east, and U.S. 191 from Wyoming and the northeast or Arizona and the south.

BY PLANE

You can fly to Moab's airport, **Canyonlands Field** (☎ 435/259–7421), from Salt Lake City on Alpine Air (☎ 801/575–2839).

BY TRAIN

Amtrak (☎ 800/872–7245) has service to Helper and Thompson Springs.

Getting Around

BY CAR

Most roads on this tour are well-maintained two-lane highways. Be sure your car is in good working order, as there are long stretches of empty road between towns, and keep the gas tank topped off.

Contacts and Resources

DOCTORS AND DENTISTS

Allen Memorial Hospital (⊠ 719 West 4th N, Moab, ☎ 435/259–7191). **Blanding Medical Center** (⊠ 930 North 400 W, Blanding, ☎ 435/678–3434). **San Juan County Hospital** (⊠ 364 West 1st N, Monticello, ☎ 435/587–2116).

GUIDED TOURS

Adrift Adventures (⊠ 378 N. Main St., Box 577, Moab 84532, ☎ 435/259–8594 or 800/874–4483, FAX 435/259–7628), **Holiday Expeditions** (⊠ 1055 E. Main St., Green River 84525, ☎ 801/564–3273 or 800/624–6323), and **Tag-A-Long Expeditions** (⊠ 452 N. Main St., Box 1206, 84532, ☎ 800/453–3292) operate guided Jeep tours into rugged wilderness areas. The **Canyonlands Field Institute** (⊠ 1350 S. U.S. 191, Box 68, Moab 84532, ☎ 435/259–7750 or 800/860–5262, FAX 435/259–2335) sponsors seminars and nature walks.

VISITOR INFORMATION

Canyonlands/North and Moab Information Center (✉ Center and Main Sts., Moab 84532, ☏ 435/259–8825 or 800/635–6622). **Canyonlands/South** (✉ 117 S. Main St., Box 490, Monticello 84535, ☏ 435/587–3235 or 800/574–4386). **Castle Country** (✉ 90 N. 100 East St., Box 1037, Price 84501, ☏ 435/637–3009 or 800/842–0789).

SOUTHWESTERN UTAH

When Mormon pioneers came to this distant corner of Utah in the early 1860s, it was determined that they could and would grow cotton. Given the warm temperatures, the crop was a viable one, and, thanks to the economic independence it promised to bring to the territory, it was to be an important one as well. After 1869, however, the newly completed transcontinental railroad provided a cheaper source of the fiber, rendering Utah's cotton farms unnecessary. Today "Utah's Dixie" still attracts people with the promise of warm weather—so much so that the largest community in the area, St. George, is also the state's fastest-growing one. In addition to this enviable climate, there is a wealth of scenic wonders, from desert to sierra, and boundless opportunities to hike, bike, and tee off.

Camping

In this region of Utah, campers have their choice from low desert to high mountain facilities. Campgrounds in Bryce, Capitol Reef, and Zion national parks fill up fast. Most of the area's state parks have camping facilities, and the region's two national forests offer many wonderful sites. In the **Dixie National Forest** (✉ 82 N. 100 East St., Cedar City 84720, ☏ 435/865–3700), the Panguitch Lake, Pine Valley, and Boulder Mountain areas are especially nice. In **Fishlake National Forest** (✉ 115 E. 900 North St., Richfield 84701, ☏ 435/896–9233), Beaver Canyon and Fish Lake are good picks. There are also more than 100 commercial campgrounds in southwestern Utah.

Fishing

A number of trout streams lace the region. These include Panguitch Creek, below the lake of the same name; Mammoth Creek, south of Hatch; the Beaver River; and the Sevier River, which flows north through Richfield and Salina. As for lake fishing, anglers favor Otter Creek Reservoir, Yuba Reservoir, and Panguitch Lake. Of course, with a name like Fish Lake, how can you go wrong? Mackinaw and rainbow trout have both made the lake famous.

While settling this portion of the state in the late 1800s, groups of Mormon pioneers would set up homes, then soon leave them to move somewhere else in the moderate climate of Utah's southwestern reaches. Modern visitors to the area often follow this same pattern. With many interesting and beautiful destinations, it is no hardship to keep moving along any plotted tour here. There are Capitol Reef, Zion, and Bryce Canyon national parks to serve as goals, but be prepared to find and enjoy many other intriguing attractions along the way.

Fillmore

56 mi from Nephi via I–15 south.

Given its central location, Fillmore was designated the territorial capital in 1851, before the town even existed. In 1855, after the first wing of the capitol was completed, the state legislature convened here, but the capital was eventually moved back to Salt Lake City because of the rapidly growing population centered there. Although the entire building was never completed, the portion that does stand is counted as Utah's oldest government building. Today it is included in the **Territorial Statehouse State Park,** which includes a collection of settlement-era relics housed in the statehouse, outdoor interpretive displays, parklike grounds, and a lovely rose garden. ✉ *50 W. Capitol Ave.,* ☎ *435/743–5316.* 🎟 *$5 per vehicle.* ⏲ *Memorial Day–Labor Day, Mon.–Sat. 8–8, Sun. 9–6; Labor Day–Memorial Day, Mon.–Sat. 9–6.*

Beaver

63 *57 mi from Fillmore via I–15 south.*

Mormons established the town of Beaver in 1856. It soon became an unsettled melting pot when gold and silver were discovered in the mountains to the west, and to keep the calm between gentile miners and pious Mormons, the army established Ft. Cameron here in 1872. The town served as the Beaver County seat from 1882 to 1975. Part of Beaver is included in a national historic district, and the old **Beaver County Courthouse** is now a museum with a large collection of pioneer tools and other antiques. ✉ *90 E. Center St.,* ☎ *no phone.* 🎟 *Free.* ⏲ *Tues.–Sat. 11–5.*

East of Beaver rise the spectacular **Tushar Mountains.** Reaching elevations of over 12,000 ft, they are Utah's third-highest mountain range, but because of their out-of-the-way location, they are not as well known as the Wasatch, Uinta, or La Sal mountains. Those who venture east from Beaver on Route 153 will find uncrowded hiking trails and campgrounds, some beautiful mountain lakes, and a small ski resort known as Elk Meadows (☞ Outdoor Activities and Sports, *below*).

Dining and Lodging

$–$$ ✕ **Garden of Eat'n.** This small-town eatery serves sandwiches, burgers, steaks, and more, and it's open for breakfast, lunch, and dinner. ✉ *324 W. 1425 North St.,* ☎ *435/438–5464. AE, D, MC, V.*

$ ✕ **Arshel's Café.** Run by the same family since the 1930s, this restaurant is a southern Utah tradition. The menu here is a list of American standards: buckwheat pancakes, tuna salad sandwiches, chicken and homemade noodles, clam chowder with chunks of potato, and chicken-fried steak with a peppery cream gravy. The good, strong coffee is the perfect accompaniment to warm peach cobbler, or a big slice of pie, baked just this morning. ✉ *711 N. Main St.,* ☎ *435/438–2977. AE, MC, V.*

$ 🏨 **Best Western Paice.** In town yet just minutes from I–15 as well as skiing and golf, this property offers convenience. Rooms are comfortable and clean, if standard. ✉ *161 S. Main St., Box 897, 84713,* ☎ *435/438–2438 or 800/528–1234,* FAX *435/438–1053. 24 rooms. Pool, indoor hot tub. AE, D, DC, MC, V.*

Outdoor Activities and Sports

Minersville State Park (✉ 12 mi west of Beaver off Rte. 21, ☎ 435/438–5472) provides boating facilities on a 1,130-acre reservoir. **Canyon Breeze** (✉ E. Canyon Rd., ☎ 435/438–9601) is a nine-hole golf course. **Elk Meadows Ski and Summer Resort** (✉ Box 511, 84713, ☎ 435/438–5433 or 888/881–7669) has 36 runs with six lifts and a vertical drop of 1,400 ft.

Brian Head

50 mi from Beaver via I–15 and Rte. 143 south.

With an abundance of biking trails and other activities, the ski-resort town of Brian Head is also a favorite summertime retreat. Five miles beyond Brian Head is one of the region's better-known scenic won-
64 ders, **Cedar Breaks National Monument.** Cutting deep into the west-

ern end of the lofty Markagunt Plateau, uplift and erosion by wind, rain, and river have etched an amphitheater awash in shades of pink, gold, and lavender. Two especially nice backcountry strolls (each 2 mi long) follow the Spectra Point and Alpine Pond trails, and although winter snows do close the road, the monument is a favorite among cross-country skiers. Road cyclists will enjoy stretches of Routes 14, 143, and 148. By the way, there are no cedars at Cedar Breaks. Rather, early pioneers misidentified junipers growing in the area. ✉ *Rte. 143,* ☎ *435/586–9451.* 🎫 *$4 per vehicle.* ⏲ *May–Oct., daily 8–sunset.*

Dining and Lodging

$$–$$$$ ✕ **The Edge.** This is the place to eat lunch and dinner in Brian Head. The Edge Burger is a half-pound monstrosity draped with cheese. Dinners include delicious steaks, seafood, soups, and salads. And, as you'd expect, the views are great. ✉ *406 S. Rte. 143,* ☎ *435/677–3343. AE, MC, V.*

$$–$$$$ 🏨 **Cedar Breaks Lodge.** On the north end of town, this hotel/condominium resort features large studio rooms in red-rock hues; hotel rooms come with kitchenettes or a wet bar, and condominiums have full kitchens. The atmosphere is casual, and the service is friendly and helpful. ✉ *223 Hunter Ridge Rd./Rte. 143, Box 190248, 84719,* ☎ *435/677–3000 or 800/272–7426,* FAX *435/677–2211. 162 units. Restaurant, bar, hot tub, exercise room. AE, D, DC, MC, V.*

Outdoor Activities and Sports

CYCLING

Brian Head is a good place to base cycling excursions. The area's most popular ride is the 12-mi Bunker Creek Trail, which winds its way through forests and meadows to Panguitch Lake. Five miles south of Brian Head, road cyclists can explore Cedar Breaks National Monument (☞ *above*) and vicinity. Brian Head Resort runs one of its ski lifts in summer, providing access to several mountain bike trails. A shuttle service takes riders to other trails on the resort property.

SKIING

Known for its abundance of snow, **Brian Head Resort** (✉ Brian Head 84719, ☎ 435/677–2035 or 800/272–7426) is a favorite among California skiers weary of the crowded megaresorts of their own state. Six lifts service 53 runs and a vertical drop of 1,707 ft. Shuttles on Sno-Cats (motorized vehicles specially equipped to groom or travel over steep terrain in snow) provide access to an extra 500 acres of double-black-diamond terrain.

Cedar City

65 *34 mi from Brian Head via Rte. 143 north and I–15 south; or 30 mi from Brian Head via Rte. 143 south, Rte. 148 south, and Rte. 14 west.*

With a population of about 14,000, Cedar City is southern Utah's second-largest community. The town was settled in 1851 by Mormons sent to mine iron-ore deposits. The going was rough, though, and very little iron was produced before a more feasible supply line was established with the East. This chapter in the town's history is today embodied at the **Iron Mission State Park.** It displays the usual collection of pioneer artifacts, plus a number of horse-drawn wagons. ✉ *635 N. Main St.,* ☎ *435/586–9290.* 🎫 *$3 per vehicle.* ⏲ *Daily 9–sunset.*

In 1897, Cedar City was awarded a branch of Utah's teacher-training school. In the years since, the school has evolved into **Southern Utah University** (✉ 351 W. Center St., ☎ 435/586–7700), offering strong programs in education, business, science, and, most conspicuously, performing arts. From late June through the first week of September, the

Utah Shakespearean Festival (☎ 435/586–7880) is held. What began in 1962 as an attempt to keep the town from dying has developed into a major production requiring hundreds of actors (students and professionals) and workers, drawing tens of thousands, and involving much more than just Shakespeare (☞ Nightlife and the Arts, *below*). The outdoor theater at Southern Utah University is a replica of the Old Globe Theatre from Shakespeare's time, showcasing Shakespearean costume and set displays during the season.

Dining and Lodging

$$–$$$$ ★ ✕ **Milt's Stage Stop.** Locals and an increasing number of tourists have discovered the terrific food and inviting atmosphere of this dinner spot in beautiful Cedar Canyon. It's known for its 12-ounce rib-eye steak, its prime rib, and its fresh crab, lobster, and shrimp dishes. In winter, deer feed in front of the restaurant as a fireplace blazes away inside. A number of hunting trophies decorate the rustic building's interior, and splendid views of the surrounding mountains delight patrons year-round. ✉ *Cedar Canyon, 5 mi east of town on Rte. 14,* ☎ *435/586–9344. AE, D, DC, MC, V.*

$–$$ **Bard's Inn Bed and Breakfast.** Rooms in this restored turn-of-the-century house are named after heroines in Shakespeare's plays—perfect for those attending the Utah Shakespearean Festival, which is within walking distance. There are wonderful antiques throughout and some unusual decorative accents: the Chinese checkerboard in the bathroom, sculptures of the Bard's most famous characters, Shakespearean costumed dolls, stained-glass windows rescued from an old church. Enjoy a full breakfast that includes fresh home-baked breads. ✉ *150 S. 100 West St., 84720,* ☎ *435/586–6612. 7 rooms. AE, MC, V.*

$ **Holiday Inn Cedar City.** This property offers perfectly adequate accommodations, plus a nice lineup of facilities. It's a convenient departure point to Bryce and Zion national parks and Cedar Breaks National Monument in summer, and to Brian Head Ski Resort in winter. ✉ *1575 W. 200 North St., 84720,* ☎ *435/586–8888 or 800/432–8828,* FAX *435/586–1010. 100 rooms. Restaurant, pool, indoor hot tub, sauna. AE, D, DC, MC, V.*

Nightlife and the Arts

The **Utah Shakespearean Festival** features several stage productions of works by Shakespeare and others; the Greenshow, with jugglers, puppet shows, and folks dressed in period costume; workshops and literary seminars; and the Royal Feaste, a popular feed for guests. Ticket reservations are strongly recommended for play performances and required for the Royal Feaste. ✉ *351 W. Center St.,* ☎ *435/586–7880 or 800/752–9849.* *$19 and up.* ⏲ *Late June–mid-Oct.*

You can scoot your boot on weekends at the **Sportsmen's Lounge** (✉ 900 S. Main St., ☎ 435/586–6552). Or, try dancing at the **Playhouse** (✉ 1027 N. Main St., ☎ 435/586–9010).

Outdoor Activities and Sports

Cedar Ridge Golf Course (✉ 200 E. 900 North St., ☎ 435/586–2970) has 18 holes.

St. George

66 *53 mi from Cedar City via I–15 south.*

Three hundred Mormon families were sent to St. George in 1861 to grow cotton. Named after the group's leader, George A. Smith, the colony faced many hardships, among them disease, drought, and floods. After the railroad rendered their cotton farms insignificant, the settlers stayed on and built a red sandstone tabernacle, which served as a meeting place for both Mormons and members of other denominations as the area's population grew. The **St. George Temple** (✉ 250 E. 400 South St., ☎ 435/673–3533) was completed in 1877. It is still in use today. From 1873 until his death five years later, Brigham Young spent his winters in a home (✉ 67 W. 200 North St., ☎ 435/673–2517) he had built for him here. Free tours of the temple grounds and the winter home are given daily. Today these venerable structures, plus many others, bring some historical perspective to a city that is growing by leaps and bounds.

St. Georgians now number over 45,000, of whom a burgeoning number are retirees. The town has many hotels and restaurants and even some interesting convention sites. The **St. George Chamber of Commerce** (✉ 97 E. St. George Blvd., ☎ 435/628–1658), is housed in the lovingly maintained Washington County Courthouse, built of adobe brick in 1876. The chamber's friendly and knowledgeable staff can help shape plans for touring the area.

Although St. George does offer a handful of interesting sights, it is the surrounding natural landscape that is the area's primary draw. Best known, of course, is Zion National Park, which lies 40 mi east. Before taking in the park, however, visit some of the less-heralded spots west and north of town. First on the list is **Snow Canyon State Park** (✉ 11 mi northwest of St. George on Rte. 18, ☎ 435/628–2255), where red Navajo sandstone walls topped by a cap of volcanic rock make for some rather scenic canyon terrain. The 50,000-acre **Pine Valley Wilderness** (☎ 435/688–3246) is 25 mi northwest of St. George via I–15 and a signed forest service road. Part of the Dixie National Forest, the wilderness provides a verdant respite from the rolling desert terrain typical of this corner of the state. The area is laced with several backcountry routes suitable for hiking and off-road bicycling, including the 6-mi Whipple National Recreation Trail and the 35-mi Summit Trail.

Beaver Dam Wash is south of the small town of Shivwits, accessible by taking Route 18 north of St. George and turning west onto a paved road that runs 12 mi, through Santa Clara to Shivwits. At 2,200 ft, this is Utah's lowest point, but more important, the area marks the spot where the Colorado Plateau, the Great Basin, and the Mojave Desert converge. In this overlapping of ecosystems, you'll find a great variety of plants and animals, especially birds.

Dining and Lodging

$$–$$$$ ✕ **Sullivan's Rococo.** Specializing in beef and seafood, this restaurant is known for its prime rib. Because it sits atop a hill overlooking town, you can enjoy spectacular views from your table. ✉ *511 Airport Rd.,* ☎ *435/628–3671. AE, D, DC, MC, V.*

$$–$$$ ✕ **Basilia's.** Mediterranean specialties fill the menu here, along with artfully arranged salads. Dine indoors, where the decor is crisp blue and white, or outside, where the evening sun bathes the surrounding red cliffs. ✉ *Ancestor Sq., 2 W. St. George Blvd.,* ☎ *435/673–7671. AE, D, MC, V.*

$–$$$ ✕ **Andelin's Gable House.** This nice sit-down restaurant features a varied menu upstairs in the Ivy and Garden rooms and five-course dinners downstairs in the Captain's Room. Entrées include fish, ribs, stir-fries, brisket, and homemade chicken potpie. ✉ *290 E. St. George Blvd.,* ☎ *435/673–6796. AE, D, MC, V.*

$–$$$ ✕ **J. J. Hunan Chinese Restaurant.** This restaurant's enduring appeal is simple: The service is good, and the dishes are tasty. ✉ *Ancestor Sq., 2 W. St. George Blvd.,* ☎ *435/628–7219. AE, D, DC, MC, V.*

$–$$ ✕ **Pancho & Lefty's.** This is a great place for Mexican cuisine. Locals like the chimichangas, *flautas* (tortillas rolled into flute shapes, stuffed, and fried), and fajitas. Those who imbibe can order margaritas. ✉ *1050 S. Bluff St.,* ☎ *435/628–4772. AE, MC, V.*

$$$$ ★ **Green Valley Spa & Tennis Resort.** Whether you want to kick-start a weight-loss plan, buff up on your tennis or golf skills, or simply enjoy the natural splendor and indulge yourself in the spa, Green Valley offers it all. A different color is used to enliven the senses each day. A red day surrounds you with red flowers, red-tinted baths, and red decor in the dining room. Native American healing traditions (resident expert Gwen Moon is a treasure) are integrated into treatments and services. The Spa's all-natural beauty potions smell and feel wonderful. The kitchen turns out low-fat, high-energy food; snacks and second helpings are offered for those less concerned with weight loss. Dozens of fitness classes are offered, and mornings begin with a beautiful hike in local red-rock canyon parks (including an optional excursion to Zion). Rooms in the Coyote Inn have beds and whirlpool tubs so decadent you'll hardly want to leave, save for the beautiful landscape moments away from your door. Jay Cooper, author of *The Body Code,* will create a food and fitness plan for you based on your genetic type. All meals, and some spa services, are included in the room rates. ✉ *1871 W. Canyon View Dr., 84770,* ☎ *435/628–8060 or 800/237–1068,* FAX *435/673–4084. 34 rooms in Coyote Inn, varying number of condos. Dining room, in-room safes, no-smoking rooms, refrigerators, 3 pools, beauty salon, spa, golf privileges, 19 tennis courts, aerobics, exercise room, hiking, jogging, laundry service, meeting rooms, airport shuttle. AE, MC, V.*

$–$$$ **Greene Gate Village Historic Bed & Breakfast Inn.** This inn is named for a gate that reportedly dates back to 1877. As legend has it, Brigham Young had the fence and gate around the St. George Temple painted green. He then gave the excess paint to church members so that they, too, could paint their own gates and fences. Local lore notwithstanding, this collection of eight vintage homes offers elegantly comfortable accommodations in downtown St. George, complete with eclectic touches such as massive antique beds and historic photographs mingled with the modern convenience of showers, Jacuzzi tubs, and fax machines. There is no smoking in the rooms, and a full breakfast is included. ✉ *76 W. Tabernacle St., 84770,* ☎ *435/628–6999 or 800/350–6999,* FAX *435/628–6989. 16 rooms. Pool, hot tub. AE, D, DC, MC, V.*

$–$$$ ★ **Seven Wives Inn.** Two historic homes and a cottage constitute this B&B. It is said that Brigham Young slept here and that one of the structures may have been used to hide polygamists after the practice was prohibited in the 1880s. Antiques are liberally used in the decor, and guest rooms, most of which boast fireplaces or wood-burning stoves, are named after the wives of a former owner's great-great-grandfather. A full breakfast is served. ✉ *217 N. 100 West St., 84770,* ☎ *435/628–3737 or 800/600–3737,* FAX *435/628–5646. 13 rooms. Dining room, pool. AE, D, DC, MC, V.*

$ **Ramada Inn.** On St. George's major thoroughfare and close to restaurants, shopping, and the historic district, this is one of the city's most convenient properties. The rooms and furnishings are up-to-date and comfortable. ✉ *1440 E. St. George Blvd., 84790,* ☎ *435/628–2828 or 800/713–9435,* FAX *435/628–0505. 136 rooms. Pool, hot tub, meeting rooms. AE, D, DC, MC, V.*

Nightlife and the Arts

The **Dixie Center** (✉ 425 S. 700 East St., ☎ 435/628–7003) hosts the **Southwest Symphony** (☎ 435/656–0434) from October to May. An intermittent **Celebrity Concert Series** lures top acts.

Tuacahn (✉ Rte. 18, south of Snow Canyon State Park, ☎ 435/652–3200 or 800/746–9882) is an outdoor amphitheater nestled in a natural sandstone cove that offers a rotating series of musicals such as *Joseph and The Amazing Technicolor Dream Coat* and *Seven Brides for Seven Brothers.*

The Blarney Stone (✉ 800 E. St. George Blvd., ☎ 435/673–9191) is a lively beer-only joint with live music on weekends. Several of the hotels in town have private clubs with live music.

Outdoor Activities and Sports

GOLF

Dixie Red Hills (✉ 645 W. 1250 North St., ☎ 435/634–5852) has nine holes. **Green Spring** (✉ 588 N. Green Spring Dr., ☎ 435/673–7888) has 18 holes. **St. George Golf Club** (✉ 2190 S. 1400 East St., ☎ 435/634–5854) is another 18-hole course. The area's newest golf course, **Entrada at Snow Canyon** (✉ 2511 W. Entrada Trail, ☎ 435/674–7500) has 18 holes and is Utah's first Johnny Miller Signature Course.

HIKING

The 50,000-acre **Pine Valley Wilderness** (☎ 435/688–3246), accessible from I–15 via a signed Forest Service road, has plenty of mountainous backcountry to explore. **Snow Canyon State Park** (☎ 435/628–2255) has several short trails and lots of small desert canyons to explore. Ask the ranger on site for suggestions. For a little urban hiking, take a brisk stroll through St. George's **Historic District,** tucked just two blocks from the city's main street. The Chamber of Commerce (✉ 97 E. St. George Blvd., ☎ 435/628–1658) has a flyer outlining a self-guided walking tour.

ROCK CLIMBING

Paragon Climbing Instruction (☎ 435/673–1709) offers professional instruction and guiding for beginners and experts.

Shopping

Zion Factory Stores (✉ 245 N. Red Cliffs Dr., I–15 Exit 8, ☎ 435/674–9800 or 800/269–8687) is southern Utah's only factory-outlet center. It has 40 manufacturers' outlets, including J. Crew and Coach Leather Goods. Across the street is the **Promenade at Red Cliff,** a retail mall.

Hurricane

13 mi from St. George via I–15 north and Rte. 9 east.

Hurricane is on the Virgin River between St. George and Zion National Park. Once a sleepy pioneer town, this area has recently experienced enormous growth, probably owing to St. George's popularity. Hurricane has one of the state's most scenic 18-hole golf courses, **Sky Mountain** (✉ 1000 N. 2600 West St., ☎ 435/635–7888). There are many fast-food chains represented here, but **The New Garden Cafe** (✉ 138 S. Main St., ☎ 435/635–9825), a restaurant that opened in 1994, still has the only espresso machine for miles. Those seeking a shopping fix will find it at the **Chums Company Store** (✉ 120 S. Main St., ☎ 435/635–9836 or 800/323–3707), the factory outlet for Hello Wear, a line of sturdy outdoor clothing designed and manufactured in Hurricane.

Zion National Park

67 *40 mi from St. George via I–15 north and Rte. 9 east.*

This wonderland of vividly hued canyons and monumental monoliths was first established as Mukuntuweap National Monument in 1909. It became Zion National Park a decade later. Now the 147,000-acre park welcomes more than 2.5 million visitors annually. Most of these visitors are accommodated in Springdale, at the park's main entrance on Route

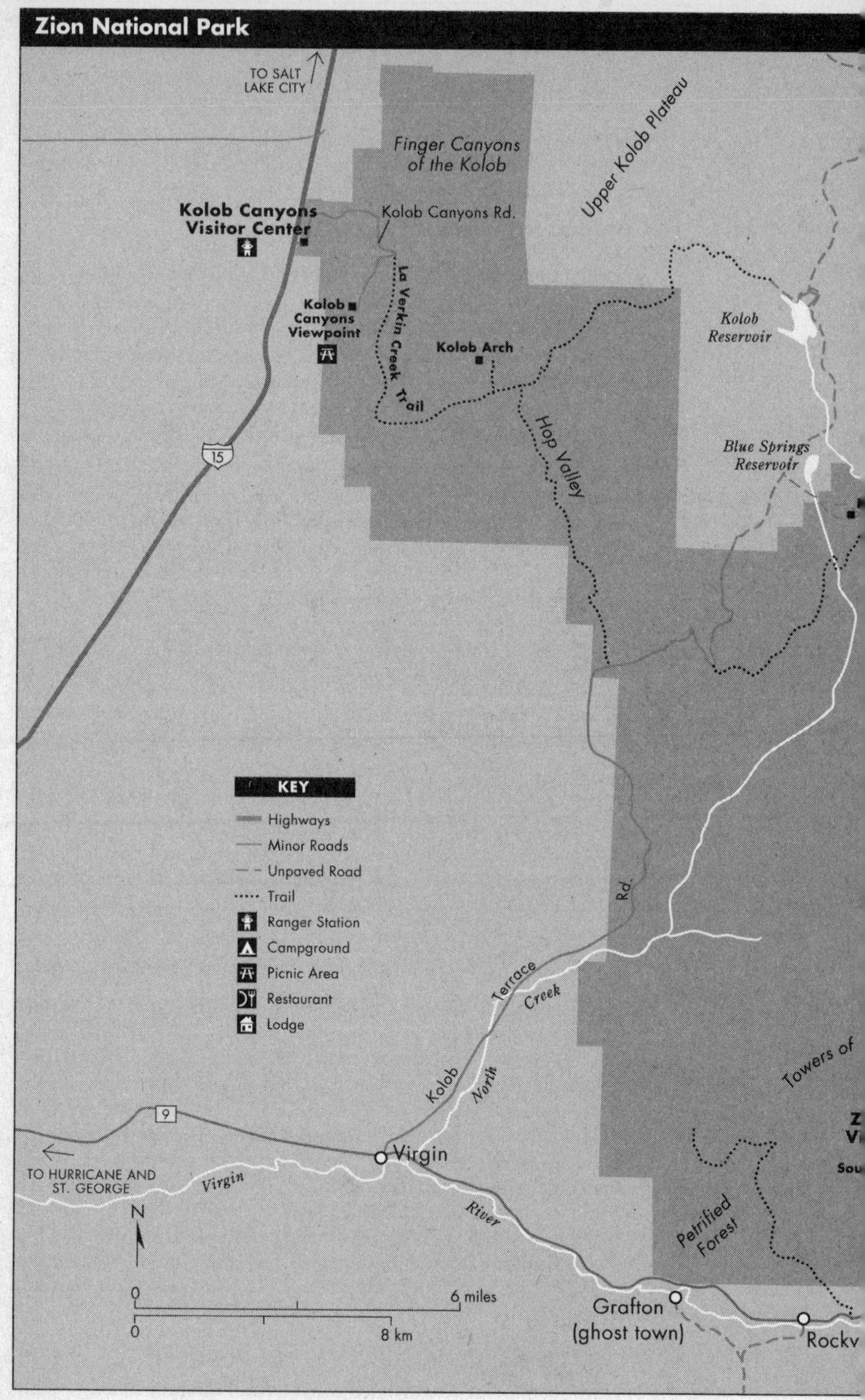

Zion National Park
TO SALT LAKE CITY
Finger Canyons of the Kolob
Upper Kolob Plateau
Kolob Canyons Visitor Center
Kolob Canyons Rd.
La Verkin Creek Trail
Kolob Canyons Viewpoint
Kolob Arch
Kolob Reservoir
Hop Valley
Blue Springs Reservoir
15
KEY
Highways
Minor Roads
Unpaved Road
Trail
Ranger Station
Campground
Picnic Area
Restaurant
Lodge
Rd.
Kolob Terrace
North Creek
Towers of
9
Virgin
TO HURRICANE AND ST. GEORGE
Virgin River
N
0
6 miles
0
8 km
Petrified Forest
Grafton (ghost town)
Rockv

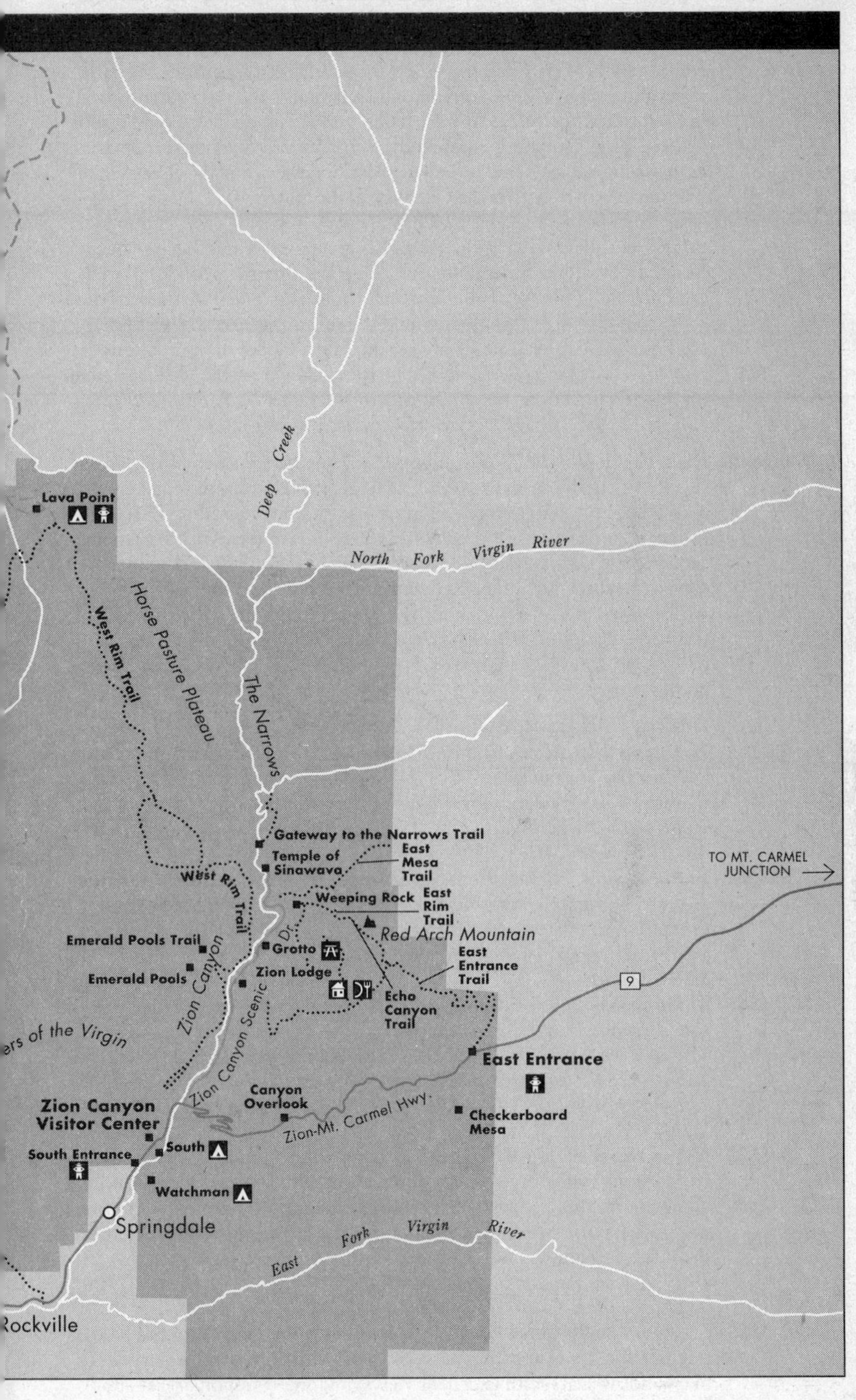

Lava Point
Deep Creek
North Fork Virgin River
Horse Pasture Plateau
West Rim Trail
The Narrows
Gateway to the Narrows Trail
Temple of Sinawava
East Mesa Trail
TO MT. CARMEL JUNCTION
West Rim Trail
Weeping Rock
East Rim Trail
Red Arch Mountain
Emerald Pools Trail
Grotto
Zion Canyon Scenic Dr.
East Entrance Trail
Emerald Pools
Zion Lodge
9
Echo Canyon Trail
Zion Canyon
ers of the Virgin
East Entrance
Canyon Overlook
Zion Canyon Visitor Center
Checkerboard Mesa
Zion-Mt. Carmel Hwy.
South
South Entrance
Watchman
Springdale
East Fork Virgin River
Rockville

9 (30 mi from I–15). Although the road through town is lined with motels, restaurants, and shops, Springdale still has an appealing feel that comes mostly from the clearly visible formations of Zion. Inside the park, front and center is **Zion Canyon,** which contains the park's main road (a 6½-mi scenic drive), an historic lodge, and a visitor center. Some 2,500 ft deep, Zion Canyon is rimmed by such naturally sculpted landmarks as the **Sentinel, East Temple,** the **Temple of Sinawava,** and the **Great White Throne.** At road's end is the **Gateway to the Narrows.** As its name suggests, the Narrows is a slender passageway, in places only a couple of dozen feet wide, carved by the Virgin River. A paved, 1-mi-long trail heads into the abyss, but hikers often wade up the stream beyond. Hikes to the **Emerald Pools** are similarly worthwhile. The trailhead is across the road from the lodge. It is 1¼ mi round trip on an easy trail to lower Emerald Pools. The middle pools are reached by a moderately strenuous 2-mi loop. The upper pools are difficult to reach. Inquire at the Visitor Center for specific directions. ✉ *30 mi east of I–15 on Rte. 9, Springdale,* ☎ *435/772–3256.* 🎫 *$10 per vehicle.* 🕒 *Daily 8–sunset.*

En Route From the depths of Zion Canyon, the **Zion–Mount Carmel Highway** (Route 9) climbs eastward. After several switchbacks, the road enters a 1-mi-long tunnel, complete with portals. Constructed in 1930, the tunnel is too small for large RVs or tour buses to pass without having rangers stop traffic; RV and bus drivers pay a fee of $10 and up for this service. Beyond the tunnel's east entrance, Route 9 continues out of the park to Mount Carmel Junction, passing through the park's slickrock territory, including Checkerboard Mesa, which resembles an enormous sandstone playing board. From here, U.S. 89 heads south for 17 mi to Kanab.

Dining and Lodging

$$–$$$ ★ ✕ **Bit and Spur Restaurant and Saloon.** This eatery serves innovative and healthy Southwestern-style Mexican food. Works by local artists fill the pine-paneled interior, while the patio features bright flowers and scents from the herb garden. ✉ *1212 Zion Park Blvd., Springdale,* ☎ *435/772–3498. MC, V.*

$$–$$$ ✕ **Flannigan's.** Named for one of Springdale's original settlement families, this intimate restaurant has views of Zion Canyon, and a collection of Everett Ruess woodcut prints. Pastas, chicken, fish, and steaks are on the menu. ✉ *428 Zion Park Blvd., Springdale,* ☎ *435/772–3244. AE, MC, V.*

$$$–$$$$ 🏨 **Cliffrose Lodge and Gardens.** Acres of lawn, trees, and gardens surround the low, rambling stucco wings of this hotel on the bank of the Virgin River, ¼ mi from Zion. The ample rooms are decorated in desert hues. ✉ *281 Zion Park Blvd., Box 510, Springdale, 84767,* ☎ *435/772–3234 or 800/243–8824,* FAX *435/772–3900. 36 rooms. Pool. AE, D, MC, V.*

$$–$$$$ 🏨 **The Harvest House.** This B&B is on the edge of Zion National Park. Along with three rooms and a suite with two bedrooms and a living room, this property has cactus gardens and a pond swimming with koi. A covered veranda winds a third of the way around the house. Breakfasts might include eggs Florentine or apple pancakes. ✉ *29 Canyon View Dr., Springdale 84767,* ☎ *435/772–3880,* FAX *435/772–3327. 3 rooms, 1 suite. Hot tub. D, MC, V.*

$$–$$$$ ★ 🏨 **Snow Family Guest Ranch.** Just minutes from Zion National Park, this B&B is a western-theme oasis filled with comfortable surprises, like window seats with excellent views, inviting common areas—both indoors and out—and breakfasts worth lingering over. ✉ *633 E. Hwy. 9, Box 790190, Virgin 84779,* ☎ *435/635–2500 or 800/308–7669. 9 rooms. Pool, hot tub. AE, D, MC, V.*

Kanab

68 *40 mi from Zion National Park's east entrance via Rte. 9 east and U.S. 89 south.*

Picturesque Kanab has considerable ties to Hollywood. The Kanab area has played a cameo role in more than 100 movies and television shows, beginning in 1922 with a Tom Mix film, *Deadwood Coach*, and continuing to productions such as the television miniseries, *How the West Was Won*. Kanab serves as a gateway to portions of the **Grand Staircase–Escalante National Monument** (☞ *below*), designated in 1996.

Lopeman's Frontier Movie Town is jam-packed with Old West movie memorabilia. Some of the buildings in its replica of a frontier town were actually used in movie sets, and photos on the walls inside reveal many familiar faces. ✉ *297 W. Center St.*, ☎ *435/644–5337.* *Free.* ⏲ *Hrs vary.*

Coral Pink Sand Dunes State Park is a giant playland of tinted sand. Big kids play on the dunes with their all-terrain vehicles, but an area has been set aside for families to explore. There is a 22-site campground. ✉ *Yellowjacket and Hancock Rds., 12 mi west of Kanab via U.S. 89,* ☎ *435/648–2800.* *$3 per vehicle.* ⏲ *Year-round.*

Dining and Lodging

$–$$ ✕ **Chef's Palace.** This restaurant is a local favorite for rib-eye steaks, prime rib, and seafood. For added cowboy atmosphere, dine in the Dude Room. ✉ *151 W. Center St.,* ☎ *435/644–5052. AE, D, DC, MC, V.*

$–$$ **Parry Lodge.** Back in the 1930s, movie stars stayed here. The names of who slept in each room are listed above the doors of the older units, and Hollywood-related photos decorate the lobby. Despite the age of the hotel, rooms are well-maintained and comfortable. ✉ *89 E. Center St., 84741,* ☎ *435/644–2601 or 800/748–4104,* FAX *435/644–2605. 89 rooms. Restaurant, pool. AE, D, DC, MC, V.*

Bryce Canyon National Park

69 *77 mi from Kanab via Rte. 9 west, U.S. 89 north (at Mount Carmel Junction), and Rte. 12 east.*

Not actually a canyon, **Bryce Canyon** is a set of amphitheaters carved into the eastern rim of the Paunsaugunt Plateau. Exposed and sculpted by erosion are pink-and-cream-color spires, or hoodoos, visible from many overlooks along the park's 35 mi of paved road. Among the stunning sights are the **Silent City**, named for the eerie rock profiles and figures, and the "chessmen" of **Queen's Garden.** Because early- and late-day sunlight casts such an unusual glow on these rock formations, many folks count Bryce as their favorite of Utah's national parks. Given its nearly 8,000-ft elevation, winter turns the area into a wonderland for cross-country skiers. The **Rim Trail** features nonstop scenery, while the **Fairyland Loop** and Queen's Garden trails lead hikers among the park's hoodoos. ✉ *Bryce Canyon, Hwy. 63,* ☎ *435/834–5322.* *$10 per vehicle.* ⏲ *Daily 8–sunset.*

Dining and Lodging

$$$–$$$$ ✕ **Bryce Canyon Lodge.** Inside the park, this historic property, designed by Stanley Gilbert Underwood for the Union Pacific Railroad and built in the mid-1920s, is a few feet from rim views. A National Historic Landmark, the lodge has been faithfully restored, right down to the lobby's huge limestone fireplace, its log and wrought-iron chandelier, and its bark-covered hickory furniture, which was built by the same company that produced the originals. Guests have their choice of motel-style rooms with the unexpected touch of balconies or porches; suites on the lodge's

Bryce Canyon National Park

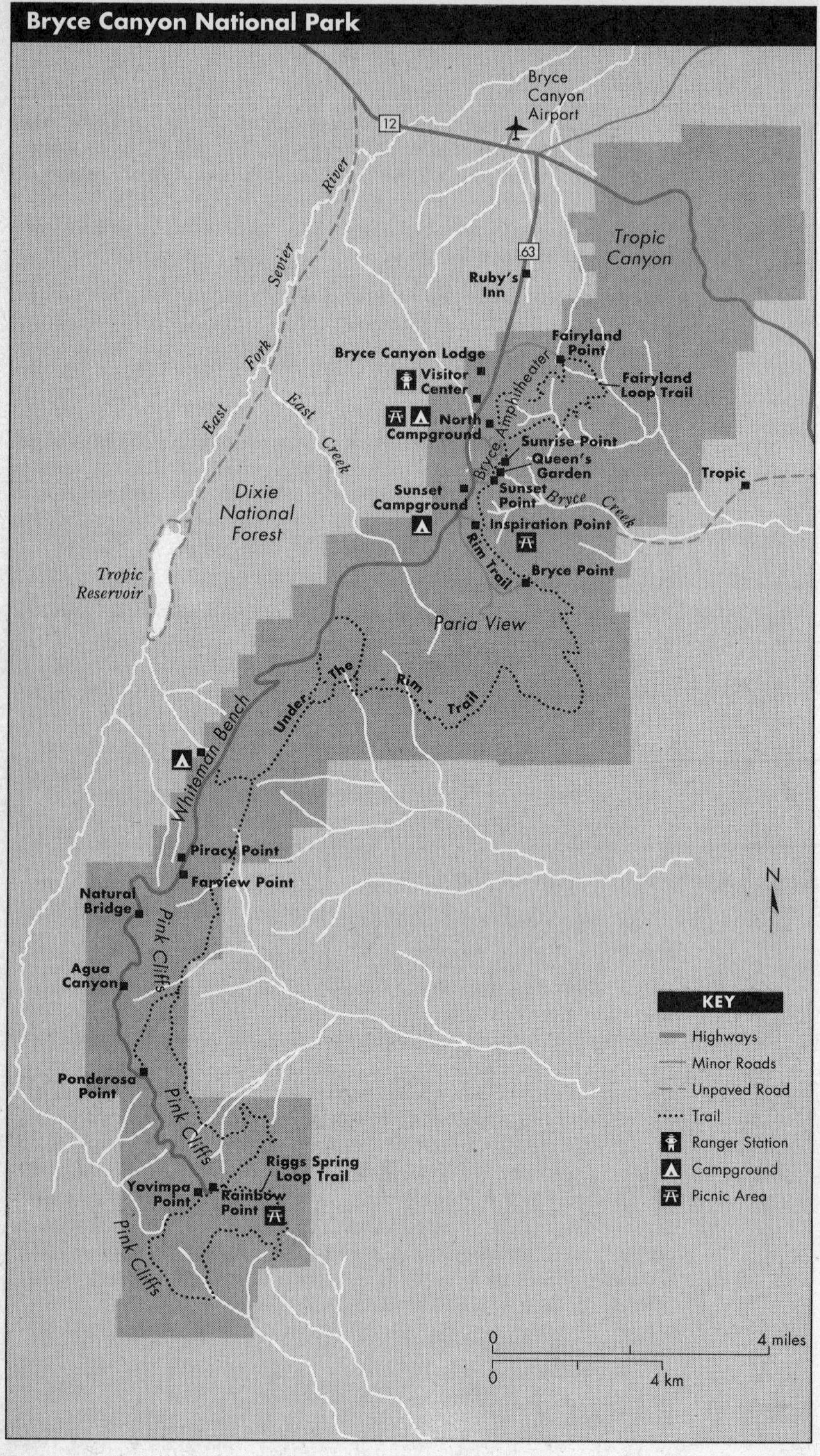
Bryce Canyon Airport
12
River
Sevier
East Fork
63
Tropic Canyon
Ruby's Inn
Bryce Canyon Lodge
Visitor Center
North Campground
Fairyland Point
Bryce Amphitheater
Fairyland Loop Trail
Sunrise Point
Queen's Garden
Sunset Point
Bryce Creek
Tropic
East Creek
Dixie National Forest
Sunset Campground
Inspiration Point
Rim Trail
Bryce Point
Tropic Reservoir
Paria View
Under The Rim Trail
Whiteman Bench
Piracy Point
Farview Point
Natural Bridge
Pink Cliffs
Agua Canyon
Ponderosa Point
Riggs Spring Loop Trail
Yovimpa Point
Rainbow Point
N
KEY
Highways
Minor Roads
Unpaved Road
Trail
Ranger Station
Campground
Picnic Area
0
4 miles
0
4 km

second level; or cozy lodgepole-pine cabins, some with cathedral ceilings and gas fireplaces. Reservations are hard to come by: Call several months ahead, or, if you're feeling lucky, call the day before your arrival—cancellations occasionally make last-minute bookings possible. The lodge also organizes horseback rides and park tours. ⊠ *2 mi south of park entrance on Rte. 63, Box 400, Cedar City 84720,* ☎ *435/834–5361, 303/297–2757 for advance reservations,* FAX *435/834–5464. 115 rooms, 3 suites. Restaurant. AE, D, DC, MC, V. Closed Nov.–Apr.*

$$–$$$$ ✕ **Best Western Ruby's Inn.** Just north of the park entrance and housing a large restaurant and gift shop, this is Grand Central Station for visitors to Bryce. A nightly rodeo takes place nearby. Rooms vary in age, with sprawling wings added as the park gained popularity. All of the guest rooms are consistently comfortable and attractive, however. The lobby, centered between the gift shop and restaurant, has rough-hewn log beams and poles, and a decor heavy on "Southwestern chic". ⊠ *Rte. 63, Box 1, 84764,* ☎ *435/834–5341 or 800/468–8660,* FAX *435/834–5265. 369 rooms. Restaurant, indoor pool, hot tub, camping, coin laundry. AE, D, DC, MC, V.*

OFF THE BEATEN PATH

KODACHROME BASIN STATE PARK – Among the spectacular but little-known geological displays at this state park are unusual petrified geysers and peculiar formations called sand pipes. The basin was named for Kodak's classic color film after pictures of it appeared in a 1949 *National Geographic* article. The park is surrounded by the Grand Staircase–Escalante National Monument (☞ Escalante, *below*). ⊠ *take Route 12 22 mi east from the eastern entrance to Bryce Canyon National Park and Kodachrome Basin Road 9 mi south,* ☎ *435/679–8562.* *$4 per vehicle.* *Daily 8–sunset.*

Escalante

 *from Bryce Canyon National Park (eastern edge) via Rte. 12 east.*

Escalante is the primary gateway community for the **Grand Staircase-Escalante National Monument;** other cities near the monument are Kanab, Boulder, and Tropic. Created in September 1996, the huge monument covers 1.7 million acres. It was named for a series of geologic steps creating a staircase effect throughout the monument, and for the scenic gorges carved by the Escalante River. There are more than 300 archaeological sites within it, as well as myriad mazelike canyons. Services and facilities inside the monument are virtually non-existent. This monument is administered by the BLM; most areas are currently free. ⊠ *755 W. Main St.,* ☎ *435/826–5499.*

Escalante is also the location of **Escalante State Park** (⊠ Rte. 12, ☎ 435/826–4466), with its collection of rainbow-color, 150-million-year-old petrified wood.

Outdoor Activities and Sports

In the northern section of the monument, east of the town of Escalante, Route 12 crosses the Escalante River, which has carved an extensive canyon system highly favored by **backpackers.** While en route to southeastern Utah in 1879, Mormon pioneers chipped and blasted a narrow passageway in solid rock, through which they lowered their wagons. This **Hole in the Rock Trail,** now a 60-mi gravel road, leads from Escalante to the **Devil's Garden Natural Area,** with **hiking** in beautiful canyons and gulches. A good long-distance **mountain-bike** ride in the isolated Escalante region follows the 44-mi **Hell's Backbone Road** from Escalante to Boulder. The grade is steep, but the views of **Box Death Hollow** make it worthwhile. Mountain bikers may want to pedal a portion of the **Burr Trail,** a 66-mi backcountry route (usable by most vehicles when dry) that crosses east through the monument into the southern portion of Capitol Reef National Park.

En Route Within the monument, heading north toward the town of Boulder, Route 12 passes the **Calf Creek Recreation Area,** highlighted by 126-ft Calf Creek Falls. The 5½-mi-round-trip hike to the falls is fairly level, but some short, sandy stretches cause briefly strenuous hiking.

Boulder

71 *29 mi from Escalante via Rte. 12 north.*

How remote is Boulder? So remote that only in the 1940s did it stop receiving its mail by mule. Today the town is home to **Anasazi State Park.** One of the largest Anasazi sites west of the Colorado River, the village predates AD 1200. ✉ *460 N. Rte. 12,* ☎ *435/335–7308.* *$5 per vehicle.* *Daily 8–sunset.*

En Route North of Boulder, Route 12 continues up and over **Boulder Mountain,** in the Dixie National Forest. As this stretch of scenic byway reaches 9,200 ft, it encounters some lush pine, spruce, and aspen forests. In addition, magnificent views of the Escalante River canyons to the south and the Henry Mountains to the east open up along the way.

Capitol Reef National Park

72 *45 mi from Boulder via Rte. 12 north and Rte. 24 east.*

Named for a sandstone formation that resembles the U.S. Capitol, **Capitol Reef National Park** extends north for 75 mi from Glen Canyon National Recreation Area. The most heavily visited corridor of the preserve follows the **Fremont River** in the northern section. Here various hikes allow for different views of the cliffs and domes in surrounding canyons (the strenuous, but short, routes to the Fremont Overlook and to Chimney Rock or the moderate Hickman Bridge Trail are good picks), and the Mormon village of Fruita offers an historical perspective on the region. Riverside orchards planted by settlers are now harvested by park visitors. Reached by high-clearance vehicles over a road that leads to the northernmost section of the park is the aptly named **Cathedral Valley.** The **Waterpocket Fold,** a giant wrinkle of rock running south for more than 100 mi, contains some spectacular hikes, especially in Muley Twist Canyon. This area is accessed by the 66-mi Burr Trail, which is passable by most cars when dry and offers motorists the chance to explore some wonderful terrain. ✉ *Hwy. 24, HCR 70, Box 15, Torrey 84775,* ☎ *435/425–3791.* *$5 per vehicle.* *Daily 8–sunset.*

Dining and Lodging

These options are in the towns of Torrey and Loa, 12 and 20 mi west of the park's east entrance, respectively, on Route 24.

$$–$$$ ✕ **Café Diablo.** Ruddy tile floors and crisp white walls make this a pleasant setting for innovative Southwestern cuisine. Offerings range from hearty *chipotle* (a kind of chili), fried ribs, or local trout crusted with pumpkin seeds, to grilled chicken with a lime and honey sauce. ✉ *599 W. Main St., Torrey,* ☎ *435/425–3070. MC, V. Closed Nov.–Apr.*

$–$$ ✕ **Capitol Reef Café.** Behind this restaurant's homey exterior, there's fabulous food to satisfy the most juvenile or jaded customer. Children love the peanut butter and honey sandwich for breakfast, lunch, or dinner. This leaves the grown-ups free to try more sophisticated fare, like the 10-vegetable salad or fillets of flaky, smoked rainbow trout caught locally. ✉ *Rte. 24, Torrey,* ☎ *435/425–3271. AE, D, MC, V. Closed Nov.–Apr.*

$$–$$$$ ★ **SkyRidge Bed and Breakfast.** Among the guest comments about this colorful, three-story inn is "I dream about SkyRidge." It is not hard to understand why. The textured walls are hung with the works of local artists. Unusual furniture—each piece chosen for its look and feel—makes the guest rooms and common areas both stimulating and comfortable. Meals here are excellent, including dinners in the winter, when area restaurants are closed. And each of the inn's windows offers an exceptional view of the desert and mountains surrounding Capitol Reef National Park. ✉ *950 E. Hwy. 24, Box 750220, Torrey 84775,* ☎ *435/425–3222,* FAX *435/425–3222. 6 rooms. Dining room, hot tub. MC, V.*

$–$$ **Road Creek Inn.** Housed in the 1912 Loa General Store building, 20 mi west of Capitol Reef National Park, this inn offers such treats as a trout pond and a game room. Guest rooms, in which there is no smoking, are decorated in Victorian-era motifs. ✉ *90 S. Main St., Box 310, Loa 84747,* ☎ *435/836–2485 or 800/388–7688,* FAX *435/836–2490. 22 rooms. Restaurant, hot tub, recreation room. AE, D, MC, V.*

Fish Lake

73 *26 mi from Loa via Rte. 24 west and Rte. 25 north.*

Fish Lake, 8,800 ft high, 1 mi wide, and 6 mi long, is known for its fishing, but you needn't have tackle box in hand to enjoy its beautiful environs. Mountain scenery and a quiet setting are the real draw. Some great hikes explore the higher reaches of the area (one trail leads to the 11,633-ft summit of Fish Lake Hightop Plateau). Cyclists enjoy fall and summer rides on forest service roads or along Route 12, a designated Scenic Byway that circles the east and north ends of the lake. There are several campgrounds as well as some wonderful lodges. The lake's depth averages 85 ft. It is stocked annually with lake trout, rainbow trout, and splake. A large population of brown trout are native to the lake. This is a destination so impressive that the 1.4-million-acre Fishlake National Forest (☎ 435/896–9233) was named after it.

Lodging

$–$$ **Fish Lake Lodge.** This large, lakeside lodge structure was built in 1932 and today exudes rustic charm and character. Guests stay in cabins—some old, others new—with an emphasis on function instead of fancy amenities. There is a dance hall and store, and the views are wonderful. ✉ *HC80, Rte. 25, 84701,* ☎ *435/638–1000. 45 rooms. Restaurant. D, MC, V. Lodge closed early Sept.–late May. Cabins open all-year.*

Richfield

43 mi from Fish Lake via Rte. 25 south, Rte. 24 north, Rte. 119 west, and I–70 south.

Route 119 winds through the fertile farmlands of the Sevier River valley to the town of Richfield. This is the most direct route to return to Salt Lake City, but not necessarily the most interesting (☞ Piute County *in* Off the Beaten Path, *below*). Richfield is a good spot from which to consider other forays into southern Utah, including those destinations to the east via I–70.

74 **Fremont Indian State Park,** 21 mi south of Richfield via I–70, in Clear Creek Canyon, has a visitor center with a museum and three interpretive trails. Originally the site included a village of pit houses, but it was obliterated in the 1980s by construction of I–70 (after archaeologists completed excavation). Most of the hundreds of rock art panels are intact and on display, making this one of the finest collections of Fremont art in the state. Several of the panels are believed to have significance

related to solstice and equinox plantings and harvests. ✉ *11550 Clear Creek Canyon Rd.,* ☎ *435/527–4631.* *$5.* *Daily 9–sunset.*

Dining and Lodging

$ **Topsfield Lodge.** Aside from Richfield's docket of national chain motels, you might try this locally owned one. In addition to basic yet clean rooms and friendly service, there is an on-site steak house ($–$$) that is quite popular among locals and visitors alike. ✉ *1200 S. Main St., 84701,* ☎ *435/896–5437. 20 rooms. Restaurant. AE, MC, V.*

OFF THE BEATEN PATH

PIUTE COUNTY – If you have the time, you might continue south from Fremont Indian State Park into tiny Piute County. Along the way, you'll pass Big Rock Candy Mountain, a colorful landmark made famous in a song by Burl Ives. Piute State Park (✉ 12 mi south of Marysvale off U.S. 89, ☎ 435/624–3268) has excellent fishing and boating on a 3,360-acre reservoir. In the town of Junction, on U.S. 89, you can't miss the bright-red Piute County Courthouse. Built in 1902, the adobe structure is on the National Register of Historic Places. Robert LeRoy Parker—alias Butch Cassidy—grew up near the small town of Circleville just south of Junction. Otter Creek State Park (✉ 4 mi north of Antimony on Rte. 22, ☎ 435/624–3268) has a 3,120-acre lake known for rainbow trout. From Junction, you can backtrack to Richfield and return to Salt Lake by way of U.S. 50 and I–15. Or, if you're up for a little adventure, you can drive Route 123 (Kimberly Scenic Backway, passable by most cars in the summer) over the Tushar Mountains to Beaver, I–15, and civilization.

Southwestern Utah A to Z

Arriving and Departing

BY BUS

Greyhound Lines (☎ 800/231–2222) runs buses along the I–15 corridor, making stops in **Beaver** (✉ El Bambi Café, 935 N. Main St., ☎ 435/438–2983), **Cedar City** (✉ 1355 S. Main St., ☎ 435/586–9465), and **St. George** (✉ McDonald's, 1235 S. Bluff St., ☎ 435/673–2933).

BY CAR

Interstate 15 is the main route into the region, from Las Vegas to the southwest and Salt Lake City to the northeast.

BY PLANE

SkyWest flies to Cedar City and St. George municipal airports. **United Express** also flies to St. George.

BY TRAIN

Milford receives limited Amtrak service at the Union Pacific facility just off Main Street.

Getting Around

BY CAR

I–15 is the main route south from Salt Lake City; I–70 heads east from I–15 below the town of Fort. Various well-maintained two-lane highways traverse southwestern Utah. Some mountain curves can be expected, and winter months may see hazardous conditions in the higher elevations. Be sure that your car is in good working order, and keep the gas tank topped off.

Contacts and Resources

DOCTORS AND DENTISTS

Beaver Valley Hospital (✉ 85 North 400 E, Beaver, ☎ 435/438–2531). **Dixie Regional Medical Center** (✉ 544 South 400 E, St. George, ☎ 435/634–4000). **Garfield Memorial Hospital** (✉ 200 North 400 E, Panguitch, ☎ 435/676–8811). **Kane County Hospital** (✉ 355 N. Main St., Kanab,

☎ 435/644–5811). **Milford Memorial Hospital** (✉ 451 N. Main St., Milford, ☎ 435/387–2411). **Valley View Medical Center** (✉ 595 South 75 E, Cedar City, ☎ 435/586–6587).

GUIDED TOURS

Boulder Mountain Lodge (✉ Box 1397, Boulder 84716, ☎ 435/335–7460 or 800/556–3446) and **Hondoo River and Trails** (✉ 95 E. Main St., Box 98, Torrey 84775, ☎ 435/425–3519 or 800/332–2696) arrange hiking and four-wheel-drive tours into portions of the Grand Staircase–Escalante National Monument. **Canyon Trail Rides** (✉ Box 128, Tropic 84776, ☎ 435/679–8665) operates mule and horseback riding tours in Bryce Canyon and Zion national parks as well as the North Rim of the Grand Canyon. **Pedal Pusher Tours** (✉ 151 W. Main St., Box 750101, Torrey 84775, ☎ 435/425–3378) offers cycling tours in Capitol Reef National Park and vicinity.

VISITOR INFORMATION

Beaver County Travel Council (✉ Box 1060, Beaver 84713, ☎ 435/438–5384). **Capitol Reef Country** (✉ Rte. 24, Box 7, Teasdale 84773, ☎ 800/858–7951). **Color Country** (✉ 906 N. 1400 West St., Box 1550, St. George 84771, ☎ 435/628–4171 or 800/233–8824). **Garfield County Travel Council** (✉ 55 S. Main St., Panguitch 84074, ☎ 800/444–6689). **Iron County Tourism and Convention Bureau** (✉ Box 1007, Cedar City 84721, ☎ 435/586–5124 or 800/354–4849). **Kane County Travel Council** (✉ Box 728, Kanab 84741, ☎ 435/644–5033). **Panoramaland** (✉ 4 S. Main St., Box 71, Nephi 84648, ☎ 435/623–5203 or 800/748–4361). **Piute Tourism Board** (✉ Piute County Courthouse, Junction 84740, ☎ 435/577–2949). **Sevier Travel Council** (✉ 220 N. 600 West St., Richfield 84701, ☎ 435/896–8898 or 800/662–8898). **Washington County Travel and Convention Bureau** (✉ 425 S. 700 East St., St. George 84770, ☎ 435/634–5747 or 800/869–6635).

UTAH A TO Z

Getting Around

By Bus

Greyhound Lines (☎ 800/231–2222) runs several buses each day through Salt Lake City. In addition, there are terminals in Beaver, Brigham City, Cedar City, Logan, Ogden, Price, Provo, St. George, Tremonton, and Vernal.

By Car

By far the best way to see Utah is by car; in fact, beyond Salt Lake City and the Wasatch Front, it's basically the only way. I–80 crosses Utah east to west, and I–15 runs the length of the state, from Idaho to Arizona. These two routes intersect in Salt Lake City. Until the summer of 2001, major renovation to I–15 between Ogden and Provo will restrict traffic to two lanes in each direction along the urban corridor of the Wasatch Front. U.S. 191 accesses eastern Utah, and U.S. 666 enters the southeast from Colorado. Front-wheel drive is suggested on the snowy roads of winter.

It is legal in Utah to make a right turn on a red light, after coming to a complete stop.

By Plane

Commuter service between Salt Lake City and smaller Utah cities, such as St. George, Cedar City, Vernal, and Moab, is available through **Alpine Air** (☎ 801/575–2839) and **SkyWest** (☎ 801/575–2508 or 800/453–9417).

By Train

Amtrak (☏ 800/872–7245) has daily service from the Rio Grande Depot in Salt Lake City and also serves Helper, Milford, Ogden, Provo, and Thompson Springs.

Contacts and Resources

Emergencies

In most towns, call **911** for police, fire, and ambulance service. In rural areas, the **Utah Highway Patrol** (☏ 801/965–4676) has jurisdiction, as do county sheriff departments.

Major towns have hospitals with emergency rooms (☞ Doctors and Dentists *in* individual A to Z sections, *above*). For nonemergencies, check in local telephone directories, with chambers of commerce, or at your lodging for names of doctors, dentists, and local pharmacies. Outside Salt Lake, pharmacies don't tend to stay open late, but major supermarket chains have pharmacy departments that are often open to 10 PM or so.

Fishing Licenses

Fishing licenses are available from the **Utah Division of Wildlife Resources** (✉ 1596 W. North Temple St., Salt Lake City 84116, ☏ 801/538–4700).

Guided Tours

GrayLine Motor Tours. (✉ 553 W. 100 South St., Salt Lake City 84101, ☏ 801/521–7060 or 800/309–2352) offers statewide tours in summer, and tours of northern Utah year round.

State Parks

Utah Division of Parks and Recreation (✉ 1594 W. North Temple St., Suite 116, Salt Lake City 84116, ☏ 801/538–7220) operates all state parks. Use fees, between $4 and $5, are charged at all state parks. Most state parks accept reservations for campsites (☏ 801/322–3770 or 800/322–3770) but also have some sites available on a first-come, first-served basis.

Visitor Information

Utah Travel Council (✉ Council Hall, Capitol Hill, Salt Lake City 84114, ☏ 801/538–1030 or 800/200–1160).

8 WYOMING

Wyoming is a land of wide-open spaces, soaring mountains, plains, prairie, high desert—and historical and cultural sites dating back thousands of years, a world-class Western museum, and the nation's first national park. Yellowstone and Grand Teton national parks and the gateway communities of Jackson and Cody are the state's greatest attractions, but Wyoming has cowboys—and rodeos—in nearly every town or city, plus miners, loggers, and high-tech business executives. Wilderness, resort, or city, the lifestyle is casual (jeans are almost always appropriate) and friendly.

By Geoffrey O'Gara and Michael McClure

Revised and updated by Candy Moulton

TOURING WYOMING'S UNPAVED ROADS BY MODEL T in the 1930s, writer Agnes Wright Spring found it easy to imagine the covered wagons and Native American bands of the 1800s. "The past presses so closely on the present!" she wrote, and even today her words hit the mark. Antelope still graze nonchalantly by highways, bull riders still bite the dust at Cheyenne's Frontier Days, and towering peaks, bearded with glaciers, stand as timeless sentinels in the West.

The closest Wyoming comes to big cities is Cheyenne and Casper, neither of which has more than 70,000 residents. Like most of the country, the state has tried to lasso high-tech industries, but you won't find General Motors or Boeing here. Even the oil and natural gas industries, centered in Casper and southwest Wyoming and long a staple of the state's economy, have declined of late. Increasingly, Wyoming residents have recognized that the state's most valuable resource is the same wild and unspoiled country that astonished explorers 50, 100, and 200 years ago. Of that, there is no shortage.

In most people's minds, wild Wyoming is synonymous with its northwest section and its cluster of parks, forests, and ski resorts. Yellowstone National Park, the most popular destination, does not disappoint. Geysers spout, elk bugle, mud pots boil, and larkspur blooms. The scars of 1988's severe fires show here and there, but park officials have capitalized on them, making the park a giant ecological classroom. As the years pass, the scars become less visible. Just to the south, the Grand Tetons rise abruptly from the Snake River plain, above the lively community of Jackson, where efforts are being made to retain working ranches and open space in the face of a tide of "second-homers."

Incomparable as the northwest is, there is much more to Wyoming. The other most-visited regions of the state, the northeast and southeast, blend mountain and plain, mine and ranch, and country towns and western cities. In the southeast, the museums, festivals, and parks of Cheyenne and Laramie ensure that Wyoming's heritage as a frontier territory has its place in contemporary life. The Bighorn Mountains in the northeast attract hikers and fishermen eager to avoid the more visited sites in the northwest.

Wyoming has fewer full-time residents (around 481,000) than any other state, but you'll find no inferiority complex. Whether they're riding the tram at Teton Village's world-class ski resort or haying the horses at a ranch in the Bighorn Mountains, Wyoming residents take ornery pride in being just specks on an uncluttered landscape, five people per square mile. They know they have something that is fast disappearing elsewhere in the world, and, with a hint of pride on a weather-beaten face, they're willing to share it.

Pleasures and Pastimes

There are no shortages of mountains and rivers and all kinds of trails for the intrepid outdoors lover. Jackson and the parks just to the north are the focus of intensive summer and winter outdoor recreation, whether it's bagging peaks in the Tetons in August or Sno-Cat skiing in the fresh powder at Grand Targhee. There is a lot of outdoors in Wyoming, however, and the adventurous visitor may want to try some less well-known areas and activities, from dude ranching around Sheridan and Cody to camping in national forests throughout the state.

Dining

The greatest variety of fine dining is in Jackson, and no other community in Wyoming comes close. There the possibilities range from a cookout with tables in tepees to an open-grilled meal in a massive log restaurant. In almost every small town, however, you'll find a place that does wonders with the regional specialties: steak and prime rib. You'll find an increasingly varied menu in most areas with such regional favorites as buffalo and trout. Some restaurants have even gained national reputations. Dining is casual; jackets and ties are not needed. Reservations, especially outside Jackson, are generally accepted but not required unless otherwise stated in reviews. A dinner in some Jackson restaurants can cost up to $50 per person with wine, but prices throughout the state are usually in the $–$$ range.

CATEGORY	COST*
$$$$	over $35
$$$	$25–$35
$$	$15–$25
$	under $15

**per person for a three-course dinner, not including drinks, tax, and tip*

Lodging

Accommodations in Wyoming range from practical roadside motels—not surprising, since most visitors come by car—to exclusive dude-ranch retreats. The *Wyoming Vacation Guide,* available from the Wyoming Division of Tourism (☞ Visitor Information *in* Wyoming A to Z, *below*) provides listings of motels, bed-and-breakfasts, dude ranches, and campgrounds and RV parks, along with major attractions. Summer traffic slackens after Labor Day, and many motels drop their fees from then until June. (In Jackson, however, prices go up again from late December through March, for the ski season.) Summer reservations for the better accommodations in Yellowstone National Park, Jackson, and Cody should be made three months in advance; Cheyenne reservations during Frontier Days should be made at least six months ahead. The accommodations available all around Yellowstone are growing exponentially, and the few remaining older, more primitive establishments (bathrooms down the hall, no air-conditioning) are being refurbished. In the Yellowstone area, lodging within the park is generally less expensive than what you'll find in nearby communities.

CATEGORY	COST*
$$$$	over $150
$$$	$100–$150
$$	$50–$100
$	under $50

**Prices are for a standard double room in high season, not including tax and* service.

Fishing

Lake and stream fishing in Wyoming is legendary. Record Mackinaw trout have been taken at Jackson Lake, and the trout population in Yellowstone Lake has been revived. Inside and outside the parks, the rivers are teeming with rainbow, native cutthroat, brook, brown, and Mackinaw trout, as well as whitefish and catfish at some lower elevations. The Snake River has its own unique cutthroat strain. Fishing aficionados often trek south into the Wind River Mountains, where glacier-fed lakes yield all of the above plus golden trout.

Exploring Wyoming

Wyoming's two national parks lie in northwest Wyoming, in the Rocky Mountains. Yellowstone National Park, with its geothermal wonders, is the state's most popular destination. Just to the south, Grand Teton National Park protects the spectacular Tetons, which jut along the skyline above the Snake River. Their adjacent gateway towns are Jackson and Dubois to the south and Cody on the east. Cheyenne, Laramie, and Saratoga along with the Medicine Bow and Snowy Range mountains anchor the southeast corner of the state; Casper is in the center. Popular areas in northern Wyoming also include Sheridan, Big Horn, and Buffalo, just east of the Bighorn Mountains, and Gillette and Devils Tower in the northeast.

Numbers in the text correspond to numbers in the margin and on the Wyoming map.

Great Itineraries

IF YOU HAVE 3 DAYS

The most popular section of Wyoming, the northwest, will more than fill a three-day trip, so plan to pack the time as completely as possible to see amazing scenery and wildlife in a unique landscape. Because it has the best air service, begin your trip in **Jackson** ① and plan to spend the first full day touring the community and **Grand Teton National Park** ④. Be sure to visit the **National Wildlife Art Museum** and the **National Elk Refuge,** where you'll see elk by the thousands in the winter and other wildlife such as trumpeter swans in the summer. Head north on U.S. 191 to **Moose.** Stop at the Grand Teton National Park visitor center, then visit **Menor's Ferry** and the **Chapel of the Transfiguration,** before continuing north on Teton Park Road to **Jenny Lake** and **Jackson Lake.** You can have a great lunch at either location. Spend the afternoon fishing, boating, or hiking. For a great view of Jackson Hole, drive to the top of **Signal Mountain** before returning to Jackson. Spend the evening in Jackson. For a western meal and program try dinner at the **Bar J Chuckwagon,** then kick up your heels at one of Jackson's great Western bars.

Early on your second day take U.S. 191 north through **Grand Teton National Park** ④ to Moran Junction, then head toward **Yellowstone National Park** ⑤. Once in the park go first to **Old Faithful.** Plan to spend the morning there, walking the geyser basin boardwalks and watching the eruption of Old Faithful. Have lunch before continuing north toward **Norris Geyser Basin.** Continue north on the Upper Loop to **Mammoth Hot Springs,** follow the figure-eight road system back to the east and Tower Junction, then head south again toward Canyon Village. It's easy to lose track of time in the geyser basins, so if you decide to spend a couple of hours exploring Norris, drive directly east to Canyon Village, skipping the Upper Loop Road entirely. Either way, expect to spend the rest of the afternoon at the **Grand Canyon of the Yellowstone.** Hike to the lookout points for the Yellowstone Falls. You can spend the night at Canyon or continue south to the elegant historic hotel at Lake Village on **Yellowstone Lake.** You'll travel about 160 mi if you take the short loop and will add 60 mi if you do the full circle.

On your third day, you have a choice to make. You may either complete the Yellowstone loop and return to **Grand Teton National Park** ④ and **Jackson** ① where shopping opportunities abound; or you may head east over Sylvan Pass and take U.S. 14/16/20 to **Cody** ⑥. If flying into Jackson and out of Cody isn't a problem or if you are driving, then heading to Cody is the recommended direction. Plan to spend the day there. Visit **Old Trail Town** in the morning, have lunch at the **Irma**

Wyoming

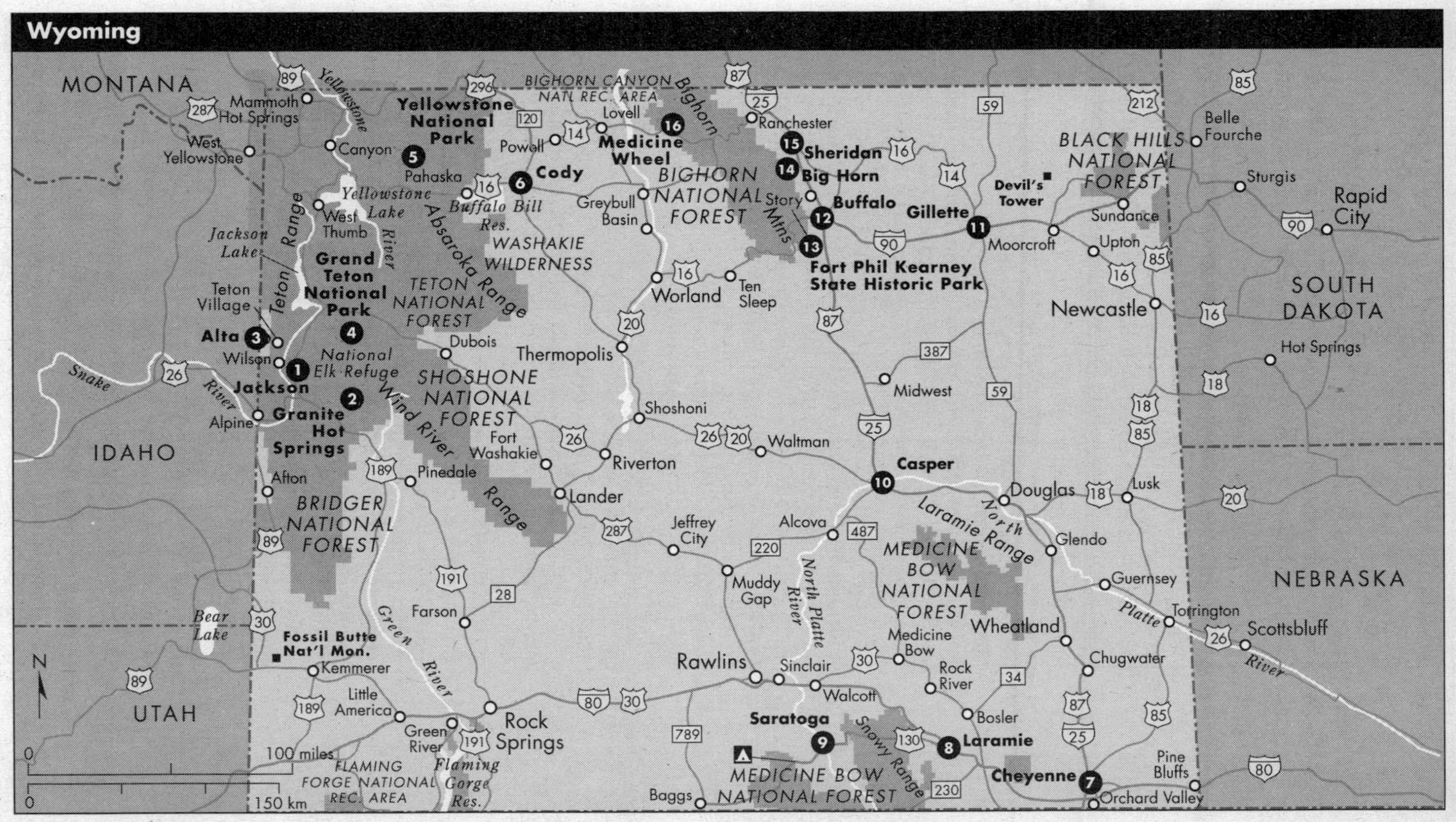
MONTANA
SOUTH DAKOTA
NEBRASKA
IDAHO
UTAH
Mammoth Hot Springs
West Yellowstone
Yellowstone
Canyon
Yellowstone National Park
5
Pahaska
Yellowstone Lake
West Thumb
River
Jackson Lake
Teton Range
Grand Teton National Park
4
Teton Village
Alta 3
Wilson
1 Jackson
National Elk Refuge
2 Granite Hot Springs
Alpine
Snake River
Absaroka Range
TETON NATIONAL FOREST
Dubois
SHOSHONE NATIONAL FOREST
Wind River Range
Afton
Pinedale
BRIDGER NATIONAL FOREST
Bear Lake
Fossil Butte Nat'l Mon.
Kemmerer
Little America
Green River
Farson
Rock Springs
Flaming Gorge Res.
FLAMING GORGE NATIONAL REC. AREA
100 miles
150 km
N
BIGHORN CANYON NAT'L REC. AREA
Powell
6 Cody
Buffalo Bill Res.
WASHAKIE WILDERNESS
Lovell
16 Medicine Wheel
Bighorn
Greybull
Basin
BIGHORN NATIONAL FOREST
Worland
Ten Sleep
Thermopolis
Shoshoni
Fort Washakie
Riverton
Lander
Waltman
Jeffrey City
Muddy Gap
Alcova
North Platte River
Rawlins
Sinclair
Walcott
Saratoga 9
MEDICINE BOW NATIONAL FOREST
Snowy Range
Baggs
Ranchester
15 Sheridan
14 Big Horn
Story
12 Buffalo
13 Fort Phil Kearney State Historic Park
Mtns
Gillette 11
Moorcroft
Devil's Tower
BLACK HILLS NATIONAL FOREST
Sundance
Upton
Newcastle
Midwest
Casper 10
Douglas
Laramie Range
North
MEDICINE BOW NATIONAL FOREST
Medicine Bow
Rock River
Bosler
8 Laramie
Cheyenne 7
Wheatland
Chugwater
Glendo
Guernsey
Lusk
Platte River
Torrington
Pine Bluffs
Orchard Valley
Belle Fourche
Sturgis
Rapid City
Hot Springs
Scottsbluff

Hotel, then devote your entire afternoon to the **Buffalo Bill Historical Center** with its four museums dedicated to Buffalo Bill, Plains Indians, firearms, and Western art.

IF YOU HAVE 7 DAYS

You can easily spend a full week exploring the sights in the three-day itinerary, spending several nights in Jackson or staying in Grand Teton before heading on to Yellowstone. If you want to see more of Wyoming's varied regions, however, we recommend that you start in Cheyenne. This suggested tour begins in southeastern Wyoming, and takes you from the area dominated by the Union Pacific Railroad to central Wyoming, marked by the ruts of the Oregon–California–Mormon trails. Then you can continue toward the northeast and the lands dominated historically by the Northern Plains Indians, before touring the two national parks.

Get to know Wyoming's cowboy and Old West heritage on your first morning in **Cheyenne** ⑦ at the **Old West Museum** and the **Wyoming State Capitol.** Then take Route 210 to **Laramie** ⑧, where you can visit the **Laramie Plains Museum** and do some shopping in the restored Landmark Square downtown. Have lunch, then continue west on the **Snowy Range Scenic Byway** (Route 130) to **Saratoga** ⑨. Have dinner at the Hotel Wolf, then spend the evening relaxing in the hot mineral **Hobo Pool.**

Leave early on your second day, taking Route 130 to I–80. Head west to Rawlins, then turn north on U.S. 287 and Route 220 toward **Casper.** Stop to visit sites on the **Oregon** and **Mormon trails,** including Independence Rock and the new Martin's Cove Visitor Center on the historic **Sun Ranch.** Depending on how much time you want to spend at the trail sites, you may want to take a lunch. It takes about three hours to drive from Saratoga to Casper, without stops. Or you can plan to have lunch in **Casper** ⑩. Spend the afternoon at **Fort Caspar Historic Site,** and exploring the city.

On your third day, venture into the region where the greatest Plains Indian wars of the 1860s occurred. Take I–25 north to **Buffalo** ⑫, where you can visit the **Jim Gatchell Memorial Museum,** an unusually interesting local institution. Have lunch in Buffalo then head 12 mi north of Buffalo to Exit 44. Three miles on U.S. 87 and Route 193 will bring you to **Fort Phil Kearny State Historic Site** ⑬. Once you've had a chance to tour the visitor center and fort location, you might want to visit nearby sites of the Fetterman Massacre and the Wagon Box Fight (the visitor center can provide detailed directions). Take U.S. 87 north to Story and detour on Route 332 to **Big Horn** ⑭, where you can visit the **Bradford Brinton Memorial,** one of the West's finest ranches. Then return to U.S. 87 and drive north to **Sheridan** ⑮. Spend the late afternoon shopping, at the museum at **King Ropes and Saddlery,** or at the **Trail End State Historic Site.**

On day four, head north on I–90 from Sheridan to Ranchester, then take scenic byway Alternate U.S. 14 west over the Bighorns. Take the time to visit the **Medicine Wheel** ⑯, a site sacred to Native Americans, from which you can see the entire Bighorn Basin. Once you've visited the Medicine Wheel, continue west down the hairpin turns of Alternate U.S. 14, possibly stopping for lunch at Lovell or Powell before heading in to **Cody** ⑥ (☞ Northwest Wyoming). The eastern part of Alternate U.S. 14 (through Bighorn National Forest) is closed in winter; then, you'll have to take the also scenic U.S. 14 from Sheridan to Cody. Plan to spend the late afternoon and evening touring the **Buffalo Bill Historical Center.**

If you like, explore Cody on the morning of your fifth day, then head toward **Yellowstone National Park** ⑤ either on U.S. 14/16/20, which is presently under construction, causing some delays; or take Route 120 north to Route 196, the **Chief Joseph Scenic Byway,** and follow it to Cooke City, Montana, and Yellowstone's northeast gate. Proceed to **Mammoth Hot Springs** for lunch, then head south toward **Norris** and **Old Faithful,** spending the afternoon exploring the two geyser basins. Spend the night at 🏨 **Old Faithful.**

On day six, backtrack to **Canyon Village** so you can experience the wonders of the **Grand Canyon** of the Yellowstone, then swing around to the southeast toward **Lake Village** before turning west and following the shore of Yellowstone Lake to West Thumb Junction. Continue south along U.S. 89/191/287 to **Grand Teton National Park** ④. Depending on your timing, you can have lunch at Lake Hotel in Yellowstone, or at the Jackson Lake Lodge in Grand Teton. Spend your afternoon exploring Grand Teton, hiking near **Jenny Lake,** boating on **Jackson Lake,** or visiting historic sites, such as **Menor's Ferry** and the **Chapel of the Transfiguration.** Arrive in 🏨 **Jackson** ① by early evening for dinner and perhaps dancing at one of the town's Western watering holes.

Spend your final day in **Jackson** ①. Visit the **Jackson Hole Museum** or the **National Wildlife Art Museum,** shop the many varied stores around the town square, or take a drive over to Wilson and the Teton Village area, where you can ride the tram to the top of the peaks for a spectacular view of the region.

When to Tour Wyoming

The best time to tour Wyoming is summer or fall, because the high mountain country gets lots of snow in the winter, and spring hardly exists. July and August are your best bets for a chance to see any particular location without fear of driving through a snowstorm, but even then be aware that it can and does snow every month of the year in the mountains. Fall can be a perfect time to visit Wyoming. Summer crowds have diminished, the days are warm and the nights are cool. Mid-September usually brings the first snowstorm of the season, followed by an Indian summer of calm days and cool temperatures. Some mountain passes, such as the Snowy Range Scenic Byway, close in the winter. Many of Wyoming's museums also close or have limited winter hours. Yellowstone National Park roads generally close by early October and don't reopen until late April or early May. Winter activities on snowmobiles, snow coaches, and cross-country skis are allowed generally from December through February. Grand Teton National Park also closes by late fall and doesn't reopen until April. Before Memorial Day, services in both parks are limited.

Summertime abounds in local celebrations and festivals. Some of the biggest are the **Cheyenne Frontier Days** in late July; nightly rodeos in Cody from June through August; and the **Cody Stampede** the Fourth of July, featuring rodeos and a parade. Most county fairs occur in August, although the Central Wyoming Fair in Casper is held in mid-July. The **Woodchoppers Jamboree** involves a rodeo and contests for lumberjacks the third full weekend in June in Encampment. Mountain men and women hold a **rendezvous** (named for the gatherings of fur trappers) along the Green River near Pinedale in mid-July and on the Blacks Fork at Fort Bridger over Labor Day. The Fort Bridger rendezvous is one of the largest in the entire Rocky Mountain region. Jackson holds festivals of varied types of art, ranging from modern to Western, during September. For snowmobilers and skiers, the winter season is the main attraction. Ice fishing is popular in January on lakes near Saratoga and Casper. In addition to fishing, the **Wild West Winter Carnival** at Boysen State Park near Shoshoni has dog races, a demolition derby, softball, and golf—all on ice.

NORTHWEST WYOMING

Yellowstone's appeal is as strong today as it was in 1872, when the region became the first national park. The numbers of people who want to visit Yellowstone is increasing in both the summer and winter seasons, leading park officials to consider future restrictions on visitation. Part of the wonder for the more than 3 million people who visit lies in the natural wonders: bubbling mud pots, spouting geysers, rushing rivers, spectacular waterfalls, and most of all, the diversity of wildlife. Long known for its elk and buffalo herds, Yellowstone in 1995 again became home for North American wolves, in an expensive, experimental repopulation program. The last wild wolves to roam the region had been killed by hunters during the 1930s, so the return of the carnivore drew worldwide attention. Although some of the wolves left the park, and were subsequently killed either illegally or by wildlife officials, the majority remained in the park, where they've formed new packs and have had new litters.

Travelers are recognizing that the wild beauty extends beyond the artificial boundaries of the park. They hike in June among the colorful explosions of wildflowers near Togwotee Pass in the Bridger-Teton National Forest north of Dubois, or ride horses in the Wapiti Valley near Cody. They raft down the white water of the Hoback River south of Jackson and shoot—with cameras—the herds of elk that gather at the National Elk Refuge.

Yellowstone's diversions aren't limited to those of the natural world. Yellowstone's so-called "gateway" towns, including Jackson to the south, Cody to the east, and Dubois to the southeast, have developed their own attractions, some of them cultural, and have improved their accommodations as well. They are also dealing with their own population explosion, as more and more people decide to relocate or build vacation homes in this country they love to visit. Attempting to cope with growth and control their destinies, communities have begun to debate how much and what kind of development is desirable. The effort to find a balance between saving the untrammeled wonders of the region and playing host to a curious, eager—and sometimes jealous—tide of visitors is one of the civic challenges here as the 21st century begins. The sites below are organized as a possible trip from Jackson and Grand Teton through Yellowstone to Cody.

Jackson

❶ *33 mi south of Grand Teton National Park's Colter Bay Visitor Center on U.S. 89/191/287.*

The largest number of visitors to Northwest Wyoming come to Jackson, which remains a small Western town, "howdy" in the daytime and hopping in the evening. For outdoor types, it's a place to stock up on supplies before heading out for white-water rafting, backpacking, mountain climbing, or, in the winter, skiing. For tourists, there's a wealth of galleries and Western-wear shops and, at night, varied cuisines and no shortage of bars and music. The lifestyle attracts visitors, and the air service to the town is the best in northwest Wyoming, with multiple flights daily.

Jackson's charm and popularity put it at risk. On busy summer days, traffic can slow to a crawl where the highway doglegs through downtown. Proposals for new motels and condominiums sprout like the purple asters in the spring, as developers vie for a share of the vacation market. Old-timers suggest that the town—in fact, the entire Teton Valley—has already lost the dusty charm it had when horses parked around the Town Square. However, with national parks and forests and state lands occupying some of the most beautiful real estate, there's only so much ground to build on. These limitations, along with the cautious approach of locals, may keep Jackson on a human scale.

Start a tour of Jackson at the **Town Square,** which has tall shade trees and, at the corners, arches woven from hundreds of elk antlers. In the winter, Christmas lights adorn the arches, and during the summer, there's a melodramatic "shoot-out" every evening at 6:30. Stagecoach rides originate here during the day.

Three miles north of town, the **National Wildlife Art Museum** (✉ 2820 Rungius Rd., ☎ 307/733–5771) is just what it sounds like. Among the paintings and sculptures of bighorn sheep, elk, and other animals of the West are works by famous artists such as George Catlin and Charles M. Russell. For local history, visit the **Jackson Hole Museum** (✉ Box 1005, corner of Glenwood and Deloney Sts., ☎ 307/733–2414).

More than 7,000 elk, many with enormous antler racks, winter in the **National Elk Refuge,** just north of Jackson. Horse-drawn sleigh rides to visit the huge herd are offered in the winter. The elk sit calmly as sleighs loaded with families and alfalfa pellets move in their midst. Dress warmly. Throughout the year, visitors drive up Refuge Road (well east of the herd in winter) for a view of Teton Valley, and sometimes camp at Curtis Creek Campground. ✉ *Elk Refuge Visitor Center, 2820 Rungius Rd., 3 mi north of Jackson at the National Wildlife Art Museum,* ☎ *307/733–0277.* 🎟 *Sleigh rides: $8.* ⏲ *Year-round; sleigh rides, Dec. 15–Apr.*

South of Jackson, concerted local and national efforts have preserved both the wildlands and the ranches that dot the Teton Valley floor. The Snake River turns west and the contours steepen; by Hoback Junction there's white-water excitement. The highway provides good views of the river's twists and turns and the life-jacketed rafters and kayakers who float the canyon. About 13 mi south of Jackson at Hoback Junction, turn east on U.S. 189/191 and follow the Hoback River south up its beautiful canyon. A tributary canyon 10 mi south of the junction is
❷ followed by a well-maintained and marked gravel road to **Granite Hot Springs,** in the Bridger-Teton National Forest, 10 mi east of U.S. 189/191 on Granite Creek Road. Visitors come for the shady, creek-side campground, the pool fed by hot springs, and moderate hikes up Granite Canyon to passes where you get panoramic views of the mountains. In the winter, there is a popular snowmobile trail from the highway.

Dining and Lodging

You can make reservations for most motels in Jackson through two **reservation services**: Central Reservations (☎ 800/443–6931) or Jackson Hole Vacations (☎ 800/223–4059).

$$–$$$ ★ ✕ **The Blue Lion.** Consistently excellent fare is served in this blue clapboard house two blocks from the Town Square. Dishes range from rack of lamb to grilled elk to fresh seafood. Having lunch on the deck is a treat in summer. The restaurant is entirely no-smoking. ✉ *160 N. Millward St.,* ☎ *307/733–3912. AE, D, MC, V.*

$$–$$$ ✕ **Mangy Moose.** Folks pour in off the ski slopes for a lot of food and talk at this two-level restaurant plus bar with an outdoor deck. The place is adorned with antiques, including a full-size stuffed caribou and sleigh suspended from the ceiling. There's a high noise level but decent food of the steaks and burgers variety at fair prices. ✉ *Teton Village,* ☎ *307/733–4913. AE, MC, V.*

$$–$$$ ✕ **Nani's Genuine Pasta House.** The ever-changing menu at this cozy, almost cramped, restaurant may contain braised veal shanks with saffron risotto or other regional Italian cooking. Almost hidden behind

a motel, it's designed to attract gourmets, not tourists. ✉ *240 N. Glenwood St.,* ☎ *307/733–3888. MC, V.*

$$–$$$ ✕ **Sweetwater Restaurant.** Mediterranean meals are served in a log cabin atmosphere, and it works. Start with smoked buffalo carpaccio or eggplant rouille; then go on to lamb dishes, mesquite chicken, or shrimp *spetses* (simmered in tomato and garlic with feta cheese). ✉ *King and Pearl Sts.,* ☎ *307/733–3553. AE, D, DC, MC, V.*

$–$$ ★ ✕ **Bar J Chuckwagon.** The best food buy in the Jackson Hole area is here, where you will get a true Western meal along with some of the best Western entertainment in the region. The meal, served on a tin plate, includes barbecued roast beef, chicken, or rib-eye steak; potatoes; beans; biscuits; applesauce; spice cake; and ranch coffee or lemonade. While eating, you'll be entertained by the Bar J Wranglers, who sing, play instruments, share cowboy stories and poetry, and even yodel. "Lap-size" children eat free. ✉ *Box 2200, 4200 Bar J Chuckwagon Rd., Wilson,* ☎ *307/733–3370. D, MC, V.*

$–$$ ★ ✕ **The Bunnery.** Lunch and dinner are served here in the summer, but it's the breakfasts that are irresistible, whether it's an omelet with Swiss cheese, mushrooms, and sautéed spinach, or a home-baked pastry. It's elbow-to-elbow inside and a brief wait to be seated on busy mornings, but any inconvenience is well worth it. ✉ *130 N. Cache St., Hole-in-the-Wall Mall,* ☎ *307/733–5474. Reservations not accepted. MC, V.*

$–$$ ✕ **Jedediah's House of Sourdough.** This restaurant, a block east of the Town Square, makes breakfast and lunch for the big appetite. There are plenty of "sourjacks" (sourdough flapjacks) and biscuits and gravy, and it has a friendly, elbow-knocking atmosphere. ✉ *135 E. Broadway Ave.,* ☎ *307/733–5671. Reservations not accepted. AE, MC, V. No dinner.*

$–$$ ✕ **Off Broadway.** Stop here for seafood and pasta (Cajun shrimp with black linguine), with a little Thai, wild game, and snazzy neon thrown in. Seating is indoors or out. ✉ *30 King St.,* ☎ *307/733–9777. AE, MC, V.*

$ ✕ **Vista Grande.** At this popular spot, you sometimes have to wait for the generous portions of Mexican-style food. Lovers of hot food will find it a little bland, and at times, it's too crowded and noisy. ✉ *Teton Village Rd. near Wilson turnoff,* ☎ *307/733–6964. Reservations not accepted. MC, V.*

$$$$ ★ 🏨 **Amangani.** Outside of town on Gros Ventre Butte, enjoying an atmosphere of Eastern simplicity and Western hospitality, this luxury resort offers beautiful views of Spring Creek Valley. The amenities here are the best in Jackson Hole and include horseback riding, tennis, and cross-country skiing and sleigh rides in winter. ✉ *1535 N. E. Butte Rd., Box 15030, 83002,* ☎ *307/734–7333 or 877/734–7333,* FAX *307/734–7332. 40 suites. Restaurant, lobby lounge, in-room data ports, in-room safes, minibars, no-smoking rooms, refrigerators, room service, outdoor pool, hot tub, massage, sauna, spa, steam room, 2 tennis courts, health club, horseback riding, cross-country skiing, sleigh rides, library, dry cleaning, concierge, meeting rooms, airport shuttle. AE, D, DC, MC, V.*

$$$$ 🏨 **Days Inn.** Like other chains, this motel is something familiar, but the lodgepole swing out front, the lobby's elk-antler chandelier, and the rooms' Teton-, Wind River–, or Snake River–range views remind you where you are. Some rooms have microwaves and fridges, and a Continental breakfast is included. ✉ *350 S. Hwy. 89, 83001,* ☎ *307/739–9010,* FAX *307/733–0044. 91 rooms. Hot tub, sauna. AE, D, DC, MC, V.*

$$$$ ★ 🏨 **Wort Hotel.** This brick Victorian hotel near the Town Square seems to have been around as long as the Tetons, but it feels fresh inside. A fireplace warms the lobby, and a sitting area is just up the stairs. Each room has locally made, Western-style furniture, including pole beds and pine dressers, with carpets, drapes, and bedcoverings in warm, muted tones

such as blues and mauves. You can sip a drink in the Silver Dollar Bar—aptly named for the 2,032 silver dollars imbedded on top of the bar—or sit down for a fine meal. Try the mixed grill of buffalo and elk medallions or the nightly veal special. ✉ *50 N. Glenwood St., 83001,* ☎ *307/733–2190 or 800/322–2727,* FAX *307/733–2067. 60 rooms. Restaurant, bar, hot tub, exercise room, meeting room. AE, D, DC, MC, V.*

$$$–$$$$ 🏨 **Alpenhof.** This small Austrian-style hotel is in the heart of the Jackson Hole Ski Resort next to the tram. The deluxe rooms have balconies, hand-carved Bavarian furniture, and cream-color walls; each has an in-room phone and televisions. Standard rooms are smaller, and don't have balconies, but they do have the hand-carved Bavarian furniture. The dining room features such entrées as wild game loaf, and Dietrich's Bar and Bistro is a relatively quiet nightclub—considering its proximity to the slopes—that also offers casual dining. ✉ *Box 288, Teton Village 83025,* ☎ *307/733–3242,* FAX *307/739–1516. 43 rooms. Dining room, bar, pool, whirlpool, massage, ski storage, nightclub. AE, D, DC, MC, V. Closed Oct., Nov., and mid-Apr.–May.*

$$$–$$$$ 🏨 **Spring Creek Ranch.** Outside town on Gros Ventre Butte, this luxury resort offers beautiful views of the Tetons and a number of amenities, including cooking in some units, horseback riding, and tennis, as well as cross-country skiing and sleigh rides in winter. Aside from 36 hotel rooms, there's a changing mix of studios, suites, and condos with lofts, called "Choates." The comfortable restaurant, the **Granary** (reservations essential), serves fine food and is slightly more expensive than the resort; lead off with Dungeness crab and Havarti cheese wrapped in phyllo dough, followed by poached salmon with a cucumber dill sauce and wild rice. ✉ *1800 Spirit Dance Rd., Box 4780, 83001,* ☎ *307/733–8833 or 800/443–6139,* FAX *307/733–1524. 36 rooms, 76 studios and suites. Restaurant, kitchenettes, outdoor pool, 2 tennis courts, horseback riding, cross-country skiing, sleigh rides. AE, D, DC, MC, V.*

$$$ 🏨 **Painted Porch Bed and Breakfast.** Cozy, clean, and comfortable, this traditional red-and-white farmhouse built in 1901 is nestled on 3½ acres of pine and aspen 8 mi out of town. There are actually four porches and a white picket fence, along with Japanese soaking tubs. Full breakfast is included. ✉ *Box 6955, 83002,* ☎ *307/733–1981,* FAX *307/733–1564. 4 rooms. Library. MC, V.*

$$–$$$ 🏨 **Pony Express.** Rooms are standard motel rooms, but some have mountain views, while others have patios. The center of town is just two blocks away. ✉ *505 Millward Ave., 83001,* ☎ *307/733–2658,* FAX *307/739–0149. 41 rooms. Hot tub. AE, D, MC, V. Closed during winter.*

Nightlife

There is never a shortage of live music in Jackson, where local performers play country, rock, and folk. Some of the most popular bars are on the Town Square. At the **Million Dollar Cowboy Bar** (✉ 25 N. Cache St., ☎ 307/733–2207), everyone dresses up in cowboy garb and tries to two-step into the Old West. The renowned Wyoming band Bruce Hauser and Sawmill Creek often performs at the **Rancher Bar** (✉ 20 E. Broadway Ave., ☎ 307/733–3886).

A special treat is down the road from Jackson at the **Stagecoach Bar** (✉ Rte. 22, Wilson, ☎ 307/733–4407), which fills to bursting Sunday when the house band—a motley bunch that includes a novelist, the first man to ski down the Grand Teton, and a changing cast of guitar aces—is playing.

Outdoor Activities and Sports

CAMPING

There's great camping in **Bridger-Teton National Forest** (✉ 340 N. Cache St., Box 1888, Jackson 83001, ☎ 307/739–5500, FAX 307/739–5010), including **Curtis Canyon,** east of the National Elk Refuge, and **Granite Creek,** just below the hot springs near the Hoback River.

CANOEING, KAYAKING, AND RAFTING

Past Jackson, where the Hoback joins the Snake River and the canyon walls become steep, there are lively white-water sections. Guided raft trips here will thrill and douse you. Experienced paddlers run the Hoback, too.

If you want instruction in the fine art of paddling, contact **Snake River Kayak and Canoe** (✉ Box 3482, Jackson 83001, ☎ 307/733–3127 or 800/529–2501). Take lessons or rent canoes and kayaks from **Teton Aquatics** (✉ 155 W. Gill Ave., Jackson 83001, ☎ 307/733–3127). If you'd rather be a passenger, traveling the peaceful parts of the river looking for wildlife, contact **Barker-Ewing Scenic Float Trips** (✉ Box 100–J, Moose 83012, ☎ 307/733–1800 or 800/365–1800). **Triangle X Float Trips** (✉ Moose 83012, ☎ 307/733–2138) also offers more subdued river trips. For wet and wild stretches of river, get in touch with **Lewis & Clark Expeditions** (✉ 145 W. Gill St., Box 720, Jackson 83001, ☎ 307/733–4022 or 800/824–5375). **Barker-Ewing Float Trips** (✉ 45 W. Broadway, Box 3032, Jackson 83001, ☎ 800/448–4204) tackles the wilder stuff. **Mad River Boat Trips** (✉ 1060 S. U.S. 89, Box 2222, Jackson 83001, ☎ 307/733–6203 or 800/458–7238), which worked on *A River Runs Through It* (directed by Robert Redford), leads a variety of white-water trips.

CYCLING

Cyclists ride the **Spring Gulch Road,** part pavement, part dirt, off Route 22, along the base of Gros Ventre Butte, rejoining U.S. 26/89/191 near the Gros Ventre River. The trip up to **Lower Slide Lake,** north of town, is also a favorite. Turn east off U.S. 26/89/191 to Kelly, and then take the Slide Lake Road. Bike rentals and sales are available at **Teton Cyclery** (✉ 175 N. Glenwood St., ☎ 307/733–4386).

GOLF

Jackson Hole Golf and Tennis Club (✉ 5000 Spring Gulch Rd., ☎ 307/733–3111) is a championship 18-hole course near the Jackson Hole Airport, with tennis, fly-fishing, horseback riding, and swimming facilities. The 18-hole **Teton Pines Golf Club** (✉ 3450 N. Clubhouse St., ☎ 307/733–1733) is just south of the Jackson Hole Ski Resort.

SKIING

Cross-country skiing and snowshoeing are permitted in parts of Yellowstone and Grand Teton national parks and surrounding forests. Among the best places is **Togwotee Pass,** east of Jackson on U.S. 26/287, in Bridger-Teton and Shoshone national forests. Lessons and groomed trails are available for a fee at **Spring Creek Ranch** (☞ Dining and Lodging, *above*). **Jackson Hole Nordic Center** (✉ Teton Village, ☎ 307/733–2292; ☞ Chapter 2) also has trails and lessons. There's downhill skiing at **Jackson Hole Ski Resort** (☞ Chapter 2).

SNOWMOBILING

Information on snowmobile rentals and guides is available from the Jackson Hole Chamber of Commerce (☞ Contacts and Resources, *below*).

Shopping

Jackson's peaceful **Town Square** is surrounded by storefronts with a mixture of specialty and outlet shops—most of them small-scale—with moderate to expensive prices. Try **Jackson Hole Clothiers** (✉ 45 E. Deloney Ave., ☎ 307/733–7211), for women's Western wear and hand-knit sweaters. **Hide Out Leather** (✉ 40 N. Center St., ☎ 307/733–2422) carries many local designs. **Cattle Kate** (✉ 120 E. Broadway Ave., ☎ 307/733–4803) produces some of the best designs in contemporary Western wear for women—based on historic styles—on the market today. The store also carries a few men's accessories.

Just north of Jackson's center, on Cache Street, is a small cluster of fine shops in **Gaslight Alley.** One of Gaslight Alley's best shops is **Valley Books** (✉ 125 N. Cache St., ☎ 307/733–4533). It ranks among the best bookstores in the region, with a big selection and salespeople who can talk Tolstoy while guiding you to the best publications on local subjects.

Jackson's art galleries serve a range of tastes. The fine nature photography of Tom Mangelson is displayed at his **Images of Nature Gallery** (✉ 170 N. Cache St., ☎ 307/733–9752). **Trailside Americana** (✉ 105 N. Center St., ☎ 307/733–3186) has more traditional Western art and jewelry.

In Teton Village (the cluster of buildings at the base of the Jackson Hole Ski Resort, 15 mi northwest of Jackson), the **Mountainside Mall,** not to be mistaken for a big suburban mall (to its credit), serves the resort crowd.

Jackson is well stocked with the best in outdoor equipment, winter and summer, including standout **Jack Dennis Sports** (✉ 50 E. Broadway Ave., ☎ 307/733–3270), Jackson's premier sports shop, an internationally known fishing and sporting headquarters. **Skinny Skis** (✉ 65 W. Deloney Ave., ☎ 307/733–6094) offers everything a cross-country skier might need. **Teton Mountaineering** (✉ 170 N. Cache, ☎ 307/733–3595) specializes in Nordic skiing, climbing, and hiking equipment and clothing. **Westbank Anglers** (✉ Box 523, Teton Village, ☎ 307/733–6483) fulfills fly-fishing dreams.

Alta

❸ *31 mi northwest of Jackson, Rte. 22 to Rte. 33 (in Idaho) to Alta cutoff (back to Wyoming).*

Alta is home to the Grand Targhee Ski and Summer Resort, famed for its deep powder and family atmosphere. The slopes never feel crowded. But to experience complete solitude, try a day of Sno-Cat skiing in untracked powder. There are three lifts and one rope tow, and a vertical drop of 2,200 ft.

Dining and Lodging

$$–$$$$ ✕🏨 **Grand Targhee Ski and Summer Resort.** Perched on the west side of the Tetons, this small but modern facility has the uncrowded, stroll-around atmosphere of a small village in the Alps. The motel-style rooms are simply furnished and clustered around common areas with fireplaces; the condominium rooms are brighter and more spacious. The resort has a handsome, natural-wood look. Expansion plans are on the drawing board, but the permit process with the U.S. Forest Service may take several years. **Skadi's** *(see below)* is the resort's foremost restaurant; the **Cactus Kitchen** has quicker, less expensive food. ✉ *Box SKI, Alta 83422,* ☎ *307/353–2300 or 800/827–4433. 97 rooms: 65 motel-style, 32 condos. 5 restaurants, pool, hot tub, outdoor hot tub, cross-country skiing. AE, D, MC, V.*

$$–$$$ ✕ **Skadi's.** This is the foremost restaurant at Grand Targhee Ski and Summer Resort. It's a relaxing, well-lighted place with Southwestern-style decor, high ceilings, and a general feel of roominess. On the menu are tenderloin beef with *poblano* chili sauce and regional game dishes including venison and pheasant. ✉ *Grand Targhee Ski and Summer Resort, Ski Hill Road, Alta,* ☎ *307/353–2300 or 800/827–4433. AE, D, MC, V.*

Grand Teton National Park

❹ *23 mi from Yellowstone National Park (south entrance) to Colter Bay Visitor Center on the John D. Rockefeller Parkway, U.S. 89/191/287.*

One might think this smaller park with a shorter history is dwarfed by its northern neighbor—Yellowstone—but nothing overshadows peaks like these. Presumably no translation of the French is necessary. The peaks—Mt. Moran, Teewinot Mountain, Mt. Owen, the Grand, and Middle Teton—form a magnificent and dramatic front along the west side of the Teton Valley. Lakes large and small are strung along the range's base, draining north into Jackson Lake, which in turn drains south into the Snake River. **Grand Teton** was put together from ranches John D. Rockefeller, Jr., bought up in the 1930s. It has a few oddities within its boundaries, such as a commercial airport and a dam to hold water for Idaho irrigators, but for fishing, hiking, climbing, boating, and rugged beauty, it's hard to match. ✉ *National Park Service, Moose 83012,* ☎ *307/739–3300 or* ☎ *TTY 307/733–2053, www.nps.gov/grte/.* 🎫 *7-day pass good for both Yellowstone and Grand Teton National Parks: $20 per motor vehicle, $10 non-motorized entry permit, $15 motorcycle or snowmobile; $40 annual permit; Golden Age and Golden Eagle permits accepted.*

Exploration of Grand Teton National Park generally occurs either from the south—Jackson—or from the north at Yellowstone National Park. For our purposes we've imagined a trip starting in Jackson. By starting from the south you can make your first stop at **Moose**, which is park headquarters and site of a visitor center, where you can get a good, quick overview of the park.

Just north of the Moose visitor center turn east to **Menor's Ferry**. The ferry on display is not the original, but it is an accurate re-creation of the one built by Bill Menor in the 1890s and demonstrates how people crossed the Snake River before bridges were built. Several cabins, including the home and store used by Bill Menor, who also operated the ferry, remain at the site; the Menor home is operated as a park gift shop. There is an historic photo collection in one of the cabins.

One parking lot serves both Menor's Ferry and the nondenominational **Chapel of the Transfiguration**, where the view of the Tetons brings couples from all over the world to say their vows.

North of Moose, Menor's Ferry, and the Chapel of the Transfiguration is **Jenny Lake**, right below the Grand Teton. You can hike on an easy–moderate trail 2 mi around the lake from the parking area at the south end to Hidden Falls. The trail is steeper from there to Inspiration Point, but then it levels off. The views are increasingly spectacular as you hike the canyon. The trail continues to Lake Solitude, but it's 9 mi from the trailhead to the lake, so be sure to allow plenty of time. You can make the walk miles shorter by taking a boat ride (☞ Outdoor Activities and Sports, *below*) from the dock near the parking area to the Cascade Canyon Trailhead.

There are many easy hikes heading off toward the mountains from Teton Park Road. (They're shown on the map in *Teewinot,* the free publication handed out at the entrances.) One of the nicest, south of Jenny Lake, is to Taggart Lake. The **Taggart Lake Trail** is an easy–moderate 1.6 mi hike from the trailhead to the lake. If you continue around the lake, the terrain is steeper near Beaver Creek and the entire loop is 4 mi. There are views of Avalanche Canyon, and you will probably see moose along the route; be sure to keep your distance. Hikers as well as canoeists enjoy **Leigh and String lakes,** which have short hikes to

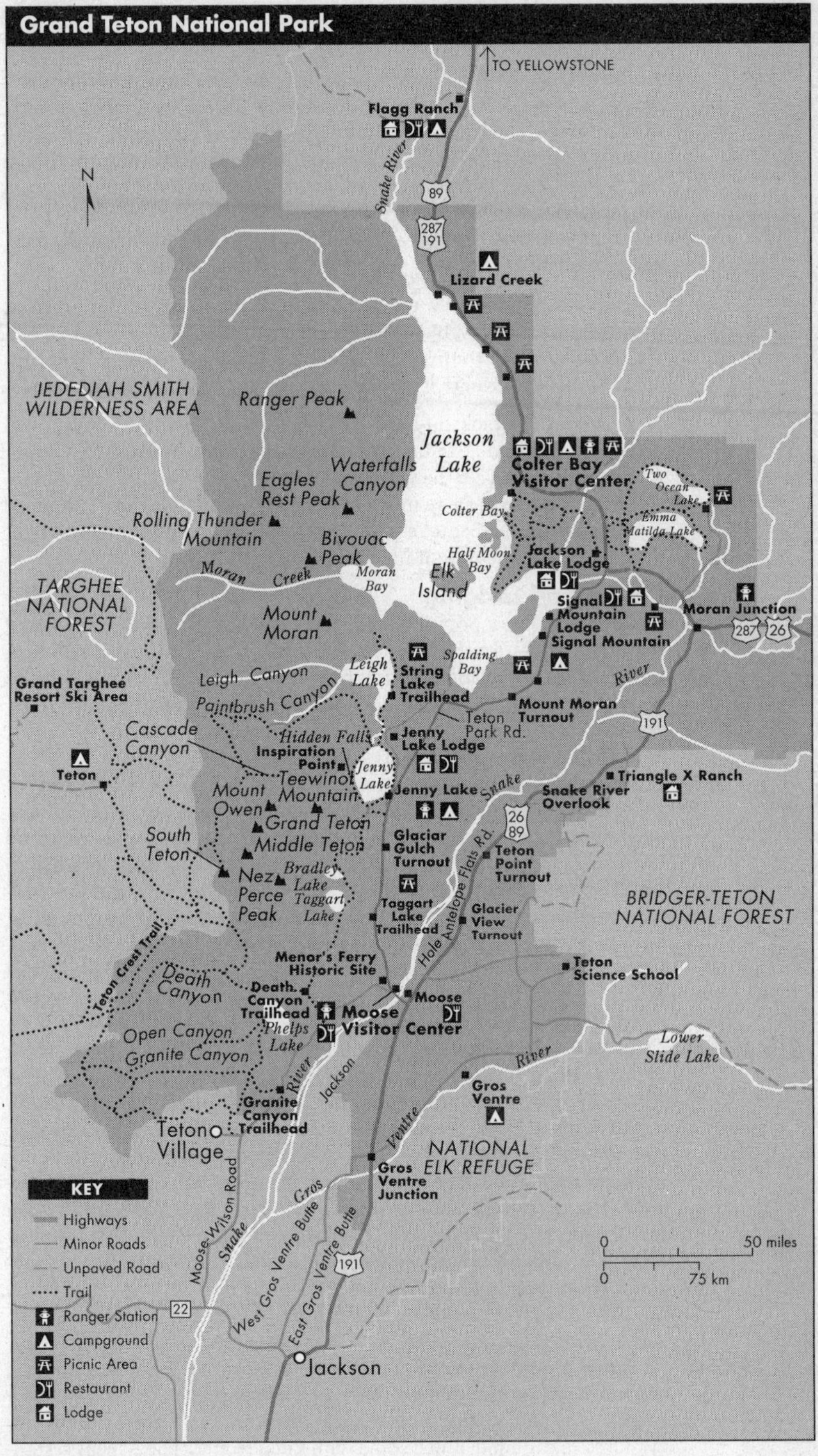
Grand Teton National Park
TO YELLOWSTONE
Flagg Ranch
Snake River
89
287
191
N
Lizard Creek
JEDEDIAH SMITH
WILDERNESS AREA
Ranger Peak
Jackson
Lake
Colter Bay
Visitor Center
Waterfalls
Canyon
Eagles
Rest Peak
Two
Ocean
Lake
Colter Bay
Emma
Matilda Lake
Rolling Thunder
Mountain
Bivouac
Peak
Half Moon
Bay
Jackson
Lake Lodge
Moran
Creek
Moran
Bay
Elk
Island
TARGHEE
NATIONAL
FOREST
Signal
Mountain
Lodge
Moran Junction
287
26
Mount
Moran
Signal Mountain
Spalding
Bay
Grand Targhee
Resort Ski Area
Leigh Canyon
Leigh
Lake
String
Lake
Trailhead
River
Mount Moran
Turnout
Paintbrush Canyon
Teton
Park Rd.
191
Cascade
Canyon
Hidden Falls
Inspiration
Point
Jenny
Lake Lodge
Teton
Teewinot
Mountain
Jenny
Lake
Triangle X Ranch
Jenny Lake
Snake
Snake River
Overlook
Mount
Owen
Grand Teton
26
89
South
Teton
Middle Teton
Glacier
Gulch
Turnout
Teton
Point
Turnout
Bradley
Lake
Nez
Perce
Peak
Taggart
Lake
Taggart
Lake
Trailhead
Antelope Flats Rd.
Glacier
View
Turnout
BRIDGER-TETON
NATIONAL FOREST
Teton Crest Trail
Hole
Menor's Ferry
Historic Site
Teton
Science School
Death
Canyon
Death
Canyon
Trailhead
Moose
Moose
Visitor Center
Phelps
Lake
Open Canyon
Granite Canyon
Lower
Slide Lake
River
Jackson
River
Gros
Ventre
Granite
Canyon
Trailhead
Teton
Village
Ventre
NATIONAL
ELK REFUGE
Gros
Ventre
Junction
KEY
Highways
Minor Roads
Unpaved Road
Trail
Ranger Station
Campground
Picnic Area
Restaurant
Lodge
Moose-Wilson Road
Snake
Gros
West Gros Ventre Butte
East Gros Ventre Butte
191
22
0
50 miles
0
75 km
Jackson

and around them, just north of Jenny Lake; turn west at North Jenny Lake Junction.

At the north end of the park is **Jackson Lake**. The biggest of the park's glacier-scooped lakes, it was made larger still by a dam, farther south, built in 1909. The lake is popular with sailors, anglers, and even windsurfers. Campgrounds and lodges dot the shore (☞ Dining and Lodging, *below*). Near Jackson Lake Junction, the Snake River emerges from the Jackson Lake Dam and winds east and then south through the park. Whether you're on the water or on shore, **Oxbow Bend**, below the dam, is an excellent place to see waterfowl and other wildlife.

U.S. 26/89/191 does run the full length of the park, with the Tetons on display all the way, but at this point (Jackson Lake Junction), a better, more leisurely route is the smaller **Teton Park Road**, which runs south to Moose, where it rejoins the highway heading to Jackson.

Not far south of Jackson Lake Junction on the Teton Park Road, you can take a brief side trip up narrow **Signal Mountain Road** to its summit, where you can see the valley and mountains on all sides. The mountain gets its name from an incident in 1891, when a local man drowned in the Snake River. Searchers looking for him agreed they would light a signal fire on the mountain when they found him.

Dining and Lodging

$–$$ ✕ **Dornan's.** This popular local hangout has Old West decor and mountain views. In the summer, it cooks up an outdoor Dutch-oven buffet (steak, ribs, and cowboy beans) and a friendly atmosphere to go with it. Meals are served outside and can be eaten at picnic tables, or inside tepees. A good wine shop is adjacent. ✉ *U.S. 191, Moose,* ☎ *307/733–2415. BYOB. MC, V.*

$$$$ ★ **Jenny Lake Lodge.** In this most exclusive of the park's resorts, elegant yet rustic cabins are bedecked with handmade quilts (and electric blankets). Overnight guests are on the American plan; two meals a day are included, as are horseback riding, bicycling, and other outdoor activities. The lodge dining room offers a set dinner menu with a choice of entrées emphasizing Rocky Mountain cuisine, including roast prime rib of buffalo or breast of pheasant with pheasant sausage. ✉ *Jenny Lake Rd., Grand Teton Lodge Co., Box 240, Moran 83013,* ☎ *307/733–3100 or 800/628–9988,* FAX *307/543–3143. 37 rooms. Restaurant, bar, horseback riding, boating, bicycles. AE, DC, MC, V. Closed mid-Oct.–early June.*

$$$–$$$$ **Jackson Lake Lodge.** Outside, the resort has a 1950s look, dark brown and low-slung. Inside, two large fireplaces adorn the lounge, Native American designs decorate the walls, and huge picture windows look out at Willow Flats, below Jackson Lake Dam. There are 30 smaller rooms in the main lodge; the others, in one-story motor-lodge-style buildings, are preferable. The lodge boasts the only swimming pool in the park. Rotating four dinner menus, the Mural Room ($$–$$$) often features buffalo, popular with the largely tourist clientele, as well as local game dishes, such as venison or antelope. ✉ *U.S. 89 north of Jackson Lake Junction, Grand Teton Lodge Co., Box 240, Moran 83013,* ☎ *307/733–3100 or 800/628–9988,* FAX *307/543–3143. 385 rooms. 2 restaurants, bar, pool. AE, DC, MC, V. Closed late Oct.–mid-May.*

$$–$$$$ **Signal Mountain Lodge.** Built of volcanic stone and pine shingles, the lodge sits on the eastern shore of Jackson Lake. The lobby has a fireplace, a piano, and Adirondack furniture, and guest rooms are clustered in cabinlike units, some with kitchenettes. The Aspens restaurant offers up views of the lake and the Tetons as well as a menu with elk medallions and shrimp linguine. ✉ *Teton Park Rd., Box 50, Moran 83013,* ☎ *307/543–2831. 79 rooms. Restaurant, bar, kitchenettes, boating. AE, DC, MC, V. Closed mid-Oct.–early May.*

$–$$$ **Colter Bay Village.** Less expensive than its posher cousins, the Colter Bay Village, near Jackson Lake, has splendid views and an excellent marina and beach for the windsurfing crowd. (You'll need a wet suit.) The cabins have a Western style. The 66 tent cabins aren't fancy and they share communal baths, but they do keep the wind and rain off. There is also a 113-space RV park. The Chuckwagon restaurant is family-oriented, serving lasagna, trout, and barbecue spare ribs, with prices in the $–$$ range. ✉ *Off U.S. 89; mailing address: Grand Teton Lodge Co., Box 240, Moran 83013,* ☎ *307/733–3100 or 800/628–9988,* FAX *307/543–3143. 166 cabins, 66 tent cabins, 113 RV spaces. 2 restaurants, bar, coin laundry. AE, DC, MC, V. Closed early Oct.–late May. (tent cabins have slightly shorter season).*

Nightlife and the Arts

Every summer the **Grand Teton Music Festival** (✉ Box 490, Teton Village Resort, 83025, ☎ 307/733–1128) presents 35 concerts featuring symphonic and chamber music. From January through March performances are held at the National Wildlife Art Museum.

Outdoor Activities and Sports

CAMPING

Grand Teton has five public campgrounds. The most popular is at **Jenny Lake** (✉ Teton Park Rd. at S. Jenny Lake). The most luxurious is **Colter Bay** (✉ On Jackson Lake, 7 mi north of Jackson Lake Lodge), which has showers, RV hookups, and laundry facilities. **Gros Ventre Campground** (✉ 4 mi east of U.S. 26/89/191 at Gros Ventre Junction), on the far eastern side of the park, is so large (360 sites) that it doesn't fill up as fast as the others. Fees range from $12 to $15 per night, but they change constantly.

CANOEING, KAYAKING, AND RAFTING

For river runners, there are peaceful, scenic stretches of the upper **Snake River** in Grand Teton National Park, including the beautiful Oxbow. You can navigate them yourself by canoe or kayak, or float as a passenger on a guided raft. Be sure to check current conditions and ability recommendations with park rangers before you launch.

ECOLOGY

The **Teton Science School** (✉ Box 68, Kelly 83011, ☎ 307/733–4765) offers ecology, park history, and wildlife courses. Contact the school for more information.

MOUNTAIN CLIMBING

Mountain climbers get a leg up in the Grand Tetons from **Jackson Hole Mountain Guides** (✉ 165 N. Glenwood St., Box 7477, Jackson, ☎ 307/733–4979). **Exum Mountain Guides** (✉ South end of Jenny Lake, Box 56, Moose, ☎ 307/733–2297) offers a variety of climbing experiences and instruction.

WATER SPORTS

You can hire canoes and powerboats at **Colter Bay Marina** (✉ North of Jackson Lake Junction, ☎ 307/733–3100). **Signal Mountain Marina** (✉ Teton Park Rd. at the south end of the lake, ☎ 307/543–2831) rents boats. Boats must be licensed by the parks. Seven-day permits, good in Grand Teton and Yellowstone parks, cost $7 for motorboats and $5 for nonmotorized boats.

For boat rides on Jenny Lake contact **Teton Boating Inc.** (✉ Box 1553, Jackson, ☎ 307/733–2703). Rides cost $4. The boats run early June–mid-September, daily 8–6.

Yellowstone National Park

❺ *52 mi from Cody (to east entrance) via North Fork Hwy. (U.S. 14/16/20).*

Few places in the world can match Yellowstone National Park's collection of accessible wonders, from grazing bison and cruising trumpeter swans to rainbow-color hot springs and thundering geysers. As you visit the park's hydrothermal areas, you'll be walking on top of the Yellowstone Caldera—a 28- by 47-mi collapsed volcanic cone, which last erupted about 600,000 years ago. The park's geyser basins, hot mud pots, fumaroles (steam vents), and hot springs are kept bubbling by an underground pressure cooker filled with magma. One geophysicist describes Yellowstone as "a window on the earth's interior." ✉ *Box 168, Yellowstone National Park, WY 82190,* ☎ *307/344–7381 or TTD 307/344–2386;* FAX *307/344–2104; www.nps.gov/yell/.* 🎫 *7-day pass good for both Yellowstone and Grand Teton National Parks: $20 per motor vehicle; $10 non-motorized entry permit; $15 motorcycle or snowmobile; $40 annual permit; Golden Age and Golden Eagle permits accepted.* ⏲ *Year-round to Mammoth; open early May–Sept. in other areas; some roads may open later or close earlier due to snowfall.*

Before you start visiting the sights, assess your desires and abilities. Would you rather hike, drive the roads, or buy a seat on a tour bus? You can sleep in solitude at a backcountry campsite or in luxury at a historic lakeside hotel. Choose between geysers and wildlife or between fishing hip-deep in the Firehole River and boating on Yellowstone Lake. If time is limited, pick a single area, such as the Grand Canyon of the Yellowstone or the Norris Geyser Basin, and don't try to do everything.

The 370 mi of public roads in the park are both a blessing and a curse. They provide access to extraordinary landscapes and wildlife but are often potholed, overcrowded, and dotted with motor homes that have been pulled over on narrow shoulders so that their occupants can photograph grazing elk or buffalo cows with calves. Some roads are under construction. As a result, roads become choked with slow-moving caravans led by big RVs. You can also expect some delays, and periodic road closures.

There are summer-staffed visitor centers throughout the park and a busy schedule of guided hikes, evening talks, and campfire programs. (Check *Discover Yellowstone,* a park newsletter available at entrances and visitor centers, for dates and times.) Pamphlets describing hot-spring basins are available for 25¢ at each site or visitor center. The park has numerous picnic areas and campgrounds, as well as restaurants and lodgings (☞ Dining and Lodging, *below*).

The **South Entrance Road** to Yellowstone National Park enters through Grand Teton National Park, passes Lewis Lake, and follows along the sometimes steep-sided path of the Lewis River. At **West Thumb,** you reach Yellowstone Lake. The park's roads are in a figure-eight pattern and you can follow them in any direction. (Each entrance road links up to the 142-mi figure-eight Grand Loop Road, which includes both the Upper Loop and Lower Loop roads.) We recommend turning toward the northwest at West Thumb and heading toward the geyser basins.

The drive over **Craig Pass,** between West Thumb and Old Faithful, was once the slowest section of the Lower Loop. A recent upgrade and widening are a significant improvement.

The **Upper Geyser Basin** and its centerpiece, **Old Faithful,** is one of Yellowstone's most popular locations, summer and winter. The mysterious plumbing of Yellowstone has lengthened the geyser's cycle somewhat in recent years, but Old Not-So-Faithful spouts a powerful 140-ft spume that pleases faithful spectators every 80 minutes or so. A visitor center nearby posts the approximate time of the next eruption. Marked trails and bridges lead across the river to **Geyser Hill.** You can wander downriver, too, away from crowds, to **Castle Geyser** and **Morning Glory Pool.** Also in the Old Faithful area are two geysers famous for huge, but very rare, eruptions: **Giantess Geyser** and **Giant Geyser.**

At the heart of the tourist development at Old Faithful is **Old Faithful Inn** (☞ Dining and Lodging, *below*), worth a visit even if you aren't staying here. An architectural marvel built in 1903 and later expanded, the log building has a six-story lobby with a huge rock fireplace and wraparound balconies high in the rafters.

Along the Lower Loop north of Old Faithful, there are two distinct geyser areas, beginning with the Old Faithful basin. The **Midway Geyser Basin** has some beautiful, richly colored, bottomless pools: former geysers Grand Prismatic Spring and Excelsior Geyser Crater. **Lower Geyser Basin** features the fumaroles, blue pools, pink mud pots, and minigeysers of **Fountain Paint Pots** (small in scale but great in variety) as well as the **Great Fountain Geyser.**

North of Lower Geyser Basin the Lower Loop follows the steaming Firehole River, providing views at times of elk and bison grazing in the distance. A one-way circuit branches off through the **Firehole River canyon,** which features a spring-warmed swimming hole. At **Madison Junction,** traffic from the popular West Entrance joins the Lower Loop Road. The Lower and Upper Loop roads join here. On the road connecting Madison Junction with the Grand Canyon of the Yellowstone you'll see the remains of the North Fork Fire, which left a moonscape on this plateau. More than a decade after the fire, the effects are still clearly visible.

At **Norris Geyser Basin,** the hottest and oldest geyser basin in the park, changes occur every year: new geysers erupt, steam vents hiss to life, hot springs suddenly stop flowing. The names of the features—Whirligig Geyser, Whale's Mouth, Emerald Spring, and Arch Steam Vent—are often apt descriptions. Walk west through **Back Basin,** where the huge, unpredictable **Steamboat Geyser** has come dramatically to life in recent years, but don't wait for it: It blows 300 ft about once a year. To the east, the smaller, colorful **Porcelain Basin** has a 1-mi boardwalk and, usually, a lot of people. You can sometimes see the whitish basin floor bulge and pulsate from underground pressure.

North of Norris on the Upper Loop is **Mammoth Hot Springs.** Many travelers skip this section of the loop, though it includes some spectacular views, including those of **Roaring Mountain,** which looks like a giant pile of melted vanilla ice cream. Mammoth is the gateway for the North Entrance. Here you'll find full services; the colony of old, stone military buildings that are now the park headquarters; and the **Horace Albright Visitor Center,** with the park's largest assemblage of information, exhibits, and publications about the park as well as historic archives for researchers. Antlered elk wander on the grass, and during the fall, bugling bulls collect their harems. The hot springs drop down terraces on the mountainside just west of the headquarters and hotel. Though the springs' flow has diminished in recent years, the **Minerva Terrace** is worth a look. You can hike a boardwalk from the top to the bottom of the huge white hot-spring constructions.

Continue clockwise on the Upper Loop. You'll pass the 60-ft **Undine Falls.** Farther along the Upper Loop, a short trail leads to the huge stump of a petrified redwood tree. Soon you reach **Tower-Roosevelt.** Here you can take the Northeast Entrance Road up the **Lamar River Valley,** a

Close-Up

THE CHANGING WORLD OF YELLOWSTONE

YELLOWSTONE IS DEFINITELY not a sleepy world of natural wonders. The park does, truly, feel alive when you see mud pots, steam vents, fumaroles, and paint pots—all different aspects of the park's geyser basins, and all intriguing. Beyond the geyser activity, changes in wildlife and vegetation make Yellowstone fascinating to visit over and over again.

Though Old Faithful continues to spew routinely, even it has changed in recent years due to various factors. The geyser now erupts about every 81 to 88 minutes (up from about every 78 minutes in 1990), and it may look different each time. Monitoring shows Old Faithful almost always spews forth the same amount of water at each eruption, but how it does so varies. Sometimes it shoots higher and faster, while other times it lasts longer, but doesn't reach so high into the sky.

Other geyser basin features aren't so reliable. The force and nature of the various geysers depends on several factors, including the complex underground plumbing at Yellowstone. Rangers say the greatest threats to the geyser basin activity are earthquakes (which occur regularly in the region, though they are usually very small tremors), and the impact caused by people. In past years, for example, people threw hundreds of coins into the bright blue Morning Glory Pool. The coins eventually clogged the pool's water vents, causing it to turn from a bright blue color to a sickly green. Though it has been cleaned and people are warned not to throw anything into it, the Morning Glory Pool has never regained its pristine color.

Besides its unique geology related to geyser basins, Yellowstone has many other faces to present to visitors. There are petrified forests and fossil remains of both plants and animals. The ongoing ecological development of the region draws widespread interest. Efforts to control movement of bison—to keep them from wandering out of the park during the winter months to seek food—and the reintroduction of wolves to the ecosystem are just two examples of issues that quickly polarize people living in, or visiting, the region around Yellowstone.

Wolves were returned to Yellowstone in 1995. They acclimated so well that they quickly formed several packs, some of which have ventured outside the park's boundaries. Though a federal judge has ruled that the reintroduction was not done properly and could order the wolves removed, for now they remain. Their presence has had lasting effects on wildlife populations. The wolves feed on both elk and buffalo, and park rangers have reported a significant decline in the Yellowstone coyote population. Since the wolves are bigger and stronger than coyotes, they may kill coyotes or force them to find a new range.

When massive fires tore through Yellowstone in 1988, some believed it would take generations to undo the destruction. In little more than a decade, however, the park has restored itself. Certainly when you visit Yellowstone now you will see reminders of those fires—vast areas of stark, dead trees. But you will also see the new growth. Lodgepole pine forests need fire to release their seeds and once seeds get a start, trees grow quickly. The new growth provides excellent hiding cover for animals, making it harder for visitors to see wildlife like elk or deer.

The constant changes in Yellowstone, created by shifts in underground plumbing at the geyser basins, the territorial movements of animals, and the regeneration of plant life, make the park a new experience every time you visit.

–Candy Moulton

favorite haunt of bison, and of wolves, which were reintroduced into Yellowstone's ecosystem in 1995.

If you drive a short way east up Chittenden Road, which intersects the Upper Loop midway between Tower-Roosevelt Junction and Canyon, you can hike 3 mi to the top of **Mt. Washburn** (10,243 ft) for an unparalleled view of the region. You'll have a view toward the Grand Canyon of the Yellowstone, the Beartooth Mountains to the northeast, and the mosaic created by forest fires in 1988. South of Chittenden Road, the Upper Loop crosses over **Dunraven Pass**; in recent years, grizzlies have often been seen in a meadow here. From the junction of the Upper and Lower loops just north of **Canyon,** you can turn south toward Yellowstone Lake or head west again to Norris and south toward Madison Junction.

The magnificent **Grand Canyon of the Yellowstone** formed where water draining from Yellowstone Lake cut deep into an ancient lava flow. Just south of Canyon is a road to the 109-ft **Upper Falls,** not as high as the more spectacular Lower Falls, but well worth a visit. You can also drive across Chittenden Bridge above the Upper Falls to view the canyon from a paved road that runs about 2 mi along the South Rim. A short hike brings you to **Artist Point,** and adventurous hikers can go farther along the South Rim on various trails. The Grand Loop Road continues along the North Rim to **Canyon,** where there is a lodge and campground. From here you can backtrack along the one-way North Rim Drive to see more of the canyon. Short paths lead to a number of scenic overlooks, including **Inspiration Point,** that provide great views of the canyon and of the breathtaking 308-ft **Lower Falls.** From Inspiration Point, you can also hike 3 mi along the **North Rim Trail,** with still more river and falls views.

The Lower Loop leads from Canyon south to **Fishing Bridge,** where the Yellowstone River drains Yellowstone Lake. Although you can't fish here anymore—it's too popular with grizzly bears—it's a nice place for a stroll. The East Entrance Road heads east from Fishing Bridge over **Sylvan Pass** to Cody. Now under construction, the road is rough in places, and you can expect delays and periodic closures. Check with the Park Service or in Cody for current conditions. In the winter, this is a favorite, if rather harrowing, entrance for snowmobilers, who come in increasing numbers to ride the park's snow-packed roads.

Yellowstone Lake was formed by glaciers. From Bridge Bay, at the lake's northern end, you can take a boat cruise (☞ AmFac Parks and Resorts *in* Guided Tours, *below*), with fine views of the Absaroka Mountains and the **Lake Yellowstone Hotel.** The hotel (built in 1891, with renovations and additions through the 1920s and a centennial restoration in 1991) is the oldest surviving lodging in any national park. Columns, gables, and decorative moldings give it a distinctive neo-Colonial air.

The Lower Loop follows the west shore of the lake south from Bridge Bay back to **West Thumb** and the South Entrance Road.

OFF THE BEATEN PATH

YELLOWSTONE INSTITUTE – This non-profit organization, housed in heated log cabins in the pastoral Lamar Valley, offers a wide range of summer and winter courses about the ecology, history, and wildlife of Yellowstone. Search with a historian for the trail the Nez Perce took in their flight a century ago, or get tips from professional photographers on how to capture a trumpeter swan on film. Facilities are fairly primitive—guests do their own cooking and camp during some of the courses—but prices are reasonable. Besides, there's no better way to get out from behind the windshield and learn what makes the park tick. Some programs

Yellowstone National Park

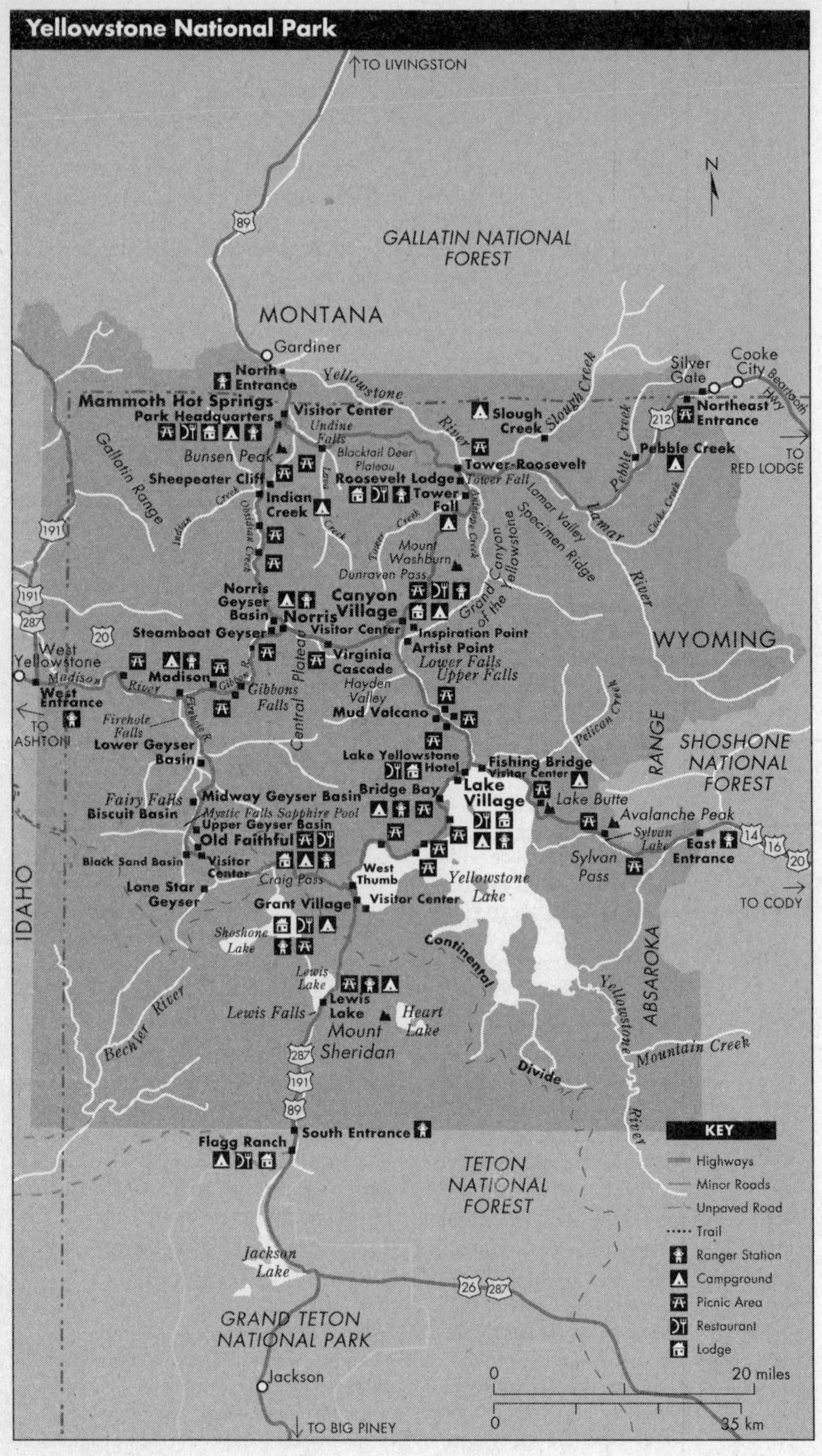
TO LIVINGSTON
GALLATIN NATIONAL FOREST
MONTANA
Gardiner
North Entrance
Mammoth Hot Springs
Park Headquarters
Visitor Center
Yellowstone River
Slough Creek
Silver Gate
Cooke City
Beartooth Hwy
Northeast Entrance
TO RED LODGE
Pebble Creek
Bunsen Peak
Undine Falls
Blacktail Deer Plateau
Tower-Roosevelt
Tower Fall
Sheepeater Cliff
Roosevelt Lodge
Indian Creek
Gallatin Range
Lamar Valley
Specimen Ridge
Lamar River
Mount Washburn
Dunraven Pass
Grand Canyon of the Yellowstone
Norris Geyser Basin
Norris
Canyon Village
Visitor Center
Inspiration Point
Artist Point
Lower Falls
Upper Falls
Steamboat Geyser
West Yellowstone
Madison River
Madison
Virginia Cascade
Gibbons Falls
Hayden Valley
Central Plateau
West Entrance
TO ASHTON
Firehole Falls
Lower Geyser Basin
Mud Volcano
WYOMING
Pelican Creek
Lake Yellowstone Hotel
Fishing Bridge Visitor Center
SHOSHONE NATIONAL FOREST
Midway Geyser Basin
Bridge Bay
Lake Village
Lake Butte
Avalanche Peak
Fairy Falls
Biscuit Basin
Mystic Falls
Sapphire Pool
Upper Geyser Basin
Old Faithful
Sylvan Lake
East Entrance
Sylvan Pass
Black Sand Basin
Visitor Center
West Thumb
Yellowstone Lake
TO CODY
Lone Star Geyser
Craig Pass
Grant Village
Visitor Center
IDAHO
Shoshone Lake
Continental Divide
Lewis Lake
Lewis Falls
Heart Lake
Mount Sheridan
Bechler River
ABSAROKA RANGE
Mountain Creek
Yellowstone River
South Entrance
Flagg Ranch
TETON NATIONAL FOREST
Jackson Lake
GRAND TETON NATIONAL PARK
Jackson
TO BIG PINEY
KEY
Highways
Minor Roads
Unpaved Road
Trail
Ranger Station
Campground
Picnic Area
Restaurant
Lodge
0
20 miles
0
35 km

are specifically designed for young people and families. ✉ *Box 117, Yellowstone National Park 82190,* ☎ *307/344–2294.*

Dining and Lodging

The park has six areas with lodges and full-scale restaurants open during the summer. They are operated by **AmFac Parks and Resorts** (✉ Yellowstone National Park, Mammoth 82190, ☎ 307/344–7901, www.ynp-lodges.com) and all accept major credit cards. Ask about size of beds, bathrooms, thickness of walls, and room location when you book, especially in the older hotels, where accommodations vary and upgrades are ongoing. Telephones have been put in some rooms, but no TVs yet.

$$–$$$ ★ ✕🏨 **Lake Yellowstone Hotel.** Built in 1889 on the north end of Yellowstone Lake, the hotel, which has neoclassical Greek columns and huge lakefront windows, is one of the oldest and most elegant park resorts. Afternoon chamber music in the sunny lobby provides a refreshing reminder of old-style luxury tourism in the "wilderness." You can stay in a somewhat primitive cabin, with pine beds and paneling, or at the hotel in a room with a brass bed and antique fixtures. The restaurant ($–$$$) is casual, with a menu that includes Thai curry shrimp and fettuccine with smoked salmon and snow peas. Restaurant reservations are required. ✉ *Lake Village. 296 rooms. Restaurant. Closed late Sept.–mid-May.*

$$–$$$ ★ ✕🏨 **Old Faithful Inn.** You can loll in front of the lobby's roaring fire and look up at wooden balconies that seem to disappear into the night sky; on those deep balconies, guests play cards, scribble at writing desks, or just relax above the hubbub. Guest-room decor ranges from brass beds to Victorian cherry wood to inexpensive motel-style furniture. More expensive rooms face the geyser. The restaurant ($–$$$) is a huge hall centered on a fireplace of volcanic stone, and it offers up shrimp scampi and chicken Forestière. Restaurant reservations are required. ✉ *Old Faithful. 327 rooms, 77 share bath. Restaurant, bar. Closed late Oct.–early May.*

$–$$ ✕🏨 **Mammoth Hot Springs Hotel.** Sharing its grounds with park headquarters, this is farther from some of the park's favorite attractions than other hotels, but it's also less crowded. Rooms are small, and cabins, four of which have hot tubs, are arranged around "auto courts," a 1950s touch. The lobby and the restaurant ($–$$$), which serves such regional American dishes as prime rib and chicken with Brie and raspberry sauce, have art deco motifs. Elk and tourists sometimes graze between the hotel and the Terrace Grill, an airy room with large windows offering fast food and cafeteria-style service. ✉ *Mammoth. 128 cabins, 4 with hot tubs; 98 hotel rooms. 2 restaurants, bar, horseback riding, cross country skiing. Closed mid-Sept.–mid-Dec., mid-Mar.–late May.*

$$$ 🏨 **Dunraven Lodge.** The park's biggest, this lodge consists of a large number of nondescript cabins and motel rooms perched above the Grand Canyon of the Yellowstone. A cafeteria fills up with a lunchtime crowd interested in sandwiches, chili, and lasagna, and the restaurant (where dinner reservations are required) features pastas, prime rib, and trout almandine. ✉ *Canyon. 599 rooms. Restaurant, bar, cafeteria, horseback riding. Closed early Sept.–early June.*

$$$ 🏨 **Old Faithful Snow Lodge.** Built in 1998, this lodge establishes a new standard for winter lodging in Yellowstone and it brings back the grand tradition of classic western park lodges with huge beams, Western furnishings, unique lighting, a fireplace in the spacious lobby and another centered between the bar and restaurant, and a long sitting room with Molesworth-style writing desks and overstuffed chairs in which to relax. The small mezzanine has wicker chairs and gives a view of the lobby; it's a great place for people watching. This is one of only two lodging facilities open during the winter months. ✉ *Off Old*

Faithful bypass Rd., next to visitor center. 100 rooms. Restaurant, bar, hiking, cross-country skiing, ski shop, snowmobiling, snowshoeing. Closed mid-Oct.–mid-Dec., mid-Mar.–mid-May.

$$ **Grant Village.** The least appetizing accommodation in the park is dull and gray and in standard motel style, but it has a view of the lake. The steak house (reservations required) serves steak, chicken, and seafood. ✉ *Grant Village. 300 rooms. Restaurant, boating. Closed mid-Sept.–May.*

$–$$ **Lake Lodge.** Less regal than its neighbor, the Lake Yellowstone Hotel, the lodge is ½ mi away along the lakeshore. Accommodations are in the lodge and in cabins, and there's cafeteria service. Pets are allowed. ✉ *Lake Village. 186 rooms. Bar, cafeteria. Closed mid-Sept.–mid-June.*

$–$$ **Roosevelt Lodge.** Near the beautiful Lamar Valley in the park's northeast corner, this is a simple, log-cabin alternative to more expensive accommodations. The dining-room restaurant dishes up barbecued ribs, Roosevelt beans, and other Western fare. ✉ *Tower-Roosevelt. 80 cabins, 8 with bath. Restaurant, bar. Closed early Sept.–early June.*

Outdoor Activities and Sports

CAMPING

The park has 11 campgrounds (under $12) and one RV park, **Fishing Bridge** ($23), open May–October with some variations. The **Grant Village** campground is as well designed as the resort (☞ Dining and Lodging, *above*) is ill designed. **Madison** is another favorite camping spot.

CYCLING

Though many people do enjoy Yellowstone via bicycle, many of the roads are narrow, with little or no shoulder and heavy traffic, making bike riding somewhat hazardous. The road from Grant Village over **Craig Pass** to Old Faithful is roomier and in better shape than most other park roads, but there is no designated bike path.

SNOWMOBILING

In Yellowstone, **AmFac Parks and Resorts** (☞ Dining and Lodging, *above*) rents snowmobiles at the Mammoth Hot Springs Hotel or Old Faithful Snow Lodge for $95 per day; there is a $15 per week user fee.

WATER SPORTS

On Yellowstone Lake, boaters embark from **Bridge Bay** (☎ 307/344–7311); rentals are available.

OFF THE BEATEN PATH

BEARTOOTH HIGHWAY – A scenic side trip outside the park at the northeast entrance is the 68-mi Beartooth Highway, U.S. 212. The highest highway in the state, it runs in and out of Montana and over 10,947-ft Beartooth Pass. To return to Yellowstone, you'll have to backtrack. Plan to spend about three hours, round trip. Switchbacks cut into steep cliffs allow cars up to spectacular views of granite peaks, snowfields, and lakes. You can make the trip even better, and longer, by taking the Chief Joseph Scenic Highway, Route 296, south from the Beartooth Highway toward Cody. There are no services, but you'll see the beautiful Sunlight Basin and the dramatic gorge carved by the Clarks Fork of the Yellowstone River.

Cody

❻ *51 mi from Yellowstone, via U.S. 14/16/20 east; 149 mi from Sheridan, via U.S. 14 west.*

Cody, founded in 1896 and named for Pony Express rider, army scout, and entertainer William F. "Buffalo Bill" Cody, lies 52 mi from the East Entrance to Yellowstone National Park. The North Fork Highway, as the route is locally known, traverses a spectacular region, following the North Fork of the Shoshone River and offering views of amazing rock formations. The road itself is rather narrow and winding, and it has some limited passing areas. Cody is within easy reach of Shoshone National Forest, the Absaroka Range, the Washakie Wilderness, and the Buffalo Bill Reservoir. A brochure with a self-guided walking tour of the town's historic sites, such as the Irma Hotel, is available from the Chamber of Commerce (☞ Contacts and Resources, *below*) for a $1 donation.

At the west end of this quiet little gateway town is one of the finest museums in the West: the **Buffalo Bill Historical Center,** sometimes called the Smithsonian of the West. The center actually houses four museums in one: the Whitney Gallery of Western Art, with works by traditional Western artists, including Charlie Russell and Frederic Remington; the Buffalo Bill Historical Center, which has memorabilia of the scout and showman; the Plains Indian Museum, housing art and artifacts of the Plains tribes; and the Cody Firearms Museum, with the world's largest collection of American firearms. ✉ *720 Sheridan Ave.,* ☎ *307/587–4771.* *$8 (2 days).* ⏲ *Apr., daily 10–5; May, daily 8–8; June–Sept., daily 7 AM–8 PM; Oct., daily 8–5; Nov.–Mar., Thurs.–Mon. 10–2.*

Cody Nite Rodeo, more dusty and intimate than such big rodeos as Frontier Days, offers children's events, such as goat roping, in additional to the regular adult events. Contact the Cody Chamber of Commerce (☞ Contacts and Resources, *below*) for information. *$10 and $12; seat prices vary with location.* ⏲ *June–Aug., daily 8:30 PM.*

On Cody's western outskirts, just off the West Yellowstone Highway, is **Trail Town,** a collection of historic buildings from Wyoming's frontier days. It features a cemetery of famous local mountain men, as well as Native American and pioneer artifacts. ✉ *1831 Demaris Dr.,* ☎ *307/587–5302.* *$4.* ⏲ *May–Sept.*

Dining and Lodging

$–$$ ✕ **Franca's Italian Dining.** Serving authentic Northern Italian food, the menu here is unique each evening. Entrées vary: pork, poultry, beef, seafood, or veal selections are offered, complemented by a wine list of some 90 selections. The small room (maximum 24) is filled with Italian art. ✉ *1421 Rumsey Ave.,* ☎ *307/587–5354. Reservations essential. No credit cards. Closed Mon., Tues., and winter. No lunch.*

$–$$ ✕ **La Comida.** Making no claim to authentic Mexican cooking, this restaurant nevertheless has received the Five Star Diamond Award as one of the top 50 Mexican restaurants in the country from the Academy Awards of the Restaurant Industry, and it has been reviewed in numerous national newspapers and magazines. The owners prefer to describe their recipes as "Cody-Mex." The decor is authentic Mexican and the atmosphere festive. ✉ *1385 Sheridan Ave.,* ☎ *307/587–9556. AE, D, DC, MC, V.*

$–$$ ✕ **Proud Cut Saloon.** At this popular downtown eatery and watering hole, owner Del Nose claims to serve "kick-ass cowboy cuisine": steaks, prime rib, shrimp, fish, and chicken. The Western decor includes paintings, vintage photographs of Cody country, and large game mounts. ✉ *1227 Sheridan Ave.,* ☎ *307/527–6905. D, MC, V.*

$$$–$$$$ ★ **Cody Guest Houses.** Lovingly restored and elegantly decorated, the Victorian guest house has lace curtains, antique furniture, and ornate decorations. The Trimmer Western Lodge, with four bedrooms, has traditional Western decor and a fireplace. ✉ *1401 Rumsey Ave., 82414,* ☎ *307/587–6000 or 800/587–6560,* FAX *307/587–8048. 8 rooms, 1 suite. AE, D, MC, V.*

$$–$$$ **Pahaska Teepee Resort.** Two miles from Yellowstone's East Entrance, these cabins, which can be a bit drafty at times, are a good base for summer and winter recreation, both inside and outside the park. This was Buffalo Bill's original getaway in the high country. ✉ *183 Yellowstone Hwy., 82414,* ☎ *307/527–7701 or 800/628–7791,* FAX *307/527–4019. 52 cabins. Restaurant, horseback riding, cross-country skiing, ski shop, snowmobiling. D, MC, V.*

$$ **Buffalo Bill Village.** This downtown development comprises three lodgings, which share many facilities. The **Buffalo Bill Village Resort,** consisting of log cabins with modern interiors, and the **Holiday Inn Convention Center,** a typical two-story brick hotel, are most noteworthy. ✉ *1701 Sheridan Ave., 82414,* ☎ *307/587–5544. Resort: 83 cabins. Inn: 184 rooms. Restaurant, bar, outdoor pool, meeting rooms. AE, D, DC, MC, V.*

$$ **Irma Hotel.** Named for Buffalo Bill's daughter, this hotel has some of the flavor of earlier days, when Buffalo Bill still ranched nearby. With brass beds and period furniture in many rooms, a large restaurant, and an elaborate cherry-wood bar, it retains its old charm. During the summer, locals stage a gunfight on the porch Tuesday–Saturday at 7 PM. ✉ *1192 Sheridan Ave., 82414,* ☎ *307/587–4221 or 800/745–4762,* FAX *307/587–4221. 40 rooms. Restaurant, bar. AE, D, DC, MC, V.*

Outdoor Activities and Sports

CANOEING, KAYAKING, AND RAFTING

Family river trips on the Shoshone River are offered by **River Runners** (✉ 1491 Sheridan Ave., 82801, ☎ 307/527–7238). **Wyoming River Trips** (✉ Buffalo Bill Village, Box 1541-TC, 82414, ☎ 307/587–6661 or 800/586–6661) also arranges Shoshone River trips.

GOLF

Olive Glenn Golf and Country Club (✉ 802 Meadow La., ☎ 307/587–5551 or 307/587–5308) is a highly rated 18-hole course open to the public; a Jacuzzi, pool, and two tennis courts are also available.

Shopping

Women shop at the **Plush Pony** (✉ 1350 Sheridan Ave., ☎ 307/587–4677) for "uptown Western clothes" ranging from the best leather belts to the most stylish skirts, jackets, and dresses. **Flight West** (✉ 1155 Sheridan Ave., ☎ 307/527–7800) offers designer Western women's wear, gifts, leather goods, and jewelry.

Wind River Hat Company (✉ 144 W. Yellowstone Ave., ☎ 307/527–5939) designs personalized hats for work or dress. Try **Creations in Leather** (✉ 1212 Sheridan Ave., ☎ 307/587–6461), which has a complete line of custom leather goods for the working cowboy; you'll find high-priced elk and deer jackets as well as shirts, vests, and skirts with matching belts and purses.

Northwest Wyoming A to Z

Arriving and Departing

BY CAR

The Yellowstone area is well away from the interstates, so drivers make their way here on two-lane highways that are long on miles and scenery. From I–80, take U.S. 191 north from Rock Springs; it's about 177 mi to Jackson. From I–90, drive west from Sheridan on U.S. 14 or 14A to Cody, and cross over beautiful Sylvan Pass to Yellowstone's East Entrance. Be forewarned, however, that construction to improve the highway has recently been causing delays in the Sylvan Pass area. Check in Cody for current road information. It's about 200 mi from Sheridan to the park. Alternatively, you can take U.S. 89 from the north or U.S. 191/287 from the west, both from Montana.

BY PLANE

East of Yellowstone, at Cody, **Yellowstone Regional Airport** (☏ 307/587–5096) is served by commuter airlines out of Denver. There is also service to the Yellowstone area through Bozeman and West Yellowstone, both in Montana.

Jackson Hole Airport (☏ 307/733–7682) lies north of Jackson in Grand Teton National Park, about 40 mi south of Yellowstone National Park. American, Delta/SkyWest, United, and United Express provide daily service, with connections in Denver, Salt Lake City, and Chicago. There are seasonal variations; for example, scheduled jet service increases during the ski season. Flights may also be booked—often at a discount—through Central Reservations (☏ 307/733–4005 or 800/443–6931).

Jackson Hole Transportation (☏ 307/733–3135) meets incoming flights at the airport, delivers guests to their accommodations, and returns for departures.

Getting Around

BY BUS

During ski season, **START** buses (☏ 307/733–4521) operate between Jackson and the Jackson Hole Ski Resort. The fare is $4 one-way. The **Targhee Express** (☏ 307/733–3101 or 800/827–4433) runs between Jackson and the Grand Targhee Ski Resort.

BY CAR

To best see the area, go by car. You can drive the road loops within the parks and stop at will for a hike or a view. Be extremely cautious in the winter when whiteouts and ice are not uncommon. If you didn't drive to Wyoming, you'll probably want to rent a car; Jackson Hole Airport has major car-rental agencies, which offer four-wheel-drive vehicles and ski racks.

Contacts and Resources

CAMPING

In the national parks, most campgrounds are open June through September. In **Grand Teton** (☏ 307/739–3300) campsites are available by advanced reservation. Fees range from $12 to $15 for developed campgrounds. You can reserve a backcountry site for a $15 nonrefundable fee, but you can also take a chance that the site you want will be open and pay no fee. For **campsite reservations** in **Yellowstone**, call **AmFac Parks and Resorts** (☏ 307/344–7311). There are no reservations taken for most campgrounds in the **Bridger-Teton National Forest** (☏ 307/739–5500) and the **Targhee National Forest** (☏ 208/624–3151), and most of these fill up more slowly than in the national parks. Reservations can be made for some **national forest campgrounds** near Jackson through U.S. Forest Reservations (☏ 800/280–2267).

CYCLING

Wyoming roads do not offer wide shoulders, but that doesn't stop cyclists from pedaling the area's two-lane highways, either in the midst of cross-country tours or on day trips. Bikers need to be alert for motorists, who are often distracted and sometimes negligent. In addition, mountain bikes are increasingly climbing the trails that hikers favor, and there are sometimes conflicts. Various outfitters guide and supply bicyclists, and provide advice and trail maps as well. (☞ Guided Tours, *below*).

DOCTORS AND DENTISTS

In Yellowstone, the **Lake Clinic and Hospital** (✉ behind the Lake Hotel, ☏ 307/242–7241) is open May 24–September 15; clinics are also in Mammoth (✉ next to the post office, Upper Mammoth, ☏ 307/344–

7965), open June–August, and at Old Faithful (✉ back of the parking lot behind Old Faithful Inn, ☎ 307/545–7325), open May 7–October 10. **Grand Teton Medical Clinic** (✉ next to Jackson Lake Lodge, ☎ 307/543–2514) is open May 23–October 3. In Jackson there's **St. John's Hospital** (✉ 625 E. Broadway Ave., ☎ 307/733–3636).

FISHING

Limits and restrictions on fishing in the parks change from year to year. A free park license is required. Outside the parks on state, private, or national forest lands, Wyoming fishing licenses are required and are usually available at sporting-goods stores and drugstores (☞ Contacts and Resources *in* Wyoming A to Z). The Wind River Indian Reservation has some of the best fishing in the Rockies. A separate license is required here. Contact **Shoshone and Arapaho Tribes** (✉ Fish and Game Dept., 1 Washakie, Fort Washakie 82520, ☎ 307/332–7207).

GUIDED TOURS

Orientation: AmFac Parks and Resorts (✉ Yellowstone National Park, Mammoth 82190, ☎ 307/344–7901) offers lodging and bus tours of Yellowstone in the summer; in the winter, packages include snowmobiling, skiing, and group tours by motorized snow coach. They also offer one-hour narrated boat tours of northern Yellowstone Lake.

Special-Interest: Absaroka Outfitters (✉ Box 929, Dubois 82513, ☎ 307/455–2275), from its scenic ranch, offers hunting and horseback-riding trips of up to seven days in the remote wilderness to the southeast of Yellowstone. **Backcountry Bicycle Tours** (✉ Box 4029, Bozeman, MT 59772, ☎ 406/586–3556) offers mountain bike tours in the area's parks and forests, mixing in rafting and hiking for variety. **Barker-Ewing Scenic Float Trips** (✉ Box 100-J, Moose 83012, ☎ 307/733–1800 or 800/365–1800) conducts gentle scenic floats or white-water trips, either half-day journeys or longer trips that include cookouts and camping. For bouncier guided white-water trips, contact **Barker-Ewing Float Trips** (✉ Box 3032, 45 W. Broadway, Jackson 83001, ☎ 800/448–4202). **Flagg Ranch Village** (✉ Box 187, Moran 83013, ☎ 307/543–2861 or 800/443–2311), between Grand Teton and Yellowstone parks, runs snowmobiling and fishing trips. **Cowboy Village at Togwotee Mountain** (✉ Box 91, Moran 83013, ☎ 307/543–2847 or 800/543–2847 outside WY) has a large snowmobile-guiding operation in the winter and switches to horse pack trips in summer.

VISITOR INFORMATION

Cody Chamber of Commerce (✉ 836 Sheridan Ave., Box 2777, Cody 82414, ☎ 307/587–2297). **Jackson Hole Chamber of Commerce** (✉ Box E, Jackson 83001, ☎ 307/733–3316). **Jackson Hole Visitors Council** (✉ Box 982, Dept. 8, Jackson 83001, ☎ 800/782–0011). **Wapiti Valley Association** (✉ 1170 Yellowstone Hwy., Cody 82414, ☎ 307/587–9595).

SOUTHEAST WYOMING

The high plains morph into the mountains in southeast Wyoming as the rolling grasslands around Cheyenne rise to the Laramie and Medicine Bow mountain ranges at the west side of the region. Communities such as Cheyenne and Laramie still have strong Western roots along with their Western names.

Cheyenne sits apart from the mountainous magnet of western Wyoming. Some detractors say it's more a part of Colorado's Front Range, which runs south across the nearby border, but the area is no Colorado wanna-be. Cheyenne is a dynamic city, thriving on a mixture of state government, the military, and new industry. The University of Wyoming, the state's only four-year university, is just over the Medicine Bow Mountains in Laramie, and outside the city limits, cattle grazing on rolling hills throughout the region are a reminder that the area's century-old ranching community still survives.

Cheyenne

7 *110 mi north of Denver, via I–25; 225 mi west of North Platte, Nebraska, via I–80.*

Born in 1867 as the Union Pacific Railroad inched its way across the plains, Cheyenne began as a rowdy camp for railroad gangs, cowboys, prospectors heading for the Black Hills, and soldiers. It more than lived up to its nickname: "Hell on Wheels." In the late 19th century, the region's enormously wealthy cattle barons, many of them English, settled in Cheyenne. They sipped brandy at the Cheyenne Club and hired hard cases like Tom Horn to take care of their competitors on the open range. Nineteenth-century Cheyenne is remembered in the area slogan "Live the Legend" and celebrated in July with western élan in Frontier Days.

During Frontier Days, Cheyenne is up to its neck in bucking broncs and bulls and joyful bluster. There are pancake breakfasts put on by locals, parades and pageantry, and parties that require the endurance of a cattle hand on a weeklong drive. The century-old event is now the world's largest outdoor rodeo extravaganza, dubbed the "Daddy of 'Em All."

The **Old West Museum** at Frontier Park has 30,000 pieces in all, including 125 carriages. Guided tours are aimed at children. During Frontier Days, the museum hosts the Governor's Invitational Western Art Show and Sale, in which top Western wildlife and landscape artists from around the country exhibit. ✉ *4501 N. Carey Ave.,* ☎ *307/778–7290.* 🎫 *$4.* ⏲ *Winter, weekdays 9–5, Sat. 11–4; summer, weekdays 8–6, weekends 10–5.*

The **Wyoming State Capitol** is a Corinthian-style structure, authorized by the Ninth Territorial Legislative Assembly in 1886 and now on the National Register of Historic Places. The dome, covered in 24-carat gold leaf and visible from all roads leading into the city, is 50 ft in diameter at the base and 146 ft high at the peak. Standing in front is a statue of Esther Hobart Morris, a proponent of women's suffrage. Wyoming is nicknamed the "Equality State" because it was the first state to give women the vote. As a result of Wyoming's small population and informal ways, it's not unusual to find the governor wandering the halls of the capitol. You can take a self-guided tour of state offices and the senate and house chambers. ✉ *Capitol Ave.,* ☎ *307/777–7220.* 🎫 *Free.* ⏲ *Weekdays 8–5; May–Aug. also Sat. 9–5.*

The **Historic Governor's Mansion** was the residence of 19 Wyoming first families from 1905 to 1976, when the state built a new residence for the governor. Ornate chandeliers in nearly every room are just some of the interesting appointments. ✉ *300 E. 21st St.,* ☎ *307/777–7878.* 🎫 *Free.* ⏲ *Tues.–Sat. 9–5.*

One of Wyoming's nicknames is the "Cowboy State," and the premiere cowboy event is **Cheyenne Frontier Days,** held the last full week of July every year since 1897. Leading contenders in the Professional Rodeo Cowboys Association compete at Cheyenne, and there are a variety of other activities including chuckwagon races, an Indian village and dancing, free pancake breakfasts that feed up to 12,000 people in two hours, and nightly concerts featuring top country entertainers. Reservations are a must. ✉ *Box 2477, Cheyenne 82003,* ☎ *307/778–7222 or 800/227–6336; 800/543–2339 in WY.*

Dining and Lodging

$$ ★ ✕ **Little Bear Steakhouse.** Locals rave about this classic American steakhouse with western decor. Try the New York strip steak or the rib eye. Non-steak eaters will also find seafood on the menu. ✉ *1700 Little Bear Rd.,* ☎ *307/634–3684. AE, D, DC, MC, V.*

$–$$ ✕ **The Albany.** Historic photos of early-day Cheyenne set the tone for this downtown icon, a place that seems as old as the city itself. It's a bit dark, and the booths a bit shabby, but the American food is solid. Now if only you could get the walls to tell their stories. No doubt they've heard it all as many of the movers and shakers in Cheyenne's past (and a few in its present) have eaten here. ✉ *1506 Capitol Ave.,* ☎ *307/638–3507. AE, D, DC, MC, V.*

$–$$ ★ ✕ **Lexie's Café.** In the oldest home in Cheyenne, a brick building more than a century old, the café has delightful breakfast and lunch menus and offers heaping platters of Mexican, Italian, and American food. ✉ *216 E. 17th St.,* ☎ *307/638–8712. AE, D, DC, MC, V. Closed Sun. No dinner.*

$ ✕ **Los Amigos.** Mexican decorations on the walls complement the south-of-the-border food at this local favorite south of downtown. ✉ *620 Central Ave.,* ☎ *307/638–8591. MC, V. Closed Sun.*

$$–$$$$ ✕🏨 **Best Western Hitching Post Inn.** State legislators frequent this hotel, known to locals as "The Hitch." It books country-western performers in the lounge. With its dark wood walls, this hotel has an elegance not found elsewhere in Cheyenne. The Cheyenne Cattle Company restaurant serves steak and other dishes in a quiet, relaxed atmosphere. ✉ *1700 W. Lincolnway, 82001,* ☎ *307/638–3301,* FAX *307/778–7194. 166 rooms, 1-2 story. Restaurant, coffee shop, lobby lounge, in-room data ports, refrigerators, indoor and outdoor pools, exercise room, meeting rooms, airport shuttle. AE, D, DC, MC, V.*

$$–$$$$ 🏨 **A. Drummond's Ranch Bed and Breakfast.** Halfway between Cheyenne and Laramie and bordered by Curt Gowdy State Park lands, this B&B is on 120 acres and has a 100-mi view of the Laramie Range and the Colorado Rockies. Guests include cross-country skiers and mountain bikers (the ranch conducts two- to six-hour tours for both), runners who want to train at the 7,500-ft elevation, and horseback riders (stalls are available to board a horse or other pet during your stay). Three meals a day can be provided for an extra charge; special diets can be accommodated. ✉ *399 Happy Jack Rd., Cheyenne/Laramie 82007,* ☎ FAX *307/634–6042. 4 rooms, 2 with bath. Dining room, outdoor hot tub, library. MC, V.*

$$–$$$ 🏨 **Little America Hotel and Resort.** At the intersection of I–80 and I–25, the resort has an executive golf course. The large rooms have double vanities, one inside the bathroom and one outside. Most guest rooms are in several buildings clustered around the swimming pool, and some are attached to the dining room, coffee shop, gift shop, lounge, and meeting rooms via a glassed-in breezeway. ✉ *2800 W. Lincolnway, 82001,* ☎ *307/775–8400 or 800/445–6945,* FAX *307/775–8425. 188 rooms. Restaurant, bar, coffee shop, refrigerators, outdoor pool, 9-hole golf course, exercise room, airport shuttle. AE, D, DC, MC, V.*

$$ 🏨 **Rainsford Inn.** Elegant surroundings and a B&B atmosphere welcome you on historic "Cattleman's Row" in the heart of downtown Cheyenne. The Cattle Baron Corner has masculine decor and overlooks 17th Street, where Cheyenne's cattle barons lived in the late 1800s. One room is suitable for people with disabilities and includes a roll-in shower. The third floor "Grandma's Attic" is a very private retreat. All rooms have whirlpool tubs, one has a gas fireplace, and a full breakfast is included. ✉ *219 E. 18th St., 82001,* ☎ *307/638–2337,* FAX *307/634–4506. 1 room with private bath, 2 rooms with shared bath, 2 suites with private baths. Dining room, no-smoking rooms, library. AE, MC, V.*

Nightlife

For an evening of live country music; two-, three-, and four-chord songs; a large dance floor; and ample beverage service, try the **Cheyenne Club** (✉ 1617 Capitol Ave., ☎ 307/635–7777). To vary the scene some, there's also live music, dancing, and drinks at the **Cowboy South** (✉ 312 S. Greeley Hwy., ☎ 307/637–3800).

Outdoor Activities and Sports

CAMPING

As everywhere in Wyoming, camping opportunities are abundant. Cheyenne has the **Terry Bison Ranch** (✉ I–25 Service Rd. near the Colorado state line, ☎ 307/634–4171). Besides a full-service campground and RV park, the bison ranch—yes, there are nearly 2,000 head on the property—has a restaurant and occasional entertainment. The **Wyoming Campground and Mobile Home Park** (✉ I–80, Exit 377, ☎ 307/547–2244) is a basic, no-frills camping area.

GOLF

Airport Course (✉ 4801 Central Ave., ☎ 307/637–6418) and **Prairie View** (✉ 3601 Windmill Rd., ☎ 307/637–6420) are two 18-hole golf courses. There's a nine-hole course at **Little America Hotel and Resort** (✉ 2800 W. Lincolnway, ☎ 307/775–8400).

Shopping

Cheyenne's **Frontier Mall** (✉ 1400 Dell Range Blvd., ☎ 307/638–2290) houses 75 specialty shops and four major department stores. It's as typical an American mall as you'll find.

Wrangler (✉ 16th and Capitol Sts., ☎ 307/634–3048) offers a full line of traditional Western clothes, ranging from Wrangler and Rocky Mountain jeans to Panhandle Slim shirts, Resistol hats, and Laredo boots. There are sizes and styles for the entire family.

En Route On your way west, midway between Cheyenne and Laramie, north of I–80 and south of Happy Jack Road (Route 210), is **Vedauwoo,** a particularly unusual area and a great place for a picnic. Springing out of high plains and open meadows are glacial remnants in the form of huge granite boulders piled skyward with reckless abandon. These one-of-a-kind rock formations, dreamscapes of gray stone, provide great opportunities for hiking, climbing, and photography.

Laramie

8 *45 mi west of Cheyenne, via I–80 and U.S. 287.*

Laramie, nestled in a valley between the Medicine Bow Mountains and the Laramie Range, was first settled when the railroad reached here in 1867. For a time it was a tough "end-of-the-rail" town. Vigilantes took care of lawbreakers, hanging them from convenient telegraph poles. Laramie today is the home of the University of Wyoming and is in the center of open-plains ranching country. Many of the historic downtown buildings have been restored and are in use as retail shops, restaurants, and the like.

Perhaps because of the bedlam of the early days, Laramie became the site of the Wyoming Territorial Prison in 1872. Until 1903, it was the region's federal and state penal facility, housing Butch Cassidy and other infamous frontier outlaws. Today the restored prison is the gem of **Wyoming Territorial Park,** giving life to the legends of frontier law and justice. In addition, the park contains a 19th-century railroad display, a U.S. marshals' museum, a replica of a frontier town, a living-history program, and the Horse Barn Dinner Theater. ✉ *975 Snowy Range Rd.,* ☎ *307/745–6161 or 800/845–2287.* 🎫 *Dinner theater: $23.95.*

Park: Memorial Day–Labor Day, daily 9–5; dinner theater: Tues.–Sun. 6–9, dark Sun. and Mon.

For more area history, visit the **Laramie Plains Museum,** in the Ivinson mansion. Built in 1892 by Edward Ivinson, a businessman and philanthropist and one of Laramie's first settlers, the estate houses a growing collection of historical artifacts from the Laramie plains area. *6th St. and Ivinson Ave., 307/742–4448. $2. June–Aug., Mon.–Sat. 9–7, Sun. 1–4; Sept.–May, weekdays 10–3, Sat. 1–3.*

The **University of Wyoming** (13th St. and Ivinson Ave.) offers year-round events—from concerts to football—and a number of attractions. The best place to start, for a tour or just for information, is the **UW Visitor Center** (14th St. and Grand Ave., 307/766–4075). Depending on your interests, you might want to visit the **Anthropology Museum** (307/766–5136), **planetarium** (307/766–6150), **Entomology Museum** (307/766–2298), **Rocky Mountain Herbarium** (307/766–2236), or other campus museums of note.

The **University of Wyoming Geological Museum,** in a building with a dinosaur statue out front, contains the skeleton of an apatosaurus 15 ft high and 75 ft long and believed to have weighed 30 tons. Other exhibits explore the dinosaur family tree, meteorites, fossils, and earthquakes. *Northwest corner of University of Wyoming campus, 307/766–4246. Free. Weekdays 8–5, weekends 10–3.*

The **American Heritage Center** houses more than 10,000 photographs, rare books, collections of papers, and memorabilia related to such subjects as American and Western history, the petroleum industry, conservation movements, transportation, and the performing arts. *2111 Willet Dr., 307/766–4114. Free. Weekdays 8–5, Sat. 11–5.*

The **Wyoming Children's Museum and Nature Center** is a hands-on place in which children and families can explore, make noise, experiment, play, imagine, discover, and invent. *Laramie Plains Civic Center, 710 Garfield St., Room 254, Laramie, 307/745–6332. $2. Tues.–Thurs. 9–5; Sat. 10–4; also Fri. 1–5 in summer.*

Dining and Lodging

$$–$$$ **Cavalryman Supper Club.** This old-fashioned restaurant with a large local clientele is on the plains, 1 mi south of Laramie on U.S. 287. Prime rib, steak, and lobster are on the menu. *4425 S. 3rd St., 307/745–5551. AE, DC, MC, V. No lunch except Jan. 1, Easter, and Thanksgiving.*

$ **Café Jacques.** This casual bar and grill serves sandwiches and 70 beers including microbrews, domestic, and imported brands. *220 Grand Ave., 307/742–5522. AE, DC, MC, V.*

$ **Overland Restaurant.** This restaurant in the historic district, right on the railroad tracks, cooks up breakfast, lunch, and dinner. Patio dining and a superb wine list enhance the food: pasta, chicken, quiche, beef, and seafood. For Sunday breakfast, you might find such entrées as yellowfin tuna and eggs, a buffalo chili omelet, or avocados Benedict. *100 Ivinson Ave., 307/721–2800. AE, D, MC, V.*

$$ ★ **Annie Moore's Guest House.** This historic home across from the University of Wyoming campus has been a fraternity, a sorority, and an apartment building, and now it's a B&B. Terra-cotta tiles, hardwood floors, the sounds of nesting owls, and a cat named Archina, who greets guests, make it cozy. Continental breakfast with homemade goodies comes with good conversation. *819 University, 82070, 307/721–4177. 3 rooms with shared bath. Dining room, recreation room, library. AE, D, MC, V.*

$$ 🏨 **Best Western Foster's Country Corner.** On the western edge of town, at the Snowy Range Road exit off I–80, is this white-brick Best Western with a convenience store, 24-hour restaurant, and liquor store. The rooms are basic, with contemporary furnishings. ✉ *Box 580, Exit 311 off I–80, 1561 Jackson St., 82070,* ☎ *307/742–8371,* FAX *307/742–0884. 112 rooms. Restaurant, bar, indoor pool, hot tub. AE, D, DC, MC, V.*

$$ 🏨 **Laramie Comfort Inn.** Laramie's newest motel has an indoor pool and hot tub, fitness room, and a full wheelchair-accessible room with the only roll-in shower in the city. One of the three suites has a whirlpool. A Continental breakfast is included in the room rate. ✉ *3420 Grand Ave., 82070,* ☎ *307/721–8856 or 800/228–5150. 55 rooms, 3 suites, 1 efficiency apartment. Indoor pool, hot tub, exercise room. AE, D, DC, MC, V.*

Nightlife and the Arts

The **University of Wyoming's fine arts program** (☎ 307/766–5249) regularly holds concerts featuring classical and popular performers. The **UW Department of Theater and Dance** also presents periodic productions on the main stage of the UW Fine Arts Center (✉ ☎ 307/766–3327).

Dinner theater is performed at the **Horse Barn Dinner Theater** (☞ Wyoming Territorial Park, *above*).

Country-and-western nightlife is found at the **Buckhorn** (✉ 114 Ivinson Ave., ☎ 307/742–3554) and the **Cowboy Saloon** (✉ 108 S. 2nd St., ☎ 307/721–3165). For rock, head to **Shooters Saloon** (✉ 303 S. 3rd St., ☎ 307/745–7676). Hang with the college students at **Mingles** (✉ 3206 Grand Ave., ☎ 307/721–2005). The younger set also congregates at the **Drawbridge Tavern** (✉ 1622 Grand Ave., ☎ 307/745–3490), which also hosts rock.

Outdoor Activities and Sports

CAMPING

Laramie has a **KOA** (✉ I–80 at Curtis St. exit, ☎ 307/742–6553). **Curt Gowdy State Park** (✉ off Happy Jack Rd.) is a good camping spot away from the city.

CYCLING

Mountain biking trails are scattered throughout the Medicine Bow National Forest and the Happy Jack recreation area, located east of Laramie. For information, trail maps, and rentals, see Mike or Doug Lowham at the **Pedal House** (✉ 207 S. 1st St., Laramie, ☎ 307/742–5533).

GOLF

Enjoy the links at the 18-hole **Jacoby Park Golf Course** (✉ off N. 30th St., ☎ 307/745–3111).

SKIING

Downhill and cross-country skiing are available 32 mi southwest of Laramie at the **Snowy Range Ski Area** (✉ 1420 Thomas St., Laramie 82070, ☎ 307/745–5750 or 800/602–7669). Cross-country trails are also scattered throughout the Medicine Bow National Forest and the Happy Jack recreation area. For information and rentals, contact **Cross Country Connection** (✉ 117 Grand Ave., Laramie 82070, ☎ 307/721–2851).

Shopping

Laramie's most unusual shopping is found along Ivinson Avenue and Grand Avenue, where a shopping district called **Landmark Square** is being created, with stores offering artwork, clothing, and hand-crafted items. In the Landmark Square area, the **Curiosity Shoppe** (✉ 206 S,

2nd St., ☎ 307/745–4760) sells antiques, pottery, and hand-embroidered and crocheted items. **A Touch of Country** features folk art, pottery, baskets, country pine furniture, and a year-round Christmas Shoppe (✉ 312 S. 2nd St., ☎ 307/721–2171).

BOOKSELLERS

The Second Story (✉ 105 Ivinson Ave., ☎ 307/745–4423), in an old, antiques-laden upstairs suite of offices in Laramie, stocks only "personally recommended books," some of them signed by visiting authors. **Chickering Bookstore** (✉ 203 S. 2nd St., ☎ 307/742–8609) features regional authors, self-help, and a good selection of children's titles. **The Grand Newsstand** (✉ 214 Grand Ave., ☎ 307/742–5127) has the best selection of Western and regional titles in the city.

SPECIALTY FOODS

Laramie's **Whole Earth Granary** (✉ 111 Ivinson Ave., ☎ 307/745–4268) sells organic whole grains and flours, 50 varieties of coffee, herbal extracts, essential oils, and fresh seafood flown in weekly, including live Maine lobster.

En Route In the summer, you can get away from the interstates by taking Route 130, the **Snowy Range Scenic Byway,** west of Laramie. This paved road in excellent condition runs over 10,847-ft Snowy Range Pass through the Medicine Bow National Forest, providing views of Medicine Bow Peak. Along the way, there are 10 campgrounds (six right on the road), 10 hiking trails (from 1½- to 8-mi long) and 100 alpine lakes and streams. The more adventurous can take any of the several gravel roads that lead into the forest. Maps are available from the U.S. Forest Service (✉ 2468 Snowy Range Rd., Laramie, ☎ 307/745–8971).

Saratoga

❾ *79 mi west of Laramie via Rte. 130, summer only; or 98 mi via I–80 west to Walcott Junction and Rte. 130/230 south.*

Tucked away in a valley formed by the Snowy Range and Sierra Madre mountains, with the North Platte River bisecting the region, Saratoga is an unknown treasure. Fine shopping and dining combine with elegant lodging facilities and outstanding recreational opportunities such as summertime river floating and fishing, and wintertime cross-country skiing and snowmobiling. The town first went by the name Warm Springs, but it was changed to Saratoga in 1884 (for Saratoga Springs, New York). It advertised itself as a place to get away to soak in the hot mineral waters and to enjoy the outdoors. It still does. The **Hobo Pool Hot Springs** and the adjacent swimming pool heated by the springs are main attractions. ✉ *201 S. River St.,* ☎ *307/326–5417.* 🎟 *Free.* ⏲ *Springs: year-round, 24-hrs; pool: Memorial Day–Labor Day, 9–8; sometimes closed for lessons.*

Dining and Lodging

$–$$ ✕ **Lazy River Cantina.** Mexican decor greets you in this downtown restaurant that also includes a banquet room and bar/lounge. The entrées include tacos, enchiladas, burritos, and chimichangas. ✉ *110 E. Bridge St.,* ☎ *307/326–8472. MC, V.*

$–$$ ✕🏨 **Wolf Hotel.** This downtown hotel, on the National Register of Historic Places, is well maintained by its caring and proud owners. The guest rooms are on the second and third floors; there is no elevator. Though some rooms are small with shared bathrooms, all have a Victorian charm. Recent renovations have put this 1893 facility back into classic condition. The downstairs dining room ($–$$$), bar, and lounge have Victorian furnishings, including antique oak tables, crystal chandeliers, and lacy drapes. There is fine dining at lunch and dinner; prime rib and steaks are real specialties. ✉ *101 E. Bridge St., 82331,* ☎ *307/326–5525. 5 rooms, 4 suites. Restaurant, bar. AE, DC, MC, V.*

$$–$$$$ **Saratoga Inn.** This is a rustic 1950s fishing, hunting, and golfing lodge that has recently undergone a complete renovation. It's now as nice as any facility in Wyoming, with classic Western decor including pole-style beds, lush leather couches, and Western art. There's a nine-hole public golf course, where cottonwoods, conifers, and the North Platte River also come into play. The dining room offers a variety of beef, chicken, and seafood entrées, with occasional barbecues and buffets. A number of activities are available including horseback riding, river fishing/floating, snowmobiling, and cross country skiing. ✉ *E. Pic-Pike Rd., 82331,* ☎ *307/326–5261,* FAX *307/326–5109. 50 rooms. Dining room, bar, outdoor hot tubs, 9-hole golf course. AE, DC, MC, V.*

Outdoor Activities and Sports

CANOEING AND RAFTING

Great Rocky Mountain Outfitters (✉ 216 E. Walnut St., 82331, ☎ 307/326–8750) offers guided canoe and raft expeditions on the North Platte River or canoe and raft guide/rental packages. River floats are available through **Platte Valley Anglers** (☞ Fishing, *below*).

FISHING

Brook trout are prevalent in the lakes and streams of Medicine Bow National Forest, but you can find rainbow, golden, cutthroat, and brown trout, as well as splake. Anglers can also drop a fly in the North Platte River. **Platte Valley Anglers** (✉ 1st and Bridge Sts., Saratoga, ☎ 307/326–5750) and **Great Rocky Mountain Outfitters** (✉ 316 E. Walnut St., Saratoga, ☎ 307/326–8750) rent tackle and runs fishing trips on the Upper North Platte.

SKIING AND SNOWMOBILING

Extensive trail networks in the Medicine Bow National Forest include opportunities for novice or experienced cross-country skiers and snowmobilers. For trail conditions, contact the **Hayden/Brush Creek Ranger District** of the Medicine Bow National Forest (☎ 307/326–5258 or 307/327–5481) or Mark Rauterkus at the Trading Post (☞ *below*).

For ski rentals, contact the **Trading Post** (✉ Hwys. 70 and 230, Encampment, 82325, ☎ 307/327–5720). Snowmobile rentals are available from **Platte Valley Outfitters** (✉ 1st St. and Bridge Ave., Saratoga, ☎ 307/326–5750).

En Route From Saratoga, travel north to I–80; take it west to Rawlins before turning north again on U.S. 287 and west on Route 220 to Casper. This brings you into the Great Divide Basin along the route of the **Oregon–California–Mormon trails,** which you generally follow from Independence Rock to Casper. On Route 220, 13 mi beyond U.S. 287, is the Martin's Cove Visitor Center on the historic **Sun Ranch.** The visitor center, opened in May 1997 by the Church of Jesus Christ of Latter-day Saints, has exhibits on Sun Ranch, the Mormon Trail, and two handcart companies (groups of pioneers pushing their belongings westward in handcarts) that became stranded by winter snows in 1856. A 3½-mi trail leads to Martin's Cove, where the pioneers found shelter from the cold. Visitors can push one of 100 handcarts up the trail and learn firsthand about this mode of transportation. The carts are loaned free, on a first-come, first-served basis; none is loaned after 3:30 and none on Sunday. ✉ *Rte. 220,* ☎ *307/328–2953. Free.* ⏲ *Daily, 8–7.*

Southeast Wyoming Area A to Z

Arriving and Departing

BY BUS

Greyhound Lines (✉ 1503 Capitol Ave., ☎ 307/634–7744 or 800/231–2222) connects Cheyenne to such hubs as Denver and Salt Lake City.

BY CAR

Cheyenne is at the intersection of I–80 and I–25.

BY PLANE

Cheyenne Airport (✉ 200 E. 8th Ave., ☎ 307/634–7071) is served by United Express (☎ 800/241–6522). Many visitors prefer to fly into Denver International Airport and drive the 90 mi north to Cheyenne.

Getting Around

BY CAR

Unless you're planning to stay put in downtown Cheyenne, you'll need to rent a car or bring your own.

BY TAXI

If you only need to get to and from the airport or bus station and the capitol area, you can make do with cabs. **Checker Cab** (☎ 307/635–5555). **Yellow Cab** (☎ 307/638–3333).

Contacts and Resources

DOCTORS AND DENTISTS

Cheyenne: United Medical Center (✉ 300 E. 23rd St., ☎ 307/634–2273).

Laramie: Ivinson Memorial Hospital (✉ 255 N. 30th St., ☎ 307/742–2141).

GUIDED TOURS

The **Cheyenne Trolley** takes a $6, two-hour tour of the historic downtown area and Frances E. Warren Air Force Base, including 20–25 minutes at the Old West Museum. The trolley runs from mid-May–mid-September, Monday–Saturday at 10 and 1:30, Sunday at 11:30. Tickets are sold at the Cheyenne Area Convention and Visitors Bureau (✉ 309 W. Lincolnway, ☎ 307/778–3133) on weekdays and at the Wrangler (✉ 16th and Capitol Sts.) on weekends.

For a self-guided walking tour of the downtown and capitol area in Cheyenne, contact the **Cheyenne Area Convention and Visitors Bureau** (☞ Visitor Information, *below*).

VISITOR INFORMATION

Cheyenne Area Convention and Visitors Bureau (✉ 309 W. Lincolnway/16th St., Cheyenne 82001, ☎ 307/778–3133 or 800/426–5009). **Laramie Area Chamber of Commerce** (✉ 800 S. 3rd St., Laramie 82070, ☎ 307/745–7339 or 800/445–5303). **Saratoga-Platte Valley Chamber of Commerce** (✉ Box 1095, Saratoga 82331, ☎ 307/326–8855).

CENTRAL WYOMING

Central Wyoming encompasses the North Platte River valley. Several emigrant trails converged along the Platte and the Sweetwater rivers and through South Pass, the easiest pass in the Rockies for covered wagons to negotiate. The North Platte River valley is one of Wyoming's important agricultural areas, but the wealth of modern central Wyoming (upon which the growth of Casper has depended) is based on its deposits of oil, uranium, and bentonite.

Casper

⑩ *157 mi from Saratoga, via Rte. 130 north and I–80 west to Rawlins, then U.S. 287 and Rte. 220 north; 214 mi from Laramie, via I–80 west, U.S. 287, and Rte. 220 north; or 178 mi north of Cheyenne via I–25.*

Located nearly in the center of Wyoming, Casper is the state's largest city. Its growth is related primarily to oil and gas exploration, although sheep and cattle ranchers run their stock on lands located all around the city.

Five major emigrant trails passed near or through Casper in the period 1843–70. The best-known are the Oregon Trail and the Mormon Trail, both of which crossed the North Platte River in the vicinity of today's Casper. The early history of the emigrant trails and the military in central Wyoming is interpreted in the museum at **Fort Caspar Historic Site.** ✉ *4001 Fort Caspar Rd.,* ☎ *307/235–8462.* *Free.* ⏲ *Site open year round. Museum: mid-May–mid-Sept., Mon.–Sat. 8–7, Sun. noon–7; mid-Sept.–mid-May, weekdays 8–5.*

Other places to enjoy when in Casper include the **Casper Planetarium** (✉ 904 N. Poplar St., ☎ 307/577–0310), with multimedia programs on astronomy and space subjects. **Werner Wildlife Museum** (✉ 405 E. 15th St., ☎ 307/235–2108), closed Sunday, has displays of birds and animals indigenous to Wyoming. The **Tate Earth Science Center and Mineralogical Museum** (✉ on the Casper College campus, ☎ 307/268–2447) has displays of fossils, rocks, jade, and the fossilized parts of a brontosaurus, plus other dinosaur bones. **The Nicholaysen Art Museum and Discovery Center** (✉ 400 E. Collins Dr., ☎ 307/235–5247) features displays by local and national artists, hands-on activities, and classes and programs.

Dining and Lodging

$–$$$ ✕ **Poor Boys Steakhouse.** Reminiscent of a frontier mining camp or Western town, this steak house at the Parkway Plaza has blue-and-white-check tablecloths and chair backs, quick service, and large portions of steak, seafood, or chicken. Salad comes in a bucket and is served with fresh, hot, white or wheat bread. Try the Moonshine Mama (grilled chicken breast smothered in mushrooms and Monterey Jack and cheddar cheeses); or enjoy a tantalizingly tender filet mignon and shrimp. For dessert there is Dutch apple pie and Ashley's Avalanche—a huge plate of ice cream, white-chocolate brownie, cherry-pie filling, chocolate sauce, and whipped cream. ✉ *123 W. "E" St.,* ☎ *307/235–1777,* FAX *307/235–8068. AE, D, DC, MC, V.*

$$ ✕ **Armor's.** A quiet atmosphere with cozy booths and tables makes this a popular place, serving steaks, prime rib, blackened and Cajun entrées, pasta, seafood, and chicken. ✉ *3422 S. Energy La.,* ☎ *307/235–3000. AE, D, DC, MC, V.*

$–$$ ✕ **El Jarro.** Usually crowded, and always noisy, this place serves hearty portions of Mexican cuisine and makes a mighty fine margarita. ✉ *500 W "F" St.,* ☎ *307/577–0538. AE, MC, V.*

$–$$ ✕ **Tommyknockers Brewery & Restaurant.** This lively spot may be a brewery, but children are welcome here in the heart of downtown. Try the pasta, pizza, calzones, steaks, and freshly brewed beers. ✉ *256 S. Center St.,* ☎ *307/473–2668. AE, D, DC, MC, V.*

$$ **Hampton Inn.** This is clean and very quiet, with coffeemakers and large cable TVs in the rooms. There's an attached Mexican restaurant. ✉ *400 W. "F" St.,* ☎ *307/235–6668,* FAX *307/235–2027. 122 rooms. Restaurant, outdoor pool, sauna. AE, D, DC, MC, V.*

$$ **Parkway Plaza.** Special winter packages make this a real bargain. The rooms are quiet and large, with double vanities, one inside the bath-

room and one outside. Furnishings are contemporary in the rooms, but Western in the public areas. ✉ *123 W. "E" St.,* ☎ *307/235–1777,* FAX *307/235–8068. 272 rooms. Restaurant, bar, coffee shop, outdoor pool, hot tub, sauna, playground, meeting rooms. AE, D, MC, V.*

$$ **Radisson.** Conveniently located just off I–25, this full-service location has everything you need under one roof. The large rooms are decorated in contemporary style with muted colors. ✉ *I–25 at N. Poplar St.,* ☎ *307/266–6000,* FAX *307/473–1010. 226 rooms. Restaurant, bar, café, indoor pool, hot tub, meeting rooms. AE, D, DC, MC, V.*

Nightlife and the Arts

Both the **Casper Symphony Orchestra** and the Casper College Theater Department perform at the Gertrude Krampert Theater (✉ Casper College, ☎ 307/268–2500). **Stage III Community Theater** (✉ 4080 S. Poplar St., ☎ 307/234–0946) provides entertainment such as plays and other dramatic performances at various times. For after-hours entertainment, try **Dillinger's Night Club,** with live music nightly above Tommyknockers Brewery & Restaurant (✉ 256 S. Center St., ☎ 307/473–2668.)

Outdoor Activities and Sports

The **Platte River Parkway path** is a hiking trail adjacent to the North Platte River in downtown Casper. Access points are at Amoco Park at 1st and Poplar streets; or at Crosswinds Park, on North Poplar Street near the Casper Events Center. **Edness Kimball Wilkins State Park** (✉ I–25, 6 mi east of Casper, ☎ 307/577–5150) is a day-use area with picnicking, swimming, fishing, and a walking path.

Central Wyoming A to Z

Arriving and Departing

BY BUS

The central part of Wyoming is well served by **Powder River Transportation** (✉ 1700 E. U.S. 14/16, Gillette, ☎ 307/682–0960). Powder River Transportation connects with **Greyhound Lines** (☎ 307/634–7744 or 800/231–2222) in Cheyenne.

BY CAR

I–25 links Casper with Cheyenne in the south and Buffalo in the north; U.S. 287 and U.S. 20/26 provide access from the west.

BY PLANE

Casper is served by **United Express** (☎ 800/241–6522) out of Denver and **Delta/Skywest** (☎ 800/221–1212) from Salt Lake City.

Getting Around

BY CAR

To get around central Wyoming, you'll have to rent a car or bring your own. Sights are spread out along and off the interstates.

Contacts and Resources

DOCTORS AND DENTISTS

The primary area hospital is the **Wyoming Medical Center** (✉ 2nd St., Casper, ☎ 307/577–7201).

VISITOR INFORMATION

Casper Chamber of Commerce (✉ 500 N. Center St., 82601, ☎ 307/234–5311 or 800/852–1889, FAX 307/265–2643). **Casper Convention and Visitors Bureau** (✉ Box 399, 82602, ☎ 307/234–5311 or 800/852–1889, FAX 307/265–2643).

NORTHEAST WYOMING

Separated from Yellowstone by the Bighorn Basin, the Bighorn Mountains should not be overlooked by lovers of high places. Topped by the 200,000-acre Cloud Peak Wilderness Area, the mountains offer good fishing, good hiking, plenty of wildlife, and some fascinating relics of ancient aboriginal residents. Friendly little towns dot the Bighorns' eastern slope, but the "big" town is Sheridan.

The area has not been heavily promoted, though it has a rich history, especially of 19th-century warfare between the cavalry and Native Americans. Even richer is its lode of coal, which lies just below the surface—mostly east of Sheridan and near Gillette—and has brought multinational companies' strip mines. It's the topsoil above the coal seams, however, that maintains the area's most characteristic and enduring element—ranches. Dude ranching had its start here, and many of the dudes were so loyal to this country that they married locals and moved west permanently.

This is the heart of energy-boom country, not far from nowhere and surrounded by coal mines and oil fields. Gillette has worked hard to make itself presentable, but you don't have to go far to find a shovel bigger than a house at one of the giant strip mines nearby. Farther to the east, the Black Hills rise from the Powder River basin and lead into South Dakota.

Gillette

⓫ *136 mi north of Casper via I–25 north to Midwest, Rte. 387 east to Reno Junction, and Rte. 59 north to Gillette.*

The route from Casper to Gillette crosses the Teapot Dome area, which gave its name to an oil-leasing scandal in the 1920s, and goes through the Thunder Basin National Grasslands. If you want to see a different source of energy for America's power plants, check out the **AMAX Belle Ayre Coal Mine,** where big shovels and haul trucks dwarf anything in a science-fiction movie. There's a surprising amount of wildlife, from falcons to deer to bobcats, dwelling in and around the huge pits. This is the first mine on the right, heading east on Bishop Road, 17 mi south of Gillette. There are free tours on summer mornings, by appointment. ✉ *1901 Energy Ct.,* ☎ *307/687–3200.*

In Gillette, check the schedule at **Camplex** (✉ 1635 Reata Dr., ☎ 307/682–0552 or 307/682–8802), a theater and convention hall with a rodeo arena, racetrack, and parks. National acts book here, but local ones fill the gaps.

Dining and Lodging

$–$$ ★ ✕ **Bailey's Bar & Grill.** This handsome, shadow-filled restaurant in an old brick building turns out delicious sandwiches in the afternoon and dinners that include some Mexican dishes. ✉ *301 S. Gillette Ave.,* ☎ *307/686–7678. AE, D, MC, V.*

$–$$ ✕ **Packard's Grill.** This family restaurant with decent food at decent prices is a cross between a brew pub and a sports bar, with sports team memorabilia on the walls. Choose from the large selection of brews. ✉ *408 S. Douglas Hwy.,* ☎ *307/686–5149. AE, D, DC, MC, V.*

$$ 🏨 **Best Western Tower West Lodge.** The biggest hotel in town is also an excellent value, with large, comfortable rooms done in beige and teal. Most rooms have cable TV and coffeemakers, and there is an on-site, 24-hour convenience store. ✉ *109 N. U.S. 14/16, 82716,* ☎ *307/686–2210,* FAX *307/682–5105. 188 rooms. Restaurant, bar, indoor*

pool, hot tub, sauna, exercise room, cabaret, nightclub. AE, D, DC, MC, V.

$$ ★ **Gillette Holiday Inn.** This is one of the best places to stay in town. Travelers with a yen for exercise will appreciate a pool of lap-swimming proportions. Rooms are decorated in soft teal and mauve. Steak and seafood are served at the Sierra Cafe. ✉ *2009 S. Douglas Hwy., 82718,* ☎ *307/686–3000 or 800/465–4329,* FAX *307/686–4018. 158 rooms. 2 restaurants, indoor pool, exercise room, sauna. AE, D, DC, MC, V.*

$$ **Quality Inn.** Right off I–90, this motel has large rooms but no frills, except for a free Continental breakfast. Antelope often graze nearby. ✉ *1004 E. U.S. 14/16, 82716,* ☎ *307/682–2616 or 800/621–2182,* FAX *307/687–7002. 80 rooms. Breakfast room. AE, D, DC, MC, V.*

Nightlife and the Arts

Pop and country performers make occasional appearances at Gillette's **Camplex** (✉ 1635 Reata Dr., ☎ 307/682–0552). A variety of horse, livestock, and rodeo events also are held at the facility.

OFF THE BEATEN PATH

DEVILS TOWER – Sixty miles east of Gillette, I–90 begins rising into the Black Hills. A side trip north takes in Devils Tower, a butte that juts upward 1,280 ft above the plain of the Belle Fourche River. Native American legend has it that the tower was corrugated by the claws of a bear trying to reach some children on top, but unimaginative geologists say it's the core of a defunct volcano. The tower was a tourist magnet long before a spaceship landed here in the movie *Close Encounters of the Third Kind.* Teddy Roosevelt made it the nation's first national monument in 1906. ✉ *Rte. 24, 6 mi off U.S. 14,* ☎ *307/467–5283.* *$4.* *Visitor center: June–Labor Day, daily 8–8.*

En Route Driving across the **Powder River basin** between Gillette and Buffalo may seem a bore and a chore to people more accustomed to four lanes of bumper-to-bumper traffic. It helps to be able to read the history in the landscape: the draws where the Sioux hunted and hid from white interlopers, the uplifts where coal seams rise to the surface, and the ranches where cattle barons once grazed their stock. If this is the sort of thing that appeals to you, you may want to take the longer route to Buffalo and forsake I–90 for U.S. 16/14. The rolling countryside may look as if it's been turned back to the deer and antelope, but on back roads such as U.S. 14/16 and around eye-blink towns such as Ucross and Spotted Horse, some of the country's wealthiest people have built ranch retreats.

Buffalo

⓬ *70 mi east of Gillette on I–90.*

Buffalo is a trove of history and a hospitable little town in the foothills below Big Horn Pass. This is the area where cattle barons who wanted free grazing and homesteaders who wanted to build fences fought it out in the Johnson County Invasion of 1892. Nearby are the sites of several skirmishes between the U.S. military and Native Americans along the Bozeman Trail. Information is available at the Fort Phil Kearny State Historic Site (☞ *below*) on both the **Wagon Box Fight** (✉ 17 mi north of Buffalo on U.S. 87, near Story) and the **Fetterman Massacre Monument** (✉ 12 mi north of Buffalo, just off I–90), where Lt. William J. Fetterman and his men died in a December 1866 battle with Lakota warriors.

The **Jim Gatchell Memorial Museum,** in Buffalo, is the kind of small-town museum that's worth stopping for. It contains Native American, military, outlaw, and ranching artifacts collected by a local druggist. ✉ *100 Fort St.,* ☏ *307/684–9331.* 🎫 *$2.* ⏲ *May–Oct., daily 9–8.*

13 The fort that once stood at **Fort Phil Kearny State Historic Site** served the military from 1866 to 1868 as a protective area for travelers en route to Montana's goldfields. Plains Indians, particularly the Lakota, claimed this as their territory, however, setting the stage for some of the greatest battles in the Plains Indian Wars. No original buildings remain, but the fort site is marked and the visitor center has good details. The site is 17 mi from Buffalo and 3 mi from I–90 Exit 44 via U.S. 87, Route 193, and County Road 195 (you can follow the signs). ✉ *County Rd. 195, 3 mi south of Story,* ☏ *307/684–7629 or 307/777–7014.* 🎫 *$1.* ⏲ *Mid-May–Sept., daily 8–6.*

Big Horn

14 *25 mi north of Buffalo via I–90, U.S. 87, and Rte. 335.*

If you're not staying at a ranch and you want to get a look at one of the West's finest, visit the **Bradford Brinton Memorial** on the old Quarter Circle A Ranch. It's near Big Horn, southwest of Sheridan via U.S. 87 and Route 335. The Brinton family didn't exactly rough it in this 20-room clapboard home, complete with libraries, fine furniture, and silver and china services. A reception gallery hangs changing exhibits from the Brinton art collection, which features such western artists as Charles M. Russell and Frederic Remington. ✉ *239 Brinton Rd.,* ☏ *307/672–3173.* 🎫 *$3.* ⏲ *May 15–Labor Day, daily 9:30–5.*

Sheridan and Big Horn are access points to the **Bighorn National Forest,** which has a variety of hiking trails and camping spots for use in the summer, and which is a popular snowmobiling area in the winter. ✉ *1969 S. Sheridan Ave., Sheridan 82801,* ☏ *307/672–0751,* FAX *307/674–2668.*

OFF THE BEATEN PATH

BIG HORN EQUESTRIAN CENTER – Continue west beyond the town of Big Horn on Route 28 and you'll come to a huge expanse of green fields where locals play polo—yes, polo—on Sunday in the summer. English and Scottish families brought polo to this area in the 1890s, and now the Big Horn Polo Club is opening its 65 acres of turf to other summer events as well, from youth soccer to bronc riding. ✉ *Near state bird farm,* ☏ *800/453–3650.*

Outdoor Activities and Sports

CAMPING

Bighorn National Forest has several campgrounds, but you can camp anywhere away from the highways for free; contact the **Bighorn National Forest** (✉ 1969 S. Sheridan Ave., Sheridan 82801, ☏ 307/672–0751, FAX 307/674–2668) for more information. Like many Wyoming towns, Sheridan makes campers welcome for a night of free tenting in **Washington Park,** along Little Goose Creek. The **Big Horn Mountain KOA Campground** (✉ 63 Decker Rd., Box 35A, Sheridan 82801, ☏ 307/674–8766) has 35 tent sites, two Kamper Kabins that sleep four, and 80 trailer slots.

Sheridan

15 *35 mi north of Buffalo via I–90.*

Sheridan is what you'd expect a Western town to be. Main Street, unlike so many downtowns, is still vital and bustling, crowded with false-front stone and brick buildings, some of which date back to the turn of the century.

The refurbished art deco **Wyo Theater** (✉ 42 N. Main St., ☎ 307/672–9048) hosts special events from time to time. A narrow storefront on Main holds **King Ropes and Saddlery** (☞ Shopping, *below*), and behind it is a free museum with a collection of cowboy memorabilia assembled by owner Don King.

Not far from the center of town is the **Sheridan Inn,** on the National Register of Historic Places, with 69 gables sprouting all over its long roof. The inn was once considered the finest between Chicago and the Pacific, luring the likes of Herbert Hoover, Will Rogers, and Ernest Hemingway. Cowboys no longer ride their horses into the bar. Lunch is now served there during the summer. There's also a gift shop, and tours are led by local volunteers. ✉ *856 Broadway,* ☎ *307/674–5440.* ⏲ *Memorial Day–Labor Day, daily 9–8; Labor Day–Memorial Day, daily 9–5.*

The **Trail End State Historic Site** is the former home of Wyoming governor, U.S. senator, and rancher John B. Kendrick and is the closest Sheridan comes to a historical museum (a surprising shortcoming in an area so rich in history). Built in the Flemish style, the 1913 house features elegant hand-carved woodwork and a third-floor ballroom. Turn-of-the-century furnishings and Kendrick's memorabilia decorate the house. Out back is a sod-roof log cabin built in 1878. ✉ *400 E. Clarendon Ave.,* ☎ *307/674–4589.* *Free.* ⏲ *June–Aug., daily 9–6; Sept.–May, daily 1–4.*

In the Bighorn Mountains, 70 mi from Sheridan along scenic U.S. 14 and Alternate U.S. 14 (the roads fork at Burgess Junction), is the
16 **Medicine Wheel,** a site sacred to Native Americans, from which you can see the entire Bighorn Basin. The origin of the Medicine Wheel is unknown. It is made of rocks arranged in the shape of a hub and spokes, and it attracts Native Americans from many tribes. To protect the area, access to the wheel is restricted to foot travel (1½-mi hike to the site), except for individuals with physical disabilities, who are allowed to drive in from the highway. Alternate U.S. 14 is open only from about June through September.

Dining and Lodging

$$–$$$$ ★ ✕ **Ciao Bistro.** Nine tables are squeezed into this European-style café's cramped quarters. There's an impressive array of fine food on the menu. Try the lamb shanks, Chilean sea bass, or horseradish-crusted halibut. ✉ *120 N. Main St.,* ☎ *307/672–2838. No credit cards.*

$ ✕ **Silver Spur.** You have to look closely to spot this breakfast place. It may appear a little dingy, but the helpings are cowboy-size and the omelets are well prepared. ✉ *832 N. Main St.,* ☎ *307/672–2749. No credit cards. No dinner.*

$$$$ **Eaton's Guest Ranch.** This is the place credited with creating the dude ranch, and it's still going strong after nearly a century as a working cattle ranch that takes guests. West of Sheridan on the edge of the Bighorn National Forest, it offers horseback riding, fishing, cookouts, and pack trips. The ranch can accommodate 125 guests, and reservations should be made by March. The facilities are a collection of cabins and the main lodge. All meals are included. ✉ *270 Eaton's Ranch Rd., Wolf 82844,* ☎ *307/655–9285,* FAX *307/655–9269. 51 rooms. Dining room, pool, hiking, horseback riding, fishing. MC, V. Closed Oct.–May.*

$$–$$$ ★ **Spahn's Big Horn Mountain Bed and Breakfast.** Ron and Bobbie Spahn have guest rooms and cabins at their soaring log home 15 mi west of Sheridan. The rooms have tongue-and-groove woodwork and peeled-log beams. Ruffled curtains and peeled-log beds complete the look. They offer far more than a traditional B&B: horseback riding, cookouts, and guided tours that include a "moose safari." Full breakfasts are provided, and other meals are available by arrangement. ✉

Box 579, Big Horn 82833, ☎ 307/674–8150. 2 rooms, 2 cabins. Dining room, horseback riding. MC, V.

$$ 🏨 **Best Western Sheridan Center Motor Inn.** A favorite with bus tours, this motel has four buildings connected by a sky bridge over Main Street. These rooms are typical motel, but some have pole furniture and blue and green tones. ✉ *612 N. Main St., 82801,* ☎ *307/674–7421,* FAX *307/672–3018. 138 rooms. 2 restaurants, bar, indoor pool, outdoor pool, sauna, spa. AE, D, DC, MC, V.*

$$ 🏨 **Mill Inn Motel.** An old mill by a bridge is incorporated into this motel on old farm grounds on the east side of town. The building has six stories, but only the first two have remodeled guest rooms with a ranch/cowboy atmosphere. The furniture came from a dude ranch, so it has a definite Western style. There are offices on the other floors. ✉ *2161 Coffeen Ave., 82801,* ☎ FAX *307/672–6401. 45 rooms. Exercise room. AE, D, MC, V.*

$$ 🏨 **Sheridan Holiday Inn.** This five-floor lodging is five minutes from the center of town. Renovations in 1995 spruced up guest rooms and added an overall Western theme to the hotel. The lobby's soaring four-story atrium is accented with plants. ✉ *1809 Sugarland Dr., 82801,* ☎ *307/672–8931 or 800/465–4329,* FAX *307/672–6388. 212 rooms. Restaurant, indoor pool, beauty salon, hot tub, sauna, putting green, exercise room, jogging, racquetball, business services, convention center, meeting rooms. AE, D, DC, MC, V.*

Shopping

The suburban malls that have drained so many downtowns are absent in Sheridan, where **Main Street** is lined with fascinating, mostly home-grown, businesses. Don't miss **King Ropes and Saddlery** (✉ 184 N. Main St., ☎ 307/672–2702 or 800/443–8919), where hard-core cowboys the world over shop for the tools of the trade. From Stetson hats to bridle bits, you can get an entire rancher's repertoire, including a hand-carved saddle costing thousands of dollars. Enormous racks in the back hold every kind of rope imaginable, and professional cowboys are often here trying out the hemp on a dummy steer. For an excellent selection of both local and general-interest books, try the **Book Shop** (✉ 117 N. Main St., ☎ 307/672–6505). Anglers will want to visit the **Fly Shop of the Big Horns** (✉ 377 Coffeen Ave., ☎ 307/672–5866).

Northeast Wyoming A to Z

Arriving and Departing

BY BUS

The northeast corner, like central Wyoming, is well served by **Powder River Transportation** (✉ 1700 E. U.S. 14/16, Gillette, ☎ 307/682–0960 or 800/237–7211).

BY CAR

Two interstates join at Buffalo: I–25 comes up from Denver, Cheyenne, Casper, and points south; I–90 comes from South Dakota and the Black Hills in the east and from Montana to the north.

BY PLANE

Sheridan and Gillette are served by **United Express** (☎ 800/241–6522) out of Denver.

Getting Around

BY CAR

To get around northeastern Wyoming, you'll have to rent a car or bring your own. Sights are spread out along and off the interstates.

Contacts and Resources

DOCTORS AND DENTISTS

Gillette: Campbell County Memorial Hospital (✉ 501 S. Burma St., Gillette, ☎ 307/682–8811). **Sheridan: Sheridan County Memorial Hospital** (✉ 1401 W. 5th St., Sheridan, ☎ 307/672–1000).

VISITOR INFORMATION

Gillette Chamber of Commerce (✉ 314 S. Gillette Ave., Gillette 82716, ☎ 307/682–3673). **Buffalo Chamber of Commerce** (✉ 55 N. Main, Buffalo 82834, ☎ 307/684–5544 or 800/227–5122). **Sheridan Chamber of Commerce** (✉ Box 707, Sheridan 82801, ☎ 307/672–2485).

WYOMING A TO Z

Getting Around

By Bus

Greyhound Lines (☎ 307/634–7744 or 800/231–2222) serves the southern tier from Cheyenne to Evanston. **Powder River Transportation** (☎ 307/682–0960 or 800/237–7211) concentrates on the northeast, including Sheridan and Gillette. There is no bus service to the northwest.

By Car

I–80 crosses Wyoming's southern tier, connecting Cheyenne to Salt Lake City; watch the weather in winter, when wind and snow can cause major problems. Entering the northeast corner from the east, I–90 passes through Gillette and Sheridan before exiting north into Montana. I–25 runs north from Denver through Cheyenne and Casper to join I–90 at Buffalo. Major natural attractions are some distance from the interstates, however, so travelers can expect to cross Wyoming's wide-open spaces on smaller, well-maintained highways. Snowplows do a Herculean job of keeping most roads clear in winter.

Making a right turn on a red light (after coming to a complete stop) is legal in Wyoming.

By Plane

An oddity of Wyoming is that you can fly directly from Jackson to Chicago, but to get a commercial flight from Jackson to Casper, within the state, requires a change of planes in Salt Lake City. Commuter airlines connect a few towns, but these intrastate routes and the airlines serving them change fairly often.

Contacts and Resources

Camping

U.S. Forest Reservations (☎ 800/283–2267). Local chambers of commerce can provide lists of guides and outfitters as well as information on camping in national and state parks.

Emergencies

In most areas, call **911** for police, fire, and medical emergencies or visit a hospital emergency room (☞ Doctors and Dentists *in* individual A to Z sections, *above*). Call the **Wyoming Highway Patrol** (☎ 800/442–9090) for accidents. For **poison control,** call ☎ 800/955–9119.

Fishing

Limits and restrictions on fishing in national parks in Wyoming change from year to year. A free national park license is required. Outside the parks, on state, private, or national forest lands, Wyoming fishing licenses are required and are usually available at sporting-goods stores and drugstores. Nonresidents can purchase a 1-day license for $5; 5-

day, $20; 10-day, $30; and season, $50. Children under 14 may fish without a license when with a licensed adult. Contact **Wyoming Game and Fish Department** (✉ 5400 Bishop Blvd., Cheyenne 82006, ☎ 307/777–4600) for information.

Guided Tours

Backcountry Tours–Wyoming (✉ Box 20103, Cheyenne 82003, ☎ 307/638–6851, FAX 307/778–6309) operates tours to remote areas of Wyoming including Adobe Town, the Red Desert, and the outlaw trail used by Butch Cassidy and the Sundance Kid. See wild horses, the Overland Trail, South Pass, and the Oregon Trail on two- or four-day, four-wheel-drive tours. **Equitour** (✉ Bitterroot Ranch, Box 807, Dubois 82513, ☎ 307/455–2778) coordinates equestrian tours the world over, but home base is in Wyoming, where trips explore areas such as Butch Cassidy's Hole in the Wall country and the route of the Pony Express.

Off the Beaten Path (✉ 27 E. Main St., Bozeman, MT 59715, ☎ 406/586–1311, FAX 406/587–4147) specializes in individualized vacations throughout Wyoming. They're well connected with the outdoor recreation community and charge $70 an hour for their services. **Rocky Mountain Holiday Tours** (✉ Box 842, Fort Collins, CO 80525, ☎ 970/482–5813 or 800/237–7211, FAX 970/482–5815) offers various packages of lodging, transportation, and tours with a range of itineraries, including Grand Teton and Yellowstone national parks.

Snowmobiling

Snowmobiling is allowed on snow-packed roads within Yellowstone Park. The state of Wyoming grooms an extensive network of trails in the forests of the northwest, including the Continental Divide Snowmobile Trail, which runs from Lander through Grand Teton. Among the bigger snowmobile operations in the northwest are Flagg Ranch Village and Togwotee Mountain Lodge. The state also grooms trails in the Bighorn mountains, in the Black Hills in northeastern Wyoming, and in the Sierra Madre and Snowy ranges in the south central part of the state. For information on trails, contact the **Wyoming State Snowmobile Program** (☎ 307/777–7550).

Visitor Information

Division of Parks and Cultural Resources (✉ Barrett Bldg., 24th St. and Central Ave., Cheyenne 82002, ☎ 307/777–7013). **Wyoming Division of Tourism** (✉ I–25 at College Dr., Cheyenne 82002, ☎ 307/777–7777 or 800/225–5996).

INDEX

D

E

T

NOTES

NOTES

NOTES

NOTES

NOTES

NOTES

NOTES

NOTES

NOTES

NOTES

NOTES

Fodor's

Looking for a different kind of vacation?

Fodor's makes it easy with a full line of specialty guidebooks to suit a variety of interests—from adventure to romance to language help.

Fodor's. For the world of ways you travel.

REPUBLIQUE FRANÇAISE
5 CENTS
CANADA
1978
DIEZ PESOS
LIBERTY
VINGT FRANCS
FB 747022 T

CONSUMER PROTECTION

Whenever shopping or buying travel services in the Rockies, **pay with a major credit card** so you can cancel payment or get reimbursed if there's a problem. If you're doing business with a particular company for the first time, **contact your local Better Business Bureau and the attorney general's offices** in your state and the company's home state, as well. Have any complaints been filed? Finally, if you're buying a package or tour, always **consider travel insurance** that includes default coverage (☞ Insurance, *below*).

➤ LOCAL BBBS: **Council of Better Business Bureaus** (✉ 4200 Wilson Blvd., Suite 800, Arlington, VA 22203, ☎ 703/276–0100, FAX 703/525–8277).

CUSTOMS & DUTIES

When shopping, **keep receipts** for all purchases. Upon reentering the country, **be ready to show customs officials what you've bought.** If you feel a duty is incorrect or object to the way your clearance was handled, note the inspector's badge number and ask to see a supervisor. If the problem isn't resolved, write to the appropriate authorities, beginning with the port director at your point of entry.

IN AUSTRALIA

Australia residents who are 18 or older may bring home $A400 worth of souvenirs and gifts (including jewelry), 250 cigarettes or 250 grams of tobacco, and 1,125 ml of alcohol (including wine, beer, and spirits). Residents under 18 may bring back $A200 worth of goods. Prohibited items include meat products. Seeds, plants, and fruits need to be declared upon arrival.

➤ INFORMATION: **Australian Customs Service** (Regional Director, ✉ Box 8, Sydney, NSW 2001, ☎ 02/9213–2000, FAX 02/9213–4000).

IN CANADA

Canadian residents who have been out of Canada for at least seven days may bring home C$500 worth of goods duty-free. If you've been away less than seven days but more than 48 hours, the duty-free allowance drops to C$200; if your trip lasts 24–48 hours, the allowance is C$50. You may not pool allowances with family members. Goods claimed under the C$500 exemption may follow you by mail; those claimed under the lesser exemptions must accompany you. Alcohol and tobacco products may be included in the seven-day and 48-hour exemptions but not in the 24-hour exemption. If you meet the age requirements of the province or territory through which you reenter Canada, you may bring in, duty-free, 1.14 liters (40 imperial ounces) of wine or liquor *or* 24 12-ounce cans or bottles of beer or ale. If you are 16 or older you may bring in, duty-free, 200 cigarettes and 50 cigars. Check ahead of time with Revenue Canada or the Department of Agriculture for policies regarding meat products, seeds, plants, and fruits.

You may send an unlimited number of gifts worth up to C$60 each duty-free to Canada. Label the package UNSOLICITED GIFT—VALUE UNDER $60. Alcohol and tobacco are excluded.

➤ INFORMATION: **Revenue Canada** (✉ 2265 St. Laurent Blvd. S, Ottawa, Ontario K1G 4K3, ☎ 613/993–0534; 800/461–9999 in Canada).

IN NEW ZEALAND

Homeward-bound residents 17 or older may bring back $700 worth of souvenirs and gifts. Your duty-free allowance also includes 4.5 liters of wine or beer; one 1,125-ml bottle of spirits; and either 200 cigarettes, 250 grams of tobacco, 50 cigars, or a combination of the three up to 250 grams. Prohibited items include meat products, seeds, plants, and fruits.

➤ INFORMATION: **New Zealand Customs** (Custom House, ✉ 50 Anzac Ave., Box 29, Auckland, New Zealand, ☎ 09/359–6655, FAX 09/359–6732).

IN THE U.K.

From countries outside the EU, including the United States, you may bring home, duty-free, 200 cigarettes or 50 cigars; 1 liter of spirits or 2 liters of fortified or sparkling wine or liqueurs; 2 liters of still table wine; 60 ml of perfume; 250 ml of toilet water; plus £136 worth of other goods, including gifts and souvenirs. If returning from outside the EU, prohibited items include meat products, seeds, plants, and fruits.

➤ INFORMATION: **HM Customs and Excise** (✉ Dorset House, Stamford St., Bromley Kent BR1 1XX, ☎ 020/7202–4227).

IN THE U.S.

Non-U.S. residents ages 21 and older may import into the United States 200 cigarettes or 50 cigars or 2 kilograms of tobacco, 1 liter of alcohol, and gifts worth $100. Meat products, seeds, plants, and fruits are prohibited.

➤ INFORMATION: **U.S. Customs Service** (inquiries, ✉ 1300 Pennsylvania Ave. NW, Washington, DC 20229, ☎ 202/927–6724; complaints, ✉ Office of Regulations and Rulings, 1300 Pennsylvania Ave. NW, Washington, DC 20229; registration of equipment, ✉ Registration Information, 1300 Pennsylvania Ave. NW, Washington, DC 20229, ☎ 202/927–0540).

DINING

Generally dining in the Rockies is casual; in a few places you may feel more comfortable wearing a jacket or tie, but for the most part anything goes. Menus are becoming more varied with such regional specialties as trout, elk, or buffalo, and more health-conscious entrées are available as well. But you can almost always order a hamburger or a steak. Dinner hours are from 6 PM–9 PM. Outside the large cities, many restaurants close by 10 PM.

The restaurants we list are the cream of the crop in each price category. Properties indicated by an ✕☒ are lodging establishments whose restaurant warrants a special trip.

RESERVATIONS & DRESS

Reservations are always a good idea: we mention them only when they're essential or are not accepted. Book as far ahead as you can, and reconfirm as soon as you arrive. We mention dress only when men are required to wear a jacket or a jacket and tie—which is almost never in the casual Rockies, except in major cities or resort areas.

WINE, BEER & SPIRITS

You'll find renowned breweries throughout the Rockies, including, of course, Coors. Although the region is not known for its wines, there are some wineries to visit, too.

DISABILITIES & ACCESSIBILITY

➤ LOCAL RESOURCES: **Denver Commission for People with Disabilities** (☎ 303/640–3056). **DREAM** (Disabled Recreation and Environmental Access Movement; ✉ The Big Mountain (no street address), ☎ 406/862–1998). **Grand Teton National Park,** (accessibility coordinator, Robin Gregory, ☎ 307/739–3300 or TDD 307/733–2053). **Relay Colorado** (☎ 800/659–3656 or TDD 800/659–2656). **Rocky Mountain National Park** (accessibility coordinator, Dana Leavitt, ☎ 970/586–1206 or TDD 970/586–8506). **Utah Travel Council** (☎ 801/538–1030). **Wilderness on Wheels** (✉ 3131 Vaughn Way, Suite 305,, Aurora, CO 80014, ☎ 303/751–3959). **Wyoming Tourist Commission** (☎ 307/777–7777). **Yellowstone National Park** (accessibility coordinator, Doug Madsen, ☎ 307/344–7381).

LODGING

When discussing accessibility with an operator or reservations agent **ask hard questions.** Are there any stairs, inside *or* out? Are there grab bars next to the toilet *and* in the shower/tub? How wide is the doorway to the room? To the bathroom? For the most extensive facilities meeting the latest legal specifications **opt for newer accommodations.**

➤ COMPLAINTS: **Disability Rights Section** (✉ U.S. Department of Justice, Civil Rights Division, Box 66738, Washington, DC 20035-6738, ☎ 202/514–0301; 800/514–0301; 202/514–0301 TTY; 800/514–0301 TTY, FAX 202/307–1198) for general complaints. **Aviation Consumer Protection Division** (☞ Air Travel, *above*) for airline-related problems. **Civil Rights Office** (✉ U.S. Department of Transportation, Departmental Office of Civil Rights, S-30, 400 7th St. SW, Room 10215, Washington, DC 20590, ☎ 202/366–4648, FAX 202/366–9371) for problems with surface transportation.